Study the whole book from India's Best Teacher of English 'Mrs Neetu Singh'

Paid Course @ 999/-

1. Please download "**KD Live App**" from "**Google Play**".
2. Please create "**New Account**" in app or click on button "**Login/ Register**" in website; Create your account by providing your name, mobile number, city etc.
3. Please fill the registration details carefully. On your registered mobile and email, you will receive "**OTP**" to activate the account.
4. Once the account is activated, you can "**Sign In**" in your account. You need to enter mobile number as username.
5. After "**Sign In**", you can see "**Redeem Coupon**" option at the bottom of "**Home Tab**" in the app
6. Please click on the same. You will reach a new page. Click on "**for KD PUBLICATION STUDENTS**" option there.
7. In the next screen, click on the book you bought. Once you have done that, you can trace the syllabus associated with this book.
8. Click on "**Buy Now**" button.
9. To get extra discount, scratch the bar on the coupon code given this page and enter the coupon code in the box and click on "**Apply Coupon**" button.
10. Click "**Pay Now**" button. Now you will be redirected to the payment gateway. Complete the process using the payment method of your choice and purchase the course at a discounted price.

AF889269

To Get Free Videos Solutions to all Questions from our App.

To Start :

Free

- Install the KD Campus E Book App after downloading it from Android Play Store App.
- Use your Phone No. to make an account.

To Enroll in the Online Book

- Open the KD Campus E Book App in your Phone
- Select the "My Books" Option in the main menu.
- Click on the "Add Book".
- Select "Add Book using Coupon code" option.
- To add your Book, scratch the strip on the Coupon code given in this page and enter the Coupon code in the box & click Redeem Now.
- Please do not give this Coupon code to anyone else you will not be able to watch online videos of this book.
- To Enroll yourself for online contents of this book, enter the Coupon code and click "Redeem Now".

To Read the Online Contents of Book

- Go directly to to my books click on the book and see your free video solution.
- To see the explanation of any question, Click on the question.
- You can watch any question later if you bookmark the question.

Tips to scan Coupon Code:

- Scratch the strip on the Coupon code.
- Go to "Add Book"option inside App, select "Add book using Coupon code" option
- Enter the Coupon code on this page in the box.
- Click Redeem Now.
- Now you can watch the videos in this App.

ENGLISH

For General Competitions

Indispensable for-
All Competitive Exams

By
Neetu Singh

Published by:
KD Publication
1997, Outram Line, Kingsway Camp, Delhi-110009

First Edition – May, 2014
Second Edition – Feb, 2015
Third Edition – Jan, 2017
Fourth Edition – Oct, 2018
Fifth Edition – Feb, 2019
Sixth Edition – June, 2020
Seventh Edition – April, 2022
Eighth Edition – May, 2023
Ninth Edition – Feb, 2025
Tenth Edition – Jan, 2026

Price: ₹ 575 /-

TYPING & DESIGNING
CHANDAN PANDIT

Dedicated to my beloved son whose time I stole to write this one

PREFACE

To the Tenth Edition

English for General Competitions *was my gift to the aspirants of competitive exams who were extremely benefitted by the approach of the book. The demand for the English version was so tremendous that I had to take the translation work on priority basis and now this book is all yours, my gift to the students especially from the North-east, South India and English Medium Schools. The numerous questions given at the end of each chapter have been carefully picked from different question papers of various competitive exams. The solution of every question has detailed explanation for easy understanding. All the latest questions especially of Passive Voice and Narration have been incorporated to help the students know the latest pattern of the questions being asked in different competitive exams. In a nutshell, I would like to say that this book is an attempt to fill the void that aspirants of General Competitions felt when it comes to preparing English for Competitive Exams. Now this book comes with video solution of all the chapters taught by me. I have also included additional concepts, synonyms and antonyms apart from what are in this book.*

The best part of the Ninth edition is that now you can get a chance to study all the 34 chapters of this book by me at a very affordable fee. I have included multiple additional concepts, new, vocabularies and roots of many words for better understanding of all the chapters in my video classes.

Our students' constructive feedback and suggestions are most welcome which have always remained and will remain our guiding light . I will be highly obliged if you message/mail me your feedback or suggestion on 8860330003 or on support@kdcampus.org.

Neetu Singh

Jan, 2026

Contents

NEETU SINGH
ENGLISH
CLASS NOTES
(Bilingual)
Download Now!

SPOKEN
ENGLISH
घर बैठे अंग्रेजी बोलना सीखें।
अब सभी करेंगे फर्राटेदार अंग्रेजी में बात, बस पढ़ लें एक बार पूरी ये किताब
By Neetu Singh

ADVANCE MATHS 360° FOR ALL EXAMS
ADVANCE
MATHS
Concepts with Theory & PYQs Till Date
BILINGUAL
360°

ARITHMETIC (BILINGUAL)
ARITHMETIC
Concepts with Theory & PYQs Till Date
BILINGUAL
360°

Abbreviations

S/ Sub	→ Subject	Adj.	→ Adjective
O/Obj	→ Object	Adv.	→ Adverb
V	→ Verb	Prep	→ Preposition
S.V	→ Singular Verb	H.V	→ Helping Verb
P.V	→ Plural Verb	$V_{b.f}$	→ Base form of Verb
S.A.	→ Singular Adjective	M.V	→ Main Verb
P.A.	→ Plural Adjective	V_1	→ First Form of Verb
N	→ Noun	V_2	→ Second Form of Verb
S.N	→ Singular Noun	V_3	→ Third Form of Verb
P.N	→ Plural Noun	Aux. Verb	→ Auxiliary Verb/ Helping verb
P	→ Pronoun	U.N	→ Uncountable Noun
S.P	→ Singular Pronoun	S.C.N.	→ Singular Countable Noun
P.P	→ Plural Pronoun	P.C.N.	→ Plural Countable Noun

CHAPTER 1

VERB (BASIC)

Any word that denotes an action or a state is **Verb**. Hence verb is also called **'doing word'/'state word'**.

➢ Verb can be classified into two categories.

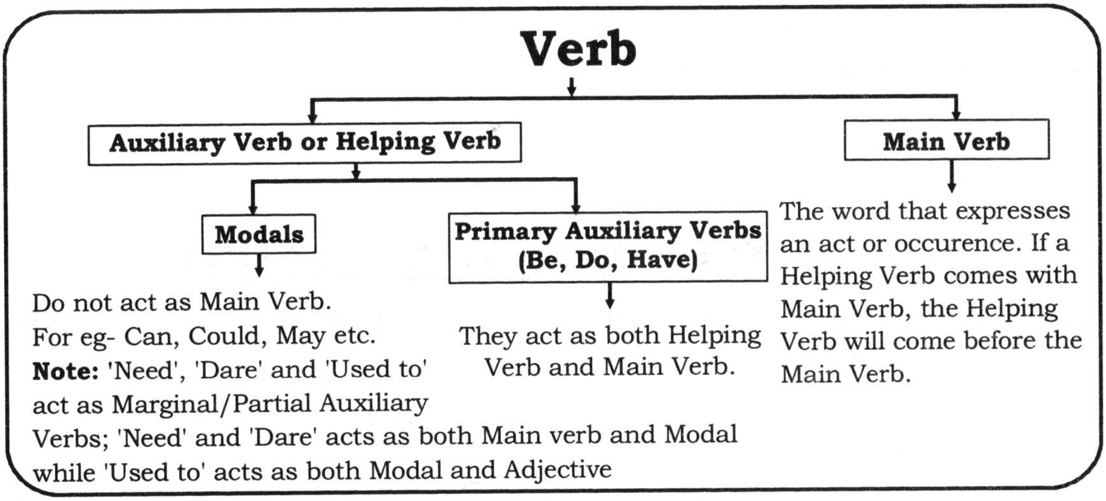

➢ **Auxiliary Verbs:** They are used in addition to other verbs. These are also called Helping Verbs.

➢ **Modal Auxiliary Verbs:** They are also called **Helping Verbs**. **Can, Could, May, Might, Shall, Will, Would, Should, Must** and **Ought to** are called Complete Modals or Modal Auxiliary Verbs.

E.g.: 1.(a) She $\underbrace{\textbf{can}}_{\textbf{Modal}}$ $\underbrace{\text{run}}_{\text{M.V.}}$ fast.

(b) You $\underbrace{\textbf{should}}_{\textbf{Modal}}$ $\underbrace{\text{study}}_{\text{M.V.}}$ English.

2. **Marginal Auxiliary Verbs: Used to**, **Need** and **Dare** are **Marginal Auxiliary Verbs**. These Modals can be used as a **Main Verb (in case of Need & Dare)** or an **Adjective (used to)** in a sentence.

- **Need & Dare** → Modal and Main Verb.
- **Used to** → Modal and Adjective

E.g.: 1. (a) I $\underbrace{\text{am}}_{\text{M.V.}}$ $\underbrace{\textbf{used to}}_{\textbf{Adjective}}$ $\underbrace{\text{sleeping}}_{\text{Gerund}}$ late at night. ***(• Here 'used to' means 'to become habitual')***

(b) I $\underbrace{\text{used to}}_{\text{Modal}}$ sleep late at night. ***(• Here 'used to' mean 'Past Routine')***

2. (a) I $\underbrace{\textbf{need}}_{\textbf{M.V.}}$ you.

(b) You $\underbrace{\textbf{need}}_{\textbf{H.V (Modal)}}$ not $\underbrace{\text{come}}_{\text{Direct Infinitive } (V_{b.f})}$ tomorrow.

3. (a) She $\underbrace{\text{does}}_{\text{H.V.}}$ not $\underbrace{\textbf{dare}}_{\textbf{M.V.}}$ $\underbrace{\text{to come}}_{\text{Infinitive } (\text{to} + V_{b.f})}$ home late.

(b) I $\underbrace{\textbf{dare}}_{\textbf{H.V (Modal)}}$ not $\underbrace{\text{enter}}_{\text{Direct Infinitive } (V_{b.f})}$ his room without permission.

4. You $\underbrace{\text{need}}_{\text{Modal}}$ not $\underbrace{\text{~~to~~ worry}}_{\text{Direct Infinitive } (V_{b.f})}$ now.

IMPORTANT POINTS ON AUXILIARY VERBS

Rule 1: **Modal Auxiliary verbs** are **not** used as **Main Verbs**. They are **used as only Helping Verbs**.

E.g.: (a) I $\underbrace{\textbf{can}}_{\textbf{H.V.}}$ $\underbrace{\text{lift}}_{\text{M.V}}$ this box. (b) He $\underbrace{\textbf{should}}_{\textbf{H.V.}}$ $\underbrace{\text{work}}_{\text{M.V}}$ hard.

Rule 2: **Modal Auxiliary Verbs** are Non-finite Verbs. Their forms do not change with **Subject, Person** or **Number**.

E.g.: (a) She **can** $\underbrace{\text{help}}_{V_{b.f}}$ you.

(b) You **should** $\underbrace{\text{understand}}_{V_{b.f}}$ your friends.

Rule 3: 'Ought' and 'used' is always followed by Infinitive **'to + $V_{b.f}$'**.

E.g.: (a) We $\underbrace{\text{ought to}}_{\text{Modal}}$ $\underbrace{\text{respect}}_{V_{b.f}}$ our parents.

(a) He $\underbrace{\text{used to}}_{\text{Modal}}$ $\underbrace{\text{come}}_{V_{b.f}}$ late.

USE OF MODAL AUXILIARY VERBS

CAN & COULD

Rule 1: **Can** denotes **power**, **ability** and **capacity**.

Could denotes past **ability**, **power** or **capacity**.

E.g: 1. He **can** lift the box.

2. I **could** not come yesterday.

Rule 2: **Can** is also used for **taking /giving permission**.

E.g: 1. You **can** go now.

2. You **cannot** enter my room.

3. **Can** I help you ?

Rule 3: **Can** denotes **theoretical possibility**.

E.g: 1. Everyone **can** make a mistake.

2. Such a pandemic **can** finish life from the earth.

Rule 4: **Could** is used to show **remote possibility**.

E.g.: There **could** be a bomb under your seat.

Rule 5: **Can** shows **friendly request** while **could** shows **formal request**.

E.g.: 1. **Can** we be friends?

2. **Could** I talk to Mr. Shukla?

Note: Both '**able to**' and '**could/can**' show **capacity**. Hence they are never used together in a sentence.

E.g.: I cannot be able to come tomorrow. (×)

(This is a superfluous sentence. The word '**superfluous**' means **more than required**. Synonyms– redundant.)

The correct sentence is:-

I **cannot** come tomorrow. (✓)

I will not be **able to** come tomorrow. (✓)

Note: **Could** expresses Past Ability but not Past Performance.

E.g.: I **Could** sing very well **(ability)** when I was young and I **was able to** perform well **(ablity + action in the past)** at the concerts.

Note: In **Negative** sentences '**could not**' and '**unable to**' mean the same.

E.g.: The doctor **could not** save the **patient.**

or

The doctor **was unable** to save the **patient.** *(Both the sentences have the same meaning.)*

Note:- *We **were able to** or **managed to** reach home safely though it was dark.

MAY, MIGHT & MUST

Rule 1: 'May' shows **possibility** .

E.g.: It **may** rain tonight. (May is used in weather forecasting – Meteorology)

Rule 2: **May** expresses wish or prayer in an Optative Sentence.

E.g.: **May** you live long!

Such sentences occur in '**Inversion**'. This means the Helping Verb comes before the Subject.

Rule 3: We use '**may**' in **subordinate clause** if **Principal clause** is in **present tense**, and the **subordinate clause** starts with **that/so that/in order that** and the subordinate clause denotes **a purpose** .

E.g.:

We eat	so that	we may live.
action-कार्य	in order that	reason–कारण

Rule 4: Might shows **less possibility**. May expresses **possibility (neither low nor high)**.

E.g.: He **might** pass the exam but seeing his intelligence, I do not have much hope.

Rule 5: **Must** shows **greater possibility**.

E.g.: He stays in five-star hotels and travels by air. He **must** be rich.

Rule 6: When '**May**' is used to show **request** with respect or to seek permission, it comes in Interrogative form?

E.g.: '**May**' I come in. Sir?

We use May in Assertive form to grant permission.

E.g.: You **may** go home now.

Note: Do not use '**Possibly**' and '**likely**' with '**May**' and '**Might**' as both indicate possibility.

E.g.: We may possibly come tomorrow. (×) *(Superfluous/ Redundant)*

We **may** come tomorrow. (✓)

We will **possibly** come tomorrow. (✓)

SHALL & WILL

Rule 1: **Shall** is used with **first person 'I' and 'we'** in future tense. All the other persons take 'will'.

E.g.: I **shall** go to college tomorrow and he **will** come with me.

In Modern English, **'will'** can be used with **'I' and 'we'** but in **interrogative sentences,** we must **use only 'shall' with 'I' and 'we'**.

E.g.: Will I go? (×)

Shall I go? (✓)

Note: **Shall** is used with **second person (You)**, **third person (He, She, It, They)**, to denote **command, promise, threat, determination, compulsion and advice.** **Will** is used with **I and We** in similar cases.

E.g.: **(a) Command**

You **shall** leave the room at once.

(b) Promise

You **shall** be awarded.

I **will help** you come what may.

* Come what may — No matter what happens

(c) Threat

Trespassers **shall** be prosecuted.

Transpasser means one who enters some one's land without permission

I **will** punish you.

(d) Determination

I **will** work hard and score good marks.

(e) Compulsion

You **shall** be here before 5 p.m for the meeting.

I **will** finish this work by tomorrow in some way or the other.

Rule (2): Imperative sentence beginning with **let us/let's,** will have '**shall we**' in the Question Tag.

E.g.: **Let us** dance together, **shall we**?

Rule (3): In the following type of sentences **shall/will** is **not used**.

E.g.: If the sentence starts with **past.**

He hoped (V_2) that he ~~will~~ **would** pass the test.

- If the sentence starts with **Past Tense,** use **would/should** and not **will/shall**.
- This rule is applicable even when **Modal or any verb** is used in place of **will/shall**.

E.g.: He said (V_2) that he ~~is~~ **was** coming.

This rule is not applicable if the 2nd part is a universal truth, habitual action, general fact, idiom or phrase.

E.g.: (1) He said that man is not a machine. (✓)

(2) Our teacher told (V_2) us that honesty is the best policy. (✓)

2. If two actions take place in future one after the other, and the first action depends on the second,
   (a) The **first action** will be in **Present Indefinite Tense.**
   (b) The **second action** will be in **Future Indefinite Tense.**

E.g.: If I ~~will~~ come (Present Indefinite (1st Action)), I will meet you (Future Indefinite (2nd Action)).

Those who ~~will~~ work hard, will pass the exam. (✓)

Note: **Future Indefinite Tense** is not used immediately after the following words. Instead **Present Indefinite Tense** is used:

If, as soon as, in case, provided, unless, until, before, after, when.

(See Chapter 'Conditional Sentence')

WOULD

Rule 1: **Would** is used to express **Past routine**. Would is used to express past routine if the action starts with Past Tense and the Verb following Would is not a Stative Verb.

E.g.: 1. When I was a kid, I **would** go to school by bus.
2. It would be a quiet street. (×)
   It used to be a quiet street. (✓)

Rule 2: Would shows **preference / choice.** Generally we use 'rather' with 'would' to express choice. If the second option is mentioned we use 'than'.

E.g.: 1. I **would** take tea.
2. He **would rather** die **than** beg.
3. I **would rather** take coffee.

Rule 3: If the sentence is in **past**, it will continue in past.

E.g.: He hoped that he ~~will~~ would pass. **(Would** is the past of **will)**

Note: We can use either '**Would**', '**used to**' or '**Past Indefinite Tense**' to express **Past Routine Action**. Would has restricted use as far as past routine is concerned.

E.g.: (1) I **used to go** (**used to + $V_{b.f}$**) to school by bus.

(2) When I was a kid, I **would go to school** (**would + $V_{b.f}$**) on foot.

(3) We **played** (**V_2**) for hours before returning home.

> If a sentence starts with Past, We can use 'would' to express Past Routine

(4) It would **be** (stative Verb) a quiet street. (×)

It used to be a quiet street. (✓)

> Would cannot come with Stative Verbs in sentences of Past Routine. Stative Verbs denote state and not action

Rule 4: Would is used in the **Principal Clause** of **Present Imagination and Past Conditional Sentences**.

E.g.: (1) If I **were** a bird, I **would** fly in the sky. (Present Imagination)

(2) If I had seen you, I would have stopped my car. (Past Conditional Sentence)

Note: In sentences of Present Imagination we use 'were' with all the subjects.

E.g.: (1) I wish, I were a bird.

(2) If I were you, I would never trust him.

Note: If sentences are of Past Imaginary, Position, we use 'had been'.

E.g.: (1) If I had been a doctor, I would have helped them.

(2) If Dr. Manmohan Singh were the Finance Minister now, the economy would be in a better condition. (Present Imagination)

(3) If Amit Shah had been the Home Minister in 1990s, Kashmir Pandits would not have faced this exile. (Past Imagination)

E.g.: I wish, as though, if, as if, would that and suppose.

Rule 5: **'Would'** is used as the past of **'will'** in indirect speech.

E.g.: He said, "He **will** go there." ***(Direct)***

He said that he **would** go there. ***(Indirect)***

Rule 6: **Would** is used for making a **'Polite request'** in an **Interrogative sentence.**

E.g.: **Would** you help me?

Rule 7: **Would** denotes **'probability'**.

E.g.: He **would** be sleeping.

Rule 8: **Would** expresses a **'wish'**.

E.g.: I **wish**, India **would** become a developed country soon.

Rule 9: **'Would like'** shows **'wish'**.

E.g.: I **would like** to talk to the manager.

SHOULD

Rule 1: **Should** is used to express **suggestion/ advice**.

E.g.: 1. You **should** study English.

2. You **should** not laugh at his mistake.

Rule 2: If **should** is used after **lest**, it shows **negative purpose**.

E.g.: He ran fast, **lest** he **should** miss the train.

Note: **Lest** can also take **'$V_{b.f}$'**.

E.g.: Take care **lest** you/he **fall**.

Note: '**Lest**' doesn't take '**not**' after it.

E.g: He doesn't take risk lest he should not lose all his money. **(Remove not)**

Rule 3: In certain Conditional Sentences, 'if' can be replaced by 'should'.

E.g.: Should you need me, let me know.

OUGHT TO

Rule 1: **"Ought to"** shows **moral obligation** or **duty**.

E.g.: We **ought to** love our country.

MUST

Rule 1: **Must** is used to denote **compulsion**.

E.g.: **Candidates must** write in ink.

Rule 2: **Must** also shows **fixed determination**.

E.g.: India **must** win the World Cup.

Rule 3: **Must** expresses **duty**.

E.g.: A soldier **must** fight for his country.

USED TO

(i) '**Used to**' denotes **Past routine/situation**.

E.g.: He **used to** study till 10 p.m.

(ii) '**Use to**' **or** '**Uses to**' does not show **present routine action**. Instead Present Indefinite Tense is used for such a purpose.

E.g.: He uses to study till 10 p.m. and then goes to bed. (×)

He **studies** till 10 p.m. and then goes to bed.(✓)

Note: **See the use of** '**used to**' in **Affirmative/Negative/Interrogative Sentence**.

(a) Affirmative : He **used to** come here.

(b) Negative : He **used not to** come here.

He **did not use to** come here.

(c) Interrogative : **Used** he to come here?

Did he use to come here?

Note: When V_1 **+ ing**, is used after **verb + used to**, it shows **habitual action**.

E.g.: I **am used to** getting (V_1 +ing) up late in the morning.

Note: In the following cases, **to +** $V_{b.f}$ is not used. Instead 'V_1 **+ ing**' is used after 'to'. Here '**to**' is not a part of **infinitive** '**to +** $V_{b.f}$'. Here '**to**' is a **preposition** and **after all the prepositions**, if we use a verb, the **verb must be in** 'V_1 **+ ing**' **form.** Some of the important phrases from which questions are asked in exams are given below.

E.g.: **Be used to, accustomed to, averse to, with a view to, addicted to, devoted to, in addition to, look forward to, object to, owing to, given to, taken to, prone to.**

E.g.: 1. He is **addicted to** smoking.

2. I am **looking forward to** meeting you.

3. He got **used to** driving on the right when he was in London.

DARE/NEED

➢ **'Dare' and 'Need'** are used as both 'Main Verb' as well as 'modal'.

➢ **Dare** expresses **challenges** or **courage**.

➢ **Need** expresses **requirements**.

E.g.: (1) He $\underbrace{\textbf{needs}}_{\textbf{M.V}}$ me.

(2) She $\underbrace{\textbf{does}}_{\textbf{H.V}}$ not $\underbrace{\textbf{dare}}_{\textbf{M.V}}$ $\underbrace{\textbf{to go}}_{\textbf{Infinitive}}$ to go there.

(3) You $\underbrace{\textbf{need}}_{\textbf{Modal}}$ not $\underbrace{\textbf{come}}_{\textbf{M.V}}$ tomorrow.

➢ Need/Dare is not used as Modal in positive sense.

E.g.: (1) $\underbrace{\text{I}}_{\text{Sub.}}$ $\underbrace{\text{need}}_{\text{modal}}$ $\underbrace{\text{help}}_{V_{b.f}}$ $\underbrace{\text{him}}_{\text{Obj.}}$. (×)

(2) I $\underbrace{\textbf{need}}_{\textbf{M.V}}$ $\underbrace{\text{to help}}_{\text{Infinitive}}$ him. (✓)

➢ **To + $V_{b.f}$ comes after need and dare**, if need and dare are used in a positive sentence.

E.g.: (1) He $\underbrace{\textbf{needs}}_{\textbf{M.V}}$ $\underbrace{\textbf{to work}}_{\textbf{to+}V_{b.f}}$ hard.

(2) He $\underbrace{\textbf{will not}}_{\textbf{H.V}}$ $\underbrace{\textbf{dare}}_{\textbf{M.V}}$ $\underbrace{\textbf{to come}}_{\textbf{Infinitive}}$ here.

➢ If **need/dare** is used in **–ve** sentence, **'not'** is followed by a **Bare Infinitive**. This means only ' **$V_{b.f}$**' and not '**to + $V_{b.f}$**'.

E.g.: (1) I **need not** come tomorrow.

(2) He **dare not** cheat anyone again.

(3) You need not ~~to~~ worry

➢ **Following Modals are used for making a request**

Modals	Use	Example
Can	Friendly request	Can we be friends.
Could	Formal request	Could I talk to Mr. Singh?
May	Request with respect	May I come in Sir?
Would	Polite Request	Would you help me?

➢ **Modals are used in the following ways in Active and Passive Voice:-**

MODALS	ACTIVE VOICE	PASSIVE VOICE
Indefinite	Sub+modal+$V_{b.f}$ +obj.	Obj + modal + be + V_3 + by + sub.
Continuous	Sub + modal + be + V_1 + ing + obj.	×××××
Perfect	Sub + modal + have + V_3 + obj.	Obj + modal + have + been + V_3+ by + sub.
Perfect Continuous	Sub + modal + have + been + V_1 + ing + obj + for / since + time.	×××××

➢ In the above mentioned chart you will find that **a modal is always followed by '$V_{b.f}$'.**

➢ See the structure given below, where Modal is used in Perfect Tense. Note the usage too.

Sub + modal + have +V_3 + obj

➢ When **some Modals are used in the structure 'Modal + have + V_3'** (e.g. should have come, could have gone, need not have seen, must have seen etc.), there is a **hidden meaning** in the sentence which is **opposite to the meaning of the sentence**.

(This is **not applicable** in case of **will, shall, would** and **might**)

E.g.: (1) I **could** score good marks. **(Meaning-I had the ability)**
(2) I **could have** scored good marks. **(Hidden meaning -I didn't score though I had the ability)**
(3) You **should** work hard. **(Just a suggestion)**
(4) You **should have** worked hard. **(Hidden Meaning - You didn't)**

PRIMARY AUXILIARY VERBS

Do, have, be are **Primary Auxiliary Verbs.** They are used as **Helping** as well as **Main Verbs.**

E.g.: **(1)** '**Do**' has the following forms: Do (V_1) Does (V_1, s/es) Did (V_2) Done (V_3)

(a) I **do** (M.V.) my work. (b) I **did** (H.V.) not know (M.V.) him.

(2) The forms of '**Have**' are :- Has/ have (V_1) Had (V_2) Had (V_3)

(i) '**Have**' demonstrates **possession.**

I **have** (M.V.) a car.

(ii) '**Have**' is used as a helping verb in **Perfect** & **Perfect Continuous Tense**.

(a) I **have** (H.V.) not seen (M.V.) him.

(b) I **had** (H.V.) been waiting (M.V.) for him for a long time.

(iii) **Have + Infinitive** denotes forced action.

(a) I **have to** work hard.

(b) She **had to** leave her job.

(3) **Be** has the following forms: Be ($V_{b.f}$) is (V_1, s/es) am are (V_1) was, were (V_2) been (V_3)

➢ Now let's see how it is used as helping and main verb.

(a) I **am** (M.V) a doctor

(b) He **was** (H.V) working (M.V) hard.

(b) He has (H.V) **been** (M.V) to London.

MAIN VERB

MAIN VERBS:-

I. Those verbs that express an action, an occurrence or a state of being and those which have $V_1/V_2/V_3$**/ing** or **/s/es** forms are called Main Verbs.

E.g.: I **know** (V_1) you.

I **knew** (V_2) you.

I have **known** (V_3) you for two years.

➢ **The forms of Main Verbs** will change if the tense of the sentence changes.

FORMS OF VERB

1. Present (1st form) **3. (3rd form)**
2. Past (2nd form) **4. (-ing form)**

Main Verbs

Regular Verbs

Where only 'ed' is needed to make verbs 'V2' & 'V3' forms.

Eg:- V_1	V_2	V_3
walk	walked	walked
talk	talked	talked
paint	painted	painted

Irregular Verbs

Here verbs to 'V2' & 'V3' forms are formed in different ways.

	All forms are the same.	Two forms are the same.	All forms are different.	
Eg:-	put	sit	go	V_1
	put	sat	went	V_2
	put	sat	gone	V_3

GROUP - I (IRREGULAR VERBS)

Present (1st Form)	अर्थ	Past (2nd Form)	(3rd Form)	– ing Form	s/es Form
Arise	उठना	arose	arisen	arising	arises
Awake	जागना	awoke	awaken	awaking	awakes
$Be_{(Vb.f)}$ (am, are) V_1	होना	was, were	been	being	is
Bear	जन्म देना	bore	born	bearing	bears
Bear	सहन करना	bore	borne	bearing	bears
Become	बनना	became	become	becoming	becomes
Begin	आरंभ करना	began	begun	beginning	begins
*Bite	दाँत से काटना	bit	bitten	biting	bites
Blow	हवा का चलना	blew	blown	blowing	blows
Bleed	खून बहना	bled	bled	bleeding	bleeds
Bind	बाँधना	bound	bound	binding	binds
Bid	आदेश देना, अभिवादन करना	bade	bidden	bidding	bids
Bid	निलामी में बोली लगाना	bid	bid	bidding	bids
Break	तोड़ना	broke	broken	breaking	breaks
Bring	लाना	brought	brought	bringing	brings
Build	बनाना/ निर्माण करना	built	built	building	builds
Burn	जलना / जलाना	burnt	burnt	burning	burns
Buy	खरीदना	bought	bought	buying	buys
Catch	पकड़ना	caught	caught	catching	catches
Choose	चुनना	chose	chosen	choosing	chooses
Cling	चिपटना	clung	clung	clinging	clings

Come	आना	came	come	coming	comes
Dig	खोदना	dug	dug	digging	digs
Do	करना	did	done	doing	does
Draw	खींचना	drew	drawn	drawing	draws
Dream	स्वप्न देखना	dreamt	dreamt	dreaming	dreams
Drink	पीना	drank	drunk/drunken$_{(Adj)}$	drinking	drinks
Drive	चलाना	drove	driven	driving	drives
Eat	खाना	ate	eaten	eating	eats
Fall	गिरना	fell	fallen	falling	falls
Feel	महसूस/ अनुभव करना	felt	felt	feeling	feels
Flee	भागना	fled	fled	fleeing	flees
Fight	लड़ना	fought	fought	fighting	fights
Find	पाना	found	found	finding	finds
Fly	उड़ना, उड़ाना	flew	flown	flying	flies
Forbid	मना करना	forbade	forbidden	forbidding	forbids
Forget	भूल जाना	forgot	forgotten	forgetting	forgets
Freeze	जमाना/जमना	froze	frozen	freezing	freezes
Get	पाना	got	got	getting	gets
Give	देना	gave	given	giving	gives
Grind	पीसना	ground	ground	grinding	grinds
Grow	बढ़ना, उगना	grew	grown	growing	grows
Hang*	लटकाना	hung	hung	hanging	hangs
Hang	फाँसी पर चढ़ाना	hanged	hanged	hanging	hangs
Have	रखना/प्राप्त करना/खाना	had	had	having	has
Hide	छिपाना/छिपना	hid	hidden	hiding	hides
Hold	थामना	held	held	holding	holds
Know	जानना	knew	known	knowing	knows
Kneel	घुटनों के बल झुकना	knelt	knelt	kneeling	kneels
Learn	याद करना, सीखना	learnt	learnt/learned$_{(Adj.)}$	learning	learns
Leave	छोड़ना	left	left	leaving	leaves
Lend	उधार देना	lent	lent	lending	lends
Lead	मार्ग दिखाना	led	led	leading	leads
Lie	लेटना	lay	lain	lying	lies
Lose	खोना/हारना	lost	lost	losing	loses
Make	बनाना	made	made	making	makes
Meet	मिलना	met	met	meeting	meets
Mean	अर्थ लगाना	meant	meant	meaning	means
Ride	सवारी करना	rode	ridden	riding	rides
Ring	बजना/बजाना	rang	rung	ringing	rings
Rise	उठना/उगना/तरक्की करना	rose	risen	rising	rises
See	देखना/ हिलना	saw	seen	seeing	sees
Seek	अपेक्षा करना/ढूँढना	sought	sought	seeking	seeks
Sell	बेचना	sold	sold	selling	sells

Send	भेजना	sent	sent	sending	sends
Shake	हिलाना/ हिलना	shook	shaken	shaking	shakes
Shine	चमकना	shone	shone	shining	shines
Shoot	फोटो निकालना/गोली मारना	shot	shot	shooting	shoots
Shrink	सिकुड़ना	shrank	shrunk/ shrunken(Adj)	shrinking	shrinks
Sing	गाना	sang	sung	singing	sings
Sink	डूबना (निर्जीव का)	sank	sunk	sinking	sinks
Sit	बैठना	sat	sat	sitting	sits
Slay	वध करना (गला काट कर)	slew	slain	slaying	slays
Speak	बोलना	spoke	spoken	speaking	speaks
Spit	थूकना	spat	spat	spitting	spits
Spend	खर्च करना	spent	spent	spending	spends
Stand	खड़ा होना	stood	stood	standing	stands
Steal	चुराना	stole	stolen	stealing	steals
Stick	चिपकना	stuck	stuck	sticking	sticks
Strike	चोट मारना	struck	struck	striking	strikes
Swear	शपथ लेना	swore	sworn	swearing	swears
Sweep	झाड़ू देना	swept	swept	sweeping	sweeps
Swim	तैरना	swam	swum	swimming	swims
Swing	झूलना	swung	swung	swinging	swings
Take	लेना	took	taken	taking	takes
Tear	फाड़ना	tore	torn	tearing	tears
Tell	कहना	told	told	telling	tells
Teach	पढ़ाना/सिखाना	taught	taught	teaching	teaches
Think	सोचना	thought	thought	thinking	thinks
Understand	समझना	understood	understood	understanding	understands
Wear	पहनना	wore	worn	wearing	wears
Weep	रोना	wept	wept	weeping	weeps
Weave	बुनना	wove	woven	weaving	weaves
Win	जीतना	won	won	winning	wins
Wind (वाइंड)	चाबी लगाना	wound(वाउंड)	wound	winding	winds
Wound (वुंड)	जख्मी करना	wounded	wounded	wounding	wounds
Write	लिखना	wrote	written	writing	writes
Wring	निचोड़ना	wrung	wrung	wringing	wrings

The following Irregular Verbs have all three forms same.

Present (1st Form)	**अर्थ**	**Past (2nd Form)**	**(3rd Form)**	**– ing Form**	**s/es Form**
Bid	बोली लगाना	bid	bid	bidding	bids
Bet	शर्त लगाना	bet	bet	betting	bets
Burst	फटना	burst	burst	bursting	bursts
Cast	फेंकना/डालना	cast	cast	casting	casts

Cost	मूल्य लगाना	cost	cost	costing	costs
Cut	काटना	cut	cut	cutting	cuts
Hurt	पीड़ा पहुँचाना	hurt	hurt	hurting	hurts
Let	करने देना	let	let	letting	lets
Put	रखना	put	put	putting	puts
Read	पढ़ना *	read	read	reading	reads
Set	अस्त होना	set	set	setting	sets
Shed	बहाना/त्याग देना	shed	shed	shedding	sheds
Shut	बंद करना	shut	shut	shutting	shuts
Spread	फैलाना	spread	spread	spreading	spreads
Thrust	ठूँसना/थोपना	thrust	thrust	thrusting	thrusts
Quit	छोड़ना	quit	quit	quitting	quits

* Read एवं Study में अंतर है। **Study का अर्थ अध्ययन करना है** जबकि **Read हम Magazine, newspaper इत्यादि को करते है।**

1. I read a novel every month.
2. I study English every day.

GROUP – II (REGULAR VERBS)

The verbs given below have the same 2nd and 3rd form.

Present (1st Form)	**अर्थ**	**Past (2nd Form)**	**3rd Form)**	**– ing Form**	**s/es Form**
Abuse	गाली देना/दुपर्योग करना	abused	abused	abusing	abuses
Act	काम करना/अभिनय करना	acted	acted	acting	acts
Add	जोड़ना	added	added	adding	adds
Admire	प्रशंसा करना	admired	admired	admiring	admires
Advise	उपदेश देना	advised	advised	advising	advises
Allow	अनुमति देना	allowed	allowed	allowing	allows
Answer	उत्तर देना	answered	answered	answering	answers
Appoint	नियुक्त करना	appointed	appointed	appointing	appoints
Appear	प्रकट होना	appeared	appeared	appearing	appears
Arrive	पहुंचना	arrived	arrived	arriving	arrives
Arrest	गिरफ्तार करना	arrested	arrested	arresting	arrests
Ask	पूछना/कहना	asked	asked	asking	asks
Attack	आक्रमण करना	attacked	attacked	attacking	attacks
Bark	भौंकना	barked	barked	barking	barks
Bathe	नहलाना	bathed	bathed	bathing	bathes
Beg	भीख माँगना	begged	begged	begging	begs
Believe	विश्वास करना	believed	believed	believing	believes
Behave	व्यवहार करना	behaved	behaved	behaving	behaves
Bless	आशीर्वाद देना	blessed	blessed	blessing	blesses

Boil	उबालना	boiled	boiled	boiling	boils
Boast	डींगें मारना	boasted	boasted	boasting	boasts
Borrow	उधार लेना	borrowed	borrowed	borrowing	borrows
Call	पुकारना	called	called	calling	calls
Carry*	ले जाना	carried	carried	carrying	carries
Clean	साफ करना	cleaned	cleaned	cleaning	cleans
Close	बंद करना	closed	closed	closing	closes
Change	बदलना	changed	changed	changing	changes
Check	रोकना/जाँच करना	checked	checked	checking	checks
Climb	चढ़ना	climbed	climbed	climbing	climbs
Clap	ताली बजाना	clapped	clapped	clapping	claps
Copy	नकल करना	copied	copied	copying	copies
Collect	इकट्ठा करना	collected	collected	collecting	collects
Complain	शिकायत करना	complained	complained	complaining	complains
Cook	पकाना	cooked	cooked	cooking	cooks
Count	गिनना	counted	counted	counting	counts
Confuse	उलझन में डाल देना	confused	confused	confusing	confuses
Consult	सलाह देना	consulted	consulted	consulting	consults
Cover	ढ़कना	covered	covered	covering	covers
Crow	बांग लगाना	crowed	crowed	crowing	crows
Cross	पार करना	crossed	crossed	crossing	crosses
Creep	रेंगना	crept	crept	creeping	creeps
Cry	चिल्लाना	cried	cried	crying	cries
Decorate	सजाना	decorated	decorated	decorating	decorates
Dance	नाचना	danced	danced	dancing	dances
Deceive	धोखा देना	deceived	deceived	deceiving	deceives
Defeat	हराना	defeated	defeated	defeating	defeats
Decide	निर्णय करना	decided	decided	deciding	decides
Desire	इच्छा करना	desired	desired	desiring	desires
Discover	खोज करना	discovered	discovered	discovering	discovers
Dip	डुबोना	dipped	dipped	dipping	dips
Die	मरना	died	died	dying	dies
Divide	बाँटना	divided	divided	dividing	divides
Dry	सुखना/सुखाना	dried	dried	drying	dries
Drown	डुबाना	drowned	drowned	drowning	drowns
Dye	रंगना	dyed	dyed	dyeing	dyes
Earn	कमाना	earned	earned	earning	earns
Enter	प्रवेश करना	entered	entered	entering	enters
Employ	काम पर रखना	employed	employed	employing	employs
Explain	समझाना	explained	explained	explaining	explains
Face	सामना करना	faced	faced	facing	faces

Fail	असफल होना	failed	failed	failing	fails
Fear	डरना	feared	feared	fearing	fears
Feed	खिलाना	fed	fed	feeding	feeds
Fell	गिराना	felled	felled	felling	fells
Finish	समाप्त करना	finished	finished	finishing	finishes
Fine	जुर्माना लगाना	fined	fined	fining	fines
Float	तैरना (सतह पर)	floated	floated	floating	floats
Graze	चरना	grazed	grazed	grazing	grazes
Gather	इकट्ठा करना/होना	gathered	gathered	gathering	gathers
Hate	घृणा करना	hated	hated	hating	hates
Hang	फांसी लगाना	hanged	hanged	hanging	hangs
Hear	सुनना	heard	heard	hearing	hears
Help	सहायता करना	helped	helped	helping	helps
Improve	सुधारना/ बेहतर होना	improved	improved	improving	improves
Invite	निमंत्रण देना	invited	invited	inviting	invites
Join	साथ में होना,	joined	joined	joining	joins
Jump	कूदना	jumped	jumped	jumping	jumps
Keep	रखना	kept	kept	keeping	keeps
Kill	जान से मारना	killed	killed	killing	kills
Knit*	बुनना	knitted	knitted	knitting	knits
Lay	रखना/(अंडा) देना, न्योछावर करना	laid	laid	laying	lays
Lie	झूठ बोलना	lied	lied	lying	lies
Laugh	हंसना	laughed	laughed	laughing	laughs
Like	चाहना	liked	liked	liking	likes
Listen	सुनना (ध्यान से)	listened	listened	listening	listens
Look	देखना	looked	looked	looking	looks
Live	रहना	lived	lived	living	lives
Love	प्रेम करना	loved	loved	loving	loves
Marry	विवाह करना	married	married	marrying	marries
Movc	हिलना	moved	moved	moving	moves
Melt	पिघलना, पिघलाना	melted	melted/ molten (Adj.)	melting	melts
Mend	सुधारना	mended	mended	mending	mends
Mix	मिलाना, मिलना	mixed	mixed	mixing	mixes
Name	नाम रखना	named	named	naming	names
Need	आवश्यकता होना	needed	needed	needing	needs
Nip	सख्ती से कुचलना	nipped	nipped	nipping	nips
Obey	आज्ञा मानना	obeyed	obeyed	obeying	obeys
Open	खोलना	opened	opened	opening	opens
Order	आदेश देना	ordered	ordered	ordering	orders

Oppose	विरोध करना	opposed	opposed	opposing	opposes
Pay	चुकाना	paid	paid	paying	pays
Play	खेलना	played	played	playing	plays
Pray	प्रार्थना करना	prayed	prayed	praying	prays
Praise	प्रशंसा करना	praised	praised	praising	praises
Preach	उपदेश करना	preached	preached	preaching	preaches
Peep	झाँकना	peeped	peeped	peeping	peeps
Plant	पौधा लगाना	planted	planted	planting	plants
Pluck	तोड़ना(जैसे फूल तोड़ते है)	plucked	plucked	plucking	plucks
Prepare	तैयार करना	prepared	prepared	preparing	prepares
Pull	खींचना	pulled	pulled	pulling	pulls
Prevent	रोकना	prevented	prevented	preventing	prevents
Punish	दण्ड देना	punished	punished	punishing	punishes
Prove	सिद्ध करना	proved	proved/proven (Adj.)	proving	proves
Promise	वचन देना	promised	promised	promising	promises
Push	धक्का देना/धकेलना	pushed	pushed	pushing	pushes
Plough	जोतना (खेत)	ploughed	ploughed	ploughing	ploughs
Quarrel	झगड़ना	quarrelled	quarrelled	quarrelling	quarrels
Rain	वर्षा होना	rained	rained	raining	rains
Reply	जबाब देना	replied	replied	replying	replies
Reach	पहुँचना	reached	reached	reaching	reaches
Receive	पाना, प्राप्त करना	received	received	receiving	receives
Refuse	इंकार करना	refused	refused	refusing	refuses
Rest	आराम करना	rested	rested	resting	rests
Resign	त्यागपत्र देना	resigned	resigned	resigning	resigns
Repair	मरम्मत करना	repaired	repaired	repairing	repairs
Remember	याद करना	remembered	remembered	remembering	remembers
Return	लौटाना, लौटना	returned	returned	returning	returns
Roar	गरजना	roared	roared	roaring	roars
Say	कहना	said	said	saying	says
Save	बचाना	saved	saved	saving	saves
Saw	आरे से चीरना	sawed	sawed	sawing	saws
Select	चुनना (छांटकर)	selected	selected	selecting	selects
Sleep	सोना	slept	slept	sleeping	sleeps
Stay	ठहरना	stayed	stayed	staying	stays
Stop	रोकना	stopped	stopped	stopping	stops
Study	पढ़ना	studied	studied	studying	studies
Slip	फिसलना	slipped	slipped	slipping	slips
Talk	बात करना	talked	talked	talking	talks

Tie	बांधना	tied	tied	tying	ties
Touch	छूना	touched	touched	touching	touches
Try	प्रयत्न करना	tried	tried	trying	tries
Trust	विश्वास करना	trusted	trusted	trusting	trusts
Use	इस्तेमाल करना	used	used	using	uses
Walk	चलना	walked	walked	walking	walks
Wash	धोना	washed	washed	washing	washes
Wait	प्रतीक्षा करना	waited	waited	waiting	waits
Work	काम करना	worked	worked	working	works
Watch	निगरानी करना	watched	watched	watching	watches
Wish	चाहना	wished	wished	wishing	wishes
Wander	घूमना/ भटकना	wandered	wandered	wandering	wanders
Waste	नष्ट करना	wasted	wasted	wasting	wastes
Wed	विवाह करना	wedded	wedded	wedding	weds
Wound	घायल करना	wounded	wounded	wounding	wounds
Worship	पूजा करना	worshipped	worshipped	worshipping	worships
Wonder	हैरान होना/ सोचना	wondered	wondered	wondering	wonders
Wrap	लपेटना	wrapped	wrapped	wrapping	wraps
Yield	झुकना/ पैदा करना	yielded	yielded	yielding	yields

CONFUSING PAIR

1.	Bear	bore	born	→ to give birth
	Bear	bore	borne	→ to tolerate
2.	Fall	fell	fallen	→ to descend freely
	Fell	felled	felled	→ to bring down
3.	Find	found	found	→ to come across
	Found	founded	founded	→ to establish
4.	Grind	ground	ground	→ to reduce to power or small pieces
	Ground	grounded	grounded	→ to bring to ground, to stop from flying
5.	Hang	hanged	hanged	→ to suspend by the neck
	Hang	hung	hung	→ to suspend from peg etc.
6.	Lie	lied	lied	→ to make an untrue statement
	Lie	lay	lain	→ to move into a horizontal position
	Lay	laid	laid	→ To sacrifice; To keep in a horizontal position; Hens lay eggs
7.	Rend	rent	rent	→ to tear or break something violently
	Rent	rented	rented	→ to grant possession in exchange of a fixed amount
8.	Rise	rose	risen	→ to get up, to progress, to ascend

	Raise	raised	raised	→ to uplift, to collect, to set upright
	Raze	razed	razed	→ to demolish
9.	See	saw	seen	→ to perceive by the eye
	Saw	sawed	sawed/sawn	→ to cut with the help of a saw which is a toothed blade used to cut trees etc.
10.	Wind	wound	wound	→ to move so as to encircle something
	Wound	wounded	wounded	→ to injure
11.	Fly	flew	flown	→ to move in air as a bird does
	Flow	flowed	flowed	→ to move in a stream just as water does

VERBS CONFUSED WITH VERB/ NOUN/ ADJECTIVE.

All the following words are very easy but meanings are given in Hindi for better understanding as far as their usage is concerned.

1.	Practice$_{(N)}$	अभ्यास
	Practise$_{(V)}$	अभ्यास करना
2.	Advice$_{(N)}$	सलाह
	Advise$_{(V)}$	सलाह देना
3.	Complain$_{(V)}$	शिकायत करना
	Complaint$_{(N)}$	शिकायत
4.	Affect$_{(V)}$	असर करना
	Effect$_{(N)/(V)}$	परिणाम/ प्रभाव में लाना
5.	Assure$_{(V)}$	तसल्ली देना
	Ensure$_{(V)}$	सुनिश्चित करना
	Insure$_{(V)}$	बीमा करना
6.	Hear$_{(V)}$	सुनना
	Listen$_{(V)}$	ध्यान से सुनना
7.	Heal$_{(V)}$	ठीक होना (घाव या जख्म का)
	Heel$_{(N)}$	ऐड़ी
8.	Prescribe$_{(V)}$	सलाह देना
	Proscribe$_{(V)}$	पाबंदी लगाना
9.	Adopt$_{(V)}$	गोद लेना
	Adapt$_{(V)}$	ढ़ालना
	Adept$_{(Adj.)}$	निपुण
10.	Allude$_{(V)}$	के संदर्भ में उल्लेख करना *(Indirectly)*
	Elude$_{(V)}$	से बचना
11.	Amend$_{(V)}$	संशोधन करना
	Emend$_{(V)}$	अशुद्धियाँ निकाल देना
12.	Bought **(V2 & V3 Form of buy)**	खरीदना
	Brought **(V2 & V3 Form of bring)**	लाना
13.	Compose$_{(V)}$	बनाना
	Comprise$_{(V)}$	बनाना/ से बना होना
14.	Deface$_{(V)}$	विकृत करना
	Efface$_{(V)}$	मिटा देना
15.	Deprecate$_{(V)}$	नापसंद करना
	Depreciate$_{(V)}$	मूल्य कम होना
16.	Envelop$_{(V)}$	ढ़कना (आवरण करना)
	Envelope$_{(N)}$	लिफाफा
17.	Excite$_{(V)}$	उत्तेजित करना
	Incite$_{(V)}$	भड़काना
18.	Flout$_{(V)}$	उल्लंघन करना
	Flaunt$_{(V)}$	दिखावा करना
19.	Hoard$_{(V)}$	छिपा कर जमा करना
	Horde$_{(N)}$	लोगों का समूह
20.	Loathe$_{(V)}$	नापसंद करना
	Loath$_{(Adj.)}$	अनिच्छुक
21.	Lose$_{(V)}$	खोना / हारना
	Loss$_{(N)}$	घाटा / हानि
	Loose$_{(Adj.)}$	ढ़ीला

22. Mitigate$_{(V)}$	बेहतर करना (कम कर के)
Militate$_{(V)}$	प्रतिकूल होना
23. Pour$_{(V)}$	उडेलना
Pore$_{(N)}$	छिद्र
Pour over$_{(Ph.V.)}$	ध्यान से पढ़ना
24. Proceed$_{(V)}$	आगे बढ़ना
Precede$_{(V)}$	से पहले आना
25. Pray$_{(V)}$	प्राथना करना
Prey$_{(V/N)}$	शिकार करना / शिकार
26. Rout$_{(V)}$	आसानी से हराना
Route$_{(N)}$	रास्ता
Root$_{(N)}$	जड़
Uproot$_{(N)}$	जड़ से उखाड़ना
27. Censure$_{(V)}$	निंदा करना
Censor$_{(V)}$	पाबंदी लगाना
28. Wave$_{(N/V)}$	लहर / लहराना
Waive$_{(V)}$	छूट देना
29. Tow$_{(V)}$	खींच कर ले जाना
Toe$_{(N)}$	पैर की अंगुलियाँ
Tiptoe$_{(V)}$	पैर की अंगुलियों पर चलना
30. Site$_{(N)}$	निर्माण स्थल
Sight$_{(N)}$	नजारा या दृष्टि
Cite$_{(V)}$	उल्लेख करना
31. Defuse$_{(V)}$	तनाव कम करना
Diffuse$_{(V)}$	फैलाना
32. Desert$_{(V/N)}$	त्याग देना / रेगिस्तान
Dessert$_{(N)}$	Meals के बाद का sweet dish
33. Sever$_{(V)}$	काट के अलग कर देना
Severe$_{(Adj.)}$	तीव्र
Sewer$_{(N)}$	नाला
34. See$_{(V)}$	देखना
Look$_{(V/N)}$	ताकना/नजर
Stare$_{(V)}$	घूरना
Peep$_{(V)}$	झाँकना, चुपके से देखना
Glare/ Glower$_{(V/N)}$	गुस्से से देखना / गुस्से से भरी नजर
Glance$_{(V/N)}$	एक झलक देखना / एक झलक
Glimpse$_{(V/N)}$	एक झलक देखना / एक झलक
35. Light $_{(Adj./ N/V)}$	हल्का/रोशनी/प्रज्वलित करना
Burn$_{(V/N)}$	जलाना / जला हुआ भाग (फफोला)
36. Catch$_{(V/N)}$	किसी गतिशील को पकड़ना / पकड़
Hold$_{(V/N)}$	ठहरी हुई चीज को थामना / पकड़ $_{(N)}$
37. Canvass$_{(V)}$	घूम-घूम के वोट मांगना
Canvas$_{(N)}$	मोटा कपड़ा (जिससे जूते एवं टेंट बनते हैं)
38. Refuse$_{(V)}$	मना करना
Deny/Refute$_{(V)}$	खंडन करना
Decline$_{(V)}$	अस्वीकार करना/ कम होना
39. Peddle$_{(V)}$	घूम-घूम के सामान बेचना
Pedal$_{(N/V)}$	साइकिल में जिस पर पैर रख कर घुमाते है। / Pedal चलाना
40. Ride$_{(V/N)}$	दोपहिये व जानवर की सवारी करना / सैर
Drive$_{(V/N)}$	चार पहिये की सवारी करना / सैर
41. Wither$_{(V)}$	मुरझाना
Weather$_{(N)}$	दिन-प्रतिदिन का मौसम
Whether$_{(Conj.)}$	या .... या ना ('Whether ... or' Co-relative है)
Whither$_{(Adj.)}$	Where (कहाँ) [पुराने काल की अंग्रेजी भाषा में] (Obsolete English)
42. Sink$_{(V)}$	डुबना (निर्जीव का)
Drown$_{(V)}$	डुबाना
43. Cease$_{(V)}$	रूकना
Seize$_{(V)}$	जब्त करना
44. Invent$_{(V)}$	अविष्कार करना
Discover$_{(V)}$	खोज करना

See how the confused words are used in the following sentences-

1. The servant **hung** the picture on the wall
   ~~hanged~~

2. Lay your books aside and **lie** down to rest.
   ~~lay~~

3. **Practice** (Noun) makes a man perfect.

4. **Practise** (Verb) the questions given in the assignment.

5. I need your **advice** (Noun).

6. Do not **advise** (Verb) me.

7. I have lodged a **complaint** (Noun) against him.

8. He **complained** (Verb) against me.

9. Bad weather **affects** (Verb) your health and the **effect** (Noun) is cough and cold

10. Many songs are not worthlistening to.(Remove 'to')
11. He **lighted** the candle and **burnt** the papers.
12. The thief **eluded** (Verb) arrest.
13. The earth's atmosphere comprises of three layers. (In active voice, comprise is not followed by 'of')
14. Mirabai **composed** many songs.
15. I **refused** to help him.
16. The thief **denied** the charges.
17. I **declined** the offer.
18. Silence **precedes** the storm.
19. This is a good **site** for a school.
20. Please **cite** an example.

SPOTTING THE ERROR

1. (a) He was so inquisitive/ (b) that he rose many/ (c) questions in the class ./ (d) No error.
2. (a) He was borne of poor parents,/ (b) but brought up/ (c) in an affluent family./ (d) No error.
3. (a) The university was/ (b) found in 1950/ (c) when India was not self dependent in many aspects./ (d) No error.
4. (a) I complaint against him/ (b) as in spite of my repeated warnings/ (c) he failed to mend his ways./ (d) No error.
5. (a) Failure must not have/ (b) permanent affect on a person/ (c)because only the tough survive./ (d) No error.
6. (a) I keep my cool/ (b) and never loose my temper/ (c) even when provoked/ (d) No error.
7. (a) He lied on the grass/ (b) for hours/ (c) enjoying the cool breeze./ (d) No error.
8. (a) During the rainy season/ (b) many rivers overflew their banks/ (c) and caused great difficulty./ (d) No error.
9. (a) He lay his luggage/ (b) aside and lay down/ (c) to rest for a while ./ (d) No error.
10. (a) When calamity fell the village,/ (b) they faced it/ (c) bravely./ (d) No error.
11. (a) The assassin was convicted/ (b) and ordered to/ (c) be hung./ (d) No error.
12. (a) If I leave now,/ (b) I will not be able to/ (c) return back before 9 p.m./ (d) No error.
13. (a) When the company offered him a purse on his retirement/ (b) he refused to/ (c) agree it ./ (d) No error.
14. (a) The timid creature was driven/ (b) into a narrow lane/ (c) where it was slewed by the kidnapper./ (d) No error.
15. (a) Being implicated in a murder case,/ (b) he was conclusively suspected/ (c) for all the unsolved murder cases./ (d) No error.
16. (a) My brother thinks/ (b) that somebody must have dared/ (c) him steal the scooter./ (d) No error.
17. (a) When I was young,/ (b) I can run/ (c) faster than Mohan./ (d) No error.
18. (a) Harish needs not/ (b) come here/ (c) as it is getting dark./ (d) No error.
19. (a) He dare/ (b) not to/ (c) go there./ (d) No error.
20. (a) I use to/ (b) play Hockey/ (c) when I was of ten years./ (d) No error.
21. (a) A soldier/ (b) could fight/ (c) for his country and save his country's honour./ (d) No error.
22. (a) I would rather/ (b) die/ (c) then beg./ (d) No error.
23. (a) Run fast/ (b) lest you/ (c) will miss the train/ (d) No error.
24. (a) He hoped/ (b) that he will/ (c) pass the exam with flying colours./ (d) No error.
25. (a) You need to work hard/ (b) but you need not/ (c) to waste time on unimportant lessons/ (d) No error.
26. (a) She would broke/ (b) a plate every day/ (c) when she came to Delhi last month./ (d) No error.
27. (a) The old lady/ (b) prayed that he/ (c) may live long./ (d) No error.
28. (a) Rama must not to/ (b) have treated his mistress/ (c) like that./ (d) No error.

29. (a) Waste material/ (b) should be recycle/ (c) if possible/ (d) No error.
30. (a) The Government cannot/ (b) be able to contain/ (c) Encephalitis by spending just 1% of GDP on Health sector./ (d) No error.
31. (a) The police think/ (b) that he may be there/ (c) yesterday at the scene of crime./ (d) No error.
32. (a) "He may live long"/ (b) his sad mother/ (c) prayed./ (d) No error.
33. (a) He returned the purse/ (b) though he could keep/ (c) it very easily./ (d) No error.
34. (a) When you had been young/ (b) you ought to learn/ (c) good habits./ (d) No error.
35. (a) If you get good marks/ (b) I shall happy/ (c) as much as you./ (d) No error.
36. (a) We ought to/ (b) honest/ (c) in our dealings./ (d) No error.
37. (a) It is very cold here/ (b) I should bring/ (c) my woolen clothes but I didn't./ (d) No error.
38. (a) Are you/ (b) used to get/ (c) up early?/ (d) No error.
39. (a) Our knowledge of history does not come to our help/ (b) and sometimes we even fail to remember/ (c) who invented America./ (d) No error.
40. (a) I think/ (b) the news/ (c) might true./ (d) No error.
41. (a) Very soon/ (b) I realised/ (c) that he is at fault/ (d) No error.
42. (a) He remembered/ (b) that his visa/ (c) will be expired in a month/ (d) No error.
43. (a) I wasn't/ (b) at the last meeting and/ (c) neither was you/ (d) No error.
44. (a) In any case no disciplinary action/ (b) are required/ (c) to be taken/ (d) No error.
45. (a) The capital of Yemen/ (b) is situating/ (c) 2190 metres above the sea level/ (d) No error.
46. (a) Owing to the heavy rains,/ (b) the ship drowned/ (c) in the middle of the ocean./ (d) No error.
47. (a) If your jogging clothes/ (b) were not made of/ (c) permeable fabric you will drown/ (d) in your sweat.

Answers with Explanation

1. (b) 'raised' is the correct word . 'Rose' means to 'get up'
2. (a) V_3 of bear (to produce offsprings) is 'born'. V_3 of bear (to tolerate) is borne.
3. (b) use 'founded' in place of 'found'. V_3 of found (to establish) is 'founded'.
4. (a) V_2/V_3 of complain is complained. Complaint is a noun. 'Complaint' means a grievance or a problem.
5. (b) Use effect$_{(N)}$ in place of affect $_{(V)}$.
6. (b) Loose $_{(Adj)}$ is not an appropriate word here. 'Lose'$_{(V)}$ is the correct word.
7. (a) Use 'lay' in place of 'lied'.
8. (b) Overflowed is the correct word here which means ' to flow out of a particular space because it has become surplus'.
9. (a) Laid is the correct word and V_2 of 'lay'.
10. (a) 'Befell' is an appropriate word here which means 'to happen (something bad) especially as if by fate'.
11. (c) Use 'Hanged' in place of 'hung'. 'Hanged' means 'to suspend by the neck'.

12. (c) Remove 'back'. The word 'back' makes 'return' superfluous.
13. (c) Use 'accept' in place of 'agree'.
14. (c) Slain is the V_3 of 'slay'. Slewed is wrong .
15. (b) 'Conclusively' means 'putting an end to a debate, question or doubt'. The word ' Suspect' doesn't go with 'conclusively' as the sentence becomes self-contradictory.
16. (c) Add 'to' before 'steal'.
17. (b) Use could (past) as the sentence is in past tense.
18. (a) Use 'need' in place of 'needs'. 'Need' is a modal here and not a main verb.
19. (b) 'dare not' is followed by 'go' and not 'to go'.
20. (a) Use 'I used to' in place of 'I use to'. 'Used to' expresses past routine action.
21. (b) Use 'must' or 'ought to' in place of 'could'.
22. (c) Use 'than' in place of 'then'
23. (c) Use 'should' in place of 'will'. 'Lest' is followed by 'should'.
24. (b) Use would (past) as the sentence is in past tense.
25. (c) 'Need not' is followed by 'V_1'. Hence remove 'to'.
26. (a) V_1 is used after all the modals . Use 'break' in place of 'broke'.
27. (c) Use 'might' (past) in place of 'may' (present) as the sentence is in past.
28. (a) Remove 'to' as the sentence must be in the formula 'must + not + have + V_3 '
29. (b) 'Should be" is followed by 'V_3' . 'Recycled' is the appropriate word.
30. (b) 'Cannot' shows ability, remove 'be able to'. If we use both 'able to' and 'can' together in a sentence, the sentence becomes superfluous.
31. (b) Change 'may' into 'might' (past). 'Yesterday' denotes 'past time'. Hence past form of 'may' must be used.
32. (a) 'May he live long' is right. In an optative sentence, 'May' comes at the starting of the sentence.
33. (b) Change 'could keep' to 'could have kept'. From the sentence we understand that the hidden meaning is - 'he did not keep the purse'.
34. (b) 'Ought to learn' should be changed to 'ought to have learnt'. From the sentence we understand that the hidden meaning is - 'he did not learn good habits'.
35. (b) Add main verb 'be' after 'shall'. A modal must be followed by a main verb.
36. (a) Add 'be' after 'ought to'. A modal must be followed by a main verb.
37. (b) Use 'should have brought'. From the sentence we understand that the hidden meaning is - 'he did not bring'.
38. (b) Change 'get' into getting' (Here 'used to' denoted a habitual action)
39. (c) Change 'invented' into ' discovered' as 'to invent' means 'to make something new that was not there before that time. 'To discover' means 'to find out something for the first time which was not in the knowledge of the people'.
40. (c) Use 'be' after 'might'
41. (c) Change 'is' into 'was'.
42. (c) Change 'will be expired' into 'would expire'.
43. (c) Change 'was into 'were'. 'You' takes 'were' and not 'was'.
44. (b) Change 'are' into 'is' because the subject "disciplinary action" is singular.
45. (b) Change 'situating' to 'situated'.
46. (b) Use sank (V_2), in place of 'drowned'. 'Sink' comes for non-living things.
47. (c) Change 'will' into 'would' as the sentence is in past tense.

CHAPTER 2

TENSE

Tense denotes the time of action/ state as well as the action/state.

TENSE

1. Present | **2. Past** | **3. Future**

Sub-Division:- **• Simple/ Indefinite • Continuous • Perfect • Perfect Continuous**

<u>Note:</u> Questions are often based on confusing pairs as well as the structure.

SIMPLE PRESENT TENSE

➢ It uses Verb 'is/ am/ are'. It describes one's identity or quality in the Present.

Structure:

+ ve → Sub + is/ am/ are + Noun/ Adjective.

– ve → Sub + is not (isn't)/ am not / are not (aren't) + Noun/ Adjective.

Ques → Is/ am/ are + sub + Noun/ Adjective?

Is → he, she, it, name, singular., **Am** → I, **Are** → You, we, they, plural

E.g.: I *am* a teacher.

She *is* not my aunt.

Are you in Delhi?

➢ Under this Tense, we include the following activities:

(1) **<u>Routine Action:</u>** **Regular Action** – I come here daily.

Irregular Action – Earthquake comes in Japan.

Habits – He smokes.

Universal Truth – The Sun rises in the east.

(2) **<u>Note:</u>** In **newspaper headlines** and **commentary of sports**, Present Indefinite Tense is used.

E.g.: (1) PM signs deal.

(2) Virat strikes the ball and off it goes across the boundary lines.

(3) Present Indefinite Tense is used to express planned action of near future.

E.g.: PM leaves for China next week.

Note: In Newspaper headlines, we avoid using Article and Helping Verbs.

Structure: **+ ve →** **Sub + V_1 + obj. (If the Sub is I, we, they, you or plural)**

- ve → **Sub + do not (don't) + V_1 + obj.**

Ques → **Do + Sub + V_1 + obj?**

Do + Sub + not+ V_1 + obj?

Don't + Sub + V_1 + obj?

+ ve → **Sub + V_1 + s/es + obj. (If sub is he, she, it, name or singular)**

- ve → **Sub + does not (doesn't) + V_1 + obj.**

Ques → **Does + Sub + V_1 + obj?**

Does + Sub + not+ V_1 + obj?

Doesn't + Sub + V_1 + obj?

➢ **Correct the following sentences:**

(1) What he **knows** about you? (×)

What **does he know** about you ? (✓)

(2) I do not know what he knows about you. (✓)

(3) The **appeal** of the victims to transfer the cases related to riots to some other states do not affect the merit of the case. (Change 'do' into 'does' as the main subject is 'appeal')

Explanation of sentences 1 & 2: In the 1st statement **'what'** is being used to raise a question. Hence interrogative form should be used after **'what'**. In the 2nd sentence **'what'** is joining two sentences hence a normal affirmative sentence should follow 'what'.

Sentence 3: [Explanation] : A verb should always agree with the main subject of the sentence. We often relate the verb with the nearest subject but this is wrong.

E.g.: The **quality** of apples **is** good.

SIMPLE PAST TENSE

➢ Verb 'was/ were' is used in this. It describes one's identity or quality of the past.

E.g.: I *was* a teacher.

She *was* not my aunt.

Were you in Delhi?

Structure:

+ ve → **Sub + was/ were + Noun/ Adjective**

– ve → **Sub + was not (wasn't) / were not (weren't) + Noun/ Adjective**

Ques → **Was / Were + Subject + Noun/ Adjective.?**

Was → I, he, she, it, name, singular. **Were** → You, we, they, plural.

- An action that is over is expressed in this Tense.

E.g.: 1. I saw you but you did not see me.

2. I meant to repair the radio but hadn't time to do it today.
(1) No error (2) to do it today. (3) I meant to repair the radio
(4) but hadn't time **(SSC CGL Tier-II Exam, 25.10.2015, TF No. 2148789)**

Ans. (4) Replace 'hadn't' with 'didn't have'.

Structure: **+ ve →** **Sub + V_2 + obj**

– ve → **Sub + did not (didn't) + V_1 + obj**

Ques → **Did + Sub + V_1 + obj ?**

Did + Sub + not + V_1 + obj ?

Didn't + sub + V_1 + obj ?

Note: If the sentence starts with **'It's time'**, **'It's high time'** or **'It's about time'** and if it is followed by a subject, the verb that will follow the subject will be in **second form (V_2)**.

E.g.: It's time you should study. (×)

1. It's time you studied (V2). (✓)

2. It's time (high time) you were (~~Was~~) at home. (✓)

- If 'It's time' is followed by 'to', '$V_{b.f}$' will be used.

E.g.: It's time to study.

Note: (1) I come here daily. (+ve)

I do not come here daily. (-ve)

You do come (V_1) here everyday. (✓)

- Use do/does + M.V (V_1) if the sentence is in Present Tense and the emphasis is on M.V.

(2) You made a mistake. (+ve)

You did not make a mistake. (-ve)

He did make (V_1) a mistake. (✓)

- Use did + M.V (V_1) if the sentence is in Past Tense and the emphasis is on M.V.

- Usually in a sentence, **'do', 'does' and 'did'** are **not used** in **positive sentences as a helping verb** but to **emphasise the main verb**, we **use 'do', 'does' and 'did' before the main verb**. In such sentences **main verb** should be in **'v_1' form**.

E.g.: (1) You **do** $\underbrace{\textbf{come}}_{V_1}$ here everyday. (✓)

(2) He **did** $\underbrace{\textbf{make}}_{V_1}$ a mistake. (✓)

- If past time is given in a sentence, the sentence must be in Past Indefinite Tense and never is Present Perfect Tense.

  E.g.: (1) I have come yesterday. (×)

  (2) I came yesterday. (✓)

SIMPLE FUTURE TENSE:

- In this, Verb 'will be/ shall be' gives an impression of one's identity or quality in the future. It describes a future identity, class or quality.

  E.g.: I *shall be* a teacher.

  She *will* not *be* my wife.

  Will you *be* in Delhi?

  Structure: **+ ve →** **Sub + shall/ will + be + Noun/ Adjective.**

  – ve → **Sub + shall/ will + not + be + Noun/ Adjective.**

  Ques → **Shall/ will + sub + be + Noun/ Adjective?**

- An action **to take place in future** comes under this **Tense**.

  E.g.: I shall meet you.

- For planned action of near future, use **Present Indefinite Tense**.

  E.g.: The train departs at 8 p.m. tonight.

  Structure: **+ ve →** **Sub + shall/ will + $V_{b.f}$ + obj**

  -ve → **Sub + shall/ will + not + $V_{b.f}$ + obj**

  Sub + shan't/ won't + $V_{b.f}$ + obj

  Ques → **Shall/will + sub + $V_{b.f}$ + obj ?**

  Shall/ will + sub + not + V_1 + obj ?

  Shan't/ won't + sub + $V_{b.f}$ + obj ?

Note: Use of shall / will is explained in Modals.

PRESENT CONTINUOUS TENSE:

- An action that is **going on at the time of speaking** comes in **Present Continuous Tense.**

  E.g.: I am studying English now.

- Sometimes some events are going on even at the time of speaking but we cannot see them, they too come in **Present Continuous Tense.**

  E.g.: (1) Coastal areas are getting submerged.

  (2) Population is increasing day by day.

Note: For officially planned action of near future, **Present Continuous Tense** is used.
The PM leaves/ will leave/ is leaving for Japan tonight.
For **Unofficial planned action of near future, do not use Present Indefinite Tense.**
E.g.: I am going to Mumbai tomorrow.

Structure: **+ ve →** **Sub + is/ am/ are + v_1 + ing+ obj**
- ve → **Sub + is/ are/ am/ + not + v_1 + ing+ obj**
Sub + isn't/ aren't/ am not + v_1 + ing+ obj
Ques → **Is/ am/ are + S + v_1 + ing+ obj?**
Is/ am/ are + S + not + v_1 + ing+ obj?
Isn't/ aren't + S + v_1 + ing+ obj?

➢ 'Am not' has **no contracted form**. In question tag **aren't** is used.
E.g.: I am fine, **aren't I** ?

➢ **Use of is / am / are**
- **Is – he/she/it/name/singular**
- **Am – I**
- **Are – you/we/they/all/plural**

Note: My father is working in a bank and my brother is studying in a school. (×)
My father works in a bank and my brother studies in a school. (✓)

➢ If the statement deals with a routine action, **Present Indefinite Tense** is used and not Present Continuous Tense but if the action is just a temporary routine action, Present Continuous Tense is used.
E.g.: I am preparing for competitive exams nowadays.

PAST CONTINUOUS TENSE:

➢ If an action was in continuation in the past, **Past Continuous Tense** is used.
E.g.: I was waiting for you.

Structure: **+ ve →** **Sub + was/were + V_1 + ing + obj**
- Ve → **Sub + was/were + not + V_1 + ing + obj**
Sub + wasn't/weren't + V_1 + ing + obj
Ques → **Was/were + Sub + V_1 + ing + obj?**
Was/were + Sub + not+ V_1 + ing + obj?
Wasn't/weren't + Sub + V_1 + ing + obj?

➢ **Use of was and were.** **Was → He / she / it / name / singular/ I**
Were → You / we / they / plural / all

➢ In **imaginary sentence**, **'were'** is used with all subjects no matter whether it is used as a helping verb or main verb.

E.g.: 1. I wish, I **were** (M.V.) a bird.

2. He walks as if he **were** (H.V.) the king of the whole world.

FUTURE CONTINUOUS TENSE:

➢ An action going on in future comes under **Future Continuous Tense.**

E.g: We shall be taking the examination at this time, next month.

Structure: + ve → **Sub + shall/ will + be + V_1 + ing + obj**
– ve → **Sub + shall/ will + not + be + V_1 + ing + obj**
Sub + shan't/ won't + be + V_1 + ing + obj
Ques → **Will/shall + Sub + be+V_1 + ing + obj?**
Will/shall + Sub + not+ be+ V_1 + ing + obj?
Won't/shan't + Sub +be+ V_1 + ing + obj?

Note: **Some verbs do not take 'ing' form**. Hence they cannot come in continuous tense.

➢ **List of such verbs:**

(1) Verbs of Perception- See, taste, smell, hear, notice, recognize.
(2) Verbs of Thinking Process- Think, know, mean, mind, remember, suppose.
(3) Verbs Showing Possession- Own, have, belong, comprise, possess, contain, consist.
(4) Verbs expressing Feelings or State of Mind- Believe, like, dislike, love, adore, want, wish, desire, hate, agree, trust, imagine, prefer, please
(5) Verbs in General- Look, seem, appear, affect, resemble, cost, require, become, hope, refuse, exist

E.g: 1. He is owning a car. (×)
He owns a car. (✓)
2. This house is belonging to me. (×)
This house belongs to me. (✓)
3. I am not meaning anything wrong. (×)
I don't mean anything wrong. (✓)
4. I am seeing a man standing there. (×)
I see a man standing there. (✓)

Note: If '**have**' denotes '**possession**', it is **not used in 'ing' form** but if '**have**' denotes '**to have fun or to eat**', 'have' **can be used in 'ing' form.**

E.g.: I am having a piece of cake. (✓)
I am having a car. (×)
I have a car. (✓)

➢ If **think, remember, feel, look, appear** etc are used to **express emotions** or the verbs given above are used in **progressive state**, they can come in 'ing' form.

E.g.: 1. I am thinking you are right. (×)
I think you are right. (✓)
2. I am thinking of you. (✓)
3. It was appearing as if they were going to kill us. (×)
It appeared as if they were going to kill us.(✓)
4. You are looking good. (✓)
5. Look ! He is smelling the rose. (✓)

- **In 'Gerund' (V_1 + ing) & 'Present Participle' (V_1 + ing), verbs are used in 'ing' form.**

  E.g.: (1) Being ill, I could not come.
  (2) Getting a job is easy now-a-days.
  (3) Seeing (Sub.) is (V) believing (Obj.).
  (4) Swimming (Sub.) is (V) a good exercise.

Note: See verb (Advance) for detailed explanation.

- If we use a **verb after a preposition**, the **verb will be in 'ing' form.**

  E.g.: (1) Bats are capable of (Prep.) hearing (V_1+ing (Gerund)) the ultrasonic waves.
  (2) He is addicted to (Prep.) drinking (V_1+ing (Gerund)).

PRESENT PERFECT TENSE:

- An action that has **recently finished** is expressed in **Present Perfect Tense.**
  E.g.: He has come to Delhi recently.
- If the action is important and not the time of action, and the time of action is not given, we use **Present Perfect Tense**.
  E.g.: We have progressed a lot.
  We have reached the moon.

Structure: **+ ve →** **Sub + has/ have + V_3 + obj**
- Ve → **Sub + has/ have + not + V_3 + obj**
Sub + hasn't/ haven't + V_3 + obj
Ques → **Has/ have + Sub + V_3 + obj ?**
Has/ have + Sub +not+ V_3 + obj ?
Hasn't/ haven't + Sub + V_3 + obj ?

- **Use of Has / Have:**
  has - With **He/ She/ It/ Name/Singular**
  have- With **I/ We/ They/ You/ Plural/ All**

See the difference:

1. Science has given us many new inventions. (✓)
2. We have reached the moon. (✓)
1. Science has given us many new inventions in the 19th century. (×)
2. We have reached the moon on 22nd Oct, 2008. (×)

- If **past time is given, use Past Indefinite Tense** and not Present Perfect Tense.

The correct sentences will be:

1. Science gave us many life saving drugs in the 19th century.(✓)
2. We reached the moon on 22nd Oct, 2008. (✓)

Note: 1. In a sentence, **any form of 'have'** can be followed by **'had'** (Here 'had' will be the Main Verb). This is because in Perfect Tense , such combinations are used.

E.g.: 1. I **have had** enough problems here. (✓)

2. He **has had** his breakfast. (✓)

2. **'Usually', 'recently', 'already', yet', 'so far'** are used in **Perfect Tense**. **'Yet'** is generally used in **negative sentences** of **Present Perfect**.

E.g.: He has not reached home **yet.** (Present Perfect)

He had not done any work **so far.** (Past Perfect)

3. If **'since'** is **followed by 'Past Indefinite Tense'** , **'since'** is **preceded by 'Present Perfect Tense'**.

E.g.: I haven't seen him (Present perfect) **since** he left India (Past Indefinite).

Note: In such sentences **the perfect form of any modal** can also be used.

E.g.: He may have grown old (Modal in perfect form) **since** she last saw him (Past Indefinite).

➢ If **since** is used at the beginning of a sentence, the formation of the sentence will be as follows-

E.g.: **Since** he joined the army (Past Indefinite), he has not taken any leave (Present perfect).

PAST PERFECT TENSE

➢ Look at the sentences given below:

1. I saw him **before** he stopped his car. (×)
   I had seen him **before** he stopped his car. (✓)
2. **Before** he understood anything the robber fled. (×)
   Before he understood anything the robber had fled. (✓)
3. I met him **after** I finished my work. (×)
   I met him **after** I had finished my work. (✓)
4. **By the time** I reached the theatre, the show started. (×)
   By the time I reached the theatre, the show had started. (✓)
5. When Anand reached his village, he found that the news about him had preceded him. (✓)
6. He lost the bicycle (2nd action = Past Indefinite) which his father had gifted him (1st = Past Perfect).

   See the sentence and the different structures in which it can be written.

   1. The student had come (1st = Present Perfect) before the teacher arrived (2nd = Past Indefinite).
   2. Before the teacher arrived, the students had come.
   3. The teacher arrived after the students had come.
   4. By the time the teacher arrived the students had come.
   5. The student had come before the teacher arrived.

➢ If **two actions take place in the past, one after the other**, the **1st action** will be in **Past Perfect Tense** and the **2nd action** will be in **Past Indefinite Tense**.

Structure: **+ ve →** **Sub + had + V_3 + obj**

- Ve → **Sub + had + not (hadn't) + V_3 + obj**

Ques → **Had + sub + V_3 + obj ?**

Had + sub +not + V_3 + obj ?

Hadn't + sub + V_3 + obj ?

Note: See the 5th sentence .

When Anand reached his village, he found that the news about him had preceded him.

EXPLANATION

➢ **'Precede'** means **'to come before'** . The **1st action** is 'the coming of the news' which must be in **Past Perfect Tense** and the **2nd action** is 'Anand going to the village' which must be in **Past Indefinite Tense**.

FUTURE PERFECT TENSE

➢ An action that will have been completed in future, comes under **Future Perfect Tense.**

E.g.: You will have finished your syllabus by the end of next month.

Note: **Look at the following sentences:**

E.g.: By the time (**By the time,**) I reach the station, (Present Indefinite) the train will have left. (Future Perfect)

➢ By the time, **Present Indefinite, Future Perfect**

Structure: **+ ve →** **Sub + will/shall + have + V_3 + obj**

- Ve → **Sub + will/shall + not + have + V_3 + obj**

Sub + won't/shan't + have + V_3 + obj

Ques → **Will/shall + Sub + have+ V_3 + obj ?**

Will/shall + Sub + not + have + V_3 + obj ?

Won't/shan't + Sub +have + V_3 + obj ?

Look at the difference:

1. **By the time** I reach the station, (Present Indefinite) the train will have left. (Future Perfect)

2. **By the time** I reached the station (Past Indefinite), the train had left. (Past Perfect)

PRESENT PERFECT CONTINUOUS TENSE:

➢ An action that has **already started** and **still going on** comes under **Present Perfect Continuous Tense.**

E.g.: I have been living in Delhi for five years.

Structure:

+ Ve → **Sub + has/ have + been + V_1 + ing + obj+ for/ since + time.**

- Ve → **Sub + has/ have + not + been + V_1 + ing + obj+ for/ since + time.**

Sub + hasn't/ haven't + been + V_1 + ing + obj+ for/ since + time.

Ques → **Has/ have + Sub + + been + V_1+ ing + obj + for/ since + time?**

Has/have + Sub +not+ been + V_1+ing + obj + for/since +time?

Hasn't/ haven't + Sub + been + V_1 + ing + obj + for/ since + time?

E.g.: I am teaching you since an hour. (×)

I have been teaching you for an hour. (✓)

- **For:** is used for a **period of time.**

  E.g.: For two hours, for last 2 years.

  For five years, for last 2 months.

  For 10 years, for last 3 weeks.

- **Since:** is used for a **point of time.**

  E.g.: Since Monday, since the beginning.

  Since 2008, since time immemorial.

  Since 7 pm, since last year.

Since
- **Calendar**
  - **Days** → Monday, Tuesday etc.
  - **Dates** → 7th May, 8th July etc.
  - **Years** → 2005, 2007 etc.
  - **Months** → May, June etc.
  - **Occasions** → Holi, Diwali etc.
- **Clock** → 7 o' clock, 8 p.m etc.
- **Stages of life** → Childhood, adolescence etc.
- **Part of each day** → Morning, last night, noon etc.

PAST PERFECT CONTINUOUS TENSE:

- An activity that started in the past, continued and finished in past comes under **Past Perfect Continuous Tense.**

  E.g.: I had been waiting for you since morning.

Structure:

+ ve → **Sub + had + been + V_1 + ing + obj + for/ since + time.**

-Ve → **Sub + had + not (hadn't) + been + V_1 + ing + obj + for/ since + time.**

Ques → **Had + sub + been + V_1 + ing + obj + for/ since + time ?**

Had + sub + not+ been + V_1 + ing + obj + for/ since + time ?

Hadn't + sub + been + V_1 + ing + obj + for/ since + time ?

FUTURE PERFECT CONTINUOUS TENSE:

➢ An action that **continues up to some future point of time** comes under **Future Perfect Continuous.**

E.g.: (1) I shall have been living in Delhi for five years by the end of this year.
(2) I shall reach my village tomorrow in the evening but my mother will have been waiting for me from morning.

Structure:

+ Ve → **Sub + shall/will + have + been + V_1 +ing + obj +for/ from+time**

- Ve → **Sub + shall/will + not + have + been + V_1 + ing + obj + for/from + time**
Sub + shan't/won't + have + been + V_1 + ing + obj + for/ from + time

Ques → **Will/shall+sub + have + been + V_1 + ing + obj + for/ from+time?**
Will/shall + sub + not + have + been + V_1 + ing + obj + for/from + time ?
Won't/shan't + sub + have + been + V_1 + ing + obj + for/ from + time ?

Note: Verbs that are not used in 'ing' form are not used in 'Continuous / Perfect Continuous Tense'.

➢ Such verbs should be used in **Indefinite Tense** instead of **Continuous Tense.**
E.g.: I am knowing you. (×)
I know you. (✓)

➢ Such verbs should be used in **Perfect Tense** instead of **Perfect Continuous tense.**
E.g.: I have been knowing him for five years. (×)
I have known him for five years.(✓)

➢ **For/since** is **used in both Perfect & Perfect Continuous Tense.**
E.g.: I have been living in Delhi for five years. (✓)
I had known him for two years. (✓)

➢ If **'for/since + time'** is used in a sentence, the sentence will be in **Perfect** or **Perfect Continuous Tense.**
E.g.: I ate nothing since morning. (×)
I have eaten nothing since morning. (✓)

➢ **'For'** is used in Indefinite Tense too.
E.g.: (i) I study for six hours daily.
(ii) I lived in Mumbai for two years.

SPOTTING THE ERROR

1. (a) I have not seen him since twenty years/ (b) and so I cannot say with certainty/ (c) whether he is alive or dead./ (d) No error
2. (a) When he did not find his cook in the kitchen/ (b) he asked his wife/ (c) where had he gone./ (d) No error
3. (a) Although I am playing cricket/ (b) for more than three years/ (c) I have not been able to score a century/ (d) No error
4. (a) I do not know where could he have gone/ (b) so early/ (c) in the morning./ (d) No error

5. (a) By the time/ (b) we got our tickets and entered the cinema theatre,/ (c) the show was already begun./ (d) No error
6. (a) By the time/ (b) we will get our tickets and enter the cinema theatre,/ (c) the show will have already begun./ (d) No error
7. (a) Gowri told me/ (b) his name after/ (c) he left./ (d) No error
8. (a) We have been/ (b) celebrating many festivals/ (c) since centuries./ (d) No error
9. (a) Old age and infirmity/ (b) had began to/ (c) catch up with him./ (d) No error
10. (a) The passer-by told us/ (b) where was the marriage hall/ (c) and even led us to it./ (d) No error
11. (a) I have passed / (b) the examination/ (c) two years ago./ (d) No error
12. (a) Since he joined/ (b) this post, he did not take/ (c) any bribe./ (d) No error
13. (a) Perhaps you know/ (b) that I have passed/ (c) the examination in 1990./ (d) No error
14. (a) He has read four plays/ (b) written by Shakespeare/ (c) by the end of his vacation./ (d) No error
15. (a) When they stole / (b) the money/ (c) and where did they hide it?/ (d) No error
16. (a) The teacher/ (b) has took/ (c) the responsibility./ (d) No error.
17. (a) For time immemorial/ (b) sea shells have been used by man/ (c) in many ways./ (d) No error
18. (a) The river is in spate/ (b) and it has overflown/ (c) its banks./ (d) No error
19. (a) The little boy/ (b) had been waiting for his turn/ (c) since a long time./ (d) No error
20. (a) This T.V. serial/ (b) is going on/ (c) for 3 years./ (d) No error
21. (a) In the early years of the renaissance of Bharatanatyam, hereditary dancers have their own set of accompanists/ (b) who lived with the dancers and travelled with them from place to place/ (c) when they gave performances./ (d) No error
22. (a) This is turned out to be/ (b) one of our most successful projects/ (c) and we have made quite/ (d) a large profit from it./ (e) No error
23. (a) He is given me/ (b) a lot of documents/ (c) to read before/ (d) the presentation tomorrow./ (e) No error
24. (a) Since the trip home/ (b) was expensive I/ (c) did not went home/ (d) during the holidays./ (e) No error
25. (a) As she is late/ (b) for work yesterday she decided/ (c) to skip breakfast and/ (d) leave for office./ (e) No error
26. (a) As soon as the CEO entered the office, the/ (b) union leaders approached him/ (c) and report the matter to him./ (d) No error
27. (a) The college/ (b) is running a computer course/ (c) since 2007./ (d) No error
28. (a) Did he tell you/ (b) why he hasn't/ (c) come yesterday?/ (d) No error
29. (a) Last night I dream/ (b) I was a Sheikh on the 169th floor/ (c) of Burj Khalifa./ (d) No error
30. (a) She and her sister/ (b) were working here/ (c) since 1983./ (d) No error
31. (a) Nobody saw him/ (b) since the fire broke/ (c) in his locality./ (d) No error
32. (a) By this time next year/ (b) Ramesh will take/ (c) his degree./ (d) No error
33. (a) The families/ (b) are living in Gulmohar Park/ (c) for the last two decades./ (d) No error

34. (a) My uncle/ (b) has left/ (c) for Bombay last Saturday./ (d) No error
35. (a) Good heavens !/ (b) How has she/ (c) grown !/ (d) No error
36. (a) I ate/ (b) nothing/ (c) since morning./ (d) No error
37. (a) He/ (b) is having/ (c) many friends here/ (d) No error
38. (a) When I went there/ (b) Charles is playing/ (c) a game of chess/ (d) No error
39. (a) The vaccine/ (b) when hit the market/ (c) is dogged by controversy/ (d) No error
40. (a) The victim tried to tell us/ (b) what has happened but/ (c) his voice was not audible./ (d) No error
41. (a) Our history can be seen as a long evolutionary dialectical development/(b) in which there have been/ (c) a painstaking forging of rational and moral self./(d) No error
42. (a) Last year two Italian prisoners of war/ (b) escapes from a prison camp/ (c) in Kenya during the war./ (d) No error
43. (a) Madhuri Dixit/ (b) is having/ (c) a large fan following./ (d) No error
44. (a) No one heard anything/ (b) about him since/ (c) he left India for good./ (d) No error
45. (a) Before the teacher/ (b) could finish the question/ (c) the students gave the correct answer./ (d) No error
46. (a) She did not prepare/ (b) her/ (c) breakfast yet./ (d) No error
47. (a) Perhaps you do not know/ (b) I am owning/ (c) a farm house besides two bungalows./ (d) No error
48. (a) When Anand reached his village/ (b) he found that / (c) the news about him preceded him./ (d) No error
49. (a) She will already return/ (b) home/ (c) when he arrives./ (d) No error
50. (a) Each one of them/ (b) has have his share/ (c) of joy and sorrow./ (d) No error
51. (a) This custom/ (b) has come down/ (c) since times immemorial./ (d) No error
52. (a) Since his arrival in India,/ (b) he is visiting as many villages as he can/ (c) to acquire a firsthand knowledge of rural India./ (d) No error.
53. (a) Believe me, I/ (b) am believing/ (c) whatever you have said./ (d) No error.
54. (a) It is time/ (b) we should have done/ (c) something useful/ (d) No error.
55. (a) Mother said,/ (b) "Son,/ (c) you have finished your homework?"/ (d) No error.
56. (a) I am going to buy/ (b) a computer/ (c) when the prices comes down./ (d) No error.
57. (a) I wish/ (b) I have learnt swimming/ (c) when I was young./ (d) No error.

Answers with explanation

1. (a) 'Twenty years' is a period of time. Hence 'for' should be used in place of 'since'.
2. (c) 'Helping verb' comes before the 'subject' in an interrogative sentence. Since this sentence is not an interrogative sentence, 'had' will come after 'he'.
3. (a) 'Am' should be changed into 'have been'. The sentence is in Perfect Continuous Tense.
4. (a)'Could' will come after 'he', since the sentence is not interrogative .
5. (c) Use 'had' in place of 'was'. If two actions take place in the past one after the other, the first action will be in Past Perfect Tense and the second action will be in Past Indefinite Tense.

6. (b) Remove 'will'. 'We get our tickets' is correct. If in a sentence two actions will have taken place one after the other in future, the first action will be in Present Indefinite Tense and the second will be in Future Perfect Tense.
7. (c) 'He had left' is the correct formation.

$\underbrace{\text{Simple Past}}_{2^{nd}\text{ Action}}$ after $\underbrace{\text{Past Perfect}}_{1^{st}\text{ Action}}$

8. (c) Use 'for' in place of 'since' because 'centuries' is a period of time.
9. (b) Use V_3 (begun) with 'had'.
10. (b) 'Was' will come after 'marriage hall' because sentence is assertive and not interrogative.
11. (a) 'I passed' (simple past) is the correct form. When a past time is mentioned, we use Past Indefinite Tense and not Present Perfect Tense.
12. (b) Use 'he has not taken' in place of 'he did not take'.

Since $\underbrace{S + V_2}_{\text{S.Past}}$ $\underbrace{S + has + V_3}_{\text{Pres.Perf.}}$ (See the last point of Present Perfect Tense.)

13. (b) 'I passed' is the correct formation. (See the explanation of question 11).
14. (a) Use 'He will have read, in place of 'he has read'. An action to be completed at certain future point of time will be in Future Perfect Tense.
15. (a) Use 'when did they steal' in place of when 'they stole' as the sentence is in interrogative form.
16. (b) Use V_3 (taken) with 'has'.
17. (a) 'Time immemorial' denotes 'point of time' and not 'period of time'. Use 'since' in place of 'for'.
18. (b) V_3 of 'overflow' is 'overflowed'.
19. (c) Use 'for' in place of 'since' because 'a long time' is a period of time.
20. (b) Use 'has been going' in place of 'is going'. The sentence is in Present Perfect Continuous Tense.
21. (a) 'early years of renaissance' shows that the sentence depicts some past time. Hence 'had' will replace 'have'.
22. (a) Change 'this is turned out' into 'this has turned out' as the sentence is of Present Perfect Tense.
23. (a) 'He has given me' should come in place of 'He is given me'.
24. (c) 'did not' is followed by 'V_1'. Use 'go' in place of 'went'.
25. (a) 'Yesterday' depicts past time. Change 'is' into 'was'.
26. (c) Change 'report' into 'reported' as the whole sentence is in past tense.
27. (b) Change 'is running' into 'has been running'. The sentence is of Present Perfect Continuous Tense.
28. (b) Change 'He hasn't into 'He hadn't'. (See the explanation of question 11).
29. (a) Last night depicts past time. Hence use V_2 of dream i.e 'dreamt' in place of 'dream' .
30. (b) Use 'had been' in place of 'were'. The sentence must be in Past Perfect Continuous Tense as 'since 1983 ' has been used in the sentence .

31. (a) 'Past Indefinite Tense' is used after 'since' if 'Present Perfect' comes before 'since'. 'Nobody has seen him' must come in place of 'nobody saw him' .
32. (b) Use 'Ramesh will have taken' in place of 'Ramesh will take'. (See the explanation of question 14).
33. (b) Use 'have been' in place of 'are'.
34. (b) Use 'left' in place of ' has left'.(See the explanation of question 11).
35. (b) Use 'she has' in place of 'has she' since the sentence is not a question.
36. (a) 'Since/for + time' can be used in Perfect / Perfect Continuous Tense only. Hence change 'I ate' into 'I have eaten'.
37. (b) Change 'is having' into 'has'. If 'have' means 'to possess', it cannot be used in 'ing' form.
38. (b) Use 'was' in place of 'is'. 'When I went there' depicts that the sentence is in past.
39. (c) 'Vaccine when hit' depicts that the sentence is in past. Change 'is into 'was'.
40. (b) Use 'had' in place of 'has'. Here an experience is being narrated by the victim. Hence the incident that took place before the subject became a victim must be in Past Perfect Tense.
41. (b) 'A painstaking forging' is singular. Hence 'has' will replace 'have'.
42. (b) Use 'escaped' in place of 'escape'.
43. (b) Use 'has' in place of 'is having'.(See the explanation of question 37).
44. (a) Use 'no one has heard' in place of 'no one heard. (See the explanation of question 12).
45. (c) Use 'the students had given' in place of 'the students gave'.

    Before $\underbrace{\text{Simple Past}}_{2^{nd}\text{ Action}}$, $\underbrace{\text{Past Perfect}}_{1^{st}\text{ Action}}$ (Past Perfect)

46. (a) Use 'she has not prepared' in place of 'she did not prepare' . 'Yet' is generally used in Present Perfect negative Tense.
47. (b) Change 'I am owning' into 'I own'.
48. (c) 'Preceded' will be replaced by 'had preceded'.
49. (a) 'Will have already returned' will replace 'she will already return'. (See the explanation of question 6).
50. (b) 'V_3' (had) will come after 'has'.
51. (c) 'time' will replace 'times'.
52. (b) 'has been' will come in place of 'is'.
53. (b) Change 'am believing' into 'believe'. 'Believe' is not used in 'ing' form.
54. (b) Change 'we should have done' into 'we did'.
55. (c) Change 'you have' into 'have you' since the sentence is interrogative.
56. (c) Use 'prices comes' will be changed to 'price comes'.
57. (b) The sentence is in past. Hence change 'have' into 'had'.

3 PASSIVE VOICE

CHAPTER

- Those forms of verb that show the '**subject doing an action**' or '**an action done on the subject**' is called voice.

Active Voice:

In active voice, the verb expresses **the action of the subject upon the object**.

General structure : **Sub + verb + obj**

Passive Voice:

In passive voice, the verb expresses **the object being acted upon**.

General structure : **Obj + Helping Verb (According to Tense) + V_3 + by + sub**

- **Passive Voice is used in the following cases:**

1. **When the subject cannot do an action.**

E.g.: Tea grows both in Assam and Ceylon. (×)
Tea is grown both in Assam and Ceylon. (✓)

2. **When the action is important and not the doer although the doer is quite known.**

E.g.: He was rushed to the hospital where he was declared brought dead.

- In the above sentence the action is more important. The people and doctor involved in the process are irrelevant.

3. **When the subject or the doer of the action is either unknown or irrelevant.**

E.g.: People were relocated from the flood affected villages.

Different Tense in Active Voice and Passive Voice:-

Indefinite Tense	**Active**	**Passive**
Present Indefinite	Sub + V_1 + obj	Obj + is/am/are + V_3 + by + sub.
Past Indefinite	Sub + V_2 + obj	Obj + was/were + V_3 + by + sub.
Future Indefinite	Sub + shall/will + $V_{b.f}$+ obj	Obj + shall/will + be+ V_3 + by + sub.
Modal (Indefinite)	Sub + modal + $V_{b.f}$ + obj	Obj + modal + be+ V_3 + by + sub.

Change the voice

	Active	Passive
E.g.	1. Police arrested him.	1. He was arrested.
	2. People speak English all over the world.	2. English is spoken all over the world.
	3. A teacher teaches English here.	3. English is taught here.
	4. No one desire riots.	4. Riots are not desired.
	5. I will not tolerate this nonsense.	5. This nonsense will not be tolerated by me.

EXPLANATION OF SENTENCES 1, 2 & 3:

- Certain actions are done by a particular subject only. In such cases 'by sub' must not be mentioned in the passive voice (See sentences 1 and 3). And if the sentence is given in Passive Voice without 'by subject', use that subject in active voice that generally does that work.

E.g.- The room was cleaned.

The cleaner cleaned the room.

- If the subject is not clear (Vague noun / indefinite pronoun),the agent (by + subject) need not be mentioned in passive voice . (See sentences 2 & 4).
- If any form of 'be' is used as main verb, the sentence cannot be turned into passive.

E.g.: 1. I am (m.v.) happy. (A.V)

2. He was (m.v.) sad. (A.V)

- The above sentences cannot be converted into Passive Voice.

CONTINUOUS TENSE

Continuous Tense	Active	Passive
Present Continuous	Sub + is/ am/ are/ V_1 + ing + obj	Obj + is/am/are + being + V_3 + by + sub
Past Continuous	Sub + was / were + V_1 + ing + obj	Obj + was/were + being + V_3 + by + sub
Future Continuous	Sub + shall/will + be + V_1 + ing + obj	Passive voice not possible
Modal Continuous	Sub + modal + be + V_1 + ing + obj	Passive voice not possible

Note:- Do not forget to use **'being' in Passive Voice of Continuous Tense.**

Change the voice

1. The committee is looking into the matter. (Active)
   The matter is **being** looked into by the committee. (Passive)

Note: Do not forget to use the preposition in Passive Voice that follows the verb in Active Voice.

2. They are laughing at you. (Active)
   You are being laughed **at** by them. (Passive)
3. The accused is being produced before the court. (Passive)
   The police are producing the accused before the court. (Active)

4. Right to protest peacefully is being demanded by the revolutionaries. (Passive)
   The revolutionaries are demanding right to protest peacefully. (Active)
5. You were not taking the exam seriously. (Active)
   The exam was not being taken seriously by you. (Passive)

PERFECT TENSE

Perfect Tense	Active	Passive
Present Perfect	Sub + has/have + V_3 + obj	Obj + has / have + been + V_3 + by + sub
Past Perfect	Sub + had + V_3 + obj	Obj + had + been + V_3 + by + sub
Future Perfect	Sub + shall/ will + have + V_3 + obj	Obj + shall / will + have + been + V_3 + by + sub
Modal Perfect	Sub + Modal + have + V_3 + obj	Obj + modal + have + been + V_3 + by + sub

Note: If passive voice is used in perfect tense, there "been" must be used.

CHANGE THE VOICE

E.g.:1. **Who** has seen him? *(Active)*
   By whom has he been seen? *(Passive)*
2. The news has surprised us. *(Active)*
   We have been surprised **at** the news. *(Passive)*
3. He will have understood your ulterior motive by that time. *(Active)*
   Your ulterior motive will have been understood by him by that time. *(Passive)*
4. The committee had looked into the matter impartially before he was found guilty.
   The matter had been looked into by the committee impartially before it found him guilty.

Note: Certain verbs take fixed preposition after them that replaces the 'by' of 'by +sub'.
known **to**, surprised **at/by**, amazed **at**, astonished **at**, startled **at**, vexed **at**, annoyed **with** somebody, annoyed **at** something, contained **in**, embodied **in**, crammed **with**, decorated **with**, filled **with**, ornamented **with**, thronged **with**, tired **of**, engulfed **in**.

Note: 'Surprised' is followed by 'at' when the action was contrary to our expectation.
Eg.: I was surprised **at** his impudent behaviour.
In all other cases 'surprised by' is used.
Eg.: I was surprised **by** his result.

E.g.:1. The fire engulfed the building.
   The building was engulfed **in** the fire.
2. This box contains ten cigars.
   Ten cigars are contained **in** this box.

PASSIVE VOICE OF INTERROGATIVE SENTENCES

➢ In the Passive Voice of Interrogative Sentences, we **start the sentence with the helping verb that goes with the object** .

Active: Have you broken the glass?

Passive: Has the glass been broken by you?

If we want **to make an Interrogative sentence of 'WH Family'** we **add the 'Wh' word before the interrogative form** of the sentence.

Active: Why have you broken the window pane ?

Passive: Why has the window pane been broken by you?

Why → Interrogative word; has the window pane been broken by you? → Interrogative form of tense

This rule is only applicable to 'why', 'how', 'when', 'where' and 'what'. In case of **who and whom**, the **rules are different** and the Passive Voice is made as illustrated below :-.

Active: Who wrote the Ramayana?

Passive: By whom was the Ramayana written?

Or

Who was the Ramayana written by?

['Whom was the Ramayana written by ?' is wrong]

Active: Whom have you invited?

Passive: Who has been invited by you?

IMPERATIVE SENTENCES

1. With obj

(i) Shut the door (A.V.)

1st way Let the door be shut. (P.V.)

Let + obj + be + V_3

2nd way You are ordered to shut the door. (P.V.)

You are ordered/ requested/ forbidden etc. + to + $V_{b.f}$ + obj.

2. Without obj

(i) Go away. (A.V.)

You are ordered to go away. (P.V.)

You are ordered/ requested/ forbidden etc. + to + $V_{b.f}$ + obj.

Moral Suggestion

(i) Help the poor. (A.V.)

The poor should be helped. (P.V.)

Obj + should + be + V_3

INFINITIVE (TO + $V_{b.f}$)

Active: **To + $V_{b.f}$**

Passive: **To + be + V_3**

1. **Active :** I am to do it.
   Passive : It is to be done by me.

2. **Active:** You are to write it in ink.
Passive: It is to be written in ink.

Note.: '**To + $V_{b.f}$**' is changed into '**to + be + V_3**' in Passive Voice **but this is not a universal rule.** If we change '**to + $V_{b.f}$**' into '**to + be + V_3**', we open the option of 'by+Sub' and if the **same subject is repeated** in the sentence **that has already come** in the sentence earlier, we **do not change** '**to + $V_{b.f}$**' into '**to + be + V_3**'

E.g.: **Active:** The teacher gave me a book **to read**.
Passive: I was given a book by my teacher **to read**.

FORCED ACTION

Active: **S + have / has/ had + to + $V_{b.f}$ + Obj**

Passive: **Obj + have / has / had + to + be + V_3 + by + sub.**

E.g.: (i) **Active:** I have to finish this work.

I	have	to	finish	this work.
↓	↓	↓	↓	↓
S	have	to	$V_{b.f}$	Obj

Passive: This work has to be finished by me

This work	has	to	be	finished	by	me
↓	↓	↓	↓	↓	↓	↓
Obj	has	to	be	V_3	by	sub

(ii) **Active:** You have to choose a dress.
Passive: A dress has to be chosen by you.

VERB- LET, BID, HELP, MAKE

➢ Verb- **Let, bid, help** and **make** are used in **Active Voice** followed by a **Bare Infinitive.**

E.g.: 1. She let me go.
2. I bade him leave the room.
3. They must help me finish the work.
4. I made him wash all the clothes

• ***Now let us see how Passive Voice of Bid, help and make is made:-***

E.g.: (1) I will make you finish the whole syllabus. → You will be made to finish the whole syllabus by me.
(2) He bade us clean the table. → We were bidden by him to clean the table.
(3) They helped us clear our doubts. → We were helped by them to clear our doubts.

➢ **Bid, help** and **make** are used in **Passive Voice** followed by **Infinitive** and not **Bare Infinitive**

E.g.: 1. I was permitted/ allowed by her to go.
2. He was bidden to leave the room by me.
3. I must be helped to finish the work.
4. He was made to wash all the clothes by me.

Note: '**Let**' is used in different sense in different sentences and the meaning of the sentence determines the Passive Voice.

E.g.: 1. Let me play (Request for permission) → I may be allowed to play.
2. Let him do this work. → Let this work be done by him.
3. Let us organize a party. (suggestion) → A party should be organized.
4. Let us help the poor. (moral suggestion) → The poor should be helped.

VERBS FOLLOWED BY ADJECTIVES.

Rose smells sweet. (Active)
Rose is sweet when it is smelt. (Passive)

Sub + verb (according to tense and number) + adjective + when + pronoun (according to number) + H.V (according to tense and number) + V_3 (M.V in V_3 form.)

E.g.: 1. Quinine tastes bitter. (Active)
Quinine is bitter when it is tasted. (Passive)

2. Those mangoes tasted sour. (Active)
Those mangoes were sour when they were tasted. (Passive)

PRACTICE SET

Directions: A sentence has been given in Active/Passive Voice. Out of the four alternatives suggested below, select the one which best expresses the same sentence in Passive/Active Voice.

1. What amused you?
(a) What you are made to amuse by?
(b) By what are you being amused?
(c) By what were you amused?
(d) By what have you been amused?

2. Smoke and flames engulfed the area and made rescue operations difficult.
(a) The area was engulfed in smoke and flames and make rescue operations difficult.
(b) The area was engulfed in smoke and flames making rescue operations difficult.
(c) The area has been engulfed in smoke and flames and made rescue operations difficult.
(d) The area was engulfed in smoke and flames and rescue operations were make difficult.

3. He asked me to finish the work in time.
(a) I was asked that I should finish the work in time.
(b) He asked me that I should finish the work in time.
(c) I was asked to finish the work in time.
(d) I was asked to finished the work in time by him.

4. Quinine tastes bitter.
(a) Quinine is bitter when it is tasted.
(b) Quinine is bitter tested.
(c) The taste of quinine is bitter.
(d) Quinine is tasted bitter.

5. The vintage cars hold a special place in the hearts of their owners.
(a) A special place in the hearts of the vintage car owners is held by them.
(b) A special place was held by the vintage cars in the hearts of their owners.
(c) A special place is held by the vintage cars in the hearts of their owners.
(d) A special place is being held by the vintage cars in the hearts of their owners.

6. The accountant took the cheque from the customer.
(a) The cheque is taken from the customer by the accountant.
(b) The cheque was taken from the customer by the accountant.
(c) The customer was taken the cheque by the accountant.
(d) The cheque had been taken from the customer by the accountant.

7. The gatekeeper refused him admittance.

(a) He was refused admittance by the gatekeeper.
(b) Admittance is refused to him by the gatekeeper.
(c) Admittance was refused by the gatekeeper .
(d) Admittance is refused him by the gatekeeper.

8. Sohan was interviewing the political leaders.

(a) The political leaders were being interviewed by Sohan.
(b) The political leader was being interviewed by Sohan.
(c) The political leaders are being interviewed by Sohan.
(d) The political leaders is being interviewed by Sohan.

9. The builders have built a perfect dam across the stream.

(a) A perfect dam has built by the builders across the stream.
(b) A perfect dam has been built by the builders across the stream.
(c) A perfect dam have been built by the builders across the stream.
(d) A perfect dam was being built by the builders across the stream.

10. They should follow all the instructions carefully.

(a) All the instructions are carefully followed by them.
(b) All the instructions should be carefully followed by them.
(c) All the instructions have to be followed by them.
(d) All the instructions can be carefully followed by them.

11. Shut the door and leave.

(a) Let the door be shut and you are ordered to leave.
(b) Let the door be shutted and you are ordered to leave.
(c) Let the door be shut and you be left.
(d) Let be the door shut and you are ordered to leave.

12. Who knows you?

(a) By whom are you known?
(b) Whom are you known by?
(c) To whom are you known?
(d) Who are you known?

13. Help others but do not expect anything in return.

(a) You are advised to help others and expect anything in return.
(b) Let others be helped and expect nothing in return.
(c) You were advised to help others and expect anything in return.
(d) You are advised to help others but forbidden to expect anything in return.

14. We are taught English here.

(a) A teacher teaches us English here.
(b) English is taught here.
(c) A lady teaches us English here.
(d) You teach us English here.

15. The news surprised us.

(a) We were surprised at the news.
(b) We were surprised by the news.
(c) We were surprised with the news.
(d) We were surprised on the news.

16. Spain expected to win the world cup.

(a) The World Cup was expected to be won by Spain.
(b) It was expected by Spain to win the World Cup.
(c) To win the World Cup has been expected by Spain.
(d) Spain expected that the World Cup be won by it.

17. After taking her to the hospital, I dropped her at her place.

(a) After being taken to the hospital, she was dropped at her place by me.
(b) After been taken to the hospital, she was dropped at her place by me.

(c) After being taken she was sent to hospital and dropped at her place by me.
(d) After being taken to the hospital, she was dropped on her place by me.

18. Have this lock broken.
(a) Break this lock.
(b) Get someone to break this lock.
(c) Let this lock be broken.
(d) Have broken this lock be.

19. Think before you speak.
(a) Let thinking be done before you speak.
(b) Let speaking be not done before you think.
(c) You are advised to think before you speak.
(d) You are requested to think before you speak.

20. The case is being investigated by the police alongwith the CBI.
(a) The police alongwith the CBI are investigating the case.
(b) The police alongwith the CBI is investigating the case.
(c) The police alongwith the CBI was investigating the case.
(d) The police alongwith the CBI were investigating the case.

21. He doesn't like people to call him cheat.
(a) He doesn't like to be called a cheat.
(b) He doesn't like to be call is a cheat.
(c) He doesn't like anyone to call him cheat.
(d) To call cheat is not liked by him.

22. At KD Campus every question is answered as we believe that even Einstein asked questions.
(a) At KD Campus every question is answered as we believe that even questions were asked by Einstein.
(b) At KD Campus every question is answered as that is believed by us that Einstein even asked question.
(c) At KD Campus we answer every question as it is believed by us that questions were asked by even Einstein.
(d) Every question is answered by KD Campus as we believe that Einstein asked even questions.

23. You must hit the nail on the head.
(a) The nail must hit on the head.
(b) The nail must be hit on the head.
(c) The nail has to be hit on the head.
(d) The nail on the head must be hit.

24. Those mangoes smell sweet.
(a) Those mangoes are sweet when they are smell.
(b) Those mangoes are sweet when they are smelt
(c) Those mangoes were sweet when those are smelt.
(d) Sweet are smelt by those mangoes.

25. The little boy asked the man the way to Athens.
(a) The man has been asked the way to Athens by the little boy.
(b) The man was asked the way to Athens by the little boy.
(c) The man was being asked the way to Athens by the little boy.
(d) The way to Athens was asked by the man from the little boy.

26. Shut the door and go away.
(a) Let the door be shut and you are ordered to go away.
(b) You are ordered to go away and shut the door.
(c) Let the door be shut and let you be gone.
(d) Shut the door and let you be gone.

27. Your proposal was objected to and everyone laughed at you.
(a) Everyone objected your proposal and laughed at you.
(b) Everyone objected to your proposal and you were laughed at.
(c) Everyone objected to and laughed at

you and your proposal.
(d) Your proposal was objected and you were laughed.

28. Let everyone be given a chance.
(a) Give everyone a chance.
(b) Give a chance for everyone.
(c) Let a chance be given to everyone.
(d) I will give up a chance.

29. Do not make a noise.
(a) Let a noise be made not.
(b) You are requested to not make a noise.
(c) You are ordered to not make a noise.
(d) You are forbidden to make a noise.

30. People are raising a hue and cry and are breaking the furniture.
(a) A hue and cry is being raised and the furniture is being broken by the people.
(b) A hue and cry is being raised and the furniture are being broken by the people.
(c) Hue and cry and the furniture is being broken.
(d) A hue and cry has been raised and the furniture has been broke.

31. The fur coats were imported from Sweden by us.
(a) Sweden imported the fur coats.
(b) Sweden was imported the fur coats.
(c) We imported the fur coats from Sweden.
(d) We had imported the fur coats from Sweden.

32. A bullet in the chest is adored by the brave.
(a) The brave adores a bullet in the chest.
(b) The brave adore a bullet in the chest.
(c) The brave adored a bullet in the chest.
(d) The brave have adored a bullet in the chest.

33. Decisions must be taken.
(a) Decisions should be taken.
(b) We must take decisions.
(c) It is good to take decisions.
(d) We should take decisions.

34. Are they not cheating us?
(a) Are we not being cheated?
(b) Are not we being cheated?
(c) Are we being not cheated?
(d) Are we being cheated?

35. The room was cleaned.
(a) The cleaner cleaned the room.
(b) The room should be cleaned.
(c) I cleaned the room.
(d) My mother cleaned the room.

36. I should have met him yesterday.
(a) He should have met by me yesterday.
(b) He should be meeting me yesterday.
(c) He should have been meeting by me yesterday.
(d) He should have been met by me yesterday.

37. One could see her lying on the flowerbeds.
(a) Flowerbeds could be seen lying on her.
(b) She could see on lying on flowerbeds.
(c) She could be seen lying on flowerbeds.
(d) She could be lying on flowerbeds seen.

38. We expect good news.
(a) Good news is expected by us.
(b) Let good news be expected.
(c) Let us expect good news.
(d) Expecting good news from them.

39. My teacher gave me a journal to read.
(a) I was given a journal by my teacher to be read.
(b) A journal to read was given to me by my teacher.
(c) A journal was given me to read by my teacher.
(d) I was given a journal by my teacher to read.

40. It is impossible to do this.
(a) This is impossible to be done.
(b) To do this by it is impossible.
(c) It is impossible to have done this.
(d) It can't be done.

41. Physically challenged people should not be laughed at by the public.
(a) Physically challenged people should not laugh at the public.
(b) The public will not be laughing at physically challenged people.
(c) The public shall not be laughing at physically challenged people.
(d) The public should not laugh at physically challenged people.

42. They say that people live on distant planets .
(a) It was said that people live on distant planets .
(b) It is being said that people live on distant planets .
(c) It is said that people live on distant planets .
(d) It is saying that people live on distant planets .

43. Can we send the parcel tomorrow?
(a) Can be the parcel sent by us tomorrow?
(b) Can we be sent by the parcel tomorrow?
(c) Can the parcel be sent by us tomorrow?
(d) Can the parcel sent by us tomorrow?

44. A detective arrested him as soon as he got home.
(a) An arrest was made by a detective as soon as he got home.
(b) He was arrested by a detective as soon as he got home.
(c) A detective was arrested by him as soon as he got home.
(d) An arrest was detected by him as soon as he got home.

45. They cooked the food and sent it to the orphanage.
(a) They cooked food was sent to the orphanage by them.
(b) The food was cooked and sent to the orphanage by them.
(c) The food was sent to the orphanage by them.
(d) The food was cooked and sent by them.

46. Where were they playing the cricket match?
(a) Where was the cricket match played?
(b) Where has the cricket match been played?
(c) Where will the cricket match be played?
(d) Where was the cricket match being played?

47. They say he can teach almost anything in this world.
(a) It is said that almost anything in this world can be taught by him.
(b) It was said that almost anything could be taught by him.
(c) They say almost anything could be taught by him.
(d) They say anything almost will be taught by him.

48. Please enter by the left door.
(a) Let the left door be entered by you.
(b) You are requested to enter by the left door.
(c) Let it be entered by the left door.
(d) The left door is requested to be entered.

49. I would advise you not to get on the wrong side of your boss.
(a) It would be advised by me not to get on the wrong side of your boss.
(b) It would be my advice not to get on the wrong side of your boss.
(c) You would be advised by me not to get on the wrong side of your boss.
(d) My advice to you would be not to get on the wrong side of your boss.

50. They have done this to defuse the crisis.
(a) The crisis has been defused by them.
(b) This has been done by them to defuse the crisis .
(c) To defuse the crisis this was done by them.
(d) To defuse the crisis this is done by them.

51. Open the door.
(a) The door must be opened.
(b) The door will be opened.
(c) The door is opened.
(d) Let the door be opened.

52. I did not trust anybody.
(a) Nobody was trusted by me.
(b) Anybody had been trusted by me.
(c) Nobody would be trusted by me.
(d) Nobody has been trusted by me.

53. Did he remember the date and time?
(a) Are the date and time remembered by him?
(b) Was he remembering the date and time?
(c) Were the date and time remembered by him?
(d) Did the date and time be remembered by him?

54. The boys were digging a hole in the ground.
(a) A hole was being dug in the ground by the boys.
(b) In the ground, the boys dug a hole.
(c) A hole in the ground has been dug by the boys.
(d) A hole in the ground has been dug by the boys.

55. We must now deal with these problems.
(a) These problems must now be dealt with by us.
(b) These problems must now be dealing with by us.
(c) These problems must now deal with by us.
(d) These problems are to be dealt with by us.

56. The audience loudly cheered the leader's speech.
(a) The leader's speech was loudly cheered by the audience.
(b) The leader's speech in loudly cheered by the audience.
(c) The audience loudly cheered the leader for his speech.
(d) The speech of the leader was loudly cheered by the audience.

57. Someone is following us.
(a) We are following by someone.
(b) We are being followed by someone.
(c) We were being followed by someone.
(d) We had been followed by someone.

58. He hasn't slept in his bed.
(a) His bed hasn't been slept in.
(b) He had not been slept in his bed.
(c) His bed had been slept in.
(d) His bed had not been slept in.

59. I was recommended another lawyer.
(a) Somebody recommended another lawyer.
(b) Somebody recommended me to another lawyer.
(c) Somebody recommended me another lawyer.
(d) Somebody recommends me another lawyer.

60. Many a person has been saved from the man-eaters by these hunters.
(a) These hunters will save many a person from the man-eaters.
(b) These hunters save many a person from the man-eaters.
(c) These hunters saved many a person from the man-eaters.
(d) These hunters have saved many a person from the man-eaters.

61. Must we cut this tree?
(a) Must this tree will cut?
(b) Must this tree be cut?
(c) Must this tree was cut?
(d) Must this tree is cut?

62. You will be looked after well.
(a) They will look after you well.
(b) They can't look after you well.
(c) They may look after well.
(d) They shall look after you well.

63. Didn't they tell you to be here by six o'clock?
(a) Weren't you told to be here by six o'clock?
(b) Haven't they told you to be here by six o'clock?
(c) You were expected to be here by six o'clock.
(d) They expected you to be here by six o'clock.

64. Don't touch this switch.
(a) This switch does not be touched.
(b) This switch must not be touched.
(c) This switch don't be touched.
(d) This switch need not be touched.

65. One cannot gather grapes from thistles.
(a) Thistles cannot be gathered from grapes.
(b) Grapes cannot be gathered from thistles.
(c) Grapes and thistles cannot be gathered by one.
(d) Grapes cannot be gathered by them.

66. They will have completed the work by the time we get there.
(a) The work will be completed by the time we get there.
(b) The work will have been completed by the time we get there.
(c) The work will have completed by the time we get there.
(d) The work will have been completed by the time we have got there.

67. You will have to pull down this sky-scraper as you have not complied with the town planning regulations.
(a) This sky-scraper will have to be pulled down as the town planning regulations have not been complied with.
(b) This sky-scraper will have to be pulled down by you as the town planning regulations have not been complied by you.
(c) This sky-scraper will be pulled down as the town planning regulations have not been complied with.
(d) This sky-scraper will have to be pulled down as the town planning regulations have not been complied.

68. He has written a poem which fascinates every one.
(a) A poem has been written by him which fascinates every one.
(b) Everyone is fascinated by the poem which has been written by him.
(c) Poem written by him fascinates everyone.
(d) Every one fascinates the poem which is written by him.

69. Will those happy days be ever forgotten by me?
(a) Will I ever forget those happy days?
(b) Shall I ever forget those happy days?
(c) Would I forget these happy days?
(d) Ever shall I forget those happy days?

70. You are requested to permit him.
(a) Please permit him.
(b) I request you to permit me.
(c) He requests to permit him.
(d) I plead you to permit him.

71. I am not going to tolerate this nonsense anymore.
(a) This nonsense is not going to be tolerated by me anymore.
(b) This nonsense is not being gone to be tolerated by me anymore.
(c) This nonsense is not being going to be tolerated by me anymore.
(d) Tolerate is not being going to be done by me of this nonsense.

72. The boys were being laughed at by the passers-by on the busy thoroughfare last evening.
(a) The passers-by laughed at the boys on the busy thoroughfare last evening.

(b) The passers-by were laughing at the boys on the busy thoroughfare last evening.
(c) The boys were laughing at the passers-by on the busy thoroughfare last evening.
(d) None of the above.

73. The police are questioning Mr. and Mrs. Sharma.
(a) Mr. and Mrs. Sharma are questioned by the police.
(b) Mr. and Mrs. Sharma have been questioning the police.
(c) Mr. and Mrs. Sharma have been questioned by the police.
(d) Mr. and Mrs. Sharma are being questioned by the police.

74. Before they invented printing, people had to write everything by hand.
(a) Before printing was invented everything had to be written by hand.
(b) Before printing was invented by them, everything had to be written.
(c) Before printing was invented people had to write everything by hand.
(d) Before printing was invented everything was written by hand.

75. Did any one ever make it clear how one operates the machine?
(a) Was it ever made clear how the machine is operated?
(b) Did any one ever make it by clear how the machine is operated?
(c) Was ever it made clear how to operate the machine?
(d) Was how to operate the machine ever made clear?

76. Why did your father refuse to give the money to you?
(a) Why was your father refused money to you?
(b) Why was the money not given to you by your father?
(c) Why was the money refused to be given to you by your father?
(d) Why the money was refused to be given to you by your father?

77. Do you expect your parents to come from Hyderabad today?
(a) Did your parents come today from Hyderabad?
(b) Were your parents expected to come from Hyderabad today?
(c) Are your parents expected to come today from Hyderabad?
(d) Do your parents are expected to come today from Hyderabad?

78. Why are you raising a hue and cry?
(a) Why are a hue and cry being raised by you?
(b) Why is a hue and cry being raised by you?
(c) Why a hue and cry are being raised by you?
(d) Why a hue and cry is being raised by you?

79. They say that there are living beings on Mars.
(a) They say that Mars has living beings.
(b) It is said that there are people living on Mars.
(c) On Mars, there are living beings.
(d) It is said that there are living beings on Mars.

80. A fortnight after he was convicted for the rape and murder of his classmate, the Delhi High Court sentenced him to death on Monday.
(a) A fortnight after he had been convicted for the rape and murder of his classmate he had been sentenced to death by the Delhi High Court on Monday.
(b) A fortnight after he was convicted for the rape and murder of his classmate he has been sentenced to death by the Delhi High Court on Monday.

(c) A fortnight after he was convicted for the rape and murder of his classmate he was sentenced to death by the Delhi High Court on Monday.
(d) A fortnight after he was been convicted for the rape and murder of his classmate he was sentenced to death by the Delhi High Court on Monday.

81. Their dog bit our neighbour yesterday.
(a) Our neighbour bit their dog yesterday.
(b) Our neighbour bitten by their dog yesterday.
(c) Our neighbour was bitten by their dog yesterday.
(d) Our neighbour were bit by their dog yesterday.

82. The MD told us about the new project.
(a) We were told about the new project by the MD.
(b) We are told about the new project by the MD.
(c) We told by MD about the new project.
(d) We had been told by MD about project.

83. The Minister had already informed his Cabinet about his decision.
(a) His Cabinet was already informed about the Minister's decision.
(b) His Cabinet has already informed the Minister about his decision.
(c) His Cabinet had already been informed about his decision by the Minister.
(d) His Cabinet will have already been informed about the Minister's decision.

84. Sayali gave the beggar an old sari.
(a) An old sari was given to Sayali by the beggar.
(b) An old sari was given to the beggar by Sayali.
(c) The beggar was being given on old sari by Sayali.
(d) The beggar had to be given on old sari by Sayali.

85. They are going to perform "Hamlet".
(a) "Hamlet" is going to be performed by them.
(b) "Hamlet" is going to perform by them.
(c) "Hamlet" is to perform.
(d) "Hamlet" has to be performed.

86. I was shocked by the letter.
(a) They shocked me with the letter.
(b) I am shocked.
(c) The letter shocked me.
(d) I shocked with the letter.

87. Somebody stole my car last week.
(a) Last week my car was steal by somebody.
(b) My car was stolen last week by somebody.
(c) My car was stolen that week by somebody.
(d) Somebody last week has stolen my car.

88. Do they sell construction material?
(a) Does construction material sold by them?
(b) Is construction material selling by them?
(c) Is construction material sold by them?
(d) Does construction material sell by them?

89. Sharma was cleaning the house.
(a) The house was cleaned by Sharma.
(b) The house will be cleaned by Sharma.
(c) The house was being cleaned by Sharma.
(d) The house is being cleaned by Sharma.

90. I bought a new shirt last week.
(a) Last week a new shirt was bought by I.

(b) Last week a new shirt is bought by I.
(c) Last week a new shirt was bought by me.
(d) Last week a new shirt had been bought by me.

91. The plants have been watered by the gardener.
(a) The gardener is watering the plants.
(b) The gardener has been watering the plants.
(c) The gardener has watered the plants.
(d) The gardener have watered the plants.

92. The children could use the place always.
(a) The place can be used by children always.
(b) The place is used by children always.
(c) The place could always be used by children.
(d) The place has been used by children always.

93. They say that the earth is round.
(a) It has been said that the earth is round.
(b) That the earth is round is said by them.
(c) It is said that the earth is round.
(d) It was said that the earth was round.

94. This machine must not be used after 5.30 p.m.
(a) You can't use the machine after 5.30 p.m.
(b) You mayn't use the machine after 5.30 p.m.
(c) You need not you the machine after 5.30 p.m.
(d) You must not use the machine after 5.30 p.m.

95. Tiny houses dot the landscape.
(a) The landscape was dotted by tiny houses.
(b) The landscape is being dotted by tiny houses.
(c) The landscape is dotted by tiny houses.
(d) The landscape has been dotted by tiny houses.

96. Dogs always chase cats.
(a) Cats are always chasing dogs.
(b) Cats have been always chased by dogs.
(c) Cats are always chased by dogs.
(d) Cats are being always chased by dogs.

97. The farmer prepared the field.
(a) The field was prepared by the farmer.
(b) The field was being prepared by the farmer.
(c) The field were prepared by the farmer.
(d) The field were being prepared by the farmer.

98. Teachers should be respected.
(a) Teachers deserve respect.
(b) Teachers are to be respected.
(c) We shall respect teaches.
(d) We should respect teachers.

99. He will do the work tomorrow.
(a) The work will be done by him tomorrow.
(b) The work would be done by him tomorrow.
(c) The work could be done by him tomorrow.
(d) The work will have been done by him tomorrow.

100. She gave me a book.
(a) I was given a book by her.
(b) She was given a book.
(c) A book is given by her to me.
(d) I was given her a book.

101. I have bought a new car.
(a) A new car was bought by me.
(b) A new car is bought by me.
(c) A new car has been bought by me.
(d) A new car had been bought by me.

102. Teachers might have given their students some concessions.
(a) Their students might have given some concessions to their teachers.
(b) Their students might be given some concessions by their teachers.
(c) Their students might be giving some concessions to their teachers.
(d) Students might have been given some concessions by their teachers.

103. You should not offer meat to vegetarians.
(a) Vegetarians should not be offered meat.
(b) Meat should be offered to non-vegetarians.
(c) Vegetarians should not offer meat.
(d) You should offer no meat to non-vegetarians.

104. You must write off all those bad debts.
(a) You must be written off by all those bad debts.
(b) All those bad debts must be written off by you.
(c) Write off all those bad debts .
(d) All those bad debts could be written off.

105. Are they receiving the chief guest at the station ?
(a) Was the chief guest being received at the station ?
(b) Is the chief guest being received at the station ?
(c) Will they be received by the chief guest at the station ?
(d) Will the chief guest be received at the station ?

106. We make butter from milk.
(a) Butter is make from milk by us.
(b) Butter is made from milk by us.
(c) Butter is make with milk by us.
(d) From milk butter is made by us.

107. I don't like people telling me what to do.
(a) I don't like being told what to do.
(b) People telling me what to do was not liked by me.
(c) I do not like being told by the people.
(d) People don't like telling me what to do.

108. The meeting has been called off by the chairman.
(a) The chairman called off the meeting.
(b) The chairman has called off the meeting.
(c) The chairman is calling off the meeting.
(d) The chairman had called off the meeting.

109. The police arrested 200 students on the University campus.
(a) 200 students had been arrested on the University campus by the police.
(b) 200 students has been arrested by the police on the University campus.
(c) 200 students were arrested by the police on the University campus.
(d) 200 students are arrested on the University campus by the police.

110. Why do you like him so much ?
(a) Why has he been liked so much by you ?
(b) Why was he liked by you so much?
(c) Why is he liked by you so much ?
(d) Why he is liked by you so much ?

111. The invitation cards will be sent today.
(a) They will sent the invitation cards today.
(b) They will have sent the invitation cards today.
(c) They will send the invitation cards today.
(d) They will be sending the invitation cards today.

112. She has baked several cakes for her friends.

(a) She has several cakes to be baked for her friends.
(b) Her friends had several cakes baked by her.
(c) Several cakes have been baked by her for her friends.
(d) Her friends baked several cakes for her.

113. We believe that God gives us misery.
(a) It was believed that God gave us misery.
(b) It has been believed that God gives us misery.
(c) It is believed that God gives us misery.
(d) It is a belief that God gives us misery.

114. A lot of saplings have been planted by the chief guest.
(a) The chief guest is planting a lot of saplings.
(b) The chief guest has planted a lot of saplings.
(c) The chief guest have planted a lot of saplings.
(d) The chief guest has been planting a lot of saplings.

115. The Prime Minister has discussed the matter with the other ministers.
(a) The matter was discussed by the Prime Minister with the other ministers.
(b) The matter is discussed by the Prime Minister with the other ministers.
(c) The matter had been discussed by the Prime Minister with the other ministers.
(d) The matter has been discussed by the Prime Minister with the other ministers.

116. The Principal will meet the students this evening.
(a) The students will be met by the Principal this evening.
(b) The students could be met by the Principal this evening.
(c) The students would be met by the Principal this evening.
(d) The students will be meeting the Principal this evening.

117. The Chief Justice of India is appointed by the President.
(a) The President of India appointed the Chief Justice.
(b) The President appoints the Chief Justice of India.
(c) The President appointed the Chief Justice of India.
(d) The appointment order of the Chief Justice of India was given by the President.

118. A meeting was convened by the Principal.
(a) The Principal convened a meeting.
(b) The Principal was convening a meeting.
(c) The Principal has convened a meeting
(d) The Principal is convening a meeting.

119. Someone has stolen my suitcase.
(a) My suitcase is stolen by someone.
(b) Someone has been stolen my suitcase.
(c) My suitcase has someone been stolen.
(d) My suitcase has been stolen by someone.

120. Anu is interviewing Radhika and Sarath Kumar.
(a) Radhika and Sarath Kumar are being interviewed by Anu.
(b) Radhika and Sarath Kumar are interviewing Anu.
(c) Radhika and Sarath Kumar were interviewed by Anu.
(d) Radhika is being interviewed by Sarath Kumar and Anu.

121. Our task had been completed before sunset.

(a) We completed our task before sunset.
(b) We have completed our task before sunset.
(c) We complete our task before sunset.
(d) We had completed our task before sunset.

122. The boy laughed at the beggar.
(a) The beggar was laughed by the boy.
(b) The beggar was being laughed by the boy.
(c) The beggar was being laughed at by the boy.
(d) The beggar was laughed at by the boy.

123. The government has launched a massive tribal welfare programme in Jharkhand.
(a) A massive tribal welfare programme is launched by the government in Jharkhand.
(b) A massive tribal welfare programme has been launched by the government in Jharkhand.
(c) Jharkhand government has launched a massive tribal welfare programme.
(d) The government in Jharkhand has launched a massive tribal welfare programme.

124. The boys were playing cricket.
(a) Cricket had been played by the boys.
(b) Cricket has been played by the boys.
(c) Cricket was played by the boys.
(d) Cricket was being played by the boys.

125. They drew a circle in the morning.
(a) A circle was being drawn by them in the morning.
(b) A circle was drawn by them in the morning.
(c) In the morning a circle have been drawn by them.
(d) A circle has been drawing since morning.

126. They will demolish the entire block.
(a) The entire block is being demolished.
(b) The block may be demolished entirely.
(c) The entire block will have to be demolished by them.
(d) The entire block will be demolished by them.

127. The burglar destroyed several items in the room. Even the carpet has been torn.
(a) Several items destroyed in the room by the burglar. Even the carpet he has torn.
(b) Several items in the room were destroyed by the burglar. He has torn even the carpet.
(c) Including the carpet, several items in the room have been torn by the burglar.
(d) The burglar, being destroyed several items in the room, also carpet has torn.

128. We must respect the elders.
(a) The elders deserve respect from us.
(b) The elders must be respected.
(c) The elders must respected by us.
(d) Respect the elders we must.

129. We have warned you.
(a) You have been warned.
(b) We have you warned.
(c) Warned you have been.
(d) Have you been warned.

130. Has anybody answered your question?
(a) Your question has been answered ?
(b) Anybody has answered your question ?
(c) Has your question been answered ?
(d) Have you answered your question ?

131. The shopkeeper lowered the prices.
(a) The prices lowered the shopkeeper.
(b) The prices were lowered by the shopkeeper.
(c) Down went the prices.
(d) The shopkeeper got down the prices.

132. One must keep one's promises.
(a) One's promises are kept.
(b) One's promises must kept.
(c) One's promises were kept.
(d) Promises must be kept.

133. The government has not approved the new drug for sale.
(a) The government approval for the sale of the new drug has not been given.
(b) The new drug has not been approved for sale by the government.
(c) For the sale of the new drug we have not been given the approval.
(d) The new drug was not approved by the government.

134. They have published all the details of the invention.
(a) All the details of the invention have been published by them.
(b) The publication of the details of invention was done by them.
(c) All the details have been invented by the publishers.
(d) All the inventions have been detailed by them.

135. He teaches us grammar.
(a) Grammar was taught to us by him.
(b) We are taught grammar by him.
(c) Grammar will be taught to us by him.
(d) We were teached grammar by him.

136. The manager could not accept the union leader's proposals.
(a) The union leader's proposals could not be accepted by the manager.
(b) The union leader's proposals were not accepted by the manager.
(c) The union leader's proposals will not be accepted by the manager.
(d) The union leader's proposals would not be accepted by the manager.

137. Prepare yourself for the worst.
(a) You be prepared for the worst.
(b) The worst should be prepared by yourself.
(c) Be prepared for the worst.
(d) For the worst, preparation should be made by you.

138. Please shut the door and go to sleep.
(a) The door is to be shut and you are to go to sleep.
(b) Let the door be shut and you be asleep.
(c) You are requested to shut the door and go to sleep.
(d) The door is to be shut and you are requested to sleep.

139. Small strokes fell great oaks.
(a) Great oaks are fallen by small strokes.
(b) Great oaks are felled by small strokes.
(c) Great oaks are fell by small strokes.
(d) Great oaks were fallen by small strokes.

140. We must take care of all living species on Earth.
(a) All living species on Earth are taken care of by us.
(b) All living species on Earth must be taken care of by us.
(c) All living species on Earth had been taken care of by us.
(d) All living species on Earth will be taken care of by us.

141. People call him a fool.
(a) He has been called a fool.
(b) He is called a fool by the people.
(c) The people have been calling him a fool.
(d) We all people have called him a fool.

142. It is being read by us.
(a) We are reading it.
(b) It will be read by us.
(c) We can read it.
(d) We have to read it.

143. He had committed a mistake.
(a) A mistake had committed by him.
(b) A mistake was committed by him.
(c) A mistake had been committed by him.

(d) A mistake has been committed by him.

144. The most useful training of my career was given to me by my boss.

(a) My boss has been giving me the most useful training of my career.
(b) My boss gives me the most useful training.
(c) My boss is giving me the most useful training.
(d) My boss gave me the most useful training of my career.

145. We have decided to open a new branch.

(a) To open a new branch was decided by us.
(b) To be opened a new branch has been decided.
(c) It has been decided to open a new branch.
(d) It may be decided to open a new branch by us.

146. The loan will be sanctioned by the bank.

(a) The bank sanctioned the loan.
(b) The bank is going to sanction the loan.
(c) The bank would sanction the loan.
(d) The bank will sanction the loan.

147. Paint the windows.

(a) Windows should be painted.
(b) Let the windows be painted.
(c) Let be the windows painted.
(d) Windows are let to be painted.

148. The traitors should be shot dead.

(a) They should have shot the traitors dead.
(b) They shall shoot the traitors dead.
(c) They should shoot the traitors dead.
(d) They shot the traitors dead.

149. Rahul is teaching the children in the slum areas.

(a) The children in the slum areas are taught by Rahul.
(b) The children are taught by Rahul in the slum area.
(c) In the slum areas the children are learning from Rahul.
(d) The children in the slum areas are being taught by Rahul.

150. One cannot expect children to understand these problems.

(a) Children cannot be expected to understand these problems.
(b) Children to understand these problems cannot be expected.
(c) Children cannot be expected to be understood these problems.
(d) To understand these problems cannot be expected from children by one.

151. Why did she break the garden wall ?

(a) Why the garden wall was broken by her?
(b) Why had the garden wall been broken by her ?
(c) Why was the garden wall broken by her?
(d) Why will the garden wall be broken by her ?

152. The students were laughing at the old man.

(a) The old man was being laughed at by the students.
(b) The old man was laughed at by the students.
(c) The old man was being laughed by the students.
(d) The old man is laughing at the students.

153. He admonished her for the error.

(a) She was admonished by him for the error.
(b) She has been admonished by him for the error.
(c) She would be admonished by him for the error.
(d) She is admonished by him for the error.

154. Can we send this big parcel by air ?

(a) Can this big parcel be sent by air?
(b) Can this big parcel sent by air ?

(c) Could this big parcel be sent by air?
(d) Could this big parcel sent by us by air?

155. The boys saved many elders from drowning.
(a) Many elders are saved from drowning by the boys.
(b) Many elders are being saved from drowning by the boys,
(c) Many elders were saved from drowning by the boys.
(d) Many elders have been saved from drowning by the boys.

156. He was refused admittance.
(a) The guards refuse him admittance.
(b) The guards refused him for admittance.
(c) The guards have refused him admittance.
(d) The guards refused him admittance.

157. You will be taken care of by me.
(a) I will be taking care of you.
(b) I would take care of you.
(c) I will take care of you.
(d) I will being take care of you.

158. Promises should be kept.
(a) You must keep the promises.
(b) We must keep their promises.
(c) Kept the promises.
(d) One should keep one's promises.

159. Circumstances forced him to resign his post.
(a) Circumstances make him to resign his post.
(b) He was forced to resign his post.
(c) He is forced to resign his post.
(d) He is forced and resigned his post.

160. He would have written this essay in time.
(a) The essay was written on time.
(b) This essay would have been written by him in time.
(c) The essay was written by him in time.
(d) He wrote the essay on time.

161. I give alms to the poor on Saturdays.
(a) Alms are given to the poor by me on Saturdays.
(b) Alms is given to the poor by me on Saturdays.
(c) Alms are given to the poors by me on Saturdays.
(d) Alms were given to the poor by me on Saturdays.

162. God helps the brave.
(a) The brave is helped by God
(b) The brave are helped by God
(c) The brave are help by God
(d) The brave helped by God

163. I haven't read Three Musketeers.
(a) Three Musketeers have not been read by me.
(b) Three Musketeers has not been read by me.
(c) Three Musketeers has been not read by me.
(d) Three Musketeers has not been readed by me.

164. I am going to buy new spectacles tomorrow.
(a) New spectacles are going to be bought by me tomorrow.
(b) New spectacles is going to be bought by me tomorrow.
(c) New spectacles are being bought by me tomorrow.
(d) New spectacles are to be bought by me tomorrow.

165. Our mothers use tongs while making chapaties.
(a) Tongs are used by our mothers while making chapaties.
(b) Tongs is used by our mothers while making chapaties.
(c) Tongs are used by our mothers while chapaties are being made.
(d) Tongs are use by our mothers while making chapaties.

166. I play Billiards during my free time.
(a) Billiards are played by me during my free time.

(b) Billiards were played by me during my free time.
(c) Billiards are being played by me during my free time.
(d) Billiards is played by me during my free time.

167. Have the car painted black.
(a) Paint the car black.
(b) I have painted the car black.
(c) Get someone to paint the car black.
(d) Black has been painted by the car.

168. Who has stolen my binoculars?
(a) By whom my binoculars have been stolen?
(b) By whom have my binoculars been stolen?
(c) By whom has my binoculars been stolen?
(d) By whom my binoculars has been stolen?

169. He has been arrested and sent to jail.
(a) The police arrested him and the court sent him to jail.
(b) The police has arrested him and the court have sent him to jail.
(c) The police have arrested him and the court has sent him to jail.
(d) The police has arrested him and the court has sent him to jail.

170. Anna and his team hope to fight corruption with Jan Lokpal Bill.
(a) It is hoped by Anna and his team that they would fight corruption by Jan Lokpal Bill .
(b) To fight corruption is been hoped by Anna and his team by Jan Lokpal Bill.
(c) To fight corruption was being hoped by Anna and his team by Jan Lokpal Bill.
(d) To fight corruption is being hoping by Anna and his team by Jan Lokpal Bill.

171. The Greeks expected to conquer Carthage.
(a) People expected the Greeks to conquer Carthage.
(b) It was expected by the Greeks to conquer Carthage.
(c) To conquer Carthage was expected by the Greeks.
(d) Carthage was expected to be conquered by the Greeks.

172. Rome was not built in a day.
(a) We did not build Rome in a day.
(b) They could not build Rome in a day.
(c) The Romans did not build Rome in a day.
(d) They have not built Rome in a day.

173. The ship is being taken to safe water by the Captain and not his crew.
(a) The Captain and not his crew is taking the ship to safe water.
(b) The Captain and not his crew are taking the ship to safe water.
(c) The Captain and not his crew have taken the ship to safe water.
(d) The Captain and not his crew is being taking the ship to safe water.

174. Strong Anti-Corruption law is liked by neither the Central Government nor the State Governments.
(a) Neither the Central Government nor the State Governments likes strong Anti-Corruption law.
(b) Neither the Central Government nor the State Governments like strong Anti-Corruption law.
(c) Neither the Central Government nor the State Governments liked strong Anti-Corruption law.
(d) Neither the Central Government nor the State Governments are liking strong Anti-Corruption law.

175. If you cannot change the master, you cannot change the destiny.
(a) The destiny cannot be changed if masters cannot change.
(b) The destiny could not be changed if masters cannot be changed.
(c) The destiny cannot change if masters cannot be changed.

(d) The destiny cannot be changed if masters cannot be changed.

176. The curd smelt sour.
(a) The curd is sour when smelt.
(b) The curd was sour when it was smelling.
(c) The curd was sour when it was smelt.
(d) The curd is sour when it was smelt.

177. People are not going to tolerate Government's despotism.
(a) Government's despotism is not going to be tolerated by people.
(b) Government's despotism was not going to be tolerated by people.
(c) Government's despotism is not being tolerated by people.
(d) Government's despotism is not to be tolerated by people.

178. He is writing a letter.
(a) A letter is being written by him.
(b) A letter is written by him.
(c) A letter has been written by him.
(d) Let a letter be written by him.

179. The man cut the tree into thin strips.
(a) The tree was cut into thin strips by the man.
(b) The tree cut itself into thin strips by the man.
(c) The tree has cut into thin strips by the man.
(d) The tree can be cut into thin strips by the man.

180. My father gave me a hundred rupee note yesterday.
(a) A hundred rupee note was given to me by my father yesterday.
(b) A hundred rupee note was being given to me by my father.
(c) A hundred rupee note had been given to me by my father.
(d) Yesterday, my father was given a hundred rupee note by me.

181. The pilot landed the plane safely.
(a) The plane had been landed safely by the pilot.
(b) The plane was landed safely by the pilot.
(c) The plane has been landed safely by the pilot.
(d) The plane was to be landed safely by the pilot.

182. Abha sent me a card.
(a) A card will be send to me by Abha.
(b) A card was sent to me by Abha.
(c) A card will be sent to me by Abha.
(d) A card is sent to me by Abha.

183. He will never forget it.
(a) It will never be forgotten by him.
(b) It can never be forgotten by him.
(c) It should never be forgotten by him.
(d) It may never be forgotten by him.

184. Let not his insulting words be minded.
(a) Don't be insulted his words.
(b) Don't mind his insulting words.
(c) Don't insult him with his words.
(d) Do mind his insulting words.

185. The students have been punished by the teacher for negligence of duty.
(a) The teacher has punished the students for negligence of duty.
(b) The teacher had punished the students for negligence of duty.
(c) The teacher punished the students for negligence of duty.
(d) The teacher have punished the students for negligence of duty.

186. The storm has destroyed twelve houses.
(a) Twelve houses had been destroyed by the storm.
(b) Twelve houses have been destroyed by the storm.
(c) Twelve houses were destroyed by the storm.
(d) Twelve houses have been stormed.

187. She is reading a novel.
(a) A novel is being read by her.
(b) A novel has been read by her.
(c) A novel is read by her.
(d) A novel was being read by her.

188. The whole village was ravaged by the man-eater.
(a) The man-eater ravages the whole village.
(b) The whole village is ravaged by the man-eater.
(c) The man-eater ravaged the whole village.
(d) The whole village is being ravaged by the man-eater.

189. The purity of justice is maintained by the reports of proceedings in the law courts.
(a) The law courts maintain purity of justice in the reports of the proceedings.
(b) The reports of the proceedings in the law courts maintain the purity of justice.
(c) Pure justice is maintained in the proceedings of the law courts.
(d) The maintenance of justice is pure in the proceedings of the law courts.

190. Newton wrote this letter yesterday.
(a) Yesterday was written letter by Newton.
(b) This letter is written by Newton yesterday.
(c) This letter was written by Newton yesterday.
(d) This letter was wrote by Newton yesterday.

191. An awareness is being created among the people by the Government about the importance of trees.
(a) The Government is creating an awareness among the people about the importance of trees.
(b) The Government are creating an awareness among the people about the importance of trees.
(c) The Government creates an awareness among the people about the importance of trees.
(d) The Government created an awareness among the people about the importance of trees.

192. Ads on TV increase the sale of any commodity.
(a) The sale of any commodity is being increased by ads on TV.
(b) The sale of any commodity are increased by ads on TV.
(c) The sale of any commodity are being increased by ads on TV.
(d) The sale of any commodity is increased by ads on TV.

193. The Indian Government is encouraging the Europeans to visit India.
(a) The Europeans are encouraged by the Indian Government to visit India.
(b) The Europeans are encouraging by the Indian Government to visit India.
(c) The Europeans are being encouraged by the Indian Government to visit India.
(d) The Europeans is being encouraged by the Indian Government to visit India.

194. He handed her a chair.
(a) She was handed a chair by him.
(b) He handed a chair to her.
(c) He will hand a chair to her.
(d) A chair will be handed to her by him.

195. Call the police at once.
(a) Let the police be called at once.
(b) The police was to be called at once.
(c) The police is to be called at once.
(d) Let the police called at once.

196. Post the letter.
(a) The letter is posted.
(b) The letter was posted.
(c) Let the letter be posted.
(d) The letter will be posted.

197. Who painted it?
(a) It was painted?
(b) Was it painted?
(c) Had it been painted by?
(d) By whom was it painted?

Answer key

1.	(c)	2.	(b)	3.	(c)	4.	(a)	5.	(c)
6.	(b)	7.	(a)	8.	(a)	9.	(b)	10.	(b)
11.	(a)	12.	(c)	13.	(d)	14.	(a)	15.	(b)
16.	(b)	17.	(a)	18.	(b)	19.	(c)	20.	(a)
21.	(a)	22.	(c)	23.	(b)	24.	(b)	25.	(b)
26.	(a)	27.	(b)	28.	(a)	29.	(d)	30.	(a)
31.	(c)	32.	(b)	33.	(b)	34.	(a)	35.	(a)
36.	(d)	37.	(c)	38.	(a)	39.	(d)	40.	(a)
41.	(d)	42.	(c)	43.	(c)	44.	(b)	45.	(b)
46.	(d)	47.	(a)	48.	(b)	49.	(c)	50.	(b)
51.	(d)	52.	(a)	53.	(c)	54.	(a)	55.	(a)
56.	(a)	57.	(b)	58.	(a)	59.	(c)	60.	(d)
61.	(b)	62.	(a)	63.	(a)	64.	(b)	65.	(b)
66.	(b)	67.	(a)	68.	(b)	69.	(b)	70.	(a)
71.	(a)	72.	(b)	73.	(d)	74.	(a)	75.	(a)
76.	(c)	77.	(c)	78.	(b)	79.	(d)	80.	(c)
81.	(c)	82.	(a)	83.	(c)	84.	(b)	85.	(a)
86.	(c)	87.	(b)	88.	(c)	89.	(c)	90.	(c)
91.	(c)	92.	(c)	93.	(c)	94.	(d)	95.	(c)
96.	(c)	97.	(a)	98.	(d)	99.	(a)	100.	(a)
101.	(c)	102.	(d)	103.	(a)	104.	(b)	105.	(b)
106.	(b)	107.	(a)	108.	(b)	109.	(c)	110.	(c)
111.	(c)	112.	(c)	113.	(c)	114.	(b)	115.	(d)
116.	(a)	117.	(b)	118.	(a)	119.	(d)	120.	(a)
121.	(d)	122.	(d)	123.	(b)	124.	(d)	125.	(b)
126.	(d)	127.	(b)	128.	(b)	129.	(a)	130.	(c)
131.	(b)	132.	(d)	133.	(b)	134.	(a)	135.	(b)
136.	(a)	137.	(c)	138.	(c)	139.	(b)	140.	(b)
141.	(b)	142.	(a)	143.	(c)	144.	(d)	145.	(c)
146.	(d)	147.	(b)	148.	(c)	149.	(d)	150.	(a)
151.	(c)	152.	(a)	153.	(a)	154.	(a)	155.	(c)
156.	(d)	157.	(c)	158.	(d)	159.	(b)	160.	(b)
161.	(a)	162.	(b)	163.	(b)	164.	(a)	165.	(a)
166.	(d)	167.	(c)	168.	(b)	169.	(c)	170.	(a)
171.	(b)	172.	(c)	173.	(a)	174.	(b)	175.	(d)
176.	(c)	177.	(a)	178.	(a)	179.	(a)	180.	(a)
181.	(b)	182.	(b)	183.	(a)	184.	(b)	185.	(a)
186.	(b)	187.	(a)	188.	(c)	189.	(b)	190.	(c)
191.	(a)	192.	(d)	193.	(c)	194.	(a)	195.	(a)
196.	(c)	197.	(d)						

EXPLANATION:-

16. (b) Option (a) cannot be the answer as it will mean that 'it was expected by the people' but in the question it is mentioned that 'Spain expected to win'. Hence option (b) is a better option.

18. (b) 'Have' is a Causative Verb here. Hence we need a subject ' someone' here.

32. (b) 'The brave' is a plural common noun. If we add 'the' before adjectives like brave, poor, rich etc, they become plural common noun and take plural verb.

35. (a) If the sentence is given in Passive Voice without 'by subject', use the subject in active voice that generally does that work.

39. (d) If we change 'to + $V_{b.f}$' into 'to + be + V_3', we open the option of 'by+Sub' and if the same subject is repeated in the sentence that has already come in the sentence earlier, we do not change 'to+$V_{b.f}$' into 'to+be+V_3'

161. (a) 'Alms' is a Plural Noun. Hence use plural verb 'are'.

164. (a) 'Spectacles' is a Plural Noun. Hence use plural verb 'are'.

165. (a) 'Tongs' is a Plural Noun. Hence use plural verb 'are'.

166. (d) 'Billiards' is plural in form but singular in meaning as it is the name of a game. Hence use singular verb 'is'.

167. (c) 'Have' is a Causative Verb here. Hence we need a subject ' someone' here.

168. (b) Binoculars is a Plural Noun. Hence use plural verb 'are'.

169. (c) Police is a Plural Noun. Hence use plural verb 'are'.

171. (b) See the explanation of question 16.

173. (a) When we join two subjects by using 'and not', the verb agrees with the first subject. 'The captain' will take 'is' with it.

174. (b) When two subjects are joined by using 'neither.....nor', the verb agrees with the second subject. 'State Governments' (Plural noun) will take a plural verb.

SPOTTING THE ERROR

1. (a) The officers/ (b) who were on inspection in this factory /(c) were discovered many discrepancies. /(d) No error.

2. (b) The teacher asked / (b) the students whether they could/(c) tell the name of the man who had been invented steam engine. / (d) No error.

3. (a) He held a bomb / (b) in his hand which was totally hiding / (c) in the long cloak that he was wearing. / (d) No error.

4. (a) I was surprise / (b) at his brazenness/ (c) as he was considered an obedient student / (d) No error.

5. (a) Had the police not/ (b) reached here / (c) on time, the traders would have robbed . / (d) No error.

6. (a)He seriously wounded / (b) during the cross fire and / (c) was rushed to hospital / (d) No error.

7. (a) Police Officers sent / (b) to the theatre and every nook and corner /(c) was thoroughly checked. /(d) No error.

8. (a) When the minister was shot dead,/ (b) people were run here and there / (c) to save themselves. /(d) No error.

9. (a) Mother's milk / (b) cannot substituted by / (c) any thing else./(d) No error.

10. (a) When the thief broke into their house / (b) they raised a hue and cry / (c) and the thief caught immediately by the people. / (d) No error

11. (a) The city / (b) was tore / (c) by riots./ (d) No error.

12. (a) It was suggested / (b) by him that the baby / (c) should be immediately taken care. / (d) No error.

13. (a) The truck driver was accused / (b) the lady for walking / (c) in the middle of the road./(d) No error.

14. (a) Some passengers / (b) were flew/ (c) to Paris on the last trip./(d) No error.

15. (a) By the time he arrived, / (b) everybody had / (c) been gone./(d) No error.

16. (a) I am extremely annoyed / (b) by/ (c) the mismanagement./(d) No error.

17. (a) The mall was / (b) engulfed/ (c) by the fire/ (d) No error.

18. (a) It believed earlier / (b) that the sun/ (c) revolved round the earth./(d) No error.

19. (a) As she was wearing / (b) skimpy clothes/ (c) she was stared./(d) No error.

20. (a) You behave in such / (b) a weird manner that / (c) everybody disgusted with you./(d) No error.

21. (a) Ten mangoes / (b) are contained / (c) by this box./(d) No error.

22. (a) A gang of robbers were arrested/ (b) by the police / (c) last night near the island./(d) No error.

23. (a) The streets of Rome / (b) were thronged/ (c) by the common people./ (d) No error.

24. (a) Everyone says that/ (b) he born / (c) of poor parents./(d) No error.

25. (a)The ship sank / (b) and everyone / (c) aboard drowned./(d) No error.

26. (a) If motorists do not observe the traffic regulations, (b) they will be stopped, ticketed / (c) and have to pay a fine. / (d) No error

27. (a) There will be no more supplies/ (b) unless all arrears of payment / (c) were cleared by next Monday. / (d) No error

28. (a) The news of his father's death / (b) was not declared / (c) so far. / (d) No error

Answers with explanation

1. (c) Remove 'were'. Since the sentence is in Active Voice of Past Indefinite Tense 'V_2' will be used in place of 'were + V_3'.
2. (c) Remove 'been'. The sentence is in Active Voice. Hence 'had + V_3' will be used and not 'had + been + V_3' which is used in Passive Voice of Past Perfect Tense .
3. (b) Turn 'hiding' into 'hidden'.
4. (a) Change 'surprise' into 'surprised'. In Passive Voice, the main verb is in 'V_3' form.
5. (c) 'Would have' will be followed by 'been'. 'Traders would have robbed' means 'the traders would have performed the act of robbing'.
6. (a) 'He seriously wounded' means 'he performed the act of harming someone grievously'. Change 'he seriously wounded' into 'he was seriously wounded'.
7. (a) Add 'were' before 'sent'.
8. (b) Change 'were run' into 'ran'. Here 'people' (the subject) performed the act of running. Hence the sentence will be in active voice.
9. (b) Use 'be' after 'cannot'. In Passive Voice 'cannot + be + V_3'is used.
10. (c) Change 'thief caught' into 'thief was caught'. 'Thief caught' means 'thief is the doer of the action'.
11. (b) Use 'V_3' after 'was'. ('torn' is the 'V_3' form of 'tear')
12. (c) Use 'of' after 'care'. Do not forget to use the preposition in Passive Voice that follows the verb in Active Voice.
13. (a) 'Truck driver' is the subject here. Hence remove 'was'. The sentence is not in passive voice.
14. (b) Use 'V_3' after 'were'. V_3 of 'fly' is 'flown'.
15. (c) Remove 'been'. The sentence is not in Passive Voice.
16. (b) Change 'by' into 'at'.

    Note: (a) Annoyed at something
    (b) Annoyed with someone
17. (c) Use 'in', in place of 'by'. 'Engulfed' takes preposition 'in'.
18. (a) Change 'it believed' into 'It was believed'.
19. (c) 'stared' takes preposition 'at'.
20. (c) Change 'everybody disgusted' into 'everybody is disgusted' .
21. (c) 'Contained' takes preposition 'in'.
22. (a) 'Gang' is a collective noun. Hence it will take singular verb 'was'.
23. (c) 'Thronged' takes preposition 'with'.
24. (b) Change 'he born' into 'he was born'.
25. (c) Add 'was' before 'drowned'.
26. (c) "and will have to" is the correct formation. The sentence is in 'Active Voice' after 'and'.
27. (c) Use 'are' in place of 'were'. Sentence is of 'Future Conditional'. If two actions take place one after the other in future, the second depending on the first, the 1st action will be in Simple Present Tense and the 2nd action will be in Simple Future Tense.
28. (b) Change 'was not declared' into 'has not been declared'. 'Yet' or 'so far' is used in the sentence . Present Perfect Tense is preferred to Simple Past Tense when 'yet' or 'so far' is used in the sentence.

4 NARRATION

CHAPTER

➢ We study 'Direct' and 'Indirect Speech' under Narration.

DIRECT SPEECH:

➢ If the sentence spoken by the speaker is written without any change, the sentence is said to be in the direct speech.

E.g.: Ram says (Reporting Verb), " I work hard (Reported Speech) ."

INDIRECT SPEECH:

➢ If the sentence spoken by the speaker is changed by the narrator following certain rules, it is called the Indirect Speech.

E.g.: Ram says that he works hard.

ASSERTIVE SENTENCES

E.g.: He says, "I work hard". (Direct Speech)

He says that he works hard. (Indirect Speech)

RULES FOR CONVERTING DIRECT INTO INDIRECT SPEECH:

➢ (1) 'Comma' and 'inverted commas' are removed and conjunction 'that' is used while changing the sentence into Indirect Speech.

➢ (2) Pronoun changes according to the following rule -

S	O	N
1	2	3

➢

Sub	Obj	No
1st Person	2nd Person	3rd Person
I, we	you	he, she, it, they

E.g.:**1.** He says, " **I** work hard"

sub. (He) — *1st Person* (I)

according to — *changes to*

He says that **he** works hard.

2. He says to me, " **You** work hard."

sub. — He; *obj* — me; *2nd Person* — You

changes to / *according to*

He tells me that **I** work hard

3. He says to me, "**She** works hard."

3rd Person — *no change*

He tells me that **she** works hard.

➢ (3) **Say/Said remains unchanged** in Indirect Speech.

'Say to' changes into 'tell' and 'said to' changes into 'told'.

E.g.: He **says to** me, "You work hard".

He **tells** me that I work hard.

Note: '**to**' is not used after '**tell**' and '**told**'. **(See page 228. The list of verbs that takes 'to' and that does not take 'to' is given.)**

➢ (4) If the **reporting verb is in 'present'** or '**future tense**', there shall be **no change in the tense of** the **reported speech**.

E.g.: He says, "I come here".

He says that he comes here.

➢ (5) If the **reporting verb is in 'past'**, and **the reported speech is a 'universal truth' / 'phrase' / 'idiom' / 'habitual action'** or '**historical fact**', the **tense of the reported speech does not change.**

E.g.: He said, "The Sun is a star".

He said that the Sun is a star.

➢ (6) If the **reporting verb is in 'past'**, and **the reported speech is not an idiom/ phrase** etc, the **reported speech changes according to the rules** given below-

E.g.: He said, "I **came here yesterday**".

He said that he **had come there the previous day**.

(1) CHANGE IN TENSE

➢ **Simple Present** (is / am / are / V_1) → **Simple Past** (was / were / V_2) → **Past Perfect** (had been / had V_3) → **No change**

➢ **Present Continuous** (is / am / are) → **Past Continuous** (was / were) → **Past Perfect Continuous** (had been) → **No change**

➢ **Present Perfect / Present Perfect Continuous** (has/ have) → **Past Perfect / Past Perfect Continuous** (had) → **No change**

(2) CHANGE OF MODALS

shall/will → ***should / would***
may → ***might***
can → ***could***

(3) CHANGE IN TIME AND PLACE

today → that day, tomorrow → the next day, yesterday → the previous day/ the day before, tonight → that night, Last → the previous, here → there, this → that, these → those, ago → before, now → then.

Examples:

1. She said, "I cannot help you at this time."
   She said that she couldn't help me at that time.
2. He said to me, "I shall come to meet you tomorrow."
   He told me that he would come to meet me the next day.
3. Ram said, "I haven't taken any exam this year but I intend to take two exams the next year"
   Ram said that he hadn't taken any exam that year but he intended to take two exams the next year.
4. He said, "Virtue is its own reward".
   He said that virtue is its own reward. (Sentence is a phrase)
5. Our teacher said, "We have to finish this work today as we know that tomorrow never comes."
   Our teacher said that we had to finish that work that day as we know that tomorrow never comes.

INTERROGATIVE SENTENCES

Questions

He said to me, "Are you coming?"

He asked me whether I was coming.

He said to me, "when are you coming?"
(Question is of wh family)

He asked me when I was coming.

➢ **Rules**

1. Change 'Said to' into **asked, questioned, inquired or interrogated.**
2. 'Question Mark (?)' should be changed into 'full stop'.
3. The sentences will not be in interrogative form in Indirect Speech. This means that helping verb is used after the subject.
4. Tense and pronoun shall be changed according to the rules.
5. If the question can be answered in yes/no, conjunction if / whether will be used. If the question is of 'wh family' no conjunction will be used.

Examples:

1. He said to me, "Do you know me?"
   He asked me if I knew him.
2. She said to him, "What are you doing now?"
   She asked him what he was doing then.
3. He said to him, "Did you intend to come with me?"
   He asked him if he had intended to come with him.
4. He said to her, "Haven't you seen this movie?"
   He asked her if she hadn't seen that movie.
5. He said to her, "Madam, can I help you?"
   She said, "No"
   He asked her respectfully if he could help her.
   She answered in the negative.
6. He said to me, "When will the train arrive?"
   He enquired of me when the train would arrive.

Explanation of Sentence 5:

- If we use 'Sir'/'Madam'/'Your Honour' or any other word of respect in the Direct Speech, such word should be replaced by word 'respectfully' in the Indirect Speech.
- If we use 'Darling'/'Dear'/'My beloved' or any other word of affection in the Direct Speech, such word should be replaced by word 'lovingly/ affectionately' in the Indirect Speech.
- If the answer is in **'yes'** or **'no'**, they must be changed into 'answered in the Affirmative/ answered in the Negative' respectively.

IMPERATIVE SENTENCES:

He said to me, "Go away".

He ordered me to go away.

- **Rules -**
  1. Change **'Said to'** into **Ordered / Respected / Forbade/ Suggested etc.**
  2. Conjunction **'to'** will replace comma and inverted commas.
  3. **'To'** is followed by **'$V_{b.f}$'**.
  4. **Tense and Pronoun** change according to rules.

Examples:

1. She said to me, "Do not come here"
   She forbade me to come there.
   or
   She ordered me not to come there.
2. He said, "call the first witness now."
   He ordered them to call the first witness then.

3. She said, "Spread the clothes in the sunlight and do not wash anything else."
   She ordered him to spread the clothes in the sunlight and not to wash anything else.
4. The captain said to the soldiers, "Stand at ease."
   The captain commanded the soldiers to stand at ease.
5. My mother said to me, "Help others but do not expect anything in return."
   My mother advised me to help others but not to expect anything in return."

EXCLAMATORY SENTENCES

She said, "Alas! I am undone".

She exclaimed with sorrow that she was undone.

Rules

1 **Said + Alas !** changes to → **exclaimed with sorrow.**

Said + Hurray ! changes to → **exclaimed with joy.**

Said + Fi ! / Ugh ! changes to → **exclaimed with despise/disgust.**

Said + Wow ! changes to → **exclaimed with joy.**

Said + Oh ! changes to → **exclaimed with surprise / regret.**

2. Conjunction **'that'** will replace comma and inverted commas.
3. **Tense and Pronoun** change according to rules.

Examples:

1. She said, "Hurray ! we have won this match."
   She exclaimed with joy that they had won that match.
2. She said, "How beautiful is the rain!"
   She exclaimed with joy that the rain was very beautiful.
3. He said, "Bravo ! you have done well."
   He applauded him saying that he had done well.
4. She said, "What a pleasant surprise!"
   She exclaimed that it was a pleasant surprise.

OPTATIVE SENTENCES

He said, "May God bless you."

He prayed that God might bless me.

Rules

1. Change '**Said**' into '**wished**' **or** '**prayed**'.
2. Conjunction **'that'** is used.
3. **Tense and Pronoun** are changed according to rules.

Examples:

1. She said, "May God pardon him".
   She prayed that God might pardon him.
2. They said, "Long live the king".
   They prayed that the king might live long.

➢ **Some Important Points:**

1. **Need not, used to, would rather, would better, had rather, had better, are not changed** when Direct Speech is changed into Indirect Speech.

E.g.: He said, "I used to go to school by bus".
He said that he used to go to school by bus.

2. If **Past Continuous** is used with **Time Clause**, the **Tense** does **not change**.

E.g.: He said to me, "While I was studying, you were playing".
He told me that while he was studying, I was playing.

3. If the **Time Clause** is mentioned, in **Past Indefinite Tense,** the **Tense** does **not change.**

E.g.: He said, "When I met him, she was playing".
He said that when he met him, she was playing.

4. If two **simultaneous actions are given in Past Indefinite Tense**, the **Tense** does **not change** when the speech in changed from direct to indirect.

E.g.: She said, "I prepared the tea and he fried the chips".
She said that she prepared the tea and he fried the chips.

5. In case of **historical** event, the **Tense** does **not change**.

E.g.: He said, "Gandhiji started the Quit India Movement".
He said that Gandiji started the Quit India Movement.

6. **Will/shall** is changed into **would/should** but the statement **will/shall**, should be changed into '**should**' if the statement is suggestive. (See example 2)

E.g.:1) He said, "I shall come tomorrow".
He said that he would come the next day.

2) Shc said to me, "What shall I do after the exam?"
She asked me what she should do after the exam.

7. **Modals** will be **changed according to the meaning of the sentence**.

E.g.1. She said, "If I get selected, I need not take any exam further".
She said that if she got selected, she would not have to take any exam further.

2. He said, "Need I send an e-mail?"
He asked me if he had to send an e-mail.

3. He said, "When I was a kid, I could not go out alone".(here 'could' is for 'permission')
He said that when he was a kid, he was not allowed to go out alone.

4. She said, "Rohit, you must be prudent".
She ordered Rohit to be prudent. (here 'must' is used for 'order')

PRACTICE SET

Directions: A sentence has been given in direct/Indirect form. Out of the four alternatives suggested, select the one which best expresses the same sentence in Indirect/Direct form.

1. "Call the first witness", said the Judge.
(a) The judge commanded to call the first witness.
(b) The judge commanded them to call the first witness.
(c) The judge commanded that the first witness be called.
(d) The judge commanded the first witness to be called.

2. The queen said to her son, "You must go to the forest and remain there till your father calls you back."
(a) The queen ordered her son to go to the forest and remain there till his father calls him back.
(b) The queen told her son that he must go to the forest and remain there till his father called him back.
(c) The queen told his son that you must go to the forest and remain there till your father called you back.
(d) The queen told her son to go to the forest and remained there till his father called him back.

3. I said to her, "All your faults will be pardoned if you confess them."
(a) I told her that all her faults will be pardoned if you confess them.
(b) I told her that all her faults would be pardoned if she confessed them.
(c) I told her that all her faults will have to be pardoned if she confessed them.
(d) I told her that all her faults would have to be pardoned if she confessed them.

4. He said to Sita, "When do you intend to pay back the money you borrowed from me?"
(a) He enquired Sita when did she intend to pay back the money she borrowed from him.
(b) He enquired Sita when she intended to pay back the money she borrowed from him.
(c) He enquired Sita when she intended to pay back the money she had borrowed from him.
(d) He enquired when Sita intended to pay back the money she borrowed from him.

5. "Let's give a party", said Jaya. "Let's not", said her husband.
(a) Jaya suggested giving a party but her husband answered in the negative.
(b) Jaya suggested giving a party but her husband opposed the idea.
(c) Jaya suggested giving a party but her husband contradicted her.
(d) Jaya suggested giving a party but her husband refused.

6. The old man of Latur said, "Alas! my only son is dead."
(a) The old man of Latur exclaimed with sorrow that his only son was dead.
(b) The old man of Latur told with pain that his only son was dead.
(c) The old man of Latur expressed with anguish that his only son was dead.
(d) The old man of Latur sorrowfully narrated that his only son was dead.

7. She said to the girl, "Did you do this?"
(a) She asked the girl that she did that.
(b) She asked the girl if she did that.
(c) She asked the girl if she had done that.

(d) She told the girl that she had done that.

8. "Many happy returns of your birthday", we said.

(a) We greeted him on his birthday.
(b) We said that many happy returns of your birthday.
(c) We wished him many happy returns of his birthday.
(d) We prayed for many happy returns of his birthday.

9. "Doctor", the patient cried, "please tell me how much time I have."

(a) The patient pleaded the doctor how much time he will have.
(b) The patient exclaimed to the doctor that how much time he had.
(c) The patient pleaded with the doctor to tell him how much time he had.
(d) The patient cried to the doctor that how much time had he.

10. "So help me Heaven!" he cried, "I will never steal again."

(a) He wanted Heaven to help him so that he would never steal again.
(b) She exclaimed to heaven that he would never steal again.
(c) He exclaimed heaven to help him that he would never steal again.
(d) He called upon heaven to witness his resolve never to steal again.

11. She said, "I'll give you Rs. 100/- to keep your mouth shut."

(a) She said that she would give him Rs. 100/- to keep his mouth shut.
(b) She offered him Rs. 100/- to keep his mouth shut.
(c) She suggested to him that she would give him Rs. 100/- to keep his mouth shut.
(d) She proposed that she would give him Rs. 100/- to keep his mouth shut.

12. From one of the windows of my flat I can see the Qutub Minar', said my friend.

(a) My friend told that from one of the windows of his flat he could see the Qutub Minar.
(b) My friend said that from one of the windows of his flat he can see the Qutub Minar.
(c) My friend said that from one of the windows of his flat he could see the Qutub Minar.
(d) My friend told that from one of the windows of his flat he can see the Qutub Minar.

13. The teacher said to the student, "Why were you absent yesterday?"

(a) The teacher asked the student why had been he absent the previous day.
(b) The teacher asked the student why had he been absent the previous day.
(c) The teacher informed the student that why he had been absent the next day.
(d) The teacher asked the student why he had been absent the previous day.

14. The teacher said to Ashok, "I shall report the matter to the Principal if you misbehave again."

(a) The teacher told Ashok that he would be reporting the matter to the Principal if he misbehaved again.
(b) The teacher warned Ashok that he would report the matter to the Principal if he misbehaved again.
(c) The teacher threatened Ashok to report the matter to the Principal if he misbehave again.
(d) The teacher cautioned Ashok about reporting the matter to the Principal if he misbehaved again.

15. "Fi! A soldier and afraid of fighting!" said Babar.

(a) Babar exclaimed with surprise that a soldier should be afraid of fighting.
(b) Addressing a soldier, Babar cursed him that he should be afraid of fighting.

(c) Babar cursed the soldier who was afraid of fighting.
(d) Babar cursed and exclaimed that a soldier should not be afraid of fighting.

16. The teacher said to Ram, "Would you like to go on a trip to Kashmir?" Ram said, "Yes."
(a) The teacher asked if Ram would like to go on a trip to Kashmir and Ram replied yes.
(b) The teacher asked Ram if he would like to go on a trip to Kashmir and Ram replied yes.
(c) The teacher asked Ram if he would have like to go on a trip to Kashmir and Ram replied in the affirmative.
(d) The teacher asked Ram if he would like to go on a trip to Kashmir and Ram replied in the affirmative.

17. Everybody said, "How well she sings!"
(a) Everybody told us that she sings very well.
(b) Everybody exclaimed that she sings very well.
(c) Everybody exclaimed that she sang very well.
(d) Everybody told us that how she sang very well.

18. "Suppose your children go out for a nice long walk", she said.
(a) She proposed that his children went out for a nice long walk.
(b) She advised that his children go out for a nice long walk .
(c) She suggested that his children go out for a nice long walk.
(d) She suggested that his children should go out for a nice long walk.

19. I said, "When it gets dark, light the lantern and hang it out."
(a) I said that when it got dark he light the lantern and hung it out.
(b) I requested that when it got dark he may light the lantern and hang it out.
(c) I said that when it got dark he should light the lantern and hung it out.
(d) I said that when it got dark he should light the lantern and hang it out.

20. "Do as you wish, but don't come and ask me for help if you get into difficulties.", he said to me
(a) He told me to do as he wished or he wouldn't come and help me if I got into difficulties.
(b) He told me to do as I wished, but not to come and ask him for help if I got into difficulties.
(c) He ordered me to do as I wished, but not to come and ask him for help if I got into difficulties.
(d) He told me that unless I did as I wished he would not come and help me if I got into difficulties.

21. "May you live long and prosper", said the old lady to her son.
(a) The old lady blessed her son with long life and wished him prosperity.
(b) The old lady prayed for her son's long life and prosperity.
(c) The old lady prayed for her son and said that he might live long and prosper.
(d) The old lady blessed her son and prayed for his long life and prosperity.

22. Socrates said, "Virtue is its own reward."
(a) Socrates said that virtue had its own rewards.
(b) Socrates says that virtue is its own reward.
(c) Socrates said that virtue is its own reward.
(d) Socrates said that virtue was its own reward.

23. He said to the interviewer, "Could you please repeat the question?"
(a) He requested the interviewer if he could please repeat the question.

(b) He requested the interviewer to please repeat the question.
(c) He requested the interviewer to repeat the question.
(d) He requested the interviewer if he could repeat the question.

24. He said, "It used to be a lovely, quiet street."
(a) He said that it used to be a lovely, quiet street.
(b) He pointed out that it had used to be a lovely, quiet street.
(c) He said that there used to be a lovely, quiet street.
(d) He inquired whether there was a lovely, quiet street.

25. The Prime Minister said that no one would be allowed to disturb the peace.
(a) The Prime Minister said, "We shall not allow any one to disturb the peace."
(b) The Prime Minister said, "We would not allow any one to disturb the peace."
(c) The Prime Minister said, "No one will disturb the peace."
(d) The Prime Minister said, "No one can disturb the peace."

26. The spectators said, "Bravo ! Well done, players."
(a) Thc spectators shouted that the players were doing very well.
(b) The spectators exclaimed with joy that the players were doing very wcll.
(c) The spectators applauded the players saying that they had done well.
(d) The spectators applauded the players joyfully to do well.

27. I said to my friend, "Good Morning. Let us go for a picnic today."
(a) I told good morning to my friend and asked to go for a picnic that day.
(b) I wished my friend good morning and proposed that we should go for a picnic that day.
(c) I wished my friend good morning and proposed that they should go for a picnic that day.
(d) I told good morning to my friend and suggested to go for a picnic today.

28. The new student asked the old one, "Do you know my name?"
(a) The new student asked the old one if he knew his name.
(b) The new student asked the old one that whether he knew his names.
(c) The new student asked the old one did he know his name.
(d) The new student asked the old one if he knows his name.

29. I warned her that I could no longer tolerate her coming late.
(a) I said to her, "You can no longer tolerate my coming late."
(b) I said to her, "I can no longer tolerate your coming late."
(c) I said to her, "He can no longer tolerate her coming late".
(d) I said to her, "I can no longer tolerate she coming late."

30. I said to my mother, "I will certainly take you to Bangalore this week."
(a) I told my mother he would certainly take her to Bangalore that week.
(b) I told my mother that I would certainly take her to Bangalore that week.
(c) I told my mother that she would certainly take her to Bangalore that week.
(d) I told to my mother that I would take you to Bangalore that week.

31. "How clever of you to have solved the puzzle so quickly!" said the mother.
(a) The mother exclaimed admiringly that it was very clever of him to have solved the puzzle so quickly.
(b) The mother expressed that he was so clever to have solved the puzzle quickly.

(c) The mother told that he was very clever in solving the puzzle so quickly.
(d) The mother exclaimed with joy that he was clever enough to solve the puzzle so quickly.

32. He said that he went for a walk every morning.
(a) He said, "I went for a walk every morning".
(b) He said, "I go for a walk every morning".
(c) He said, "I will go for a walk morning".
(d) He said, "he went for a walk every morning".

33. I reiterated, "I don't care about the job".
(a) I reiterated I didn't care about the job.
(b) I said again and again I didn't care about the job.
(c) I reiterated that I did not care about the job.
(d) I repeatedly said that I cared about the job.

34. I said to my brother, "Let us go to some hill station for a change."
(a) I suggested to my brother that they should go to some hill station for a change.
(b) I suggested to my brother that we should go to some hill station for a change.
(c) I suggested to my brother that let us go to some hill station for a change.
(d) I suggested to my brother that let them go to some hill station for a change.

35. I wondered how many discoveries went unheeded.
(a) I said, "How many discoveries have gone unheeded?"
(b) I said, "How many discoveries went unheeded?"
(c) I said, "Do discoveries go unheeded?"
(d) I said, "How many discoveries go unheeded?"

36. Gopan said to me, "Can you do these sums for me?"
(a) Gopan asked me if I could do those sums for him.
(b) Gopan asked me if I can do those sums for him.
(c) Gopan asked me if I can do those sums for him.
(d) Gopan asked if I could do these sums for him.

37. The boss said, "It's time we began planning our work".
(a) The boss said that it was time they had begun planning their work.
(b) The boss said that it was time we had began planning our work.
(c) The boss said that it was time they began planning their work.
(d) The boss said that it was time we began planning his work.

38. He said to the judge, "I did not commit this crime."
(a) He told the judge that he did not commit the crime.
(b) The told the judge that he had not committed the crime.
(c) He told the judge that he had not committed that crime.
(d) He told the judge that he had not committed this crime.

39. Rahul said, "I will do it now or never".
(a) Rahul said that he will do it now or never.
(b) Rahul said that he will now or never do it.
(c) Rahul said that he would do it then or never.
(d) Rahul said that he would now or never do it.

40. My father once said to me, "If I can't trust my people, then I don't want to be doing this."
(a) His father once told him that if he couldn't trust his people then he didn't want to be doing that.

(b) My father once told me that if he couldn't trust his people then he didn't want to be doing that.
(c) My father once told me that if he couldn't trust my people then he didn't want to be doing that.
(d) My father once told me that if he couldn't trust his people then he didn't want to be doing this.

41. Doshi said to his wife, "Please select one of these necklaces."
(a) Doshi requested his wife to select one of these necklaces.
(b) Doshi said to his wife to please select one of these necklaces.
(c) Doshi told his wife to please select one of these necklaces.
(d) Doshi requested his wife to select one of those necklaces.

42. He wrote in his report, "The rainfall has been scanty till now."
(a) He reported that the rainfall has been scanty till now.
(b) He reported that the rainfall had been scanty till now.
(c) He reported that the rainfall has been scanty till then.
(d) He reported that the rainfall had been scanty till then.

43. "Govind," said the manager sternly, "I command you to tell me what the old man said."
(a) The manager sternly commanded Govind to tell him what the old man had said.
(b) The manager commanded sternly to Govind to tell him what the old man had to say.
(c) The manager commanded Govind to tell him what the old man said.
(d) The manager told Govind to tell him what the old man said.

44. He says, "I am going to the market now."
(a) He says that he is going to the market now.
(b) He said that he was going to the market then.
(c) He says that he was going to the market then.
(d) He said that he was going to the market now.

45. She said to Rita, "Please help me with my homework."
(a) She requested Rita to help her in her homework.
(b) Rita requested her to help her with her homework.
(c) She requested Rita to help her with her homework.
(d) She requested Rita to help her homework.

46. He said to me, "Do not run after money and then you will see money running after you."
(a) He told to me that I did not run after money and then I would see money running me.
(b) He advised me not to run after money and then I would see money running after me.
(c) He warned me not to run after money and then I will see money running after me.
(d) He warned me not to run after money and then money would run after me.

47. He said to me, "Do you know English?"
(a) He asked me if I did know English.
(b) He asked me if I knew English.
(c) he asked me that if I know English.
(d) He asked me if I know English.

48. My father said to me, "Bravo! You have done well."
(a) My father applauded me saying that I had done well.
(b) My father applauded me saying that I have done well.
(c) My father applauded me saying that I did well.
(d) My father applauded me saying that you had done well.

49. Tom said that he had had a strange experience the day before.

(a) Tom said, "I have a strange experience yesterday."
(b) Tom said, "I have had a strange experience yesterday."
(c) Tom said, "I had a strange experience yesterday."
(d) Tom said, "I had had a strange experience yesterday."

50. Our teacher said to us, "I am not going to tolerate your nonsense anymore."
(a) Our teacher warned us that she is not going to tolerate our nonsense anymore.
(b) Our teacher warned us that she was not going to tolerate our nonsense anymore.
(c) Our teacher told us that she was not going to be tolerate our nonsense anymore.
(d) Our teacher said that she was not going to tolerate our nonsense anymore

51. Sheela said, "I am going to finish this work now before I start a new work tomorrow."
(a) Sheela told me that she was going to finish that work then before she started a new work the next day.
(b) Sheela said that she was going to finish that work then before she started a new work the next day.
(c) Sheela said that she is going to finish that work then before she started a new work the next day.
(d) Sheela told that she was going to finish that work then before she started a new work the next day.

52. "Do you suppose you know better than your own father?" shouted her angry mother.
(a) Her angry mother shouted and asked that she supposed whether she knew better than her own father.
(b) Her angry mother shouted and asked that she supposed that she knew better than her own father.
(c) Her angry mother shouted whether she supposed that she known better than her own father.
(d) Her angry mother shouted and asked her whether she supposed that she knew better than her own father.

53. "So help me, Heaven !" he cried "I will never drive recklessly".
(a) He called upon Heaven to see his resolve never to drive recklessly.
(b) He called upon Heaven to witness his resolve never to drive recklessly.
(c) He called upon Heaven to witness his resolved never to drive recklessly.
(d) He ordered Heaven to witness his resolve never to drive recklessly.

54. The dwarf said to her, "Promise me that when you are a queen you will give me your first-born child."
(a) The dwarf advised her to promised that when she was a queen she would give him her first born child.
(b) The dwarf requested her to promise that when she had been a queen she would give him her first born child.
(c) The dwarf requested her to promise that when she is a queen she would give him her first born child.
(d) The dwarf asked her to promise him that when she was a queen she would give him her first born child.

55. "Dear bird", she said, stroking its feathers, "have you come to comfort me in my sorrow?"
(a) Stroking the bird's feathers, she asked affectionately that she had come to comfort her in her sorrow.
(b) Stroking the bird's feathers, she asked affectionately whether it had come to comfort in her sorrow.
(c) Stroking the bird's feathers, she asked affectionately whether they had come to comfort her in her sorrow.

(d) Stroking the bird's feathers, she asked affectionately whether it had come to comfort her in her sorrow.

56. He said, "My God ! I am ruined."

(a) He exclaimed sadly that he was ruined.
(b) He exclaimed that he was ruined.
(c) He exclaimed sadly that he had been ruined.
(d) He exclaimed sadly that he ruined.

57. "Ah me!" exclaimed the man, "What a rash and bloody deed you have done!"

(a) The man exclaimed that he had done a very rash and bloody deed.
(b) The man exclaimed sadly that he had done a very rash and bloody deed.
(c) The man exclaimed with sorry that you had done a very rash and bloody deed.
(d) The man exclaimed with sorrow that they had done a very rash and bloody deed.

58. Bhishma said, "Boys! Boys! Remember you are playing a game. If it be Arjuna's turn let him have it."

(a) Bhishma asked the boys to remembered that they were playing a game. If it was Arjuna's turn he must have it.
(b) Bhishma asked the boys to remembered that they were playing a game. If it is Arjuna's turn he must have it.
(c) Bhishma asked the boys to remember that they were playing a game. If it was Arjuna's turn he must have it.
(d) Bhishma asked the boys to remember that we were playing a game. If it was Arjuna's turn he must have it.

59. "What are you doing, grandma?"said the little boy. "I'm planting saplings, my little prince." "Ah, how interesting! Let me try , if I can also do so."

(a) The little boy said to his grandma what she was doing. She replied affectionately that she was planting saplings. The boy exclaimed that it was very interesting and wanted to try if he could also do so.
(b) The little boy asked his grandma what she was doing. She replied affectionately that she was planting saplings. The boy exclaimed that it was very interesting and wanted to try if he could also do so.
(c) The little boy asked his grandma that she was doing. She replied affectionately that she was planting saplings. The boy exclaimed that it was very interesting and wanted to try if he could also do so.
(d) The little boy asked his grandma what was she doing. She replied affectionately that she was planting saplings. The boy exclaimed that it was very interesting and wanted to try if he could also do so.

60. "You say," said the judge, "that the bag you lost contained one hundred and ten pounds". "Yes, your honour," replied the cheat. "Then as this one contains one hundred pounds it cannot be yours."

(a) The judge asked the cheat if the bag he had lost contained one hundred and ten pounds. The cheat replied respectfully in the affirmative. Then the judge concluded that as that one contained one hundred pounds it could not be his.
(b) The judge ordered the cheat if the bag he had lost contained one hundred and ten pounds. The cheat replied respectfully in the affirmative. Then the judge concluded that as that one

contained one hundred pounds it could not be his.

(c) The judge ordered the cheat that the bag he had lost contained one hundred and ten pounds. The cheat replied respectfully in the affirmative. Then the judge concluded that as that one contained one hundred pounds it could not be his.

(d) The judge asked the cheat that the bag he had lost contained one hundred and ten pounds. The cheat replied in the affirmative. Then the judge concluded as this one contained one hundred pounds it could not be his.

61. The child said, 'Mommy, can you bring the moon for me?' Mommy said, 'No.'

(a) The child asked his mommy if she could bring the moon for him. Mommy replied in the negative.

(b) The child told his mommy if she could bring the moon for him. Mommy replied in the negative.

(c) The child asked his mommy if she could bring the moon for him. Mommy replied no.

(d) The child said to his mommy that she could bring the moon for him. Mommy replied in the negative.

62. He said, "Fi!" and vomited

(a) He exclaimed with disgust and had vomited

(b) He exclaimed with disgust and vomited

(c) He exclaimed with sorrow and vomited

(d) He exclaimed with disgust and then had vomited

63. The captain said to the soldiers, "Stand at ease."

(a) The captain commanded the soldiers to stand at ease.

(b) The captain said the soldiers to stand at ease.

(c) The captain told the soldiers to stand at ease.

(d) The captain commanded the soldiers that they stand at ease.

64. "I can show no mercy," said the king, "except permitting you to choose what kind of death you wish to die."

(a) The king asked that he could show no mercy except permitting him to choose what kind of death he wished to die.

(b) The king advised that he could show no mercy except permitting him to choose what kind of death he wished to die.

(c) The king ordered that he could show no mercy except permitting him to choose what kind of death he wished to die.

(d) The king said that he could show no mercy except permitting him to choose what kind of death he wished to die.

65. Kausalya said to Rama, " Do not desire, O my child, to possess the stars, because they are thousands of miles off."

(a) Kausalya forbade her child Rama to desire to possess the stars because they were thousands of miles off.

(b) Kausalya requested her child Rama to desire to possess the stars because they were thousands of miles off.

(c) Kausalya ordered her child Rama to not desire to possess the stars because they were thousands of miles off.

(d) Kausalya said to her child Rama not to desire to possess the stars because they were thousands of miles off.

66. "What a stupid fellow you are!" she remarked.

(a) She exclaimed that what a stupid fellow he was.

(b) She exclaimed that he was a very stupid fellow.
(c) She exclaimed in disgust how he could be so stupid.
(d) She asked him what a stupid fellow he was.

67. The police said to the thief, "Don't move."
(a) The police ordered the thief not to move.
(b) The police ordered the thief that he should not move.
(c) The police told the thief that he did not move.
(d) The police ordered to the thief to not move.

68. He said, "I am going to college just now."
(a) He said that he was going to college just now.
(b) He asked that he was going to college just then.
(c) He said that he was going to college just then.
(d) He asked that he was going to college just now.

69. The teacher said to the student "Can you explain this?"
(a) The teacher asked the student whether he can explain this.
(b) The teacher asked the student whether he can explain that.
(c) The teacher asked the student whether he could explain this.
(d) The teacher asked the student whether he could explain that.

70. Ramu said, "My master is planning to build a huge house in Khandala."
(a) Ramu said that his master planned to build a huge house in Khandala.
(b) Ramu said that his master is planning to build a huge house in Khandala.
(c) Ramu said that his master's plan is to build a huge house in Khandala.
(d) Ramu said that his master was planning to build a huge house in Khandala.

71. Nandita said to Nitin, "Can you solve this sum?"
(a) Nandita asked Nitin if could he solve this sum.
(b) Nandita asked Nitin if could he solve that sum.
(c) Nandita asked Nitin if he could solve this sum.
(d) Nandita asked Nitin if he could solve that sum.

72. He said, "How lovely the scene is!"
(a) He exclaimed that the scene is very lovely.
(b) He exclaimed that how the scene was lovely.
(c) He exclaimed that the scene was very lovely.
(d) He exclaimed that the scene is indeed lovely.

73. Bill said, "I am here to help you all."
(a) Bill said that he is here to help you all.
(b) Bill said that he was there to help us all.
(c) Bill said that he was here to help us all.
(d) Bill said that he is there to help us all.

74. The kids yelled in a loud voice, "We love our family."
(a) The kids yelled loudly that they love our family.
(b) The kids yelled in a loud voice that they loved their family.
(c) The kids yelled in a loud voice that they loved our family.
(d) The kids were shouting loudly that they loved their family.

75. He said to me, "Please visit my company tomorrow".
(a) He said to me to visit his company tomorrow.
(b) He requested me to visit his company tomorrow.
(c) He requested me to visit his company the next day.
(d) He said to me to visit his company the next day.

76. He said, "My parents are arriving tomorrow".

(a) He said that his parents are arriving the next day.
(b) He said that his parents were arriving the next day.
(c) He said that his parents are arriving tomorrow.
(d) He said that his parents have arrived the next day.

77. He said, "How cruel of him!"

(a) He remarked that it was very cruel of him.
(b) He remarked on his great cruelty.
(c) He remark that it was very cruel of him.
(d) He remarked that it is very cruel of him.

78. "How did it get here?" she wanted to know.

(a) She wanted to know how did it get here.
(b) She wanted to know how it had got there.
(c) She wanted to know how did it got there.
(d) She wanted to know how it get there.

79. The author said, "It took me three years to finish the novel."

(a) The author said that it took him three years to finish the novel.
(b) The author said that it had taken me three years to finish the novel.
(c) The author said that it would take him three years to finish the novel
(d) The author said that it had taken him three years to finish the novel.

80. "Go away!" she said to the man, "do not trouble your family anymore".

(a) She asked the man to go away and not trouble the family any more.
(b) She asked the man not to trouble the family that was away, any more.
(c) She asked the man not to trouble your family any more and go away.
(d) She asked the man to go away and not to trouble his family any more.

81. He asked me, "Have you finished reading the magazine?"

(a) He asked me whether I had finished reading the magazine.
(b) He asked me if had I finished reading the magazine.
(c) He asked me if I have finished reading the magazine.
(d) He asked me whether I finished reading the magazine.

82. He said, "We have done our work."

(a) He said that he had done his work.
(b) He said that they have done their work.
(c) He said that they had done their work.
(d) He said that they should do their work.

83. "I'm sorry I'm unable to repay the loan in time," said the customer.

(a) The customer regrets that he was unable to repay the loan in time.
(b) The customer regretted that he is unable to repay the loan in time.
(c) The customer regretted that he was unable to repay the loan in time.
(d) The customer said that he could be unable to repay the loan in time.

84. "Please, take me to the officer," said the visitor.

(a) The visitor requested them to take him to the officer.
(b) The visitor told them to take him to the officer.
(c) The visitor requested for the officer to be taken.
(d) The visitor wanted the officer to take him there.

85. Nitin said, "What a pleasant atmosphere this place has!"

(a) Nitin exclaimed with joy that that place was a pleasant atmosphere.
(b) Nitin exclaimed with joy that was a pleasant atmosphere in that place.

(c) Nitin exclaimed with joy that that place had a pleasant atmosphere.
(d) Nitin exclaimed with joy that what a pleasant atmosphere that place had.

86. Aarti said, "I am in a hurry today."
(a) Aarti said that she was in a hurry that day.
(b) Aarti said that I am in a hurry today.
(c) Aarti said that she is in a hurry today.
(d) Aarti said that she is in a hurry that day.

87. They said, "We are practising for the next match."
(a) They said that they are practising for the next match.
(b) They said that they practised for the next match.
(c) They said that they were practising for the next match.
(d) They said they were going to practise for the next match.

88. He said, " May you live long."
(a) He suggested that my life might be long.
(b) He prayed that my life might be long.
(c) He prayed that my life may be longer.
(d) He declared that my life is longer.

89. "When did you meet my brother?" she asked me.
(a) She wanted to know when did I meet her brother.
(b) She asked when did I meet my brother.
(c) She asked me when I had met her brother.
(d) She wants to know when I had met my brother.

90. Ruby requested me to lend her Rs. 1000 the next day.
(a) Ruby said to me, "Please lend me Rs. 1000 the next day."
(b) Ruby said to me, "Please lend her Rs. 1000 the next day."
(c) Ruby said to me, "Please lend her Rs. 1000 tomorrow."
(d) Ruby said to me, "Please lend me Rs. 1000 tomorrow."

91. "You'd better leave the dog alone," the man said.
(a) The man said to me to leave the dog alone.
(b) The man told me to better leave the dog alone.
(c) the man warned me to leave the dog alone.
(d) The man said I should leave the dog alone.

92. "I'd have enjoyed the journey more if the man next to me hadn't snored all the time," said John.
(a) John said that he enjoyed the journey but the man next to me snored.
(b) John said that he would have enjoyed the journey more if the man next to him hadn't snored all the time.
(c) John said that he would have enjoyed the journey if the next man hadn't snored all the time.
(d) John said that he would have enjoyed the journey if the man next to him did not snore.

93. A poet said, "The night is dark and I am far from home."
(a) A poet said that the night was dark and he was far from home.
(b) A poet told his friend that the night is dark and that he is far from home.
(c) The friend was told by the poet that the night was dark and he was far from home.
(d) A poet said that the night is dark and he is far from home.

94. The players reported that the spectators were cheering while they were playing.
(a) "The spectators have been cheering while we played", said the players.

(b) "The spectators cheered while we were playing", said the players.
(c) "The spectators were cheering while we were playing", said the players.
(d) "The spectators played while we cheered", said the players.

95. She requested the boys to listen to what she was saying.
(a) She said to the boys, "Please listen to what I am saying."
(b) I said to the boys, "Listen to what I am saying."
(c) She said, "Boys, listen to what I was saying."
(d) She said, "I requested you to listen to what I am saying."

96. "Do you want balloons ?" he said to the child.
(a) He asked the child if it wanted balloons.
(b) He asked the child whether it had wanted balloons.
(c) He asked the child did it want balloons.
(d) He asked the child if it would want balloons.

97. She said, "How ugly I look in this dress!"
(a) She said that how ugly she was looking in that dress.
(b) She exclaimed how ugly she looked in that dress.
(c) She expressed how ugly she looked in that dress.
(d) She exclaimed that she looked very ugly in that dress.

98. She said "You can leave the books here."
(a) She said that they can leave the books there.
(b) She said that they could leave the books there.
(c) She said that they can leave the books here.
(d) She said that they could leave the books here.

99. My friend said, "I am leaving today."
(a) My friend said that he is leaving today.
(b) My friend said that he was leaving today.
(c) My friend said that he leaves today.
(d) My friend said that he was leaving that day.

100. Mukta said to Puneet, "My mother is a good cook."
(a) Mukta told Puneet that her mother was a good cook.
(b) Mukta told Puneet that my mother was a good cook.
(c) Mukta told to Puneet that her mother is a good cook.
(d) Mukta asked Puneet that her mother is a good cook.

101. The commander said to the army, "March forward".
(a) The commander asked the army march forward.
(b) The commander ordered the army to march forward.
(c) The commander requested the army to go forward.
(d) The army requested the commander to march.

102. He promised, "I will do it tomorrow."
(a) He promised that he will do it tomorrow.
(b) He promised that he will do it the next day.
(c) He promised that he would do it tomorrow.
(d) He promised that he would do it the next day.

103. Geeta said, "I did not do this deliberately."
(a) Geeta said that I had not done that deliberately.
(b) Geeta said that she had not done that deliberately.
(c) Geeta said that she has not done this deliberately.
(d) Geeta said that I have not done this deliberately.

104. She said, "I'm afraid we are rather late!"
(a) She exclaimed that they were frightened of being late.
(b) She exclaimed that she was afraid that they were rather late.
(c) She shouted that they were scared that they would be late.
(d) She screamed that she was worried that they would all be late.

105. She said to me, "What can I do for you ?"
(a) She asked me what she could do for me.
(b) She asked me what can she do for me.
(c) She asked me what she can do for me.
(d) She asked me whether she can do anything for me.

106. He said, 'Alas! I am undone !'
(a) He said that it was his undoing.
(b) He exclaimed pathetically that he was undone.
(c) He stated that he was undone.
(d) He cried that he was being undone.

107. "I shall unlock the secrets of their success," he said.
(a) He said that he shall unlock the secrets of their success.
(b) He said that he should unlock the secrets of their success.
(c) He said that he would unlock the secrets of their success.
(d) He said that he will unlock the secrets of their success.

108. "I wonder what he wants of us," said Quint.
(a) Quint said that he was wondering what he wanted of them.
(b) Quint said that he wondered what he wanted of us.
(c) Quint said he wondered what he wants of them.
(d) Quint said that he wondered what he wanted of them.

109. Dinesh said, "I want to eat a good mango one of these days."
(a) Dinesh said he wants to eat a good mango one of these days.
(b) Dinesh said that he wanted to eat a good mango one of those days.
(c) Dinesh said that he wants to eat a good mango one of those days.
(d) Dinesh said that he wanted to eat a good mango one of these days.

110. He said, "I intend to leave for Delhi tonight."
(a) He said that he will intend to leave for Delhi tonight.
(b) He said that he should intend to leave for Delhi that night.
(c) He said that he intended to leave for Delhi that night.
(d) He said that his intention is to leave for Delhi tonight.

111. He said, "The Sun rises in the east."
(a) He said that the Sun rised in the east.
(b) He said that the Sun rises in the east.
(c) He said that the Sun will rise in the east.
(d) He said that the Sun may rise in the east.

112. Ram asked Krishna, "Where are you going today?"
(a) Ram asked Krishna where he was going that day.
(b) Ram asked Krishna as to where he was going on the previous day.
(c) Ram asked Krishna where was he going the next day.
(d) Ram asked Krishna where was he going the day before.

113. He said, "What a fool Tom is!"
(a) He exclaimed that he was a big fool.
(b) He exclaimed that Tom was a big fool.
(c) He wondered what kind of a fool Tom was.
(d) He claimed that Tom was a big fool.

114. "What kind of scheme do you have?" Amit said to the insurance agent.

(a) Amit asked the insurance agent what kind of scheme he/she had.
(b) Amit asked the insurance agent what kind of scheme he/she has.
(c) Amit asked the insurance agent what kind of scheme he/she is having.
(d) Amit asked the insurance agent what kind of scheme he/she was having.

115. The doctor said to the patient, "Take complete rest."
(a) The doctor told to the patient that take complete rest.
(b) The doctor advised the patient to take complete rest.
(c) The doctor suggested the patient to take complete rest.
(d) The doctor asked the patient take complete rest.

116. Mini said to me, "I have bought this flat for my mother."
(a) Mini told that she had bought that flat for her mother.
(b) Mini said that she bought that flat for her mother.
(c) Mini said she has bought that flat for her mother.
(d) Mini told me that she had bought that flat for her mother.

117. He said, "I will come again."
(a) He said that he will come again.
(b) He says he is coming again.
(c) He says he'll come again.
(d) He said that he would come again.

118. "Don't do any more work until you have had a rest," her mother said to her.
(a) Her mother advised her not to do any more work until she has had a rest.
(b) Her mother advised her not to do any more work until she had had a rest.
(c) Her mother advised her that she not do any more work until she had had a rest.
(d) Her mother advised her that she need not do any more work until she had had a rest.

119. "Make me another suit like this," he said to the tailor.
(a) He asked the tailor to make him another suit like this.
(b) He asks the tailor to make him another suit like this.
(c) He told the tailor to make him another suit like that.
(d) He told the tailor to make me another suit like this.

120. My Principal told me, "Don't conduct any test tomorrow."
(a) My Principal told to me not to conduct any test tomorrow.
(b) My Principal told me not to conduct any test tomorrow.
(c) My Principal ordered me don't conduct any test.
(d) My Principal ordered me not to conduct any test the next day.

121. Kiran said to me, "Did you see the cricket match on television last night?
(a) Kiran asked me if I saw the cricket match on television the earlier night.
(b) Kiran asked me if I had seen the cricket match on television the previous night.
(c) Kiran asked me did I see the cricket match on television last night.
(d) Kiran asked me whether I had seen the cricket match on television last night.

122. David said to Anna, "Mona will leave for her native place tomorrow."
(a) David told Anna that Mona will leave for her native place tomorrow.
(b) David told Anna that Mona left for her native place the next day.
(c) David told to Anna that Mona would be leaving for her native place tomorrow.

(d) David told Anna that Mona would leave for her native place the next day.

123. I said to him, "Why are you working so hard ?"

(a) I asked him why he was working so hard.
(b) I asked him why was he working so hard.
(c) I asked him why he had been working so hard.
(d) I asked him why had he been working so hard.

124. Pooja said, "Ridhi, do you want another cake?"

(a) Pooja asked Ridhi do you want another cake.
(b) Pooja asked Ridhi if she wanted another cake.
(c) Pooja said to Ridhi you wanted another cake.
(d) Pooja said if you wanted another cake.

125. The tailor said to him, "Will you have the suit ready by tomorrow evening?"

(a) The tailor asked him that he will have the suit ready by the next evening.
(b) The tailor asked him that he would had the suit ready by the next evening.
(c) The tailor asked him if he would have the suit ready by the next evening.
(d) The tailor asked him if he will like to have the suit ready by the next evening.

126. He ordered his servant to do as he was told.

(a) He ordered his servant, "Do as you are told."
(b) He said to his servant, "Do as you are told."
(c) He said to his servant, "Do as I told you."
(d) He said to his servant, "Do as you were told."

127. He said, "Be quiet and listen to my words."

(a) He urged them to be quiet and listen to his words.
(b) He urged them and said be quiet and listen to words.
(c) He said they should be quiet and listen to his words.
(d) He said you should be quiet and listen to my words.

128. He said to me, "I have often told you not to play with fire."

(a) He said that he has often been telling me not to play with fire.
(b) He told me that he had often told me not to play with fire.
(c) He reminded me that he often said to me not to play with fire.
(d) He said to me that he often told me not to play with fire.

129. "I have seen the film before" Sunita says.

(a) Sunita said that she had seen the film before.
(b) Sunita says that she has seen the film before.
(c) Sunita said that the film was seen by her before.
(d) Sunita said that she saw the film earlier.

130. Pawan said to me, "If I hear any news, I'll phone you."

(a) Pawan told me that if he heard any news, he will phone me.
(b) Pawan told me that if he will hear any news, he will phone me.
(c) Pawan told me if he had heard any news, he would phone me.
(d) Pawan told me that if he heard any news, he would phone me.

131. The teacher said to Mahesh, "Congratulations ! Wish you success in life."

(a) The teacher congratulated Mahesh and said wish you success in life.
(b) The teacher wished congratulations and success in life to Mahesh.

(c) The teacher said congratulations to Mahesh and wished him success life.
(d) The teacher congratulated Mahesh and wished him success in life.

132. The poor examinee said, "O God! take pity on me."
(a) The poor examinee prayed God to take pity on him.
(b) The poor examinee, invoking God, implored him to take pity on him.
(c) The poor examinee exclaimed that God take pity on him.
(d) The poor examinee asked God to take pity on him.

133. "Where will you be tomorrow," I said, "in case I have to ring you ?"
(a) I asked where you will be the next day in case I will ring him.
(b) I asked where he would be the next day in case I had to ring him.
(c) I said to him where he will be in case I have to ring him.
(d) I enquired about his whereabouts the next day in case I would have to ring up.

134. Seeta said to me, "Can you give me your pen ?"
(a) Seeta asked me can I give her my pen.
(b) Seeta asked me if I can give me your pen.
(c) Seeta asked me if I could give her my pen.
(d) Seeta asked me if I gave her my pen.

135. The father warned his son that he should be beware of him.
(a) The father warned his son, "Beware of him !"
(b) The father warned his son, "Watch that chap !"
(c) The father warned his son, "Be careful about him."
(d) The father warned his son, "Don't fall into the trap."

136. Manna said to Rohan, "Have you sat in a trolley bus before ?"
(a) Manna asked Rohan whether he had sat in a trolley bus earlier.
(b) Manna asked Rohan had he sat in a trolley bus before.
(c) Manna asked Rohan-if he sat on a trolley bus before.
(d) Manna asked Rohan if he has ever sat in a trolley bus

137. Farhan said to Geeta, "Could you lend me a hundred rupees until tomorrow ?"
(a) Farhan asked Geeta whether she could lend him a hundred rupees until tomorrow.
(b) Farhan asked Geeta whether she could lend him a hundred rupees until the next day.
(c) Farhan asked Geeta whether she could lend me a hundred rupees until the next day.
(d) Farhan asked whether Geeta could lend me a hundred rupees until the next day.

138. "What about going for a swim," he said, "It's quite fine now."
(a) He asked me what about going for a swim as it was quite fine then.
(b) He proposed going for a swim as it was quite fine.
(c) He suggested going for a swim as it was quite fine.
(d) He advised me to go for a swim as it was quite fine.

139. "You can't bathe in this sea," he said to me, "it's very rough."
(a) He said that I can't bathe in this sea because it's very rough.
(b) He said that you couldn't bathe in that sea if it was very rough.
(c) He said that I couldn't bathe in that sea as it was very rough.
(d) He said that you can't bathe in this sea since it was very rough.

140. Jagdish said, "We passed by a beautiful lake when we went on a trip to Goa."
(a) Jagdish said that they passed by a beautiful lake when they had gone on a trip to Goa.

(b) Jagdish said that they had passed by a beautiful lake when they went on a trip to Goa.
(c) Jagdish said that they had passed by a beautiful lake when they had gone on a trip to Goa.
(d) Jagdish said they passed by a beautiful lake when they went on a trip to Goa.

141. He said to me, "I expect you to attend the function."
(a) He told me that he had expected me to attend the function.
(b) He told me that he expected me to attended the function.
(c) He told me that he expected me to have attended the function.
(d) He told me that he expected me to attend the function.

142. He said, "Why didn't you send your application to me ?"
(a) He enquired why I had not sent my application to him.
(b) He enquired why I did not send my application to him.
(c) He enquired why had I not sent my application to him.
(d) He enquired why did I not send my application to him.

143. Dinesh asked, "Are you going to the party tomorrow, Eliza ?"
(a) Dinesh asked whether Eliza was going to the party the next day.
(b) Dinesh asked Eliza whether you are going to the party the next day.
(c) Dinesh asked Eliza whether she was going to the party the next day.
(d) Dinesh asked Eliza are you going to the party tomorrow.

144. John said, "How long will it take to travel from Germany to South Africa?"
(a) John asked how long it will take to travel from Germany to South Africa.
(b) John asked how long would it take to travel from Germany to South Africa.
(c) John asked how long it would take to travel from Germany to South Africa.
(d) John was asking how long must it take to travel from Germany to South Africa.

145. "What did you see at the South Pole?" Ashok asked Anil.
(a) Ashok asked Anil if he saw anything at the South Pole.
(b) Ashok asked Anil what he had seen at the South Pole.
(c) Ashok asked Anil what did he see at the South Pole.
(d) Ashok asked Anil that he saw anything at the South Pole.

146. "Do you want some more sweets ?" asked my friend.
(a) My friend asked me if I want some more sweets.
(b) My friend said to me if I wanted some more sweets.
(c) My friend asked me whether I wanted some more sweets.
(d) My friend asked me that I wanted some more sweets.

147. I said to my sister, "I brought you a doll yesterday."
(a) I told my sister that I brought you a doll the previous day.
(b) I told my sister that I had brought her a doll the previous day.
(c) I told my sister that I had brought her a doll yesterday.
(d) I told my sister that I brought her a doll yesterday.

148. The captain said to the army, "March forward, now."
(a) The captain said to the army that march forward now.
(b) The captain ordered the army to march forward then.
(c) The captain ordered the army to march on that day.
(d) The captain ordered the army to attack the enemy.

149. They said, "We've lived here for a long time."

(a) They said that they have lived there for a long time.
(b) They said that they lived here for a long time.
(c) They said that they had lived there for a long time.
(d) They said that they have lived for a long time.

150. "Would you open the door please ?" She said'
(a) She asked me to please open the door.
(b) She requested me to open the door.
(c) She requested me to please open the door.
(d) She asked me open the door.

151. The teacher said, "Gandhiji was born in India."
(a) The teacher said that Gandhiji had been born in India.
(b) The teacher says that Gandhiji was born in India.
(c) The teacher said that Gandhiji had born in India.
(d) The teacher said that Gandhiji was born in India.

152. "Where do you live ?" asked the stranger.
(a) The stranger asked where I lived.
(b) The stranger enquired where I was living.
(c) The stranger questioned where did live.
(d) The stranger wanted to know where I live.

153 .I said to him, "How do you know this?"
(a) I asked him how I knew that.
(b) I asked him that how he knew that.
(c) I told him how I knew that.
(d) I asked him how he knew that.

154. He said, "We are all humans."
(a) He said that we are all humans.
(b) He said they were all humans.
(c) He said that he was a humans.
(d) He said all were humans.

155. "Would you mind taking off your shoes before entering the house ?" he said to the foreigner.
(a) He requested the foreigner to take off his shoes before entering the house.
(b) He told the foreigner that he must take off his shoes before entered the house.
(c) He said the foreigner that to take off his shoes before entered the house.
(d) Before entering the house he said that shoes must be taken off.

156. "I lost my book yesterday", she said to her teacher.
(a) She admitted to her teacher that she had lost her book the previous day.
(b) To her teacher she was admitted that she has lost her book the previous day.
(c) She admitted losing her book to her teacher yesterday.
(d) She said to her teacher that I have lost my book the previous day.

157. They said, "The boy will soon be found and we will bring him."
(a) They said that boy would be found and brought.
(b) They said that the boy would soon be found, and that they would bring him.
(c) They informed him that the boy would soon be found, and they ought to bring him.
(d) They told that the boy will be found soon and they will bring him.

158. "Stop talking children," said the teacher.
(a) The teacher ordered the children to stop talking.
(b) The teacher asked the children to stop talking.
(c) The teacher told to the children to stop talking.
(d) The teacher said the children to stop talking.

159. The teacher said that the Earth moves round the Sun.

(a) The teacher stated: "The Earth has been moving round the Sun.
(b) The teacher said, "The Earth is moving round the Sun."
(c) The teacher said, "The Earth will move round the Sun."
(d) The teacher said, "The Earth moves round The Sun."

160. The lady said that they had been witnessing the programme.
(a) The lady said, "We were witnessing the programme."
(b) The lady says, "We are witnessing the programme."
(c) The lady said, "We witnessed the programme."
(d) The lady says, "We had witnessed the programme."

161. The Principal told us, "Wait here till I return."
(a) The Principal told us wait here till her return.
(b) The Principal told us to wait there till he returned.
(c) The Principal told us to wait there till I return.
(d) The Principal told us please wait here till he returned.

162. My mother said to me, "Who is your best friend?"
(a) My mother questioned me as to who my best friend was.
(b) My mother asked me who was my best friend.
(c) My mother asked me who my best friend was.
(d) My mother asked me who my best friend is.

163. The teacher said to the boys, "If you do your best you will surely pass."
(a) The teacher asked the boys to work hard so that they can pass.
(b) The teacher told the boys that unless they work hard they will not pass.
(c) The teacher requested the boys that if they work better, they will surely pass.
(d) They teacher told the boys that if they did their best they would surely pass.

164. The boy pleaded that he had not stolen the book.
(a) The boy said, "I don't steal the book."
(b) The boy said, "I didn't steal the book."
(c) They boy said, "I hadn't stolen the book."
(d) The boy said, "I haven't stolen the book."

165. Kavitha said, "I saw the photograph."
(a) Kavitha told that she saw the photograph.
(b) Kavitha said that she had seen the photograph.
(c) Kavitha said that the photograph was seen by her.
(d) Kavitha said that she has seen the photograph.

166. The king said to his men, "Put the men in prison."
(a) The king implored his men to put the man in prison.
(b) The king commanded his men to put the man in prison.
(c) The king requested his men to put the man in prison.
(d) The king informed his men to put the man in prison.

167. He said, "I have made a kite."
(a) He says that he made a kite.
(b) He will say that he had made a kite.
(c) He said that I had made a kite.
(d) He said that he had made a kite.

168. Dravid's neighbour said, "Do you like to play golf?"
(a) Dravid's neighbour questioned him and said if he liked to play golf.
(b) Dravid's neighbour asked him to like golf.
(c) Dravid's neighbour asked him if he would like to play golf.
(d) Dravid's neighbour asked him if he liked to play golf.

169. She announced that they had selected Pradeep as their leader.
(a) She said, "Pradeep is our leader."
(b) She announced, "We have selected Pradeep as our leader."
(c) She announced, "Let us select Pradeep as our leader."
(d) She declared, "Pradeep had been selected as our leader."

170. He told the boy not to sit there.
(a) "Didn't sit here," he said to the boy.
(b) "Don't sit there," he said to the boy.
(c) "Didn't sit there," he said to the boy.
(d) "Don't sit here," he said to the boy.

ANSWER KEY

1.	(b)	2.	(b)	3.	(b)	4.	(c)	5.	(b)
6.	(a)	7.	(c)	8.	(c)	9.	(c)	10.	(d)
11.	(b)	12.	(c)	13.	(d)	14.	(b)	15.	(d)
16.	(d)	17.	(c)	18.	(a)	19.	(d)	20.	(b)
21.	(c)	22.	(c)	23.	(c)	24.	(a)	25.	(a)
26.	(c)	27.	(b)	28.	(a)	29.	(b)	30.	(b)
31.	(a)	32.	(a)	33.	(c)	34.	(b)	35.	(d)
36.	(a)	37.	(c)	38.	(c)	39.	(c)	40.	(b)
41.	(d)	42.	(d)	43.	(a)	44.	(a)	45.	(c)
46.	(b)	47.	(b)	48.	(a)	49.	(c)	50.	(b)
51.	(b)	52.	(d)	53.	(b)	54.	(d)	55.	(d)
56.	(a)	57.	(b)	58.	(c)	59.	(b)	60.	(a)
61.	(a)	62.	(b)	63.	(a)	64.	(d)	65.	(a)
66.	(b)	67.	(a)	68.	(c)	69.	(d)	70.	(d)
71.	(d)	72.	(c)	73.	(b)	74.	(b)	75.	(c)
76.	(b)	77.	(a)	78.	(b)	79.	(d)	80.	(d)
81.	(a)	82.	(c)	83.	(c)	84.	(a)	85.	(c)
86.	(a)	87.	(c)	88.	(b)	89.	(c)	90.	(d)
91.	(c)	92.	(b)	93.	(a)	94.	(c)	95.	(a)
96.	(a)	97.	(d)	98.	(b)	99.	(d)	100.	(a)
101.	(b)	102.	(d)	103.	(b)	104.	(b)	105.	(a)
106.	(b)	107.	(c)	108.	(d)	109.	(b)	110.	(c)
111.	(b)	112.	(a)	113.	(b)	114.	(a)	115.	(b)
116.	(d)	117.	(d)	118.	(b)	119.	(c)	120.	(d)
121.	(b)	122.	(d)	123.	(a)	124.	(b)	125.	(c)
126.	(b)	127.	(a)	128.	(b)	129.	(b)	130.	(d)
131.	(d)	132.	(b)	133.	(b)	134.	(c)	135.	(a)
136.	(a)	137.	(b)	138.	(a)	139.	(c)	140.	(c)
141.	(d)	142.	(a)	143.	(c)	144.	(c)	145.	(b)
146.	(c)	147.	(b)	148.	(b)	149.	(c)	150.	(b)
151.	(d)	152.	(a)	153.	(d)	154.	(a)	155.	(a)
156.	(a)	157.	(b)	158.	(a)	159.	(d)	160.	(a)
161.	(b)	162.	(c)	163.	(d)	164.	(d)	165.	(b)
166.	(b)	167.	(d)	168.	(d)	169.	(b)	170.	(d)

Explanations

1. (b) Commanded must be followed by an object (them).

5. (b) Sentence starting with 'let' shows suggestion or idea. Hence, it will be appropriate to change 'let us not' into 'opposed the idea'.

10. (d) Change 'So help me Heaven' into called upon. 'Call upon Heaven' almost gives the same meaning as 'help me heaven'. And 'I never steal' again is showing strong determination here, Hence use of resolve (fixity of purpose) is correct. Use of 'Called upon' and 'resolve' together make the option 'd' the most appropriate.

11. (b) This question is Mood based. Choose the option that indicates the intention of the speaker.

18. (a) It seems that there is a hidden proposal in the sentence. Hence use of 'propose' is the most appropriate.

23. (c) Use of 'Please' after 'requested' will make the sentence superfluous. Could is also being used here in the sense of request. Hence use of 'requested ' and 'Could' will also make sentence superfluous.

24. (a) The sentence is of past routine. If sentence is of 'present routine' or 'past routine' action, than it remain same in direct speech.

25. (a) While changing into Indirect speech the voice of sentence is also being changed.

32. (a) The sentence is of past routine. Hence it will not be changed. According to rule option 'd' is not wrong.

49. (c) According to rule: have had $\xrightarrow{\text{changes into}}$ had had (option 'b')
had (V_2)had had (had + (V_3))(option 'c')
had had (V_2)had had (option 'd')
Option 'b' is wrong. Because we do not use yesterday (Past tense) with have had (Present perfect). Option 'd' is wrong because we use past

perfect before any past action. Change Simple past (had) into past perfect (had V_3).

53. (b) See the explanation of question No.10

62. (b) Here 'Vomited' will not be changed into 'had vomited' because 'vomited' is not under inverted Commas.

94. (c) When two Simultaneous actions are in simple past and past continuous, then there will be no change of tense in indirect speech.

132. (b) Use of invoking [to ask for aid or protection) and implored (to make a very serious or emotional request to (someone)] make the option (b) is the most appropriate.

154. (a) The sentence is a Universal truth.

164. (d) Here work is important. Hence the use of Present Perfect tense is the most appropriate.

SPOTTING THE ERROR

1. (a) He said/ (b) that / (c) he will come. / (d) No error

2. (a) He said/ (b) that / (c) I shall work hard if I want to pass. / (d) No error

3. (a) He asked me/ (b) that if / (c) I was fine./ (d) No error

4. (a) He asked me/ (b) that what / (c) had happened./ (d) No error

5. (a) He asked me/ (b) what / (c) did I say about him./ (d) No error

6. (a) He told to me / (b) that / (c) the Sun is a star./ (d) No error

7. (a) The king commanded to / (b) call the/ (c) first witness./ (d) No error

8. (a) The judge asked me / (b) if I knew the / (c) accused or not./ (d) No error

9. (a) Ram was telling / (b) that everyone / (c) was happy with the bonus./ (d) No error

10. (a) My teacher said that / (b) a bad carpenter / (c) fights with his tools./ (d) No error

11. (a) She ordered the servant shut / (b) the door /(c) and leave the room./ (d) No error

12. (a) She exclaimed with surprise / (b) that / (c) how tall has she grown./ (d) No error

13. (a)The teacher asked the little boy/(b) if he knows the / (c) correct answer to the question./(d) No error

14. (a) Mother allowed me to / (b) go wherever/ (c) I want./ (d) No error

15. (a) The father forbade his son / (b) not to make the / (c) same mistake again./ (d) No error

16. (a) He exclaimed with sorrow / (b) that his father died just two / (c) months before. / (d) No Error.

17. (a) She requested him/ (b) to take her to the doctor / (c) as she has very high fever. / (D) No Error

18. (a) When my boss said / (b) that he was coming to see / (c) me the next day, I wondered what problems he will have with me. / (d) No Error

19. (a) I suggested that she should / (b) stay at home if it / (c) rained but she does not give any answer. / (d) No Error

20. (a) He asked me / (b) why had I gone to office / (c) when I knew there would be fewer buses on road that day. / (d) No Error

21. (a) My friend asked me / (b) what could she do/ (c) for me in that critical situation. / (d) No Error

22. (a) The Government warned the multiplexes that if / (b) they continue charging prices higher than MRP , their / (c) licences would be cancelled. / (d) No Error

23. (a) My father told me / (b) that if I work for the / (c) betterment of mankind, God would certainly do good to me . / (d) No Error

24. (a) My teacher wanted to know / (b) if I had done / (c) the homework or not. / (d) No Error

25. (a) She says, "I studied / (b) hard so that I / (c) may get good marks/ (d) No Error

26. (a) She said that she was going to / (b) theatre and wanted to know that I could / (c) accompany him. / (E) No Error

27. (a) She requested me / (b) to wait for her / (c) until she returns from school. / (d) No Error

28. (a) The players exclaimed / (b) with joy that / (c) they have won the match / (d) No Error

29. (a) The Principal said / (b) that the gates should / (c) be locked as the classes have started. / (d) No Error

30. (a) He told us / (b) that / (c) he has not read the book. / (d) No Error

Answers with explanation

1. (c) Change 'will' into 'would'. Said (reporting verb) is in past. Hence the reported speech is also in past.
2. (c) Change 'shall' into 'should' and 'want' into 'wanted'. (Explanation is given in 1).
3. (b) Remove 'that'. If an interrogative sentence is not of 'Wh' family, conjunction 'if/whether' is used.
4. (b) Remove 'that'. If an interrogative sentence is of 'Wh' family, no conjunction is used.
5. (c) In reported speech, an interrogative form is not used. Hence 'did I say' will change into 'I said'.
6. (a) 'To' doesn't come with 'tell/told'.
7. (a) 'Commanded' must be followed by an object.
8. (b) Change 'if' into 'whether'. 'Whether ..... or' is the correct correlative . 'If..... or' is not the correct correlative.
9. (a) 'Telling' must be followed by an object.
10. (d) The sentence is correct. The reported speech given here is an idiom. Hence tense will not change.
11. (a) Add 'to' before 'shut'. In an imperative sentence conjunction 'to' is used.
12. (c) 'How tall has she grown' is interrogative form of a sentence as 'has' has come before subject 'she'. Change 'How tall has she grown' into ' she had grown very tall'.
13. (b) Change 'knows' into 'knew'.
14. (c) Change 'I want' into 'I wanted'. The sentence is in past tense.
15. (b) Remove 'not'. 'Not' is not used with 'forbade'. Other words that do not take 'not' with them are - unless, until, deny, prohibit, lest, hardly, barely, rarely, scarcely and both.
    Note: Not is not used with both as in place of 'both....not', we use 'neither of'.
    E.g.: Both of them did not go. (×)
    Neither of them went. (✓)
16. (b) 'Had' will come before 'died'. 'Simple Past Tense' changes into 'Past Perfect Tense'.
17. (c) Replace 'has' with 'had'. In indirect speech 'Simple Present Tense' changes into 'Simple Past Tense'.
18. (c) Change 'will' into 'would'. In indirect speech 'will/shall' changes into 'would/ should'.
19. (c) Change 'does not' into 'did not'. 'Simple Present Tense' changes into Simple Past Tense'.
20. (b) Use 'had' after 'I'. In indirect speech a sentence is in assertive form and not in interrogative form.
21. (b) 'could' will come after 'she'. In indirect speech a sentence is in assertive form and not in interrogative form.
22. (b) Past of 'continue' is 'continued'. In Indirect Speech 'Simple Present Tense' changes into 'Simple Past Tense'.
23. (b) Change 'work' to 'worked'. In Indirect Speech 'Simple Present Tense' changes into Simple Past Tense'.
24. (b) Change 'if' into 'whether'. 'Whether ..... or' is the correct pair . 'If..... or' is not the correct correlative.
25. (c) Change 'may' into 'might'.
26. (b) Change 'that' into 'if'.
27. (c) Change 'returns' into 'returned'.
28. (c) Change 'have' into 'had'.
29. (c) Change 'have' into 'had'.
30. (c) Change 'has' into 'had'.

5

CHAPTER

QUESTION TAG

Ram works hard, **doesn't he** ?

He is not coming, **is he** ?

➢ A **short question** following a sentence is called a Question Tag.

Rules for making Question Tag

1. The **sentence** and the **Question Tag** must be in the **same Tense**.
2. If the **sentence is Positive, the Question Tag must be Negative** and vice versa.
3. Always use **Pronoun** in the Question Tag.
4. For Negative Question Tag, use the **Contracted form of 'Helping Verb' and 'not'** .

E.g. didn't, hadn't, won't etc.

SOME IMPORTANT RULES:

(1) There is no contracted form of 'am not' but **'aren't'** is used in Question Tag.

E.g.: I am fine, aren't I ?

(2) **Each, Every, Everyone, Everybody, No one, Nobody, None** are **Singular** and hence will **take Singular Verb/Singular Pronoun/ Singular Adjective** with them but their **Question Tag will take Plural Verb** and **Plural Pronoun**.

E.g.: a. Everyone has come, hasn't he ? (×)

Everyone has come, **haven't they** ? (✓)

b. None of your friends likes her, do they ? (✓)

Everyone can speak English, **can't they** ? (✓)

(3) **Collective Noun takes Singular Verb and Singular Pronoun** in Question Tag.

E.g.: The jury has (S.V.) taken its (S.A.) decision, **hasn't it**?

(4) If we talk about **the individual members** of the collective noun or if **there is a difference in opinion** among the members of the collective noun, **Plural Verb and Plural Pronoun** are used.

E.g.: a. The committee are (P.V.) divided in their (P.A.) opinion, **aren't they**?

b. The audience have (P.V.) taken their (P.A.) seats, **haven't they**?

(5) Some words are **negative in meaning**. For e.g.- **hardly, barely, seldom, scarcely, rarely, barely, no, not and never**. If we find such a word in a sentence, we need a **positive question** tag.

E.g. (a) He hardly does any work, **does he** ?

(b) He found barely anything to eat, **did he** ?

(c) He is seldom absent, **is he** ?

(6) If the sentence starts with **'let us/let's'** , **'shall we'** is used in the question tag.

E.g.: Let us go to party tonight, **shall we** ?

(7) (a) In **Imperative Sentences**, question tag **'won't you'** is used.

E.g.: Come in, **won't you**?

(b) If in a Imperative Sentence, somebody is being offered anything, or if someone is being asked to do something, **'will you/would you'** is used in the Question Tag.

E.g.: (i) Open the door, would you?

(ii) Have some more tea, would you?

(c) **'Can't you'** is used in the question tag to express **Impatience**.

E.g.: Shut your mouth, Can't you?

(d) In **Negative Imperative** sentence, **'will you ?'** is used in the Question Tag.

E.g.: Do not worry, **will you**?

(8) If a **sentence starts with 'There'**, the question tag will have **'there' in the place of Pronoun.**

E.g.: There is no water, **is there**?

There were no good schools in the town, **were there**?

(9) Question Tag is always **made in accordance with the main part of the sentence**.

E.g.: I think, he is right, **isn't he**? (Here 'I think' is not important and hence it is not the main part of the sentence)

(10) **Little** and **few** means **'not equal to'**. If they are used in a sentence, the sentence becomes negative in meaning. Such sentences will have positive **Question Tags**. (Note: A little and A few do not make the sentence negative because they mean at least some.)

E.g.: (1) Few people turned up for the show, **did they**?

(2) Little hope is left now, **is it**?

(3) They have a little information, **don't they**?

Note: I have a car

The Question Tag is 'don't I'. The sentence is of Present Indefinite Tense so it needs helping verb 'do'.

PROVIDE SUITABLE QUESTION TAG FOR THE FOLLOWING SENTENCES

Find the meaning of the difficult words and learn them by heart

1. I am happy,
2. I don't write letter,
3. I didn't go to college yesterday,
4. It is very cold,
5. You haven't eaten anything,
6. She doesn't drive carelessly,
7. I have called him up,
8. The boys are quite boisterous,
9. My friend Ram is an egoist,
10. God is Omnipotent, omnipresent and Omniscient,
11. The mob killed the District Magistrate,
12. Bhim was a glutton,
13. We see somnambulists in movies very often,
14. Bhagat Singh was a martyr,
15. We see conjurors in circus,
16. Asthma is not a contagious disease,
17. We used to see epidemic in villages earlier,
18. Sanjivini was considered to be a panacea,
19. We find too many monologues in Shakespeare's plays,
20. We hadn't got any remuneration,
21. Polygamy has been banned in many countries,
22. Charles Shobraj was an imposter,
23. Hindus practise idolatry,
24. My nephew is an ambidextrous,
25. He is a pessimist,
26. Everyone has come late today,
27. The mob has lynched the thief,
28. The audience have taken their seats,
29. Have some more tea,
30. Wait for me,
31. Let's go out for a walk,
32. He has barely anything to wear,
33. Somebody entered the room,
34. I think, you are right,
35. I feel, he is hungry,
36. There are many boys in this school,
37. Nobody bothers,
38. It hardly rains here,
39. The jury was unanimous in its decision.
40. I am tired,
41. Few people came forward to help him.
42. Little could be done.
43. Nothing seems amiss.
44. Nothing can be done now.
45. Something seems queer.

Answers

1. aren't I?
2. do I?
3. did I?
4. isn't it?
5. have you?
6. does she ?
7. haven't I?
8. aren't they?
9. isn't he?
10. isn't he?
11. didn't it
12. wasn't he?
13. don't we?
14. wasn't he.
15. don't we?
16. is it?
17. didn't we?
18. wasn't it?
19. don't we?
20. had we?
21. hasn't it?
22. wasn't he?
23. don't they?
24. isn't he?
25. Isn't he?
26. haven't they?
27. hasn't it?
28. haven't they?
29. will /would you?
30. will you?/can you?
31. Shall we?
32. does he?
33. didn't they?
34. aren't you?
35. Isn't he?
36. aren't there?
37. do they?
38. does it?
39. wasn't it?
40. aren't I?
40. aren't I?
41. did they ?
42. could it?
43. does it?
44. can it?
45. doesn't it?

CHAPTER 6

SUBJECT–VERB AGREEMENT

- In a sentence, the **verb must agree with the subject**. In other words we can say that the **Verb used is according to the person/ thing and the number of persons/ things etc**. This is called Subject–Verb Agreement.

1. $\underbrace{\text{He}}_{\text{S.S}}$ $\underbrace{\text{comes}}_{\text{S.V}}$. (If the **Subject** is **Singular,** the **Verb** must also be **Singular**.)
2. $\underbrace{\text{They}}_{\text{P.S}}$ $\underbrace{\text{come}}_{\text{P.V}}$. (If the **Subject** is **Plural,** the **Verb** must also be **Plural**.)

- We need to be familiar with Singular and Plural Verbs.

Singular Verb	Plural Verb
is	are
has	have

Singular Verb	Plural Verb
was	were
V_1+s/es (plays, goes etc.)	V_1 (play, go etc.)

Difference between Verb and Noun:

Noun + s/es → Plural Noun (Noun become Plural when s/es is added)

Verb + s/es → Singular Verb (Verb becomes Singular when s/es is added)

Rule - 1

- If two subjects are joined by **'and'**, **Plural Verb** will be used .

E.g.: Ram **and** Shyam $\underbrace{\text{are}}_{\text{P.V}}$ coming.

Rule - 2

- If two or more than two **Nouns or Adjectives** are joined by **'and'** but **only one person or thing or idea is discussed**, singular verb is used.

E.g.: My friend, philosopher and guide have come. (change 'have' into **'has'**)
Slow and steady win the race. (change 'win' into **'wins'**)
Fish and chips **is** my favorite dish.(✓)

- If **two Uncountable Nouns** are joined by **'and'** and if **two different subjects** are discussed, **Plural Verb** will be used.

E.g.: Poverty (U.N) **and** misery (U.N) **come** (P.V) together. (✓)

Rule - 3

- If the subject is joined by **'as well as', 'with', 'alongwith', 'together with', 'and not', 'In addition to', 'but', 'besides', 'except', 'rather than', 'accompanied by', 'like', 'unlike', 'no less than', 'nothing but'**, the **Verb** will agree with the **first subject.**

E.g.: (1) Ram (S. S.) **as well as** his parents **is** (S.V.) coming.

(2) The Captain (S. S.) **along with** the sailors **was** (S.V.) drowned.

(3) My father (S.S.) **unlike** my uncles **is** (S.V.) very strict.

Rule - 4

- If an **Article** is placed just **before the 1st subject**, it means the **person/thing is the same** for which two Nouns are used. Hence **Singular Verb** will be used. Similarly if only one person or thing is discussed, we use Article before the first Noun only.

E.g.: 1. **A** white and black gown **was** (S.V.) bought by her.

2. Churchill was a great orator and a great politician of his time. (×)
   Churchill was a great orator and politician of his time. (✓)

- But if an **Article** is used **before every subject**, it refers to **different people/things**. Hence **Plural Verb** will be used.

E.g.: **The** director and **the** producer **have** (P.V.) come.(✓)

Rule - 5

- If two subjects are joined by **'neither.........nor', 'either........or', 'not only'........'but also', 'nor', 'or', 'none-but'** ,the **verb** will **agree** with the **nearest subject**.

E.g.:

(1) **Neither** Ram **nor** Shyam (S. S.) **has** (S.V.) come.

(2) **Either** Ram **or** his friends (P. S.) **have** (P.V.) come.

(3) **Has** (S.V.) Ram (S.S.) **or** Shyam come?

Rule - 6

- **'Neither of'** means **'not either of the two things or people'**.
  Neither of the two roads leads to the station.
- **'None of'** means **'not one of the group of things or people'**.

E.g.: Neither of his four sons looked after him. (×)
None of his four sons looked after him. (✓)

- **'Either of'** means ' **one of the two things or people'**.

E.g.: Either of the five members is at fault. (×)
One of the five members is at fault. (✓)
Either of the twins will be made the trustee.(✓)

Note: **'Not'** is **not** used with **'both'**. For this purpose **'neither of'** is used.

E.g.: Both of them did not take the exam. (×)
Neither of them took the exam. (✓)

Rule -7

- Certain Nouns are **Plural in form but Singular in meaning**. Hence they take **Singular Verb**.

E.g.: (a) **Names of diseases** : **Measles, Mumps, Rickets, Shingles etc.**
(b) **Names of games** : **Billiards, Darts, Draughts etc.**
(c) **Names of countries** : **The United States, The West Indies etc.**
(d) **Names of books** : **The Arabian Nights, Three Muskeeters etc.**
(e) **Names of subjects** : **Physics, Economics, Civics, Statistics, Politics, Linguistics.**

E.g.: (1) Mathematics **is** (s.v.) an interesting subject.

(2) Politics **is** (s.v.) not my cup of tea.

Note: If **'Statistics'** means **'data'**, **'Mathematics'** means **'Calculations'** and **'Politics'** means **'Political thoughts'**, **Plural Verb** is used.

E.g.: Statistics **have** (P.V.) revealed multiple scams in the organisation of the Commonwealth Games.

Rule - 8

- Usually we **match the Verb with the nearest subject** but this is wrong. Match the Verb with the main subject of the sentence.

E.g.: (1) The quality of apples **is** good.

(2) He and not his parents **is** guilty.

(3) The appeal of the victims for the transfer of the cases related to riots to some other States **has** been accepted.

Rule - 9

➢ **Collective Nouns** always take **Singular Verb**.

E.g.: (1) The **herd** (S.S.) of cows **is** (S.V.) grazing in the field.

(2) The committee (S.S.) **has** (S.V.) unanimously taken **its** (S.A.) decision.

➢ If there is a **division** among the members of the collective noun or we **talk about the members** of the collective noun, **Plural Verb and Plural Pronoun** are used.

E.g.: (1) The jury **are** (P.V.) divided in **their** (P.P.) opinion.

(2) The audience **have** (P.V.) taken **their** (P.A.) seats.

Rule - 10

➢ **Plural numbers** always take **Plural Verb**.

E.g.: Hundred boys **are** (P.V.) in my class.

Note:- If **Plural Noun** is used **after cardinal Adjectives** (one, two, three, four etc.) and if Plural Noun denotes certain **amount, weight, height** or **period,** Singular Verb will be used.

In other words we can say that **Plural number** used as a **Singular unit** will take **Singular Verb**.

E.g.: (1) Hundred rupees **is** (S.V.) in my pocket.

(2) Ten miles **is** (S.V.) a long distance to cover on foot.

➢ **Note the difference:**

Five thousand (Numeral (Adj.)) rupees (P. N.) **is** (S.V.) a handsome amount.

Five thousand (Numeral (Adj.)) rupees (P. N.) **have** (P.V.) been spent on different useful commodities.

Rule - 11

➢ **Each, Every, Everyone, Someone, Somebody, Nobody, None, One, Any, Many a, More than one** are Singular. Hence they will take Singular Verb, Singular Noun and Singular Pronoun.

E.g.: (1) **Each** student **has** come.

(2) **Each** boy and **each** girl **has** come.

(3) **One** must tolerate **one's** friend as well as ~~**his**~~ (**one's**) enemy.

(4) **Many a** student ~~have~~ (has) not done ~~their~~ (his) home work.

(5) **More than one man** (S.N) **was** (S.V) present there.

Note: **Many** is used in the following ways:

(1) **Many a** man (S.N.) has (S.V.) come.

(2) **Many** men (P.N.) have (P.V.) come.

(3) **A great/ A good many** men (P.N.) have (P.V.) come.

Rule - 12

➢ If **'of'** is used after **each, one** etc, the **Noun or Pronoun that comes immediately after 'of'** will be **Plural** in form. However **the Verb, Pronoun, Adjective etc that comes in the latter part of the sentence will be Singular** in form.

E.g.: One of the boys/them (Noun/Pronoun (Plural)) has (S.V.) done his (S.A.) work.

Rule - 13

➢ If **'each'** is used **after Plural Noun or Plural Pronoun**, **Plural Verb** is used.

We (P.S.) each **have** (**P.V.**) a duty towards our nation. (✓)

Rule -14

➢ If a **Subject** and the **Verb** are **joined by a Relative Pronoun**, the **Verb** used will **agree with the antecedent** to the Relative Pronoun.

E.g.: (1) She is one of the noblest **women** that (R.P) ~~has~~ (**have**) ever lived on this earth.

(2) I am not one of **those** **who** (**R.P**) will trust everyone whom ~~I meet~~ (**they meet**) .

Note: Try to understand the meaning of the sentence in this type of questions.

Rule - 15

➢ If Indefinite Pronoun **'One'** comes as the **Subject** of a sentence, it takes **Singular Verb** and **Singular Pronoun 'one'**, **'one's'**, and **'oneself'** and not 'he', 'him', 'his' or 'himself'.

E.g.: **One** should keep his promise. (×)
One should keep **one's** promise. (✓)

Rule - 16

➢ If a sentence states an **Imaginary Position**, it starts with **if, as if, as though, suppose, I wish, in case, would that** etc. In such sentences **'were'** is used as the verb irrespective of the number of the subject.

E.g.: I wish, **I were** a bird.
If he **were** rich, he would help others.

Rule - 17

➢ In **Optative Sentences, all subjects** takes **Base form of verb**.

E.g.: (1) $\underbrace{\text{God}}_{S.S.}$ $\underbrace{\textbf{save}}_{V_{b.f}}$ the king. (2) Long $\underbrace{\textbf{live}}_{V_{b.f}}$ $\underbrace{\text{the Queen}}_{S.S.}$.

Rule - 18

➢ **'A number of' / 'a large number of' / 'a great number of'** is used with **Plural Countable Noun**. Hence they will take **Plural Verb** .

E.g.: A number of $\underbrace{\textbf{students}}_{P.S.}$ $\underbrace{\textbf{were}}_{P.V.}$ present. (✓)

Note: **'The number of'** denotes the number of Plural Countable Noun. It will **take Singular Verb.**

E.g.: The number of $\underbrace{\text{boys}}_{P.S.}$ $\underbrace{\text{are}}_{P.V.}$ fifty. (×)

The number of $\underbrace{\textbf{boys}}_{P.S.}$ $\underbrace{\textbf{is}}_{S.V.}$ fifty. (✓)

Rule - 19

➢ With Uncountable Nouns we use '**Amount of / Quantity of'** followed by a **Singular Verb** .

E.g.: **The amount of** $\underbrace{\text{money}}_{U.N.}$ $\underbrace{\text{are}}_{P.V.}$ not sufficient.(×)

The amount of $\underbrace{\text{money}}_{U.N.}$ $\underbrace{\textbf{is}}_{S.V.}$ not sufficient. (✓)

Note:-

A number of, Numerous, A lot of, Lots of, Plenty of, Some, Few, Money, Majority come with P.C.N	Quantity of, A lot of, Lots of, Plenty of, A great deal of, Some, Little, Much comes with U.N	Amount of comes with Money

Rule - 20

➢ **'All'** can be used in both **Countable** and **Uncountable** sense. When used as **Uncountable**, it takes **Singular Verb** and when used as **Countable**, it takes **Plural Verb**.

E.g.: (1) **All** $\underbrace{\textbf{is}}_{S.V}$ well that $\underbrace{\textbf{ends}}_{S.V}$ well.

(2) **All** $\underbrace{\textbf{are}}_{P.V}$ well at home. (✓)

Rule - 21

➢ **Furniture, advice, work, evidence, equipment, news, information, luggage, baggage, percentage, poetry, knowledge, dirt, dust, traffic, electricity, music, breakage, stationery, scenery, confectionery, pottery, bakery, crockery, behaviour, hair, business, mischief, bread, wastage, money, Jewellery, word(when used in sense of Message and Promise) Fuel and Cost** are Uncountable Nouns and hence will take **Singular Verb**. These Nouns will not take Article **'A/ An'**, **'many'**, **'few'**, **'number of' and 'Plural Form'**.

E.g.: (1) The **scenery** (S.N.) of Kashmir **has** (S.V.) enchanted us.

(2) I have no **information** about her residence.

(3) The **mischief** committed by him is unpardonable.

(4) His **hair** is black.

➢ Such Nouns have no Plural form but sometimes we need the Singular/Plural form of some of these Nouns. The **Singular/ Plural form is made by adding certain words before the Uncountable Nouns**.

E.g.: (a) He gave me **a piece of** information.

(b) **All pieces of** information given by her were reliable.

(c) **Many kinds of** furniture are available in that shop.

(d) I want **a few Articles of** jewellery.

(e) He ate **two slices of** bread.

Note: **Monies** is the **plural of money** which means **amounts of money**.

E.g.: Monies have been collected and handed to the women's welfare society.

Rule - 22

➢ Certain **Nouns** exist in **Plural Forms** only. Thus, '**s**' cannot be removed from such Nouns to make then **Singular**. They take Plural Verb with them.

(I) **CLOTHES AND ACCESSORIES:** Jeans, Pants, Trousers, Shorts, Braces, Sunglasses, Reading glasses, Goggles, Spectacles

(II) **INSTRUMENTS:** Binoculars, Forceps, Handcuffs, Scissors, Tongs, Gloves, Pliers, Bellows, Pincers

(III) **OTHERS:** Gallows, Arrears, Fangs, Archives, Congratulations, Thanks, Fireworks, Savings, Riches, Embers, Outskirts, Regards, Shambles, Remains, Surroundings, Tidings, Troops, Tactics, Valuables, Belongings, Eatables, Fetters, Tethers, Entrails, Nuptials, Proceeds, Ashes, Goods, Premises, Auspices, Alms, Contents, Whereabouts, Wages, Dues, Assets

E.g.: (a) Where are my **pants**?

(b) Where are the **tongs**?

(c) The **proceeds** were deposited in the bank.

(d) All his **assets** were seized.

➢ **Note:-** Wages can be used in both Singular and Plural form. See the following sentences:

	Meaning	Form	E.g.:
Wages	Labour	Plural	Wages are paid in cash.
	Result	Singular	Wages of hard work is sweet.

Rule - 23

News, Innings, Politics, Summons, Physics, Economics, Ethics, Mathematics, Mumps, Measles, Rickets, Shingles, Billiards, Athletics, Civics, Linguistics are certain **Nouns** that are **Plural in form** but **Singular in meaning.** They take **Singular Verb.**

E.g.: (a) No **news** is good news.
(b) **Politics** is a dirty game.
(c) **Economics** is an interesting subject.
(d) **Ethics** demands honesty.

Rule - 24

- **Cattle, Cavalry** (Soldiers of horses), **Infantry** (Soldiers on foot), **Poultry** (hens and ducks), **Peasantry** (Farmers), **Children, Gentry** (High class people), **Police** and **People** are certain **Nouns** that are **Singular in form** but **Plural in meaning**. They take **Plural Verb**.

  's' is never used with these nouns.

E.g.: (a) **Cattle** are grazing in the field.
(b) Our **infantry** have marched forward.
(c) **Police** have arrested the thieves.

Note: **'People'** means **'a number of men'** while **'peoples'** means **'people of different races'**.

E.g: The Greek peoples were brave. (Here we are talking about only one race. Therefore the use of 'peoples' is wrong. Write 'the Greeks' or 'the Greek people'.)

Rule - 25

- **Deer, Sheep, Series, Species, Fish, Crew, Team, Jury, Aircraft, Counsel** are certain Nouns that are used in **both Singular and Plural** forms. If they are used in **Singular sense, they take Singular Verb** and if they are used in **Plural sense, they take Plural Verb.**

E.g.: (a) Our team **is** the best.
(b) Our team **are** trying their new uniform.
(c) There are two fish in the pond.
(d) There are many fishes in the aquarium. (Here the word 'fishes' refers to different species of fish)

Look at the table given below:

Rule - 26

S.N	WORDS	+NOUN/PRONOUN	VERB
1.	No	+ U. N	Singular Verb
2.	No	+ S. C. N	Singular Verb
3.	One-third of / Three-fourths of / The rest of / A quarter of / Part of / Ten percent of / Twenty Percent of	+ U. N.	Singular Verb
4.	One-third of / Three-fourths of/ Part of / Ten percent of / Twenty percent of	+ P. C. N.	Plural Verb
5.	Most of / Some / Some of / Half of/ Enough / Enough of / Not enough of/ Plenty of / A lot of/ Lots of	+ U. N.	Singular Verb
6.	Most of / Some / Some of /Half of/ Enough / Enough of / Not enough of/ Plenty of / A lot of/ Lots of	+ P. C. N.	Plural Verb
7.	The percentage of	+ U.N./P.C.N.	Singular Verb
8.	More than one	+ S. C. N.	Singular Verb
9.	More than two/three. etc.	+ P. C. N.	Plural Verb
10.	More	+ P. C. N. + than one	Plural Verb

The following sentences show how the rules given in the table are followed

1. No air is present on Mars.
2. No student was interesting in taking the exam.
3. One-third of the work has been finished.
4. One-third of the students have passed.
5. Ninety percent of the work is done.
6. Most of the knowledge is gained by experience.
7. Most of the girls are absent today.
8. Ninety percent of the students have passed the exam with flying colours.
9. Half of the candidates have passed with flying colours.
10. Some of the students have not taken the exam.
11. The percentage of successful candidates is less.
12. More than one city was ruined.
13. More cities than one were in ruins.
14. More than two thieves have been caught.
15. More plans than one were made.

Note: See the difference between sentence 12 and 13.

SPOTTING THE ERROR

1. (a) Neither of them/ (b) are going to attend/ (c) the party on 10th October./ (d) No error
2. (a) He walked five miles which are really a great distance/ (b) for a man like him who is not only old but also ill./ (d) No error
3. (a) Either my colleague/ (b) or a peon are coming home/ (c) with the material today./ (d) No error
4. (a) The rise and fall/ (b) of the tide are due/ (c) to lunar influence./ (d) No error
5. (a) Many a man/ (b) have succumbed/ (c) to this temptation./ (d) No error
6. (a) The introduction of tea, coffee/ (b) and such other beverages/ (c) have not been without some effect./ (d) No error
7. (a) The newer type of automatic machines/ (b) wash/ (c) clothes faster./ (d) No error
8. (a) Each of the students in the computer class/ (b) has to type/ (c) their own research paper this semester./ (d) No error
9. (a) Everyone of the films/ (b) you suggested/ (c) are not worth seeing./ (d) No error
10. (a) The Secretary and Principal of the college/ (b) are attending/ (c) the District Development Council Meeting at the Collectorate./ (d) No error
11. (a) There is/ (b) only one of his novels/ (c) that are interesting./ (d) No error
12. (a) Knowledge of/ (b) at least two languages/ (c) are required to pass the examination./ (d) No error
13. (a) It is I/ (b) who is to blame/ (c) for this bad situation./ (d) No error
14. (a) Romanticism of melancholy/ (b) in art and literature are the reason/ (c) for insensitivity to those suffering from depression./ (d) No error

15. (a) Patience as well as perseverance (b) are necessary/ (c) for success./ (d) No error
16. (a) In Singapore/ (b) my brother-in-law with his wife/ (c) were present at the function./ (d) No error
17. (a) A hot and/ (b) a cold spring/ (c) was found near each other./ (d) No error
18. (a) Either of the roads/ (b) lead/ (c) to the park/ (d) No error
19. (a) One of my desires/ (b) are to become/ (c) a doctor./ (d) No error
20. (a) The whole block of flats/ (b) including two shops were/ (c) destroyed in fire./ (d) No error
21. (a) The sum and substance/ (b) of his poem/ (c) are as follows./ (d) No error
22. (a) Neither of the/ (b) five accused/ (c) could be convicted./ (d) No error
23. (a) The strain of all/ (b) the difficulties, vexations and anxieties/ (c) were more than he could beat./ (d) No error
24. (a) Everybody/ (b) it must be admitted/ (c) has their ups and downs./ (d) No error
25. (a) Every woman in the world/ (b) fervently hopes that their child/ (c) will be a normal and healthy baby/ (d) No error
26. (a) Neither of them/ (b) sent their papers/ (c) in time for the last seminar/ (d) No error
27. (a) This is a strange world/ (b) where each one pursues their own golden bubble/ (c) and laughs at others for doing the same./ (d) No error
28. (a) If it were possible to get near when/ (b) one of the volcanic eruptions take place/ (c) we would see a grand sight./ (d) No error
29. (a) A rise in rents and wages/ (b) have been found/ (c) to go together./ (d) No error
30. (a) He is one of those few post-colonial writer who believes/ (b) that this talk about colonialism has gone too far/ (c) and has turned into a cliche./ (d) No error
31. (a) One of the peculiarities/ (b) which distinguishes the present age/ (c) is the multiplication of books/ (d) No error
32. (a) Neither of them/ (b) are going to have/ (c) any doubt as far as malpractices are concerned/ (d) No error
33. (a) Ten miles are/ (b) a long distance / (c) to cover on foot./ (d) No error
34. (a) If Mahatma Gandhi/ (b) was alive, he would feel sorry for the poor and downtrodden who/(c) still struggle everyday to make both ends meet. / (d) No Error
35. (a) Having acquired some experience/ (b) she is no longer one of those who believes/ (c) every explanation they are given./ (d) No error
36. (a) With regard to implementation of the/ (b) details of the proposal, the committee was divided/ (c) in their opinion./ (d) No error
37. (a) Most of the funds/ (b) we get from/ (c) America is used to build roads and bridges./ (d) No error
38. (a) The tiger was not/ (b) the only dangerous animal/ (c) in the forest, there was hyenas too./ (d) No error
39. (a) She immediately quit/ (b) the job in which/ (c) neither skill nor knowledge were required./ (d) No error
40. (a) The type of qualities you acquire/ (b) depend upon your company/ (c) and so you associate yourselves with simple and good natured people./ (d) No error

41. (a) Our success or our failure/ (b) largely depend/ (c) upon our actions./ (d) No error
42. (a) He is/ (b) one of the tallest boy/ (c) in the class./ (d) No error
43. (a) That day when they brought her back for the last time/ (b) there was many old-timers/ (c) who were shocked and fearful./ (d) No error
44. (a) A computer virus works exactly/ (b) like the biological variety/ (c) which invade the human body./ (d) No error
45. (a) Many a boy/(b) have not done their/ (c) homework properly./ (d) No error
46. (a) Two miles beyond/ (b) that building was seen dozens/ (c) of antisocial elements./ (d) No error
47. (a) Along the northern frontier/ (b) of India is seen/ (c) the beautiful and mighty Himalayas./ (d) No error
48. (a) A body of volunteers/ (b) have helped in/ (c) making this celebration a great success./ (d) No error
49. (a) There appears/ (b) a number of problems/ (c) and I really do not know how to solve them. (d) No error
50. (a) Shingles are a disease/ (b) in which a person develops/ (c) lots of inflamed spots round the waist./ (d) No error
51. (a) Whether she should get married/ (b) or whether she should remain/ (c) single are her personal problem./ (d) No error
52. (a) Two and two/ (b) makes/ (c) four./ (d) No error.
53. (a) Many a men/ (b) attended the meeting/ (c) last night./ (d) No error.
54. (a) The perquisite/ (b) to this job makes it/ (c) even more attractive than the salary indicated./ (d) No error.
55. (a) Either you/ (b) or he/ (c) are happy./ (d) No error.

Answers with explanations

1. (b) Use 'is' in place of 'are'. The Noun / Pronoun following 'neither' is Plural, but the Verb following the Noun / Pronoun must be Singular.
2. (a) Here, 'five miles' is Singular as it is taken as a Singular unit. Hence Singular Verb 'is' will be used.
3. (b) Use 'is' in place of 'are'. When two subjects are joined by 'either or' , 'neither nor', 'or' or 'nor', the Verb will agree with the nearest subject.
4. (b) "The rise and fall" is a Singular subject. Hence Singular Verb 'is' will be used.
5. (b) 'Many a' is Singular and will take Singular Noun, Verb and Pronoun.
6. (c) The Verb must agree with the main subject. 'Introduction' is a Singular subject and hence will take Singular Verb 'has'.
7. (b) The Verb must agree with the main subject. 'Newer type' is a Singular subject and hence will take Singular Verb 'washes'.
8. (c) Use 'his' in place of 'their'. The Noun / Pronoun following 'each of...' is Plural, but the Verb following the 'Noun / Pronoun' must be Singular.
9. (c) Verb will be according to the subject, 'everyone'. 'Everyone' is Singular. Thus Singular Verb 'is' should be used.

10. (b) Here 'the' is used only before 'secretary'. This means the same person is the secretary as well as principal. Hence Singular Verb will be used.
11. (c) Use 'is' in place of 'are', because ' only one' of the novels is interesting.
12. (c) Here 'Languages' is not the main subject. Rather 'knowledge is the main subject. Hence Verb used must agree with 'knowledge'. Use 'is' in place of 'are'.
13. (b) Change 'is' into 'am'. If a subject and the Verb are joined by a Relative Pronoun, the Verb used will agree with the antecedent to the Relative Pronoun.
14. (b) Change 'are' into 'is' because the main subject 'romanticism' is Singular.
15. (b) When two subjects are joined by 'as well as', the Verb agrees with the 1st subject. 'Patience' is a Singular subject and hence will take Singular Verb 'is'.
16. (c) When two subjects are joined by 'with', the Verb agrees with the 1st subject. 'Brother in law' is a Singular subject and hence will take Singular Verb 'was'.
17. (c) Use 'were' in place of 'was'. If two subjects are joined by 'and' and if article is used before both the subjects, Plural Verb will be used.
18. (b) If 'of' is used after each, every, one etc, the Noun or Pronoun that comes immediately after 'of' will be Plural in form. However the Verb, Pronoun etc that come in the latter part of the sentence will be Singular in form.

    Either of the **roads/ them leads** to the park.

↓	↓	↓
Plural Noun	**Plural Pronoun**	**Singular Verb**

19. (b) Change 'are' into 'is'.(See sentence 18 for explanation)
20. (b) Change 'were' into 'was'. 'Block' is the main subject here and is Singular in form. The Verb must agree with the main subject.
21. (c) 'The sum and substance' means 'gist'. Moreover 'the' is used before the '1st subject' only. Hence change 'are' into 'is'.
22. (a) Change 'neither of' into 'none of'. The word 'neither' means not any of the 'two'.
23. (c) Change 'were' into 'was'. 'Strain' is the main subject here and is Singular in form. The Verb must agree with the main subject.
24. (c) 'Everybody' is Singular. Hence Singular Pronoun 'his' will be used.
25. (b) 'Every woman' is Singular and hence will take Singular Pronoun. Change 'their' into 'her'.
26. (b) Change 'their' into 'his'. If 'of' is used after 'neither' the Noun or Pronoun that comes immediately after 'of' will be Plural in form. However the Verb, Pronoun etc that come in the latter part of the sentence will be Singular in form.
27. (b) 'Each one' is Singular and hence will take Singular Pronoun 'his'.
28. (b) Use Singular Verb with 'one of'. 'Takes' will come in place of 'take'. Since the sentence is in past, 'took' will be used.
29. (b) Change 'have' into 'has'. 'Rise' is the main subject here and is Singular in form. The Verb must agree with the main subject.

30. (a) 'one of' will be followed by a Plural Noun. Hence 'writers' will replace 'writer'. Verb will follow the antecedent (writers) to the Relative Pronoun (who). Change 'believes' into 'believe'.
31. (b) The antecedent of 'which' is 'peculiarities' which is Plural. Hence change distinguishes (Singular) into distinguish (Plural).
32. (b) Change 'are' into 'is'.(See sentence 18 for explanation)
33. (a) 'Ten miles is Plural in form but used a Singular unit. Hence Singular Verb 'is' should be used.
34. (b) The sentence is of imaginary position. Change 'was' into 'were'.
35. (b) 'Those' is the antecedent of who (Relative Pronoun).Hence Verb will match with 'those'. Use Plural Verb 'believe'.
36. (b) Change 'was' into 'were' because collective Noun 'the committee' is divided here.
37. (c) Change 'is' into 'are'. 'Funds' is the main subject which is Plural. Hence Verb used must agree with 'funds'.
38. (c) Change 'was' into 'were'. 'Hyenas' is the main subject which is 'Plural'. Hence Verb used must agree with 'hyenas'.
39 (c) Change 'were' into 'was'. When two subjects are joined by 'neither..... nor', the Verb agrees with the nearest subject.
40. (b) The type (Singular) will take Singular Verb 'depends'.
41. (b) Change 'depend' into 'depends'. If two subjects are joined by 'or', the Verb agrees with the nearest subject.
42. (b) 'One of...' takes Plural Noun. Change 'boy' into 'boys'.
43. (b) Use Plural Verb 'were' with 'many old timers'.
44. (c) The antecedent of which is 'variety' which is Singular and hence will take Singular Verb 'invades'.
45. (b) Singular Noun/ Pronoun/Verb will follow 'many a'. Change 'have' and 'their' into 'has' and 'his'.
46. (b) Use 'were' in place of 'was'. 'Dozens of antisocial elements' is the main subject here and hence Plural Verb will be used.
47. (b) Change 'is' into 'are'. Here 'is seen' is used for 'the Himalayas' and not 'India'. Hence 'are seen' must be used.
48. (b) Collective Nouns like 'body', 'group', 'class' etc takes 'Singular Verb'. Change 'have' into 'has'.
49. (a) Change 'appears' into 'appear'. 'A number of problems' is Plural .
50. (a) 'Shingles' is Plural in form but Singular in meaning. Thus Singular Verb 'is' is used.
51. (c) Change 'are' into 'is'.
52. (b) Change 'makes' into 'make'.
53. (a) 'Many a' takes Singular Noun 'man'.
54. (b) Change 'makes' into 'make'. 'perquisites' is the main subject here which is Plural.
55. (c) Change 'are' into 'is'.

CHAPTER

7 CONDITIONAL SENTENCES

➢ When **two actions take place one after the other**, the second depending on the first, it is called a **conditional sentence.**

E.g.: You will succeed provided you work hard.

Here your success depends on your hard work.

➢ **Look at the following words.**

1. If	2. Provided	3. As soon as	4. No sooner ... than
5. Unless	6. Until	7. When	8. In case

These words generally come in Conditional Sentences.

➢ **Conditional sentences have two parts:-**

1. **If Clause or Subordinate Clause**
2. **Main Clause or Principal Clause**

Conditional sentences are of three types:-

A. **'If clause' in present tense. (Type 1)**
B. **'If clause' in past tense. (Type 2)**
C. **'If clause' in past perfect tense. (Type 3)**
D. **Other types of conditional sentences.**
E. **Conditional Sentences of Universal Truth. (Type 0).**

A. 'IF CLAUSE' IN PRESENT TENSE

General structure:- **If + Present Indefinite, Future Indefinite**

➢ In such sentences **'If clause'** is in **Present Indefinite Tense** and the **'main clause'** in **Future Indefinite Tense.**

Eg.: If I will come to Delhi (1st Action), I will meet you (2nd Action) - (×)

If I come to Delhi (1st Action, Present Indefinite), I will meet you (2nd Action, Future Indefinite). (✓)

➢ If **two actions take place one after the other in future**, and **if the second action depends on the first action, the first action is in Present Indefinite Tense** and **the second action is in Future Indefinite Tense**.

E.g.: 1. She will come to meet you as soon as you will reach Delhi. (×)
She will come to meet you **as soon as** you reach Delhi. (✓)

2. If the government will become strict, corruption will surely finish. (×)
   If the government becomes strict, corruption will surely finish. (✓)
3. I will help him provided he will mend his ways. (×)
   I will help him **provided** he mends his ways. (✓)
4. Unless he will not take care of his health, he will not recover. (×)
   Unless he takes care of his health, he will not recover. (✓)
5. There will be rush at the platform when the train will arrive. (×)
   There will be rush at the platform **when** the train arrives. (✓)

➢ In the above sentences, **'will/shall/would/'** will not come with the part that consists of **'If'**, **as soon as, provided, before, after, until, unless, in case, when** and **lest.**

➢ 'Not' is **not used** with clause comprising '**until/unless**'. See sentence 4.

➢ In **Conditional Sentences, 'will/shall'** will not come with '**when**'. (see sentence 5) But if the sentence is **completely in present tense,** both the **'if clause'** and the **'main clause'** will be in **Present Indefinite Tense**.

E.g.: 1. If it rains, the school remains closed.
2. If you heat water, it turns into steam.

➢ If a **probability** is expressed in a sentence, **may/might** will come in place of "**will**".

1. If it rains, the students **may** not come for class.
2. If the fog stays for long, the flights **may** get late.

➢ If the sentence is regarding permission, '**may**' will come in place of 'will'.

E.g.: If you have finished your work, you **may** go home.

➢ If the sentence is related to a suggestion, '**should / must**' will come in place of 'will'.

1. If you want to remain healthy, you **should** exercise daily.
2. If you do not know him, you **must** not open the door.

➢ In sentences related to requests with respect, '**could/may**' comes.

E.g.: If you meet him, **could** you tell him to call me up?
If you come to Delhi, **would** you come to meet me?

➢ In '**if clause**' **Present Continuous Tense can be used** in place of Present Indefinite Tense.

E.g.: If you are waiting for the bus, you should take a taxi.
If you are not reading the newspaper, you **should** let others read it.

➢ In **'If clauses' Present Perfect Tense can be used.**

E.g.: 1. If you have finished the work, you **may** leave.
2. If they have bought tickets, they **will** surely go to watch the movie.

PRESENT CONDITIONAL

B. 'IF' CLAUSE IN 'S + V_2' (V_2 cannot be 'was')

General Structure— **If + Sub + V_2 (any V_2 Except 'was'), Subject + would + $V_{b.f}$**

E.g.: If I had money, I would lend it to you.

➢ Conditional of this type is used when we talk about something which is purely imaginary.

- In the above sentence '**If I had money**' shows that the subject had no money.

C. 'IF' CLAUSE IN PAST PERFECT TENSE

General Structure— **If + Past Perfect, Sub + would + have + V_3**

E.g.: If I had seen you, I would have stopped my car.

- Conditional sentences of this type are used when something did not happen because a certain condition was not fulfilled.

  "**If**" I had seen you, means "**I had not seen you.**"
- In such sentences we can also replace '**If**' with '**had**'. This will not change the meaning of the sentence.

Had + Subject + V_3 + obj, Subject + would + have + V_3

E.g.: Had I seen you, I would have stopped my car.

THREE IMPORTANT STRUCTURE

- **If + Present Indefinite** , **Future Indefinite**
- **If + S + had + V_3** , **S + would + have + V_3**
- **If + S + V_2 (Except 'was')** , **S + would + $V_{b.f}$**

D. OTHER TYPES OF CONDITIONAL SENTENCES

(i) Sentences related to Present imaginary position.

General Structure— **If + subject + were, subject + would + $V_{b.f}$**

E.g.: If I were a bird, I would fly in the sky.

- For Present Posts, **were** is used with all subjects.
- '**was**' is not used with the following words since they usually denote imaginary position/action.

  If, as though, in case, as if, would that and I wish.

E.g.: He scolds me as if he was my father. (×)

He scolds me as if he were my father. (✓)

- **If clause**, can also take '**unless, so long as, soon as, when, provided, in case, but for**' etc.

E.g.: Unless you work hard, you will not pass.

Note: "**Not**" is not used with unless/until.

Unless + affirmative = If + negative

E.g: 1. Unless you work hard, you will not pass.

2. If you do not work hard, you will not pass.

Other examples of Conditional Sentences

1. I shall support him **so long as** I am alive.
2. **As soon as** the train comes, passengers will rush for seats.
3. **When** he comes to Delhi, I will go to meet him.

SPOTTING THE ERROR

1. (a) If he were you / (b) I would have given/ (c) him my car. / (d) No error
2. (a) Had he invited me / (b) I would have attended / (c) the function. / (d) No error
3. (a) If he had called me up (b) I would inform/ (c) him ./ (d) No error
4. (a) If he will work hard / (b)/ he will surely / (c) get the job of his choice. / (d) No error
5. (a) Unless I do not / (b) see his ticket, / (c) I will not let him sit here. / (d) No error
6. (a) Before the police will come / (b) you should better / (c) get the anticipatory bail. (d) No error
7. (a) We will come to know the truth / (b) after / (c) the investigation finished. / (d) No error
8. (a) Until the train will not get the signal , (b) it will not / (c) leave the platform. / (d) No error
9. (a) If I had money/ (b) I will have lent / (c) it to her. / (d) No error
10. (a) If I was you/ (b) I would not tolerate him / (c) for a moment. / (d) No error
11. (a) Suppose she does not agree/ (b)what could/ (c) we do ? / (d) No error
12. (a) Supposing if you do not reach / (b) the station in time,/ (c) what will you do? / (d) No error
13. (a) If you saw a tiger / (b) what will your / (c) reaction be?/ (d) No error
14. (a) If I had two houses, / (b) I would have given / (c) one to you./ (d) No error
15. (a) If we will heat dry ice / (b) it turns / (c) to vapour. / (d) No error
16. (a) Suppose if you are / (b) late, you will be / (c) in trouble. / (d) No error.
17. (a) Unless / (b) he will not understand the concept/ (c) he will not be able to solve the questions. / (d) No error
18. (a) If he tried again,/ (b) he can pass the exam/ (c) with flying colours. / (d) No error
19. (a) I will wait for you / (b) unless / (c) you come. / (d) No error
20. (a) If I was you / (b) I would teach/ (c) him a lesson. / (d) No error
21. (a) If I were the Prime Minister of India / (b) I will work for the / (c) welfare of the poor. / (d) No error
22. (a) If she would have come to me / (b) I would have given her the / (c) money she needed / (d) No error
23. (a) If he drove fast/ (b) he can reach the station / (c) in time / (d) No error
24. (a) If I was a millionaire/ (b) I would support / (c) the millennium project / (d) No error
25. (a) If both of you stood / (b) on the table/ (c) it would have broken./ (d) No error
26. (a) If she would have worked hard , / (b) she would / (c) have passed. / (d) No error
27. (a) If you had seen me, / (b) you should have stopped your car / (c) and come to help me. / (d) No error
28. (a) If the Government will make strict law/ (b) the law and order situation / (c) will improve. / (d) No error
29. (a) But for his help / (b) the patient would / (c) have died. / (d) No error
30. (a) But for his prompt action / (b) many people would/ (c) have lost their savings. / (d) No error
31. (a) I will not come / (b) in case / (c) it will rain. / (d) No error
32. (a) Had the river overflown its bank,/ (b) flood would / (c) have come. / (d) No error
33. (a) Had I known him, / (b) I would allow him / (c) to enter my house. / (d) No error
34. (a) You will not get well / (b) unless you will not / (c) follow the doctor's instructions. / (d) No error

35. (a) Supposing if he refuses / (b) to meet you, / (c) what will you do? / (d) No error
36. (a) I shall take you for a long drive /(b) after you /(c) will return from the meeting. / (d) No error
37. (a) When you complete your service / (b) you will be / (c) retired on pension. / (d) No error
38. (a) Were she I, / (b) she will not allow/ (c) you to go anywhere at this time of crisis./ (d) No error
39. (a) I told her when / (b) she came to Delhi,/ (c) I would show her all historical monuments. / (d) No error
40. (a) You can scale this high peak, / (b) provided you/ (c) will wear the right kind of shoes. / (d) No error
41. (a) Had you / (b) worked hard/ (c) you will have passed./ (d) No error
42. (a) When I shall see him/ (b) I shall/ (c) tell him/ (d) No error
43. (a) He will tell you/ (b) about it when/ (c) he will come back./ (d) No error
44. (a) When I will get back/ (b) I shall pay back/ (c) the money that I borrowed from you last month /(d) No error
45. (a) I will/ (b) meet him/ (c) when he will come./ (d) No error
46. (a) Had I realized/ (b) your house was such a long way off, / (c) I would take a taxi./ (d) No error

Answers with explanation

1. (c) Change 'I would have given' into 'I would give'.
2. (d)
3. (b) Change 'I would inform' into 'I would have informed'. If the 'If clause' is 'subject + had + V_3', the main clause is 'subject + would + have + V_3'.
4. (a) Change 'If he will work hard' into 'If he works hard '. 'Will' is not used in the 'If clause'.
5. (a) Remove 'do not'. 'Not' doesn't come after unless.
6. (a) Change 'before the police will come' into 'before the police come '. 'Will' is not used in the 'If clause'.
7. (c) Change 'investigation finished' into 'investigation has finished'. If the 2nd action takes place after the 1st action has already finished, the 1st action will be in present perfect tense.
8. (a) Remove 'will not'. 'Not' and 'will' do not come after 'unless'. Change 'get' into 'gets'
9. (b) Change 'will have lent' into 'would lend'. See the given structure-

   If + S + V_2 , **S + would + $V_{b.f}$**

10. (a) Change 'was' into 'were'. 'Was' is not used in imaginary position.
11. (b) Change 'could' into 'can'. The sentence is not of past ability.
12. (a) Remove 'if'. 'supposing' and 'if' mean the same. when used together, they make the sentence superfluous.
13. (b) Change 'will' into 'would'. (see sentence 9)
14. (b) Change 'I would have given' into 'I would give'.
15. (a) Remove 'will'. (see question 4)
16. (a) Remove 'if'. 'Suppose' and 'if' mean the same. when used together, they make the sentence superfluous.
17. (b) Change 'he will not understand' into 'he understands'.'Not' and 'will' do not come after 'unless'.
18. (b) Change 'can' into 'could'. The sentence is in past.
19. (b) Change 'unless' into 'until'. Until is time oriented whereas unless is action oriented.

20. (a) Change 'was' into 'were'. 'Was' is not used in imaginary position.
21. (b) Change 'will' to 'would'. The sentence is in past.
22. (a) Change 'If she would have come to me' into 'If she had come to me'. See the given formula-

    If + S + had + V_3,

    S + would + have + V_3
23. (b) Change 'can' into 'could'. The sentence is in past.
24. (a) Change 'was' into 'were'. 'Was' is not used in imaginary position.
25. (c) Change 'would have broken' into 'would break'. The sentence fits in the formula given below-

    If + S + V_2, **S + would + $V_{b.f}$**
26. (a) Change 'If she would have worked hard' into 'If she had worked hard'. The sentence fits in the formula given below-

    If + S + had + V_3,

    S + would + have + V_3
27. (d)
28. (a) Change 'If the Government will make' into 'If the Government makes '. 'Will' is not used in the 'If clause'.
29. (d) here 'but for' means 'without'.
30. (d) here 'but for' means 'without'.
31. (c) Change 'It will rain' into 'it rains'.
32. (a) V_3 of 'overflow' is 'overflowed'.
33. (b) Change 'I would allow' into 'I would have allowed'. The sentence fits in the formula given below-

    Had + S+ V_3,

    S + would + have + V_3
34. (b) Remove 'will not'. 'Not' and 'will' do not come after 'unless'.
35. (a) Remove 'if'. 'Supposing' and 'if' mean the same. Together they make the sentence superfluous.
36. (c) Change 'will return' into 'have returned'. If the 2nd action takes place after the 1st action has already finished, the 1st action will be in Present Perfect Tense.
37. (a) 'When you have completed your services' is correct. If the 2nd action takes place after the 1st action has already finished, the 1st action will be in Present Perfect Tense.
38. (b) Change 'will' into 'would'. The sentence is in past.
39. (a) Add 'that' after 'I told her' because a sentence is connected to the other sentence with the help of a conjunction.
40. (c) Change ' will wear' into 'wear '. 'Will' is not used in the 'If clause'.
41. (c) Change 'will' into 'would'. The sentence is in past.
42. (a) 'When I see him' is correct. 'Will' is not used in the 'If clause'.
43. (c) Change 'he will come' into 'he comes'.
44. (a) Change 'when I will get back' into 'when I get back'.
45. (c) Change 'when he will come' into 'when he comes'.
46. (c) Change 'I would take' into 'I would have taken'.

CHAPTER 8 VERB (ADVANCE)

KINDS OF VERBS

1. Finite Verbs
2. Non-finite Verbs
3. Transitive Verbs
4. Intransitive Verbs

1. **Finite Verbs:** Verbs that are **limited by number and person** are known as **finite verbs.**

E.g.: He **is** playing.
They **are** playing.
Here the subjects 'he' and they' decide whether we need to use 'is' or 'are'. Hence here 'is and 'are' are finite verbs

2. **Non-finite Verbs:** Verbs that are **not limited by number and person** are known as **infinite verbs.**

E.g.: I like **watching** T.V.
She wants **to go** abroad.
Here 'watching and 'to go' will not change if we change the subject of the sentence. This means they are not limited by number and person.

Non-finite Verbs are of the following three types:

(a) **Infinitive**
(b) **Gerund**
(c) **Participle**

A. **Infinitive :** It is denoted by '**to + $V_{b.f}$**'. It acts as a **noun** and a **verb**. Hence infinitive is also called **Verb - Noun**.

E.g.: 1. **To err** is human.
2. I want **to study**.
3. I want **to study** English.

- **Look at the sentences given above:**
- In sentence 1, '**To err**' is used as a **subject (to + $V_{b.f}$)**.
- In sentence 2, '**to study**' is used as an **object**. **(to + $V_{b.f}$)**.
- '**To study**' is the **object** of '**want**' (verb), but if '**English**' acts as an **object**' '**to study**' acts as a verb.
- Thus, '**to + $V_{b.f}$**' acts as both **noun and verb**.

B. **Gerund:** It is denoted by 'V_1+ing'. It acts as a **noun** and a **verb**. Hence **Gerund** is also called **Verb - Noun**.

E.g.:1. **Swimming** is a good exercise.
2. I learnt **driving**.
3. I like **watching** television.

- In sentence 1, '**Swimming**' **(V_1 + ing)** acts as **subject**.
- In sentence 2, '**Driving**' **(V_1 + ing)** is **object**.
- In sentence 3, '**Watching**' is the **object** of verb '**like**' but if television is taken as an object, then "**watching**" acts as **verb**. Thus **V_1 + ing** is **both noun and verb**.

Note: With the following verbs/adjectives/phrases '**V_1 + ing**' is used after 'to'.

E.g.: **Verb + used to, accustomed to, averse to, with a view to, addicted to, devoted to, in addition to, look forward to, object to, owing to, given to, taken to, prone to.**

E.g.:1. He is **addicted to** smoking.
2. I am **looking forward to** meeting you.
3. He was **used to** driving on the right when he was in London.

In other words, after all the prepositions (including 'to') , if a verb comes, the verb has to be in 'V_1 + ing'

E.g.:(a) I am looking forward to meeting (V_1+ing) you.

(b) He is given to drinking (V_1+ing).

(c) He is prone to making (V_1+ing) the same mistake again and again.

(d) He got used to driving (V_1+ing) on the right when he was in London.

- But in modals '**V_1**' comes after 'used to'.

(e) I used to drive (V_1) on the right.

- **Difference between d & e**

Sentence (d)		Sentence (e)	
(1)	If verb comes before 'used to', ' V_1+ing' comes after used to.	(1)	If verb does not comes before 'used to' 'V_1' comes after 'used to'.
(2)	It denotes a habit	(2)	It denotes a routine action of past .
(3)	It can be used in any tense. The verb and its form that precedes 'used to' determines the tense of the sentence.	(3)	It can be used only in Past tense.

C. **Participle:** A word that acts as a **verb** as well as **adjective** is called a participle.

(i) **Present Participle (V_1 + ing)**

1. **Hearing** the noise, we rushed out of the restaurant.
2. **Thinking** all is well, he went to bed.

➢ In the above sentences, **'V_1 + ing'** denotes an action going on or an incomplete action.

(ii) **Past Participle (V_3)**

1. **Driven** by poverty, he committed suicide.
2. **Deceived** by his best friend, he was left in the lurch.

➢ In the above sentences **'V_3'** shows **an** action already completed before the second action took place . **'V_3'** is called **Past Participle**.

(iii) **Perfect Participle (Having V_3)**

1. **Having done** with it, they got down to work.
2. **Having rested**, they started their journey again.

➢ The above sentences show an action being **completed** in past. **'Having + V_3' (Perfect Participle)** is used for such purpose.

➢ **Transitive Verb:** If a verb **requires an object** after it, it is called a **Transitive verb**.

E.g.:1. I $\underbrace{\text{write}}_{\text{V}}$ $\underbrace{\text{essays}}_{\text{obj.}}$.

2. Children $\underbrace{\text{fly}}_{\text{V}}$ $\underbrace{\text{kites}}_{\text{obj.}}$.

➢ **Intransitive Verb:** If a verb does not require an object after it, it is called an Intransitive Verb.

E.g.: Birds $\underbrace{\text{fly}}_{\text{v}}$.

She $\underbrace{\text{slept}}_{\text{v}}$.

E.g.:1. He killed (What ?)

He $\underbrace{\text{killed}}_{\text{t.v.}}$ a $\underbrace{\text{rabbit}}_{\text{obj.}}$.

2. I helped (?)

I $\underbrace{\text{helped}}_{\text{t.v.}}$ $\underbrace{\text{him}}_{\text{obj.}}$.

A sentence with transitive verbs will need an object otherwise the sentence will not make a complete sense.

➢ **Causative Verbs: Have, get** and **make** are causative verbs.

In a normal sentence, the subject does the verb on the object.

E.g.: He (Sub.) helps (Verb) the poor (obj.).
Sub. does → Verb on → obj.

➢ But if, subject **(S_2)** induces another subject **(S_1)** to do the verb on the object, causative verb is used.

E.g.:1. He got caught.
2. The environment gets polluted due to our ignorance.

➢ See the sentences given below to understand the use of causative verbs.

E.g.:1. I (S_2) made ('Make' according to tense) him (S_1) do ($V_{b.f}$) the whole work (obj.).

2. We (S_2) got ('Get' according to tense) him (obj.) arrested (V_3) by the police (S_1).

3. Have ('Have' according to tense) the box (obj.) opened (V_3).

4. We (S_2) have to make ('make' according to tense) the system (S_1) work ($V_{b.f}$).

5. I (S_2) cannot get ('get' according to tense) your work (obj.) done (V_3) by him (S_1).

Note: Difference between Make and Have/Get

1. **S_1** is **optional** in sentences that have causative verbs **'get/have'**. If **S_1 is present it comes in 'by + S_1' after the use of Get/Have.**

   But **S_1** is **mandatory** when **'make'** is used as a causative verb.

2. The **main verb** comes in **V_3** form when **'Get/Have'** is used as a **causative verb.**

   The **main verb** comes in **V_1** form when **'Make'** is used as a **causative verb.**

3. In a sentence, **Get/Have/Make** changes according to tense.

➢ See the patterns given below and understand how a verb is used in them.

Pattern - 1 | **Subject + Verb**

➢ This is the most simple pattern. In such a sentence, an **Intransitive verb** is used after the subject. The meaning of the sentence is clear even without an object. Such sentences cannot be changed into Passive Voice.

E.g.:

S.N	Subject	Verb
1.	Birds	fly.
2.	The moon	is shining
3.	The baby	is sleeping.
4.	I	was going

Pattern - 2 **Subject + verb + subject complement**

➢ In such sentences, the complement is either a noun, a pronoun or an adjective. Sentences of this pattern too cannot be changed into Passive Voice.

E.g.

S.N.	Subject	Verb	Subject Complement
1.	This	is	a pen.
2.	It	is	I
3.	He	looks	happy.
4.	My father	got	angry.

Pattern - 3 **Subject + verb + direct object**

➢ Transitive Verbs need an object for the sentence to make a complete sense. The sentence of this type follows the pattern given below.

E.g.:

S.N.	Subject	Verb	Direct Object
1.	I	know	him.
2.	She	opened	the door.
3.	You	should help	yourself.

Pattern - 4 **Subject+verb + indirect object + direct object**

➢ It a sentence has two objects, the indirect object comes first and then the direct object. The indirect object is the receiver and the indirect object is the thing received.

E.g.:

S.N.	Subject	Verb	Indirect Object	Direct Object
1.	I	gave	her	my book.
2.	I	bought	her	a purse
3.	He	showed	me	his notes.

Pattern - 5 **Subject + verb + direct object + preposition + prepositional object**

➢ If the direct object comes first, it is followed by a preposition and then comes the indirect object.

E.g.:

S.N.	Subject	Verb	Direct Object	Preposition	Prepositional object
1.	I	gave	my book	to	her.
2.	I	bought	a purse	for	her.
3.	He	showed	his notes	to	me and my friends.

- Pattern 5 is preferable if the direct object is less important or if the indirect object is long.

Pattern - 6 **Subject + verb + noun/ pronoun + adjective**

- In this type of sentences, the adjective denotes the situation that is created by the verb or if the noun and the adjective together make the object.

E.g:

S.N.	Subject	Verb	Direct Object	Adjective
1.	He	pushed	the door	open.
2.	She	washed	the plates	clean.
3.	I	like	my tea	strong.
4.	I	bought	this shirt	cheap.

- The verbs used in this pattern are given below:

get, keep, beat, drive, make, paint, leave, turn, find, like, wish.

Pattern - 7 **Subject + verb + preposition + prepositional object.**

E.g.:

S.N.	Subject	Verb	Preposition	Prepositional object
1.	This car	belongs	to	me.
2.	She	met	with	an accident.
3.	He	succeeded	in	his attempt.

Pattern - 8 **Subject + verb + to-infinitive (as object of the verb)**

S.N.	Subject	Verb	Infinitive	
1.	She	wants	to sleep.	
2.	He	forgot	to take	his medicine.
3.	I	hoped	to pass	the exam.

- The verbs used in this pattern are given below:

Like, love, prefer, begin, start, agree, try, attempt, choose, continue, intend, propose, desire, wish, want, hate, dislike, hope, expect, promise, fear, remember, forget, offer, learn.

Pattern -9 **Subject + verb + noun/ pronoun + infinitive.**

E.g.:

S.N.	Subject	Verb	Noun/ Pronoun	Infinitive + etc.
1.	I	want	you	to help him.
2.	The doctor	advised	him	to rest.
3.	I	allowed	Rohit	to go.

➤ The verbs used in this pattern are given below:

Ask, tell, order, command, persuade, encourage, urge, want, wish, request, intend, expect, force, tempt, teach, invite, help, warn, like, love, hate, allow, permit, remind, cause, mean, dare.

Pattern - 10 **Subject + verb + Gerund.**

Here **Gerund** acts as the **object**.

E.g.:

S.N.	Subject	Verb	Gerund, etc.
1.	She	started	singing.
2.	He	has finished	talking.
3.	I	love	teaching.

➤ The verbs used in this pattern are given below:

Begin, start, love, like, hate, stop, finish, enjoy, prefer, fear, remember, forget, mind, miss, suggest, practise, try, understand, keep, admire, avoid, consider, intend, delay, deny, detest, cannot help, rest, defer, worth, risk, it is no good, propose, regret, anticipate.

Pattern - 11 **Subject + Verb + Noun/ Pronoun + Present Participle.**

E.g.:

S.N.	Subject	Verb	Noun/ Pronoun	Present Participle
1.	I	saw	him	crossing the bridge.
2.	I	heard	him	shouting
3.	You	kept	me	waiting

➤ The verbs used in this pattern are given below:

See, hear, smell, feel, watch, notice, find, observe, listen, get, catch, keep, leave, set, start.

Pattern - 12 **Subject + Verb + Noun/ Pronoun + Plain Infinitive.**

E.g.:

S.N.	Subject	Verb	Noun/ Pronoun	Plain Infinitive
1.	I	will not let	you	go
2.	We	made	him	finish the work.
3.	I	bade	the boy	leave the room.

➤ The verbs used in this pattern are given below:
See, watch, notice, observe, hear, listen, feel, make, let, help, bid.

➢ **Important rules related to verb:**

1. a. Being ill, I could not come. (✓)

b. Being a rainy day, I could not come. (×)

c. Walking along the road, my pen fell down. (×)

➢ In the 1st sentence, if the subject is not mentioned before '**being**' in the first part of the sentence, subject '**I**' of the 2nd part becomes the **common subject** of both the parts but the meaning of the sentence comes out to be correct.

➢ In the second sentence, if '**It**' is not used before '**being**', '**I**' becomes the subject of 'rainy day' and this gives a wrong meaning to the sentence. Thus '**It being a rainy day**' must be used.

➢ Similarly, in the 3rd sentence use proper subject before '**walking**' otherwise '**my pen**' will become the subject of 'walking'.

Thus '**While I was walking along the road**' is the correct formation.

2. (i) The girls watched intently as the model applied her make-up with a practiced hand.(×)

➢ Here verb (V_3) must come as an adjective and not a noun. '**Practised' (verb)** should be used. in place of 'practiced' (Noun). Practice is a noun.

E.g.: **Spoken** English
Revised edition
Written document

➢ But if the action is shown in **continuous** form or we talk about any state of being, **'ing'** form of verb is used.

E.g: **Rising** prices.
Developing country
Steaming cup of tea
Barking dogs

3. If the verb is used as a noun, '**ing' (Gerund) form** / '**to +** V_1' **(infinitive)** form is used.

E.g.: Smoking (obj) is prohibited here.

Swimming (sub) is a good exercise.

To err (Sub.) is human.

4. **Adverb of manner** explains **how a verb is done**. Adverb of manner generally ends in **'ly'** .

E.g.: He works (Verb) honestly (Adv).

He talks (Verb) politely (Adv).

Note: I bought this shirt Cheaply.(×)
I bought this shirt Cheap.(✓)

- If the **verb** is related to our five senses, an **adjective** is used after it and not an **adverb**.

E.g.: He **looks** (Verb) honest (Adj).

He **sounds** (Verb) polite (Adj).

- **The verbs of sensation are given below:**
Look, seem, sound, appear, smell, taste and **feel**
- Besides the verbs of sensation **'be'** , **'become'**, **'turn'**, **'get'**, **'grow'**, **'keep'**, **'make'** and **'prove'** are qualified by an adjective and not by an adverb.

E.g.: When he heard the news, he **became** sad (adj).

5. We adapt to the environment. (×)
We adapt **ourselves** to the environment. (✓)

- Following verbs will also take reflexive pronoun after them:
Acquit (to do better than expected), absent, avail, reconcile (to accept a situation reluctantly), amuse, resign (to accept something as inevitable) , avenge, enjoy, exert, apply (to work hard on something), adapt, adjust, pride

1. The officer **acquitted themselves** well during the crisis.
2. She has **reconciled herself** to the demands of her in laws.
3. The students exert **themselves** a lot at the time of examination.
4. You will have to **apply yourself** to this task heartedly.
5. I **pride myself** on being able to work smoothly under pressure too.
6. You should **avail yourself** of this opportunity.
7. He **resigned himself** to yet another day without food.

Note: They **enjoyed** the party (no need of reflexive pronoun as an object is present)
They enjoyed during vacation. ('themselves' is used after 'enjoyed' as an object is not present)

- If 'enjoy' is followed by an object, reflexive pronoun is not used but if the object is not mentioned, reflexive pronoun is used.
- If '**absent**' is used as **a verb**, **it will be followed by a Reflexive Pronoun** .
He was **absent**. (✓)
He **absented** himself. (✓)

Note: ➢ If **'acquit'** means **to decide in court that one is not guilty**, reflexive pronoun is not used.

E.g.: The court acquitted him.
If '**acquit**' means **to do better than expected**, a reflexive pronoun is used.

E.g.: The police **acquitted themselves** well during the riot.

- If '**reconcile**' means **to settle a matter or resolve**, reflexive pronoun shall not be used.

Eg.: I reconciled with him after the bitter argument.

- If '**reconcile**' means **to accept a situation reluctantly**, a reflexive pronoun follows it.

E.g.: He reconciled himself to the arrogant attitude of his boss.

➢ **Note:** In short we can say that if the subject becomes the receiver of the action, the verbs given above will take a reflexive pronoun.

E.g.: (i) Keep yourself away from bad company. (×)
Keep away from bad company. (✓)
(ii) He hid himself in the room. (Drop 'himself')

List of verbs that do not take Reflexive Pronoun:
Keep, stop, turn, qualify, bathe, move, rest, hide

6. A verb either does not take any preposition or takes a fixed preposition .

(i) I prefer tea than coffee. (×)
I **prefer** tea **to** coffee. (✓)

(ii) He invited me on/for tea.(×)
He **invited** me **to** tea. (✓)

7. If an infinitive (**to sleep, to write etc.**) qualifies a noun (**bed, pen, etc.**), the infinitive takes a suitable preposition after it. (**in, with etc.**)

(i) The poor had no bed to sleep **in.**
(ii) He had no pen to write **with.**
(iii) Do you have a chair to sit **on?**

8. If we need two forms of a verb in a sentence, we must use both of the forms.

(i) I have never and will never cheat you. (××)
I have never $\underbrace{\text{cheated}}_{V_3}$ and will never $\underbrace{\text{cheat}}_{V_1}$ you. (✓)

(ii) Nothing has or will be more tragic than his demise. (×)
Nothing has $\underbrace{\text{been}}_{V_3}$ or will $\underbrace{\text{be}}_{V_1}$ more tragic than his demise. (✓)

9. **'Were'** is used for **Present imaginary posts.**

E.g.: If he was a millionaire, he would help the millennium project. (×)
It he were a millionaire, he would help the millennium project. (✓)

10. In **optative sentences**, **Base forms of verb** are used with singular subjects too.

Long $\underbrace{\text{live}}_{V_{b.f}}$ the $\underbrace{\text{king}}_{S.S.}$! (✓)

11. A number of verbs can act as a noun if an article is used with them .

E.g. (i) He is $\underbrace{\text{walking}}_{\text{Verb}}$.
(ii) He is going for a $\underbrace{\text{walk}}_{\text{Noun}}$.
(iii) He $\underbrace{\text{rides}}_{\text{Verb}}$ a horse.
(iv) He went for a $\underbrace{\text{ride}}_{\text{Noun}}$.

12. If different verbs need different prepositions, use all the prepositions.

E.g.: (i) Amphibians can live **on** land and **in** water.
(ii) He was acquitted **of** and absolved **from** all the charges of corruption.

13. There are certain verbs that generally do not come in 'ing' form:-

(1) Verbs of Perception- See, taste, smell, hear, notice, recognize, look, appear.

(2) Verbs of Thought- Think, know, mean, mind, remember, suppose.

(3) Verbs of Possession- Own, have, belong, comprise, possess, contain, consist.

(4) Verbs of Feeling or State of Mind- Believe, like, dislike, love, adore, want, wish, desire, hate, agree, trust, imagine, please

(5) Verbs in General- affect, resemble, cost, require, become, hope, refuse, prefer, exist

(for detail explanation, see Continuous Tense)

E.g.: I am having car. (×)

I have a car. (✓)

14. Adverb 'as' is used with the following verbs:

Regard, describe, define, treat, view, know

➢ **Adverb 'as' can not be used with the following verbs:**

Name, elect, think, consider, call, appoint, make, choose

E.g.:
1. I **regard** him my brother. (Add 'as' after 'him')
2. Biology has been **defined** the study of organism. (Add 'as' after 'defined')
3. She is **considered** as the best student of my class. (Drop 'as' after 'considered')
4. The teacher **called** him as stupid. (Drop 'as')
5. The principal **appointed** him as a lecturer. (Remove 'as')
6. He **thinks** her as a fool. (Remove 'as')

15. If '**It's high time**'/ '**it's time**'/'**it's about time**' is used in a sentence, '$\mathbf{V_2}$' comes in the sentence.

E.g.: It's high time you **did** something.

16. A **few nouns take a definite verb** before them that sounds the most appropriate.

Have —lunch etc.	**take** —an exam	**make** —a demand	**Other examples**
a good time	advantage	a gesture	**Launch** scheme
a shower	an action	a noise	**Render** help
a dream	risk	a promise	**Impart** education
a conversation	your time	a request	**Levy** tax
		a mistake	**Impose** tax/fine
			Level charges (See Classroom Notes for more examples)

17. All the prepositions (including 'to') take '$\mathbf{V_1}$ + ing' after them.

E.g.:
1. He is afraid **to** $\underbrace{\textbf{do}}_{V_{b.f}}$ anything against his boss.
2. He is afraid **of** $\underbrace{\textbf{going}}_{V_1+ing}$ out after sunset.
3. He is addicted $\underbrace{\textbf{to}}_{Prep.}$ $\underbrace{\textbf{smoking}}_{V_1 + ing}$.

SPOTTING THE ERROR

1. (a) Walking along the road/ (b) a car knocked/ (c) him down./(d) No error.
2. (a) Having done my homework/ (b) my mother allowed me/ (c) to go out and play./(d) No error.
3. (a) Being a rainy day,/ (b) I had to cancel/ (c) all my appointments./ (d) No error.
4. (a) A few selfish leaders/ (b) are bent to harm/ (c) the very foundation of democracy./ (d) No error.
5. (a) As I have worked hard,/ (b) I am confident to pass/ (c) with flying colours ./ (d) No error.
6. (a) We went to that place/ (b) with a view to help/ (c) the earthquake victims./ (d) No error.
7. (a) You should avoid/ (b) to go to school/ (c) as you have severe eye infection./ (d) No error.
8. (a) I have/ (b) no achievement/ (c) to boast./ (d) No error.
9. (a) One must avail of/ (b) every opportunity/ (c) that comes in life./ (d) No error.
10. (a) Have the letter/ (b) send/ (c) by someone who is trustworthy./ (d) No error.
11. (a) Would you please order/ (b) for tea and buiscuits/ (c) for all of us./ (d) No error.
12. (a) Everyone considered him as/ (b) a brave man/(c) but he fled from the battlefield./ (d) No error.
13. (a) My father does not mind/ (b) to be disturbed/ (c) while he is reading the newspaper./ (d) No error.
14. (a) Perhaps you do not know/ (b) I am having a car and a jeep/ (c) besides a big house in a good locality./ (d) No error.
15. (a) The lawyer asked me/ (b) if it were worth to take/ (c) the matter to court./ (d) No error.
16. (a) I bade him/ (b) to submit all the important documents/ (c) before he left the job./ (d) No error.
17. (a) He thinks/ (b) himself/ (c) as a great scholar ./ (d) No error.
18. (a) All the candidates/ (b) will give/ (c) a test on Friday./ (d) No error.
19. (a) Mrs Dorai would rather/ (b) spend a quiet evening/ (c) than attending a party./ (d) No error.
20. (a) The audience/ (b) watched the clowns/ (c) performed their act ./ (d) No error.
21. (a) The life-guard would not/ (b) let the children/ (c) to swim at the deep end of the pool ./ (d) No error.
22. (a) He denied/ (b) to help/ (c) me./ (d) No error.
23. (a) Walking along the/ (b) bank of the river/ (c) the road began to rise./ (d) No error.
24. (a) It is time you/ (b) decide on your next/ (c) course of action ./ (d) No error.
25. (a) As I was feeling sleepy/ (b) I asked for/ (c) a steamed cup of tea./ (d) No error.
26. (a) I remember/ (b) meet him/ (c) five years ago./(d) No error.
27. (a) I have always/ (b) and will always/ (c) be faithful to you./ (d) No error.
28. (a) I am afraid/ (b) I did a mistake/ (c) in the calculation./ (d) No error.
29. (a) The lights went out/ (b) while we/ (c) took the examination./ (d) No error.

30. (a) His assistants have and/ (b) are still doing/ (c) excellent work for the organization./ (d) No error.
31. (a) After the teacher had told the boys/ (b) how to pronounce the word/ (c) all of them in one voice repeated the word again ./ (d) No error.
32. (a) The company is not doing well./ (b) Isn't it time you/ (c) sell off your shares in it ?/ (d) No error.
33. (a) He caught the boy/ (b) steal/ (c) the parcel./ (d) No error.
34. (a) I declined the invitation/ (b) not because I did not want to go,/ (c) but because I have no time./ (d) No error.
35. (a) It is a known fact/ (b) that time does not return back/ (c) once it is lost./ (d) No error.
36. (a) Even after sixty years of independence/ (b) lakhs of people/ (c) do not have beds to sleep./ (d) No error.
37. (a) The dinosaurs could not/ (b) adapt to the/ (c) changing environment./ (d) No error.
38. (a) The students were/ (b) looking forward to/ (c) meet the eminent scientist./ (d) No error.
39. (a) The lady made the/ (b) little boy to wash/ (c) all the clothes./ (d) No error.
40. (a) We must get this letter/ (b) send/ (c) as soon as possible./ (d) No error.

Answers with Explanations

1. (a) Add 'while he was' before 'walking' or 'a car' will become the subject of the first part and the sentence will give a wrong meaning.
2. (a) Use 'I' before 'having' or 'my mother' will become the subject of the first part and the sentence will give a wrong meaning.
3. (a) Use 'it' before 'being'.(Reason same as that of 1 and 2)
4. (b) Change 'bent to harm' into 'bent on harming'. 'Bent on' means 'determined to do'.
5. (b) Use 'confident of passing'. 'Of' is used with 'confident', and $\mathbf{V_1}$ **+ ing** (gerund) is used after all prepositions.
6. (b) $\mathbf{V_1}$ **+ ing** comes after 'with a view to'. Change 'help' into 'helping'.
7. (b) Change 'to go' into 'going'. Gerund comes after 'avoid'.
8. (c) Add 'of 'after 'boast'. If an infinitive comes after a noun, an appropiate preposition should come after the infinitive.
9. (a) Add reflexive pronoun 'oneself' after 'avail'.'Avail'(when used as a verb) is followed by a reflexive pronoun.
10. (b) Use 'V_3' of 'send' i.e 'sent'. If 'get' and 'have' are used as causative verbs,the main verb is in third form.

    Eg: 1.Have it $\underbrace{\text{painted}}_{V_3}$ red. 2. Get it $\underbrace{\text{done}}_{V_3}$.

11. (b) Remove 'for' .'Order' as a verb does not take 'for' after it.
12. (a) Remove 'as'. 'Considered' is not followed by 'as'.
13. (b) 'Gerund' will come after 'mind'. Change 'be' into 'being'.

14. (b) Change 'having' into 'have'. When 'have' means 'to possess', it does not take 'ing' form.
15. (b) 'V_1 + ing' should follow 'Worth'. 'Worth taking' is correct.
16. (b) 'Bade' (V_2 of bid) takes 'plain infinitive' (V_1) after it and not 'infinitive' (to + V_1). Change 'to submit' into 'submit'.
17. (c) Remove 'as'.'Think' is not followed by 'as'.
18. (b) 'take test' is correct. Students/candidates take a test and teachers give a test to the students.
19. (c) Use 'attend' after 'than'. Because 'would rather' is followed by 'V_1' and after 'than' the same form 'V_1' will come .
20. (c) ' V_1 + ing' or 'V_1' comes after 'watch'. Hence use 'performing / perform'.
21. (c) Use V_1 after 'let'. Remove 'to'.
22. (b) Change 'help' into 'helping'. Gerund comes after 'deny'.
23. (a) Add 'while I was' before 'walking alone'.
24. (b) Change 'decide' into 'decided'. 'V_2' comes after 'it is time + subject'.
25. (c) 'Steamed' expresses 'a complete action'. 'V_1 + ing' is used as an adjective to show an action still going on. 'Steaming' is the correct form here.
26. (b) Change 'meet' into 'meeting'. Gerund comes after 'remember'.
27. (a) 'V_3' comes after 'have' and 'V_1' comes after 'will'. 'Will' is followed by 'be'. Hence 'V_3' will follow 'have'.
28. (b) We make a mistake. Hence change 'did' into 'made'.
29. (c) Change 'took' into 'were taking' . 'while' denotes a continuous activity.
30. (a) Add 'done' after 'have' .Different forms of verbs should be used in a sentence if needed.
31. (c) Remove 'again'. 'Repeat' should not be followed by 'again' because this will make the sentence superfluous.
32. (c) Change 'sell' to 'sold'.'V_2' comes after 'it is time + subject'.
33. (b) Change 'steal' to 'stealing'.See pattern 11.
34. (c) Change 'have' to 'had'. The sentence is in past.
35. (b) Remove 'back'.'Return' should not be followed by 'back' because this will make the sentence superfluous.
36. (c) Add 'in' after 'sleep' .If 'infinitive' is used after 'noun' then appropriate preposition should follow 'infinitive'.
37. (b) Add 'themselves' after 'adapt'.
38. (c) 'Looking forward to' is followed by 'V_1+ing'.
39. (b) Remove 'to'.'Plain infinitive' (V_1) comes after 'make'.
40. (b) Change 'send' to 'sent' .'V_3' comes after 'Get'.

CHAPTER 9

VERB AS A NOUN/ GERUND

Let us see how a 'verb' can work as a 'noun'. This can be done in three ways.

1. By adding an article before a verb, many **verbs** become **Noun**.
2. In the form of **'V_1+ing' (Gerund)**, a verb can act as a noun.
3. In the form of **'to+$V_{b.f}$' (Infinitive)** too a verb can act as a noun.

But before discussing the above three in detail, let us see when we can say that a 'verb' can be called a 'noun'.

Let us see an example.

Ms. Neetu Singh (Sub) teaches English (Obj).

It is clear from the above example that a noun can come in place of a subject or an object. Noun is the name of a person, place or thing and in the example given above the names of a woman and a language are nouns.

This means if we can prove that a verb can come in place of a noun, it can be called a noun-verb. Now let us see the three given above one by one.

1. **When a verb is preceded by an article.**

(a) I went for **a walk**.

(b) She has gone to see **a play**.

(c) The cunning agent took me for **a ride**.

(The phrase 'to take someone for a ride' means 'to fool.') Here 'walk', 'play' and 'ride' are preceded by an article and have been used as a noun. Here I would like to make it clear that it is an essential feature of 'article' that it comes with a 'noun'. Hence in all the example given above a verb-noun has come in place of noun. Apart from this if we see the example given below, it will become clear that as a noun, they can come in place of both subject and object.

E.g. I saw a play (Obj). The play (Sub) was very thought-provoking.

See an interesting example given below.

A bachelor degree is **a must** for applying for the post of manager.

Just see how 'must' which is a 'modal' works as a noun here when it is preceded by an article but retains the meaning of 'must' which is used in the sense of 'a necessity' in modals too.

2. **V_1+ing form** – 'V_1+ing' form of a verb is called a Gerund when it works as a noun. Let us first find out whether it really works as a noun or not. To do so we need to put it in the place of subject and object.

Eg. 1. **Swimming** (Sub) is a good exercise.

2. We prohibit **smoking** (Obj).

The examples given above prove that 'V_1+ing' can work as a noun. But why do we call them verb-noun when it is functioning as a noun. The reason is that originally it is a form of verb and apart from this, it exhibits the qualities of a verb too. The example given below can help us examine the qualities of a verb.

If a verb is transitive, it must be followed by an object for the sentence to make a complete sense. Apart from this a verb is qualified by an adverb.

Now let us see an example of gerund whether a gerund retains the characteristics of a verb or not.

Eg. 1. I prefer **working** (gerund) hard (adverb).

In this sentence 'hard' qualifies 'working'. This means an adverb can qualify a gerund.

2. He loves **playing** (gerund) cricket (obj).

In this sentence playing is acting as a transitive verb and the meaning of the sentence is clear only when cricket i.e. an object comes in the sentence. Now we have understood why Gerund is called 'Noun-verb'.

But the most important issue is how questions based on gerund are asked in the exam. This has been discussed below.

★ There are certain verbs which are followed by the Gerund and not infinitive.

List of such verbs	Examples
1. Admit	He admitted **cheating** me.
2. Appreciate	I would appreciate your **talking** softly.
3. Avoid	I avoid **travelling** by bus.
4. Verb + accustomed to	He got accustomed to **drinking**.
5. Verb + used to	I am used to **getting** up late.
6. Can't help	I can't help **laughing** at his jokes.
7. Consider	I considered **moving** to Mumbai.
8. Tolerate	I tolerated **being** shouted at.
9. Deny	He denied **stealing** my watch.
10. Like/ dislike	I like/ dislike **getting** up late.
11. Enjoy	I enjoy **watching** television.
12. Feel like	I feel like **helping** all the needy people.
13. Finish	He finished **saying** his prayers.
14. Imagine	Just imagine **living** in a wonderland.
15. Keep	We kept **waiting** for him.
16. Look forward to	I am looking forward to **meeting** you.
17. (Not)mind	He doesn't mind **getting** disturbed.
18. Miss	I miss **going** to India Gate.
19. Postpone	He postponed **returning** to Delhi.
20. Practise	I practised **writing** fast.
21. Recommend	He recommends **taking** stairs and not an elevator.
22. Regret	I regret **going** to party with him.
23. Resent	I resent **being** ill sometimes.
24. Resist	He resisted **asking** for help.
25. Risk	I risked **being** all alone at home.
26. Suggest	I suggested **staying** in a resort.

ऐसे verbs की सूची	Example
27. Advise	Doctors advise **drinking** low fat milk.
28. Can't stand	He couldn't stand **getting** insulted.
29. Permit	We don't permit **smoking** here.
30. Quit	He quit **smoking**.

Verbs followed by either Gerund or Infinitive

1. Begin	I began **playing** Cricket. I began **to play** Cricket.
2. Continue	I continued **working** hard. I continued **to work** hard.
3. hate	I hate **getting** up early in the morning. I hate **to get** up early in the morning.
4. Intend	I intend **working** hard. I intend **to work** hard.
5. (dis) like	I like **going** out for a stroll. I dislike **to go** out alone.
6. love	I love **watching** television. I love **to watch** television.
7. Neglect	I neglected **taking** care of my health. I neglected **to take** care of my health.
8. Prefer	I **prefer** to go to college by bus. I **prefer** getting up late.
9. Propose	He proposed **going** to party with me. He proposed **to go** to party with me.
10. Remember	I remember **going** to the zoo when I was a kid. Please, do remember **to post** my letter.
11. Start	I started **working** hard. I started **to work** hard.
12. Stop	I stopped **playing** cricket. I stopped **to play** cricket.

See the difference in meaning →

The 2nd sentence means 'I stopped somewhere to play cricket' but the 1st sentence means' action of playing cricket was stopped by me'

Now see some questions based on the rule discussed

1. Children enjoy_________outdoor games
   (A) play (B) playing
   (C) to play (D) played
2. I am looking forward _________you.
   (A) to meeting (B) meet
   (C) meeting (D) No improvement
3. (A) My father doesn't mind /(B) to be disturbed /(C) any time /(D) No error.

4. (A) Do you think/(B) it's worth to taking / (C) too much risk/(D)No error.
5. I miss __________my favourite shows after moving to India.
   (A) watching (B) watch
   (C) to watch (D) to watching

Answer-key

1. (B) 2. (A)
3. (B) being disturbed 4. (B) worth taking
5. (A)

★ **If verb comes after a preposition, it is in Gerund form.**

1. He is fond of **singing.**
2. She was good at **swimming.**
3. I am tired of **making** excuses.
4. They are addicted to **smoking** .
5. He was accused of **stealing** my watch.

★ **A Gerund is preceded by a possessive adjective**

1. (A)I am sorry for (B)/ mine being /(C) too rude./(D) No error.
2. She was not sure of _________passing the exam.
   (A) his (B) him
   (C) he (D) himself
3. I am confident of ____________winning the case.
   (A) my (B) mine
   (C) me (D) myself
4. She didn't like _________helping strangers.
   (A) my (B) mine
   (C) me (D) myself
5. Owing to my ______a girl, I was given fewer rights and facilities.
   (A) be (B) to be
   (C) being (D) been

Answer-key

1. (B); Change 'mine' into 'my'.
2. (A); 3. (A);
4. (A); 5. (C);

Heinous Crime

A girl was raped, I heard in news,
Thanks it's not I, I happily mused.
Why should I bother ,why should I care,
I am a good girl, never there.
I have my villa and a personal plane,
The low girls travel by buses and train.
Then came an uncle and few of his friends,
To my villa and played a game.
My soul was shattered, my body bruised.
I felt dirty, pained and misused
I am a girl in Man's world, The heinous of all crimes,
I should have understood this before high time.

by
Neetu Singh

CHAPTER 10

INFINITIVE

Infinitives are nouns with certain qualities of a verb that is either in the form of '**to + $V_{b.f}$**' **(Infinitive)** or '**$V_{b.f}$**' **(Direct Infinitive)**.

Infinitives can **come after another verb, subject, object** or **complement** of a sentence.

See the following examples-

1. I want (Verb) to go (Infinitive) home. *(Infinitive after a Verb)*
2. It's not easy (Adjective) to learn (Infinitive) swimming. *(Infinitive after an Adjective)*
3. We need some time (*Noun*) to sort (Infinitive) out the issues. *(Infinitive after a Noun)*
4. To err (subject) is human, to forgive divine. *(Infinitive as the subject)*
5. He likes (Verb) to sing (Object). *(As object of a transitive Verb)*
6. His greatest pleasure is to gamble. *(Infinitives as the complement of Verb)*

Infinitive are Noun but has not left the qualities of a verb.

Now let us see how we can say infinitives are verb-noun.

Infinitives
- **Verb** - A Verb takes an object if it is transitive.
  - A Verb is qualified by an Adverb.
- **Noun**- A Noun comes in place of a subject and an object.

If by the help of examples, we can prove that infinitives can show the qualities of both, we can comfortably say that infinitives are verb-noun.

Examples-

1. To err (subject) is human.
2. I love to dance (object).
3. To respect women is our moral duty.
   In this sentence 'to respect' is a noun as it comes in the place of subject but like a verb, it takes an object 'women'.

4. I decided to teach English.

In this sentence 'to teach' like a Noun is the object of the Verb 'decided' but like a Verb it takes an object 'English'.

5. I decided to leave the job immediately.

In this sentence 'to leave' is an object of the verb 'decided' but like a verb it takes an object 'job' and is also modified by an adverb 'immediately' .

From the examples given above we can comfortably say that infinitives act as both noun and verb.

Forms of Infinitives-

1. I come here **to study**. **(Active voice— to $V_{b.f}$)**
2. She wanted **to be flattered**. **(Passive voice— to be V_3)**
3. He admitted **to have misused** his rights. **(Perfect Infinitive— to have V_3)**
4. He seemed **to have been cheated**. **(Perfect Infinitive Passive Voice— to have been V_3)**
5. They pretended **to be running** out of time. **(Continuous Infinitive— to be V_1+ ing)**
6. He admitted **to have been mistreating** his wife since their marriage. **(Perfect Continuous — to have been + V_1 + ing)**
7. I will not let him **go** (Bare Infinitive) $V_{b.f}$.

From the examples given above, we can say that Infinitives can be used in both Active and Passive Voice and in all types of Tenses.

➢ When Infinitives are used to express manner, the full form of the Infinitive is '**how to+$V_{b.f}$**'. We can use any 'Wh + to + $V_{b.f}$' too in other cases.

The Verbs are- **Ask, explain, discover, know, learn, teach, wonder.**

E.g: 1. I **wondered what to do.**

2. I **know how to swim.**
3. He **taught me how to speak** Japanese.
4. I **forgot what to write** in the application.

➢ If a Noun is followed by an Infinitive, we need to use an appropriate Preposition (if needed) after the Noun .

See the examples given below:

1. I have no bed (Noun) to sleep (Infinitive) in (Prep.) .

2. She needed a chair (Noun) to sit (Infinitive) on (Prep.) .

Direct or Bare Infinitive: Infinitives without 'to' is called 'direct' or 'Bare Infinitives'.

➢ **'Direct Infinitives' are used after- 'had sooner', 'had better', 'had rather', 'would rather', 'sooner than' and 'rather than'**.

E.g: 1. You **had better leave** now.

2. I **would rather die than beg**.
3. They **had sooner sort** out their differences **than** part ways.

- **Direct Infinitive are used after the following Verbs when they are used in Active voice - 'Bid', 'make', 'help', 'feel', 'see', 'watch', 'hear'**

  ('make' — as Causative Verb)

E.g: 1. I **bade** him go (Direct infinitive) out.

2. My mother **made** me do (Direct infinitive) the home work.

3. I **watched** him go (Direct infinitive).

When **make** and **bid** are used **in Passive Voice they take 'to +$V_{b.f}$' (Infinitive)** and not 'V_1' (Direct Infinitive) after them.

E.g: 1. I was **made** to wash (infinitive) all the clothes.

2. I was **bidden** to leave (infinitive) the room at once.

Remember:- Bid (V_1) bid (V_2) bid (V_3) (when 'bid' means 'to pay a certain price in an auction')

E.g: He bid (V_2) $2000 for the painting.

Bid (V_1) (to command, to greet) bade (V_2) bidden (V_3)

E.g: I bade (V_2) him leave the room.

- **'Let' takes direct infinitives** in both active and passive voice.

E.g: 1. I will not **let** him go (Direct infinitive). **(Active voice)**

2. Bad habits must be **let** go (Direct infinitive). **(Passive voice)**

'Need' and **'Dare'**

- ***See these examples:***

1. You need not to worry. (×)

You need not worry. (✓)

2. We dare not to disobey the traffic rules.(×)

We dare not disobey the traffic rules. (✓)

3. Need I to take this exam? (×)

Need I take this exam? (✓)

From the examples, we can say that **'Need'** and **'Dare'** take Direct Infinitives when they are used **as Modals in negative and interrogative sentences.**

However we know that **Modals take '$V_{b.f}$'** after them. ***(See Chapter –1 'Verb' of Volume –1)***

Hence in Positive Sentences **Need** and **Dare** are not used as Modals.

E.g: You need work hard. (×)

You need to work hard. (✓)

➢ **'Why not' take direct infinitives.**

E.g: 1. Why not <u>stop</u> (Direct infinitive) now ?

➢ When **'have+ object'** is used in the sense of expressing wish, it is **followed by Direct Infinitives.**

E.g: 1. I will **have him speak** the truth.

➢ **Perfect Infinitives** ⇒ Perfect infinitives should come if the action expressed by the infinitive precedes the action of the finite verb.

E.g: He **admitted** (Finite Verb (2nd action)) **to have violated** (1st action) anti-corruption law many times.

Here the action of 'violating anti-corruption' law is prior to the action of 'admitting'.

➢ **Split Infinitive ('to' and '$V_{b.f}$' separated from each other by an Adverb, Conjunction etc)** ⇒ Though many grammarians believe that splitting Infinitives is wrong, it is imperative to mention here that it is completely acceptable in modern English.

See the examples given below:-

1. **To boldly** (**adverb**) **go,** where no man has gone before, requires a lot of guts.

   (Here adverb 'boldly' splits the infinitive 'to go')

2. The population is expected **to more than double** in the next ten years.

   (Here more than one word 'more than' split the infinitive 'to double')

➢ **See the following examples to understand how the use of 'Infinitive' and 'Gerund' changes the meaning of the sentence.**

1. Go on

(a) Go on + 'V_1 + ing' → Means to continue.

E.g: He went on talking.

(b) Go on + 'to+ $V_{b.f}$' → Refers to a change of activity.

E.g: He stopped talking about the problems and went on to describe the possible solutions.

2. Regret

(a) Regret + 'V_1 + ing'- This form looks back at the past repenting something.

E.g: He regrets leaving his job.

(b) Regret +'to+$V_{b.f}$' → used mostly in announcement of undesirable news.

E.g: We regret to inform you that the flight has been cancelled due to bad weather.

3. Advise, prohibit, allow, permit and **forbid.**

If these verbs are followed immediately by an object, an infinitive is used otherwise 'V_1 + ing' form will follow.

E.g: 1. We **prohibit smoking** here.

2. We **prohibit** people (object) **to smoke** here.

3. I wouldn't **advise taking** the car to Chandi Chowk.

4. I wouldn't **advise** anyone (object) **to take** the car to Chandi Chowk.

4. See, watch and **hear**

If these verbs are followed by **'V_1 + ing'** form, it suggests that one pays attention to 'events' or 'actions' that are already going on.

E.g: I **saw the old man crossing** the road.

If these verbs refer to **'complete events or actions'** which are seen or heard from beginning to end, direct infinitive will follow.

E.g: I **saw the old man cross** the road and disappear in the moor.

5. Like, love, hate and **prefer**

These verbs are followed by both **'V_1 + ing'** and **'to+$V_{b.f}$'** form without much difference in meaning.

E.g: 1. I **love to take** hot shower bath after a day long work.

2. Children **enjoy watching** television.

But after **would + like /prefer /love /hate, infinitives are preferred**.

E.g. 1. I **would like to meet** the manager.

2. I **would love to do** it if you permit me.

6. Stop

(a) Stop + 'V_1 + ing'- Means to stop doing the activity mentioned.

E.g: I stopped playing cricket.

(b) Stop + 'to + $V_{b.f}$' → Means to stop in order to do the activity mentioned.

E.g: I stopped to play cricket.

Exercise

Exercise based on Infinitive & Gerund.

1. I feel like (A)/ to go (B)/ to a movie (C)/ No error (D)
2. It isn't wrong(A)/to defend (B)/oneself (C) No error (D)
3. I think (A)/defending (B)/oneself is the right thing to do (C)/if one is not wrong. /No error (D)
4. I can't imagine______out of a flying plane.
   (A) To jump (B) jumping
   (C) jump (D) to be jumped
5. I feel (A)/ like to eat (B)/something now.(C)/ No error (D)
6. They are relieved____the traffic_________more easily.
   (A) to find, flowing (B) to find, to flow
   (C) find, following (D) find, flow

7. On 17th February 2003, a congestion charge for ______in Central London was introduced. The aim was _____ the number of vehicles in the city of London.
   (A) drive, to reduce
   (B) driving, to reduce
   (C) to drive, to reduce
   (D) driving, reducing
8. I wonder, is it right to charge people to driving in the city.
   (A) Charging, driving
   (B) to charge, for driving
   (C) Charge, drive
   (D) No improvement
9. I Look forward at meeting the President of America.
   (A) to meeting (B) to meet
   (C) meet (D) No improvement
10. Do you object to mine working on Sundays?
   (A) my (B) me
   (C) I (D) no improvement
11. I am not used to get up early in the morning.
   (A) to got (B) to getting
   (C) about getting (D) No improvement
12. I prefer to take metro than driving.
   (A) taking, to
   (B) take, over
   (C) about taking, than
   (D) No improvement
13. I regret__________the exam due to illness.
   (A) missing (B) to missing
   (C) missed (D) about missing
14. I regret________ you that your son has been detained.
   (A) to informing
   (B) to inform
   (C) about informing
   (D) No word needed.
15. ________and______cannot go together.
   (A) drinking, drive
   (B) drinking, driving
   (C) to drink, to drive
   (D) drink, drive
16. I wouldn't advise you taking the car to Janpath.
   (A) to take (B) take
   (C) to taking (D) No improvement
17. She enjoys______Science fiction.
   (A) reading (B) to read
   (C) having reading (D) read
18. Sheela suggested ___ a movie after work.
   (A) to watch (B) watching
   (C) about watching (D) to watching
19. Where did you learn______German ?
   (A) speaking (B) to speak
   (C) speak (D) to speaking
20. Would you mind ___ me write an application?
   (A) to help (B) helping
   (C) help (D) to helping
21. The models practised walking with a book balanced on their heads.
   (A) to walk (B) to walking
   (C) walk (D) No improvement
22. My friend promised________care of my pet while I was on vacation.
   (A) to take (B) taking
   (C) take (D) to have taken care
23. Witnesses reported_______the bank robbers while they were scaling the wall.
   (A) to see (B) to have seen
   (C) to seeing (D) saw
24. I dislike him(A)/eavesdropping habits (B)/ so much that I cannot stand it any more. (C)/ No error (D)
25. We must avoid(A)/to use cell phones(B)/ while we are in court rooms.(C)/ No error.
26. I don't mind(A)/cooking(B)/ when my servant is not well.(C)/ No error (D)
27. I would like (A)/to try (B)/ a new look now. (C)/ No error (D)
28. I wasn't sure of him(A)/contesting (B)/ the Lok Sabha election. (C)/ No error (D)

29. I can't stand _______ all the time.
  (A) he complaining
  (B) him complaining
  (C) his complaining
  (D) him complain

30. Our teacher won't allow us to use calculators.
  (A) using (B) to using
  (C) use (D) No improvement

31. She prefers__________dinner as she is not good at cooking.
  (A) my making (B) me making
  (C) me to make (D) me make

32. I hope you don't mind___while you sleep.
  (A) my listening to music
  (B) me listening to music
  (C) me to listen music
  (D) mine listening to music

33. She likes to go__________.
  (A) fishing (B) surfing the internet
  (C) learning foreign language
  (D) missing

34. The passing marks(A)/that we needed (B)/ seemed a distant dream for most of us. (C)/ No error (D).

35. He said that(A)/his wife didn't have (B)/ dressing sense. (C)/No error (D).

36. I remember (A)/to go for trekking (B)/ when I was a kid.(C)/No error (D).

37. Your hair needs ______ .
  (A) Cutting (B) to cut
  (C) cut (D) to be cut down

38. I tried lifting (A)/the suitcase but it (B)/ was too heavy. (C)/No error (D).

39. Due to me (A)/being an unknown face (B)/ I was refused admittance. (C)/No error (D).

40. I don't have (A)/a pen(B)/ to write.(C)/No error (D).

41. She has (A)/no bed (B)/ to sleep.(C)/No error (D).

42. This project is not (A)/ worth to risk (B)/all your money.(C)/No error (D).

Answer-key

1. (B); Change 'to go' into 'going'
2. (D); 3. (D); 4. (B);
5. (B); Change 'to eat' into 'eating'
6. (A); 7. (B); 8. (B); 9. (A);
10. (A); 11. (B); 12. (A); 13. (A);
14. (B); 15. (B); 16. (A); 17. (A);
18. (B); 19. (B); 20. (B); 21. (D);
22. (A); 23. (B);
24. (A); Change 'him' into 'his'. We use a Possessive Adjective before a noun.
25. (B); Change 'to use' into 'using'. 'Avoid' is followed by a Gerund.
26. (D);
27. (D); 'like' is followed by a 'gerund' but 'would like' is followed by an infinitive.
28. (A); 'Contesting' (a gerund) will be preceded by a Possessive Adjective (his) and not a Pronoun (him).
29. (C); 30. (D); 31. (A);
32. (A); 33. (A);
34. (A); Change 'passing marks' into 'pass marks'. 'Passing marks' is wrong English.
35. (C); Change 'dressing sense' into 'dress sense'. 'Dressing sense' is wrong English.
36. (B); Change 'to go' into 'going'. 'Remember' is followed by a gerund.
37. (A);
38. (A); Change 'lifting' into 'to lift'.
39. (A); Change 'me' into 'my'. 'Being' is preceded by a Possessive Adjective (my). 'Due to' is acceptable in modern English though a sentence should start with 'owing to' if we strictly follow traditional English.
40. (C); Add 'with' after 'write'. If a noun is followed by an infinitive, an appropriate preposition must follow.
41. (C); Add 'in' after 'sleep'.
42. (B); Change 'to risk' into 'risking'. 'Worth' is followed by a 'Gerund'.

11 PARTICIPLE

CHAPTER

"A Participle is a word formed from a verb that is partly a verb and partly an Adjective."

There are three forms of Participle-

	(1) Present Participle	(2) Past Participle	(3) Perfect Participle
Form⟶	V_1 + ing	V_3	having + V_3

Now let as see how the meaning changes when we use different participles.

Present Participle

Form → V_1 + ing

Eg – Laughing loudly, he rolled on the sofa.

Usage – Here both the action went on together. Here we want to emphasise that the second action took place when the first was still going on.

Past Participle

Form → V_3

Eg – Blinded by the sudden jet of pepper spray, the assailant groped for the exit.

Usage – Here the actions took place one after the other. The second action started after the 1st action and also as the result of the Ist action. If the 1st action is in Passive Voice, use this structure.

Perfect Participle

Form → Having + V_3

Eg – Having rested for the whole night, the travellers resumed their journey.

Usage – Here the second action started after the first action had finished.

It is also used when the first action has been going on for a period of time when the second action started or some time had passed before the 2nd action started.

Eg– 1. Having lived there for more than two decades, he did't want to leave his hometown.

Eg– 2. Having been a good dancer in my school days, I found it easier to learn the new dance moves.

There are certain verbs with two distinct V_3 forms. In such cases only one is usually used as an adjective form.

List of such Verbs

	V_1	V_2	V_3
1.	Prove	proved	proved/proven
2.	Shear (to the cut hair off)	sheared	sheared/shorn
3.	Shrink (to become smaller in size, amount etc)	shrank	shrunk/shrunken
4.	Drink	drank	drunk/drunken
5.	Melt	melted	melted/molten
6.	Telecast	telecast	telecast
7.	Broadcast	broadcast	broadcast
8.	Forecast	forecast	forecast
9.	Get	got	got/gotten

Eg:- As verb

1. I have proved him wrong.
2. I have scored good result.

3. The news of infiltration was broadcast.
4. He had drunk a lot before the police arrested him.

Eg:- As adjective

proven fact, shrunken eyes, ill-gotten money, drunken driving, molten chocolate, shorn sheep.

Note: 1

We use Past Participle to describe how we feel and Present Participle to describe what caused the feelings.

Eg –1. Exciting movie.
Excited spectators.

2. Interesting story.
Interested candidates.

Note: 2

Participle as Adjective – Past and Present participle often function as adjectives that describe nouns.

Eg –1. crying baby
2. broken arm
3. bleeding knees
4. developed country
5. smiling woman
6. swollen head

Note : 3

Participle as Adverb – Participles can function as adverbs too that describe how the verb was done.

Eg – 1. He came screaming out of the room.
2. He came home crying.

Note : 4

Meaning and use of Participle Clauses– Participle Clauses give information about condition, reason, result or time.

Condition- (In place of an 'if-condition').

Eg- Looked after carefully, the dog will live long.

Meaning- If you look after the dog carefully, it will live long.

Reason- (In place of words like 'so' or 'therefore').

Eg- Wanting to speak, he cleared his throat and garnered courage.

Meaning- He wanted to speak so he cleared his throat and garnered courage.

Time- (In place of words like 'when', 'while' or 'as soon as').

Eg- Sitting at the table, I suddenly realised water flowing under my chair.

Meaning- While I was sitting at the table, I suddenly realised water flowing under my chair.

Participle Clauses:-

Participle Clauses are forms of adverbial clause which enables us to convey information in a more economical way. We can use Participle Clauses when the Participle and the Verb in the main clause have the same subject.

Eg- 1. Being ill, I didn't go to office. (✓)

2. Being a rainy day, I didn't go to office. (×)
Hence the Participle 'being' and the verb in the main clause 'didn't go' have different subjects.
It being a rainy day, I didn't go to office. (✓)

4. Driving on the motorway, the baby began to cry. (×)
While I was driving on the motorway, the baby began to cry. (✓)

☞ Participle clauses can be formed with the Present Participle or Past Participle. Participle clauses with Past Participles have a passive meaning.

Eg- 1. (a) Shouting loudly, he walked out.
(He was shouting –Active)

(b) Shouted at loudly, he walked out.
(Someone else shouted at him –Passive)

Eg- 2. (a) Crying bitterly, he narrated the incident.
(He was crying –Active)

(b) Driven by poverty, he committed suicide.
(poverty pushed him to commit suicide –Passive

Exercise

Fill in the correct participle form of the verbs given in the bracket (Present Participle, Past Participle or Perfect Participle)

1. He was sitting in his bed ________ a newspaper. (read)
2. __________in the same industry for years, we knew each other well. (work)
3. The glass ____with water was kept on the table. (fill)
4. ______for around ten years, they had a lot to talk about. (not meet)
5. ______to poor parents, he had to work hard to make both ends meet. (bear)
6. _____________a spoit child, he often behaved in an affected manner. (be)
7. _______his words , he apologized and withdrew his statement. (Regret)
8. ________the car, he went to the police station to lodge his complaint. (Park)
9. __________the movie many times, he knew the dialogues by heart. (See)
10. A girl ________a red dress opened the door. (wear)
11. Tea ________in Assam, is exported all over the world. (produce)
12. She works in a bakery __________pies and cakes. (make)
13. The house _______to the poet was sold for a song. (belong)
14. Picture _________by Hussain sold for millions of dollars. (paint)
15. A truck ________vegetables ran into a bus. (carry)
16. __________by my work, my boss gave me a hike in my salary (impress)
17. ___________enough for his exam, he couldn't pass the final semester. (not study)
18. _________, I cannot come to meet you (An assignment, finish)
19. _______________a good dancer in my school days, I found it easier to learn the new steps. (Be)
20. It is a__________fact that insects too communicate. (Prove)

Answer Key

1.	Reading	8.	Having parked	15.	carrying
2.	Having worked	9.	Having seen	16.	Impressed
3.	filled	10.	Wearing	17.	Not having studied
4.	Not having met	11.	produced	18.	Having an assignment to
5.	born	12.	making	19.	Having been
6.	Being	13.	belonging	20.	proven finish
7.	Regretting	14.	painted		

12 INVERSION

CHAPTER

Inversion is the reversal of the normal word order in a sentence or a phrase.

These are two types of inversion.

1. **Subject-verb inversion (Complete Inversion** – Where the subject and the main verb switch positions and the word order becomes **verb + subject**. Generally this order is used when a sentence starts with an Adverb of place.

   E.g.:- Here $\underbrace{\text{comes}}_{\text{Verb}}$ $\underbrace{\text{the rain}}_{\text{Subject}}$.

2. **Subject–auxiliary verb inversion (Partial Inversion)**:– Where the subject and the auxiliary verb switch positions and the word order becomes **'Auxiliary verb + subject + main verb'.**

   E.g.: Never $\underbrace{\text{did}}_{\text{Auxiliary verb}}$ $\underbrace{\text{I}}_{\text{Sub}}$ $\underbrace{\text{go}}_{\text{Main verb}}$ there.

Inversion is used in the following types of sentences-

1. **Interrogative sentences:-**

   E.g.: 1. $\underbrace{\text{Do}}_{\text{A.V}}$ I $\underbrace{\text{know}}_{\text{Main Verb}}$ him ?

   2. $\underbrace{\text{Isn't}}_{\text{A.V}}$ he $\underbrace{\text{working}}_{\text{Main Verb}}$ hard ?

If the sentence is of **imaginary position**, it is of the following structure-

Ex- $\underbrace{\text{If}}_{\text{If+}}$ $\underbrace{\text{I}}_{\text{Sub}}$ $\underbrace{\text{were}}_{\text{Main Verb}}$ a bird , $\underbrace{\text{I}}_{\text{Sub}}$ $\underbrace{\text{would}}_{\text{would}}$ $\underbrace{\text{fly}}_{V_1}$.

But if we remove 'if' from such imaginary sentences, 'were' which is the main verb here, comes before the subject and then the structure of the sentence is-

Ex- $\underbrace{\text{Were}}_{\text{Main Verb}}$ $\underbrace{\text{I}}_{\text{+Sub}}$ a bird , $\underbrace{\text{I}}_{\text{Sub}}$ $\underbrace{\text{would}}_{\text{H.V}}$ $\underbrace{\text{fly}}_{V_1}$.

3. **Conditional Sentences:-** Conditional sentences of past is generally of the following formation.

   E.g.: $\underbrace{\text{If}}_{\text{If+}}$ $\underbrace{\text{I}}_{\text{Sub}}$ $\underbrace{\text{had}}_{\text{H.V.}}$ $\underbrace{\text{seen}}_{V_3}$ $\underbrace{\text{you}}_{\text{obj}}$, $\underbrace{\text{I}}_{\text{Sub+}}$ $\underbrace{\text{would}}_{\text{H.V.}}$ $\underbrace{\text{have}}_{\text{have}}$ $\underbrace{\text{stopped}}_{V_3}$ $\underbrace{\text{my car}}_{\text{object}}$.

But if we remove 'if' from such Imaginary Sentences, 'had' which is an auxiliary verb here comes before the subject and then the structure of the sentence is-

E.g.: - $\underbrace{\text{Had}}_{\text{H.V.}}$ $\underbrace{\text{I}}_{\text{Sub}}$ $\underbrace{\text{seen}}_{V_3}$ + $\underbrace{\text{you}}_{\text{obj}}$, $\underbrace{\text{I}}_{\text{Sub}}$ $\underbrace{\text{would}}_{\text{H.V.}}$ $\underbrace{\text{have}}_{\text{have}}$ $\underbrace{\text{stopped}}_{V_3}$ $\underbrace{\text{my car}}_{\text{object}}$.

- '**Should**' can come in place of 'if' in Conditional Sentences (of real or open condition).

  E.g.: 1. Should you need my help, do call me.

4. **Short Answers-**Short answers start with **'So' if the answer is positive** and **'Neither' if the answer is negative**. If a sentence starts with 'So' or 'Neither' the auxiliary verb comes before the subject.

E.g.: 1. I don't like playing football.

Short Answer-Neither do I.

2. I am tired.

Short Answer- So am I.

In the same way there are certain other examples though they do not fall in the category of short answers.

E.g.: Wheat is not native to India and neither is Barley. (✓)

Wheat is not native to India and Barley isn't either. (✓)

Note: How inversion *i.e.* **'is' before 'Barley'** comes if the sentence starts with neither but a normal sentence *i.e.*

Barley (Sub) + isn't (verb) comes if the sentence starts with a **'subject'** .

5. **Optative Sentences** – In Sentences of **'wish' and 'prayers'**, the **'verb'** comes before the 'subject'.

E.g.:1. May (H.V) god (sub) bless (V_1) you (obj).

2. Long (Adv) live (H.V.) the king (Sub).

6. **Introductory Comparative** :- If a sentence starts with a comparative degree, the sentence will be in inversion.

E.g.: 1. More important than our personal view is (verb) the students' opinion (sub).

2. No less beneficial than the invention of the telephone was (Verb) that of the telegraph machine (sub).

Note:- We can use the form of Inversion here only when the verb is a **'be-verb'** .

7. **Introductory 'V_3/ing' verb** :- Inversion follows when the sentence starts with 'V_3/ing' form of a verb.

E.g.:1. Lost among the old clothes was my new favourite shirt which I had been looking for a long time.

2. Located between San Francisco and Marin County is the Golden Gate Bridge.

3. Burning out of control was a dense forest of Australia.

8. **Negative Introductory:-** Inversion follows **when a sentence starts with 'no', 'not' or 'never'** or when such a word is used at the starting of a sentence that is negative in meaning such as **rarely, hardly, seldom, barely, little** or **scarcely**.

Eg. 1. Nowhere else in the world do (H.V.) we (sub) find (Main Verb) such diversity in culture.

2. Never in the history of India, did (H.V.) we (sub) see (Main Verb) such a shrewd mentor like Chanakya.

3. Not a word did (H.V.) our Prime Minister (sub) speak (Main Verb) when the opposition heaped him with accusations.

4. Hardly had (H.V.) I (sub) reached (Main Verb) the main road when the rain started.

9. **Adverbial Introductory** :- Inversion follows when a sentence starts with an Adverb.

E.g.: 1. On a hill lived (Main Verb) an old saint (sub).

2. Under a tree was (H.V.) seated (Main Verb) a cunning fox (sub).

3. Only when the virus introduces its nucleic acid into a cell does (H.V.) a disease (sub) occur (Main Verb).

4. Along the border was (H.V.) deployed (Main Verb) the Indian army (Obj).

10. Inversion follows if in a sentence the following Correlatives are used.

So.......... that
Not only.......... but also
No sooner.......... than
Hardly.......... when
Scarcely.......... when

In such sentences Inversion follows only when the sentence starts with the first part of the correlatives given above.

Eg. :1. So tired was (M.V.) I (sub) that I was unable to walk.

2. Not only does (H.V.) he (sub.) know (M.V.) me but also my parents.

3. Scarcely had (H.V.) I boarded (M.V.) the train when it departed.

11. Complete Inversion follows if a **sentence starts with 'here' , 'there', 'away', 'out', 'in', 'down', or 'up' followed by a noun.**

E.g.:1. Up goes (Main Verb) the water vapour (Noun) and down comes (Main Verb) the rain (Noun).

2. Here comes (Main Verb) our chief guest (Noun).

3. There goes (Main Verb) the plane (Noun).

But if a sentence starts with the words given above but followed by a pronoun, a normal sentence will follow.

Eg.: 1. Here he (Pronoun) comes (Verb).

2. There it (Pronoun) is (verb).

12. See some common phrases given below. These phrases will be followed by Inversion.

- **Under no circumstance**
- **In no way**
- **On no account (means – under no circumstance)**
- **On no condition (means – absolutely not.)**
- **At no time.**
- **Only yesterday/only last week/only day before yesterday etc.**
- **Round the corner (means- soon to take place)**
- **Five miles beyond the..... /ten metres above the sea level etc.**
- **To such an extent.**
- **To such a degree**
- **So well/so absurdly (So + adverb of manner)**

E.g.: 1. Round the corner is (M.V.) your examination (sub.).

2 . So well was (H.V.) the work (obj) done (M.V.) that I could not point out even a single mistake.

3. Ten miles beyond the hill was (H.V.) seen (M.V.) a ferocious tiger (obj).

4. Only yesterday did (H.V.) I (verb) meet (Main Verb) him.

5. To such an extent was (H.V.) the car (obj) damaged (Main Verb) that it couldn't be repaired.

CORRECT THE UNDERLINED PART IF NEEDED

1. Not a word he spoke when he heard the news of his son's demise.
2. Round the corner your exam is.
3. Never in the history of India we find such a feeling of nationalism.
4. Under a tree a cunning fox was seated.
5. Here the rain comes.
6. There our chief guest comes.
7. There lived a saint and on a hill his tiny hut was.
8. Twenty miles beyond the terrain, a bridge was built.
9. Little we know about his miserable condition.
10. To such an extent the condition has aggravated that no one can solve it.
11. Only the day before yesterday we saw him.
12. She will not do anything and neither her brother will.
13. Hardly I saw him intently when he ran away.
14. Not only he knows me but also my parents.
15. Under no circumstance we can allow such blatant act of corruption.
16. Seldom we go to our native village.
17. If I came to know the truth, I would have helped him with all that he needed.
18. I haven't been to any European country and neither my parents have.
19. Never I go to his place and I find him very egoist and self-praising.
20. No sooner the government enacted the Hindu Marriage Act than the condition of Hindu women started getting better.
21. Along the border several rounds of firing were heard.
22. Down the stream went rumbling.
23. Seldom I have seen such a beautiful monument.
24. Hardly he knows anything about the political situation of his native state.
25. Under no circumstance I can accept your proposal.
26. On no condition , I will sell my land.
27. Only by taking some amount of money on loan, I can buy this bungalow.
28. Here the train comes.
29. So well he organized the party that everyone was left spell-bounded.
30. So rudely he spoke that I felt extremely offended.

Answer-key

Change:

1. 'He spoke' into 'did he speak'.
2. 'Your exam is' into 'is your exam'.
3. 'We find' into 'do we find'
4. 'A cunning fox was seated' into 'was seated a cunning fox'.
5. 'The rain comes' into 'comes the rain'.
6. 'Our chief guest comes' into 'comes our chief guest'.
7. 'His tiny hut was' into 'was his tiny hut'.
8. 'A bridge was built' into 'was a bridge built'.
9. 'We know' into 'do we know'.
10. 'The condition has aggravated' into 'has the condition aggravated'.
11. 'We saw him' into 'did we see him'.
12. 'Her brother will' into 'will her brother'.
13. 'I saw' into 'did I see' or 'had I seen him'.
14. 'He knows' into 'does he know'.
15. 'We can' into 'can we'.
16. 'We go' into 'do we go'.
17. 'If I came' into 'If I had come' or 'Had I come'.
18. 'My parents have' into 'have my parents'.
19. 'I go' into 'do I go'.
20. 'The government enacted' into 'did the government enact'.
21. 'were heard several rounds of firing' is the correct structure.
22. 'Down the stream went' into 'Down went the stream'.
23. 'I have seen' into 'have I seen'.
24. 'He knows' into 'does he know'.
25. 'I can' into 'can I'.
26. 'I will' into 'will I'.
27. 'I can buy' into 'can I buy'.
28. 'The train comes' into 'comes the train'.
29. 'He organized' into 'did he organize'.
30. 'He spoke' into 'did he speak'.

CHAPTER 13 MOOD

It indicates the mood or intention of the speaker.

There are three moods in English :

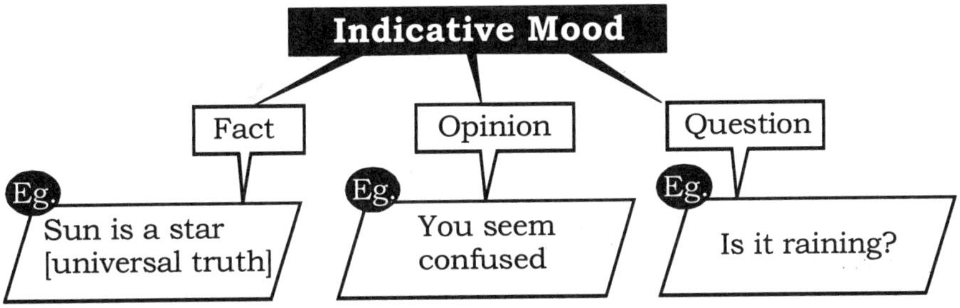

- Remember that facts come in universal truth which is in Present Indefinite Tense.

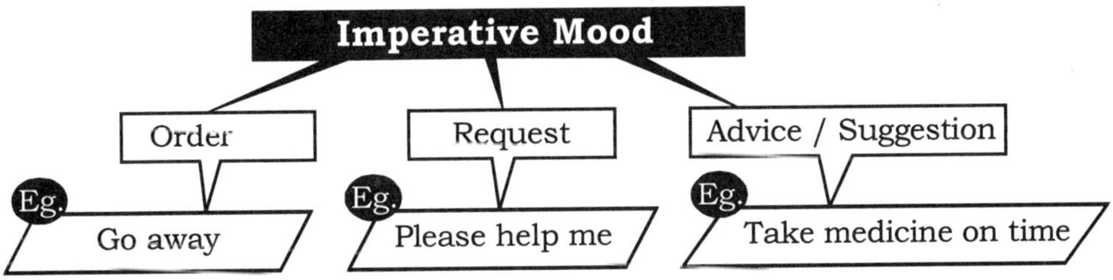

How Mood influences Narration:

1. He said, "Babies drink milk." [Universal truth]
   He said that Babies drink milk.

- No change of tense takes place if a universal truth is changed into indirect speech.

2. He said, "Babies, drink milk." [imperative sentence]
   He ordered the babies to drink milk.

(Here just a comma (,) changes the mood of the sentence)

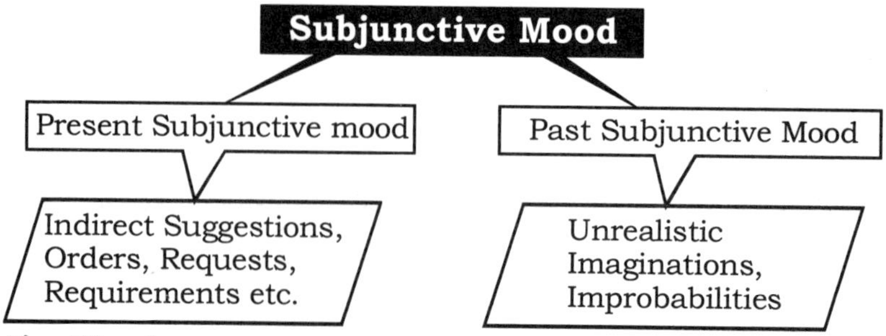

Past Subjunctive Mood

We use 'V_2' (except 'was') in Past Subjunctive Mood. It expresses improbabilities.

1. If I _____ you, I would beat him black and blue. (be)
2. What would you do if you ______ a dinosaur? (see)
3. It's time you _______ in bed. (be)
4. He talks as if he was the Prime Minister. (Change 'was' into 'were'.)
5. He walks as if the whole earth belongs to him. (Change 'belongs' into 'belonged')

Answers: 1. were 2.saw 3.were

Present Subjunctive Mood

We use the base form of verb in Present Subjunctive Mood. It expresses indirect suggesstions, orders etc.

1. This civil case doesn't require that he is present. (Change 'is' into 'be')
2. In this criminal case, it is imperative that he remains present in the court. (Change 'remains' into 'remain')
3. According to a fable, Savitri prayed to the Almighty that her husband be brought back to life. (No error)
4. Our teacher suggested to us that every one of us ________ our best shot.
   (i) to give (ii) should give (iii) gives (iv) give Ans. (iv)
5. The cabin crew advised that every passenger fasten his seat belt. (No error)
6. I would rather he stay at home. (Change 'stay' into 'stayed')
7. I had rather tell him the truth. (No error)
8. The staff demanded that they be paid the Diwali bonus. (No error)
9. God saves the world ! (Change 'saves' into 'save')
10. May God bless him ! (No error)
11. Long live the king ! (No error)
12. It is necessary that every boarder informs him parents. (Change 'informs' into 'inform')

Explanation of 6 & 7: Would rather, Had rather, Had Sooner, Had better express wish or strong desire. They take second form of verb (V_2) after them but if followed by another subject (as in 6), and base form if no such subject follows (as in 7).

Eg. The bank would rather you paid by cheque but you had rather pay in cash.

CHAPTER 14

NOUN

Naming word is called Noun.

➢ They are 5 types of Noun:-
1. **PROPER NOUN**
2. **COMMON NOUN**
3. **COLLECTIVE NOUN**
4. **MATERIAL NOUN**
5. **ABSTRACT NOUN**

(1) PROPER NOUN

Proper noun is the name of a **particular person, place or thing**.

E.g.: Ram, Delhi, Geeta etc

(a) **Ram** is my friend

(b) I live in **Delhi.**

(2) COMMON NOUN

Common noun is the **name given in common** to every person or thing of the same class or kind.

E.g.: Boy, city, country etc.

(a) The **boy,** said that the nearest **town** was very far.

(b) The **girls** are going to the nearest **village.**

(3) COLLECTIVE NOUN

A collective noun is the **name of a number (or collection**) of persons or things taken together and spoken of as a whole.

E.g.: Team, Committee, Army, Jury etc.

Usually collective noun is used as **Singular**. They can be used as **Plural if there is a division** among the members of the collective noun or **the members are being talked about.**

E.g.: **(a)** The **flock** of geese **spends** (S.V.) most of its time in the pasture.

(b) The **jury** **is** (S.V.) deciding the matter.

(c) The **committee** **meets** (S.V.) every week.

(d) The **team** **are** (P.V.) divided over the issue of captainship. (मतभेद)

(e) The **jury** **have** (P.V.) taken **their** (P.P.) seats. (प्रत्येक व्यक्ति)

(4) MATERIAL NOUN

➢ The **Noun** from which such a substance can be understood from which other things are made is called **Material Noun**.

Eg:- Silver, iron, wood etc.

(a) The necklace is made of **gold.**

(b) She has purchased a tea set of **silver.**

(c) He got his furniture made of teak **wood.**

➢ **Material Nouns** are not ***Countable*** i.e. cannot be counted. They can be measured or weighed. Usually ***Singular verb*** is used with them and ***Article*** does not come before them.

(5) ABSTRACT NOUN

➢ *Abstract Noun,* represents such qualities, feelings, actions and states that cannot be touched or seen, but can only be felt.

Eg:- Honesty, bravery, hatred (quality), laughter (action), poverty, youth (state).

➢ ***Abstract Noun*** is commonly used in ***Singular form***.

Eg:- **(a)** People respect his **sincerity.**

(b) Honesty is the best policy.

➢ **Noun can be divided into (A) Countable and (B) Uncountable:-**

(A) COUNTABLE NOUNS

➢ **Countable Noun** is the **Noun** that can be counted.

Eg:- (a) We bought **six** tables.

(b) I have a **few** friends.

(c) She watched **many** movies last month.

(B) UNCOUNTABLE NOUNS

➢ **Uncountable Noun** is the **Noun** that cannot be counted.

Eg:- (a) J. Priestly discovered **oxygen.**

(b) They decided to sell the **furniture.**

(c) Much **money** was wasted on the show.

	Countable Noun	Uncountable Noun
Eg:-	Stars, Seconds, Rupees etc.	Money, time, knowledge etc.
Verb-	Singular with Singular Noun; Plural with Plural Noun	Singular Verb
Adjective-	Many, few, a number of, the number of.	Much, little, quantity of etc.
Article -	A/An/ the can be used.	only 'the' can be used

IMPORTANT POINTS

RULE - 1:- Certain **nouns** exist in **plural forms** only. Thus, "**s**" cannot be removed from such nouns to make them **singular** in form.They take plural verb with them.

E.g.: **Scissors, tongs, pliers, pincers, bellows, trousers, pants, pajamas, shorts, spectacles, goggles, binoculars, sunglasses, gallows, fangs, Alms, amends, archives, arrears, auspices, congratulations, embers, fireworks, lodgings, outskirts, particulars, proceeds, regards, riches, remains, savings, shambles, surroundings, tidings, troops, tactics, thanks, valuables, wages, belongings, handcuffs, forceps, braces, etc.**

Eg.: (a) Where are my **pants**?
(b) Where are the **tongs**?
(c) The **proceeds** were deposited in the bank.
(d) All his **assets** were seized.
(e) **Alms** were given to the beggars.

➤ **Note:-** Wages can be used in both singular & plural form. See the following sentences:-

	Meaning	Form	E.g.:
Wages	Labour	Plural	Wages are paid in cash.
	Result	Singular	Wages of hard work is sweet.

RULE - 2:- News, Innings, Politics, Summons, Physics, Economics, Ethics, Mathematics, Mumps, Measles, Rickets, Shingles, Billiards, Athletics, Linguistics are certain **Nouns** that **are Plural in form but Singular in meaning. They take Singular Verb.**

E.g.: (a) No **news** is good news.
(b) **Politics** is a dirty game.
(c) **Economics** is an interesting subject.
(d) **Ethics** demands honesty.
(e) Two **summonses** have been received. (Plural of 'summons' is 'summonses')

RULE - 3:- Cattle, Cavalry (Soldiers of horses), **Infantry** (Soldiers on foot), **Poultry** (hens and ducks), **Peasantry** (Farmers), **Children, Gentry** (High class people), **Police** and **People** are certain **Nouns** that are **Singular in form** but **Plural in meaning**. They take **Plural Verb**.

'**s**' is never used with these nouns.

Eg.: (a) **Cattle** are grazing in the field.
(b) Our **infantry** have marched forward.
(c) **Police** have arrested the thieves.

Note: '**People**' means '**a number of person**' while '**peoples**' means '**people of different races**'.

RULE - 4:- Furniture, advice, work, evidence, equipment, news, information, luggage, baggage, percentage, poetry, knowledge, dirt, dust, traffic, electricity, music, breakage, stationery, scenery, confectionery, pottery, bakery, crockery, behaviour, hair, business, mischief, bread, wastage, money, Jewellery, word(when used in sense of 'Message' and 'Promise') Fuel and Cost are uncountable nouns and hence will take **singular verb**. These nouns will not take '**A/An**', '**many**', '**few**', '**number of**' and '**plural form**'.

E.g.: (a) The **scenery** (S.N.) of Kasmir **has** (S.V.) enchanted us.

(b) I passed the exam but the **percentage** (S.N.) of marks **was** (S.V.) not good.

(c) The **mischief** committed by him is unpardonable.

(d) His **hair** is black.

(e) I have some **equipment** that I needed for the project.

➢ Such nouns have no plural form but sometimes we need the Singular/plural form of these nouns. The **Singular/ Plural form is made by adding certain words before the Uncountable Nouns**.

E.g.: (a) He gave me **a piece of** information.

(b) **All pieces of** information given by her were reliable.

(c) **Many kinds of** furniture are available in that shop.

(d) I want **a few articles of** jewellery.

(e) He ate **two slices of** bread.

(f) Please show me **some items of** office stationery.

(g) The Police have found **a strand of** hair in the car.

Note: **Monies** is the **plural form of money** which means **amounts of money**.

E.g.: Monies have been collected and handed to the women's welfare society.

RULE 5 :- **Deer, Sheep, Series, Species, Fish, Crew, Aircraft, Counsel** are certain Nouns that are used in **both Singular and Plural** forms. If they are used in **Singular sense, they take Singular Verb** and if they are used in **Plural sense, they take Plural Verb.**

E.g.: (a) A sheep **is** grazing in the field.

(b) Two sheep **are** grazing in the field.

(c) There **are** two fish in the pond.

(d) There **are** many fishes in the aquarium. (Here the word '**fishes**' refers to **different species of fish**)

RULE 6 :- **Hyphenated Noun** does not have plural form.

E.g.:(a) He gave me two **hundred-rupees** notes. (change 'rupees' into 'rupee')

(b) He stays in **five-stars** hotels. (change 'stars' into 'star')

RULE 7 :- Certain nouns/words are used in colloquial English in India which is wrong as the word is literally translated from English to Hindi.

E.g.:

Wrong	Correct
1. Cousin brother / Cousin sister	**1. Cousin**
2. Pick pocketer	**2. Pick pocket**
3. Good name	**3. Name**
4. Big blunder	**4. Blunder (means a big mistake)**
5. Strong breeze	**5. Strong wind (Breeze is always light and gentle)**
6. Bad dream	**6. Nightmare**
7. Proudy	**7. Proud**
8. According to me	**8. In my opinion**
9. Cheater	**9. Cheat**

➢ **We generally get confused while using the following Nouns:-**

(a) **Floor** (the flat surface of a room) (a) **Ground** (surface of the earth)

(b) **Skill** (we acquire it by learning) (b) **Talent** (A natural ability)

(c) **Envy** (a wish to possess that the other person has.) (c) **Jealousy** (a feeling that arises out of fear of losing that you have.)

RULE 8 :- When a **Definite Numeral Adjective** is added before the following Nouns, they take **Singular form.**

E.g.: **Pair, score, gross, stone, hundred, dozen, thousand, million, billion etc.**

E.g.(a) I have **two hundred** rupees only.

(b) She purchased **three dozen** pencils.

(c) He has already donated **five thousand** rupees.

➢ If **'of'** is used with them, such nouns are used in **Plural** form.

E.g.: **dozens of women, hundreds of people, millions of dollars**.

(a) **Hundreds of people** came to see the fair.

(b) He donated **millions of rupees**.

(a) I have two **pairs** of shoes. (Pairs take 'of'. 'Two pair shoes' is wrong)

RULE 9 :- If a **Preposition** comes after a **Noun** and then the same **Noun is repeated**, the Noun should be used in Singular form.

E.g.:(a) **Town after town** was devastated.

(b) **Ship after ship** is arriving.

(c) The BJP organized **door to door** campaign.

Towns after towns, rows upon rows, doors to doors, or ships after ships must not be used.

RULE 10 :- Nouns like **teacher, student, child, clerk, advocate, worker, writer, author, leader, musician** etc are common gender Nouns. They are used for both male and female. They are also called dual genders. Thus **'His/he/him'** is used for such Nouns (When such Nouns are used in Singular).

(1) Every **leader** should perform **his** duty.

(2) A **teacher** should practise what **he** preaches.

Words Denoting Groups

1. A **band** of musicians.
2. A **board** of directors, etc.
3. A **bevy** of girls, women and officers
4. A **bunch** of grapes, keys, etc.
5. A **bundle** of sticks and hay.
6. A **caravan** of merchants, pilgrims, travellers.
7. A **chain/range** of mountains or hills.
8. A **choir** of singers.
9. A **class** of students.
10. A **retinue** of servants/ attendants.
11. A **clump/grove** of trees.
12. A **code** of laws.
13. A **constellation or galaxy** of stars.
14. A **battalion/regiment/army** of soldiers.

15. A **convoy** of ships, cars etc. moving under an escort.
16. A **course** or **series** of lectures.
17. A **crew** of sailors.
18. A **crowd/mob** of people.
19. A **curriculum** of studies.
20. A **flight** of steps, stairs, flying birds
21. A **fleet** of ships or motorcars.
22. A **flock** of geese, sheep and birds.
23. A **gang** of robbers, labourers.
24. A **garland/bunch/bouquet** of flowers.
25. A **heap** of ruins, sand, stones.
26. A **herd** of cattle.
27. A **litter** of puppies.
28. A **pack** of hounds, cards.
29. A **pair** of shoes, scissors, spectacles trousers.
30. A **series** of events.
31. A **sheaf** of corn, arrows.
32. A **swarm** of ants, bees or flies.
33. A **train** of carriages, followers etc.
34. A **volley/ fusillade/ salvo** of shots, bullets
35. A **forum** of people (discussing issues)
36. A **congregation** of people (discussing religious issues)
37. A **shoal/ school** of fish.

Noun Gender

A shoal/ school of fish

Gender is divided into four categories:-

1. **Masculine Gender:** denotes male gender.

E.g.: **Tiger, Father, Lion** etc.

2. **Feminine Gender:** denotes female gender.

E.g.: **Tigress, Woman, Lioness, Mother, Sister, Goddess**, etc

3. **Common Gender:** denotes both male and female.

E.g.: **Child, baby, teacher, servant, student, cousin, infant, thief, neighbour** etc.

4. **Neuter Gender:** used for non-living things. It has no gender. (It is neither male nor female)

E.g.: **Copy, Book, Room, Paper, Television, Box**

Rules for changing Masculine Nouns into Feminine Nouns:-

RULE 1:- Some Masculine Nouns change into Feminine when '**ess**' is added at the end.

Masculine	**Feminine**	**Masculine**	**Feminine**
Author	Authoress	Host	Hostess
Jew	Jewess	Mayor	Mayoress
Poet	Poetess	Tutor	Tutoress
Shepherd	Shepherd	Giant	Giantess
Heir	Heiress	Lion	Lioness
Priest	Priestess	Tailor	Tailoress

RULE 2:- In case of some Nouns **'ess'** is added but after removing the last vowel.

Masculine	Feminine	Masculine	Feminine
Actor	Actress	Benefactor	Benefactress
Hunter	Huntress	Prince	Princess
Waiter	Waitress	Ambassador	Ambassadress
Negro	Negress	Tiger	Tigress
Director	Directoress		

RULE 3:- In some cases the Masculine Noun is changed a bit and then **'ess'** is put at the end to make it Feminine.

Masculine	Feminine	Masculine	Feminine
Emperor	Empress	Governor	Governess
Duke	Duchess	God	Goddess
Master	Mistress	Sorcerer (Magician)	Sorceress

RULE 4:- In some cases the 1st or the 2nd word of compound Masculine Noun are changed.

Masculine	Feminine	Masculine	Feminine
Man-servant	Maid-servant	Washerman	Washerwoman
Buck Rabbit	Doe-Rabbit	Brother-In-Law	Sister-In-Law
He-bear	She-bear	Jack-ass	Jenny-ass
Head master	Head mistress	Milkman	Milkmaid
Post master	Post mistress	Peacock	Peahen
Landlord	Landlady	Step father	Step mother
He-goat	She-goat	Cock-sparrow	Hen-sparrow
Dog-wolf	Bitch-wolf	Step-brother	Step-sister
Grandson	Granddaughter	Bull-calf	Cow-calf
Father-in-law	Mother-in-law		

RULE 5:- Masculine / Feminine Gender of a few words are given below. They are not changed according to any special rule.

Masculine	Feminine	Masculine	Feminine
Administrator	Administratrix	Executor	Executrix
Lad	Lass	Prosecutor	Proscutrix
Boar	Sow	Brother	Sister
Colt	Filly	Dog	Bitch
Buck	Doe	Monk	Nun
Gander	Goose	Horse	Mare
King	Queen	Man	Woman
Sheep	Ewe	Son	Daughter
Uncle	Aunt	Fox	Vixen
Ox/Bull	Cow	Hero	Heroine
Testator	Testatrix	Bachelor	Maid
Boy	Girl	Cock	Hen
Drake	Duck	Father	Mother
Bridegroom	Bride	Gentleman	Lady
Husband	Wife	Lord	Lady
Male	Female	Nephew	Niece
Sir	Madam	Widower	Widow
Wizard	Witch		

Noun-Number (Singular-Plural)

Singular Noun:- denotes **one place, person, thing**. E.g.: Boy, girl, table, chair etc.

Plural Noun:- denotes **more than one place, person or thing**. E.g.: cities, boys, tables, chairs, etc.

➢ **Changing singular into plural**

RULE 1:- Some Nouns are made plural by adding '**s**'.

E.g.: boy, girl, kite, telephone etc.

RULE 2:- Some Nouns which have **s, ss, ch, sh, z or x at the end,** their Plural forms are made by adding "**es**" at the end.

Singular	Plural	Singular	Plural
Bus	Buses	Watch	Watches
Ass	Asses	Fix	Fixes
Church	Churches	Fox	Foxes
Switch	Switches	Canvas	Canvases
Class	Classes	Quiz	Quizzes
Tax	Taxes	Box	Boxes
Dish	Dishes	Coach	Coaches

➢ **A few exceptions**

Stomach	Stomachs	Locus	Loci
Radius	Radii	Ox	Oxen

RULE 3:- Nouns that end in '**O**' and have a 'consonant' preceding it are made Plural by adding '**es**'.

Singular	Plural	Singular	Plural
Hero	Heroes	Mango	Mangoes
Cargo	Cargoes	Potato	Potatoes
Mosquito	Mosquitoes	Echo	Echoes

Exceptions

Singular	Plural	Singular	Plural
Dynamo	Dynamos	Ratio	Ratios
Solo	Solos	Memento	Mementos
Piano	Pianos	Photo	Photos
Studio	Studios	Embryo	Embryos

RULE 4 :- Nouns ending with double vowel are made Plural by adding '**s**'.

Singular	Plural	Singular	Plural
Bee	Bees	Tree	Trees
Portfolio	Portfolios	Zoo	Zoos
Radio	Radios	Woe	Woes

RULE 5:- Nouns that end in '**Y**' and have consonant' preceding 'y' are made Plural by changing 'y' into '**ies**' .

Singular	Plural	Singular	Plural
Cry	Cries	Family	Families
City	Cities	Lorry	Lorries
Country	Countries	Pony	Ponies
Reply	Replies	Dictionary	Dictionaries

RULE 6:- Nouns that end in '**Y**' and have a vowel before 'y' are made Plural by adding '**s**'.

Singular	**Plural**	**Singular**	**Plural**
Key	Keys	Ray	Rays
Way	Ways	Toy	Toys
Donkey	Donkeys	Monkey	Monkeys
Valley	Valleys	Storey	Storeys

RULE 7:- Nouns that end in '**f/fe**' are made Plural by changing '**f/fe**' into '**ves**'.

Singular	**Plural**	**Singular**	**Plural**
Calf	Calves	Wife	Wives
Wolf	Wolves	Leaf	Leaves
Shelf	Shelves	Half	Halves
Thief	Thieves	Life	Lives
Knife	Knives	Loaf	Loaves

Exception:

Singular	**Plural**	**Singular**	**Plural**
Belief	Beliefs	Cliff	Cliffs
Safe	Safes	Turf	Turfs
Chief	Chiefs	Dwarf	Dwarfs
Gulf	Gulfs	Roof	Roofs
Scarf	Scarfs	Brief	Briefs
Grief	Griefs		

RULE 8:- Compound Nouns are made Plural by adding '**s**' to the main word.

Singular	**Plural**
Brother-in-law	Brothers-in-law
Bed-room	Bed-rooms
Commander-in-chief	Commanders-in-chief
Step-daughter	Step-daughters
Maid-servant	Maid-servants
Pea-hen	Pea-hens
Peacock	Peacocks
Mother-in-law	Mothers-in-law
Sister-in-law	Sisters-in-law
Member of Parliament	Members of Parliament
Man hater	Man haters
Woman lover	Woman lovers
Man lover	Man lovers

Note: Plural form is Handfuls, Mouthfuls and Spoonfuls of Handful, Mouthful and Spoonful.

RULE 9:- In the following Nouns, the inner vowels are changed to make them Plural in form.

Singular	**Plural**	**Singular**	**Plural**
Man	Men	Foot	Feet
Mouse	Mice	Goose	Geese
Woman	Women	Tooth	Teeth
Oasis	Oases	Louse	Lice

RULE 10:- In the following Nouns '**en**' is added to change them into Plural.

Singular	Plural
Child	Children
Ox	Oxen

RULE 11:- Some Nouns have two Plural forms, which have different meanings.

1. **Brother** (a) **Brothers** - sons of the same parents
   (b) **Brethren** - members of society/community/religious group.
2. **Cloth** (a) **Cloths** - unstitched cloth
   (b) **Clothes** - stitched clothes (garments)
3. **Die** (a) **Dies** - stamps for printing and coining.
   (b) **Dice** - small cubes used in games.
4. **Index** (a) **Indexes** - tables of contents in a book.
   (b) **Indices** - signs used in algebra.

➢ **Some typical Plural Nouns**

(a) Some Nouns (of Latin origin) ending in '**um**' are Singular. They are made Plural by replacing '**um**' by '**a**'

Singular	Plural (of Plural form)	Singular	Plural (of Plural form)
Datum	Data	Ovum	Ova
Dictum	Dicta	Memorandum	Memoranda
Stratum	Strata	Agendum	Agenda

Note:

Some Nouns (of Latin origin) end in '**um**' but '**s**' is added at their end to change them into Plural form.

Singular	Plural (of Plural form)	Singular	Plural (of Plural form)
Asylum	Asylums	Museum	Museums
Premium	Premiums	Forum	Forums
Pendulum	Pendulums		

(b) Some Nouns (of Latin origin) end in '**us**'. They are made Plural by replacing '**us**' by '**i**'.

Singular	Plural
Radius	Radii
Syllabus	Syllabi

(c) Some Nouns (of Greek origin) end in '**is**'. They are made Plural by changing '**is**' into '**es**'

Singular	Plural	Singular	Plural
Analysis	Analyses	Crisis	Crises
Hypothesis	Hypotheses	Basis	Bases
Thesis	Theses	Oasis	Oases

(d) Some Nouns ending in '**on**' are made Plural by replacing '**on**' by '**a**'.

Singular	Plural
Phenomenon	Phenomena
Criterion	Criteria

(e) Nouns of a single letter, a digit or some words:

Singular	Plural	Singular	Plural
If	Ifs	5	5s
BA	BAs	But	Buts
10	10s	MA	MAs
I	I's	P	P's
ATM	ATMs	T	T's
MP	MPs	UPC	UPCs

(f) Singular and Plural forms of a few Nouns have entirely different meanings. Hence they must be used carefully.

Singular	Plural	Meaning (of plural form)
Air	Airs	False way of behaving
Return	Returns	Calculation of income
Iron	Irons	Shackles
Sand	Sands	Desert
Abuse	Abuses	Evil words
Good(adj)	Goods	Movable property
Water	Waters	Sea
Work	Works	Literary pieces
Fruit	Fruits	Result
Wit	Wits	Intelligence
Pain	Pains	Trouble taking

(g) Some Nouns take one more meaning when changed into plural form.

Singular	Plural	Meaning(In plural form)
Custom	Customs	Duty, beliefs
Manner	Manners	Ways, etiquette
Quarter	Quarters	¼, residence
Letter	Letters	Alphabet, literature, letter

➢ **Use of 'of'/ 'apostrophe' with Nouns**

(A) Apostrophe is used in the following ways to express possession.

Living things

E.g.: (a) Mohan's book (b) A cow's horn (c) A woman's purse

(B) **If a Plural Noun ends in 's/es', 's' is not added while using apostrophe** with the Plural form.

E.g.: (a) Boys' college (b) Girls' school (c) Working women's hostel

Note: If Plural form is different from Singular form, 's' comes with both the forms.

E.g: (a) Child's play, Children's school. (b) Man's duty, Men's wear.

(C) When **Noun ends in hissing sound**, **'s' is not added after apostrophe**.

E.g.: (a) For peace' sake
(b) For conscience' sake
(c) For goodness' sake
(d) Ganesh' idol
(e) For Jesus' sake

Note:- God's sake

(D) Apostrophe is **not** used with **Possessive Pronouns** (his, hers, yours, ours, theirs)

E.g.: yours faithfully, yours truly

(E) Apostrophe can come only at the end of the Compound Nouns.

E.g.: (a) **Commander-in-chief's** orders.
(b) My **son-in-law's** sister.

(F) Apostrophe is not used with non-living things. We use 'of'.

E.g.: Table's leg (×)
Leg of table (✓)

Exceptions:

(1) **When a non-living thing is personified**

E.g.: (a) Sun's fury (b) Nature's love

(2) **Nouns related to 'time/weight/place'**

E.g.: (a) a day's leave (b) arm's length
(c) a pound's weight (d) 7 O'clock

(3) **With respectable Nouns**

E.g.: (a) Court's order (b) At duty's call

(4) **With Phrases**

E.g.: (a) at wit's end (b) within a stone's throw

(5) **With heavenly objects**

E.g.: (a) Earth's atmosphere

(G) Do not use double apostrophe.

E.g. (a) My wife's secretary's mother has expired. (×)
The mother of my wife's secretary has expired. (✓)

(H) "**s**' is used with anybody / nobody /everybody /somebody/ anyone/someone/no one/everyone.

E.g.: (a) Everyone's concern is no one's concern.
(b) Everybody's business is nobody's business.

➢ If 'else' is used with anybody/ nobody etc, 'apostrophe' will be used.

E.g.: (a) I can rely on your words, not **somebody else's.**
(b) I obey your orders and **nobody else's.**
(Here, it will be wrong to write somebody's else/nobody's else.)

SPOTTING THE ERROR

1. (a) My sister / (b) has read / (c) pages after pages of the Bible./ (d) No error
2. (a) I went to the temple / (b) with my parents, aunts / (c) and cousin sisters. / (d) No error
3. (a) He / (b) takes pain / (c) over his work./ (d) No error
4. (a) The Manager put forward / (b) a number of criterions / (c) for the post./ (d) No error
5. (a) I like / (b) the poetries / (c) of Byron and Shelley./ (d) No error
6. (a) The beautiful / (b) surrounding of the place / (c) enchanted me./ (d) No error
7. (a) No porter being available/ (b) he carried / (c) all his luggages himself./ (d) No error
8. (a) The table's legs / (b) have been / (c) elaborately carved./ (d) No error
9. (a) The sceneries / (b) of Kashmir / (c) is very charming./ (d) No error
10. (a) The driver showed / (b) great talent in keeping / (c) the damaged car under control./ (d) No error
11. (a) When I entered the bedroom / (b) I saw a snake crawling / (c) on the ground./ (d) No error
12. (a) Alms / (b) are given/ (c) to the poors./ (d) No error
13. (a) Lasers are / (b) indispensable tools / (c) for the delicate eyes surgery./ (d) No error
14. (a) If you have a way with words / (b) a good sense of design and administration ability / (c) you may enjoy working in high pressure world of advertising./ (d) No error
15. (a) Last week's sharp hike in the wholesale price of beef / (b) is a strong indication for / (c) higher meat costs to come./ (d) No error
16. (a) Whenever he goes to Mumbai / (b) he stays in/ (c) five-stars hotels./ (d) No error
17. (a) The company has ordered / (b) some / (c) new equipments./ (d) No error
18. (a) A strong breeze / (b) blew his / (c) cap off./ (d) No error.
19. (a) One of the firmest belief among the Hindus is that/ (b) Karma affects their / (c) life and also the life after death./ (d) No crror
20. (a) He was advised to take/ (b) two spoonsful of / (c) medicine three times a day./ (d) No error
21. (a) It is a big blunder/(b) but we had /(c) to ignore it/(d)No error
22. (A) The police have received / (b) two important informations / (c) that can help them solve the triple murder case (E) No error
23. (a) The sheafs / (b) of the wheat plants were too heavy / (c) for the weak farmer to carry them on his head./ (d) No error
24. (a) The population of India /(b) is divided into two classes- / (c) Haves and Haves not./ (d) No error
25. (a) All his sister-in laws /(b) are extremely co-operative / (c) and she doesn't miss her real sisters at all./ (d) No error
26. (a) Envy strikes a woman / (b)when she sees her husband / (c) talking to another woman./ (d) No error

27. (a) Two summons have been issued by the court / (b) but he has not / (c) yet appeared before the court./ (d) No error
28. (a) The Vaidya's / (b) have been living here / (c) for about a decade./ (d) No error.
29. (a) You are among those/ (b) man who earned name and fame not by / (c) chance but by hard work ./ (d) No error
30. (a) Children are playing / (b) and making mischiefs/ (c) as their holidays have started./ (d) No error.
31. (a) Sheeps are economically useful/ (b) and so they are reared/ (c) for wool and meat./ (d) No error.
32. (a) I read the letter/ (b) and made him aware/ (c) of its content./ (d) No error.
33. (a) I shall not go to party tonight/ (b) since I have many works to complete/ (c) before I give presentation tomorrow./ (d) No error.
34. (a) One must be always/ (b) true to one's words/ (c) if one wants to get respect from everyone./ (d) No error.
35. (a) Even after the enactment of several Acts and Provisions /(b) we can see five years old boys/ (c) working in hazardous factories./ (d) No error.
36. (a) The fan's blade / (b) has broken/ (c) and we must buy a new fan before disposing it of./ (d) No error.
37. (a) She wears spectacle/ (b) and so she was unable to see the gangster/ (c) that attacked her last night./ (d) No error.
38. (a) All the furnitures have been/ (b) sold for a song/ (c) as we were in a hurry to leave the town./ (d) No error.
39. (a) The angry mob/ (b) attacked the police officers/ (c) when they came to raze the illegal construction./ (d) No error.
40. (a) They left/ (b) their luggages/ (c) at home by mistake and went to the railway station./ (d) No error.
41. (a) The car could not/ (b) ascend the steep hill/ (c) because it was in the wrong gears./ (d) No error.
42. (a) The ticket window/ (b) remained closed / (c)throughout the day./ (d) No error.
43. (a) Satyajit Ray, who conceived, co-authored / (b) and directed a number of good films, was/ (c) one of India's most talented film maker./ (d) No error.
44. (a) I think this/ (b) is not your book. / (c) It is some body's else./ (d) No error.
45. (a) You should not put/ (b) your sign on any paper / (c) that you haven't read./ (d) No error.
46. (a) Towns after towns were/ (b) conquered / (c) by him but he found no peace./ (d) No error.
47. (a) When we reached the fair/ (b) we found that there / (c) was no place to stand./ (d) No error.
48. (a) All the evidences were/ (b) against him and he was / (c) held guilty./ (d) No error.
49. (a) My cousin brother is a cheater/ (b) and he / (c) cheats his family members and friends too./ (d) No error.
50. (a) The committee/ (b) could not come to/ (c) a final conclusion./ (d) No error.

51. (a) The cattle in the meadow/ (b) was terrified to hear/ (c) the roar of a lion which appeared to be wild with anger./ (d) No error.
52. (a) There should be/ (b) no furnitures/ (c) in my room./ (d) No error.
53. (a) That house/ (b) is built of/ (c) stones./ (d) No error.
54. (a) Santosh lives/ (b) by the principals/ (c) he professes./ (d) No error.
55. (a) The astronomer/ (b) who predicts the future/ (c) has arrived./ (d) No error.
56. (a) He told me that/ (b) it was/ (c) his friend's Sankar's house./ (d) No error.

Answers with explanation

1. (c) If a noun comes on the either side of a preposition, the noun will come in singular form. 'Page after Page' is correct.
2. (c) Change 'cousin sisters' into 'cousins'.
3. (b) 'take pains' is correct. It means 'to work hard'.
4. (b) 'Criteria' is plural of 'criterion'.
5. (b) 'Poetry' is an uncountable noun. Hence it is singular and it does not have any plural form.
6. (b) Surrounding is the 'ing' form of verb 'surround'. Use 'Surroundings'. It means the area around someone or something.
7. (c) Change 'luggages' into 'luggage'. It is an uncountable noun. Hence it must be in singular form.
8. (a) 'Table's legs' should be changed into 'legs of table'. ' 's' is generally not used with non-living things.
9. (a) Change 'sceneries' into 'scenery'. Scenery is an uncountable noun.
10. (b) Change 'talent' into 'skill'. 'Talent' is the natural ability to do something. 'Skill' requires special training and knowledge.
11. (c) 'Ground' means the surface of earth. Change 'ground' into 'floor'.
12. (c) Change 'the poors' into 'The poor'. 'The poor' means the deprived class.
13. (c) 'Eyes surgery' should be changed into 'eye surgery'. 'Eyes'(noun) when used as an adjective should not be used in plural form.
14. (b) 'Administration' is a noun. We need an adjective form here which is 'administrative'.
15. (c) Change 'costs' into 'cost'. Cost as noun is uncountable and it has no plural form.
16. (c) 'Five-star' is a hyphenated noun which is not used in plural form.
17. (c) 'Equipment' is an uncountable noun and has no plural form.
18. (a) 'Breeze' is gentle. 'Strong wind' is the appropriate word here.
19. (a) The 'noun' that comes after 'one of the' must be plural. 'One of the firmest beliefs' is the correct form.
20. (b) Use 'spoonfuls'.
21. (a) 'Blunder' means 'big mistake'. Hence 'big blunder' is superfluous.
22. (b) 'Information' is an uncountable noun. To make it countable and plural use 'pieces of information'.
23. (a) Plural form of 'sheaf' is 'sheaves' and not 'sheafs'.

24. (c) 'Have nots' is a coined word which means 'deprived class'.
25. (a) 'Sisters-in-law' is the correct plural form of 'sister-in-law'.
26. (a) 'Jealousy' is the fear to lose the person/thing that we have. Envy means 'resentful desire of something possessed by someone else'.
27. (a) 'Summons' is singular in form. Its plural is 'summonses'.
28. (a) Use 'Vaidyas' as we are talking about the members of the family with their last name 'Vaidya' . Remove 'apostrophe'.
29. (b) 'Those' being plural will take plural noun 'men'.
30. (b) 'Mischief' is an uncountable noun. It has no plural form.
31. (a) 'Sheep' has no plural form but can be used in plural sense.
32. (c) Change 'content' into 'contents'. It means 'that are contained in a piece of writing or speech'.
33. (b) 'Work' is an uncountable noun. 'Many pieces of work' is the correct usage.
34. (b) 'True to one's word' should be used.
35. (b) Use 'five year old boys'. Here 'year' will be in singular form as it qualifies noun 'boys' and acts as an adjective.
36. (a) Change 'fan's blade' into 'blade of fan'.
37. (a) Change 'spectacle' into 'spectacles'.
38. (a) Change 'furnitures' into 'furniture'.'Furniture' being an uncountable noun will take singular verb.
39. (a) 'Angry mob' is superfluous. 'Mob' means 'angry group of people'.
40. (b) Change 'luggages' into 'luggage'.
41. (c) Use 'wrong gear'. Only one gear is functional in a car at a time.
42. (a) Change 'window' into 'counter'.
43. (c) The noun after 'one of' is plural in form. Hence 'one of the film makers' is correct.
44. (c) 'Somebody else's' is correct.
45. (b) 'Sign' is a verb. Use noun 'signature' here.
46. (a) 'Town after town' is the correct form. See sentence 1.
47. (c) Use 'no room'. 'Room' means 'enough empty space for people or things to be fitted in'.
48. (a) 'Evidence' is an uncountable noun. It has no plural form. Use singular verb 'was'.
49. (a) Use 'cousin' and 'cheat'. 'Cousin brother' and 'cheater' are words formed in India due to Indianization of English language.
50. (c) Remove 'final'. 'Conclusion' is always final.
51. (b) 'Cattle' is a plural noun. Change 'was' into 'were'.
52. (b) 'Furniture' has no plural form. Remove 's'.
53. (c) Change 'stones' into 'stone'.
54. (b) Change 'principals' into 'principles'.
55. (a) Change 'Astronomer' into 'astrologer'. 'Astrologer' is one who predicts future.
56. (c) Change friend's into friend. Double apostrophe cannot be used in a sentence.

CHAPTER 15 PRONOUN

- A **word used in place of Noun** is called a **Pronoun.**
- In order to **avoid repetition of a noun** in a sentence, pronoun is used.

E.g.: Mrs. Shukla, being a good teacher, she is liked by all the students. (**remove 'she'**) 'She' is a Pronoun and must be used in place of the Noun (Mrs. Shukla) and not with the noun.)

TYPES OF PRONOUNS :

1. **Personal Pronouns** :Pronouns that stands for the three persons (explained later) I, me, we, us, you, he, him, she, her, it, they, them.
2. **Possessive Pronouns** : Pronouns that show possession.

   Mine, ours, yours, his, hers, theirs
3. **Demonstrative Pronouns** : Words used for Nouns to point at something/someone.

   This, that, these, those
4. **Distributive Pronouns** : Words used for individuals or objects referring to them as one at a time.

   Each, either, neither, every, none etc.
5. **Reciprocal Pronouns** : each other, one another.
6. **Reflexive Pronouns** : Myself, ourselves, yourself, yourselves, himself, herself, itself, themselves, oneself
7. **Emphatic or Emphasizing Pronouns** : Such pronouns are used to lay stress on the subject. Examples:- Myself, ourselves, yourself, yourselves, himself, herself, itself, themselves, oneself

E.g.: You, **yourself** are responsible for your problems.
He hurt **himself.**

8. **Indefinite Pronouns** : Words used for nouns in vague or general meaning.

   Everybody, somebody, nobody, anybody, everybody, someone, no one, anyone, everything, something, nothing, anything, all, some, any, both, another, much, few, little.
9. **Relative Pronouns** :Words used for nouns to show them 'relating to'.

   Who, whom, whose, which, what, that etc.

The Case of Personal Pronouns		Subject	Object	Possessive Adjective	Possessive Pronoun
First Person	Singular	I	me	my	mine
	Plural	We	us	our	ours
Second Person	Singular/ Plural	You	you	your	yours
Third Person	Singular	She, He, It	her, him, it	her, his, its	hers, his, ---
	Plural	They	them	their	theirs

10. **Interrogative Pronouns**:- Words used for nouns to ask questions.
    Who, whom, whose, which etc.

- **Now let us see all the Pronouns in detail:**

1. **Use of Personal Pronoun:**
   They are used as **first person**, **second person** and **third person**. They are called **personal pronouns**.

PERSONAL PRONOUN

Nominative Case	Objective Case	Nominative Case	Objective Case
I	me	He	him
She	her	It	it
They	them	You	you
We	us		

Rule 1:-

- Verb is Preceded by the **nominative form** of Pronoun and followed by the **Objective case**.

E.g.: I teach him. (Active Voice)
Sub. Verb Obj.
before after

He is taught by me. (Passive Voice)
before after

Rule 2:-

- If all the three persons or two out of three persons come in a single sentence, the order is 231.

1. **You, he** and **I** shall study for the exam. (231)
2. **He** and **I** have finished our work. (31)
3. **You** and **he** have done a great job. (23)

Rule 3:-

- If all the three persons or two out of three persons come in a single sentence and something wrong is talked about or some mistake done by the persons has been accepted, the order is 123.

E.g.: (1) **I, you** and **he** have made a mistake. (123)

(2) **You** and **he** have done this mischief. (23)

Rule 4:-

- If Pronouns are in plural form, the order should be 123.

E.g.: **We, you** and **they** should now get down to work.

Rule 5:-

- An objective case comes after **'let', 'like', 'between....and' , 'but', 'except' and 'all prepositions'**.

E.g.:
1. **Let me** do this work.
2. There is no problem between she and I. (×)
   There is no problem **between her and me.** (✓)
3. Everybody but **him** was present for the meeting. (✓)
4. He laughed at I. (×)
   He laughed **at me**. (✓)
5. Everyone attended the party except he. (×)
   Everyone attended the party **except him**. (✓)

Rule 6:-

- If there is a comparison between two pronoun, the Pronoun of the same case is used after as/than.

E.g.:
1. He is **as** fast **as** me (Objective Case) .(×)
2. He is **as** fast **as** I (Nominative Case) .(✓)
3. I run faster **than** him (Objective Case) .(×)
4. I run faster **than** he (Nominative Case) .(✓)
5. I know you **as** much **as** him. (✓)

Sentence 5 means that 'I know you as much as I know him'.

- From the above examples it is clear that a subject is compared with subject and an object is compared with object.

Rule 7:-

- If a sentence starts with '**It**' followed by any form of '**be**' the pronoun that follows 'be' must be in '**nominative case**'.

E.g.: It is **I** (Nominative case) who am to blame.

Use of it-

Rule 1:-

- '**It**' is used for non-living things, animals, infants and insects. 'They' is the plural form of 'it'.

E.g.: 1. America is a developed country. **It** is a super power.
2. Sri Lanka and Pakistan are developing countries. **They** are facing internal terrorism.

Rule 2:-

- '**It**' is used to denote **time, weather, climate, temperature, distance** or any other natural event. It is used only as an **introductory subject**. In this case 'it' is called 'empty/dummy it' as it has no meaning.

E.g.: It is raining. It is morning.
It is winter. It is 6 o'clock.
It is March. It is Monday.

Rule 3:-

- It is also used in place of **Infinitive clause** and **Gerund.**

E.g.: **It** is easy to solve it.
It is humane to err.

Rule 4:-

- '**It**' is used in a sentence as a subject to emphasize the Noun or the Pronoun.

E.g.: **It** was he (Pron.) who made this mistake.

Rule 5:-

- "**It**" is used to introduce a phrase/clause.

E.g.: **That the record will break today** (Clause) is probable.

Meaning- It is probable that the record will break today.

- **Difference between 'This' and 'It'.**

'This' is used to point towards a **person or thing or for the introduction of a person or when the singular object or person is placed at a near distance.** Here 'It' will not come.

E.g.: **This** is a book.
This is a pen.
This is Rohan, my cousin.

- It denotes **distance/time/weather** etc. Here '**this**' is not used for such purpose.

E.g.: **It** is 10 a.m.
It is winter.
It is night.

Note: A Noun can be used after 'this'.

E.g.: **This** book (Noun) is mine.

- **'It'** is a Pronoun and hence a Noun cannot be used after 'it' as 'Pronoun' and 'Noun' cannot come together.
- **It** book is mine. (×)
  It is my book. (✓)
- **'It'** is used for singular noun/non-living thing or an infant.

E.g.: 1. **It** is a splendid moment.
2. The baby is cute but **it** is crying a lot.

Nominative Case	Possessive Adjective	Possessive Pronoun
I	my	mine
We	our	ours
You	your	yours
He	his	his
She	her	hers
It	its	×
They	their	theirs

Rule 1:-

- Possessive pronouns are not used before nouns.

E.g.: Ours school (Noun) was closed for four days. (×)

Our school was closed for four days. (✓)

Note: (i) Possessive adjectives are used before nouns.

E.g.: This is **my book**.

(ii) If the noun has already been mentioned, possessive pronoun is used to avoid repetition.

E.g.: This book is **mine.**

Possessive pronouns	Meaning (Possessive Adjective + Noun)
Mine	My + noun
Ours	Our + noun
Yours	Your + noun
His	His + noun
Hers	Her + noun
Theirs	Their + noun

(iii) 'His' is used as both Possessive Adjective and Possessive Pronoun.

(iv) 'Its' is used as Possessive Adjective but not as Possessive Pronoun.

Rule 2:-

- **Possessive Pronoun** can be used in any sentence **as the subject** of the verb.

E.g.: (a) **Yours** is (S.V.) a new car.

Meaning - Your car is a new car.

(b) **Hers** is (S.V.) a beautiful house.

Meaning - Her house is a beautiful house.

Rule 3:-

- **Possessive Pronoun** can be used **as the object** of a verb.

E.g.: (a) He has lost (Verb) **my books** as well as **yours**.

Meaning - He has lost my book as well as your book.

(b) Save **your time** and mine (Obj.) too.

Meaning - Save your time and my time too.

Rule 4:-

- Possessive Pronoun can be used as the **object of a preposition**.

E.g.: (1) I prefer your help to (Prep.) her (Obj.). (×)

I prefer your help to (Prep.) **hers** (**Obj.**).(✓)

(2) Your house is better than (Prep.) my (Obj.). (×)

Your house is better than (Prep.) **mine** (**Obj.**). (✓)

Rule 5:-

- We do not use possessive adjective with **separation, leave, excuse, mention, report, pardon, sight, favour.**

Eg.: (a) Your separation is very painful to me. (**Use 'separation from you'**)

(b) At his sight the robbers fled. (**'At the sight of him' is right**)

(c) I need your favour please. (**'I need a favour from you' is correct**)

Rule 6:-

- In Possessive Pronouns apostrophe is not used before 's'.
  The use of your's, her's, it's is wrong.

E.g.: The bear had a ring around it's nose. (×)

The bear had a ring around its nose. (✓)

Rule 7:-

Gerund is used after Possessive Adjective. In such cases never use Possessive Pronoun or Objective case of Pronoun.

E.g.: (a) I was confident of **my** winning the match.

(b) She was not confident of **her** doing well in the examination.

(c) She is sure of my/my/me/mine helping others ('my' is the correct choice)

➢ **Use of Reflexive Pronouns:**

E.g.: The poor man poisoned **himself** and his children.

Rule 1:-

➢ Use **Reflexive Pronoun after acquit, avail, reconcile, amuse, resign, avenge, exert, apply, adapt, adjust, pride, absent and enjoy**.

E.g.:
1. We **adapt ourselves** to the changing climate.
2. The officers **acquitted themselves** well during the crisis.
3. She has **reconciled herself** to the demands of her in-laws.
4. The students **exert themselves** a lot at the time of examination.
5. You will have to **apply yourself** to this task whole-heartedly.
6. I **pride myself** on being able to work smoothly under pressure too.
7. You should **avail yourself** of this opportunity.

Note: Look at the sentences below-

(a) They enjoyed the party. (**no need of reflexive pronoun**)

(b) They enjoyed during vacation. **(Use 'themselves' after 'enjoyed')**

➢ If 'enjoy' is followed by an object, we do not use a reflexive pronoun, but if the object is not mentioned, we use a reflexive pronoun.

Note: Look at the sentence below:

(a) He was absent. (✓)

(b) He absented himself. (✓)

➢ If **absent** is used as a verb, a **reflexive pronoun** is used.

Rule 2:-

➢ **Keep, stop, turn, qualify, bathe, move, rest** and **hide do not take a reflexive pronoun after them.**

E.g.: (a) You should keep yourself away from bad boys. **(remove yourself)**

(b) He hid himself in the room. **(remove himself)**

Rule 3:-

➢ Reflexive pronoun cannot be used as a subject or an object of a sentence unless a noun/pronoun comes before it.

E.g.: (a) Myself Ram from Delhi. ('I am Ram from Delhi' is correct)

(b) Yourself and he reached there in time. (Use 'you' in place of 'yourself')

(c) I myself did this work. (✓)

(d) Rohit will do the work for myself. (Use me)

USE OF DISTRIBUTIVE PRONOUN:

Rule 1:-

- **Either** denotes **choice between two**.

E.g.: Either of these three friends is naughty. (×)
Either of these two pens is red. (✓)

Note: **'Any'** or **'One'** is used to choose, between many persons or things.

E.g.: One of these boys is naughty. (✓)

Rule 2:-

- **Neither** denotes 'none out of two things/persons'.

E.g.: **Neither** of the two girls is active. (✓)

- **None** denotes 'none out of more than two things/persons'.

E.g.: Neither of his four sons looked after him. (×)
None of his four sons looked after him. (✓)

USE OF RECIPROCAL PRONOUN:

'Each other' and 'one another' are called Reciprocal Pronouns. They denote mutual relationship.

Rule 1:-

- **Each other** denotes mutual relationship between people/things while one another denotes mutual relationship among more than two things/persons.

E.g.:(a) He was so afraid that his knees knocked **one another**. (use each other in place of one another)

(b) After the farewell the students of Class XII bade **each other** good bye. (use 'one another' in place of 'each other')

USE OF DEMONSTRATIVE PRONOUN:

- Demonstrative case is used to point towards a noun/nouns.

E.g.: **This, that, these, those, such, the same.**

- If they come before a noun, they are called demonstrative adjectives.

Rule 1:-

- **'This'** is used for a singular object /person that is placed closer. 'This' is singular'.'These' is plural.
  'These' is used for more than one object /person that are placed far.

E.g.: **This** is a $\underbrace{\text{cat}}_{\text{S. N.}}$.

These are $\underbrace{\text{cats}}_{\text{P. N.}}$.

Rule 2:-

- **'That'** is used for a distant thing/person. 'That' is singular.

'Those' is used for more than one distant thing/person. 'Those' is plural.

E.g.: **That** is a book (S. N.).

Those are books (P. N.).

➢ To avoid repetition of singular noun 'that' is used. In case of a plural noun 'those' is used.

E.g.:(a) The climate of Pune is better than **that of** Mumbai (it means climate of Mumbai).

(b) The streets of Delhi are wider than **those of** Mumbai. (it means the streets of Mumbai).

Rule 3:-

In a sentence 'one' is used to avoid the repetition of a singular countable noun. 'Ones' is used to avoid the repetition of plural countable nouns.

Do not use one's in place of ones.

E.g.:

(1) **This** is the new version, that is an old **one**.

(2) **These** are new books but those are old **ones**.

USE OF RELATIVE PRONOUNS:

Those pronouns that connect a clause or phrase to a noun or a pronoun is called a Relative Pronoun.

E.g.: **who, whom, which, that and what.**

E.g.: I met Veena, **who** was returning from school.

Rule 1:-

➢ Relative Pronouns **(who/which/that)** are used as a **subject in subordinate clause**.

E.g.: The boy who (Subj.) came here is a player.

Rule 2:-

➢ **Relative Pronouns (whom/which/that)** are used an **object in subordinate clause**.

E.g.: I have a son whom (Obj.) I love (Verb) very much.

Rule 3:-

➢ If two **antecedents** are joined by **'and'** one being a human and the other being a non living thing / animal, a **relative pronoun 'that'** is used.

E.g.: The man and his dog **that** I saw yesterday have been kidnapped.

Rule 4:-

- **'That'** is used after a superlative degree.

E.g.: Mr. Mishra is the most laborious man **that** I have ever seen.

Rule 5:-

- If **'All'** denotes people and is used as a subject, '**who**' **or** '**that**' is used and not '**whom/which**'.

E.g.: All **who/that** are interested to do this work can start now.

Rule 6:-

- If **'all'** denotes non living things, **'that'** is used and not **'who** or **'whom'.**

E.g.: All **that** glitters is not gold.

All is well **that** ends well.

Note: All + uncountable noun is followed by **'that'.**

E.g.: All the money **that** I gave her has been spent.

Rule 7:-

- **Everything, nothing, the only, any, all, everyone, none, no, nobody, much, little, the same, the few, the little will take** '**that**' after them.

E.g.: (a) My father has given me **everything that** I needed.

(b) This is **the only** pen, **that** I bought yesterday.

(c) My wife has spent **the little** money **that** I gave her.

(d) This is same dress **that** I had chosen.

Rule 8:-

- If the verb is mentioned, **'the same + noun'** is followed by **'that'** .

E.g.: This is the same man **that** deceived me.

Verb (**clearly given**)

- If the verb is not given use **'as'**.

E.g.: This is the same dress **as** mine.

USE OF INTERROGATIVE PRONOUNS:

Pronouns used for asking questions are called **Interrogative Pronouns.**

E.g.: Who, whom, whose, which etc.

Rule 1:-

- Look at the examples given below-

(A) **Who** is used for the subject.

Who is playing?

(B) **Whom** is used for the object.

Whom has he invited ?

(C) **'Whose'** is used to find out the owner.

Whose book is this?

Rule 2:-

➢ '**Preposition + whom**' can be used but not '**preposition + who**' .

E.g.: (a) **By whom** was the Ramayana written ?

(b) **To whom** are you known?

Note:- If preposition is used at the end of the sentence, 'who' comes at the starting of the sentence.

E.g.: (a) **Who** was the Ramayana written by?

(b) **Who** are you known **to**?

See the difference:

1. Who are (V) you (sub.) ? (✓)
2. I don't know who are you. (×)

   I don't know who you (sub.) are (V). (✓)

➢ Interrogative form of a sentence comes after '**wh**' family (See sentence1). This means, helping verb comes before the subject. If a '**wh**' family word is used to join two sentences, i.e. it is used as a relative pronoun, assertive form of sentence follows the 'wh' family word (See sentence 2). Helping verb is used after the subject.

Rule 3:-

➢ If a choice is to be made between two or more, **which** is used.

E.g.:(a). Who is your brother in the crowd ? (×)

Which is your brother in the crowd ? (✓)

(b). Who of the servants do you want ? (×)

Which of the servants do you want ? (✓)

Rule 4:-

➢ '**Whose**' is not used for non-living things.

E.g.: 1. Whose book is this ? (✓)

2. This is the flyover whose inauguration was done by the transport minister. (×)

This is the flyover, the inauguration of which was done by the transport minister. (✓)

➢ **Pronoun in Relation to Sub–Verb agreement.**

Questions related to Pronoun are also asked under Subject-verb Agreement.

POSSESSIVE PRONOUN:

Rule 1:-

➢ When two subjects are joined by **'as well as', 'with', 'alongwith', 'together with', 'and not', 'in addition to', 'but', 'besides', 'except', 'rather than', 'accompanied by', 'like', 'unlike', 'no less than', 'nothing but'**, the Possessive Adjective will agree with the **1st subject**.

E.g.:(a) Rita **as well as** her friends has done **her** work.

(b) My friend Reena **along with** her sister is doing **her** job at Delhi.

Rule 2:-

➢ When two **subjects** are joined by **'either.... or', 'neither.....nor', 'not only.....but also', 'none.....but',** the possessive adjective/ pronoun agrees with the **nearest subject**.

E.g.: **Neither** the staff members **nor** the manager was taking his task seriously.

Rule 3:-

➢ When **'each, neither, either, anyone, every one, every body, someone, somebody, no one, nobody, none'** is used as subject, 3rd person singular is used as the possessive case.

E.g.: (a) Everyone has done his work himself.

(b) **Neither** of the two brothers has brought their luggage. **(Change 'their' into 'his')**

Rule 4:-

➢ If collective noun like **Jury, army, fleet, crew** etc are used as the subject of the sentence , it denotes a **group** and hence **Singular Pronoun and Adjective** like **it, its, itself** is used.

E.g.: The jury has given their verdict. (×)

The jury **has** given **its** verdict. (✓)

Rule 5:-

➢ If **Collective Noun** is used as the **subject** and it denotes **separate individuals** or a **division** is shown among the members, it is considered **plural** and hence **plural pronoun** and **plural adjective/pronoun they, them, their, theirs, themselves** are used with them.

E.g.: The team are divided in **its** opinion. (×)

The team are divided in **their** opinion. (✓)

Rule 6:-

➢ If two or more than two **singular nouns** are joined by **'and'**, **plural pronoun** and **plural adjective they, them, their, theirs, themselves** are used.

E.g.: Ram **and** Shyam do **their** work. (✓)

Rule 7:-

➢ If two **singular nouns** are joined by **'and'** and if an **article** is used **before the first singular noun**, it denotes **'one person/thing'**. Here **singular pronoun** and **adjective - he, him, his, himself** will come for human beings and **it, its, itself** will come for non living things.

E.g.: **The** secretary and treasurer is negligent of their duty. (×)

The secretary and treasurer is negligent of **his** duty. (✓)

Rule 8:-

➢ If two nouns are joined by **'and'** and an **article** or a **Possessive Adjective** is used before each noun, it denotes many persons or things. Here **Plural Pronouns** and **Adjectives** will be used.

They, them, their, theirs, themselves will be used as per requirement.

E.g.: The secretary and treasurer did not do his work. (×)

The secretary and the treasurer did not do their work. (✓)

Rule 9:-

➢ If two or more than two nouns are joined by **'and'** and **each/ every** is used before each noun, **singular pronoun, singular adjective** and **singular verb** will follow.

E.g.: (a) **Every** soldier and **every** sailor was in their place.

(b) **Every** soldier and **every** sailor was in **his** place. (✓)

Rule 10:-

➢ If **many a/an + singular noun** is used with the **subject** of the sentence, singular pronouns and singular adjectives are used.

E.g.: **Many a** soldier (S. N.) has (S.V.) met his (S.P.) death in the battlefield. (✓)

DISTRIBUTIVE PRONOUNS:

Rule 1:-

➢ **Plural Noun / Pronoun** is used after **each of/either of/neither of**.

E.g.: **Each of** the boys (P. N.) has a note book.(✓)

Rule 2:-

➢ When the sentence starts with **each of/either of/neither of, each, either, neither, 'the'** is used before the plural noun/ plural pronoun but **singular adjective singular verb and singular pronoun are used** in the latter part of the sentence.

E.g.: 1. Each of the boys has their own book. (×)

Each of the boys (P. N.) has (S.V.) his (S.V.) own book. (✓)

2. None of them (P. P.) knew how to do the fitting himself (S. P.)

Rule 3:-

➢ If 'each' comes after the subject, the auxiliary verb/main verb will be used that agrees the subject .

E.g.: We have each advised him to give up smoking. (×)

We (Sub.) **each** have (Aux. Verb) advised him to give up smoking. (✓)

<u>**Note:**</u> In such sentences, the verb must agree with the subject.

Rule 4:-

➢ 'Both' is used for **two people or things**.

E.g.: All of the two students are guilty. (×)

Both of the two students are guilty. (✓)
'**Both**' is not used in negative sense.

E.g.: Both of them are not going. (×)
Neither of them is going. (✓)

USE OF INDEFINITE PRONOUNS:

Rule 1:-

➢ If '**one**' is used as the subject, Possessive case **one's** and Reflexive Pronoun - '**oneself**' is used.

E.g.: (a) **One** should do **one's** duty **oneself**.
(b) **One** should keep **one's** promise.

Note: Read '**Question Tag**' carefully. Some questions related to 'pronoun' come under 'question tag'.

SPOTTING THE ERROR

1. (a) Unless two or more members object/ (b) to him joining the club, we shall have to/ (c) accept his application for membership./ (d) No error.
2. (a) I was surprised and pleased (b)/ when I was informed of me (c) winning the contest./ (d) No error.
3. (a) Our dog may look/ (b) fierce but/ (c) that wouldn't hurt a fly./ (d) No error.
4. (a) No one can/ (b) challenge destiny,/ (c)isn't it?/ (d) No error.
5. (a) All the doubts are cleared/ (b) between/ (c) you and I./ (d) No error.
6. (a) The front page story was about a school girl/ (b) that had hurt herself/ (c) while saving a child in an accident./ (d) No error.
7. (a) The last thing that the fond mother/ (b) gave her only son/ (c) was his blessing./ (d) No error.
8. (a) It is not/ (b) I who is/ (c) to blame./ (d) No error.
9. (a) I shall avail of/ (b) this opportunity/ (c) to meet you there./ (d) No error.
10. (a) Put you in my position/ (b) and you will realise/ (c) the problems faced in my profession./ (d) No error.
11. (a) Each of them/ (b) has to understand/ (c) their responsibility/ (d) No error.
12. (a) We are proud to announce/ (b) that every one of us have earned/ (c) a good name./ (d) No error.
13. (a) Here is/ (b) the man whom I think/ (c) committed the crime./ (d) No error.
14. (a) He took/ (b) his younger sister/ (c) with himself./ (d) No error.
15. (a) The company is in debt/ (b) and has been unable/ (c) to pay their employees' salaries/ (d) for the past six months./ (e) No error.
16. (a) The company has appointed/ (b) consultants to help them/ (c) increase its revenue and/ (d) improve its financial position./ (e) No error.
17. (a) You cannot change/ (b) people, but you/ (c) can definitely/ (d) change own./ (e) No error.
18. (a) Governments and business houses must reduce/ (b) its own energy use/ (c) and promote conservation/ (d) to their citizens and employees./ (e) No error.
19. (a) Even those which/ (b) have no previous/ (c) work experience have/ (d) applied for this job./ (e) No error.
20. (a) He talked on the phone/ (b) for hours together/ (c) who really irritated/ (d) his parents a lot./ (e) No error.

21. (a) Instead of laying off/ (b) the workers, the company/ (c) decided to ask them/ (d) to avail voluntary retirement./ (e) No error.
22. (a) The two sisters shouted/ (b) at one another/ (c) in public./ (d) No error.
23. (a) We must supplement/ (b) our diet with vitamins and minerals/ (c) in order to keep/ (d) oneself fit/(e) No error.
24. (a) Mrs. Pratap, being a good teacher/ (b) she is selected/ (c) for the National Award./ (d) No error
25. (a) The poor man/ (b) poisoned him/ (c) and his own children./ (d) No error.
26. (a) It was in 2006/ (b) that we first flew/ (c) to the United States./ (d) No error.
27. (a) I was driving under the bridge/ (b) as a football/ (c) hit my window./ (d) No error.
28. (a) Many a student/ (b) have passed/ (c) the I.I.T. examination./ (d) No error.
29. (a) It was me who was/ (b) responsible for/ (c) making all the arrangements for the successful completion of his studies./ (d) No error.
30. (a) I wonder/ (b) why are you tinkering with the wire./ (c) You might get a shock./ (d) No error.
31. (a) John, I and Hari/ (b) have finished/ (c) our studies./ (d) No error.
32. (a) He doesn't/ (b) know/ (c) to swim./ (d) No error.
33. (a) All the dresses/ (b) looked good and so I/ (c) bought all of it./ (d) No error.
34. (a) Those people who/ (b)do not work hard/ (c) they do not succeed in life./ (d) No error.
35. (a) He bathed himself/ (b) in/ (c) a river./ (d) No error.
36. (a) She could not/ (b) bear/ (c) his separation./ (d) No error.
37. (a) If you want this job/ (b) you will need/ (c) his favour./ (d) No error.
38. (a) Both of them will not/ (b) refute/ (c) the charges./ (d) No error.
39. (a) She is the kind / (b) of woman whom every body knows/ (c) is benign and magnanimous./ (d) No error.
40. (a) The master did not know/ (b) who of the servants/ (c) broke the expensive dinner set./ (d) No error.
41. (a) The Congress Party stood/ (b) for implementation of the Nuclear Liability Bill/ (c) and was ready to stake their political existence./ (d) No error.
42. (a) He is not one of those/ (b) who will help every Tom, Dick and Harry/ (c) whom he meets./ (d) No error.
43. (a) My teacher/ (b) did not object/ (c) to me using the calculator./ (d) No error.
44. (a) He, You and I/ (b) shall arrange everything/ (c) and shall not ask them for help./ (d) No error.
45. (a) Was it me/ (B) who had to face/ (c) the music ?/ (d) No error.
46. (a) The audience/ (b) are requested/ (c) to be in its seats and stay away from the track./ (d) No error.
47. (a) The number of vehicles/ (B) plying on the roads of Delhi/ (c) is more than on the roads of Bangalore./ (D) No error.
48. (a) Being a destitute/ (b) I admitted him/ (c) to an orphanage./ (d) No error.
49. (a) One should keep/ (b) his promise/ (c) if one wants respect from both friends and enemies./(d) No error.
50. (a) Last summer I went to Shimla/ (b) and enjoyed very/ (c) much./ (d) No error.
51. (a) If I were him/ (b) I would teach/ (c) him a lesson./ (d) No error.

52. (a) Being a/ (b) rainy day I/ (c) could not go to school/ (d) No error.
53. (a) One of them/(b) forgot to take their passport/ (c) and found himself in a difficult situation/(d) No error.
54. (a) Mr. Sharma, our representative,/ (b) he will attend the meeting/ (c) on our behalf./ (d) No error.
55. (a) Each girl was/ (b) given a packet of sweets/ (c) and she was happy./ (d) No error.
56. (a) Myself and he/ (b) will manage/ (c) everything./ (d) No error.
57. (a) The Ganga is a river/ (b) whose origin/ (c) has always been a matter of speculation./ (d) No error.
58. (a) My friend/ (b) is laborious and intelligent, (c) isn't it ?/ (d) No error.
59. (a) It is difficult to say/ (b) who is the better/ (c) of the two players./ (d) No error.
60. (a) It is the best/ (b) which the government can do/ (c) for the downtrodden./ (d) No error.
61. (a) Neither of the two friends/ (b) has got their money back/ (c) from the company./ (d) No error.
62. (a) This is the road/ (b) whose inauguration/ (c) was done by the President./ (d) No error.
63. (a) Many women/ (b) reconcile to the/ (c) demands of their in-laws./ (d) No error.
64. (a) May I know/ (b) to who/ (c) I am speaking ?/ (d) No error.
65. (a) The person who/ (b) I met yesterday/ (c) was my classmate./ (d) No error.
66. (a) Owing to me being a new comer/ (b) I was unable/ (c) to get a good house./ (d) No error.
67. (a) A good friend of/ (b) me has been/ (c) in London for twenty years./ (d) No error.
68. (a) It was him/ (b) who came running/ (c) into the classroom./ (d) No error.
69. (a) I and Raju/ (b) left for Delhi/ (c) last summer./ (d) No error.
70. (a) I will certainly/ (b) avail of your offer/ (c) when the occasion arises./ (d) No error.
71. (a) The book/ (b) is well illustrated/ (c) and attractively bound/ (d) making altogether an attractive volume/(e) No error.
72. (a) Besides me/ (b) many other/ (c) were present./ (d) No error.
73. (a) My house/ (b) is farther/ (c) than her's./ (d) No error.
74. (a) He is the person,/ (b) whom, everyone thought,/ (c) has stolen the ring./ (d) No error.

Answers with explanation

1. (b) Change 'him' into 'his'. A possessive adjective comes before a gerund (joining).
2. (b) Change 'me' into 'my'. A possessive adjective comes before a gerund (winning).
3. (c) Use 'it' (pronoun) for 'dog'.
4. (c) Use 'can they' in place of 'isn't it'. See Question Tag.
5. (c) 'Between..........and' takes objective form of pronoun. Change 'I' into 'me'.
6. (b) Change 'that' into 'who'. 'School girl' is the subject which will take relative pronoun 'who'.
7. (c) 'Mother' will take possessive adjective 'her'.
8. (b) Change 'is' into 'am'. The verb that follows the relative pronoun should match with the antecedent to the relative pronoun.(Here 'I' is the antecedent of 'who').
9. (a) Use a reflexive pronoun with 'Avail'. Use 'myself' after 'avail'.

10. (a) Change 'you' into 'yourself'.
11. (c) Change 'their' into 'his'. 'Each' takes singular adjective/pronoun.
12. (b) 'has' is used with 'everyone'.
13. (b) 'The man' is the subject here that will take relative pronoun 'who'.
14. (c) Change 'himself' into 'him'.
15. (c) 'Company' is a singular noun. Singular possessive adjective 'its' will be used with it.
16. (b) 'Company' is a singular noun and will take 'it' in place of 'them'.
17. (d) Change 'own' into 'yourself'.
18. (b) Change 'its' into 'their'. Government and business houses being plural will take plural adjective 'their'.
19. (a) Change 'which' into 'who'.
20. (c) Use 'which' in place of 'who'. 'Talking on telephone' is not a person but an activity and hence takes 'which' and not 'who'.
21. (d) Avail is followed by a reflexive pronoun and preposition 'of'. Add 'themselves of' after 'avail'.
22. (b) Change 'one another' into 'each other'.
23. (d) Remove 'oneself'. Reflexive pronoun doesn't come with 'keep'.
24. (b) Remove 'she'. In a single sentence a noun and a pronoun for the same noun cannot come together.
25. (b) Change 'him' into 'himself'.
26. (b) Change 'that' into 'when' because '2006' is time.
27. (b) Change 'as' into 'when'. Here the time is important.
28. (b) 'Many a' is singular and will take singular verb 'has'.
29. (a) Use 'It was I'. Sub form 'I' will follow 'It + was (form of be).
30. (b) Use 'are' after 'you'. Sentence is not interrogative.
31. (a) According to rule 231, 1st person should come last. 'John, Hari and I' is the correct order.
32. (c) 'Wh' family will come after 'know' and 'wonder' if the verbs are followed by 'to+V_1 . Change 'to swim' into 'how to swim'.
33. (c) Change 'it' into 'them' as 'dresses' is a plural noun.
34. (c) Remove 'they'. In a sentence 'those people' and 'they' will not come together.
35. (a) Remove 'himself'. A reflexive pronoun will not be used after 'bathe'.
36. (c) 'His separation' is wrong as possessive case is not used with word 'separation'. Change 'his separation' into 'separation from him'.
37. (c) Change 'his favour' into 'favour from him'.
38. (a) Do not use 'not' with 'both'. Change 'both of them will not' into 'neither of them will'.
39. (b) Use 'who' in place of 'whom'.'Woman' who is the subject here will take 'who'.
40. (b) Change 'who' into 'which'. 'Of' is preceded by 'which' and not 'who/whom'.
41. (c) Change 'their' into 'its'. 'Congress Party' is singular and will take singular adjective 'its'.
42. (c) Change 'he meets' into 'they meet'.'Those' will take 'they' and not 'he'.
43. (b) Change 'me' into 'my'. A possessive adjective comes before a gerund (joining).
44. (a) According to rule 231 rule you, he, and I is the correct order.
45. (a) 'was it I' is the correct formation. This is the interrogative form of

'It was $\underbrace{\textbf{I}}_{\text{Nominative case}}$'

46. (c) Change 'its' into 'their'. For individual persons/things, plural pronoun and plural verb are used.
47. (c) Add 'that of' before 'on'. 'That of' refers to 'the number of vehicles'.
48. (a) 'Being' should be preceded by 'he'. If 'He' is not made the subject of destitute, I becomes the subject of destitute and the meaning of the sentence becomes wrong.
49. (b) Use one's in place of 'his'. 'Ones' is the possessive case of 'one'.
50. (b) Add 'myself' after enjoyed. If there is no object after the verb 'enjoy', a reflexive pronoun follows the verb.
51. (a) Change 'him' into 'he'. Here 'him' is not an object.
52. (a) Add 'It' before being to make the sentence meaningful. See sentence 48.
53. (b) Change 'their' into 'his'. 'one' is a singular pronoun and hence will take singular possessive case 'his'.
54. (b) Remove 'He'. Noun has already been used in this sentence.
55. (c) Change 'she' into 'they'. Here the sentence changes after 'and' and hence plural pronoun 'they' will be used as now all the girls are being referred to.
56. (a) Change 'myself' into 'I'. Reflexive pronoun cannot come in place of subject.
57. (b) Change 'whose origin' into 'the origin of which' because 'whose' is not used for 'non-living things'.
58. (c) Change 'isn't it ?' into 'Isn't he ?'. See Question Tag.
59. (b) Change 'who' into 'which'. 'Who/whom' cannot come before 'of'.
60. (b) Change 'which' into 'that'. A superlative degree is followed by 'that'.
61. (b) Change 'their' into 'his'. 'Neither of' / 'either of' / 'each of' etc take plural pronoun or noun after them but verb/pronoun in the latter part of the sentence is always singular.

E.g.: Neither of the $\underbrace{\text{two friends}}_{\text{Plural Noun}}$ $\underbrace{\text{has}}_{\text{Singular Verb}}$ got $\underbrace{\text{his}}_{\text{Singular Pronoun}}$ money back.

62. (b) Change 'whose inauguration' into 'the inauguration of which'. 'Whose' is not used for 'non-living things'.
63. (b) A 'reflexive pronoun' must follow reconcile. Add 'themselves' after 'reconcile'.
64. (b) Change 'who' into 'whom' because we need a relative pronoun for an object.
65. (a) Change 'who' into 'whom' because we need a relative pronoun for an object.
66. (a) Change 'me' into 'my'(possessive case) before Gerund 'being'.
67. (b) Change 'me' into 'mine'.
68. (a) Change 'him' into 'he'.
69. (a) According to rule 231, 'Raju and I' is the correct order.
70. (b) Reflexive pronoun 'myself' must follow 'avail'. Subject is 'I' and reflexive pronoun must be 'myself'.
71. (c) Use 'it' after 'making' as the pronoun for 'book' will be 'it'.
72. (b) 'Many' is plural in meaning . Hence it must be followed by 'others' (Plural).
73. (c) Change 'her's' into 'hers'.
74. (b) Change 'Whom' into 'who'.

16 ADJECTIVE

CHAPTER

Adjective –

An adjective is a word that qualifies a noun or a pronoun.

Ram is a good boy.

He is intelligent.

In the above sentences 'good' and 'intelligent' qualify 'Ram' and tell us the qualities of 'he'. Adjectives come before a noun and after a verb.

Types of Adjectives-

There are eight types of Adjectives

1. **Adjective of quality**
2. **Proper adjective**
3. **Adjective of number**
4. **Demonstrative adjective**
5. **Distributive adjective**
6. **Interrogative adjective**
7. **Adjective of quality**
8. **Possessive adjective**

1. **Adjective of quality** – **Adjectives** that show **the kind or quality** of a person or thing.

E.g.: An **honest** man.

Adjective of quality is used in two ways.

(a) **Attributive use** – When an adjective is used before noun, it is said to be used attributively.

E.g.: Solomon was a **wise** king (Noun).

Here wise is used before a noun (king) so it is attributive.

(b) **Predicative use** – When **an adjective is used after verb**, it is said to be used predicatively.

E.g.: The weather is (Verb) **pleasant**

2. **Proper Adjective** – An adjective which is **formed from proper nouns** is called known as proper adjective.

E.g.: **Buddhist** monastery, **British** rule.

Here '**Buddhist**' and '**British**' are proper adjectives.

3. **Adjective of quantity** – An Adjective that shows **how much** of a thing is meant.

E.g.: **Some** milk, **enough** oil, **sufficient** sugar, **no** manners.

Here **some, enough, sufficient** and **no** are adjective of quantity.

4. **Adjective of number** – An Adjective that shows **how many** persons or things are meant or in what order a person or thing stands.

It is of two types:-

(i) **Definite**

(ii) **Indefinite**

(i) **Definite-** Definite denotes an exact number.

E.g.: **Five** boys, **fifth** row.

(ii) **Indefinite:** Indefinite does not denote an exact number.

E.g.: **Few** girls, **several** boys.

(a) **Cardinal Adjective** – **Definite numbers** like **one, two, three, four** are Cardinal adjectives.

E.g.: He has **four** pens.

She has **two** books.

(b) **Ordinal Adjectives** – **Definite order** like **first, second, last** are Ordinal adjectives.

E.g.: The **first** chapter of this book is on verb.

Note: 1. Article **'the'** is used before Ordinal and not before Cardinal.

E.g.: Lesson **one** is on verbs.

The **first** chapter of this book is on verbs.

2. When both Ordinal and Cardinal adjectives come together in a sentence, they are in the order '**OC**'. This means **first 'Ordinal' and then 'Cardinal**.'

E.g.: We will revise the lessons in the **last two** classes.

(5) **Demonstrative Adjective** – The adjective that **points out which person or thing** is meant is known as the demonstrative adjective.

E.g.: **This** boy, **that** group, **these** people, **those** countries.

Note: If **this, that, these** or **those** are immediately followed by a **noun**, these words are called **demonstrative adjectives** and if these words are immediately followed by a **verb,** these words are known as **demonstrative pronouns.**

E.g.	**Demonstrative Adjective**	**Demonstrative Pronoun**
	This girl is good.	**This** is a good girl.
	That pen is new.	**That** is a new pen.
	These shirts are white.	**These** are white shirts.

(6) **Distributive Adjective** – The **Adjective** which refers to each one of the number is known as **distributive adjective.**

E.g.: **Each** candidate is honest.

Every boy is present today.

Note: **If each, every, either** or **neither** is immediately followed by **noun**, it is known as **Distributive Adjective** and if **each, every, either** or **neither** is followed by **some other word**, it is known as **Distributive Pronoun**.

E.g.	**Distributive Adjective**	**Distributive Pronoun**
	Each boy took the test.	**Each** of the boys took the test.

(7) **Interrogative Adjective** – **What, which** and **whose** are interrogative adjectives when they are used with a noun.

E.g.: **Which** room is hers?

Whose book is this?

Note: If '**what**', '**which**', '**whose**' is followed by a noun, these words are interrogative adjectives and if it is followed by a verb, it is known as interrogative pronoun.

E.g.:	**Interrogative Adjective**	**Interrogative Pronoun**
	What colour is your bag?	**What** did you do?

(8) **Possessive Adjectives** – **Adjectives** that shows possession is called possessive Adjective.

E.g.: **My** book, **our** class

COMPARISON OF ADJECTIVES

- An **Adjective** comes in **three degrees** - **positive, comparative** and **superlative degree.**
- **Positive degree** denotes **the quality** of a person, thing or group. It is used when **no comparison** is made.

E.g.: He is a **good** boy.

- When **two things or sets of things are compared**, comparative degree is used.

E.g.: He is **better** than you.

- **Superlative degree** is used to choose **one out of a group or many**.

E.g.: He is the **best** student of my class.

WAYS TO CHANGE POSITIVE INTO COMPARATIVE AND SUPERLATIVE DEGREE

Rule 1

- To change an **adjective** into **comparative degree** '**er**' is added to the **positive degree** and '**est**' is added to change it into **superlative degree.**

Positive	Comparative	Superlative
Bold	Bolder	Boldest
Deep	Deeper	Deepest
High	Higher	Highest
Strong	Stronger	Strongest
Thick	Thicker	Thickest
Weak	Weaker	Weakest

Rule 2

- If **'e'** is present at the end of a **positive degree**, **'r'** is added to change it into a **comparative degree** and **'st'** to change it into **superlative degree.**

Positive	Comparative	Superlative
Able	Abler	Ablest
Brave	Braver	Bravest
Fine	Finer	Finest
Noble	Nobler	Noblest
True	Truer	Truest
Wise	Wiser	Wisest

Rule 3

- If the **positive degree** ends in a **consonant** and a short vowel comes before it, the last consonant is doubled and then '**er**' and '**est**' are added to change it into **comparative** and **superlative degree** respectively.

Positive	Comparative	Superlative
Big	Bigger	Biggest
Fit	Fitter	Fittest
Hot	Hotter	Hottest
Sad	Sadder	Saddest
Thin	Thinner	Thinnest
Wet	Wetter	Wettest

Note: If last consonant is preceded by two vowels, the consonant is not doubled.

Sweet	Sweeter	Sweetest

Rule 4

- When a **positive degree** ends in '**y**' and a **consonant** is present before '**y**', the **'y'** is converted into '**i**', and then '**er**' and '**est**' are added respectively.

Positive	Comparative	Superlative
Dry	Drier	Driest
Happy	Happier	Happiest
Heavy	Heavier	Heaviest
Pretty	Prettier	Prettiest
Merry	Merrier	Merriest
Sweet	Sweeter	Sweetest

Note: If the last consonant is preceded by two vowels, 'er' and 'est' are added without doubling the consonant.

Note: If a vowel is present before **'y'** , only **'er'** and **'est'** should be added.

Positive	Comparative	Superlative
Grey	Greyer	Greyest

Rule 5

➢ Adjectives that are of **more than two syllables**, are changed to **comparative** and **superlative** degree by adding **more** and **most** respectively.

Positive	Comparative	Superlative
Beautiful	more beautiful	most beautiful
Courageous	more courageous	most courageous
Intelligent	more intelligent	most intelligent
Pleasant	more pleasant	most pleasant

Note: Certain **adjectives do not follow any rule**. They get changed completely.

Positive	Comparative	Superlative
Good/well	better	best
Bad/ill	worse	worst
Little	less/lesser	least
Fore	former	foremost/first
Late	later/latter	last/latest
Far	farther	farthest
Near	nearer	nearest/next
Old	older/elder	oldest/eldest
Much/many	more	most

Note: * Well & ill are adverbs

* Less means 'smaller in amount' while lesser means 'of less strength or importance'.

➢ **Correct use of some adjectives**

(1) Use of **'some'** and **'any'**

Some/any means a little but the use is different.

(a) **Some** is used in affirmative sentence before uncountable nouns to denote the quantity and it is used before plural countable nouns to denote number.

E.g.: I have **some** water (U.N.).

I have **some** friends (P.C.N.).

➢ 'Some' is generally used in positive sentences. 'Any' is generally used in negative sentences and questions.

E.g.:(1) I have **some** problems.

(2) I do not have **any** problem.

(3) Do you have **any** problem?

➢ When an answer is expected in 'yes' , 'some' is used in questions too.

E.g.: Do you have some water?

Note:- 'no any' cannot be used together

2. **Use of few, little, much and many,**

Countables

Few — many

little — much

Uncountable

Few
- Few- Hardly any.
- A few- Some but not many.
- The few- Not many but all available.

Little
- Little- Hardly any.
- A little- Some but not much.
- The little- Not much but all that is available.

➢ **Fill in the blanks using few/little, a few / a little or the few / the little**

1. _____ knowledge is a dangerous thing.
2. The doctor advised him to rest for _____ days.
3. _____ water I kept for you has been finished by him.
4. The show was cancelled as ____ people turned up to see it.
5. I cannot prepare tea for you. There is ____ milk in the refrigerat[illegible]

Answers:-

(1) A little (here the sentence means that incomplete knowledge is a [illegible]erous thing. Here we mean that knowledge is available but not much.)

(2) A few ('days' is a countable noun, hence a few is used and not litt[illegible]. A doctor will advise us to rest for atleast some days, hence 'a few' is appropriate.)

(3) The little (water is uncountable and here it means the small quantity of water that I had kept for you, hence 'the little' is appropriate.)

(4) Few (If very few people come, the show gets cancelled, hence 'few' is appropriate here which means 'hardly any'.)

(5) Little (when milk is in negligible quantity, tea cannot be prepared).

➢ **Little** & **few** cannot be used with **quantity & number**. Instead **'small'** is used with them.

E.g.: Little quantity of food was wasted. (×)

Small quantity of food was wasted. (✓)

SOME CORRECT USES OF ADJECTIVE

Rule 1

- **Positive degree of adjective / adverb** comes in between **'as......as'** and **'so.....as'**.

E.g.: He is **as** good (Adj.) **as** his brother

He ran **as** fast (Adv.) **as** he could.

Rule 2

- **'Adjective + er .... than'** indicates the presence of a **comparative degree**. Comparative degree comes before '**than**'.

E.g.: He is better **than** his brother.

'**Than**' may or may not come after a comparative degree.

E.g.: Today I am feeling **better.**

Rule 3

- **'The'** is used before a superlative degree.

E.g.: He is **the best** player of the team.

Rule 4

- When **one is chosen out of two**, we use a **comparative degree preceded by** '**the**' **and followed by** '**of**'.

E.g.: She is the best of two sisters. (×)

She is **the better of** two sisters. (✓)

- If **one is chosen out of** '**more than two**' **or** '**all**', **superlative degree** is used **preceded by** '**the**' and **followed by** '**of**'.

E.g.: He is **the best of** the three/all the players.

Rule 5

When **two qualities** of a noun or a pronoun are compared with each other, **more + positive degree** is used instead of a comparative degree.

E.g.: He is wiser than intelligent.(×)

He is **more wise** than intelligent. (✓)

Rule 6

- If **one is compared with all the others** of the same variety, '**any other**' is used to **exclude the former**.

E.g.: Gold is more precious than any metal. (×)

Gold is more precious than **any other** metal. (✓)

Look at the following sentences:

Diamond is more precious than any metal. (✓)

The above sentence is correct because diamond is not a metal.

Rule 7

- Adjectives that end in **'ior'** are followed by **'to'** and not **'than'.**

E.g.: **Superior, inferior, senior, junior, prior, anterior, posterior.**

He is senior than me. (×) (Replace 'than' by **'to'**)

Rule 8

- **Adjectives** like '**interior**', '**exterior**', '**ulterior**', '**major**', '**minor**', '**empty**', '**excellent**', '**circular**', '**extreme**', '**chief**', '**entire**', '**complete**', '**perfect**', '**final**', '**last**', '**unique**', '**universal**', '**round**', '**square**', '**triangular**', '**eternal**', '**everlasting**', '**ideal**', '**absolute**', '**impossible**' **and** '**supreme**' '**free**' and '**vacant**' are **not used in comparative degree or superlative degree**.

E.g.:
1. Good deeds are more everlasting. (Remove more)
2. This is the most unique creation. (×)
   This is a unique creation. (✓)

Rule 9

- Some adjectives are used in **only positive and superlative degree** and not in comparative degree.

Positive	**Superlative**
Top	Topmost
Bottom	Bottomost
Northern	Northernmost
Southern	Southernmost
Eastern	Easternmost
Western	Westernmost

Rule 10

- Adjective '**preferable**' is used in only **comparative degree.**
- '**Preferable**' is followed by '**to**' and not '**than**' or '**more**'. **Prefer**' (verb) is followed by '**to**' and not '**than**'.

E.g.: This is more preferable **to** that. (×)

This is preferable **to** that. (✓)

Rule 11

- If two adjectives are used for a single noun or pronoun and if both adjectives are connected by a conjunction, both the adjectives must be in same degree.

E.g.: Gandhiji was noblest and wiser of all the leaders. (×)

Gandhiji was the **noblest** and **wisest** of all the leaders. (✓)

Rule 12

- If '**the**' is used before an adjective, the adjective becomes a plural common noun. It will hence take a plural verb.

E.g.: **rich, poor, needy, aged, blind, dead, meek, wicked** etc.

1. **The rich** (rich people) usually exploit **the poor**. (poor people)
2. **The honest are** rewarded.

Rule 13

- Verbs are modified by adverbs.

E.g.: He works (V) honestly (adv.).

- 'ly' is added to an adjective to convert it into an adverb (except in some cases)

E.g.:

Adjective	Adverb
Polite	Politely
Bad	Badly
Sincere	Sincerely

- But **verbs of sensation (seem, look, appear, feel, taste, sound and smell)** is followed by an **adjective and not** an **adverb.**

E.g.: He feels badly. (×)

He feels **bad.** (✓)

The soup smells deliciously. (×)

The soup smells **delicious.** (✓)

- Apart from **verbs of sensation 'be', 'become', 'turn**', '**get**', '**grow**', '**keep**', '**make**' '**stay**', '**remain' and** '**prove**' are also modified by adjective and not adverbs.

E.g.: When he heard the news, he became sad (adj).

Rule 14

- Many nouns are a part of **Hyphenated or compound adjectives**. They never come in plural form.

E.g.: I delivered a two hours lecture. (×)
I delivered a **two-hour** lecture. (✓)
He gave me two hundred-rupees notes. (×)
He gave me two **hundred-rupee** notes. (✓)

Rule 15

- If a **noun works as an adjective**, it **cannot** be in **plural form.**

E.g.: 1) Lasers are indispensable tools for delicate eyes surgery. ('eye' in place of 'eyes')
2) He has undergone knee surgery.

Rule 16

- Some adjectives are confusing in their meaning. Hence they should be used carefully.

(1) **Farther and Further** – Farther means 'at a greater distance'.

E.g.: She lives at the **farther** end of the lane.
Further means 'in addition'

E.g.: I did not receive any **further** order.

(2) **Last and latest**
Last means 'after all others'.

E.g.: The **last** ruler of Mughal Empire was Bahadur Shah Jafar.
Latest means 'newest or recent'

E.g.: What is the **latest** score?

(3) **Elder and older** – **Elder/eldest** means **'of earlier birth'**. It shows blood relation.
E.g.: He is my **elder** brother.
Older/Oldest means **'of earlier time'**.
E.g.: He is **older** than his uncle.

(4) **Nearest and next**
Nearest means **'within a short distance'.**
E.g.: Which is the **nearest** hospital?
Next means '**immediately adjacent**'.
E.g.: The bank is in the **next** building.

(5) **Later and latter**
Later means 'at some time subsequent to a given time'.
E.g.: I will call you later.
Latter means 'second of the two'.
E.g.: The **latter** part of the movie was boring.
Note- **Former** is the opposite of **latter.**

(6) **Less and Lesser**
Less means 'smaller in quantity'.
E.g.: There is **less** rainfall in this area.
Lesser means 'of less strength, quality, or importance'.
E.g.: There are many **lesser** gods in Hinduism.

Rule 17

➢ Possessive case comes after **'All'** and **'Both'** and not before them.

E.g.: 1. My all friends have got selected. (×)
All my friends have got selected. (✓)
2. **Both my** brothers are in Delhi.

Rule 18

➢ If both **positive and comparative degree** of an **adjective** are used in a single sentence, both **'as....as'** & **'than'** will be used.

➢ **Positive degree** is used with **'as ....as'** and **'so....as'** and **comparative degree** is used with **'than'**.

E.g.: 1. He is **as** intelligent **as** if not more **than** his brother.
2. She is not **so** beautiful **as** though fairer **than** you.

Rule 19

➢ Comparative degree does not come with the word **'times'/ 'twice'/ 'thrice'**.

E.g.: My house is four times bigger than yours. (×)
My house is four times as big as yours. (✓)

Rule 20

➢ If **adjective of size, colour, age** etc. come together in a sentence, they should be used in the following order:

Number (1) → **Opinion** (2) → **Size** (3) → **Age** (4) → **Shape** (5) → **Colour** (6) → **Origin** (7) → **Material** (8) → **Purpose** (9) noun

E.g.: 1. I bought **beautiful** (opinion), **tiny** (size), **heart-shaped** (shape), **purple** (colour), **American** (origin), **diamond** (material) for my **wedding** (purpose) ring.

2. The thief flashed a **big** (size) **sharp** (shape) knife and asked the cashier to fill the **black** (colour) **leather** (material) bag with money.

We can remember the order as **NOSASCOMP**.

Number- one, many
Opinion- beautiful, pretty , ugly etc.
Size- big, small, tiny, minute etc.
Age- old, new, recent etc.
Shape- round, oval, heart-shaped etc.
Colour- Blue, red, pink etc.
Origin- Indian, German etc.
Material-wooden, leather etc.
Purpose- wedding, dining, sleeping etc.

Note:- 'Tall, dark and handsome' or 'fair and beautiful' are such common examples that have opinion after colour.

Rule 21

➢ Two **comparative** and two **superlative degrees** never come together as the sentence will become superfluous.

E.g.:1. He is the most cleverest of all the officers. (×)
He is the cleverest of all the officers. (✓)
2. This is more better than that. (×)
This is better than that. (✓)

Rule 22

➢ If different **prepositions** are needed with different **adjectives,** suitable **prepositions** must be used with each of them.

E.g.: He is senior and more experienced than you. (×)
He is senior to and more experienced than you. (✓)

SPOTTING THE ERROR

1. (a) Anurag is eclipsed by his wife, / (b) who is cleverer and / (c) amusing than he is. /(d) No error
2. (a) The two first to arrive / (b) were the lucky recipients / (c) of a surprise gift. /(d) No error
3. (a) Of the billions of stars in the galaxy, (b) how much are / (c) suitable for life? / (d) No error
4. (a) A few word of / (b) gratitude are enough / (c) to express your / (d) feelings sincerely. / (e) No error.
5. (a) He feels his troubles / (b) as much or / (c) even more than they. / (d) No error
6. (a) The recently hike / (b) in the price of petroleum products / (c) will hit / (d) household budgets severely.
7. (a) There is not many traffic / (b) along the street / (c) where I live. / (d) No error
8. (a) The police arrived and discovered / (b) a large number of hoarded sugar/ (c) in his shop. / (d) No error
9. (a) As a dramatist / (b) Shaw is superior than / (c) any other twentieth century writer. / (d) No error
10. (a) Of the two great cities/ (b) the former is / (c) biggest. / (d) No error
11. (a) A non banking financial company is a / (b) financial institution similarly to a bank / (c) but it cannot issue cheque books to customers. / (d) No error
12. (a) Everyone agrees that / (b) the Ganga is the holiest / (c) of all other rivers of India. / (d) No error.

13. (a) Krishna ran to the / (b) nearing grocery store to / (c) buy biscuits as his parents were expecting guests. / (d) No error
14. (a) While giving a loan/ (b) you must check / (c) if the borrower has sufficiently collateral to repay it. / (d) No error
15. (a) Although his speech / (b) was not very clearly everyone understood / (c) the underlying meaning. / (d) No error
16. (a) He is the most / (b) intelligent and also / (c) the very talented student of the college. / (d) No error
17. (a) Having been found / (b) guilty of the theft / (c) Sunny was sentenced to five year's imprisonment. / (d) No error
18. (a) The Railways have made / (b) crossing the tracks / (c) a punished offence. / (d) No error
19. (a) Alms / (b) are given / (c) to the poors. / (d) No error
20. (a) Lasers are / (b) indispensable tools / (c) for the delicate eyes surgery. / (d) No error
21. (a) The number of applications has risen / (b) this year by / (c) as many as 50%. / (d) No error
22. (a) Two lakh of people / (b) attended the meeting / (c) held in the parade ground. / (d) No error
23. (a) These sort of men / (b) attain success by hook or by crook / (c) so they do not deserve any applause. (d) No error
24. (a) Can you tell me how / (b) many eggs and / (c) milk he has brought / (d) No error
25. (a) Whole the chapter / (b) is full of printing errors which are the outcome / (c) of the proof reader's carelessness. (d) No error
26. (a) Her black long / (b) hair adds / (c) glamour to her looks. (d) No error
27. (a) I trembled when I saw / (b) a sharp long knife / (c) in his hand. / (d) No error
28. (a) I saw / (b) an anxious pale girl / (c) who was fidgetting near the ICU / (d) No error
29. (a) Mumbai is / (b) further from / (c) Delhi than / (d) Patna. (e) No error
30. (a) This book is / (b) undoubtedly preferable than / (c) that and its printing / (d) is also comparatively good. (e) No error
31. (a) You can trust / (b) this channel/ (c) for the last news of this hour. (d) No error
32. (a) Everybody knows / (b) that Radha is the most unique / (c) singer of this college / (d) No error
33. (a) The faster he completes / (b) the work given to / (c) him, the largest will be his profit. / (d) No error.
34. (a) He does not have / (b) some money to buy a new machine so he is / (c) anxious / (d) No error
35. (a) This young lady is / (b) more beautiful but not so cultured / (c) as her sister. (d) No error
36. (a) Now-a-days, / (b) the weather / (c) is getting cold and colder. / (d) No error
37. (a) This photograph / (b) was comparatively better / (c) than that which he had kept in his purse. / (d) No error
38. (a) Ram is as good, / (b) if not better than / (c) they./ (d) No error
39. (a) Gopal felt happily / (b) to learn that I / (c) had got a job in the Bank./ (d) No error
40. (a) He is comparatively / (b) weaker / (c) in maths / (d) No error.
41. (a) Many a / (b) boys are / (c) absent today / (d) No error.
42. (a) Honest are / (b) rewarded / (c) sooner or later / (d) No error.

43. (a) My all / (b) friends will come / (c) tomorrow to meet me / (d) No error.
44. (a) He is wiser / (b) enough to / (c) understand your trick / (d) No error.
45. (a) Ramayana is more / (b) sacred than / (c) all the mythologies of Hindus / (d) No error.
46. (a) He offered / (b) me a / (c) steamed cup of tea / (d) No error.
47. (a) I will buy / (b) the book when / (c) the revise edition comes / (d) No error.
48. (a) He ran so fastly / (b) that he reached / (c) the destination in just two minutes. / (d) No error.
49. (a) I am sure that / (b) all my monthly expenses / (c) would exceed the income if I do not economise. / (d) No error.
50. (a) I am more lonelier/ (b) here than/ (c) I was in the USA./ (d) No error.
51. (a) To me it appears that/ (b) Anthropology is the more interesting/ (c) of all the subjects./ (d) No error.
52. (a) The circulation of The Statesman/ (b) is greater than/ (c) that of any newspaper/ (d) No error.
53. (a) In the garden/ (b) were the more beautiful flowers/ (c) and silver bells./ (d) No error.
54. (a) In his old age,/ (b) a person is likely to get/ (c) more weak day by day./ (d) No error.

Answers with explanation

1. (c) Add 'more' before 'amusing'. Both 'more amusing' and 'cleverer' must be in the same degree because both the adjectives are joined by a conjunction.
2. (a) 'Two first' should be converted to 'first two'.
3. (b) Change 'much' into 'many' as 'stars' come under countable noun. Stars are not uncountable but are rather countless.
4. (a) Change 'word' into 'words' because 'a few' is followed by plural countable noun.
5. (b) Correct use is 'as much as'. If both positive and comparative degree of an adjective are used in a single sentence, both 'as....as' & 'than' will be used.
6. (c) We need an Adjective 'recent' to qualify the Noun (hike) here. 'Recently' is an Adverb.
7. (a) 'Traffic' is an uncountable noun. Hence change 'many' into 'much'.
8. (b) 'Sugar' is an uncountable noun. Hence change 'number' into 'quantity'.
9. (b) 'Superior' is followed by 'to' and not 'than'.
10. (c) Change 'biggest' to ' the bigger'. When one is chosen out of two, a comparative degree is used.
11. (b) 'Similarly' is an adverb, that qualifies a verb. 'Similar' must come here because an adjective qualifies a noun.
12. (c) Change 'all other rivers' into 'all the rivers'.
13. (b) Change 'nearing' into 'nearby' or 'nearest'.
14. (c) Sufficient (adjective) explains the quality of 'collateral' which is a noun. 'Sufficiently' is an adverb.
15. (b) 'Clearly' is an adverb, which qualifies a verb. Clear (adjective) explains the quality of speech (noun).
16. (c) Change 'very' into 'most'. If two adjectives are joined by a conjunction, both the adjectives should be in the same degree. Hence use 'most intelligent' with 'most talented'.
17. (c) Hyphenated adjective is always in singular form. 'Five-year imprisonment' is the correct form.
18. (c) 'Punishable' is the adjective form of 'punish'.

19. (c) 'The poor' means 'the deprived people'.
20. (c) 'Eyes' a noun atcs as an adjective in 'eyes surgery' because here 'eyes' qualifies 'surgery'. If a noun works as an adjective, it must be in singular form. Change 'eyes' into 'eye'.
21. (c) 'Much' will come with 50%. Here a plural number is used as a singular unit.
22. (a) 'Of' doesn't come with definite numeral adjective.
    E.g.: Two lakh people.
    Indefinite numeral adjective takes 'of'.
    E.g.: Lakhs of people.
23. (a) 'These' is plural and hence will take 'sorts' and not 'sort'.
24. (c) 'Milk' being uncountable noun will take 'how much'.
25. (a) 'The' is used before 'whole'.
26. (a) 'Long black' is the correct order. 'Adjective of size' comes before 'adjective of colour'.

    Long (Adj. of size) black (Adj. of colour) hair.
27. (b) 'Long sharp knife' is the correct order according to OSASCOMP.
28. (b) Adjective of human emotion/ personality comes after adjective of colour.

    a pale (Adj. of colour) anxious (Adj. of emotion) girl.
29. (b) The correct word is 'farther' (denotes distance)
30. (b) 'to' comes with 'preferable'.
31. (c) Change 'last' into 'latest'.
32. (b) 'Unique' does not come in superlative or comparative degree. Change 'the most unique' into 'a unique'.
33. (c) 'The larger' will come with 'the faster'.
34. (b) Change 'some' into 'any' as the sentence is negative.
35. (b) Add 'than' after 'more beautiful'.
36. (c) Change 'cold' into 'colder'. To show a gradual change, we use adjectives in comparative degree.
37. (b) Change 'better' into 'good'. Comparative degree doesn't come with the word 'comparatively'.
38. (a) Add 'as' after 'as good'.
39. (a) 'happy' (Adjective) will come in place of 'happily'(adverb). Adjectives come with verbs of sensation.
40. (b) The word 'comparatively' is not used with a comparative degree. Change 'weaker' into 'weak'.
41. (b) 'Many a' takes 'singular noun' and 'singular verb'. Change 'boys are' into 'boy is'.
42. (a) 'Honest' is an adjective but becomes a plural common noun when article 'the' is used before it. 'The honest' means honest people.
43. (a) Change 'My all' into 'all my'.
44. (a) Change 'wiser' to 'wise'. 'Enough' takes positive degree before it.
45. (c) 'All other mythologies' is more appropriate as this will exclude 'Ramayana'.
46. (c) Change 'steamed cup' into 'steaming cup'.
47. (c) Change 'revise' to 'revised'.
48. (a) Change 'fastly' into 'fast'.
49. (b) Do not use 'all'. 'Monthly expenses' includes 'all the expenses'.
50. (a) Remove 'more'. Two comparative degrees do not come together.
51. (b) Use superlative degree most.
52. (c) Use 'any other newspaper'. 'Any newspaper' includes 'The Statesman' too.
53. (b) Change 'more' into 'most'.
54. (c) Change 'more weak' into 'weaker'.

17 CONJUNCTION

CHAPTER

- **Conjunction** is a **word**, or a **group of words** which **connects** two or more than two **words, phrases, clauses, sentences etc.**

Eg.:1. **Ram** and **Shyam** will come.

↑___Words___↑

2. **People's ignorance** and **population explosion** are two inter-related problems.

↑____Phrases____↑

3. **She said** that **she would come**.

↑____Clauses____↑

- In sentence (1) **'and'** joins two words '**Ram**' and '**Shyam**'. In sentence (2) **'and'** joins two phrases '**people ignorance**' and '**population explosion**' and in sentence (3) **'that'** joins two sentences 'she said' and 'she would come'. Hence 'and' as well as 'that' are conjunctions.
- **Some common conjunctions are**

And	**As well as**
Otherwise, or, else	**So, hence**
Therefore, hence	**Either.....or**
Consequently	**Both.... and**
Neither... nor	**Too....to**
So....that	**As........as**
So.......as	**As...........so**
Whether......or	**But**
As soon as	**No sooner.......than**
Or...........	**Scarcely.......when**
Not only........but also	**Hardly.........when**
Where	
Wherever	**When**
Whenever	**Until/Unless....,**
While	**Because**
As.... ,	**Lest......should**
Such.....that	**If**
Provided	**As if**
Though ... yet/ ,	**Although ... yet/ ,**
Whereas	**Nevertheless**
As though	**As far as**

TYPES OF CONJUNCTION

Conjunctions are of two types:-

1. Co-ordinating conjunction
2. Sub-ordinating conjunction

1. CO-ORDINATING CONJUNCTION:- Read the following sentences-

1. He read the notes **and** returned it to me.
2. He came to meet me, **but** I was not at home.
3. She worked hard **yet** she failed.
4. He is foolish (Adj.) and miserly (Adj.).
5. He is foolish and miserly.

Co-ordinating Conjunctions join words of equal rank i.e., Adjective with Adjective, Adverb with Adverb and so on.

➢ **Co-ordinating conjunctions are of four types:**

(i) **Cumulative Conjunctions:**

'And', **'also'**, **'both ..... and'**, **'as well as'**, **'now'**, **'too'**, **'no less than'**.

➢ These conjunctions connect two nouns, pronouns etc.

E.g.: 1. He is rich (adj.) **and** happy (adj.).

2. Ram (Noun) **as well as** Shyam (Noun) is coming.

(ii) **Alternative Conjunctions:**

'Either .... Or', 'Neither .... Nor', 'else' or 'otherwise'

➢ Where we have to choose one out of two given alternatives, we use alternative conjunctions.

E.g.:(1) **Either** sit quietly **or** go away.

(2) You must run fast **else** you will miss the train.

(iii) **Adversative Conjunctions:**

'But', **'yet'**, **'still'**, **'only'**, **'however'**, **'nevertheless'** are used to join such nouns, pronouns, sentences etc that denote that the result is opposite to the action.

E.g.:(a) He is rich **but** he is not happy.

(b) He is industrious **still** he does not get good marks.

(iv) **Illative Conjunctions:** Illative conjunctions join two actions in which one action is the result of the other action.

E.g.: I was ill **so** I could not come.

2. SUB-ORDINATING CONJUNCTIONS: Read the following sentences.

(a) **If** you work hard, you will succeed.

(b) **Since** I was busy, I could not call you up.

- In these sentences, conjunctions like '**if**', '**since**' etc join two clauses. If sentence are divided into clauses, one will be the **principal clause** and the other the **subordinate clause.** Here the subordinate clause depends on the principal clause.
- The conjunction which joins a subordinates clause is called subordinating conjunction. Here the conjunction is needed to make the sentence meaningful.
- The following Subordinating conjunction are used depending on the meaning of the sentence.

(i) Time : When, whenever, till, until, before, since, while, as soon as, as long as, just as.

1. **When** I saw him, I stopped my car.
2. **As soon** as it rains, the farmers will sow the seeds.

(ii) Place : Where, wherever,

1. We found frogs **where** we found insects.

(iii) Cause : Since, because, as,

1. She came **because** I called her up.
2. **As** he is a miser, no one likes him.

(iv) Purpose : That, so that, in order that, lest

1. We eat **so that** we may live.
2. Run fast **lest** you **should** miss the train.

(v) Result : So . . . . . that, such . . . that

1. He is **so** weak **that** he cannot even stand.
2. He is **such** a fool **that** he doesn't understand anything.

(vi) Condition : If, unless, provided.

1. He cannot succeed **unless** he works hard.
2. I will help him **provided** he mends his ways.

(vii) Manner : As, as if, as though, as far as.

1. He scolds me **as if** he were my father.

Note : If'**as'** denotes the reason, it is not followed by '**so**'

As I was ill, so I could not come (Remove 'so')

'Since' is also not followed by '**so**'.

Since he is a liar , so I do not trust him. (Remove 'so')

(viii) Comparison : As, as ..... as, so......as, than

1. A wise enemy is better **than** a foolish friend.
2. He is **as good as** she at English.

Note:

(1) **So ..... as/as........as** is used to make a comparison between two person or things.

(A) **So... as** is used in **negative** Sentences.

E.g.: He is not **so** good **as** you. (Negative)

➢ But **As .... as** is used in both **Affirmative** and **Negative** sentences.

E.g.: He is **as** good **as** you. (Affirmative)

He is **not as** good **as** you. (Negative)

(ix) **Contrast (Difference): however.**

(a) I tried very hard **however** I could not win the race.

(3) **Correlative Conjunction:**

Conjunctions that appear in pair are correlative conjunction.

E.g.: **'Either ... or', 'neither ... nor', both .... and, not only .... but also, though .... yet, whether ... or.**

E.g.: **Neither** his friends **nor** his parents knew about his evil intention.

I do not know **whether** he will come **or** not.

(4) **Compound Conjunction:**

A group of words used as a conjunction is called **Compound conjunction.**

In order that: The announcement was made **in order that** all might know the new date of exam.

On condition that: I will give you money **on condition that** you will not misuse it.

Even if: She will succeed in life **even if** she faces some initial failures.

So that: We eat **so that** we may live.

Provided that: You can take any dress **provided that** you return it after the party.

As though: He shows off **as though** he were a king.

As well as: Ram **as well as** his friends has come to the party.

As soon as: The farmers will sow the seeds **as soon as** it rains.

As if: He scolds me **as if** he were my father.

➢ Questions are frequently asked from the following rules -

Rule 1

(1) **And** (2) **As well as**

(3) **Both .... and** (4) **Not only .... but also**

➢ These co-relatives are used to join nouns, pronouns etc. but as far as adjectives are concerned, they join two desirable or two undesirable adjectives but not a desirable adjective with an undesirable one.

E.g.: He is **both** intelligent **and** hard working.

He is **not only** dishonest **but also** lazy.

Rule 2

➢ If two subjects are joined by **'as well as'/'with'/'alongwith'/ 'and not'/ 'in addition to'/ 'but'/'besides'/'except'/ 'rather than'/'accompanied by',** the verb agrees with the first subject.

E.g. **Ram as well as** his friends is coming.

He and not his parents is guilty.

Rule 3

➤ Many times conjunctions are used at wrong places. In a sentence, the conjunction must not be misplaced.

E.g.: Not only he cheated his friends but also his parents. (×)

He cheated **not only** his friends (1st Noun) **but also** his parents (2nd Noun). (✓)

➤ In this sentence 'his friends' and 'his parents' are the two nouns we are talking about. 'Not only' should come before 'his friends' and 'but also' should come before 'his parents'.

Other examples:-

1. Sit either quietly or go away. (×)
2. Neither the poor villagers grow nor eat vegetables. (×)

➤ Both the sentences are wrong because when conjunctions are in pairs (co-relative), the position of the conjunction matters.

E.g.:(1) **Either** sit (1st Verb) quietly **or** go (2nd Verb) away. (✓)

(2) The poor villagers **neither** grow (1st Verb) **nor** eat (2nd Verb) vegetables. (✓)

Rule 4

➤ When conjunction are in pairs, the pair must be correct.

Some Common Conjunctions	**Some Common Conjunctions**
And	**As well as**
Otherwise, or else	**So, hence**
Therefore,	**Either.....or**
Consequently	**Both.... and**
Neither... nor	**Too....to**
So....that	**As........as**
So.......as	**As...........so**
Whether......or	**But**
As soon as	**No sooner.......than**
Or............	**Scarcely.......when**
Not only........but also	**Hardly.........when**
Where	**Wherever**

When	**Whenever**
Until/Unless....,	**Doubt ... if/ whether (In Positive sentences)**
While	**Doubt ... that (in Negative and Interrogative sentence)**
Because	
As.... ,	**Lest......should**
Such.....that	**If**
Provided	**As if**
Though	**Although**
Whereas	**Nevertheless**
As though	**As far as**

E.g.: (1) Though he worked hard but he failed. (×)
Though he worked hard **yet** he failed. (✓)
(2) He is both intelligent as well as industrious. (×)
He is **both** intelligent **and** industrious. (✓)
(3) The party is **between** 7 p.m **to** 9 p.m. (×)
(4) The party is **from** 7 p.m **to** 9 p.m. (✓)
(5) I have **no other** aim but to succeed in life. (×)
(6) I have **no other** aim **than** to succeed in life. (✓)
(7) Nothing **else but** arrogance ruined him. (✓)
(8) He asked me if I was coming or not. (×)
(9) He asked me **whether** I was coming or not. (✓)

Rule 5

So ... that
Too .... to

E.g.: (1) I am so happy. (×)
I am **very** happy. (✓)
(2) He is **so** tired **that** he cannot walk. ('too ... to' can be used in place of so... that)
He is **too** tired **to** walk.
(3) It is **too** hot **to** go out.
It is **so** hot **that** we cannot go out.
(4) She is **so** weak **that** she cannot walk.
She is **too** weak **to** walk.
(5) This problem is **so** complicated **that** no one can solve it.
This problem is **too** complicated for anyone **to** solve.

➢ Explanation to sentence 5 If **'any one'** is not mentioned before **'to solve',** 'this problem' becomes the subject of 'solve' and the meaning of sentence will become wrong. Always remember that if the subject changes the **2nd** subject must be mentioned before **'to + $V_{b.f}$'.**

(6) It is **so** expensive **that** I cannot buy it.
It is **too** expensive for me **to** buy.

- Another method: In sentences 5 and 6, the second part of sentence can be converted into **passive voice,** and the 2nd subject can be mentioned in 'by + subject'.

  The **2nd sub** which is different from the **1st sub** comes in 'by+sub' and then the meaning of sentence becomes correct.

  Infinitive- **To + V_1** (active voice).

  - **To + be + V_3** (passive voice).

- This problem is too complicated **to be solved**.
- It is too expensive **to be bought** by me.

Rule 6

Neither ..... nor (none of the two)

Either .... or (one of the two)

Neither Ram **nor** Shyam (S.S.) has (S.V.) come.

Neither Ram **nor** his friends (P.S.) have (P.V.) come.

Has (S.V.) Ram (S.S.) **or** his friends come?

- If two subjects are joined by **'neither ... nor', 'either .... or', 'nor' and 'or'** the verb agrees with the nearest subject.

Rule 7

- **'Neither of'** means '**none of the two**'. If '**more than two persons or things**' are present, '**none of**' is used.
- **Either of ....** means **'one of the two'**. If **more than two persons or things** are present, '**one of**' is used.

E.g.: **None of** his four sons looked after him. (✓)

Either of the students of your class has done this mischief. (×)

One of the students of your class has done this mischief. (✓)

Rule 8

As soon as ....

As soon as he will come, I will call you up. (×)

As soon as he comes, I will call you up. (✓)

If **two actions take place one after the other in future** and **if the second action depends on the first**, the **first action will be in Present Indefinite Tense** and the **second action will be in Future Indefinite Tense**. (see Future conditional sentences)

Rule 9

Note: '**If/when**' is **not** followed by '**then**'.

E.g.: When I come, ~~then~~, I will meet you.

- Similarly '**since / as / because**' are not followed by '**so/therefore/ hence/ that's why**'.

E.g.: Since I was ill, I could not come.

Note: 'As you sow, so shall you reap' (a phrase where 'as' is followed by 'so')

Rule 10

No sooner ..... than

Hardly ....when

Scarcely........ when

Note: (1)Always use the correct pair.

E.g.: 1. **No sooner** did he see me, when he ran away. (Replace 'when' by '**than**')

2. No Sooner had the thief seen the police then he ran away. (Replace 'then' by '**than**')

(2) These three **co-relatives** are used only in **past tense.**

(3) If a sentence starts with 'Hardly', 'Scarcely' , ' No sooner', 'Not only', 'Neither' etc., the sentence formation following these conjunctions will be in inverted form i.e. '**helping verb + sub + main verb' (here 'Had + S + V_3' or 'Did + S + V_1')** but this does not make the sentence interrogative in meaning.

E.g.: Hardly I saw him when I stopped my car. (×)

Hardly did I see him **when** I stopped my car. (✓)

Rule 11

Lest .... Should

.... or ......

..... otherwise .....

- **Use the correct pair.**

Run fast lest you will miss the train. (×)

Run fast **lest** you **should** miss the train.(✓)

Note: 'Lest' can also take simply '**V_1**' after it.

Take care lest he fall.(✓)(Not 'falls')

Rule 12

'Unless', 'until' and 'till'

1. There is a difference between **'until'** and **'unless'.** 'Until' is 'time oriented' and 'unless' is 'action oriented'.

E.g.: **Until** the light turns red, no one will stop.

Unless you work hard, you won't succeed.

2. We do not begin a sentence with **'till'.**

E.g.: **Till** the train gets the signal, it will not proceed. (×)

('**till**' must be converted into 'until')

Rule 13

- 'Until/unless' is not followed by 'not'.

E.g.: **Until** the train will not get the signal it will not run. (×)
Until the train gets the signal, it will not run.
Note: **'Will/would/shall'** does **not** come after '**until**' and '**unless**'. (✓)

E.g.: Unless the Government will not take action, corruption will not stop. (×)
Unless the Government takes action, corruption will not stop. (✓)

Rule 14

- In **affirmative sentences** '**doubt**' and '**doubtful**' are followed by '**if/whether**'. In **negative** or **interrogative** sentences '**doubt**' and '**doubtful**' are followed by '**that**'.

E.g.:

Affirmative sentence	Negative / Interrogative
Doubt __ if / whether	**Doubt __ that**
Doubtful __ if / whether	**Doubtful __ that**

E.g.:1. He doubts that she will help him. (×)
He **doubts if/whether** she will help him.*(Affirmative sentence)*
2. I have no doubt if/whether he will cheat me.(×)
I have **no doubt that** he will cheat me. *(Negative sentence)*
3. I am doubtful that my parents will allow me to go to the party. (×)
I am **doubtful if/whether** he will allow me to go to the party. (*Affirmative sent.*)
4. He is not doubtful if/whether I will finish his work in time (×)
He is **not doubtful that** I will finish his work in time. (*Negative sentence)*

Rule 15

- **'The same'** is followed by '**that**' or '**as**' .
- **'The same'** is followed by '**that**' if a verb comes after '**the same**'.

E.g.:(i) This is **the same** book **that** I wanted (Verb).

(ii) He is **the same boy that** met (Verb) me in the market

- But **'the same'** is followed by **'as'** if there is no verb after **'as'**.

E.g.: This is the same book as mine.

Rule 16

- (i) '**As .... as**' and '**so .... as**' are used for comparison. '**As .... as**' is used in positive as well as negative sentences and '**so ... as**' is used in **Negative** sentences.

E.g.:(1) He is as intelligent as you. (positive sentence)
(2) He is not as intelligent as you. (negative sentence)
(3) He is not so intelligent as you. (negative sentence)

(ii) Only the positive degrees of **Adverbs** and **Adjectives** can be used with '**As .... as**' and '**so ... as**'.

E.g.: (1) He ran **as** faster **as** he could (change faster into **fast**)
(2) He is **as** better **as** you. (change better into **good**)

SPOTTING THE ERROR

1. (a) You are quite cynical/ (b) when you say that the reason why we have/ (c) such a large turnout is because we are serving refreshments./ (d) No error.
2. (a) That store/ (b) hadn't hardly/ (c) any of those goods./ (d) No error.
3. (a) I needed that money/ (b) so desperately, it was/ (c) like manna from heaven when it arrived./ (d) No error.
4. (a) The period/ (b) between 1980 to 1990/ (c) was very significant in my life./ (d) No error.
5. (a) No sooner had the hockey match started/ (b) when it began/ (c) to rain./ (d) No error.
6. (a) She is very/ (b) beautiful/ (c) but intelligent./ (d) No error.
7. (a) Your success in the IAS examinations depends not only on/ (b) what papers you have selected/ (c) but on how you have written them/ (d) No error.
8. (a) No sooner had/ (b) he arrived then/ (c) he was asked to leave again./ (d) No error.
9. (a) I haven't been/ (b) to New York before and/ (c) neither my sister./ (d) No error.
10. (a) Scarcely had/ (b) I arrived than/ (c) the train left./ (d) No error.
11. (a) The reason why/ (b) he was rejected/ (c) was because he was too young./ (d) No error.
12. (a) Unless you do not give/ (b) the keys of the safe/ (c) you will be shot./ (d) No error.
13. (a) None of the diplomats at the conference/ (b) was able either to/ (c) comprehend or solve the problem./ (d) No error.
14. (a) I have found that he is/ (b) neither willing/ (c) or capable./ (d) No error.
15. (a) We are extremely pleased/(b) for excited as well to invite you/(c) to attend the meeting./(d) No error.
16. (a) When her son got a job/ (b) then she was/ (c) very happy./ (d) No error.
17. (a) Bread and butter/ (b) is/ (c) all we want./ (d) No error.
18. (a) The cost of the new/ (b) machines is likely to/ (c) be so high as ten/ (d) times the existing ones./ (e) No error.
19. (a) He walked as faster/ (b) as he could so that/ (c) he would not miss the train to work./ (d) No error.
20. (a) She was running/ (b) a very high fever/(c) and thus her mother takes her to the doctor./(d) No error.
21. (a) No sooner the teacher/ (b) enter the class/ (c) than the students stood up./ (d) No error.
22. (a) Unless/ (b) you will work hard,/ (c) you cannot pass./ (d) No error.

23. (a) Keep him at an arm's length/ (b) lest you may not repent/(c) in the long run./ (d)No error.
24. (a) The briefing/ (b) will be held/ (c) between 2pm. to 3pm./ (d) No error.
25. (a) Unless you do not meet/ (b) all the requirements/ (c) your application will be rejected./ (d) No error.
26. (a) Not only he/ (b) bakes cakes/ (c) but also sells them./ (d) No error.
27. (a) No sooner she had realized/ (b) her blunder than she began/ (c) to take corrective measures./ (d) No error.
28. (a) She was not/ (b) so well versed in/ (c) English that we had expected./ (d) No error.
29. (a) Mr. Sinha, my friend, philosopher and guide not only stopped coming/ (b) here but also going to any place/ (c) which is related to his wife's life./ (d) No error.
30. (a) Neither the doctor nor the nurses/ (b) were asleep when/ (c) the injured was brought to the hospital./ (d) No error.
31. (a) As soon as the peon rings the bell, then all/ (b) the students come to the assembly room/ (c) for prayer./ (d) No error.
32. (a) Hardly had he come out of the bus/ (b) then the bomb exploded/ (c) and shattered the bus into pieces./ (d) No error.
33. (a) Scarcely had I bought/ (b) the ticket when the train/ (c) left the platform with a hissing sound./ (d) No error.
34. (a) Many of the freedom fighters/ (b) are so respectful as Gandhiji/ (c) if not more. / (d) No error.
35. (a) This is perhaps the same place who/ (b) was chosen by us/ (c) for the picnic./ (d) No error.
36. (a) She asked me that why I was/ (b) not preparing for the/ (c) Civil Service Examinations./ (d) No error.
37. (a) Run fast/ (b) lest you will/ (c) lose the race/ (d) No error.
38. (a) As Amir Khan is a perfectionist,/ (b) so he always insists/ (c) on retakes till he is satisfied with the shot./ (d) No error.
39. (a) You must either/ (b) work hard/ (c) else be prepared to lead a miserable life./ (d) No error.
40. (a) I don't know if any of the students/ (b) of our school is going/ (c) to pay any heed to the principal's order or not./ (d) No error.
41. (a) This is not such a/ (b) complicated problem who cannot be solved/ (c) with determination./ (d) No error.
42. (a) Although these books/ (b) are not useful but the students buy them/ (C) because their seniors did so./ (d) No error.
43. (a) He did not/ (b) succeed in the examination,/ (c) yet he had worked hard and had adopted the right strategy./ (d) No error.
44. (a) He has lots/ (b) of money and/ (c) he will not help any one/ (d) No error.
45. (a) Because he is intelligent,/ (b) therefore he gets good/ (c) marks in all the examinations./ (d) No error.

46. (a) Both the rich along with/ (b) the poor are affected equally/ (c) when prices of petrol and diesel increase./ (d) No error.
47. (a) I cannot say/ (b) if he has paid/ (c) the fee or not./ (d) No error.
48. (a) Ten years have passed/ (b) that I returned from/ (c) America and settled in India./ (d) No error.
49. (a) It was almost/ (b) ten years ago since he wrote/ (c) a letter to me enquiring about my well being./ (d) No error.
50. (a) He would not/ (b) have died when you had/ (c) helped him in time./ (d) No error.
51. (a) Scarcely we had/ (b) reached the office/ (c) when it started raining cats and dogs./ (d) No error.
52. (a) The labourers/ (b) relax/ (c) between 4.00 p.m. to 5. 00 p.m./ (d) No error.

Answers with explanation

1. (c) 'Because' doesn't come with 'the reason why' because then the sentence becomes superfluous.
2. (b) 'Hardly' is negative in meaning. 'Not' doesn't come with 'hardly'. 'Had' will come in place of 'hadn't'.
3. (b) 'So' must be followed by 'that'. 'That' will come after 'so desperately'.
4. (b) 'Between' is followed by 'and' and not 'to'. ('from' is followed by to)
5. (b) 'No sooner' is following by 'than' and not when.
6. (c) Change 'but' into 'and'.
7. (c) 'But also' follows 'not only'. Add 'also' after 'but'.
8. (b) 'No sooner' is followed by 'than' and not 'then'.
9. (c) 'Neither' is followed by 'helping verb' and then the subject. 'Neither has my sister' is the correct sentence form.
10. (b) 'Scarcely' is followed by 'when' and not 'than'.
11. (c) 'Because' cannot come with 'the reason why' because then the sentence becomes superfluous.
12. (a) 'Unless' is not followed by 'not'. The sentence must be 'unless you give'.
13. (b) In the given sentence 'comprehend' and 'solve' are the two verbs. Either must come before 'comprehend' because 'or' has been used before 'solve'. Hence put 'either' after 'to'.
14. (c) 'Neither' is followed by 'nor' and not 'or'.
15. (b) Change 'for' into 'and'.
16. (b) 'When' is not followed by 'then'.
17. (c) Add 'that' after 'all'.
18. (c) 'So ..... as' is used in negative sentences. Here 'as .... as' must be used.
19. (a) With 'as .... as' the adjective/adverb will come in their positive degree. Change 'faster' into 'fast'.

20. (c) Change 'thus her mother takes' into 'so her mother took'.
21. (a) 'No sooner' is followed by a 'helping verb' and then the 'sub'. 'No sooner did the teacher enter' will be the correct way of writing this sentence.
22. (b) Will/shall/would do not come with 'unless'/'if'/'until'/'provided'/'before'/'after'/'in case' and 'as soon as'. 'You study hard' must come in place of 'you will study hard'.
23. (a) Change 'may not' into 'should'
24. (c) 'Between' is followed by 'and' and not 'to'. Here we need 'from ... to' as period is given.
25. (a) 'Unless' is not followed by 'not'. 'Unless you meet' will be the correct sentence formation.
26. (a) Put 'not only' after 'he'. It is a question of misplaced conjunction.
27. (a) 'Had' must come after 'no sooner' and then the subject must follow.
28. (c) 'So .... as' is the right pair. 'As' must come in place of 'that' here as category is given here.
29. (a) 'Not only' has come here at the wrong place. It is a matter of misplaced conjunction. 'Not only' must come before 'coming'.
30. (d)
31. (a) 'Then' cannot' come with 'as soon as'.
32. (b) 'Hardly' is followed by 'when' and not 'then'.
33. (d)
34. (b) 'So ... as' is used in negative sentences. Use 'as ... as' in this sentence.
35. (a) 'The same' is followed by 'that' and moreover 'who' is not used for 'places'.
36. (a) The use of 'that' before 'wh family' is wrong when the sentence is in interrogative form in indirect speech. Remove 'why'.
37. (b) 'Lest is followed by 'should' and not 'will'.
38. (b) 'As' is not followed by 'so'.
39. (c) Change 'else' into 'or'. 'Either .... or' is the correct co-relative.
40. (a) Change 'if' into 'whether'.'Whether....or' is the correct pair of conjunction.
41. (b) 'Such is followed by 'that'. Change 'who' into 'that'.
42. (b) 'Although' is not followed by 'but'.
43. (c) Change 'yet' into 'though'.
44. (b) Change 'and' into 'but'.
45. (b) 'because'/'as'/'since' are not followed by 'therefore'.
46. (a) 'Both' is followed by 'and' and not 'along with'.
47. (b) Change 'if' into 'whether'.
48. (b) 'Since' must come in place of 'that'.
49. (b) 'When' will come after 'ago' as a point of time is denoted.
50. (b) Change 'when' into 'if'.
51. (a) Change 'we had' into 'had we'.
52. (c) 'Between' is followed by 'and' and not 'to'.

CHAPTER 18

ARTICLE

'**A**', '**An**', '**The**' are called Articles.

'A' and 'An' 'are' called **Indefinite Articles** while '**the**' is called **Definite Article**.

ARTICLE

↓

Indefinite-A/An | **Definite-The**

➢ A/An are used before singular countable nouns when they are indefinite and introduced for the first time.

(a)	This is book.	(×)	This is **a** book.	(✓)
(b)	She sang song.	(×)	She sang **a** song.	(✓)
(c)	This is umbrella.	(×)	This is **an** umbrella.	(✓)

➢ Where are articles used ?

She is ____excellent. (Here no article will come because there is no noun after excellent. An article needs a noun in absence of which, we cannot use any article.

She is an excellent student.(✓)

➢ An 'article' comes before a 'noun'.

E.g.: She is **a** $\underbrace{\text{student}}_{\text{noun}}$.

➢ If an adjective qualifies the noun, the 'article' comes before the 'adjective'.

E.g.: She is **an** $\underbrace{\text{excellent}}_{\text{adj}}$ $\underbrace{\text{student}}_{\text{noun}}$.

➢ If an 'adverb' qualifies the 'adjective' qualifying the 'noun', the 'article' comes before the 'adverb'.

E.g.: She is **a** $\underbrace{\text{very}}_{\text{adv}}$ $\underbrace{\text{good}}_{\text{adj}}$ $\underbrace{\text{student}}_{\text{noun}}$.

- **Use of A/An**

1. **A/An** are used before **indefinite singular countable nouns.**

   A/An are called indefinite articles.

E.g.: (a) I have **a** car. (c) This is **an** orange.

(b) He sang **a** song. (d) Ram is **a** student.

- **(A) An** is used only before vowel sounds. Remember **'a,e,i,o,u'** do not necessarily produce vowel sound. We must see the Hindi letters if we are comfortable in Hindi because the vowels of Hindi letters (अ, आ, इ, ई, उ, ऊ, ए, ऐ, ओ, औ) can be helpful else we need to learn phonetics.

- **(B)** If the word starts not with vowel sound but with consonant sound, article **'A'** is used.

E.g.: **An** umbrella **A** university **A** union

A year **A** one rupee note **An** honest man

In abbreviation too take care of the pronunciation.

E.g.: (a) He is **an** MLA/ MP (b) He lodged **an** FIR.

(c) He is **an** IAS officer. (d) He is **an** SHO.

(e) I have **an** x-ray machine. (f) She in **an** LL.B graduate.

(g) I have been waiting for **an** hour. (h) He is **an** heir to the throne.

(i) Ram is **an** honest person.

- **Other Examples**

1. **An** hour.
2. **An** honour.
3. **An** honourable person.
4. **An** honest man
5. **An** heir.
6. **A** house
7. **An** honorarium.
8. **A** historical monument.
9. **A** young man.
10. **A** ewe.
11. **An** eagle.
12. **A** European.
13. **A** university.
14. **A** unit.
15. **A** union.
16. **An** Umbrella
17. **A** unique planet.
18. **A** useful book.
19. **A** year.
20. **A** one-rupee note.
21. **A** one-eyed man.
22. **An** orange
23. **An** F.O.
24. **A** forest officer.
25. **An** M.P
26. **A** Member of Parliament.

USE OF INDEFINITE ARTICLE A/AN

1. **A/An** is used before **singular countable nouns** which means that **can be counted.**

E.g.: (a) I have **a** pen.

(b) She has **a** car.

(c) Ram has **an** umbrella.

(d) She is **a** housewife.

Note: Noise is an **uncountable** noun, yet it takes '**a**' before it.

E.g.: (a) Do not make **a** noise.

2. In **exclamatory sentences**, **A/An** is used after '**what**' and '**how**' and before the singular countable noun that comes in the sentence. Check the position of 'Article'.

E.g.: (a) What **a** grand building!
(b) What **a** pretty girl!
(c) How grand **a** building it is!
(d) How pretty **a** girl she is!

3. **In place of 'per'**, **'a/an'** can be used.

E.g.: (a) This car runs twenty kilometres **a** litre.
(b) I earn ten thousand **a** month.
(c) This train runs 27 kilometres **an** hour.

4. With a few words that denote the number of countable nouns such as '**hundred**', '**thousand**', '**million**', '**dozen**', '**couple**' etc '**a**' is used.

E.g.: (a) **A** dozen apples.
(b) I have **a** hundred pens.

5. '**A**' is used before fractions and **half/fractions.**

(a) $2\frac{1}{4}$ m - Two and **a** quarter metre.

(b) $3\frac{1}{2}$ km - Three and **a** half metre.

(c) She has to run **half a** mile everyday.

6. When a verb is used as a noun, it takes article '**A/An**' before it.

E.g.: (a) He goes for **a walk** daily.
(b) He has gone for **a ride.**
(c) I had **a talk** with them.

7. If **many/rather/quite/such** takes a singular noun after them, '**A/An**' is used before the noun.

(a) Many **a** citizen would welcome such a change.
(b) It is rather **a** pity.
(c) It was quite **an** impossible task.
(d) It was such **a** foolish decision.

➢ In a few **phrases A/An** are used. Some of these phrases are-

In a fix, in a hurry, in a nutshell, make a noise, make a foot, keep a secret, as a rule, within a stone's throw, a short while ago, at a loss, take a fancy to, take an interest in, take a liking, a pity, tell a lie.

E.g.: (a) Never tell **a** lie.
(b) Do not make **a** noise.
(c) Twelve inches make **a** foot.

➢ In a few **phrases A/An** are not used. Some of these phrases are-

To lose heart, to set foot, to give ear, at home, last but not least, to catch fire, in hand, set on fire, by car/bus etc, at last, by mistake, in danger, to take heart.

E.g.: (a) I am at home.
(b) The house was set on fire.
(c) I go to college by bus.

Where do we omit '**A/An**' ?

- It should **not** be used with a **plural noun.**

E.g.: A boys have come (×)
(boys = pl.n.)

Boys have come (✓)

The boys have come (✓)

- **A/An is not used with uncountable nouns.**
Advice, Accommodation, Baggage, Luggage, News, Permission, Progress, Scenery, Weather, Traffic, Knowledge, Music, Wine, Equipment, Information, Poetry, Furniture, Hair, Business, Mischief, Bread, Stationery Crockery, Postage, Wastage, Money, Jewellery, Breakage, Work, Evidence.

E.g.: (a) He gave me an advice (remove *'an'*)
(b) I will buy a furniture today (remove *'a'*)

- **NOTE:** A few words are used before certain uncountable nouns to make them countable.

E.g.:(a) I have **a piece of information** for you.
(b) I had **a slice of bread.**
(c) He gave **me a piece of** work to do.

- Articles are not used before the nouns, in sentences, starting with '**what kind of**', '**what sort of**', '**what type of**' and '**what variety of**'.

E.g.:(a) What sort of a man is he ! (×)
What sort of man he is ! (✓)

USE OF DEFINITE ARTICLE 'THE'

- '**The**' is used before **definite nouns** towards which we can **point out**; the nouns that we can **visualize** or that has **already been introduced.** '**The**' is hence called **Definite article.**

E.g.:(a) Once upon a time, there lived **a king. The king** was very kind. One day, he met **an old man**. **The old man** was very poor.

In the first sentence '**a king**' is introduced. In the second sentence, we have become familiar with the character '**king**' and hence '**the**' comes before '**king**'. In the third sentence '**an old man**' is introduced and in the fourth sentence after we have become familiar with the character '**old man**', '**the**' comes before 'old man'.

(b) **The** man in white shirt is my brother.

(c) **The** boy standing near the gate is my brother. In sentence (b)& (c),'the' is used to be specific about the noun we are talking about.

USE OF ARTICLE WITH DIFFERENT KINDS OF NOUN

PROPER NOUN

1. Article **never comes with the names of any person or place**.

E.g.: Ram was an obedient son.

Rome is an ancient city.

Exceptions:-

In the following cases article **A/An** is **used** before **proper nouns**.

E.g.:(a) **A** Mr. Sharma has come to meet you.

(b) This book is written by **a** Dinesh Mishra.

In sentences (a) and (b), the nouns '**Mr. Sharma**' and '**Mr. Dinesh Mishra**' are not known to the speaker and he knows only the name that has been conveyed to him, so **A** is used before '**Mr. Sharma** and '**Mr. Dinesh Mishra**'

➢ When **a person or place** is mentioned in a sentence for **comparative purpose**, '**the**' comes before that proper noun.

(a) He is **the Ram** of modern India.

(b) He is **a Hitler**.

(c) Jaipur is **the Rome** of India.

➢ '**The**' comes before the **names of a few places**.

E.g.: **The** Ukraine

The Great Britain

The Netherlands

The Hague.

2. '**The**' does **not** come with the **names of States**. Exception- '**The Punjab**'.

3. '**The**' is **not** used with the **name of any country**.

E.g.: America, Russia, China etc.

However, if '**Union**', '**United**', '**Republic**' or '**Kingdom**' comes with the names of the country, '**the**' is used.

E.g.: The U.S.A., The Soviet Union, The Irish Republic.

4. '**The**' comes before the **names of mountain ranges**.

E.g.: '**The** Himalayas', '**The** Alps'.

Note: ' **Aravali**' is **not** a mountain range. Hence '**the**' **doesn't come** before it.

➢ '**The**' **doesn't** come before the names of **mountain peaks**.

E.g.: Mt. Everest, Mt. Abu.

5. '**The**' comes before '**nationality**' but **not** with the name of any '**language**'.

E.g.: **The** English speak English.

The English defeated **the** French.

6. Article does **not** come before the **name of any disease**.

Exceptions: The Measles, **The** Rickets, **The** Mumps, **The** Plague, **The** Flu.

7. '**The**' is used with the following **Proper Nouns:-**

(i) **Names of Rivers: The** Yamuna, **the** Ganga, **the** Godawari, **the** Sutlej.

(ii) **Names of Seas: The** Arabian sea, **the** Caribbean sea.

(iii) **Names of Oceans: The** Indian Ocean, **the** Pacific Ocean, **the** Atlantic Ocean.

(iv) **Names of Groups of islands**: **The** Lakshadweep, **the** Andaman and Nicobar Islands.

(v) **Names of Heavenly Objects**: **The** Sun, **the** Venus,

(vi) **Names of Bays: The** Bay of Bengal.

(vii) **Names of Deserts** : **The** Sahara Desert.

(viii) **Names of Canals** : **The** Suez Canal.

(ix) **Names of Newspapers** : **Th**e Hindu, **The** Times of India.

(x) **Names of Movements**: **The** Quit India Movement

(xi) **Names of Union**: **The** U.N.

(xii) **Names of Airways/ Trains**: **The** Jet Airways, **the** Intercity, **the** Rajdhani Express.

(xiii) **Names of Political Parties**: **The** BJP, **the** Congress.

(xiv) **Names of Statutes/Acts** : **The** Indian Penal code, **The** Legislature.

(xv) **Names of Musical Instruments**: **The** flute, **the** violin.

(xvi) **Names of Religion**: **The** Hindus, **the** Muslims, **the** Sikhs

(xvii) **Names of Inventions**: **The** telescope, **the** telephone.

(xviii) **Names of Clubs** : **The** Lions Club,

(xix) **Names of Dynasty**: **The** Marathas, **the** Peshwas.

(xx) **Names of body parts** : Only when a possessive adjective is replaced by any article otherwise articles don't come before parts of body.

E.g.: He was wounded in **his/the** eye.

(xxi) **Dates**: **The** 10th of May.

(xxii) **Army/Police**: **The** Army, **the** Police.

(xxiii) **Names of planets**: **The** Venus, **the** Mars.

(xxiv) **Names of hotels**: **The** Taj Hotel.

(xxv) **Names of trophies/Cups**: **The** World Cup.

(xxvi) **Names of Era, Revolutions & Wars**: **The** Middle Ages, **The** French Revolution.

(xxv) **Names of things that are unique: The** world, **The** universe, **the** environment, **the** atmosphere.

9. '**The**' comes before **space** only when it means '**room**'.

E.g.:(a) He tried to park his car but **the** space was not enough.

(b) Many astronauts dream of going to space.

10. '**The**' is used before directions - **The** East, **The** West.

If direction comes before the name of any place, '**the**' is **not** used.

E.g.: West Bengal

Article does not come before **Northern, Southern, Eastern, Western** as they are adjectives and will not take any article unless followed by a suitable noun.

E.g.: **Western** India

Some more examples-

1. He is going to **North America.**
2. Sweden is in **Northern Europe.**

11. **Before the names of holy books**: **The** Ramayana, **The** Bible.

12. **Before the names of monuments** : **The** Taj Mahal, **the** Red fort.

__Note:__ **'The'** does not come before the names of **buildings, monuments** and **sacred books** if the name comprises two or more words out of which **one is the name of a person or place**,

E.g.: Delhi Airport, Victoria Palace, London Zoo, Jai Singh Palace, Indira Gandhi Airport, Valmiki's Ramanyan, Banabhatt's Kadambiri.

13. **Names of movements**: **The** Quit India Movement.

14. **Names of Posts**: **The** chairman, **The** director

Here A/An can also be used before the names of the posts if we are talking about one out of many similar posts.

E.g.: She is **a** director of many companies.

➢ **Articles do not come with :**

(i) **Names of months** : July, September etc.

(ii) **Names of days**: Sunday, Monday etc.

(iii) **Names of subjects**: Maths, Physics etc.

(iv) **Names of roads**: Mall road, M. K. Road etc.

(v) **Names of meals**: Lunch, Dinner etc.

(vi) **Names of languages**: English, Hindi etc.

(vii) **Names of Hobbies**: Gardening, Singing etc.

(viii) **Names of Games**: Hockey, Cricket etc.

(ix) **Names of Lakes**: Wular Lake

(x) **Names of Continents**: Asia

(ix) **Before Noun Complement**: appoint, make, elect, select.

E.g.: They elected him ~~**the**~~ president.

(x) '**The**' is **not** used before '**Heaven**', '**Hell**', '**God**' and '**Parliament**'.

E.g.: (i) Go to hell.

(ii) God resides in heaven.

(iii) The bill was passed in Parliament.

COMMON NOUN:

1. If an object is **already known** to both the speaker and the listener, article **'The'** is used before it.

E.g.: (a) Kindly return **the** book . (That I gave you)

(b) Can you turn off **the** light. (The light in the room)

2. If an **article** comes before a **singular common noun**, it can represent the **entire species.**

E.g.: **A** dog is a faithful animal.

NOTE: **Man** doesn't come under this rule because the word 'man' means a human being.

E.g.: Man is mortal.

3. When we talk about a **personality present inside a person**, article comes with the name of that personality.

E.g.: (a) **The** judge (moral of judge) in him, prevailed upon **the** father (love of father for his son) and he sentenced his son to death.

(b) **A** mother (feelings of motherhood) was born in her when she saw the baby.

4. If **Schools, colleges, Temple** are denoted in reference to their primary purpose, article is not used.

E.g.: Children should go to school.

I go to temple every morning.

➢ An article is used if school, college, temple etc. denotes a place or a building and not its primary purpose.

E.g.: My house is behind **a** school.

The college is next to **the** temple.

ABSTRACT/MATERIAL NOUN:

No Article is generally used with abstract nouns. They are uncountable **nouns** hence **A/An** cannot be used with them.

E.g.: Gold is precious.

Honesty is the best policy.

➢ **Note**:If nouns are followed by 'of' an article **precedes** the noun.

Article + Noun + of + ...

(1) **The** cotton **of** Egypt is known for its superior quality.

(2) **The** honesty **of** this boy is liked by all.

USE OF ARTICLE WITH ADJECTIVE:

(1) 'The' is often used before **superlative degree.**

(a) He is **the best** student of our class.

(b) She is **the most** beautiful girl of the town.

Note: Article 'A/An' can also be used if we talk about one out of many nouns qualified by superlative adjectives.

E.g.: This is a most useful book needed for competitive exams.

(2) **'The'** is used before **the comparative degree,** when two comparative degrees are shown to be directly or inversely proportional to each other.

E.g.: (a) **The more** electricity you use, **the higher** your bill will be.

(b) **The higher** you climb, **the harder** you fall.

(3) If one out of two are chosen, a comparative degree is used **preceded by 'the'** and **followed by 'of'**.

E.g.: (a) He is **the stronger** of the two players.

(b) He is **the better** of the two wrestlers.

➢ But if one out of many are chosen, a Superlative degree is used, **preceded by 'the'** and **followed by 'of'**.

E.g.: She is the best of all the players.

(4) When 'the' is used before **adjectives** like **honest, rich, poor, meek** etc., it denotes the entire class and becomes plural common noun. Such nouns take plural verb.

E.g.: (a) **The honest** are always rewarded.

(b) **The rich** exploit the poor.

(c) **The young and the old, the poor and the rich**, all demand corruption free India.

(5) When any **adjective** or a **noun** qualifies a **proper noun**, article **'the'** is used with the proper noun.

E.g.: Ashoka **the great,**

The great Akbar,

Napoleon, **the warrior.**

(6) '**The**' is used before **Ordinal** numbers **(first, second, third** etc). **Cardinal** numbers such as **one, two, three** do not take any article before them.

E.g.: (a) Chapter **two** of this book is very difficult.

(b) **The second** chapter of this book is very difficult.

(c) Volume **one** is on Grammar.

(d) **The first** volume is on Grammar.

(7) '**The**' is used **before** adjective '**same**' and '**whole**' and **after** '**all**' and '**both**'.

E.g.: (a) He is **the same** boy that met me in the market.

(b) **The whole period** was wasted.

(8) **When Article 'a' or 'the' is used with few and little, the sentence takes a different meaning.**

Few (a) A few - Not equivalent to zero.
(b) Few - Equivalent to zero but not equal zero.
(c) The few - All that is available.

Little (a) A little - Not equivalent to nothing.
(b) Little - Equivalent to nothing but not equal to nothing.
(c) The little - All that is available.

This has been given in detail in chapter Adjective.

(9) If **so, as, too, how** and **quite** are used before **adjectives, A/An** is used if the **noun that follows the adjective is singular.**

E.g.: (a) It is too heavy **a** box for me to carry.

(b) Rohit is not so famous **a** businessman as you think.

USE OF ARTICLE ACCORDING TO SUBJECT – VERB AGREEMENT

➢ If an **article** is placed **before the 1st subject only**, it means the **person/thing is the same** for which two nouns are used. Hence **singular verb** will be used.

E.g.: (a) **A** white and black gown **was** (S.V.) bought by her.

(b) Churchill was a great orator and a great politician of his time. (×)
Churchill was a great orator and politician of his time. (✓)

➢ But if an **article** is used **before every subject**, it refers to **different people/things**. Hence **plural verb** will be used.

E.g.: (a) **The** director and **the** producer **have** (P.V.) come.(✓)

(b) The secretary and the treasurer were present there.
Here secretary & treasurer are different individuals.

➢ **Difference between A/An and One:**

1. **A** and **An** are **articles. One** is an **adjective**

2. '**A**' is used in the sense of '**per**' as in per day, per week, per kg etc.

E.g.: Ten rupees a kilo, four times a day, sixty kilometres an hour, twelve rupees a dozen.

3. Use of '**A**' and '**One**' gives different meanings to a sentence when used before a noun.

E.g.: **One** cow is not enough for our joint family (we need two or more as the consumption of milk is huge.)

A cow is a useful animal. (cows are useful)

4. **One** can be used with **another/other** but '**a**' cannot be used.

E.g.: (a) One student wants to study, another wants to play.
(b) One day he comes, the other day he does not.

5. '**One**' comes before **day/week/month/year/summer/winter** etc., when we are referring to an incident on **that particular** day/week etc.

(a) One night, there was a terrible storm.

(b) One day, Ravana came to Sita's cottage.

6. Use of '**one day**' does not point to any particular day.

E.g.: (a) One day, you will realize your mistake.

(b) One day, you will feel sorry for what you have done.

7. '**One**' can be used as **a /an pronoun** too.

E.g.: (a) Did you get any berth? Yes, I managed to get one.

Note: Plural of 'one' is 'some'.

E.g.: Did you get berths for your party workers ? Yes, I managed to get some.

8. To **Avoid repetition** of a 'noun' we use pronoun 'one'.

E.g.: This car is better than that one.

SPOTTING THE ERROR

1. (a) The loss of jobs/ (b) is regarded by some as an necessary evil/ (c) in the fight against inflation./ (d) No error.
2. (a) It is a/ (b) quarter to ten/ (c) by my watch./ (d) No error.
3. (a) Gita doesn't usually/ (b) wear jewellery but yesterday/ (c) she wore ring./ (d) No error.
4. (a) The police asked us/ (b) about our movements/ (c) on a night of crime./ (d) No error.
5. (a) In science the credit goes to a man/ (b) who convinces the world,/ (c) not to the man to whom the idea first occurs./ (d) No error.
6. (a) It is only after/ (b) the match is over/ (c) that people realize/ how exciting it is./ (d) No error.
7. (a) Of the two/ (b) sisters, she/ (c) is better./ (d) No error.
8. (a) It is unfortunate enough/ (b) to lose few friends we make/ (c) during our school days./ (d) No error.
9. (a) There were a number of intelligent gentlemen at the party/ (b) but it was Mr. Subramaniam, an eminent scientist,/ (c) who remained a centre of attraction./ (d) No error.
10. (a) I have been/ (b) informed that/ (c) Mr. Sharma, the director and the chairman will visit Patna the following month./ (d) No error.
11. (a) He is/ (b) the best worker/ (c) of the factory but unfortunately least paid./ (d) No error.
12. (a) He has come out/ (b) with an unique proposal/ (c) for his friends (d) No error.
13. (a) When the house was/ (b) set on the fire, all the people/ (c) started shouting at the top of their voices./ (d) No error.
14. (a) Little knowledge/ (b) of medicine that he possessed/ (c) proved to be a blessing for him when he was in great pain./ (d) No error.
15. (a) It was/ (b) by a mistake/ (c) that he injured her hand./ (d) No error.
16. (a) These orders of/ (b) the Manager/ (c) may put the lives of two thousand workers in a danger./ (d) No error.
17. (a) I inspired him/ (b) to take the heart/ (c) in all adverse situations and deserve to be called a real hero./ (d) No error.
18. (a) The most happy/ (b) marriage is/ (c) a union of a deaf man and a blind woman./ (d) No error.
19. (a) John suggested to/ (b) the children of his village that they should/ (c) go to the school regularly and do their home work sincerely./ (d) No error.
20. (a) Some people say that/ (b) her husband is in the jail/ (c) and so she lives alone./ (d) No error.
21. (a) The Greek peoples/ (b) arc considered/ (c) very brave/ (d) No error.
22. (a) His father/ (b) asked him to go/ (c) to the temple every morning/ (d) No error.
23. (a) There was little/ (b) milk in the refrigerator and she gave it/ (c) to her crying son./ (d) No error.
24. (a) He leads/ (b) a very luxurious life / (c) so he goes to every part of India by a car./ (d) No error.
25. (a) Thanks to an effort/ (b) and persistence of the doctors, the victims of the blast/ (c) have been able to start a normal life again./ (d) No error.

26. (a) In a hour's time/ (b) I will be back/ (c) but now I have to go./ (d) No error.
27. (a) Terrorist organizations/ (b) kill innocent people/ (c) to spread a violence./ (d) No error.
28. (a)Whole world is/ (b) today facing the threat of extinction/ (c) due to the inventions of Science./ (d) No error.
29. (a) The answer/ (b) to all the sufferings of / (c) human beings lies in the Science./ (d) No error.
30. (a) The police should exercise/ (b) their authority with little/ (c) bit of sensitivity and humanity./ (d) No error.
31. (a) This is/ (b) most important/ (c) chapter which we will have to study very carefully./ No error.
32. (a)The Ganges/ (b) is for North India/ (c) what Krishna is for South India./ (d) No error.
33. (a) I like to travel/ (b) by the air as/ (c) I am a very busy person./ (d) No error.
34. (a) The Chairman and the Trustee/ (b) was removed from his/ (c) post because he had misappropriated the fund./ (d) No error.
35. (a) She found/ (b) herself in a trouble/ (c) when she saw the stalker following her persistently./ (d) No error.
36. (a) All the people/ (b) of India know that/ (c) Gandhi ji was a very wise and a noble soul./ (d) No error.
37. (a) The man/ (b) is the only creature/ (c) that is endowed with the art of humour./ (d) No error.
38. (a) It is very difficult/ (b) to find out the number of/ (c) the creatures living on the earth./ (d) No error.
39. (a) While climbing/ (b)the hill, to his amazement , the/ (c) poor man found the box of pearls./ (d) No error.
40. (a) The blast derailed the lives / (b)of many people but in an year/ (c) time leavingapart the victims, no one remembered anything/ (d) No error.
41. (a) Cowards die/ (b) several times,/ (c) the braves die but once/ (d) No error.
42. (a) Akbar became a heir/ (b)to the throne at/ (c) a young age of thirteen/ (d) No error.
43. (a) The both brothers/ (b) are safe now/ (c) and are recuperating./ (d) No error.
44. (a) When the principal entered the classroom/ (b) all boys shook/ (c) in their shoes/ (d) No error.
45. (a) Father in him/ (b) could not bear the condition of/ (c) his ailing daughter/ (d) No error.
46. (a) Let judge in you/ (b) decide what/ (c) punishment should be given to him/ (d) No error.
47. (a) My teacher said that/ (b) Sun is a/ (c) star/ (d) No error.
48. (a) Due to its beauty/ (b) Kashmir is known as/ (c) Switzerland of India/ (d) No error.
49. (a) Most of the people of Southern India/ (b) do not know/ (c) the Hindi/ (d) No error.
50. (a) He went for the lunch/ (b) at 1 p.m. and then/ (c) returned/ (d) No error.
51. (a) The honesty/ (b) is/ (c) a virtue./ (d) No error.
52. (a) Every morning the Sun/ (b) rises/ (c) in east/ (d) No error.
53. (a) He is/ (b) best player/ (c) in India./ (d) No error.
54. (a) When I met him/ (b) the couple of days back/ (c) he was writing a new book,/ (d) No error.

Answers with explanations

1. (b) Use 'a' before the word 'necessary' , 'Necessary' starts with a consonant sound.
2. (a) Remove 'a'.
3. (c) 'Ring' is a singular uncountable noun and is being introduced here in the sense of 'one'. It will hence take indefinite article 'a'.
4. (c) Change 'a' into 'the'. Here 'night of crime' is definite as it was the night when the crime that the speaker is talking about took place. Hence definite article 'the' will be used.
5. (a) Change 'a' into 'the'. The person who convinced the world is definite. Hence definite article 'the' will be used.
6. (b) Change 'the' into 'a'. Here we are not talking about any definite match. Hence definite article 'a' will be used.
7. (c) Add 'the' before better. When one is chosen out of two, a comparative degree is used preceded by 'the' and followed by 'of'.
8. (b) Add 'the' before 'few'. Here we are talking about 'the friends we make during school days'. Hence definite article 'the' will be used.
9. (c) Here one person is the centre of attraction. When only one is chosen out of all, article 'the' is used,
10. (c) Here Mr. Sharma holds two posts. Hence 'the' will come before only the first noun 'director'. (see subject-verb agreement)
11. (c) Add 'the' before least, Article 'the' comes before superlative degree of an adjective.
12. (b) Unique does not start with vowel sound. Use 'a' in place of 'an'.
13. (b) 'Set on fire' is the appropriate phrase.
14. (a) Here 'little' denotes 'small quantity' and not 'negligible quantity'. Here 'the' is best suited before 'little'.
15. (b) 'By mistake' is the correct phrase.
16. (c) 'In danger' is the correct phrase.
17. (b) 'To take heart' is the correct phrase. It means to be optimistic.
18. (c) Here we are talking about the union that is between a deaf man and a blind woman. Hence 'the' will be used.
19. (c) Here 'school' is mentioned in relation to its primary purpose. Hence no article will be used.
20. (b) Here 'jail' is mentioned in relation to its primary purpose. Hence no article will not be used.
21. (a) 'Peoples' denotes 'people of different races'. 'The word 'Greek' denotes only one race. Hence the use of 'the Greeks' or 'the Greek people' must replace 'the Greek peoples'.
22. (c) Here 'temple' is mentioned in relation to its primary purpose. Hence 'the' will not be used.
23. (a) Add 'a' before 'little'.
24. (c) 'By car' is the correct phrase.

25. (a) Here we are talking about the efforts and persistence shown by the doctors. Hence we need definite article 'the' before 'effort'.
26. (a) 'Hour' starts with a vowel sound. Hence use 'an' before 'hour'.
27. (c) 'Violence' is an uncountable noun. Hence 'a' will not be used. 'Spread violence' is the correct phrase.
28. (a) Add 'the' before 'whole world'.
29. (c) 'The' is not used with the name of any subject.
30. (b) Add 'a' before 'little'. Here we mean that the police must have some amount of sensitivity.
31. (b) 'Most' is a superlative degree. Hence add 'the' before 'most'.
32. (c) Add 'the' before 'Krishna'. Article 'the' comes with the names of rivers.
33. (b) 'By air' is the correct phrase.
34. (a) Remove 'the' that has been used before 'chairman'. Both the positions are held by the same person.
35. (b) Remove 'a'. 'Trouble' is an uncountable noun.
36. (c) Remove 'a'. Both the adjectives have been used for the same person.
37. (a) Remove 'the'. The word 'man'. is sufficient which means human being.
38. (c) Remove 'the'.
39. (c) The poor man is unaware of the box of pearls. Hence 'a' will be used before 'box of pearls'.
40. (b) 'Year' does not start with vowel sound. Hence 'year' will be preceded by 'a'.
41. (c) 'Brave is an adjective, it cannot be made plural by adding 's'. It becomes a plural common noun if 'the' is added before it.
42. (a) 'Heir' starts with a vowel sound. Change 'a' into 'an'.
43. (a) Add 'the' after 'both'.
44. (b) Add 'the' after 'all'.
45. (a) Add 'the' before 'father'. When we talk about the personality present inside a person, we use article 'the' before the name of the personality.
46. (a) Add 'the' before 'judge'. When we talk about the personality present inside a person, we use article 'the' before the name of the personality.
47. (b) Add 'the' before 'sun' as it is the name of a heavenly body.
48. (c) Add 'the' before 'Switzerland' . When the name of a person or place is used due to its quality and as an example, an article precedes the proper noun.
49. (c) Remove 'the'. We do not use any article with the names of languages.
50. (a) Remove 'the'. Names of meals do not take any article.
51. (a) Remove 'the'. Article is not used before 'abstract nouns'.
52. (c) Add 'the' before 'East'. The names of directions take article 'the'.
53. (b) Add 'the' before 'best' which is a superlative degree.
54. (b) Change 'The' into 'a'.

19 PREPOSITION

CHAPTER

Preposition, are those words, which are used before a **noun** or **pronoun** and denote the **relation between the noun / pronoun and the other part of the sentence.**

E.g: (i) There is a cat sitting **under** the table.

(ii) We need a roof **over** us.

(iii) I go to school **by** bus

Note: Prepositions are placed usually before noun / pronoun, but not always.

E.g.(i) Who was he talking **to** ?

(ii) He does not have a pen to write **with.**

CONFUSING PREPOSITIONS

Between - Among	**Beside - Besides**	**For - Since**
Across - Through	**on - upon**	**on - over**
in - into	**in - within**	**by - with**
before - in front of	**at - in**	**in spite of - despite**

➢ **Among is used in reference to the association with or in company of more than two.**

E.g. 1. A lot of co-operation is needed among (~~between~~) the different states to combat Naxalism.

2. Alms were distributed **among** the beggars.

3. The teacher distributed sweets **among** them.

➢ **Between is used in reference to the association of two.**

E.g. The match will be played between (~~among~~) India and Australia-

➢ **Between can be used in reference to more than two when.**

(1) We talk about a definite number of people etc no matter whether there are two or more things /persons and.

(2) when we talk about mutual relationship/co-operation etc.

E.g. (i) There is a tournament to be played **between** India , Australia and New Zealand.

(ii) There is an alliance **between** the three **European nations.**

➢ **'Between' is followed by 'and'. ('Between......and' is a correlative)**

E.g. The meeting will be held **between** 10 a.m. **and** 4 p.m.

➢ **'Between..... and' takes Objective case of Pronoun .**

E.g. There is no enmity **between him** and **me** (not He & I.)

➢ Plural **noun / pronoun** comes with **'Between'.**

E.g:(i) Between **the countries**
(ii) Between **the students**
(iii) Between **them**
(iv) Between **us**

➢ **'Each / Every' cannot be used after 'Between'.**

E.g.:(i) **Between each** boy. (×)
(ii) **Between every** girl. (×)
(iii) There are ten millimetres **between each** centimetre. (×)

➢ **Amongst** and **Among** mean the same though **slightly different** from each other.

(i) Amongst comes before **'The'**

E.g.: There was no co-operation amongst **the** boys.

(ii) **Among** is used before **consonant sound,** while **amongst** is used before vowel sound.

E.g.:(a) among them. ('them' starts consonant sound)
(b) amongst us. ('us' starts vowel sound)

However in modern English, we do not follow this rule. Wherever 'amongst' goes with the rhythm of the sentence, we use 'amongst'.

➢ **Amid/Amidst** is used for **more than two**. The difference here is the same as above. 'Amid/Amidst' **can be used before uncountable nouns** too.

E.g.(i) The bill was passed **amid** pandemonium.
(ii) You are sitting **amidst** us and talking against us.

2. Beside and **Besides**

Beside	and	**Besides**
Adjacent		apart from

Eg.:(i) He sat **beside** me
(ii) **Besides** his children his nephews and nieces were also present at the ceremony.

3. For and **Since**

For	and	**Since**
Denotes period of time		denotes point of time

E.g:(a) I have eaten nothing **for** a long time.
(b) She has been living here **for** ten years.
(c) I have been living here **since** 2009.

Since, is also used to denote **'reason'.**

Eg.:- Since I was unwell, I didn't take the test .

'since', 'because' and **'as'** are not followed by **'So'/'therefore'/'that's why'.**

Since ...., (✓) As/Because/Since ..... so/therefore/that's why (×)
As ....(✓)
Because ...., (✓)

Note: **As** you sow, **so** you shall reap (a phrase where 'as' is followed by 'so'.)

For-Indicates the purpose.

E.g:- The police are **for** our safety.

4. Across

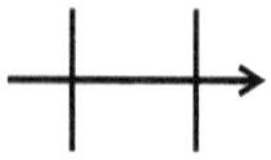

from one to the other side.

I swam **across** the river.

Through

Via (medium)/Indicates movement from one end to the other end.

1. The message was conveyed to me by him **through** her.
2. The train passed **through** the tunnel.

➢ **Across has two other meanings too -**

(a) **On the opposite side**

Eg.: He is waiting for me **across** the road.

(b) **Both sides**

E.g: A tree fell **across** the railway line that caused an accident.

1. Come across (to meet by chance/ suddenly)

When I was going to college, I suddenly came across my childhood friend. (×)

Note:- **Come across** means to **meet suddenly or by chance**. Hence **'suddenly' or 'by chance' cannot come with 'come across'.**

2. '**With**' cannot be used with **'come across'.**

E.g:(i) I came across **with** him. (×)

(ii) I came across him. (✓)

5. on upon

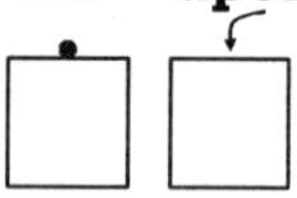

E.g.:(i) The books is **on** the table. **(placed in contact)**

(ii) The cat jumped **upon** the rat. (**in motion**)

6. over

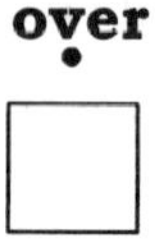

Motion or position higher than but no physical contact

E.g: The fan is **over** my bed. **(no physical contact)**

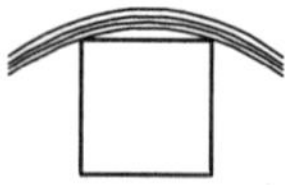

So as to cover the whole surface no matter whether there is physical contact or not.

Eg.:(i) The bridge was built **over** the river.

(ii) Put a blanket **over** the baby.

7. Over Under

'Over' and 'under' respectively indicate **placed 'higher' or 'below'** something.

Eg.:(i) There is a fan **over** your bed.

(ii) A cat is sitting **under** the table.

8. In Into

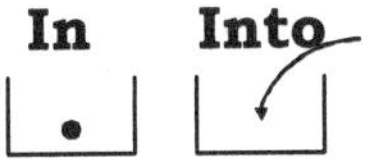

Eg.:(i) We are sitting **in** the classroom. (**located inside** or **within**)

(ii) The boy jumped **into** the river .(Indicates **entry** or **insertion**)

Note: 'Into' is not used with 'enter' as the sentence becomes superfluous.

E.g:(i) He entered into the room. (Remove 'into')

(ii) He threw the ball into the well. (use 'in' place of 'into')

Note: Enter into any agreement/alliance, & enter on/upon (to undertake) is correct.

9. On time	**In time**
on scheduled time	**in the given time span**

E.g:(i) We reached the examination centre **in** time.

(ii) The examination starts **on** time.

(iii) We thought that the train would be late but it arrived exactly in/on time.('on' is the appropriate preposition here.)

10. By	**With**
Indicates the doer	**Indicates the means/ equipment.**

E.g.:(i) The paper was signed **by** him **with** a Parker pen **in** black ink.

(ii) The snake was killed **by** him **with** a stick.

(iii) You cannot catch a big fish **with** a small rod.

11. Before	**In front of**
In advance/at an earlier time	**Directly before or ahead of**

Eg.:(i) I came **before** you.

(ii) India raised the issue of cross-border terrorism **before** the U.N.

(iii) Don't park your car **in front of** my gate.

12. At	**In**
Used with a relatively smaller place	**Used with a relatively bigger place**

Eg.: I live **at** Mukherjee Nagar **in** Delhi.

13. In spite of **Despite**

Regardless of/notwithstanding/nevertheless

Eg.: **In spite of** working hard, he failed.

Note: Do not use 'of' with 'despite'.'Despite' and 'inspite of' mean the same.

Eg: **Despite** being rich, he is not happy.

14.	By	In
	Mode of transportation takes preposition when it comes with 'go'/'come'/'travel'/'arrive' etc.	**Indicates within limits/inclusion.**

Eg.: (i) I am sitting **in** the car. (✓)

(ii) I am going **in** car. (×)

(iii) I am going **by** car. (✓)

'On foot' means **'walking'.**

Eg.: I go to college **on foot.**

15.

Exact time (hour)	Month	Year	Day	Date
at	in	in	on	on

E.g:- **I reached Delhi at 7 o' clock.**

in May

on Monday

in 2005

on the 7th of September

➢ **'At'** is used with the following:

at dawn, **at** dusk, **at** day break, **at** sunrise, **at** noon, **at** sunset, **at** night, **at** midnight etc.

Note: **'In'** is used with **'morning'/'evening'**. If **date/day** is mentioned with **morning/ evening** , **'on'** comes before the date/day.

Eg.:(i) **in** the morning.

(ii) **in** the evening.

(iii) **on** Sunday morning.

(iv) **on** the evening of May, the 2nd.

➢ **Today, tomorrow, yesterday, the following day, the next day, yesterday evening, yesterday afternoon, last night, this morning, this afternoon, tonight, tomorrow morning, tomorrow evening do not take preposition** before them.

E.g:(i) He will go there **on tomorrow.** (remove **'on'**)

(ii) They arrived here **on last night.** (remove **'on'**)

16. After (later in time or place) and Before (preceding in time)

E.g:(i) He came to India **after** a long time.

(ii) I left America **before** Christmas.

17. Till / until is used for **'point of time'.** They are usually interchangeable and **'till' is not the contracted form of 'until'**. 'Till' is rather the older form.

E.g:(i) The government will not pass any bill **until/till** next session.

18. **By** is used for '**point of time**' as a **preposition of time.**

E.g:(i) We shall have finished the syllabus **by** the end of next month.

19. **During** denotes **at some point of time in the course of some action.**

E.g:(i) **During** the strike, many people died.

➢ **Up** **Down** **Upto**

E.g.(i) He climbed **up** the tree.

(ii) He ran **down** the stairs.

(iii) Children can get free education **upto** the age of 14. (**Upto** indicates **extension as far as a specific place**)

A FEW OTHER PREPOSITIONS-

1. '**To**' denotes **destination.**

E.g:(i) Ram is going **to** college

(ii) Send him **to** school.

2. '**Towards**' denotes '**in the direction of**'.

E.g.:(i) He is going **towards** the college.

3. **For** can indicate **goal** or **destination** too.

E.g:-(i) He is leaving **for** America tonight.

4. **Along- In the line matching the length or the direction of/parallel .**

E.g:(i) I walked **along** the railway line.

(ii) He walks **along** the road. (not 'on the road')

➢ **Along with- Together with someone or something.**

E.g:- Come **along with** me.

5. **Against-**

(a) **In opposition to / contrary to.**

E.g:- It is difficult to sail **against** the current.

(b) **Hostility to**

Eg:- I am **against** terrorism.

(c) **In contact with**

Eg:- Do not stand **against** the railing. You may fall down.

6. **Onto**

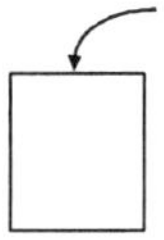

'to a position on'

E.g:- He jumped **onto** his horse and rode away.

7. With

Indicates 'combination, accompaniment or addition'.

E.g:- I am **with** you through thick and thin.

8. Beyond

Out of the reach or sphere of

E.g:- The case is **beyond** the jurisdiction of the court.

9. About

(a) **Concerning**

E.g: I know **about** him.

(b) **Approximately**

E.g: It is **about** 100 kilometres away from Delhi.

(c) **about + infinitive** (To indicate '**intention to do action**')

E.g: I am **about to** start a new lesson.

➢ '**about + to+$V_{b.f}$**', '**going + to+$V_{b.f}$**' and '$\underbrace{\textbf{be}}_{\text{any form}}$ **+ to + $V_{b.f}$**' mean the same.

E.g: (a) I am **going to** start a new lesson now.

(b) The minister **is to** deliver a speech.

10. Above - Means to a **higher position than a level / standard / mark**. '**Below**' is the **opposite of 'above'.**

E.g:(i) The river is flowing **above** the danger level.

(ii) His English is **below** average.

(iii) The selling price of every commodity in the multiplex is **above** MRP.

(vi) The score was **below** hundred when the team lost its last wicket.

11. 'Of

(a) Indicates '**belonging to/possession**' **for non-living things**.

E.g:- 1. Table's wood (×)
Wood **of** table (✓)

2. Chair's leg (×)
Leg **of** chair (✓)

(b) Indicates **Origin**

E.g:(i) He comes **of** a royal family.

(c) Reason

➢ die **of** disease.

➢ die '**from**' reason.

E.g:(i) He died **of** cancer.

(ii) He died **from** thirst.

(d) Indicates **characteristics**

E.g:(i) The problems **of** Delhi.

12. 'Off'- Indicates **physical separation**

E.g:- (i) Keep the dog **off** the flower beds.

13. Behind- In, towards the back or **later in time.**

E.g:(i) The police are running **behind** the thief.

(ii) She hid **behind** the curtain.

(iii) The train was behind time.

MORE ABOUT PREPOSITION

(a) Objective case comes after a preposition.

E.g:(i) I do not depend on (Prep.) him (Objective Case).

(ii) She relies on (Prep.) me (Objective Case).

(b) If two **verbs/ adjectives** etc **take two different prepositions**, **we must mention both the prepositions**, we cannot simply use one preposition with the last verb/ adjective.

E.g:(i) I was **surprised at** as well as **pleased with** her performance.

(ii) He is senior and older **than** I. (Use '**to**' after 'senior')

(iii) His watch is different and cheaper **than** mine. (Use '**from**' after 'different')

(iv) She is younger and taller **than** her brother. (✓)

(c) 'To' is followed by 'V_1' in case of Infinitive but **when 'to' is used as a preposition, it is followed by 'V_1+ing,** if a verb comes after the preposition.

E.g: (i) I am **looking forward to going** (V_1+ing) to London.

(ii) He is afraid **of going** (V_1+ing) out after sunset

<u>**Note:**</u> **The following phrases end in 'to' and are followed by 'ing' form of a verb.** Questions based on these phrases are generally asked.
Be used to, accustomed to, averse to, with a view to, addicted to, devoted to, in addition to, look forward to, object to, owing to, given to, taken to, prone to.

E.g:- I am **looking forward to going** (V_1+ing) to London

➢ No Preposition is used before '**home**, if any of the following verbs (verbs of motion) is used.
Bring, go, come, arrive, reach, get.
(i)I went home by car.
<u>**Note:**</u> If **Possessive Adjective or a Noun with an apostrophe** is used before '**home**', '**to**' is used **before** '**home**' only when specific verbs are used. (Not 'arrive' and 'reach')

E.g: (i) I went **to his home.**

(ii) I decided to go **to Ram's home.**

➢ **Stress, emphasise, investigate, comprise, accompany, consider, violate, pervade, precede, succeed, invade, resist, enter, eschew, direct, join, sign, affect, ensure, board, discuss, describe, reach, order, tell, demand, attack, control, resemble** and **ridicule,** are not followed by any preposition if they are used in active voice.

E.g:(i) The teacher emphasised on the need of discipline in life. (Drop 'on').
(ii) I have ordered for a cup of tea. (Drop 'for')
(iii) I shall discuss about the problem with you. (Drop 'about')
(iv) (a) He described/ (b) about the incident/ (c) in his story./ (d) No error
(Remove about)

➢ 'To' should not be used with the following verbs when followed by an Indirect Object. Such verbs are - **advise, tell, ask, beg, command, encourage, request, inform, thank, welcome, warn, forbid, order, remind, congratulate, compliment**.

E.g:(i) I advised ***to*** him to go. (Drop 'to')
(ii) I informed ***to*** the police of the accident. (Drop 'to')
(iii) I was told to postpone the meeting. (✓)

➢ **'To'** is used after **say, suggest, propose, speak, reply, explain, complain, talk, listen, write, report, pray** and **describe** if the object is a person.

E.g:(i) You **suggested to him** that he should leave the place.
(ii) She **said to me** that she would help me.
(iii) He did not **reply to** me.

➢ **Object of the verbs (direct object/indirect object) in the following cases, decides the preposition that follows the verb**. Such verbs are -**Furnish, Entrust, Present, Provide, Supply** etc.

E.g:(i) I provided him money. (×)
I provided him **with** money. (✓)
Or
I provided money **to** him.(✓) (See Classnotes for more explanation)

(ii) **Compensate, Explain, Fine, Propose, Recommend, Rob, Suggest take preposition according to the object** of the sentence.

E.g:(i) Rob a person **of** something.
(ii) We informed the police **of** an accident.
(iii) I explained the matter **to** him.
(iv) He robbed her **of** her jewellery.

SOME PHRASE PREPOSITION:

(1) According to - as stated by
E.g. **According to** the terms and conditions, he will have to finish it in two days.

(2) By dint of - by force of, because of
E.g:- I passed the exam **by dint of** hard work.

(3) In case of - in the event of
E.g:- **In case of** emergency, call 100.

(4) By virtue of - by the authority of
E.g:- The judge can pass the order **by virtue of** his powers.

(5) Owing to - due to

'Owing to' means **'due to'** but there are a few differences.

(a) A sentence should start with **'owing to'** and not **'due to'**.

E.g:- Due to heavy rains, I could not come. (×)

Owing to heavy rains, I could not come.(✓) (**Note:** SSC accepts that a sentence can start with 'due to')

This rule is not important as far as modern English is concerned.

Note: **'Due to'** comes after different forms of **'be'**

E.g:- The accident was (form of 'be') owing to heavy rains.(×)

The accident was (form of 'be') due to heavy rains.(✓)

(6) With reference to - in context of

E.g:- **With reference to** your letter, dated 27th July 2023, I hereby submit my reply.

(7) In order to - for the purpose of

E.g:- We vacated the premises **in order to** avoid litigation.

(8) In course of - during

E.g:- **In course of** time, I faced many problems.

(9) On behalf of - as a representative of

E.g:- He came to receive the award **on behalf of** his brother.

(10) Agreeably to - willing

E.g:- **Agreeably to** the terms of the agreement, we will pay you Rs. 1 lakh.

(11) By means of - through the use of

E.g:- He amassed a lot of money **by means of** sharp practices.

(12) For the sake of - indicates purpose

E.g:- Save plants atleast **for the sake of** your children.

(13) In favour of - to the benefit of

E.g:- He voted **in favour of** his friend.

(14) In lieu of - in the place of

E.g:- He got fifty thousand rupees **in lieu of** his claim.

(15) On account of - by reason of

E.g:- **On account of** his negligence, the company has suffered heavy loss.

(16) In relation to - in connection with

E.g:- There are some rules **in relation to** the organization of the match.

➢ **See the difference**

1. I actcd **according to** your order.
   I acted **in accordance with** your order.
2. Mother Teresa had **affection for** all.
   Mother Teresa was **affectionate to** all.
3. He has **ambition for** fame.
   He is **ambitious of** fame.
4. I am **capable of** doing hard work.
   I have **capacity for** doing hard work.
5. I have **confidence in** myself.
   He is **confident** of his son's success.
6. He has **desire for** money and fame.
   He is **desirous of** money and fame.

FIXED PREPOSITION

'TO' COMES WITH FOLLOWING WORDS :

Words	Meaning in English	Meaning in Hindi
Abhorrent *to*	causing or deserving strong dislike	घिनौना
Access *to*	reach	पहुँच
Accountable *to*	obliged to accept responsibility	उत्तरदायी
Accustomed *to*	usual or regular	आदी होना
Addicted *to*	unable to stop using, habitual	लत लगना
Adhere *to*	to cause to stick fast	पालन करना, जुड़े रहना
Adjacent *to*	sharing a border	सटा हुआ
Affectionate *to*	feeling or showing love and affection	स्नेही
Agreeable *to*	ready or willing to agree	सहमत
Allegiance *to*	loyalty to a person, country, group, etc.	निष्ठा
Alternative *to*	substitute	विकल्प
Answerable *to*	required to explain actions or decisions to someone	जवाबदेह
Antidote *to*	a substance that stops the harmful effects of a poison	विष नाशक
Attention *to*	notice, interest, or awareness	ध्यान
Attune *to*	to bring into harmony	लय में करना
Averse *to*	having a feeling of dislike	प्रतिकूल
Beneficial *to*	producing good or helpful results or effects	फायेमंद
Blind *to*	unable to see (fault etc)	(के प्रति) अंधा
Comparable *to*	being similar or about the same	तुलनीय
Complement *to*	to complete something else or make it better	पूरक
Conform *to*	to obey or agree to something	अनुरूप
Detrimental *to*	causing damage or injury	हानिकारक
Devoted *to*	completely loyal	भक्त
Disgrace *to*	to cause to lose respect or be humiliated	अपमान
Due *to*	because	के कारण
Enmity *to*	a very deep unfriendly feeling	शत्रुता
Equal *to*	same	बराबरी
Equivalent *to*	almost same	लगभग बराबर
Essential *to*	extremely important and necessary	आवश्यक
Exception *to*	a case where a rule does not apply	अपवाद
Favourable *to*	showing approval	अनुकूल
Given *to*	habitual	आदी होना
Harmful *to*	causing or capable of causing damage or harm	नुकसान पहुंचने वाला

Heir *to*	a person who has the legal right to receive the property of someone who dies	वारिस
Immune *to*	not capable of being affected by a disease	प्रतिरक्षा
Important *to*	having serious meaning or worth	जरूरी
Incidental *to*	happening as a minor part or result of something else	आकस्मिक
Indebted *to*	owing something (such as money or thanks) to someone or something	ऋणी
Indifferent *to*	not interested in or concerned about something	उदासीन
Indigenous *to*	produced, living, or existing naturally in a particular region or environment	स्वदेशी
Injurious *to*	causing injury	हानिकारक
Key *to*	to make something correspond to something else	मौलिक
Look forward *to*	anticipated with satisfaction	संतुष्टि के साथ आशा करना
Loyal *to*	having or showing complete and constant support for someone or something	निष्ठावान
Obstruction *to*	something that blocks	बाधा
Opposite *to*	not agree	के विरूद्ध
Postscript *to*	a note or series of notes added at the end of a letter, article, or book	परिशिष्ट भाग
Preface *to*	an introduction to a book or speech	प्रस्तावना
Prefer *to*	to like (someone or something) better than someone or something else	के तुलना में ज्यादा पसंद करना
Preferable *to*	better or more desirable	बेहतर
Profitable *to*	producing good or helpful results or effects	लाभदायक
Prone *to*	likely to do, have, or suffer from something	से ग्रस्त होने की संभावना
Reduced *to*	to make (something) smaller in size, amount, number, etc.	को कम करना
Relevant *to*	relating to a subject in an appropriate way	प्रासंगिक
Repugnance *to*	a strong feeling of dislike or disgust	घृणा
Resign oneself *to*	to accept something reluctantly because you cannot change it	बेमन से ही पर स्वीकार कर लेना
Sensitive *to*	likely to cause people to become upset	संवेदनशील
Sequel *to*	a book, movie, etc., that continues a story begun in another book, movie, etc.	का अगला भाग
Similar *to*	almost the same	समान
Stick *to*	to hold to	लगे रहना
Submission *to*	something that is submitted	प्रस्तुत
Submit *to*	yield or accept to a superior force	के आगे झुकना

Subscribe *to*	to pay money to get a publication or service regularly	सदस्यता लेने के लिए
Succumb *to*	to stop trying to resist something	मर जाना/ हार मान जाना
Supplement *to*	to add something to (something) in order to make it complete	पूरक बनना
Surrender *to*	to give the control or use of (something) to someone else	समर्पण करना
Susceptible *to*	easily affected, influenced, or harmed by something	ग्रहणक्षम
Swing *to*	to move with a smooth, curving motion	झूलना
Taken *to*	to begin to like something	पसंद करना शुरू करना
Tantamount *to*	equal to something in value, meaning, or effect	समान
Temptation *to*	a strong urge or desire to have or do something	प्रलोभन
True *to*	faithful	वफादार होना

'OF' COMES WITH FOLLOWING WORDS :

Abhorrence *of*	strong hatred	घृणा
Accused *of*	one charged with an offence	अभियुक्त
Afraid *of*	filled with fear	डरा हुआ
Ambitious *of*	having a desire of	महत्वाकांक्षी
Anxious *of*	causing or showing fear or nervousness	चिंतित
Ashamed *of*	feeling shame, guilt, or disgrace	शर्मिंदा
Assurance *of*	the state of being sure or certain about something	आश्वासन
Aware *of*	knowing that something (such as a situation, condition, or problem) exists	अवगत
Bereft *of*	no longer having it, deprived	वंचित
Beware *of*	to be careful	सावधान रहना
Boast *of*	a reason to be proud	डींग मारना
Capable *of*	able to do something	सक्षम
Cautious *of*	careful about avoiding danger or risk	सर्तक
Certain *of*	not having any doubt about something	पक्का होना
Charge *of*	to make a person responsible for something	के प्रभारी
Composed *of*	calm and in control of your emotions	शांत
Consist *of*	to be made up of (something)	से बना हुआ
Confident *of*	showing that you have confidence	आश्वस्त होना
Conscious *of*	aware	जागरूक
Convicted *of*	to prove or find guilty	अपराधी ठहराया हुआ
Convinced *of*	to cause (someone) to believe that something is true	यकीन करना

Deprived *of*	not having the things that are needed for a good or healthy life	वंचित
Devoid *of*	lacking	वंचित
Diffident *of*	lacking confidence	आत्मविश्वासहीन
Disapprove *of*	to officially refuse to approve or accept (something)	अस्वीकार करना
Dispose *of*	to get rid of something	छुटकारा पाना
Embarrassed *of*	ashamed	शर्मिंदा
Envious *of*	feeling or showing a desire to have what someone else has	ईष्यालु
Fond *of*	to have liking of	के शौकीन
Formed *of*	organized in a way characteristic of living matter	का गठन
Frightened *of*	to cause to become afraid	डरा हुआ
Get rid *of*	to become free from something	छुटकारा पाना
Guilty *of*	responsible for committing a crime or doing something bad or wrong	अपराधी
Lack *(N)*	deficient	की कमी
Need *(N)*	to require	जरूरत
Proof *of*	something which shows that something else is true or correct	प्रमाण होना
Scared *of*	to be frightened or worried	डरा हुआ
Shortage *of*	a condition in which there is not enough of something needed	कमी होना
Sure *of*	ascertain	निश्चित होना
Void *of*	null or containing nothing	रिक्त
Want *(N)*	to need (something)	की इच्छा होना
Wary *of*	marked by being cautious	सावधान
Worthy *of*	deserving respect, attention	के योग्य

'FOR' COMES WITH FOLLOWING WORDS :

Affection *for*	a feeling of liking for someone or something	के लिए स्नेह
Affection *for*	feeling or showing love and affection	स्नेही
Ambition *for*	a particular goal or aim	महत्वाकांक्षा
Anxiety *for*	fear or nervousness about what might happen	चिंता
Appetite *for*	a physical desire for food	भूख
Aptitude *for*	a natural ability to do something or to learn something	योग्यता
Atone *for*	to make amends or reparation	हरजाना देना
Capacity *for*	the ability to hold or contain	क्षमता

Compassion ***for***	a feeling of wanting to help someone who is sick, hungry, in trouble, etc.	सहानुभूति
Compensation ***for***	something that is done or given to make up for damage, trouble, etc.	मुआवजा, हर्जाना
Contempt ***for***	a feeling that someone or something is not worthy of any respect or approval	अवमानना
Canvass ***for***	to ask (the people in an area) what they think about a candidate, project, idea, etc.	मत माँगना
Craving ***for***	a very strong desire for something	तृष्णा
Desire ***for***	to want or wish for (something)	इच्छा
Hope ***for***	expect	आशा
Liking ***for***	a feeling of regard or fondness	पसंद करना
Yearn ***for***	to desire very much	के लिए लालसा करना

'FROM' COMES WITH FOLLOWING WORDS :

Abstain ***from***	to choose not to do or have something	परहेज करना
Abstinence ***from***	the practice of not doing or having something that is wanted	परहेज करना
Debar ***from***	to officially prevent (someone) from having or doing something	निषेध करना
Derive ***from***	to take or get (something) from (something else)	से निकालना या हासिल करना
Descent ***from***	an act of coming or going down in location or condition	से नीचे जाना
Desist ***from***	to stop doing something	करना बंद कर देना
Deviate ***from***	to do something that is different or to be different from what is usual or expected	(रास्ते से) हटना
Emerge ***from***	to become known or come from	उभरना
Escape ***from***	to get away from a dangerous place or situation	सुरक्षित निकल जाना
Exemption ***from***	permission not to pay or do something	छूट
Prevent ***from***	to stop (something) from happening or existing	रोकना
Prohibit ***from***	to order (someone) not to use or do something	निषेध
Protect ***from***	to keep (someone or something) from being harmed	बचाना
Recover ***from***	to become healthy after an illness or injury	स्वस्थ होना
Refrain ***from***	to stop yourself from doing something	परहेज करना
Resign ***from***	to give up (a job or position) in a formal manner	त्यागपत्र देना
Respite ***from***	relief	राहत

'ON' COMES WITH FOLLOWING WORDS :

Comment ***on***	to make a statement about someone or something	टिप्पणी करना

Deliberate ***on***	to think about or discuss something very carefully in order to make a decision	विचार करना
Depend ***on***	to be subject to determination by the situation	पर निर्भर
Dwell ***on***	to live in a particular place	में रहना
Embark ***on***	to begin a journey	यात्रा शुरू करना
Encroach ***on***	to gradually move or go into an area that is beyond the usual or desired limits	अतिक्रमण करना
Impose ***on***	to cause (something, such as tax) to affect someone or something by using your authority	कर लगाना
Insist ***on***	to demand that something happen or that someone do something	आग्रह करना
Intrude ***on***	to come or go into a place where you are not wanted or welcome	पर अतिक्रमण करना
Trample ***on***	to cause damage or pain by walking or stepping heavily on something or someone	पैर तले कुचलना
Acquaintance ***with***	so	
Absorbed ***in***	having one's attention wholly engaged or occupied	अवशोषित
Accomplished ***in***	very skillful, having or showing the skill of an expert	निपुण
Assiduous ***in***	very hard working	परिश्रमी
Bigoted ***in***	blindly devoted to some creed, opinion, or practice	धर्मांध, कट्टर व्यक्ति
Dabble ***in***	to take part in an activity in a way that is not serious	शौकिया तौर पर कुछ करना
Deficient ***in***	not good enough, lacking	अपूर्ण, कमी
Diligent ***in***	showing steady and earnest care and hard work	मेहनती
Excel ***in***	to be better than others	श्रेष्ठ होना
Experienced ***in***	having knowledge or skill in a particular field	अनुभवी
Indulge ***in***	to allow (yourself) to have or do something as a special pleasure	लिप्त होना
Interested ***in***	wanting to learn more about something or to become involved in something	रूची
Involved ***in***	connected with something	शामिल होना
Persist ***in***	to continue to occur or exist beyond the usual, expected, or normal time	लगे रहना
Presevere ***in***	to continue doing something though it is difficult	लगे रहना
Proficient ***in***	good at doing something	कुशल
Remiss ***in***	not showing enough care and attention	बेपरवाह
Versed ***in***	skilled in something	निपुण

'WITH' COMES WITH FOLLOWING WORDS :

Acquaintance ***with***	someone who is known	जान-पहचान
Afflicted ***with***	caused pain or suffering	पीड़ित
Alliance ***with***	a union or association	संधि
Associate ***with***	to combine or unite with another for mutual benefit	सहयोगी
Bear ***with***	to suffer	सहना
Beset ***with***	to cause problems or difficulties for (someone or something)	(किसी के लिए) परेशानी उत्पन्न करना
Busy ***with***	full of activity or work	व्यस्त रहना
Clash ***with***	a short fight	टकराव
Coincide ***with***	to happen at the same time as something else	एक समय पर होना
Compatible ***with***	capable of existing together in harmony	अनुकूल
Compliant ***with***	inclined to agree with others	आज्ञाकारी
Conformity ***with***	the fact or state of agreeing with or obeying something	अनुपालन
Contrasted ***with***	to be different especially in a way that is very obvious	विषम
Conversant ***with***	to be familiar with	परिचित
Cope ***with***	to endure something unpleasant	सामना करना
Correspond ***with***	to be similar or equal to something	अनुरूप
Disgusted ***with***	a feeling of revulsion or profound disapproval	घृणा
Drenched ***with***	to make (someone or something) completely wet	भीगना
Endowed ***with***	to give a large amount of money to a school, hospital, etc.	संपन्न
Gifted ***with***	having great ability	प्रतिभाशाली
Intimacy ***with***	a state marked by emotional closeness	आत्मीयता
Intimate ***with***	to say or suggest (something) in an indirect way	सूचित करना
Popular ***with***	liked or enjoyed by many people	लोकप्रिय
Quarrel ***with***	to fight	लड़ाई करना
Remonstrate ***with***	to disagree and argue or complain about something	प्रतिवाद करना
Replete ***with***	having much or plenty of something	परिपूर्ण
Satiated ***with***	to satisfy (a need, desire, etc.) fully	तृप्त
Satisfied ***with***	to cause (someone) to be happy or pleased	संतुष्ट
Sympathize ***with***	to feel sorry for someone who is in a bad condition	के साथ सहानुभूति रखना

SPOTTING THE ERROR

1. (a) He took/ (b) leave of/ (c) four days./ (d) No error.
2. (a) Children/ should always/ (b) listen the advice of their elders/ (c) and well wishers./ (d) No error.
3. (a) He will not/ (b) listen/ (c) what you say./ (d) No error.
4. (a) Nobody denies/ (b) that my ideas/ (c) are different than yours./ (d) No error.
5. (a) It was I who was responsible of/ (b) making all the arrangements for the/ (c)successful completion of his studies./ (d) No error.
6. (a) She was in the courtyard/ (b) when the burglars/ (c) entered into her house./ (d) No error.
7. (a) Our teacher/ (b) emphasised on/ (c) the use of correct grammar./ (d) No error.
8. (a) On the time/ (b) of the opening ceremony of the theatre/ (c) a large crowd had assembled./ (d) No error.
9. (a) While they were returning/ (b) from school,/ (c) a stalker attacked on them with a knife./ (d) No error.
10. (a) The decline of his moral values/ (b) has caused a lot/ (c) of pain to his parents/ (d) No error.
11. (a) Without thinking/ (b) for a moment he/ (c) entrusted me in all the responsibilities./ (d) No error.
12. (a) Sudha fell in/ (b) the well and nobody / (c) tried to save him./ (d) No error.
13. (a) I / (b) prefer coffee/ (c) than tea/ (d) No error.
14. (a) Suresh is busy / (b) in his work/ (c) for his presentation./ (d) No error.
15. (a) While crossing the road/ (b) an old man was/ (c) run out by a bus./ (d) No error.
16. (a) Amphibians / (b) can live / (c) in water as well as land./ (d) No error.
17. (a) My mother is fond off/ (b) cooking different / (c) types of dishes./ (d) No error.
18. (a) Our teacher/ (b) cannot/ (c) control on the students./ (d) No error.
19. (a) The lawyer has been waiting/ (b) for the prisoner / (c) since two hours. / (d) No error.
20. (a) Mr. Bacon has / (b) great affection to/ (c) his family./ (d) No error.
21. (a) Rekha has a great/ (b) enmity for her/ (c) brother's friend./ (d) No crror.
22. (a) He threw the bucket/ (b) into the river/ (c) and returned home without any water./ (d) No error.
23. (a) There appears/ (b) to be very little/ (c) understanding among the two brothers. / (d) No error.
24. (a) She was/ (b) angry on me because I/ (c) had not invited her to the party./ (d) No error.
25. (a) He got a prestigious job though/ (b) he was not worthy/ (c) for it./ (d) No error.
26. (a) He described about/ (b) the incident/ (c) in a very interesting way./ (d) No error.
27. (a) My father/ (b) deals/ (c)with garments./ (d) No error.
28. (a) I cannot / (b) deal from/ (c) those unruly students./ (d) No error.
29. (a) Despite of / (b)working hard/ (c) he failed./ (d) No error.
30. (a) Ashok/ (b) married with/ (c) Rekha last month./ (d) No error.
31. (a) The earth's atmosphere/ (b)comprises of/ (c) three layers/ (d) No error.
32. (a) The court held/ (b) the local MLA responsible/ (c) for the loss or damage to any public property./ (d) No error.

33. (a)He was debarred to attend/ (b) the monsoon session/ (c)of the Parliament./ (d) No error.
34. (a) We will have to await for/ (b) the result/ (c) as the managent is on strike./ (d) No error.
35. (a) He should refrain/ (b) to associate himself with any party/ (c) because people have faith in his integrity./ (d) No error.
36. (a) The songs of / (b) the old movies are/ (c) worthlistening to./ (d) No error.
37. (a) It should be obvious to you/ (b)that if you persist bothering him,/ (c) he will get angry with you/ (d) No error.
38. (a) I certainly/ (b) differ with you/ (c) in this matter (d) No error.
39. (a)He had a suspected fracture, / (b) so he was/ (c)admitted into the hospital/ (d) No error.
40. (a) If you put your / (b) heart to it,/ (c) you will be a winner/ (d) No error.
41. (a) He walked/ (b) ten miles/ (c) by foot/ (d) No error.
42. (a) He is good / (b) in mathematics/ (c)but his friend isn't./ (d) No error.
43. (a) Those who are in power/ (b) have to be sensitive of/ (c)the sufferings of the poor/ (d) No error.
44. (a) Which newspaper/ (b) do you/ (c) subscribe for?/ (d) No error.
45. (a) We thought that the train/ (b) would be late but/ (c) it arrived exactly in time./ (d)No error.
46. (a) Despite of repeated warnings, / (b) he touched a live electric wire,/ (c) and was electrocuted./ (d) No error.
47. (a)It is my pleasure / (b) to congratulate you for your success/ (c) in the Civil Services Examination/ (d) No error.
48. (a) I will avail/ (b) myself with/ (c) this golden opportunity/ (d) No error.
49. (a) It is half/ (b) past two/ (c) in my watch/ (d) No error.
50. (a) She can / (b) cope up with any difficult situation/ (c) as she is a braveheart./ (d) No error.
51. (a) Ravi/ (b) told to his friend/ (c) to buy a car./ (d) No error.
52. (a) He is/ (b) accused with/ (c) committing the murder./ (d) No error.
53. (a) The poet/ (b) described about/ (c) the spring season./ (d) No error.
54. (a) The atmosphere/ (b) comprises of/ (c) many inert gases also./ (d) No error.
55. (a)We disposed off / (b) our old furniture/ (c) before moving to Mumbai./ (d) No error.
56. (a)He was/ (b) bereft from / (c) all his possession./ (d) No error.
57. (a) He assented of/ (b) my proposal/ (c) as it was very attractive./ (d) No error.
58. (a) A large sign near/ (b) the entrance warns the visitors/ (c) to beware about bears./ (d) No error.
59. (a) The teacher was tense/ (b) when he entered/ (c) the class which comprised of/ (d) a hundred students./(e) No error.
60. (a) There is no rule/ (b) regarding the length of a precis/ (c) with relation to/ (d) that of the original passage./(e) No error.
61. (a) He/ (b) is suffering/ (c) with flu./ (d) No error.
62. (a) He wanted to go/ (b) to home/ (c) as he was sick./ (d) No error.

Answers with Explanation

1. (b); 'leave for four days' is the correct form.
2. (b); 'listen' is followed by 'to'.
3. (b); 'Listen' is followed by 'to'.
4. (c); 'different' is followed by 'from'.
5. (a); 'responsible' is followed by 'for'.
6. (c); 'entered' is not followed by 'into'.
7. (b); 'emphasised' is not followed by 'on'.
8. (a); 'On' will be replaced by 'at'.
9. (c); 'attack' is not followed by 'on'.
10. (a); 'decline' is followed by 'in'.
11. (c); 'entrusted' is followed by 'with'.
12. (a); 'fell into' is the correct form here.
13. (c); 'than' must be replaced by 'to'. 'Prefer' takes 'to' after it.
14. (b); busy' is followed by 'with' and not 'in'.
15. (c); 'run out' must be replaced by 'run over'. 'Run over' means 'to come under the wheels of'.
16. (c); 'Land' will be followed by 'on'.
17. (a); 'Fond' is followed by 'of'.
18. (c); If 'control' is used as a verb, it is not followed by 'on'.
19. (c); 'Since' must be replaced by 'for'. 'Two hours' is a period.
20. (b); 'affection' is followed by 'for' and not 'to'.
21. (b); 'enmity' is followed by 'towards' and not 'for'.
22. (b); Here 'threw' will be followed by 'in' and not 'into'.
23. (c); 'among' must be replaced by 'between'.
24. (b); 'angry' is followed by 'with' is a person comes in place of object.

    Note-angry with someone.
    angry at something.
25. (c); 'worthy' is followed by 'of' and not 'for'.
26. (a); 'describe' is not followed by any preposition.
27. (c); 'Deal in' means 'to trade'.
28. (b); 'Deal with' means 'to tackle.'
29. (a); 'Despite' is not followed by 'of'.
30. (c); Remove 'with'.
31. (b); In active voice, a 'Comprise' is not followed by 'of'.
32. (c); 'Loss' is followed by 'of'.
33. (a); 'debarred from attending' is the correct form.
34. (a); 'await for' must be replace by 'wait for'.
35. (b); 'Refrain' is followed by 'from' and not 'to'.
36. (c); 'listen is followed by 'to' but 'worthlistening' is not followed by any preposition.
37. (b); 'persist' is followed by 'in'.
38. (b); 'differ' is followed by 'from' and not 'with'.
39. (c); 'admitted to' will be the correct form here.
40. (b); 'put your heart into it' is the correct form which means 'to do something with sincere efforts and energy'.
41. (c); 'on foot' must be used here'.
42. (b); 'Good' is followed by 'at'.
43. (b); 'Sensitive' is followed by 'to'.
44. (c); 'subscribe' is followed by 'to'.
45. (c); The word 'exactly' makes 'On time' a more suitable option.
46. (a); 'Despite' is not followed by 'of'.
47. (b); 'Congratulate' is followed by 'on'.
48. (b); 'avail' is followed by 'of'. 'Avail myself of this' is the correct form.
49. (c); 'in' must be replaced by 'by'.
50. (b); 'Cope with' is the correct form which means 'to handle'.
51. (b); 'told' and its forms do not take 'to'.
52. (b); 'accused' is followed by 'of'.
53. (b); 'described' is not followed by 'about'.
54. (b); If the sentence is in active voice, 'comprise' is not followed by 'of'.

55. (a); 'disposed' is followed by 'of' and not 'off'.
56. (b); 'bereft' is followed by 'of'.
57. (a); 'assented' is followed by 'to" and not 'of'.
58. (c); 'beware' is followed by 'of' and not 'about'.
59. (c); In active voice, a 'Comprise' is not followed by 'of'.
60. (c); 'with relation to' must be changed into 'in relation to'.
61. (c); 'with must be changed into 'from'. 'Suffer' is followed by 'from'.
62. (b); Remove 'to'.

FILL IN THE BLANKS WITH APPROPRIATE PREPOSITION

1. He drove from Maharashtra ______ Karnataka without stopping to rest.
(a) is (b) to
(c) into (d) towards.
2. Bill's fight ______ hunting put 26 professional hunting companies out of jobs.
(a) towards (b) for
(c) over (d) against
3. The court has absolved him _____ all the charges leveled against him.
(a) off (b) with
(c) in (d) of
4. You are welcome to partake ________ their light refreshment.
(a) in (b) for
(c) at (d) of
5. We met a lot of people ______ our holidays.
(a) on (b) in
(c) during (d) at
6. The firm has been dealing ______ luxury goods for more than two decades.
(a) in (b) with
(c) out (d) on
7. Today students should be reconciled _______ the way things are changing.
(a) with (b) to
(c) for (d) at
8. That week the dollar dropped _____ its lowest levels.
(a) to (b) at
(c) into (d) by
9. He went _______ sea alone.
(a) in (b) to
(c) into (d) on
10. Everyone in this world is accountable to God _____ his actions.
(a) actions (b) for
(c) to (d) over
11. Speed is ____ essence in a project of this type.
(a) in (b) for
(c) about (d) of
12. A wise man profits _____ the mistakes of others.
(a) through (b) from
(c) with (d) by
13. Ram agreed _____ my proposal.
(a) with (b) for
(c) on (d) to
14. He is addicted _____ smoking.
(a) to (b) with
(c) on (d) for
15. He sat ____ the shade of a tree.
(a) under (b) into
(c) in (d) on
16. There is something wonderful _____ him
(a) of (b) about
(c) for (d) in side
17. When will you hand _____ your assignment?
(a) in (b) back
(c) down (d) into
18. A new minister has taken ______ after the election.
(a) to (b) over
(c) off (d) down
19. There is a bridge ______ the river.
(a) over (b) on
(c) down (d) across
20. Please make yourself ____ home.
(a) with (b) at
(c) in (d) on

21. The brave youth immediately jumped _____ the river to save the drowning child.
(a) in (b) into
(c) inside (d) to

22. We can make no progress if we continue working ______ these conditions.
(a) into (b) with
(c) under (d) for

23. Keep your dog ____ the flower beds. It may damage the flowers.
(a) out (b) from
(c) beside (d) off

24. _______ a moment she felt disappointed for no stockings hung from the fire place.
(a) just (b) for
(c) at (d) since

25. We were completely taken ____ by the estate agent who turned out to be a crook.
(a) for (b) on
(c) off (d) in

26. Dr. Sharma concluded his speech ______ explaining the importance of charity.
(a) by (b) with
(c) at (d) in

27. Shivaji Maharaj fought _____ every kind of aggression.
(a) against (b) to
(c) with (d) at

28. Don't depend _____ others; you must stand on your own feet.
(a) at (b) on
(c) to (d) for

29. Our life promises a lot ______ pleasure and we must learn to enjoy it.
(a) with (b) for
(c) of (d) at

30. He travelled all ______ the world when he was eighty years old.
(a) in (b) over
(c) with (d) of

31. My father lives ______ Delhi.
(a) in (b) at
(c) inside (d) on

32. Madhav is good ______ English.
(a) in (b) at
(c) on (d) with

33. Naina did not disclose the fact ______ her husband.
(a) to (b) before
(c) from (d) on

34. The child did not approve ______ the father's plan.
(a) to (b) by
(c) of (d) with

35. The tribes lived ______customs different from the English had ever seen.
(a) on (b) by
(c) off (d) with

36. The strike has been called ______ .
(a) of (b) at
(c) off (d) by

37. We warned her ______the danger
(a) from (b)about
(c) against (d) of

38. We laughed ______ the affair.
(a) over (b) about
(c) for (d) on

39. Put a blanket _____ the baby.
(a) over (b) about
(c) at (d) on

40. Stay______ your limits.
(a) within (b) in
(c) at (d) on

41. She was happy to partake ___ the festivities.
(a) in (b) of
(c) at (d) for

42. I can cope ______ any problem.
(a) up with (b) with
(c) up (d) from

43. His manners ______ him.
(a) speak of (b) speak out
(c) speak up (d) speak for

44. A thorough search of the aircraft was carried ______ in the airport.

(a) out (b) off
(c) on (d) along

45. Discrimination ______ any form should be avoided.
(a) of (b) by
(c) from (d) in

46. A large number of people have fallen victim ______ dengue fever.
(a) to (b) of
(c) from (d) with

47. She scoffed ______ the idea of revolution.
(a) for (b) at
(c) about (d) on

48. This work of art is worthy ______ praise.
(a) of (b) for
(c) for (d) to

49. It is our duty to get ______ the truth.
(a) to (b) over
(c) into (d) at

50. For a child, a blow ______ self-esteem is a terrible thing.
(a) of (b) with
(c) to (d) on

51. He is a descendent ______ the Mughal royalty.
(a) of (b) from
(c) in (d) for

52. Fate smiled ______ him in all his ventures.
(a) above (b) below
(c) on (d) at

53. Don't put ______ until tomorrow what you can do today.
(a) up (b) of
(c) on (d) off

54. The train is arriving ______ platform number 4.
(a) at (b) on
(c) before (d) upon

55. The criminal was totally taken ______ when the police recognized him.
(a) aback (b) up
(c) for (d) away

56. The examination will begin ______ Monday.
(a) from (b) in
(c) at (d) on

57. You must apologise ______ him for this.
(a) with (b) to
(c) of (d) for

58. She seems cursed ______ bad luck.
(a) by (b) with
(c) for (d) on

59. He was brought ______ by his aunt as his mother had died when he was just a lad.
(a) up (b) put
(c) off (d) with

60. As she became tired, errors began to creep ______ her work.
(a) with (b) into
(c) off (d) up.

61. Small pox has been eradicated ______ India.
(a) in (b) from
(c) within (d) out of

62. I complimented him ______ his success.
(a) about (b) for
(c) on (d) at

ANSWER KEY

1.	(b)	2.	(d)	3.	(d)	4.	(d)	5.	(c)
6.	(a)	7.	(a)	8.	(a)	9.	(b)	10.	(b)
11.	(d)	12.	(b)	13.	(d)	14.	(a)	15.	(c)
16.	(b)	17.	(a)	18.	(b)	19.	(a)	20.	(b)
21.	(b)	22.	(c)	23.	(d)	24.	(b)	25.	(d)
26.	(a)	27.	(a)	28.	(b)	29.	(c)	30.	(b)
31.	(a)	32.	(b)	33.	(a)	34.	(c)	35.	(b)
36.	(c)	37.	(d)	38.	(a)	39.	(a)	40.	(a)
41.	(a)	42.	(b)	43.	(d)	44.	(a)	45.	(d)
46.	(a)	47.	(b)	48.	(a)	49.	(d)	50.	(c)
51.	(a)	52.	(c)	53.	(d)	54.	(a)	55.	(a)
56.	(d)	57.	(b)	58.	(b)	59.	(a)	60.	(b)
61.	(b)	62.	(c)						

CHAPTER 20

ADVERB

AN ADVERB IS A WORD THAT QUALIFIES-

(a) **A verb**

Eg.: He works (verb) **hard** (**Adv.**)

(b) **An adjective**

E.g.: He is very (Adv.) good (Adj.)

(c) **An adverb**

E.g.: She works **very** (**Adv.**) hard (Adv.).

(d) **A preposition**

E.g.: The helicopter hovered **exactly** (**Adv.**) over (Prep.) his house.

(e) **A conjunction**

E.g.: He likes her **simply** (**Adv.**) because (Conj.) she has a clear conscience.

(f) **A complete sentence**

E.g.: **Fortunately,** (**Adv.**) no one was hurt (Sentence).

ADVERBS ARE OF THREE TYPES

1. **Simple Adverb**
2. **Relative Adverb**
3. **Interrogative Adverb**

1. **Simple Adverb**

It denotes **time, place, number, frequency of manner, reason, degree, affirmation or negation.**

(a) **Adverb of Manner : - An adverb of manner tells us how a verb is done.**

E.g.: He works **honestly.**

He walks **slowly.**

Remember: The adverb ending in **'ly'** generally comes under adverb of manner.

Adjective	**Adverb**
Slow	Slowly
Glad	Gladly
Honest	Honestly

➢ **Miser, niggard, scholar** and **coward,** are a few nouns in which we often get confused between their **adjective** and **adverb** forms.

Noun	Adjective Form	Adverb Form
Coward	Cowardly	In a cowardly manner
Niggard	Niggardly	In a niggardly manner
Miser	Miserly	In a miserly manner
Scholar	Scholarly	In a scholarly manner

➢ **Look at the following sentences:**

1. He is miser. (×) (Add 'a' before miser which is a noun)
2. He is a miser man. (×) (use adjective 'miserly' to qualify man which is a noun)

   He is a miserly man.(✓)
3. He behaved miserly. (×) ('behave' is a verb, and adverb of 'miser' will be used to qualify the verb)

   He behaved in a miserly manner.(✓)

Remember:

➢ A few words have the same adverb and adjective forms.

E.g.: '**Fast, straight, outright, direct, hard, late, high, safe** and **quiet.**

E.g.:

Adverb	**Adjective**
He works **hard.**	This is a **hard** task.
He wakes up **early.**	He came by an **early** flight.
Run **fast.**	He is a **fast** runner.
He waited **long** for me.	He went on a **long** journey.
Come **near.**	He is of my **near** relation.

➢ A few adverbs have **different meanings in 'ly'** form.

(a)

Late	**Lately**
After the usual or proper time	**Recently/of late**

E.g.: (i) I haven't seen Akila **lately.**

(ii) He came **late** for the meeting.

(b)

Hard	**Hardly**
With great effort	**with difficulty**

E.g.: (i) She works **hardly** to make both ends meet. (×)

(ii) She works **hard** to make both ends meet. (✓)

(iii) He **hardly** does any work. (✓)

(c)

Free	**Freely**
Without charge	**with freedom**

E.g.: (i) We can move about **freely** in India.

(ii) Rides are provided **free** in this water park.

➢ **Both 'loudly'** and '**aloud**' are adverbs but different in meaning.

Loudly means '**in high volume**'.

Aloud means '**audibly**'.

E.g.: (i) Please speak **aloud**. The students sitting on the last bench are unable to hear you.

(ii) We cannot play music **loudly** in this park.

➢ **Adverb of Time**

after, ago, early, late, now, then, soon, today, tomorrow etc are adverbs of time.

It shows **when the action took place.**

E.g.: I came **late**.

➢ **Adverb of Place**

Here, there, in, out, up, down, within, above, below etc.
Shows **where the action took place.**

E.g.: I could not find him **anywhere**.

➢ **Adverb of Frequency:**

Adverb of frequency / number: **Once, twice, thrice, always, seldom, often, frequently** etc

It shows **how often.**

E.g.: I can **never** behave in such a reckless manner .

She **seldom** goes there.

She **often** comes to meet me.

➢ **Adverb of Degree:**

very, much, too, quite, little, almost etc.

It shows **how much.**

E.g.: This work is **almost** complete.

I am **quite** well.

➢ **Adverb of Reason:**

So, hence, therefore, on account of, consequently etc.

Adverb of Reason shows **why the action took place.**

E.g.: I could not come **because** I was not well.

I don't like him **since** he has cheated many people.

➢ **Adverb of Affirmation**

surely, certainly, truly, indeed, definitely etc.

E.g.: A friend in need is a friend indeed.

I will **surely** repay the loan.

➢ **Adverbs of Negation**

E.g.: **no, not, never**, etc.

E.g.: He did **not** reply to my letter.

I have **never** cheated anybody.

➢ **RELATIVE ADVERBS: when, where, why and how**.

Relative Adverbs joins sentences. It points towards its **antecedents** (noun/pronoun) and **denotes place, reason or manner**.

E.g.: I don't know **where** he has gone.

He will come **when** I call him.

➢ **INTERROGATIVE ADVERBS: why, when, where, how.**

E.g.: **Why** are you surprised ?

Where has she seen me?

- **COMPARISON OF ADVERBS**

	Positive	Comparative	Superlative
(a)	Hard	harder	hardest
	Fast	faster	fastest
	Soon	sooner	soonest
	Near	nearer	nearest
	Early	earlier	earliest
(b)	Beautifully	more beautifully	most beautifully
	Carefully	more carefully	most carefully
	Swiftly	more swiftly	most swiftly
	Slowly	more slowly	most slowly
	Wisely	more wisely	most wisely
(c)	Ill, Badly	worse	worst
	Forth	further	furthest
	Far	farther	farthest
	Late	later	latest, last
	Little	less	least
	Much	more	most
	Well	better	best

- **POSITION OF ADVERB**

Adverb is always placed adjacent to the word that it modifies. If the position of adverb is changed, the meaning of the sentence changes.

E.g.: **Only** she saw my dress. (Dress was seen by just one person)
She **only** saw my dress. (She did not do anything else)
She saw **only** my dress. (She did not see the dress of any other person)
She saw my **only** dress. (I had just one dress)
She saw my dress **only.** (Not my shoes, accessories etc.)

- Adverbs can come **at the beginning of a sentence** :

(i) **Interrogative Adverb is always used in the beginning of a sentence.**

E.g.: **When** are you returning home ?

(ii) **In order to modify a complete sentence, an adverb is used at the beginning of a sentence.**

E.g.: **Surely**, I will take care of you.

(iii) **To emphasize the adverb, it is used in the beginning.**

E.g.: **Off** it goes.
Here comes the chief guest.

- Adverbs can come **at the middle of a sentence** :

(i) **Adverb of frequency (always, never, ever, often, seldom, sometimes) are used before the verbs that they modify**.

But if these adverbs come at the beginning of the sentence, the sentence takes inversion form which means the verb/helping verb comes at the beginning of the sentence.

1. Seldom he comes to Delhi. (×)
   Seldom does he come to Delhi. (✓)
2. Never I'll go there. (×)
   Never shall I go there. (✓)
3. No sooner she reached the station than the train left. (×)
   No sooner did she reach the station than the train left. (✓)
4. Hardly she had reached the station when the train arrived. (×)
   Hardly had she reached the station when the train arrived. (✓)
5. So quickly she ran that she overtook her friends. (×)
   So quickly did she run that she overtook her friends. (✓)
6. His wife comes here and **so** does he. (✓)
7. He doesn't know any one here and **neither** do I.(✓)

➢ **If both the auxiliary verb and the main verb come in a sentence, the adverb of frequency/ degree is put between the auxiliary verb and the main verb.**

E.g.: He will (H.V.) **never** come (M.V.) here.

I have (H.V.) **seldom** gone (M.V.) there.

(iii) **No matter whether 'to be' and its forms are used as a helping verb or a main verb, the adverb of frequency/degree comes always after 'be'.**

E.g.: She is (M.V.) **always** happy.

I am (M.V.) **never** sad.

He is (H.V.) **always** praised (M.V.) for his sweet voice.

➢ **See the following sentences:**

1. He comes often every Sunday. (place often before comes)
2. He goes usually to shop every Sunday. (place usually before goes)
3. He is always happy. (✓)

➢ **USE OF SOME ADVERBS:**

1. Difference between very and much-

(a) **very is used with positive degree**.

E.g.: very good, very wise, very lucky, very honest.

Much is used with comparative degree.

E.g.: Much better, much wiser, much luckier, much more honest.

Note:

(a) **Very much + comparative degree** is also used in a sentence.

E.g.: Very much better, very much wiser, very much luckier etc.

(b) **Very/much is used with superlative degree** too.

E.g.: The (The+) very (very+) best (Sup.) boy.

(c) **Very is used before Present Participle.**

E.g.: very interesting, very daring, very confusing, very surprising, very entertaining.

(d) **Much is also used with past participle.**

E.g.: much surprised, much grieved, much admired .

(e) **Very is not used with Past Participle, but it is used with the following past participles.**

E.g.: Very tired, very dejected, very contented, very discontented, very pleased, very drunk, very limited, very delighted.

2. 'Quite' means 'perfectly/completely' or 'almost'.

(1) I am **quite well**.

(2) You are **quite right** but you have missed some important points.

3. Fairly and Rather

A. **Fairly** is used with **positive degree.**

E.g.: fairly wise, fairly good.

Rather is used with **positive** and **comparative degree**.

E.g.: rather bad, rather difficult, rather worse, rather hotter.

B. **'Fairly'** is **not followed** by **'too'**. In such sentences use **'Rather'** in place of 'fairly'.

E.g.: Fairly too good. (×)

Rather too good.(✓)

C. **Desirable Adjectives** are used after **'fairly'**.

E.g.: fairly wise, fairly beautiful.

➢ **Unpleasant adjectives are used after 'rather'.**

E.g.: Rather wicked, rather difficult, rather troublesome, rather dull .

Note: Rather amusing, rather good, rather clever, rather pretty, rather beautiful are also correct.

4. (a) **'Too'** means **'also' but 'too' usually takes the place of 'also' when needed after some clause or subject.**

E.g.: I also was invited for tea.(×)

I too was invited for tea.(✓)

(b) It **too** means **more than required.** Hence **'too' should not be used with pleasant adjectives.**

E.g.: **too bad, too naughty, too wicked, too fat, too dull etc**.

E.g.: I am too glad to meet you (×)

I am **very glad** to meet you.(✓)

(c) **'Too....to' can take pleasant adjectives** too.

E.g.: He is **too** intelligent **to** be cheated.

The sentence given above means 'he is so intelligent that he cannot be cheated'.

More examples of **'too + adjective'**

(i) He is **too** tall. (He is awkwardly tall)

(ii) She is **too** slim. (She is awkwardly slim)

(iii) It is **too** cold. (It is bitterly cold)

5. **'So' cannot be used in place of 'very'**.

E.g.: (1) I am **so** happy. (×)

(2) I am **very** happy.(✓)

(3) I am **so** happy **that** I am unable to control my feeling. (✓) ('So...that' is a place of conjunction)

6. **Enough:** It **acts as both an adjective** and **an adverb**. If it works as adverb, it is used after adjective which it modifies. When used as an adjective it is placed before a noun. **Enough precedes a noun but follows an adjective**.

E.g.: (1) She is wise **enough** to understand your intention.

(2) He has **enough** money to buy this car.

➢ **Positive degree of adjective / adverb is used before enough**.

E.g.:(1) (A) He is/ (B) faster enough/ (C) to defeat/ (D) you./ (E) No Error. (×)

(2) (A) He is bravest/ (B) enough to be/ (C) selected for/ (D) NDA./ (E) No Error. (×)

➢ In sentence 1, use 'fast' in place of 'faster' and in sentence 2, use 'brave' in place of 'bravest'

7. **<u>Yet:-</u>** means-**up to the moment/ time of speaking**. It is used in interrogative / negative sentences. It is placed after verb or verb + obj.

8. **Too much** and **Much too.**

➢ **Uncountable Noun is used after 'Too Much'**. E.g., Anxiety, tension, tiredness but Adjective is used after **Much too.** E.g.,– Anxious, tensed, tired

E.g.: 1. He is too much worried (adj) (×)

He is much too worried (✓)

2. I have too much work (noun) to do (✓)

<u>Note:</u> It is generally used in present perfect negative sentence not in past tense.

E.g.: (i) The postman did not come yet. (×)

(ii) The postman has not come yet. (✓)

(iii) Didn't the postman come yet ? (×)

(iv) Hasn't the postman come yet ? (✓)

Some rules relating to Adverb-

<u>Rule 1</u>:

➢ **'Else' is followed by 'but'.** and **'than' follows 'rather', 'other' and 'otherwise'**.

E.g.: (i) I would rather die than beg.

(ii) It is nothing else than sheer foolishness. (Use 'but' in place of 'than')

(iii) Rahul had no other alternative but to work hard. (Use 'than' in place of 'but')

(iv) Rohit has no one else to talk to except his wife. (Use 'but' in place of 'except')

Rule 2:

➢ Adverbs, **seldom, never, nowhere, nothing, hardly, scarcely, neither, barely, rarely** are negative in meaning.

E.g.: (i) I **rarely** went to meet nobody. (Use **'anybody'** in place of 'nobody')
(ii) She **hardly** knows nothing about me. (Use **'anything'** in place of 'nothing')
(iii) I **hardly** know somebody in the city. (Say **'anybody'** in place of 'somebody')

Rule 3:

➢ Negative words like **not/never** is not used with **deny, forbid, both, unless, until, lest, hardly, scarcely, rarely, seldom and too.....to.**

E.g.:

(i) She denied that she had not done anything wrong. (Delete 'not')
(ii) Both of us are not going there. (×)
Neither of us is going there. (✓)
(iii) Unless he will not come, I will not go. (×)
Unless he comes, I will not go. (✓)

Note: He did not deny that he was not present at the scene of crime (✓)
[**Meaning** - He accepted that he was present there]

Rule 4:

➢ (A) **Adverb 'as' can be used with -Regard, describe, define, treat, view, know.**
(B) **Adverb 'as' cannot be used with-Name, elect, think, consider, call, appoint, make, choose.**

E.g.: (i) I **regard** him my brother. (Add 'as' after 'him')
(ii) Biology has been **defined** the study of organisms. (Add 'as' after 'defined')
(iii) She is **considered** as the best student of my class. (Drop 'as' after 'considered')
(iv) The teacher **called** him as stupid. (Drop 'as')
(v) The principal **appointed** him as lecturer. (Remove 'as')
(vi) He **thinks** her as a fool. (Remove 'as')

RULE 5

➢ **If the sentence starts with an 'Adverb', 'Helping Verb' should come before the 'Subject'.** ***(See Inversion)***

1. Seldom he comes to Delhi. (×)
Seldom does he come to Delhi. (✓)
2. Never I'll go there. (×)
Never shall I go there. (✓)
3. No sooner she reached the station than the train left. (×)
No sooner did she reach the station than the train left. (✓)
4. Hardly she had reached the station when the train arrived. (×)
Hardly had she reached the station when the train arrived. (✓)
5. So quickly she ran that she overtook her friends. (×)
So quickly did she run that she overtook her friends. (✓)
6. His wife comes here and **so** does he. (✓)
7. He doesn't know any one here and **neither** do I. (✓)

Rule 6:

- **'Too'**, **'as well'** is used as **'Besides'**, **'in addition to'**or **'also'** in affirmative sense. **'Also'** should not be used at the end.

E.g.: She found her bag and money **too/as well.**

Rule 7:

- **'Seldom or never'**, **'seldom, if ever'**, **'little or nothing'**, **'little, if anything'** are correct but it is wrong to say **'seldom or ever'** or **'little or anything'.**

E.g.: He **seldom or never** goes to see movies.

Rule 8:

- **Verbs of sensation (Taste, Smell, Feel, Appear, Seem, Sound, and look)**, should **take adjective and not adverb** after them.

E.g.: I look (Verb of sensation) honest. (Adjective)   I work (ordinary verb) honestly. (adverb)

I felt (verb of sensation) bad. (adj)   I sing (Ordinary verb) badly. (Adv)

- **be, become, turn, get, grow, keep, make, stay, remain and prove** are also certain verbs **that take adjective and not adverb** after them.

E.g.: He got angry (adj) .

RULE 9:

- **Manly, masterly, slovenly, friendly, miserly, niggardly, cowardly, scholarly, orderly, gentlemanly, sickly** are adjectives. They must not be mistaken as adverbs just because they end in 'ly'.

E.g.: He behaved friendly. (×)
He behaved in a friendly manner. (✓)

SPOTTING THE ERROR

1. (a) A soldier is/ (b) taught never to/(c) fight cowardly./(d) No error.
2. (a) A man of fifty/ (b) cannot be called/ (c) as young./ (d) No error.
3. (a) He is being/(b) very politely/ (c) for the reason best known to him. /(d) No error.
4. (a) He is enough tall/(b) to be selected as Sub Inspector/ (c) in Delhi Police./(d) No error.
5. (a) He is niggard/ (b) and saves each/(c) and every paise./(d) No error.
6. (a) I am full of energy/(b) today because I /(c) soundly slept last night./(d) No error.
7. (a) I did not know hardly/(b) anyone in the college/ (c) and so I felt lonely all the time./(d) No error.
8. (a) I have never seen/ (b) a coward man /(c) like Sohan./(d) No error.

9. (a) I never remember/(b) to have met a more intelligent/(c)man in my life./(d) No error.
10. (a) I refused to accompany him/(b) because he was/(c) so boring./(d) No error.
11. (a) I refused to consider/(b) him as an honest boy /(c) as he had cheated many people./(d) No error.
12. (a) I see him often/(b) at the/(c) bus terminal./(d) No error.
13. (a) Mangoes taste /(b) more sweetly than /(c) any other fruit of this world./(d) No error.
14. (a) My father /(b) is very quicker than/(c) I at chess./(d) No error.
15. (a) Never in the history/(b) there has been/ (c) as shrewd a mentor as Chanakya./ (d) No error.
16. (a) Outright rejection/(b) of my plea /(c) disappointed me./(d) No error.
17. (a) She did her job/ (b) as better as she/(c) could do./(d) No error.
18. (a) She does her/(b) work good as she/(c) is a trained nurse./(d) No error.
19. (a) She had barely/(b) nothing to wear/(c) when she came to me for help./(d) No error.
20. (a) This question is/(b) quite too simple,/ (c) for me/(d) to answer.
21. (a) She knows/(b) riding/ (c) a horse./(d) No error.
22. (a) Great leaders tried / (b) to eradicate social evil practices/(c)with tooth and nail./(d) No error.
23. (a) It rained/ (b)like cats and dogs/ (c)throughout the night./(d) No error
24. (a) The State Government/(b) appointed him as /(c) officer-in-charge./(d) No error.
25. (a) The teacher asked/ (b) the students to/(c) talk loudly./(d) No error.
26. (a) Though he was brave,/ (b) he could not face the ups and downs/(c) of life manly./(d) No error.
27. (a) We must try /(b) to save our hardly /(c) earned money./(d) No error.
28. (a) We seldom or ever/(b) go out these days /(c) because it is too hot now-a-days./ (d) No error.
29. (a) We should /(b) keep our belongings/(c) orderly./(d) No error.
30. (a) Vijay could not scarcely conceal/ (b) his happiness /(c) at my resignation./(d) No error.
31. (a) When I read his biography,/(b) I hardly found something/(c)in his character that I could admire./(d) No error.
32. (a) When she received the good news,/ (b) she ran straightly /(c) to call up her parents./(d) No error.
33. (a) You always /(b) come lately/ (c) to class./(d) No error.
34. (a) You have /(b) acted nobler than/(c) all of us./(d) No error.
35. (a) You should have/(b) sufficiently collateral/(c) to pay back the loan. (d) No error.
36. (a) Veena worked /(b)very hardly /(c)as she wanted to be a surgeon./(d) No error.
37. (a) She sounded /(b)very sadly after /(c)the death of her pet/(d) No error.
38. (a) Her speech was not clearly /(b)but we understood /(c)the underlying meaning./ (d) No error
39. (a) All the pupils/ (b) stood up respectively/ (c) as the teacher entered the room./ (d) No error.

Answers with explanation

1. (c) 'In a cowardly manner' is the correct form. 'Cowardly' is an adjective. 'Fight' is a verb and needs an adverb to qualify it.
2. (c) Remove 'as'.
3. (b) Change 'Politely' into 'polite' because an adjective follows 'be' and its forms.
4. (a) 'Enough' comes after an 'adjective'. Put 'enough' after 'tall'.
5. (a) Add 'a' before 'niggard' (noun)
6. (c) Slept (verb) will take 'soundly'(adverb) after it.
7. (a) Hardly cannot take 'not' after it.
8. (b) Man (noun) must be qualified by an adjective 'cowardly'.
9. (a) 'Never' will come after 'remember'.
10. (c) Replace 'so' with 'very'.
11. (b) Remove 'as'. Consider is not followed by 'as'.
12. (a) 'Often' will come before the main verb 'see'.
13. (b) 'Taste' is a verb of sensation that takes an adjective and not an adverb. Change 'more sweetly' into 'sweeter'.
14. (b) 'Much' will come with 'quicker (comparative degree)
15. (b) Never (adverb) will be followed by a helping verb (has) first and then the subject.
16. (d)
17. (b) 'As..........as', will take the positive degree of adjective/adverb in between them. 'As well as' is the correct form here.
18. (b) 'Good' is an adjective. Use adverb 'well' here.
19. (b) 'Barely' will not take 'nothing' after it. Change 'nothing' into 'anything'.
20. (c) Remove 'quite' Adverb 'quite' and 'too' together make the sentence superfluous.
21. (b) 'Knows how to ride' is the correct form here.
22. (c) Remove 'with'.
23. (b) Remove 'like'.
24. (b) Remove 'as'. 'Appoint' is not followed by 'as'.
25. (c) Change 'loudly' into 'aloud' (audible).
26. (c) Change 'manly' into 'manfully'. 'Manly' is adjective. It means 'brave/strong'.
27. (b) Change 'hardly' into 'hard'.
28. (a) 'Seldom' is followed by 'never'.
29. (c) 'Orderly' is an adjective. 'In an orderly manner' is correct.
30. (a) Scarcely cannot be used with 'not'.
31. (b) 'Hardly' will come with 'anything'.
32. (b) 'Straight' is both adverb and adjective . 'Straightly' is a wrong word.
33. (b) 'Lately' means 'recently'. 'Late' is the correct word here.
34. (b) Use 'more nobly'. 'Nobler' is an adjective and here we need an adverb.
35. (b) 'Collateral' is a noun and hence will be qualified by an adjective 'sufficient'. 'Sufficiently' is an adverb.
36. (b) 'Hard' must replace 'hardly' here.
37. (b) 'Sound' (verb of sensation) will be qualified by 'sad'
38. (a) 'Speech (noun) will be qualified by an adjective 'clear'.
39. (b) Change 'respectively'(in the order given) into 'respectfully' (marked by respect).

CHAPTER 21
PARALLELISM

Parallelism means similarity in value, construction and position. A sentence with parallel structure contains words that are parallel or similar in form and function. In fact sentences with parallel structure are balanced and easy to read as a noun balanced by a noun and a verb by a verb. In other words we can say that all must have grammatical form.

(A) **Words** are balanced with **words**.

example :

(i) **Snakes, Crocodiles** and **lizards** are reptiles.

(ii) Traditional methods of food preservation include **drying**, **smoking** and **pickling.**

(iii) Like mother, like daughter.

(B) **Phrases** are balanced with **phrases**.

example :

(i) In Shimla it is colder **in January** than **in February**.

(C) **Clauses** are balanced with **clauses.**

example :

(i) Psychologists study **how we think** and **why we act**.

3. I wondered **what was in the packet, where it came from, who had sent it** and **why it had not been delivered**.

How to correct faulty Parallelism

To correct a sentence containing faulty parallelism. it usually takes only a few moments of thinking and rewriting and of course some knowledge of the parts of speech.

Rule 1 : Correcting Non-parallel Words

In a series of words, each word should be of the same part of speech. You should be careful not to match a series of words with a phrase or a clause.

1. The qualities of a good soldier are **loyalty**, **honesty** and **being brave**. (×)
   The qualities of a good soldier are **loyalty**, **honesty** and **bravery**. (✓)
2. A soldier obeys his senior **willingly**, **completely** and **with speed**. (×)
   A soldier obeys his senior **willingly completely** and **quickly**. (✓)
3. The trainees **analyzed, discussed** and **they raised questions about** the new rules. (×)
   The trainees **analyzed, discussed** and **questioned** the new rules. (✓)
4. He is foolish and miser. (×)
   He is foolish (adj.) and miserly (adj.). (✓)
5. He acted honestly but miserly. (×)
   He acted honestl (adv.) but in a miserlymanner (adv.). (✓)

Rule 2 : Correcting Non-parallel Phrases

Non-parallel Phrases : When ideas are presented in a series of phrases, make sure that each phrase is of same type.

1. A woman always finds time for **doing** her chores, **enjoying** leisure time, and talk about her neighbours. (×)
   A woman always find time for **doing** her chores, **enjoying** leisure time and **talking** about her neighbours. (✓)
2. They travelled to **Delhi, to Agra** and **visited Shimla**. (×)
   They travelled **to Delhi, Agra** and **Shimla**. (✓)

3. I faced the trial **believing** in my own innocence and I **desired** the truth to prevail. (×)
   I faced the trial **believing** in my own innocence and **desiring** the truth to prevail. (✓)

Rule-3 : Correcting Non-parallel Clauses

Non-parallel Clauses : When a series of subordinate clauses is presented, each clause should be of the same type.

1. Our **lawyer** accepts cases **that are worthy** and **if she thinks** she will win. (×)
   Our **lawyer** accepts cases **that are worthy** and **that she thinks** she will win. (✓)

Rule-4: Correcting Non-parallel Comparisons

1. My essay received a low grade **more for its** grammatical mistakes **than what was said in it**. (×)
   My essay received a low grade **more for its** grammatical mistakes **than for its content**. (✓)
2. **Giving** an oral presentation requires more preparation than **to write** a term paper. (×)
   Giving an oral presentation requires more preparation than **writing** a term paper. (✓)
3. I **like** television as much as **reading** books. (×)
   I like **watching** television as much as **reading** books. (✓)

Rule-5 : Correcting Non-parallel with Coordinate Conjunctions

We use Coordinate Conjunctions (and, but, or, yet, for, nor) to join equal expressions. In fact these Conjunctions can join Nouns, Verbs, Adjectives and Coordinate Clauses *i.e.* clauses of equal ranks.

To use them correctly we must make sure that what is on one side of these coordinate conjunctions must be parallel to what is on the other side.

1. He **likes to go** fishing during the day, but my brother **prefers catching** fish at night. (×)
   He **likes to go** fishing during the day but my brother **prefers to catch** fish at night. (✓)
2. **Eating** healthy food, **resting** and **to drink** a lot of fluid is advisable. (×)
   Eating healthy food **resting** and **drinking** a lot of fluid is advisable. (✓)

Rule-6 : Correcting Non-parallel Structure with Correlative Conjunctions

The paired Correlative Conjunctions both....and either....or, neither....nor, not only....but also and whether....or are used to join equal expressions.

1. She is not only **an excellent** student but also **she is a superb singer.** (×)
   She is only **only an excellent student** but also **superb singer.** (✓)
2. We **not only want to visit** the Taj Mahal **but also the Agar Fort.** (×)
   We want to visit **not only the Taj Mahal but also the Agra Fort.** (✓)

Let us see how we can balance correlatives in different ways. The only thing we have to keep in mind is that correlative conjunction requires equal grammatical units after both the parts of conjunction.

1. Not only **did** he buy flowers for his mother but also **purchased** the same for his wife (verb 'did' balanced by verb purchased).
2. He bought flowers not only **for his wife** but also **for his mother.** ('for his + Noun' balanced by 'for his +Noun')

Note:- He was paid 5000/- for boarding and lodging. (×) (Here we need **board and lodging** which means the meals and room that are provided when someone pays to stay somewhere). Board and lodging does not follow the rule of Parallelism

Exercise

1. (A) I like/(B) shopping /(C) and to eat out./(D) No error.
2. (A) Public transit/(B) such as buses or a train/ (C) can help reduce air pollution./ (D) No error.
3. (A) He swiftly/(B) and with efficiency /(C) controlled the damaged car./(D) No error.
4. (A) We spent the whole day (B)/ loitering here and there /(C) eating pizzas and we wiggled on the sofas./(D) no error.
5. (A) Not only he bought flowers for his wife/(B) but also/(C) for his mother./(D) No error.
6. (A)My friends took me/(B) to a dancing show/(C) and then to a baby show./(D) No error.
7. (A) I would rather/(B) pay for my fooding and lodging/(C) than assistance from my parents./(D) No error.
8. (A) The school campus has space /(B)for a new playground /(C) but not a computer lab./(D) No error.
9. (A) It's time /(B) not for words /(C) but action. /(D) No error.
10. (A) My income is /(B) less than/(C) my wife. /(D) No error.

Answers

1. (C); Change 'to eat' into 'eating'. 'Shopping' (Gerund) has to be balanced by 'eating' (gerund).
2. (B); Change 'a train' into 'trains'. 'Buses' (Plural noun) has to be balanced by 'trains' (Plural noun).
3. (B); Change 'with efficiency' into 'efficiently'. 'Swiftly' (adverb) has to be balanced by 'efficiently' (adverb).
4. (C); Change 'we wiggled' into 'wiggling'. 'Loitering' and 'eating' (both Gerunds) have to be balanced by 'wiggling' (a gerund).
5. (A); Shift 'not only' before 'for his wife' because the other part of correlative 'Not only.. but', also (i.e 'but also') is before 'for his mother'.
6. (B); Change 'dancing show' into 'dance show' to balance it with 'baby show'.
7. (C); Add 'take' before assistance. 'Pay' (a verb) has to be balanced by 'take' (a verb).
8. (C); Add 'for' before computer lab.
9. (C); Add 'for' before 'action'.
10. (C); Change 'my wife' into 'my wife's'. 'My income' has to be balanced by 'my wife's income'.

22 SUPERFLUOUS EXPRESSIONS

CHAPTER

'**Superfluous**' means '**more than what is needed**'. Generally we use such expressions in our sentences because we are habitual of translating them from Hindi to English. For example we say 'return back' even when we know that 'return' means 'to come back' or 'go back'.

Let us see all about superfluous one by one.

- *We must not use '**not**' after the following words as the use of 'not' makes the sentence superfluous. The given words comprise 'not' in their meaning and hence the use of 'not' makes them superfluous.*

Until, Unless, Rarely, Hardly, Scarcely, Seldom, Barely, Forbid, Deny, Prohibit, Without, But for (means 'without'), Lest.

Eg:-
1. He did not deny that he had not stolen my watch.(Change 'not stolen' into 'stolen')
2. Unless you will not work hard, you will not succeed. ('will not work' into 'work')
3. Not until the train gets the signal, will it leave the platform. (✓) (Here 'Not at the starting of the sentence is of the 2nd part of the sentence and due to negative introductory, the 2nd part of the sentence is in inversion. (See chapter Inversion)

- *We must not use '**back**' after the following words as the use of 'back' makes the sentence superfluous. The meaning of the given words already comprises 'back'.*

Recede, Return, Retract, Retreat, Withdraw, Recall, Reimburse.

Eg:-
1. He did not return back my watch.(Remove 'back')
2. The water of the river receded back after the flood.(Remove 'back')
3. Maruti recalled back many cars due to a technical fault in the new model.(Remove 'back')

- *We must not use '**again**' after the following words as the use of 'again' makes the sentence superfluous. 'Re' means 'again'.*

Repeat, Recapitulate, Recall, Reborn, Rebuilt.

Eg:-
1. I recapitulated the lessons again before taking the exam. (Remove 'again')
2. Ram was reborn again as Krishna in the Dwapar yug. (Remove 'again')
3. The bridge was rebuilt again after the earthquake had devastated the whole town. (Remove 'again')

- *We must not use '**more or most** with the following adjectives as the use of 'more' or 'most' makes the sentence superfluous. The meaning of the following adjectives is complete in their real sense and hence cannot be used in comparative and superlative degrees.*

Interior, Exterior, Ulterior, Major, Minor, Empty, Excellent, Circular, Extreme, Chief, Entire, Complete, Perfect, Final, Last, Unique, Universal, Round, Square, Triangular, Eternal, Everlasting, Ideal, Absolute, Impossible, Supreme.

Eg:- 1. This is a more unique feature of this flora. (Remove 'more')
2. Corruption is a more universal problem. (Remove 'more')
3. You have done the most excellent piece of work. (Remove 'the most' and add 'an')

• *When we use two of the following words together, the sentence becomes superfluous as all mean the same.*

Suppose, If, In case, Would that, Should (When 'should' means 'if')

Eg:- 1. Suppose if I do not come, what will you do ? (Remove either 'suppose' or 'if')
2. Should you if need my help, do let me know.(Remove 'if')

• ***Two Comparative or two Superlative Degrees cannot come together as the sentence will become superfluous.***

Eg:- 1. He is more faster than his brother. (Remove 'more'.)
2. This is the most best example of evolution. (Remove 'most')

• ***There are many such words that become superfluous when we add a subsequent word of more or less the same meaning.***

WORD/PHRASE	ADDITIONAL WORD THAT MAKES IT SUPERFLUOUS
May/Might	possibly/likely to/probably
Can/Could	able to/capable of
7 p.m./9.30 p.m. etc	evening
8 a.m./11a.m. etc	morning
Despite	of
Cousin	sister/brother
Consensus	opinion
Consort/spouse	husband/wife
Sibling	brother/sister
During	the period/while
Await	for
Kindly	please
Request	please/kindly
Rain cats and dogs	like
Bag and baggage	with
Tooth and nail	with
Flee	away
Coward	man/boy etc ('Coward' is a noun hence no Noun will follow it)
Twins/ Triplet etc	two/ three
Friend	mutual(use word 'common') ('Mutual friend' that you see on facebook is wrong English)
Agreement	mutual
Relatively/Comparatively	better/faster etc. (use a positive degree and not a comparative degree)
The reason why	because
Blunder	big/huge (even 'slight/small' etc too cannot be used with 'blunder' as they will mean the opposite)
Tell/Told	to (See Preposition. Certain 'verbs' are followed by 'to' when an object follows and certain verbs do not)
On the contrary	but
Enter	into (Except when it means 'to make oneself a party to')

Exceed	more than
Related to/concerned with	regarding
Breeze	light (Do not use 'strong breeze' as 'breeze' means 'light, gentle wind')
Come across	with
Come across	suddenly
Universally	every where/ubiquitous/omnipresent/everywhere
Approach	near
Throughout	whole
Illustrate	about
The thing or any other noun	What ('What' is not preceded by any antecedent)
Sufficient	enough
Quite	all/completely
Period	of time
Funeral	service
Enough	very
Comprise	of (In active voice)
Family	member
Reception	party

Correct the following sentences

1. (A) Shyam Yadav, being a philanthropist/ (B) and altruist,/(C)he is liked by all the people of his village./(D) No error.
2. (A) Those people who do not perform their duty,/(B) they should not make/(C) a hue and cry for their rights/(D) No error.
3. (A) When I was going to market,/(B) I suddenly came across/(C) my childhood friend/(D) No error.
4. (A) We usually come across with/(B) difficulties but we have to/(C) cope with them./(D) No error.
5. (A) A cool light breeze was blowing/(B) and it soon put the child/(C) to sleep./(D) No error.
6. (A) Do you have sufficient/(B) enough money to buy/(C) this dress ?/(D) No error.
7. (A) When we entered into/(B) the hall, everyone stood up/(C) and gave us a warm welcome./(D) No error.
8. (A) To our amazement/(B) the speed of the car increased/(C)when it approached near the toll tax counter./(D) No error.
9. (A) The essay on women empowerment/(B) should not exceed/(C) more than five hundred words./(D) No error.
10. (A) Corruption is such a problem/(B) that is found/(C) universally everywhere/(D) No error.
11. (A) Suppose if the driver doesn't come,/(B) how shall/(C) we go home?/(D) No error.
12. (A) The rain kept pouring/(B) throughout the/(C) whole day./(D) No error.
13. (A) It rained/(B) like cats and dogs/(C) during the weekends and we had to stay indoors./(D) No error.
14. (A) When Alexandar saw that/(B) his army was exhausted/(C) he decided to retreat back./(D) No error.
15. (A) The thing what/(B) attracted me towards her/(C) was her simplicity./(D) No error.
16. (A) The judge dismissed the case because/ (B) the plaintiff was hell bent on/ (C)withdrawing back his complaint./(D) No error.
17. (A) The robbers forbade the passengers/(B) not to make/(C) a noise./(D) No error.
18. (A) He left India/(B) with bag and baggage/ (C) for good./(D) No error.
19. (A) Niharika, my cousin sister/(B) will contest the next/(C) Lok Sabha election./(D) No error.
20. (A) We will organize a blood donation camp/ (B) at 8 a.m./(C) tomorrow morning./(D) No error.
21. (A) We cannot illustrate about/(B) the process of evolution/(C) as any such process involves thousands of years/(D) No error.

22. (A) I didn't mean to insult you/(B) but on the contrary/(C) I had come here to congratulate you./(D) No error.
23. (A) No consensus opinion/(B) could be reached/(C) on women's reservation bill./(D) No error.
24. (A) The magistrate warned the witness,/(B) "Once your statement is recorded,/(C) you cannot retract back from it."/(D) No error.
25. (A) Despite of being a meritorious student/(B) he failed to prove/(C) his mettle./(D) No error.
26. (A) Any act of terrorism/(B) is universally condemned /(C) by all./(D) No error.
27. (A) Time and opportunity, once lost,/(B) never/(C) return back./(D) No error.
28. (A) She looked very elegant and presentable enough/(B) to get the job/(C) of air hostess very easily./(D) No error.
29. (A) She said,/(B) "Delhi is comparatively/(C) Colder than Mumbai."/(D) No error.
30. (A) The Mughal Empire made/(B) a big blunder/(C) by letting the British set up the East India Company./(D) No error.
31. (A) My English is equally/(B) as good as/(C) yours./(D) No error.
32. (A) He is a coward man/(B) as he is not able to face/(C) the ups and downs of life manfully./(D) No error.
33. (A) No matter how much you spend,/(B) we will reimburse back/(C) all your expenditure./(D) No error.
34. (A) The victim was persuaded/(B) to recall back what had happened with her/(C) but she was unable to recollect anything./(D) No error.
35. (A) The students have already taken the exam/(B) and the result is being/(C) awaited for./(D) No error.
36. (A) The thief fled away/(B) as the night was dark/(C) and the roads were deserted with not a single check post placed anywhere./(D) No error.
37. (A) You are requested to kindly/(B) submit all the documents/(C) before the 30th of next month./(D) No error.
38. (A) She requested the senior executive/(B) if he could repeat the data/(C) as she was unable to note them down./(D) No error.
39. (A) Even after many rounds of talks/(B) India and Pakistan could not reach at/(C) a mutual agreement on the issue of Kashmir./(D) No error.
40. (A) I prefer staying at home/(B) more than going/(C) to parties./(D) No error.
41. (A) A deed of kindness has/(B) a more everlasting/(C) effect on every creature living on this planet./D) No error.
42. (A) He is /(B) more wiser/(C) than all his friends./(D) No error.
43. (A) He has the right/(B) to receive an annual sum/(C) out of the income every year./(D) No error.
44. (A) Before translating the sentence word for word/(B) it is worth first asking/(C) Whether it can be literally translated or not./(D) No error.
45. (A) This cup of steaming coffee/(B) is too hot to/(C) drink it./(D) No error.
46. (A) He was too drunk/(B) to know/(C) where he was going to./(D) No error.
47. (A) You must mend your ways/(B) lest you should/(C) not fall in any trap./(D) No error.
48. (A) The pre-recorded/(B) statement of the witness/(C) was produced before the court./(D) No error.
49. (A) Dr. Radha Krishnan/(B) was an educated/(C) man of letters./(D) No error.
50. (A) His speech was/(B) vaguely ambiguous as/(C) we could not understand what was the exact topic of his speech./(D) No error.

Answer-key

1. (C)	2. (B)	3. (B)	4. (A)	5. (A)	6. (B)	7. (A)	8. (C)
9. (C)	10. (C)	11. (A)	12. (C)	13. (B)	14. (C)	15. (A)	16. (C)
17. (B)	18. (B)	19. (A)	20. (C)	21. (A)	22. (B)	23. (A)	24. (C)
25. (A)	26. (C)	27. (C)	28. (A)	29. (B)	30. (B)	31. (A)	32. (A)
33. (B)	34. (B)	35. (C)	36. (A)	37. (A)	38. (B)	39. (C)	40. (B)
41. (B)	42. (B)	43. (C)	44. (B)	45. (C)	46. (C)	47. (C)	48. (A)
49. (C)	50. (B)						

Solution

1. (C) 'He' must be omitted. A pronoun is used in place of a noun and not in addition to a noun.
2. (B) 'They' must be omitted. A pronoun is used in place of a noun and not in addition to a noun.
3. (B) 'Suddenly' should be omitted.
4. (A) 'With should be omitted.
5. (A) 'Light' must be omitted. 'Breeze' means 'light, gentle wind.'
6. (B) 'Enough' should be omitted. 'sufficient' means 'enough'.
7. (A) 'Into' should be omitted. 'Enter' means 'to come into'
8. (C) 'Near' must be omitted. 'Toll' and 'tax' mean the same hence remove 'tax'.
9. (C) 'More than' should be omitted. 'Exceed' means 'to be more than' .
10. (C) 'Every where' must be omitted.
11. (A) 'If' must be omitted.
12. (C) 'whole' should be removed.
13. (B) 'like' should be removed.
14. (C) 'Back' must be omitted. 'Retreat' means 'going backward'.
15. (A) 'that' must replace 'what' . 'An antecedent' doesn't come before 'what'
16. (C) 'Back' must be omitted.
17. (B) 'Not' should be removed.
18. (B) 'with' should be removed.
19. (A) 'Sister' should not be used. 'Cousin sister' is a superfluous expression.
20. (C) 'Morning' should not be used. 'a.m'. refers to 'morning '.
21. (A) 'About' should be removed.
22. (B) 'But' should be removed.
23. (A) 'Opinion' should not be used. 'Consensus opinion' is a superfluous expression.
24. (C) 'back' must be omitted.
25. (A) 'of' should not be used.
26. (C) 'by all' will not be used here. 'Universally is sufficient'.
27. (C) 'back' will be omitted.
28. (A) 'very' must be removed.
29. (B) 'Comparatively' must be removed as 'colder' itself is a comparative degree.
30. (B) 'big' must be omitted. Blunder means 'A big mistake'.
31. (A) 'equally' must be removed. 'as + positive degree + as' is used for comparison .
32. (A) 'Man' must be removed. 'Coward' a noun cannot be followed by another noun.
33. (B) 'Back' will be omitted.
34. (B) 'Back' will be omitted.
35. (C) 'for' will be omitted.
36. (A) 'away' will be omitted. 'fled' means 'to run away'.
37. (A) 'kindly' will be removed. 'request' and 'kindly' mean the same.
38. (B) Change 'if he could repeat' into 'to repeat'. Here 'request' should not be followed by 'could' which gives the meaning of 'request' in this statement. We know that 'could' is used for 'formal request' too.
39. (C) 'Mutual' will not be used. 'Mutual agreement' is a superfluous expression.
40. (B) 'to' must replace 'more than'.
41. (B) 'More' must be omitted.
42. (B) 'More' must be removed. Double comparative degrees are not used in a sentence.
43. (C) 'Every year' will be removed. 'Annual' has been already used here.
44. (B) 'First' must be removed.
45. (C) 'It' should not be used here. In one sentence both noun 'This cup of steaming coffee' and pronoun 'it' cannot come together.
46. (C) 'To' will be omitted.
47. (C) 'Not' will be removed.
48. (A) 'Pre' will be removed. Recording is something that is 'pre-' (before than).
49. (C) 'of letters' will be removed. 'Man of letters' means an educated man.
50. (B) 'Vaguely' will be removed as 'ambiguous' and 'vaguely' carry the same meaning i.e 'unclear'.

CHAPTER

23 PHRASAL VERBS

S.No.	Phrasal verb	Meaning in English	Meaning in Hindi
1.	**Account for (something)**	To explain the reason for	जबाव देना (का कारण बताना)
	E.g You are accounted for your misdemeanour.		
2.	**Add up**	To join or unite so as to increase in size, quantity, quality or scope	में जुड़ जाना जिससे माप/भार में बढ़ोतरी हो जाए
	E.g Add up these words to your word bank.		
3.	**Answerable for**	To be responsible for	जवाबदेह होना
	E.g I am not answerable for this mistake.		
4.	**Ask after**	to make inquiries about the health of (someone)	किसी के सेहत के बारे में पूछताछ करना
	E.g I met Alka and she was asking after you.		
5.	**Ask for (something)**	to demand	किसी वस्तु की माँग करना
	E.g She was asking for a hike in her salary.		
6.	**Attend on**	To serve	सेवा करना
	E.g Radhika has many servants to attend on her.		
7.	**Back off**	To retreat/ to choose not to take action	दावा छोड़ देना/ पीछे हट जाना
	E.g Finally she backed off from her claim on the property.		
8.	**Back out**	To withdraw from something before completion/to fail to keep promise	कार्य पूरा होने से पहले पीछे हट जाना/ वादे से मुकर जाना
	E.g You should not back out now as you had promised to help me.		
9.	**Back up**	To support	सहायता देना
	E.g "We need back up because the soldiers are getting exhausted", the command or commander said.		
10.	**Bank upon/ Count on**	To rely on	विश्वास करना या निर्भर होना
	E.g You cannot bank upon him as he may take you in any time.		
11.	**Bear down**	To overthrow or crush by force	परास्त कर देना
	E.g We have to bear down our enemies.		
12.	**Bear upon**	To be relevant	संबंधित होना/प्रासंगिक होना
	E.g Will the new law bear upon the outcome of the case?		
13.	**Bear out**	To support the truth/substantiate	सही साबित करने में सहायक होना
	E.g This document will bear out your claim on this building.		

14.	**Bear up**	To withstand stress or difficulty	सहना
	E.g Everyone has to bear up some difficulties.		
15.	**Bear with**	To tolerate with someone	बर्दाश्त करना
	E.g Our server is down. Kindly bear with us.		
16.	**Become of**	To happen	घटित होना (किसी व्यक्ति के साथ)
	E.g I wonder, what became of my old friends.		
17.	**Boil down to**	To be reduced to its essentials.	सार निकालना/संक्षिप्त करना
	E.g Every business boils down to just one thing i.e profit.		
18.	**Branch out**	To spread	फैल जाना
	E.g We are going to branch out our business soon.		
19.	**Break down (of machine)**	To stop working	काम करना बंद कर देना
	E.g The bus broke down on the way so I could not reach the station in time.		
20.	**Break down (of person)**	To lose control (emotionally or mentally)	हिम्मत/हौसला खो देना
	E.g We should not break down in adverse situation.		
21.	**Break forth**	To come to view/to appear suddenly	अचानक उजागर होना
	E.g Chaos might break forth if the police fail to control the situation.		
22.	**Break in on**	To interrupt a conversation or discussion/ to intrude.	खलल डालना
	E.g The conversation between Ali and Sona was going on when Rahul broke in on it.		
23.	**Break into**	To enter or open a place or vehicle forcibly	जबरदस्ती प्रवेश करना
	E.g The thief broke into the house.		
24.	**Break off**	To stop suddenly/ to end a relationship.	सहसा रूक जाना/ संबंध खत्म करना
	E.g He broke off in the middle of his lecture yesterday.		
	E.g They broke off their business relationship		
25.	**Break out**	To start suddenly (disease, war etc.)	अचानक फैलना
	E.g Dengue has broken out in Delhi.		
26.	**Break up**	To end/disperse	भंग होना
	E.g Seeing the police the crowd broke up.		
27.	**Break up**	To separate (of a relationship etc.)	अलग हो जाना
	E.g They have broken up and now marriage is not on the cards.		
28.	**Breakthrough**	To discover a secret	रहस्य की खोज करना
	E.g There is no breakthrough in the robbery case.		
29.	**Bring about**	To cause to happen	होने का कारण होना
	E.g The sound economic policies brought about a revival of the company.		
30.	**Bring along**	To take someone/something	साथ लाना
	E.g Bring your son along with you when you come here.		
31.	**Bring down**	To overthrow (a government)/to reduce in position	सत्ता से नीचे गिराना/ पद में कम करना
	E.g The sting operation, exposing the corrupt ministers, can bring down the government.		

32.	**Bring forth**	To give birth to/produce	उत्पन्न/ पैदा करना
	E.g *Corruption brings forth poverty.*		
33.	**Bring forward**	To present	प्रस्तुत करना
	E.g *The judge asked me to bring forward some proof against him.*		
34.	**Bring in**	To produce, yield or earn	कमाई कराना/पैदा करना
	E.g *Our company will bring in huge profit this month.*		
35.	**Bring off**	To carry to a successful conclusion	करने से सफल होना
	E.g *The government has brought off changes in the Land Bill.*		
36.	**Bring on**	To cause to happen	का कारण बनना
	E.g *The new law will surely bring on positive changes in the society.*		
37.	**Bring out**	To present to the public/to make some quality noticeable	प्रस्तुत करना/कुछ विशेष जानकारी में लाना
	E.g *His evidence has convincingly brought out several facts before the court.*		
38.	**Bring over**	To bring someone to one's side	अपने पक्ष में करना
	E.g *We should not try to bring him over as he is not a reliable person.*		
39.	**Bring round**	To bring to one's senses/to make one agree to one's opinion	होश में लाना/अपने अनुकूल बनाना
	E.g *The Trade Union succeeded in bringing the management round to their point of view.*		
40.	**Bring under**	To control	वश में करना
	E.g *The East India company brought many provinces under its control.*		
41.	**Bring up**	To raise/ to rear/to increase	उठाना (मुद्दा इत्यादि)/ पालन-पोषण करना/ बढ़ाना
	E.g *She was brought up in a very poor family.*		
42.	**Call on**	To visit (a person)	मुलाकात करना (किसी से)
	E.g *The PM will call on the flood victims tomorrow.*		
43.	**Call at**	To visit (a place)	मुलाकात करना (किसी के घर/ ऑफिस इत्यादि जाकर)
	E.g *Last Sunday I called at your home but you were not at available.*		
44.	**Call for**	To demand (answer, explanation)	मांग करना
	E.g *This irresponsible behaviour calls for strict actions against her.*		
45.	**Call forth**	To produce (a reaction)elicit	प्रतिक्रिया पैदा करना
	E.g *The arbitrary Bill called forth a strong reaction.*		
46.	**Call in**	To summon/ send for	बुलावा भेजना
	E.g *She is too ill to call in a doctor.*		
47.	**Call off**	To cancel	रद्द करना
	E.g *The meeting was called off without any reason.*		
48.	**Call up**	To recall	याद करना
	E.g *The victim tried to call up the actual sequence of the incidents b[illegible]ouldn[illegible]*		
49.	**Call upon/on**	To invite to do something	कुछ करने [illegible] के लिए आमंत्रित करना
	E.g *I call upon you to furnish the details of your income and expenditure.*		

50.	**Carry away**	To arouse too much emotion/ zeal	उत्तेजित करना/भावुक करना
	E.g *I was carried away by the emotional scenes of the movie.*		
51.	**Carry off**	To execute	कार्यान्वित करना
	E.g *He carried off the responsibility successfully.*		
52.	**Come by**	To get	मिलना/प्राप्त करना
	E.g *It is difficult to come by a good job now-a-days.*		
53.	**Carry on**	To continue	जारी रखना
	E.g *You must carry on with your charitable work.*		
54.	**Carry out**	To complete or fulfil/to execute	किसी कार्य या आदेश को पूरा करना
	E.g *We must carry out the orders of the court.*		
55.	**Carry through**	To sustain/ to persist	बनाए रखना
	E.g *I carried through the feelings that I had for him to the present.*		
56.	**Catch on**	To understand/to become popular	समझना/ लोकप्रिय होना
	E.g *Work hard if you want to catch on the syllabus.*		
	E.g *The fashion will soon catch on.*		
57.	**Catch up with**	To stop being behind	बराबरी पर आ जाना
	E.g *Work hard to catch up with them.*		
58.	**Chance upon**	To meet/get by chance	अचानक मिल जाना
	E.g *I chanced upon one of my friends when I was going to market.*		
59.	**Clear of**	To free from blame	आरोप मुक्त करना
	E.g *He was cleared of the charges.*		
60.	**Close in**	To encircle closely	चारों तरफ से घेरना
	E.g *The police personnel closed in on the suspect.*		
61.	**Come about**	To happen	घटित होना
	E.g *How did this huge loss come about?*		
62.	**Come across**	To find (unexpectedly) or meet by chance	अचानक मिल जाना
	E.g *I came across my childhood friend yesterday.*		
63.	**Come down**	To become lower or cheaper	नीचे आना/सस्ता होना
	E.g *The price of petrol is supposed to come down soon.*		
64.	**Come forward**	To offer help	सहायता के लिए आगे आना
	E.g *Several people came forward to offer help to the flood victims.*		
65.	**Close down**	To stop operating	बंद हो जाना
	E.g *All the petrol pumps of Reliance closed down.*		
66.	**Come in for**	To receive/subjected to	सामना करना
	E.g *His misdemeanour comes in for harsh criticism.*		
67.	**Come of**	To originate, to be the result of something	उत्पन्न होना
	E.g *Nothing came of his efforts though he tried his best.*		
68.	**Come off**	Happen/succeed	होना/सफल होना
	E.g *The deal did not come off despite my best efforts.*		

69.	**Come out**	To come into public view, happening ***E.g*** *The investigating team must come out with the truth as soon as possible.*	बाहर आना/जाहिर होना
70.	**Come round**	To accept someone's opinion ***E.g*** *He took some time to come round to my side but now he agrees to my opinion.*	दूसरे की बात मानकर विचार बदल लेना
71.	**Come through**	To do what is needed or expected or to become communicated ***E.g*** *The message of the PM came through loud and clear.*	जो जरूरी हो वो करना/ संप्रेक्षित करना
72.	**Come down**	To fall/ to pass by as tradition ***E.g*** *These customs have come down from time immemorial.*	नीचे आना/एक से दूसरे पीढ़ी में जाना
73.	**Come to senses**	To gain consciousness or to recover/ to get result. ***E.g*** *He came to his senses after a short while.* ***E.g*** *You will come to nothing if you keep on fighting.*	होश में आना/ नतीजा होना
74.	**Come up**	Raised for discussion ***E.g*** *The issue of safety came up twice during the meeting.*	उठाना (मुद्दा)
75.	**Come upon/across**	To meet by chance ***E.g*** *I came upon/ across this beautiful piece of art while I was looking for some decorative items.*	अचानक मिलना
76.	**Count on**	To depend on, to rely on ***E.g*** *I cannot count on them.*	विश्वास करना या निर्भर रहना
77.	**Crop up**	To happen unexpectedly (usually problem) ***E.g*** *A number of problems cropped up suddenly.*	अचानक होना
78.	**Cut across**	to pass through the shortest way/ to affect many. ***E.g*** *The issue of health care cuts across all the strata of our society.*	सबसे छोटे मार्ग से गुजरना/ कई को प्रभावित करना
79.	**Cut down on**	To curtail ***E.g*** *We need to cut down on the intake of salt.*	कटौती करना
80.	**Cut in**	to interrupt ***E.g*** *You should not cut in when your boss speaks.*	हस्तक्षेप करना
81.	**Cut out for**	To be suitable for ***E.g*** *I am cut out for the profession of teaching.*	किसी कार्य के लिए उपयुक्त होना
82.	**Dawn upon**	To understand ***E.g*** *It dawned upon me that I had been cheated.*	समझ में आना (कोई बात)
83.	**Deal in**	To have business of something ***E.g*** *She deals in garments.*	का व्यवसाय करना
84.	**Deal with**	To handle ***E.g*** *I cannot deal with the stupid people.*	निपटना
85.	**Die down**	To gradually disappear, to lose strength or power ***E.g*** *The rumours will die down.*	धीरे-धीरे कम हो जाना, शक्ति क्षीण होना

86.	**Die for**	To have a great wish	इच्छा या चाह रखना
	E.g We die for those chocolate cakes now.		
87.	**Die out**	To get extinct	विलुप्त/खत्म हो जाना
	E.g Several species died out because of climate change.		
88.	**Dispose of**	To sell off/ to get rid of	बेचना/ छुटकारा पाना
	E.g I want to dispose of some old furniture.		
89.	**Do away with**	To abolish	समाप्त कर देना
	E.g We should do away with such evil practices.		
90.	**Do without**	To manage without	किसी चीज के बिना काम चलाना
	E.g I cannot do without my books.		
91.	**Drag on**	To stretch	लम्बा खींचना
	E.g The court cases drag on for years.		
92.	**Drive out**	To make someone run away	भगा देना
	E.g Drive out the cattle from the field.		
93.	**Drop in**	To come suddenly	अचानक पहुँचना
	E.g Some guest dropped in yesterday.		
94.	**Dwell on**	To keep thinking or talking about or rely on something	किसी बात के बारे में बोलते या सोचते रहना या उसी पर निर्भर रहना
	E.g It is no use dwelling on your misfortunes.		
95.	**Eat into**	To weaken	खोखला करना
	E.g Corruption is eating into our system.		
96.	**Enter into**	To start or get involved in	किसी कार्य में सम्मिलित हो जाना
	E.g You are advised not to enter into this agreement.		
97.	**Fall apart**	To break into pieces	बिखर जाना
	E.g Every part of this movement is falling apart.		
98.	**Fall back**	To retreat	पीछे हट जाना
	E.g The invading army was forced to fall back due to continuous firing.		
99.	**Fall back on**	To use as a last resort	कठिनाई के समय में किसी चीज की सहायता लेना
	E.g I have no one to fall back on.		
100.	**Fall flat**	Fail to produce any effect	कोई असर पैदा न करना
	E.g His advice fell flat on us.		
101.	**Fall for**	To fall in love with, to become a victim of	प्यार होना, शिकार होना
	E.g He fell for her simple behaviour.		
102.	**Fall in**	To sink inward/ collapse	अंदर धँस जाना
	E.g The roof fell in killing five people.		
103.	**Fall in with**	To agree with	सहमत होना
	E.g I fall in with you on this matter.		
104.	**Fall off**	To become less, decrease	कम होना
	E.g Stock prices have fallen off.		

105.	**Fall out (with)**	To quarrel with, to happen	झगड़ा होना, घटना
	E.g We should not fall out with them without any rhyme or reason.		
106.	**Fall through**	To fail	असफल होना
	E.g The plans fell through due to your misdemeanour.		
107.	**Feel like**	To be excited to do something	किसी काम को करने का इच्छुक होना
	E.g I feel like going to school.		
108.	**Figure out**	To understand	समझ पाना
	E.g I am unable to figure out the meaning of his ambiguous statement.		
109.	**Fish for**	To seek something by probing	पाने का प्रयास करना (सूचना इत्यादि)
	E.g The reporter tried to fish for some information.		
110.	**Fly open**	To open suddenly	अचानक खुल जाना
	E.g The doors flew open when the storm came.		
111.	**Follow up**	To pursue	करना (किसी कोर्स/मकसद को पूरा करने हेतु)
	E.g You must follow up this routine for better result.		
112.	**Gain on**	To come close to someone or something that you are chasing	नजदीक आना (उसके, जिसे पाने के प्रयासरत हो)
	E.g I am gaining on them in my business. Soon I will leave them behind.		
113.	**Get about/ around**	Spread, move around or be socially active	फैल जाना, इधर-उधर घूमना या सामाजिक रूप से सजग होना
	E.g Good news about upcoming vacancies is getting about.		
114.	**Get at**	to understand, to reach successfully	समझ जाना, तक पहुँचना
	E.g I am doing my best to get at the truth.		
115.	**Get away with**	To do something wrong or illegal without getting caught or punished	कोई गलत काम करना और पकड़े जाने या सजा से बच जाना
	E.g The thieves got away with all my belongings.		
116.	**Get back**	To return	लौटना
	E.g I will get back to you soon.		
117.	**Get along**	have smooth relations	अच्छा संबंध होना
	E.g He and his wife are not getting along well these days.		
118.	**Get down**	To direct attention towards something	किसी कार्य के तरफ ध्यान लगाना
	E.g Please get down to your work.		
119.	**Get off**	To leave work with permission	काम से अधिकारिक अवकाश मिलना
	E.g *You can get an off tomorrow.*		
120.	**Get on**	To make progress, to be on harmonious terms	प्रगति करना, अच्छा संबंध होना
	E.g He gets on well with all his neighbours.		
121.	**Get over**	To overcome	पार पाना/ उबर जाना
	E.g Finally I got over the difficulties and court cases.		

122.	**Get rid of**	To dispose of/to leave	छुटकारा पाना
	E.g *I want to get rid of my bad habits.*		
123.	**Get round (a problem)**	To evade or avoid a problem	किसी समस्या से बचने के लिए रास्ता ढूंढ लेना
	E.g *He will get round your problems in some way or the other.*		
124.	**Get round (someone)**	To persuade someone to do what you want	किसी को कुछ करने के लिए मना लेना
	E.g *You will have to get them round to join your team.*		
125.	**Get through**	To finish or assist in finishing	कोई कार्य पूरा करना या पूरा कराने में सहायता करना
	E.g *If you work hard, you will get through this task in a week.*		
126.	**Get up**	to wake up	जागना
	E.g *I get up at 6 am everyday.*		
127.	**Give away**	To distribute	बाँटना
	E.g *The Chief guest gave away the prizes.*		
128.	**Give in**	To agree, to surrender, to submit	मान जाना, समर्पण कर देना, सौंपना
	E.g *The daughter-in-law gave in to her in-laws' demands.*		
129.	**Give up**	To leave, to stop doing something/ to yield	छोड़ देना, त्याग देना, हार मान जाना
	E.g *She has given up smoking.*		
130	**Go ahead**	To start or continue to do something	किसी कार्य को शुरू करना या जारी रखना
	E.g *Go ahead with your demands.*		
131.	**Go along**	To cooperate	सहयोग देना
	E.g *I will go along with them on this issue.*		
132.	**Go at**	to attack especially with energy	हमला करना (पूरे उर्जा के साथ)
	E.g *The bull went at the audience and this led to stampede.*		
133.	**Go back on**	To break a promise	वादे से मुकर जाना
	E.g *Why did you go back on your promise?*		
134.	**Go by**	To work accordingly	नियमानुसार कार्य करना, गुजरना (समय इत्यादि का)
	E.g *(1) We should go by the traffic rules.* *(2) Time went by.*		
135.	**Go down**	To be accepted	विश्वास करना/ स्वीकार करना
	E.g *The theory of evolution did not go down well initially.*		
136.	**Go down in history**	To get registered in history	इतिहास में नाम दर्ज कराना
	E.g *Ashok went down in History due to his religious work.*		
137.	**Go for**	To attack, to try to attain, to choose	आक्रमण करना, पाने की कोशिश करना या चुनना
	E.g *(1) I will go for this dress. (2) If you want it, go for it.*		

138.	**Go off**	explode *E.g The bomb went off and people ran helter-skelter.*	फटना (बम का)/बन्दूक से गोली छूटना
139.	**Go on**	To continue doing something *E.g She went on reading the book.*	जारी रखना
140.	**Go over**	To gain acceptance *E.g The film went over well.*	स्वीकार होना
141.	**Go through**	To pass through a time, to read *E.g Let me go through this book.*	किसी दौर से गुजरना,पढ़ना
142.	**Go up**	Increase *E.g Price of foodgrains went up due to famine.*	बढ़ना
143.	**Go with**	To select or choose *E.g I cannot go with this brand.*	चुनना
144.	**Hear of**	To get the news about *E.g I haven't heard of any such haunted house.*	समाचार मिलना
145.	**Hit on/upon**	To come to mind suddenly *E.g An idea hit upon me when I was reading the story.*	अचानक दिमाग में आना
146.	**Hold back**	To retain in one's possession, to restrain oneself *E.g Please hold back your emotions.*	(व्यक्त करने) से रोकना, खुद को रोकना किसी कार्य से
147.	**Hold down**	To prevent, to limit *E.g The militants were held down by the Indian army.*	रोकना, नियंत्रित करना
148.	**Hold on**	To maintain one's grip, to continue to do something despite difficulties, to wait for something wanted or requested. *E.g Please hold on while we transfer your call to our executive.*	पकड़कर रखना, जारी रखना (कठिनाई के बावजूद), इंतजार करना
149.	**Hold with**	Approve of/agree with *E.g I cannot hold with them on this matter.*	सहमत होना
150.	**Hunt down**	To pussue successfully by diligent searching and chasing. *E.g The militants were hunted down at the border.*	खोज, निकालना
151.	**Hush up**	To hide *E.g They hushed up this scam.*	छिपाना
152.	**Impress (idea) on**	To convince someone or impart a strong impression in the mind of someone *E.g She can impress upon the clients easily.*	छाप छोड़ना (कोई बात का किसी व्यक्ति के दिमाग पर)
153.	**Iron out**	To ease a problem *E.g We need to iron out our differences.*	समस्या की गंभीरता कम करना
154.	**Jump at (conclusion)**	To draw conclusion in a hurry *E.g You should not jump at any conclusion.*	जल्दबाजी में निष्कर्ष निकालना
155.	**Keep on**	Continue *E.g He kept on talking.*	जारी रखना

156.	**Keep up**	to maintain	कायम रखना
	E.g Keep up your confidence in every situation.		
157.	**Kick against**	To fight against people in authority	विरोध करना
	E.g We cannot kick against the authority as we may be booked for sedition.		
158.	**Knock about/around**	To wander about aimlessly	इधर-उधर घूमना बिना किसी मकसद के
	E.g He knocked about as he was jobless.		
159.	**Knock someone about /around**	To behave violently towards someone	किसी के साथ उग्र तरीके से व्यवहार करना
	E.g We cannot knock him about without any rhyme or reason.		
160.	**Knock down**	To bring to the ground with a blow	कुचल देना, धक्का मार कर गिरा देना
	E.g He was knocked down by a speeding car.		
161.	**Lap up**	To receive very eagerly	अत्यंत उत्सुकता के साथ प्राप्त करना
	E.g Let us lap up the victory.		
162.	**Laugh at**	To make fun of	मजाक उड़ाना
	E.g We should not laugh at others.		
163.	**Laugh off/away**	To make something seem less important or serious	हँसी में किसी गंभीर बात को उड़ा देना
	E.g He laughed off/ away his troubles.		
164.	**Lay aside/by**	To make savings for future use.	बचत करना
	E.g Please lay some money aside for the rainy days.		
165.	**Lay down**	To give up for future use or surrender	हथियार डाल देना या समर्पण कर देना
	E.g There is no alternative but to lay down your weapons.		
166.	**Lay in**	To store for future use	जमा करना (भविष्य के लिए)
	E.g The ants lay in food for the winter season.		
167.	**Lay off**	To terminate the service of	काम से निकाल देना
	E.g The company is going to lay off some workers.		
168.	**Lay out**	To arrange according to plans	व्यवस्थित करना
	E.g Lay out your plans before investing money.		
169.	**Leave off**	To stop, cease	बंद करना
	E.g We leave off working as soon as the clock strikes five.		
170.	**Leave/let alone**	to refrain from disturbing or interfering	दखल देने से बचना
	E.g Leave me alone. I am sick of your interference.		
171.	**Let someone down**	To disappoint someone	निराश करना
	E.g Trust me, I will not let you down.		
172.	**Let on**	Share a secret	गुप्त बात सांझा करना
	E.g No one will let on about the surprise party.		
173.	**Let in**	Allow to enter	प्रवेश करने देना
	E.g We cannot let those people in.		
174.	**Let something off**	To make something such a bomb explode or fire a gun	किसी बम/ गोली को फूटने या चलने देना
	E.g The police cannot let the bomb off, as the place is heavily crowded.		

175.	**Let someone off**	To allow to get away without the expected punishment	गलती के लिए दंड दिए बिना छोड़ देना
	E.g The court cannot let them off as the crime is serious.		
176.	**Let out**	To allow someone or something to leave a place	बाहर निकालने देना
	E.g Who has let the dogs out?		
177.	**Let up**	To slow down, to become less severe	कम होना/ तीव्रता कम करना
	E.g We will stay here until the storm lets up.		
178.	**Lie behind**	To be the hidden cause	छिपा हुआ कारण होना
	E.g Every one knows what lies behind this cold-blooded murder.		
179.	**Lie in**	Exist in something	किसी चीज में होना
	E.g Beauty lies in the eyes of the beholder.		
180.	**Light on/upon**	To think/find something unexpectedly	अचानक सूझना
	E.g She lighted upon a new way of solving the problem.		
181.	**Light up**	To brighten/to become cheerful	चमकना/ खुश हो जाना
	E.g The good news will light up her face.		
182.	**Live by**	Follow manners/means in life	मान्यताओं/सिद्धान्तों को मानना
	E.g We should live by principles.		
183.	**Live upto**	To live or act in accordance with	उम्मीदों पर खरा उतरना
	E.g I couldn't live upto my parents' expectations.		
184.	**Live with**	To put up with, resign oneself	सहन करना
	E.g She cannot live with this tension for a long time.		
185.	**Live through**	To endure, survive	बर्दाश्त करना
	E.g He lived through the rainy days and this made him strong.		
186.	**Look after**	Take care of	ध्यान रखना
	E.g He looked after his ailing father.		
187.	**Look back on**	To think of	बीते समय के किसी अनुभव या बात के बारे मे सोचना
	E.g I keep looking back on those happy days.		
188.	**Look down on/upon**	To regard as inferior	नीची निगाह से देखना
	E.g We should not look down upon the poor.		
189.	**Look for**	To try to find	खोजना
	E.g I am looking for a suitable match for my son.		
190.	**Look forward to**	Expect with pleasure	खुशी के साथ इन्तजार करना
	E.g I am looking forward to meeting you soon.		
191.	**Look in on/call on**	To visit	किसी से मिलने जाना
	E.g I will look in on/ call on you soon.		
192.	**Look into**	investigate	जाँच पड़ताल करना
	E.g The police will look into the matter.		

193.	**Look on/upon**	To consider	मानना
	E.g She looked on this serious matter as a joke.		
194.	**Look out**	beware/ watch out	सावधान होना
	E.g Look out, the train is coming.		
195.	**Look something/ someone up**	To seek information about	कोई जानकारी खोजना
	E.g I looked up the number of the hospital on Google.		
196.	**Look to**	To expect	कोई आशा करना
	E.g I look to hearing from her within a week.		
197.	**Look up for**	To search	ढूँढ़ना
	E.g I am looking up for a job.		
198.	**Look up to**	To admire	पसंद करना
	E.g I look up to my teachers.		
199.	**Look up**	To improve	बेहतर होना
	E.g Even after the government has changed, things are not looking up.		
200.	**Make do**	To manage with limited means.	काम चलाना/(जितना हो उसी से)
	E.g They had to make do with limited resources.		
201.	**Make for**	To make possible	किसी बात में सहायक होना
	E.g Internet makes for better communication.		
202.	**Make of**	To understand, to produce or construct from	अभिप्राय को समझना, से बना होना
	E.g What do you make of this news?		
203.	**Make off**	To run away with	किसी चीज को लेकर भाग निकलना
	E.g He made off with all my money.		
204.	**Make out**	To understand	समझना
	E.g I cannot make out the head or tail of your statement.		
205.	**Make over**	convert, redo, renovate	परिवर्तित
	E.g This place needs a complete makeover.		
206.	**Make the most of**	To use to the greatest advantage	पूरा-पूरा लाभ उठाना
	E.g We will make the most of this opportunity.		
207.	**Make up**	Invent something like excuse or story/ to compensate for	बनाना/रचना (कहानी/बहाने इत्यादि)/ क्षतिपूर्ति करना
	E.g (1) He made up an excuse for coming late. *(2) They paid him four million dollars to make up for the loss.*		
208.	**Make up one's mind**	Determine	निर्णय कर लेना
	E.g You will have to make up your mind whether you want to accept the offer or not.		
209.	**Meet with**	To experience or undergo	अनुभव करना
	E.g He met with an accident.		
210.	**On the make**	In the process of forming	बनने की क्रिया में
	E.g. Seeing this child artist, I can say that a very good actor is on the make.		

211.	**Mess around**	To spend time without any purpose or plan just in a playful way	समय बिताना (बिना किसी विशेष उद्देश्य के या मजाक में)
	E.g *They mess around at the park annoying the elderly people.*		
212.	**Mess up**	to make a mistake	गल्ती करना
	E.g *They messed up and suffered huge loss.*		
	Mess (something) up	To make something disorderly or untidy	अस्त-व्यस्त करना
	E.g *They messed up my beautiful carpet.*		
213.	**Mess with**	To alter something improperly, to deceive or confuse someone	अस्त-व्यस्त करना/उलझा देना
	E.g • *Don't mess with the sitting arrangement.* • *Don't try to mess with me.*		
214.	**Move in**	To enter a new house/ place business	नये घर/ ऑफिस में प्रवेश करना
	E.g *I moved in but found the house not safe.*		
215.	**Move on**	To concentrate one's emotions or attention on other matter in recovering from a setback or difficulty.	आगे बढ़ना (पुरानी बुरी यादें व परेशानियों को भुला कर)
	E.g *Control your emotions and move on in life.*		
216.	**Move out**	To leave a house	रहने का स्थान छोड़ देना
	E.g *I moved out of the government allotted flat.*		
217.	**Nose out**	To defeat by a narrow margin, to move cautiously out of some place	बहुत कम अंतर से हराना, सावधानी से निकलना
	E.g • *She nosed out her competitor.* • *She nosed out of her room while the building was shaking hoping she wouldn't be hurt.*		
218.	**Note down**	To write something so that you don't forget it	लिखना (याद रखने हेतु)
	E.g *Please note down the important points.*		
219.	**Occur to**	To come to mind	ध्यान में आना
	E.g *It suddenly occurred to me that my purse was missing.*		
220.	**Part from**	To separate from someone.	छोड़ देना (व्यक्ति को)
	E.g *I cannot part from my son.*		
221.	**Part with**	To separate from something.	छोड़ देना (वस्तु को)
	E.g *I cannot part with my books.*		
222.	**Pass away**	To die	मर जाना
	E.g *He passed away in sleep.*		
223.	**Pay for**	To suffer for making some mistake.	गलती का हर्जाना भरना
	E.g *We have to pay for our sins.*		
224.	**Play at**	To do without interest or half-heartedly.	बिना रूचि के कोई काम करना
	E.g *She is just playing at her husband's business.*		
225.	**Play down**	To make something appear less important, to belittle	किसी बात के महत्व को कम करके आंकना
	E.g *He played down my efforts.*		

226.	**Play on**	To take advantage of	का लाभ उठाना
	E.g He played on her emotions.		
227.	**Put aside**	To stop using until later/ to disregard.	भविष्य के लिए बचाकर रखना/ उपेक्षा करना
	E.g Put aside some money for the rains days.		
228.	**Put down**	To suppress/to criticize	दमन करना/ निंदा करना
	E.g Never put down your friends in public.		
229.	**Put off**	To postpone/ to repel	स्थगित करना/ विकर्षित करना
	E.g • The meeting was put off due to heavy rain. • The smell of tobacco puts her off.		
230.	**Put on**	Assume/ to clothe oneself	ग्रहण करना/पहनना
	E.g Put on your sweater.		
231.	**Put out**	To extinguish	बुझा देना
	E.g Put out the fire.		
232.	**Put through**	To make someone experience something unpleasant	किसी को मुसीबत या परेशानी में डालना
	E.g He put me through many problems.		
233.	**Put up**	To stay	ठहरना
	E.g Where are you putting up in Delhi?		
234.	**Put up**	To erect or built	निर्माण करना
	E.g We will put up a tent at night.		
235.	**Put together**	To construct or create	बनाना
	E.g We need to put together the models for our physics assignments.		
236.	**Pay-off**	to be successful	फलदायक होना
	E.g Hard work pays off.		
237.	**Run down**	become weak/to criticise	कमजोर होना/हरा देना/ आलोचना करना
	E.g (i) Do not run down your spouse in public. (ii) He looks run down.		
238.	**Run into**	To face/to meet by chance	सामना होना/ अचानक मुलाकात करना
	E.g I ran into my childhood friend in the market.		
239.	**Run off**	To run away	भाग जाना
	E.g He ran off with his master's money.		
240.	**Run out**	To become used up, be exhausted	खत्म होना
	E.g He ran out of money while he was in the U.S.		
241.	**Run over**	to crush beneath	कुचल जाना
	E.g The old man was run over by a speeding bus.		
242.	**Run short of**	exhaust	कम पड़ जाना
	E.g We ran short of money at the mall.		
243.	**Run through**	to look at/ examine especially quickly	सरसरी निगाह डालना
	E.g Please run through the important points.		
244.	**See through**	To realise the truth	सच्चाई भांप जाना
	E.g I saw through his evil intention.		

245.	**See to**	To attend	निपटाना
	E.g The work has to be completed on time. Please see to it.		
246.	**See off**	To take leave of	बिदा लेना
	E.g I went to the station to see off my friends.		
247.	**Send for**	To call, summon	बुलावा भेजना
	E.g Please, send for a doctor.		
248.	**Set about**	To initiate	प्रारंभ करना (किसी कार्य को)
	E.g He set about solving the problems one by one.		
249.	**Set apart**	To reserve for a specific use	आरक्षित करना
	E.g Some fund was set apart for public welfare.		
250.	**Set aside**	To reject or discard	रद्द करना
	E.g The order of the lower court was set aside by the High Court.		
251.	**Set forth**	To present for consideration, to express in words	विचार हेतु रखना, शब्दों में बताना
	E.g Set forth your proposal before the committee.		
252.	**Set in**	To begin to happen	शुरू होना
	E.g Problems soon set in and all felt uneasy.		
253.	**Set off**	To occur, to explode	शुरू करना/ फट जाना
	E.g • The bombs set off ripping apart the bus. *• We set off for Manali in the morning.*		
254.	**Set up**	To establish	स्थापित करना
	E.g He set up a new business.		
255.	**Set upon**	To attack violently	उग्रता के साथ आक्रमण कर देना
	E.g Our army set upon the intruders.		
256.	**Shoot down**	To defeat, disappoint	हरा देना, निराश करना
	E.g He shot down his opponent.		
257.	**Shoot up**	To grow rapidly	तेजी से बढ़ना
	E.g Prices shoot up during inflation.		
258.	**Sit on**	To suppress or postpone	दबा देना/ टालते रहना
	E.g The court sat on the case for years.		
259.	**Smart under**	To be afflicted with	पीड़ित होना
	E.g He smarted under the blow of the lash.		
260.	**Smile on**	To bless	प्रसन्न होना
	E.g Fate smiled on him.		
261.	**Sort out**	To find a solution	समस्या को सुलझाना
	E.g Please sort out the problems.		
262.	**Stand by**	To remain loyal/to be ready	वफादार रहना/के लिए तैयार करना
	E.g I will stand by you through thick and thin.		
263.	**Stand for**	To represent or mean/to support	अर्थ होना/किसी विचार को समर्थन देना
	E.g • White flag stands for surrender. *• I stand for truth in all circumstances*		

264.	**Stand out**	To be noticeable or distinct	तुलनात्मक रूप से विशिष्ट होना
	***E.g** Owing to her efficiency, she stands out among all the employees.*		
265.	**Stand up to**	To defend or challenge, confront fearlessly	से मुकाबला करना
	***E.g** You will have to stand up to the cause.*		
266.	**Stand down**	To resign, to withdraw	पद त्याग देना/ दावा छोड़ देना
	***E.g** He stood down and withdrew his candidature.*		
267.	**Stand up**	To remain valid	सही होना (जैसे दावा का)
	***E.g** His defence will not stand up in the court.*		
268.	**Step aside**	To resign from a post	पद से इस्तीफा देना
	***E.g** He stepped aside giving way to his subordinate.*		
269.	**Step down**	To resign from a high post	उच्च पद से नीचे उतरना
	***E.g** He stepped down after being chargesheeted.*		
270.	**Step in**	To intervene	दखल देना
	***E.g** The boss stepped in when the fight turned ugly.*		
271.	**Step out**	To quit	छोड़ देना
	***E.g** Step out of my way.*		
272.	**Step up**	To increase	बढ़ाना
	***E.g** We need to step up the production of our goods.*		
273.	**Stick out**	To be prominent	दिखना,ध्यान आकर्षित करना
	***E.g** His funny dress made him stick out of the crowd.*		
274.	**Strike down**	To nullify	निरस्त करना
	***E.g** The Supreme Court struck down sec 303 of IPC.*		
275.	**Taken aback (used in passive only)**	To be surprised	अचंभित हो जाना
	***E.g** I was taken aback by his audacity.*		
276.	**Take after**	To resemble a close or an older relative	(घर के बड़ों की तरह) दिखना या करना
	***E.g** He has taken after his father.*		
277.	**Take down**	To write down	लिख लेना
	***E.g** Please take down the important points.*		
278.	**Taken in (used in passive only)**	To deceive	धोखा देना
	***E.g** He was taken in by the crook.*		
279.	**Take off**	To remove, to leave the ground (of a plane)	निकाल लेना/उड़ना/प्रस्थान करना
	***E.g** (i) Take off your shoes.* *(ii) The plane took off.*		
280.	**Take over**	To take responsibility for or control of	पद-भार संभालना
	***E.g** The minister has taken over the key position.*		
281.	**Take someone for**	Think one to be someone else	किसी को कोई और मान लेना
	***E.g** I took him for my nephew as the room was poorly lit.*		

282.	**Take to**	To become addicted *E.g He has taken to drinking.*	लत लगना
283.	**Take up**	To begin to pursue *E.g He has taken up MBA course after graduation.*	किसी काम को शुरू करना
284.	**Tone down**	To lessen the intensity *E.g Tone down your voice. I am not your servant.*	तीव्रता में कमी करना
285.	**Touch upon/on**	To deal with (a topic) in passing *E.g He touched upon the important aspects of socialism in his speech.*	संक्षिप्त में बताते हुए निकल जाना
286.	**Touch up**	To improve by making minor correction *E.g The artists touch up their makeup before the camera is switched on.*	सुधारना
287.	**Toy with**	To think of (something) briefly and not very seriously *E.g You are toying with my dream project.*	किसी योजना पर अनमने ढ़ंग से विचार करना
288.	**Try on**	To wear something briefly (to check if it fits or not) *E.g I tried on this new dress but it didn't fit me.*	पहनकर देखना (सही माप का है या नहीं)
289.	**Turn down**	To refuse or reject *E.g He turned down my offer.*	अस्वीकार कर देना (अनुरोध आदि)
290.	**Turn out to be**	To prove to be *E.g He turned out to be a crook.*	साबित होना
291.	**Turn out**	To come to a meeting or to form a crowd *E.g Many party workers turned out for the rally.*	किसी कार्यक्रम में शामिल होना
292.	**Turn up**	To arrive *E.g Many students turned up for the test.*	कहीं पहुँचना
293.	**Wait on**	To serve the needs of, visit *E.g The hosts waited on the guests.*	सेवा करना
294.	**Wear off**	To lose effect *E.g Soon the polish started wearing off.*	हल्का या कमजोर पड़ जाना
295.	**Wear out**	To tire greatly/to get damaged *E.g The labourers started wearing out.*	बहुत थका देना, घिस जाना
296.	**Weigh down**	To make anxious, to burden *E.g He was weighed down with added responsibilities.*	किसी बोझ या निराशा से दब जाना
297.	**While away**	To spend time leisurely *E.g Don't while away your time.*	बेफिक्री से समय बिताना
298.	**Work up**	To intensify gradually *E.g I am slowly working up to 50 sit-ups every day.*	धीरे-धीरे तीव्रता बढ़ाना
299.	**Write off**	To disregard as inconsequential *E.g The critics wrote off the author soon after the release of his first novel.*	महत्वहीन करार देना

24 SENTENCE IMPROVEMENT

CHAPTER

Sentence Improvement comprises different types of questions which are mainly based on Grammar, Vocabularies and the best way of presenting a sentence. Let us see the different types under which sentence improvement can be categorised.

Type-1: Grammar Based – Generally we do not have to prepare this type of questions separately. This type of questions gets ready alone with **detecting errors** without taking any extra pains. The only difference is that in **detecting error,** we mark that part which is not correct and in **sentence improvement,** we have to mark the correct option out of the given alternatives that will replace the incorrect underlined part of the sentence. If there is no error, we choose the option 'No improvement'.

Examples

1. Nisha is more funnier than Natasha.
   (A) funnier (B) funniest
   (C) quite funny (D) No improvement
2. Either Vijay or Vimal are going to be selected for the watch.
   (A) has (B) is
   (C) have been (D) No improvement
3. My uncle presented me the more expensive watch.
   (A) much (B) more
   (C) most (D) No improvement
4. The two brothers shared the property beside themselves.
   (A) among (B) between
   (C) amidst (D) No improvement
5. The office staff members wished each other on New Year's Day.
   (A) one other (B) one another
   (C) each another (D) No improvement
6. His speech was broadcasted over the radio last Thursday
   (A) was broadcast
   (B) had been broadcast
   (C) has been broadcast
   (D) No improvement
7. Both the mother-in-laws welcomed the newly weds with garlands of flowers
   (A) mothers-in-laws
   (B) mother-in-law
   (C) mothers-in-law
   (D) No improvement
8. Did there bus come on time?
   (A) their's (B) theirs
   (C) their (D) No improvement
9. Mayank was working overtime for the last two weeks.
   (A) is working (B) is being working
   (C) has been working
   (D) No improvement
10. Most children are liking ice-cream.
    (A) likes (B) like
    (C) were liking (D) No improvement
11. Supposing if he comes, what should I do?
    (A) if he comes
    (B) in case he will come
    (C) in the event of his being come
    (D) No improvement
12. Children like to eat sweets, isn't it ?
    (A) do they ? (B) is it ?
    (C) don't they? (D) No improvement.
13. He was so afraid that his knees knocked one another.
    (A) one against (B) each other
    (C) both (D) No improvement.
14. She had read Oliver Twist when she had been fourteen years old.
    (A) had became (B) has become
    (C) was (D) No improvement.
15. All the candidates will give a test on Friday.
    (A) appear (B) take
    (C) accept (D) No improvement.
16. When are you starting to write to your friend?

(A) wanting (B) going
(C) thinking (D) No improvement

17. If I was you I would not sign the document.
(A) If I have been you (B) If I were you
(C) If I had been you
(D) No improvement

18. I prefer to ride than to walk.
(A) ride to walk
(B) riding than walking
(C) riding to walking
(D) No improvement

19. They were astonished through his failure in the examination.
(A) from (B) at
(C) with (D) No improvement

20. He returned the book after he read it.
(A) was read (B) reading
(C) had read (D) No improvement

21. As he was a braveheart, Rakesh decided to join the army.
(A) though he was a braveheart
(B) although he was a braveheart
(C) while he was a braveheart
(D) No improvement

22. She hurt her back while she worked yesterday.
(A) worked out (B) had worked
(C) was working (D) No improvement

23. My friend lamented that though a complete report was sent to the department a month ago no action is being taken so far.
(A) no action has been taken.
(B) no action was taken.
(C) no action had taken.
(D) No improvement.

24. Kari left the house before Shyarn got there.
(A) will leave (B) had left
(C) leaves (D) No improvement

25. The company is not doing well. Isn't it time you sell off your shares in it ?
(A) sold (B) selling
(C) give (D) No improvement

26. Although Pandas eat bamboo almost exclusively, they are also carnivorous.
(A) until (B) as soon as
(C) not only (D) No improvement

27. He was weary of failure, Didn't he ?
(A) Isn't he ? (B) Wasn't he ?
(C) Doesn't he ? (D) No improvement

28. What you have been doing since the workshop last month ?
(A) have you done
(B) you have done
(C) have you been doing
(D) No improvement

29. No sooner had the teacher entered the room and the boys rushed to their seats.
(A) when (B) than
(C) but (D) No improvement

30. We have already disposed our old house.
(A) disposed off (B) disposed out
(C) disposed of (D) No improvement

31. We can buy anything in this shop, Can we?
(A) Isn't it? (B) Can't we?
(C) Don't we? (D) No improvement

32. If I had followed your advice, I would not regret today.
(A) will not regret (B) had not regretted
(C) would not have regretted
(D) No improvement

33. Somebody must be made to answer for the security scam.
(A) to (B) after
(C) upon (D) No improvement

34. Corruption is the most serious problem in India.
(A) the more serious
(B) the seriouser
(C) serious (D) No improvement

35. They reached at Calcutta on Monday last.
(A) reached to Calcutta
(B) reached on Calcutta
(C) reached Calcutta
(D) No improvement

36. I did not saw my cousin in Madras.
(A) not seen (B) did not see
(C) did not seen (D) No improvement

37. He behaves like coward.
(A) cowardly
(B) in a cowardly manner
(C) as if he was a coward
(D) No improvement

38. Neither of them went to the cinema.
(A) both of them did not go
(B) both did not go
(C) neither went
(D) No improvement

39. I used to have very thick hair.
(A) use to have (B) used to having
(C) used to had (D) No improvement

40. She usually does not leave for work until she finished all her chores.
(A) finishes
(B) has finished
(C) had finished
(D) No improvement

41. The article should not exceed more than hundred words.
(A) exceed beyond
(B) exceed than
(C) exceed
(D) No improvement

42. He may be poor now but he appears to be rich.
(A) seem rich
(B) rich to be
(C) to have been rich
(D) No improvement

43. The only way to solve the racial problem is by education.
(A) because of (B) thanks to
(C) on account of (D) No improvement

44. Did you finish the work yet ?
(A) Had you finished.
(B) Haven't you finished
(C) Would you finish
(D) No improvement

45. I'll tell you as soon, as I'll know.
(A) I would know (B) I can know
(C) I know (D) No improvement

46. How are you going to have your car painted? I am going to have it red painted.
(A) paint it red
(B) have it painted red
(C) paint
(D) No improvement

47. The job wasn't interesting, but on the contrary it was well-paid.
(A) on the whole
(B) on the other side
(C) on the other hand
(D) No improvement

48. The postman comes twice a day, don't he?
(A) doesn't he (B) does he
(C) do he (D) No improvement

49. We met a lot of people at our holidays.
(A) on (B) in
(C) during (D) No improvement

50. People whom are outdoors for long periods of time need to protect themselves to avoid the harmful effects of too much sunlight.
(A) who (B) how
(C) whose (D) No improvement

51. The department has been running this programme for the past two years.
(A) from the past two years
(B) since the past two years
(C) the last two years
(D) No improvement

52. She paid close attention to the man sitting besides her.
(A) beside to (B) beside
(C) beside of (D) No improvement

53. I shall see him only if he agreed to bear the cost.
(A) agrees (B) might agree
(C) had agreed (D) No improvement

54. I can accept anything than dishonesty.
(A) anything other than
(B) any other thing than
(C) anything more than
(D) No improvement

55. One must obey his parents.
(A) his own parents
(B) parents
(C) one's parents
(D) No improvement

56. No sooner had she heard the news when she fainted.
(A) that she fainted
(B) than she fainted
(C) and she fainted
(D) No improvement

57. At the very moment they were showing signs of growing nervousness, isn't it ?
(A) wasn't it (B) weren't it
(C) weren't they (D) No improvement

58. One hour in the week was set aside by him for the reception of whomsoever chose to visit him.
(A) whomever (B) whosoever
(C) who (D) No improvement

59. Rahul has lived in Delhi for three years when his parents came there.
(A) was living (B) has been living
(C) had been living
(D) No improvement

60. He said that he saw him last year, to discuss the documents.
(A) met (B) had seen
(C) seen (D) No improvement

61. Kalidasa is the Shakespeare of India.
(A) Shakespeare (B) a Shakespeare
(C) like Shakespeare
(D) No improvement

62. He is addicted to alcohol and exerts a bad influence for his family.
(A) on (B) in
(C) about (D) No improvement

63. Them shoes are mine.
(A) Those (B) That
(C) Their (D) No improvement

64. No sooner had she realized her blunder than she began to take corrective measures.
(A) then she began to take
(B) than she began taking
(C) when she began to take
(D) No improvement

65. I will be with you in one quarter of an hour.
(A) a quarter of one hour
(B) a quarter of an hour
(C) a quarter of hour
(D) No improvement

66. He ordered me open the window.
(A) asked (B) bade
(C) requested (D) No improvement

67. Do you know to prepare the Balance Sheet?
(A) Do you know to balance
(B) Do you know to make
(C) Do you know how to prepare
(D) No improvement

68. Neither plants nor animals, can survive without oxygen.
(A) Plants can neither
(B) Neither can plants
(C) Plants, neither
(D) No improvement

69. The light went out while I read.
(A) was reading (B) am reading
(C) had read (D) No improvement

70. She said me about her holiday in Kerala.
(A) told about (B) said about
(C) had read (D) No improvement

71. Why do you prefer the theatre than the cinema?
(A) for (B) against
(C) to (D) No improvement

72. He is the only man I know, who can laugh at himself.
(A) whose (B) whom
(C) which (D) No improvement

73. He won't hear you provided you shout.
(A) unless (B) in case
(C) as long as (D) No improvement

74. The ship is at the anchor and the sailors are now at ease.
(A) at anchor (B) at an anchor
(C) at its anchor (D) No improvement

75. The music show already began when we arrived in the hall.
(A) had already begun
(B) had already began
(C) would begin
(D) No improvement

76. My group of tenth-graders are well behaved.
(A) is so well behaved
(B) are so well behaved
(C) is well behaved
(D) No improvement

77. My admonishing to him will not change his mind.
(A) admonishing at him
(B) admonishing him
(C) admonishing for him
(D) No improvement

78. Surbhi's father did not want her to have spent all her money at the fair.
(A) to be spending
(B) to have been spending
(C) to spend
(D) No improvement

79. Basmati rice is more superior than most other varieties of rice.
(A) superior than (B) more superior to
(C) superior to (D) No improvement

80. Those were the days when we would all go out together.
(A) will all go out
(B) will be going out
(C) would have been going
(D) No improvement

81. Beside being a poet, he is also a famous singer.
(A) Besides being
(B) Besides becoming
(C) Beside becoming
(D) No improvement

82. A large number of people have fallen victim to dengue fever.

(A) of (B) from
(C) with (D) No improvement

83. The stranger asked the little girl what is her name.
(A) what her name is
(B) what her name was
(C) what was her name
(D) No improvement

84. She scoffed on the idea of revolution.
(A) for (B) at
(C) about (D) No improvement

85. The Minister denied reports that prices will rose after the budget.
(A) would rise after
(B) will now rise
(C) is rising up
(D) No correction required

86. His life is an example of how the human will can flourish even in harsh conditions.
(A) what the human will can
(B) how the human can and will
(C) when the human will can
(D) No correction required

87. Enlightenment were a state of relaxed awareness.
(A) had (B) has
(C) is (D) No improvement

88. I complimented him for his success in the examination.
(A) about (B) on
(C) at (D) No improvement

89. He should not had ignored his friend.
(A) should not have
(B) should have not
(C) should not has
(D) No improvement

90. It was quite clear that the runner could be able to improve upon his own record.
(A) will be able (B) should be able
(C) would be able (D) No improvement

91. This work of art is worthy to praise.
(A) for (B) of
(C) about (D) No improvement

92. Rakesh didn't knew my address.
(A) didn't known (B) didn't have
(C) didn't know (D) No improvement

93. Mary would not go to the market unless I go with her.
(A) shall go (B) went
(C) would go (D) No improvement

94. Flowers embellishment the beauty of our surroundings.
(A) replenish (B) enhance
(C) destroys (D) No improvement

95. The cheapest electronic good are manufactured in China.
(A) electronical good (B) electrical good
(C) electronic goods
(D) No improvement

96. I have been living in Delhi from 1989.
(A) ever since (B) since
(C) in (D) No improvement

97. The student who will score the maximum marks, will be awarded a certificate.
(A) who score the maximum marks
(B) who would score the maximum marks
(C) who would be scoring the maximum marks
(D) No improvement

98. She congratulated him on his success in the examination.
(A) about (B) for
(D) at (D) No improvement

99. The team has been practising from the past two months.
(A) since the past
(B) for the past
(C) for past
(D) No improvement

100. Her brother may have aged when she last saw him.
(A) since she last saw him
(B) from when she last saw him
(C) before she last saw him
(D) No improvement

101. She is really looking forward to interact with the poet.
(A) looking forward for interacting
(B) looking forward to interacting
(C) looking forward towards interacting
(D) No improvement

102. Frank stood beside to Harry.
(A) beside (B) besides
(C) besides to (D) No improvement

103. If I will go there, I shall buy the book.
(A) I went (B) I shall go
(C) I go (D) No improvement

104. It took her a long time to get past her failure in the medical examination.
(A) through (B) over
(C) by (D) No improvement

105. When we came out of the restaurant it was half past eleven.

(A) When we had come out of the restaurant
(B) After we came out of the restaurant
(C) When we have come out of the restaurant
(D) No improvement

106. I did not agree with him; he appeared to be so bigoted for me to concur.
(A) much (B) very
(C) too (D) No improvement

107. As soon as she noticed the workmen, she asked them what they have been doing.
(A) have done (B) had been doing
(C) are doing (D) No improvement

108. I worked in this office since 2005.
(A) have worked (B) have been working
(C) am working (D) No improvement

109. That was not quite all what I did during the holidays.
(A) that (B) which
(C) how (D) No improvement

110. Since he had studied very hard, Ramesh had little hope of passing his examination.
(A) Despite (B) Although
(C) However (D) No improvement

111. He wants to buy a new shirt as he has no money.
(A) since (B) but
(C) because (D) No improvement

112. His house has no furnitures yet.
(A) have no furniture yet
(B) had no furniture yet
(C) has no furniture yet
(D) No improvement

113. If I were in the hospital, would you visit me?
(A) will you visit me?
(B) are you visiting me?
(C) you will visit me?
(D) No improvement

114. He throwed it out of the window.
(A) threw (B) throw
(C) thrown (D) No improvement

115. It's obvious that they are trying to cheat, isn't it?
(A) are they? (B) aren't they?
(C) is it? (D) No improvement

116. He is not only known for his wealth but also for his learning.
(A) not only known for his learning
(B) only known for his wealth
(C) known not only for his wealth
(D) No improvement

117. My friend lives in a nearby street whose name I have forgotten.
(A) the name of which
(B) which name
(C) of which name
(D) No improvement

118. We generally select one of the most intelligent student of the school for this award.
(A) one of the most intelligent students of the school
(B) one of the intelligent most students of the school
(C) one of the intelligent most student of the school
(D) No improvement

119. He both won a medal and a scholarship.
(A) He won a medal and a scholarship both.
(B) Both he won a medal and a scholarship.
(C) He won both a medal and a scholarship.
(D) No improvement

120. No sooner had the dividend been declared, the notices were sent out.
(A) The company had hardly declared the dividend till the notices were sent for mailing.
(B) They had no sooner declared the dividend then the notices were sent out.
(C) Hardly had the dividend been declared when the notices were sent out.
(D) No improvement

121. We had a grand party and we enjoyed very much.
(A) We had a grand party and enjoyed very much.
(B) We had a grand party to enjoy very much.
(C) We had a grand party and we enjoyed ourselves very much.
(D) No improvement

122. Every morning I get up at 4 O'clock, but today I get up at 7 O'clock.
(A) got up (B) was getting up
(C) am getting up (D) No improvement

Type- 2: <u>Based on Vocabularies</u> – Normally when a student memorizes vocabularies, he is under an impression that questions based on vocabularies come only in synonyms and antonyms. Questions based on vocabularies come in sentence improvement too where the student is tested not only for his knowledge of the meaning of the given words but also how they should be used in the given sentence. The student is expected to be capable enough to choose the most appropriate word from the given options and improve the language of the sentence. Apart from this some questions are also based on One Word Substitution.

Examples

1. The relatives <u>comforted</u> the old man whose wife had died.
(A) sympathized with
(B) pitied
(C) consoled (D) No improvement
2. They obtained the top-secret information by <u>wrong</u> means
(A) clever (B) fraudulent
(C) bad (D) No improvement
3. He took <u>disadvantage</u> of the situation and cheated many people.
(A) chance (B) advantage
(C) disapproval (D) No improvement.
4. The increasing sale of luxuries is an <u>index</u> of the country's prosperity.
(A) appendix (B) pointer
(C) mark (D) No improvement
5. He kept us all in <u>suspension</u> regarding his future plans.
(A) suspending (B) suspense
(C) suspicion (D) No improvement
6. During the recent floods, we <u>waded through</u> waist-deep water for almost half a kilometer.
(A) shuffled through (B) walked over
(C) skipped through
(D) No improvement
7. In Gujarat, communal violence and rioting <u>ignited</u> up twice in the late seventies and early eighties.
(A) flared (B) burned
(C) took (D) No improvement
8. The <u>underlining</u> assumption is that the amount of money available is limited.
(A) undermining (B) underlying
(C) underwhelming
(D) No improvement
9. He is <u>one who gives money or helps others</u> who has been instrumental in the upliftment of many. poverty stricken people.
(A) a philosopher
(B) a philatelist
(C) a philanthropist
(D) No improvement
10. When those whom he had injured accused him of being a <u>charlatan</u> he retorted curtly that he had never been a quack.
(A) libertine (B) sycophant
(C) plagiarist (D) No improvement
11. You must <u>remind me</u> to post the letters.
(A) remember me
(B) have remind me
(C) have remembered me
(D) No improvement
12. Suddenly a pigeon <u>faltered</u> out of the rubble.
(A) fluttered (B) flustered
(C) frittered (D) No improvement
13. I do not like <u>these kind</u> of novels.
(A) this kind (B) those kind
(C) this kinds (D) No improvement
14. Unity in diversity is the most <u>noticeable</u> quality of India.
(A) popular (B) remarkable
(C) famous (D) no improvement
15. Sordid and sensational books tend to <u>vitiate</u> the public taste.
(A) divide (B) distract
(C) distort (D) No improvement
16. His Master's thesis <u>was highly estimated</u> and is now being prepared for publication.
(A) was highly discussed
(B) was highly commended
(C) is highly appraised
(D) No improvement
17. The <u>false appearance</u> of the building erected for the function was blown away in the storm.
(A) Exterior (B) Facade
(C) Skeleton (D) No improvement

18. She has decided to canvas for the Conservative Party.
(A) advertise (B) canvass
(C) canvassing (D) No improvement

19. The policeman captured the first car that approached and ordered the driver to take the injured child to the hospital.
(A) caught (B) commandeered
(C) interrupted (D) No improvement

20. They objected to the plan on the grounds that it was too expensive.
(A) refused (B) declined
(C) disagreed (D) No improvement

21. The people criticized the terrorist attack.
(A) condoned (B) condemned
(C) conceded (D) No improvement

22. The judge asked the lawyer to be consistent with proof in the case.
(A) corroboration (B) documents
(C) evidence (D) No improvement

23. I grew up in a tiny town called Alwar.
(A) a minute town
(B) a humungous town
(C) a small town (D) No improvement

24. The boy wanted to ask his father for money, but waited for a propitious occasion.
(A) protective (B) prophetic
(C) prospective (D) No improvement

25. The host offered me tea but I denied it.
(A) said no (B) rejected
(C) refused (D) No improvement

26. How can anyone sympathize with you when what you say is hardly gullible?
(A) credible (B) incredible
(C) credulous (D) No improvement

27. Poisonous waste from the industrial plants is hazardous to the environment.
(A) toxic (B) troublesome
(C) effluent (D) No improvement

28. Owing to the close affinity of the architect and the builder, the project was completed ahead of schedule.
(A) termination (B) cooperation
(C) collaboration (D) No improvement

29. The servant was disturbed as her son was now out of sight due to bad company.
(A) out of bounds (B) out of control
(C) out of reach (D) No improvement

30. The Japanese are hardly working people.
(A) a hard working people
(B) a hardly working people
(C) hard working people
(D) No improvement

Type 3: Based on the use of the best verb/ word in the given action/sentence – This type of questions is easier for students who develop reading habits. Due to regular reading habit, they choose the most appropriate word conveniently. For eg: In the sentence 'I did a mistake' , they can easily locate the mistake and will point out that 'made' will come in the place of 'did' as we normally say, "I made a mistake". In the same way, 'All of a at once' is wrong as they, time and again, while reading have come across 'all of a sudden'. Here, I feel, that it is mandatory to mention that reading is a fruitful habit. We imbibe the meaning and usage of many words automatically if we make reading a habit.

Examples

1. Keats says the idea very well in his poems.
(A) speaks (B) describes
(C) expresses (D) No improvement

2. The enemy soldiers went back hastily.
(A) returned (B) retreated
(C) retrenched (D) No improvement

3. I will be giving blood in the hospital at 9.00 a.m. tomorrow.
(A) exchanging (B) contributing
(C) donating (D) No improvement

4. The suspected couple was taken away from the airport through a side entrance to the police station for interrogation.
(A) whisked (B) rushed
(C) guided (D) No improvement

5. The transport workers have organised a strike asking for more salary.
(A) demanding (B) begging
(C) requesting (D) No improvement

6. It was mere affection that stopped him from beating his son:
(A) great (B) much
(C) filial (D) No improvement

7. The British superiority all over Africa and Asia collapsed in the first half of the twentieth century.
(A) domicile (B) residence
(C) dominion (D) No improvement

8. Since setting up, the club has produced so many players.
(A) since its inception
(B) since have been set up
(C) Being set up
(D) No improvement

9. I hope I am going to get fever soon.
(A) fear (B) feel afraid
(C) doubt if (D) No improvement

10. When we came out of the cinema, it was falling with rain.
(A) pouring (B) descending
(C) dropping (D) No improvement

11. Serious charges of corruption were levied against him.
(A) put (B) levelled
(C) made (D) No improvement

12. A lot of bloodshed could have been saved, had the administration taken timely action.
(A) protected (B) prevented
(C) eschewed (D) no improvement

13. The professor has agreed to take remediable classes for the weaker students.
(A) redressal (B) remedial
(C) practice (D) some

14. My foot is paining.
(A) aching (B) ailing
(C) hurting (D) No improvement

15. She gave most of her time to dance.
(A) lent (B) spent
(C)devoted (D) No improvement

16. Work at the request of your conscience.
(A) behest (B) desires
(C) orders (D) No improvement

17. Raju requested me to his birthday party tomorrow.
(A) indulged (B) invited
(C) inspired (D) No improvement

18. The Prime Minister established a commission to look after the plight of the widows.
(A) formed (B) created
(C) set up (D) No improvement

19. The monkey was seated at the foot of a tree.
(A) bottom (B) end
(C) root (D) No improvement

20. He decided to reveal the corruption in his department to the media.
(A) show (B) disclose
(C) expose (D) No improvement

21. My friend won me at tennis.
(A) succeeded me (B) outran me
(C) beat me (D) No improvement

Type- 4: Based on best way of expressing an action – Many times, we are able to convey what we mean but the listener finds it difficult to interpret the meaning of the sentence and then with the help of his common sense, he tries to reason it out. In every language, it is essential that the speaker adopts the most lucid way of expressing his thoughts, ideas and opinions. For eg- In the sentence, 'I gave the dog biscuit' the meaning is clear but the sentence will be more lucid and well expressed if we say, "I gave biscuits to the dog".

Examples

1. The courtiers used to tell the King how efficient an administrator he was all day long.
(A) The courtiers all day long used to tell the King how efficient an administrator he was.
(B) The courtiers used all day long to tell the King how efficient an administrator he was.
(C) The courtiers used to tell the King all day long how efficient an administrator he was.
(D) No improvement

2. There followed an awkward silence after Ram declared his love to her.
(A) No improvement
(B) Embarrassing silence
(C) Clumsy silence
(D) A period of embarassment

3. Sleeping, resting and fluids are the best ways to care for a cold.
(A) and that drinking fluids
(B) and drinking fluids
(C) which drank fluids
(D) No improvement

4. By studying AIDS has engaged many researchers in the last decade.
(A) Important study
(B) Now that the study
(C) The study of
(D) No improvement

5. A good scholar must be precise and possess originality.
(A) must be precise and original
(B) must be possess precision and original
(C) must be precision and possess originality
(D) No improvement

6. Can any spiritually dead man be so as to have no love for his native country?
(A) Can any man be so spiritually dead as to have no love for his native country ?
(B) Can any native man be so dead as to have no love for his spiritual country ?
(C) Can any dead man be so as to have no spiritual love for his native country ?
(D) No improvement

7. Whenever I doubt about the meaning of a word, I look up my dictionary.
(A) whenever I have a doubt
(B) Whenever I am in doubt
(C) The moment I doubt
(D) No improvement

8. I in black and white must have your terms down.
(A) I must have in black and white your terms down.
(B) I must have your terms in black and white down.
(C) I must have your terms down in black and white.
(D) No improvement

9. We have been credibly informed that the murderer has given himself up.
(A) We have been informed that the murderer has credibly given himself up.
(B) We have been informed that the murderer has given credibly himself up.
(C) We have been informed that credibly the murderer has given up himself.
(D) No improvement

10. The man whom I thought was thoroughly honest proved to be a swindler.
(A) The man whom I thought was thoroughly honest proved a swindler.
(B) The man who I thought was thoroughly honest proved to be a swindler.
(C) The man to whom I thought was thoroughly honest proved to be a swindler,
(D) No improvement

11. Riding upon his horse, the tiger jumped at him.
(A) Riding upon the tiger, the horse jumped at him.
(B) The tiger jumped at him while he was riding upon his horse.
(C) The tiger rode at him while he was jumping upon his horse.
(D) No improvement

12. What do you for go to school ?
(A) For what do you go to school?
(B) What do you go for to school?
(C) What do you go to school for?
(D) No improvement

13. He pleased the directors and this completed his report in good time.
(A) He pleased the directors in good time and this completed his report,
(B) He completed his report in good time and this pleased the directors.
(C) He pleased the directors and completed his report and this in good time.
(D) No improvement

Type- 5: Based on good manners:- Many times the given sentence is correct in all aspects whether it is the grammar of the sentence or the vocabularies used but good manners and etiquettes forbid us to use such sentences. 231 and 123 rules of Pronoun are also based on good manners. There is a saying 'The donkey comes the last'. It means 'I' comes last. 123 Rule says that first the 2nd person, then the third person and then the 1st person must come in a sentence (See Pronoun in Volume-1)

Examples

1. He asked me if I had a disease.
(A) was unwell
(B) is unwell
(C) have a disease
(D) No improvement

Type-6: Based on Synonyms – Many times the underlined word of the question has its synonym given in one of the options. We must keep in mind that synonym has not been asked and if the given option does not improve the sentence in any way, we must choose no improvement as our answer.

Examples

1. She left the room feeling contrite.
   (A) sorry for what she had done
   (B) rather ill
   (C) extremely irritated
   (D) No improvement
2. To alleviate the pain of losing his only son, he took up meditation.
   (A) lessen (B) minimalise
   (C) lesson (D) No improvement

Type 7: Certain common sentences of day-to-day use comprise 'phrases' and 'sayings'. Hence sentences based on Phrasal Verbs, Idioms and Phrases are also asked in sentence improvement.

Examples

1. The workers looked run down
   (A) Happy (B) Relaxed
   (C) Exhausted (D) No improvement
2. She did not hand in her homework after the summer vacation.
   (A) hand over (B) hand out
   (C) handed (D) No improvement
3. Two children were knocked down by a speeding truck.
   (A) turned down (B) pulled down
   (C) brought down (D) No improvement
4. Geeta said that she had never viewed across a book she liked so much.
   (A) come across (B) come through
   (C) come round (D) No improvement
5. The opposition members in the legislative assembly have decided to oppose any bill put forward by the ruling party.
   (A) keep in (B) render
   (C) offer (D) No improvement
6. There will be black murder when she hears this.
   (A) red (B) blue
   (C) pink (D) No improvement
7. If you put your heart to it, you will be a winner.
   (A) in it (B) into it
   (C) on it (D) No improvement
8. Owing to emergency conditions, the army was asked to stand up.
   (A) stand out (B) stand in
   (C) stand by (D) No improvement

Type- 8: We are generally confused in the meaning of certain words and hence misuse them. Questions based on such words too are asked in sentence improvement.

Examples

1. When the police peeped through the window , a baby was seen playing on the ground.
   (A) floor (B) grounds
   (C) surface (D) No improvement
2. The chief guest was invited on stage and amidst a round of applause he stood.
   (A) stood up (B) got off
   (C) stand up (D) No improvement
3. John, wear your jacket as it is getting very cold.
   (A) get on (B) put on
   (C) take on (D) No improvement
4. The strong breeze blew his hat away.
   (A) The strong air (B) The strong breath
   (C) The strong wind
   (D) No improvement

Type- 9: Certain sentences are correct as far as the meaning of the sentence, vocabularies used and the grammar are concerned but these sentences are incomplete legally or otherwise. To have a clear meaning of the sentence, we need to use clear and unambiguous language.

1. The judge passed an order that the convict must be hanged to death.
   (A) hanged till death
   (B) hung till death
   (C) hanged into death
   (D) No improvement

TYPE – 1 :- Answers

1.(A) Two comparative degrees never comes together.
Change 'more funnier' into 'funnier'.
Moreover 'than' is preceded by a comparative degree. So all other options here cannot be considered.

2.(B) If two subjects are joined by either....or, the Verb will agree with the nearest subject.
Change 'are' into 'is'.

3.(C) Article 'the' comes before 'superlative degree of Adjectives' and not with 'comparative degree'.
Change 'more' into 'most'.

4.(B) 'Between' is used for 'two'.
Change 'beside' into 'between'

5.(B) Each other – denotes mutual relationship between two people or thing.
One another – denotes mutual relationship among more than two things or persons.
Change 'each other' into 'one another'.

6.(A) 'Broadcast' as a Verb remains the same in 2nd and 3rd form.
Change 'was broadcasted' into 'was broadcast'.

7.(C) Change 'mother-in-laws' into 'mothers-in-law'.

8.(C) Possessive Adjective 'their' must be used here as it is followed by a Noun 'bus'. 'Theirs' is inappropriate as 'theirs' is a Pronoun and it cannot be followed by a Noun 'bus'.
Change 'there' into 'their'.

9.(C) 'For'/'since' + 'time' in used in 'Perfect' and 'Perfect Continuous Tense'.
Change 'was working' into 'has been working'.

10.(B) Simple Present Tense is used for present routine action.
Change 'are liking' into 'like'. Moreover 'like is generally not used in 'ing' form.

11.(A) 'Suppose' and 'if' never come together as this will make the sentence superfluous.
Superfluous means 'more than what is necessary'.
Change 'Supposing if he comes' into 'If he comes'.

12.(C) The 'sentence' and the 'question tag' must be in the same Tense.
Change 'isn't it' into 'don't' they'.

13.(B) 'Each other' denotes 'mutual relationship between two persons/ things'.
'One another' denotes 'mutual relationship among more than two persons or things'.
Change 'one another' into 'each other'.

14.(C) If 'past time' is given in a sentence, the sentence is in 'Simple Past Tense'.
Change 'had been' into 'was'. Here both the 'state' and 'action' are of the same Tense. Hence both will be in simple past Tense.

15.(B) Teachers give a test.
Students take a test.
Change 'give' into 'take'.

16.(B) Change 'starting' into 'going'.

17.(B) 'Was' is not used with any subject if the sentence is imaginary.
Change 'If I was you' into 'If I were you'.

18.(C) Prefer is followed by 'to' not 'than'. Moreover 'prefer' is followed by both a 'Gerund' and 'Infinitive'.
Change 'to ride than to walk' into 'riding to walking' because 'to walk' looks awkward after 'to'.

19.(B) 'Astonished' is followed by Preposition 'at'.
Change 'through' into 'at'.

20.(C) If 'two sentences' are joined by 'after', the 1st action is in Past Perfect Tense and the 2nd action is in Simple Past Tense.

$\underbrace{\text{2nd action}}_{\text{Simple past}} + \text{after} + \underbrace{\text{1st action}}_{\text{Past perfect}}$

Change 'read' into 'had read'.

21.(D) The 2nd action is the outcome of the state of being (to be a braveheart). Hence 'as' is an appropriate option here.

22.(C) Change 'worked' into 'was working'. 'While' shows that the 2nd action was going on when the 1st action took place.

23.(A) 'Yet' and 'so far' mean 'upto the time when the sentence was spoken' and are generally used in Present Perfect Tense. Hence 'Present Perfect' is the most appropriate Tense here.

24.(B) If two sentences are joined by 'before', the first action is in Past Perfect Tense and the 2nd action is in Simple Past Tense.

$\underbrace{\text{1st action}}_{\text{Past perfect}} + \text{after} + \underbrace{\text{2nd action}}_{\text{Simple past}}$

Change 'left' into 'had left'.

25.(A) If the sentence starts with 'It's time' or It's high time', and if it is followed by a subject, the Verb will be in second (V_2) form.
Change 'sell' into 'sold'.

26.(D) The 2nd action/state is opposite to the 1st one. Hence 'although' is best suited here.

27.(B) The 'sentence' and 'question tag' must be in the same Tense.
Change 'didn't he' into 'wasn't he'.

28.(C) Sentence is in Interrogative form.
Change 'you have been doing' into 'have you been doing'. Helping Verb will come before the subject.

29.(B) 'No sooner' is followed by 'than'.
Change 'and' into 'than'.

30.(C) The fixed Preposition that comes with 'disposed' is 'of'.
disposed of – to get rid of – छुटकारा पाना

31.(B) If the sentence is positive, the question tag must be negative.
Change 'can we' into 'can't we'.

32.(C) The structure of Conditional Sentence of past is–
If + Sub + had + V_3, Sub + would + have + V_3.

33.(D) Answer to (a person) – को जवाब देना
Answer for (something some act) – का जवाबदेह होना

34.(D)

35.(C) Change 'reached at Calcutta' into 'reached Calcutta'. 'Reach' does not take any Preposition if it is followed by a destination.

36.(B) '1st form of Verb is used with did' as two V_2 cannot come together.
Change 'did not saw' into 'did not see'.

37.(B) 'Behave' is Verb and we know that an adVerb qualifies the Verb
Change 'like coward' into 'in a cowardly manner'.
'Cowardly' is an Adjective.

38.(D) Note: 'Both....... not' is not correct to use. For '0 out of two' we use 'neither of'.

39.(D) For past routine action, we use 'used to + base form of Verb'.

40.(B) If the 2nd action starts after the 1st action is over, the 1st action will be in Present Perfect Tense and the second action will be in Simple Present Tense.
Change 'finished' into 'has finished.'

41.(C) 'Exceed' and 'more than' together make a sentence superfluous. Change 'exceed more than' into 'exceed'.

42.(C) Change 'to be rich' 'into have been rich'.
It seems that he was rich earlier.

43.(D)

44.(B) 'Yet' is generally used in present perfect negative sentences.
Change 'did you finish' into 'haven't you finish'.

45.(C) Simple future is never used immediately after 'as soon as'.
Change 'I'll know' into 'I know.'
Moreover if two actions take place one after the other in future, the 1st action is in simple present Tense and the 2nd is in simple future Tense.

46.(B) Change 'have it red painted' into 'have it painted red'.
The action is of causative Verb.

47.(A) 'But' and 'on the contrary' if used together, make the sentence superfluous.
Change 'on the contrary' into 'on the whole.'

48.(A) The sentence and the question tag must be in the same person. The postman being singular will take 'does' and not 'do'.
Change 'don't he' into 'doesn't he'.

49.(C) Change 'at' into 'during'. Here we are talking about a period of time at a stretch. 'At' denotes a point of time.

50.(A) Who is used for the subject.
Change 'whom' into 'who'.

51.(D) 'For' is used for a period of time.

52.(B) 'Beside' means 'Next to (के बगल में)' and 'Besides' means 'apart from' (के अलावा). Change 'besides' into 'beside'.

53.(A) In Future Conditional Sentences, the 1st action is in simple present Tense.

54.(A) Change 'anything than' into 'any thing other than'

55.(C) 'One' always takes 'one's' as possessive Adjective. Change 'his parents' into 'one's parents'.

56.(B) 'No sooner' is followed by 'than'. Change 'when she fainted' into 'than she fainted'.

57.(C) The sentence and the question tag must be in the same Tense. Change 'isn't it' into 'weren't they'.

58.(B) Whomsoever — (जिस किसी को भी) is used as an object. Whosoever – (जो कोई भी) is used as a subject. Change 'whomsoever' into 'whosoever'.

59.(C) for/since + time is used in perfect or perfect continuous Tense but the sentence is still incorrect as the action 'parents came' shows that it is of past. Hence change 'has lived' into 'had been living'.

60.(B) Change 'saw' into 'had seen'. Sentence is of 'Indirect speech'.

61.(D) When a proper Noun is used as an example to compare some other proper Noun with it, the proper Noun is preceded by an article.

62.(A) Change 'for' into on'.

63.(A) 'Those' is used for more than one distant thing/person. Change 'them' into 'those'. 'Them' cannot be followed by a Noun 'shoes' as 'them' is a Pronoun. We know that Pronoun comes in place of a Noun and not with a Noun.

64.(B) 'Begin' is followed by a gerund.

65.(B) Change 'in one quarter of an hour' into 'a quarter of an hour'. One is used in place of a/ an only when we need to emphasise 'one'.

66.(B) Bid is followed by a bare infinitive in active voice. Change 'ordered' into 'bade' because if we use 'ordered', 'asked' or 'requested', we will need 'to open' and not just 'open' which is given in the sentence.

67.(C) Know always takes 'wh' family, if it is followed by 'to + base form of Verb'. Change 'do you know to prepare' into 'do you know how to prepare'.

68.(D) 'Neither.....nor' is the correct pair of corRelative.

69.(A) Change 'read' into 'was reading'. 'While' shows that the action was in continuation.

70.(B) 'Said' takes 'to' if it is followed by an object. Change 'said me about' into 'said about'.

71.(C) 'Prefer' is followed by 'to'. Change 'than' into 'to'.

72.(D)

73.(A) Change 'provided' into 'unless'. 'Provided' here means 'in case'. 'He won't hear you provided you shout' is an absurd sentence.

74.(A) Change 'at an anchor' into 'at anchor'. Here no article is needed as 'at anchor'. 'At anchor' means to hold something (such as ship) firmly in place — (जहाज में) लंगर लगाना

75.(A) The first action is in past perfect and the 2nd action is in simple past Tense. Change 'already began' into 'had already begun'.

76.(C) Main subject of this sentence is 'My group'. Verb is used according to the main sub. Change 'are well behaved' into 'is well behaved'.

77.(B) Change 'admonishing to him' into 'admonishing him'. Verb 'admonish' does not take any Preposition.

78.(C)

79.(C) Superior becomes superfluous with 'more' and Adjectives that end in 'ior' takes 'to' and not 'than'. Change 'more superior than' into 'superior to'.

80.(D) Here 'would' will come and not 'will' as the sentence is in past.

81.(A) Beside – By the side of, adjacent – के बगल में
Besides – Apart from – के अलावा
Change 'beside being' into 'besides being'.

82.(D) Victim of – का पीड़ित होना (Eg: She is a victim of child abuse)
fall victim to - शिकार हो जाना (Eg: She fell victim to human trafficking)

83.(B) 'What' has been used as a Relative Pronoun in this sentence. The sentence is not interrogative. Hence helping Verb will come after the subject. Moreover the sentence is in past.
Change 'what is her name' into 'what her name was'.

84.(B) Change 'on into at'.
Scoffed at – to ridicule — मजाक उड़ाना

85.(A) Change 'will rose after' into 'would rise after'.
The sentence is in past. Hence 'will' cannot be used. Modals are followed by 'base form of Verb'.

86.(D) Here 'human will' means 'human determination'.

87.(C) Change 'were' into 'is'. Here the subject 'Enlightenment' is a singular subject and hence will take a singular Verb.

88.(B) Change 'for' into 'on'.
Eg:- Complimented on his success
(2) Complimented for his new house.

89.(A) Change 'should not had' into 'should not have'. Base form of Verb comes after all modals.

90.(C) Both 'able to' and 'could/can' show capacity. Hence they are never used together in a sentence.
Change 'could be able' into 'would be able'.

91.(B) Worthy of (trust, etc.) — के लायक
Change 'to' into 'of'.

92.(C) First form of Verb is used with 'did'.
Change 'didn't knew' into 'didn't know'.

93.(B) Sentence is in past. (Here 'would' is V_2 form of will')
Change 'go' into 'went'

94.(B) Change 'embellishment' into 'enhance'.
'Embellishment' is a Noun. Its Verb form is 'embellish'.

95.(C) Good (Adj) – अच्छा
Goods (Noun) – Movable property – सामान
Change 'electronic good' into 'electronic goods'.

96.(B) Both 'since' and 'from' are used for 'point of time' but 'since' is preferred to 'from' if the point of time is of past.

97.(A) In future conditional sentences, the first action is in simple present Tense and the 2nd action is in future Tense.
Change 'who will score the maximum marks' into 'who scores the maximum marks'.

98.(D) 'Congratulate' takes Preposition 'on' — पर बधाई देना

99.(B) 'For' is used for 'duration'.

100.(A)

Pres. Perf. — Since — S. Past

See Present Perfect Tense (last point) of Volume 1. If 'since' is followed by simple past, it is preceded by present perfect Tense. Here the action is a possibility. 'may have V_3' is best suited.

101.(B) 'Look forward to' is followed by a 'gerund'.
Change 'looking forward to interact' into 'looking forward to interacting'.

102.(A) Beside – By the side of — के बगल में
Change 'beside to' into 'beside'.

103.(C) Double future sentences never come together if one action is followed by the other action. The 1st action is in simple present Tense.
Change 'I will go' into 'I go'

104.(B) Change 'past' into 'over'.
Get over means 'to overcome'. We overcome our failures.

105.(D) The action is of past. Hence the use of 'we came' is appropriate.

106.(C) 'Too........to' is the correct corRelative.
Change 'so' into 'too'.

107.(B) Sentence is in past. Change 'have been doing' into 'had been doing'.

108.(B) If 'for/since + time' is used in a sentence, the sentence will be in Perfect or Perfect Continuous Tense.
Change 'worked' into 'have been working'.

109.(A) 'All' is followed by 'that'.
Change 'what' into 'that'.

110.(B) Although is used for two sentence when the result is not in accordance with the action.
Change 'since' into 'although'.

111.(B) 'But' shows contradiction.
Change 'as' into 'but'.

112.(C) 'Furniture' is an uncountable Noun. It is always used in singular form and takes singular Verb.
Change 'has no furnitures yet' into 'has no furniture yet'.

113.(D) The sentence is of Present imaginary position. Formula: If + Sub + were......., Sub + would + V_1 and since it is an interrogative sentence, 'sub' is preceded by helping Verb 'would'.

114.(A) Forms of throw –

1st	2nd	3rd
Throw	threw	thrown.

Change throw' into 'threw'.

115.(B) The sentence and the question tag must be in the same Tense.
Change 'isn't it' into 'aren't they'.

116.(C) Many times conjunctions are used at wrong places.
Change 'not only known for his wealth' into 'known not only for his wealth'. If 'but also', is followed by 'his learning', 'not only' should be followed by 'his wealth'. He is known will come before 'not only'.

117.(A) Change 'whose' into 'the name of which'.
'Whose' is not used with non living things.

118.(A) We choose 'one' out of plural countable Noun. Hence 'students' will come in place of 'student'.

119.(C) In this sentence, we are talking about both medal and scholarship.
Hence 'both' will come after 'won'. This sentence is of misplaced conjunction.

120.(C) The correct pair is given in option 'C' only (Hardly .... when)

121.(C) Reflexive Pronoun comes with enjoy if there is no object after 'enjoy'. 'Enjoyed' here must be followed by 'ourselves'.

122. (A) Change 'get up' into 'got up'. Today the event did not take place as usual.
So, Past Indefinite Tense should be used to get the correct meaning in the sentence.

TYPE – 2 :- Answers

1.(C) Change 'comforted' into 'consoled'.
When a person is very sad, weeping or mourning, we console him.

2.(B) Change 'wrong' into 'fraudulent'.
Fraudulent – Done to trick someone for the purpose of getting something valuable – कपटपूर्ण

3.(B) Change 'disadvantage' into 'advantage'.
'Disadvantage' means 'shortcomings'.
'Undue advantage' is a more appropriate word for this sentence.

4.(D)

5.(B) Suspense – A feeling of excitement caused by wondering what will happen
Suspension – The act of making something invalid usually for a short period of time.
Suspicion – A feeling of doubt.
Change 'suspension' into 'suspense'.

6.(D) Waded – to walk through water – पानी में चलना
Shuffled – to rearrange to produce random order – उलट-पलट करना
Skipped – to pass by or leave out – छोड जाना

7.(A) Change 'ignited' into 'flared'.
Ignite – to set on fire.
'Flare-up' means a sudden occurrence or expression of anger or an occurrence in which something (such as violence) suddenly begins – भड़कना (गुस्सा, हिंसा या आग का)

8.(B) Underlying – used to identify the idea, cause, problem.
Underlining – To draw a line under.
Change 'underlining' into 'underlying'.

9.(C) One who gives money or helps others – A philanthropist.

10.(D) Charlatan – A person who falsely pretends to know or be something in order to deceive people – धोखेबाज
Sycophant – A person who praises powerful people in order to get their approval – चापलूस

Libertine - A person who leads an immoral life – अनैतिक जीवन जीने वाला
Both 'charlatan' and 'quack' mean the same. Hence we need no improvement.

11.(D) Remind- To make someone think about something again – याद दिलाना
Remember – To have in your mind – याद रखना

12.(A) Fluttered – to move or flap the wings quickly without flying – फड़फड़ाना
Faltered – to begin to walk or move in an unsteady way – लड़खड़ाना
Flustered – to make (someone) nervous and confused – घबड़ा देना
Frittered – to break into small fragment – टुकड़े करना
Change 'faltered' into 'fluttered' as pigeons flutter their wings.

13.(A) 'These' and 'those' will take plural Nouns (Kinds). 'This' and 'that' will take singular Noun (kind). Hence only option (A) is correct.

14.(B) Noticeable – Able to be easily seen or noticed Remarkable-unusual or surprising.
Change 'noticeable' into 'remarkable' which is a better option.

15.(D) Distract – to take attention away from someone or something – ध्यान भटकाना
Distort – to change something so that it is no longer of the same shape or size or true or accurate – रूप बिगाड़ना
Vitiate – to ruin or spoil something – भ्रष्ट करना
Sordid – Immoral – अनैतिक

16.(B) Change 'was highly estimated' into 'was highly commended'.
Commended – express approval of– तारीफ करना
Appraise – to estimate the value of – आकंलन करना

17.(B) Facade - the front of a building –किसी इमारत का सामने का भाग

18.(B) Canvas – Coarse cloth – मोटा कपड़ा
Canvass–Visit houses to get political support– घूम-घूम कर वोट माँगना
Change 'canvas' into 'canvass'.

19.(B) Commandeered – To take by force especially for military purposes.
Change 'captured into commandeered'
Here the purpose was not to seize or impound but to take the injured child to the hospital.
Hence commandeered is the best option.

20.(D) Decline – Refuse to accept an offer
Refuse – show unwillingness towards.
But both 'decline' and 'refuse' are not followed by 'to'. Hence 'no improvement' is the best option.

21.(B) Condemned – Express strong disapproval of change 'criticized' into 'condemned' which is a stronger word.

22.(C) Evidence – material that is presented to a court of law to help find the truth about something – सबूत
Change 'proof' into 'evidence'

23.(C) Change 'a tiny town' into 'a small town'.
Tiny – very small — बहुत छोटा/ सुक्ष्म
Humongous – very large — विशालकाय

24.(D) Propitious — likely to have or produce good results – शुभ
Prophetic – correctly stating what will happen in the future – भविष्यवक्ता या भविष्यवाणी संबंधित

25.(C) Deny – To declare untrue – किसी बात की सत्यता का खंडन करना
Refuse – Show unwillingness towards – मना करना
Change 'denied' into 'refused'.

26.(A) 'Hardly credible' means 'that cannot be believed'.
Gullible – easily deceived – आसानी से बेवकूफ बनने वाला
Credible – capable of being believed – विश्वास करने योग्य
Incredible-that cannot be believed – अविश्वसनीय
Change 'gullible' into 'credible'.

27.(A) Change 'poisonous' into 'toxic'.
Effluent - liquid (such as sewage) that is released as waste – गन्दा बहने वाला पानी
Toxic – containing poisonous substance – जहरीला
'Toxic waste' is used more and is hence a common and better option.

28.(C) Change 'affinity' into 'collaboration'.
Affinity – An attraction to something – आकर्षण
Collaboration – To work with another person – सहयोग/साथ में

29.(B) Change 'out of sight' into 'out of control'
We get out of control if we are in bad company.

30.(C) (As adVerb) Hardly – Rarely – मुश्किल से
Hard - with effort – मेहनत से
Change 'hardly working people' into 'hard working people'.

TYPE – 3 :- Answers

1.(C) We express our ideas.
We don't speak or describe ideas.

2.(B) Retreated – movement by soldiers away from an enemy – मोंचा छोड़ना
Change 'went back' into 'retreated'.

3.(C) Change 'giving' into 'donating'
We donate blood.

4.(A) Whisked – to move or take someone or something to another place very quickly – जल्दी से हटा लेना
Change 'taken away' into 'whisked'.

5.(A) 'Asking for' means 'demanding' but 'demanding' is a stronger word and suits the context of the sentence.
Change 'asking for' into 'demanding'.

6.(C) Filial – of or relating to a son or daughter – संतान-संबंधित
Mere – to denote that something is unimportant. – महत्वहीन
Change 'mere' into 'filial'.

7.(C) Dominion – the power to rule control a country– अधिराज्य
Change 'superiority' into 'dominion'.

8.(A) Change 'since setting up' into 'since its inception'. 'Since its setting up' would have been correct but 'its' was missing.

9.(A) Change 'hope' into 'fear'. He hope for something good and we fear of something bad that may happen.

10.(A) Change 'falling with' into 'pouring'.

11.(B) Change 'levied' into 'levelled'.
Levied – An amount of money that must be paid and that is collected by a government – कर इत्यादि का लगाना
Levelled — to aim or direct
Eg:- to level a charge of fraud.

12.(B) Change 'saved' into 'prevented'.
We prevent bloodshed to save people.
Eschew – to avoid (something) especially because one does not think it is right, proper etc – परहेज करना

13.(B) Remediable – capable of being solved or cured – उपचार योग्य
Remedial – Done to make something better – सुधारात्मक
Change 'Remediable' into 'Remedial'.

14.(A) We have stomach ache or head ache.
'Ache' is a common word for body pain.

15.(C) Change 'gave' into devoted'
He devote time to learn some art or skill. Devote 'to' dance is the correct sentence formation.

16.(A) Behest – An authoritative order or urgent prompting
Change 'request' into 'behest'.
We do something good at the behest of our conscience.

17.(B) Change 'requested' into 'invited'.
Indulge – to allow to do something स्वीकृति देना
Inspire – to make someone want to do something – प्रेरणा देना

18.(C) A commission is set up.

19.(D) 'Foot of the tree/mountain' means 'at the lower end of or the bottom' of the tree or mountain.

20.(C) Expose – To reveal (something hidden, dishonest, etc)
Change 'reveal' into 'expose'.

21.(C) 'To beat someone' means 'to defeat'.

TYPE – 4 :- Answers

1. (C)	2. (A)	3. (B)	4. (C)
5. (D)	6. (A)	7. (A)	8. (C)
9. (D)	10. (B)	11. (B)	12. (C)
13. (B)			

TYPE – 5 :- Answers

1.(A) The given sentence is grammatically correct but it is not good etiquette wise.

TYPE – 6 :- Answers

1.(D) Contrite – Sorry for what she had done. Since meaning is same, no improvement is necessary.

2.(D) Alleviate – To reduce the pain or trouble of – दु:ख कम करना
Lessen – To become less or to cause to become less – कम करना
Since meaning is same, no improvement is necessary.

TYPE – 7 :- Answers

1.(D) Run down - Exhausted /to decline in physical condition or vigour
Exhausted means the same.

2.(D) 'Hand in' means 'to submit' – जमा करना/सौंपना

3.(D) Knock down – to strike to the ground with a sharp blow – कुचल देना

4.(A) Come across – To meet by chance – अचानक मुलाकात होना
Change 'Viewed across' into 'come across'.

5.(D)

6.(B) Blue murder – An extravagantly loud outcry.
Change 'black' into 'blue'.

7.(B) Change 'to it' into 'into it'.
To 'put your heart into it' means 'to do it whole-heartedly'

8.(C) 'Stand by' means 'to be or to get ready to act' – कार्य करने के लिए उपस्थित होना।

TYPE – 8 :- Answers

1.(A) Floor is the surface of a room on which we stand (फर्श), ground is outside of a house (जमीन).

2.(A) To 'stand up' means 'to rise up from a sitting posture' – खड़े होना

3.(B) Wear – to have something on one's body – पहने हुए होना
Put on-to dress – पहनना
Change 'wear' into 'put on'.

4.(C) 'Strong' never comes with 'breeze'. 'Breeze' is always gentle.
Change 'the strong breeze' into 'the strong wind'.

TYPE – 9 :- Answers

1.(A) A convict is hanged till he is dead. 'Hanged to death' is grammatically correct but 'hanged till' death is legally a better option.

CHAPTER 25

WORD OFTEN CONFUSED & MISUSED

S.N.	WORD	हिन्दी में अर्थ	Meaning in English
1.	**Accept**	स्वीकार करना	To receive a thing.
	Except	के अलावा	Leaving apart or excluding.
2.	**Expect**	उम्मीद करना	To hope
	Suspect	आशंका करना	To apprehend
3.	**Adopt**	अपनाना/गोद लेना	To accept/to take another person's child legally.
	Adept	निपुण	Proficient
	Adapt	ढ़ालना	To change accordingly.
4.	**Allude**	उल्लेख करना	Refer to
	Elude	बचना	To escape
5.	**Alternate**	एक छोड़ कर एक	One after another.
	Alternative	विकल्प	Available instead /substitute
6.	**Aural**	कान से संबंधित	Of ear
	Oral	मौखिक	Verbal
7.	**Access**	पहुँच	Approach
	Excess	प्रचुरता में	More than due.
8.	**Averse**	नापसंद करना	To dislike
	Adverse	विपरीत	Unfavourable
9.	**Advice (N)**	सलाह	An opinion
	Advise (V)	सलाह देना	To offer an opinion.
10.	**Affect (V)**	असर करना	To influence
	Effect (N)	परिणाम	Result
11.	**Apposite**	उपयुक्त	Proper
	Opposite	के सामने/विपरीत	In front of/ contrary
12.	**Amend**	संशोधन करना	To improve
	Emend	अशुद्धियाँ निकाल देना	To remove the mistakes
13.	**Amoral**	नीतिहीन	Having no moral sense.
	Immoral	अनैतिक	Not conforming to moral standards.
14.	**Antics**	हँसाने के लिए की गई हरकत	Tricks
	Antiques	प्राचीन कला की वस्तुऐं	Ancient pieces of art.

15.	**Appraise**	मूल्यांकन करना	Assess the quality/ value of.
	Apprise	सूचित करना	Inform
16.	**Allusion**	संदर्भ में (अप्रत्यक्ष रूप से)	Indirect reference
	Illusion	भ्रम	Deception
17.	**Beside**	के बगल में	By the side of
	Besides	के अलावा	Apart from
18.	**Bridle**	लगाम	Headgear of horse
	Bridal	दुल्हा/दुल्हन से संबंधित	Related to bride/ bridegroom
19.	**Beneficial**	लाभदायक	Useful
	Beneficiary	लाभान्वित व्यक्ति	One who receives benefit.
20.	**Boar**	सुअर	A pig
	Bore	बर्दाश्त करना/ पैदा करना	To tolerate or to produce (V_2 of bear)
21.	**Bought**	खरीदना	V_2 and V_3 of buy.
	Brought	लाना	V_2 and V_3 of bring.
22.	**Catch**	गतिशील को पकड़ना	To take hold of something when it is moving.
	Hold	थामना	To take hold of something when it is static.
23.	**Childish**	बेवकूफी भरा	Foolish
	Childlike	मासूम	Innocent
24.	**Continual**	नियमित रूप से	Happening repeatedly
	Continuous	लगातार	Without break
25.	**Credible**	विश्वसनीय	Believable
	Creditable	सम्मानीय	Praiseworthy, honourable
26.	**Censure**	निन्दा करना	To criticise
	Censor	प्रतिबन्धित करना	Official licensing of films etc.
27.	**Canon**	नियम	Rule
	Cannon	तोप	A powerful gun fixed to wheels.
28.	**Canvas**	मोटा कपड़ा	Coarse cloth
	Canvass	घूम-घूम के वोट माँगना	Visit houses to get political support.
29.	**Cemetery**	कब्रगाह	A burial place
	Symmetry	एक सा	Harmony
30.	**Casual**	उदासीन, अनौपचारिक	Not formal, not taking much interest.
	Causal	कारक संबंधी	Relating to cause
31.	**Climactic**	उत्कर्ष से संबंधित	Relating to climax
	Climatic	जलवायु संबंधित	Relating to climate
32.	**Coarse**	भद्दा/ मोटा/ समतल नहीं	Rough
	Course	किसी कार्य का सिलसिलेवार रास्ता	A line of action.
33.	**Confidant**	राजदार	A person who is entrusted with secrets.
	Confident	आत्मविश्वास के साथ	Sure and certain.
34.	**Contagious**	बिमारी जो छूने से फैले	A disease that spreads by contact.
	Contiguous	सिमांत	Near
	Infectious	बिमारी जो हवा एवं पानी से फैले	A disease that spreads by air or water.

35.	**Corps**	सेना की टुकडी	A division of army.
	Corpse	मृत शरीर (इंसान का)	A dead body.
	Carcass	किसी बड़े जानवर का मृत शरीर	The dead body of a large animal.
36.	**Conscious**	अवगत	To know
	Conscientious	ज़मीरवाला	With a sense of duty.
37.	**Complain (V)**	शिकायत करना	To say that something is wrong or not satisfactory.
	Complaint (N)	शिकायत	A report of a problem.
38.	**Complacent**	आत्म संतुष्ट	Self-satisfied.
	Complaisant	आज्ञाकारी	Obedient and compliant.
39.	**Complement**	पूरक	N-a thing that completes or improves. V-add to something in a way that it improves.
	Compliment	तारीफ	A remark of admiration.
40.	**Custom**	सामाजिक नियम	Social usage.
	Habit	आदत	Personal usage.
41.	**Compose**	बनाना	Make up the whole.
	Comprise	से बना होना	Consist of.
42.	**Career**	पेशा	Course through life.
	Carrier	सामान ढ़ोने की गाड़ी	That which carries.
43.	**Credible**	विश्वसनीय	Believable
	Credulous	जो आसानी से विश्वास कर ले	Too ready to believe.
44.	**Discreet**	(सचेत ताकि किसी को व्यवहार या भाषा से चोट न पहुँचे)	Careful not to cause offence by speech or behaviour.
	Discrete	(पृथक)	Separate, distinct.
45.	**Disease**	बिमारी	Ailment or illness.
	Decease	मृत्यु	Dcath.
46.	**Decent**	सभ्य	Nice, respectable.
	Descent	ढ़लान	Downward motion.
	Dissent	मतभेद	Difference of opinion.
47.	**Dual**	दोहरा	With two parts.
	Duel	द्वंद्व युद्ध	A fight between two persons using guns or swords.
48.	**Deface**	विकृत करना	Disfigure.
	Efface	मिटा देना	Wipe out.
49.	**Deny**	खंडन करना	To declare untrue.
	Decline	अस्वीकार करना	Refuse to accept an offer.
	Refuse	इन्कार करना	Show unwillingness towards.
	Refute	खंडन करना (सबूत के साथ)	Prove wrong.
50.	**Defy**	उल्लंघन करना	To break the law.
	Deify	ईश्वर बना देना	To make someone or something a god.

51.	**Defuse**	तनाव कम करना	Remove the tension.
	Diffuse	फैलाना/अस्पष्ट	Spread out; not clear or concise.
52.	**Desert**	N- रेगिस्तान, V- त्याग देना	N- An area where there is little rain. V- To leave someone.
	Dessert	भोजन के बाद का मीठा व्यंजन	Sweet dish eaten at the end of a meal.
53.	**Depression**	गड्डा/अवसाद	Hollow/ A mental state of despair.
	Depreciation	मूल्य कम होना	Undervalue.
54.	**Disinterested**	निष्पक्ष	Impartial.
	Uninterested	दिलचस्पी ना होना	Not interested.
55.	**Delightful**	प्रसन्नतादायक	Very pleasant.
	Delicious	स्वादिष्ट	Pleasing to taste.
56.	**Deprecate**	नापसंद करना	To hate.
	Depreciate	मुल्य कम करना	To reduce in value.
57.	**Defective**	त्रुटिपूर्ण	Having a certain imperfection.
	Deficient	कमी होना	Lacking something.
58.	**Decided**	निर्णय किया हुआ (निश्चित)	Clear and definite.
	Decisive	निर्णायक	Deciding.
59.	**Effective**	असरदार	Producing effect.
	Efficacious	जो निश्चित ही उत्तम परिणाम दे	Able to produce the desired result.
	Efficient	कार्यकुशल	Competent.
60.	**Elicit**	उत्पन्न कर पाना	To get or produce something.
	Illicit	अवैध	Illegal or disapproved of by society.
61.	**Economical**	कम खर्च वाला	Involving less expenditure.
	Economic	अर्थव्यवस्था सम्बन्धित	Relating to economy.
62.	**Enduring**	लम्बे समय तक कायम	Existing for a long time.
	Endurable	सहन करने लायक	Bearable.
63.	**Emigrant**	प्रवासी	A person who leaves his country to settle in another.
	Immigrant	अप्रवासी	One who comes to another country.
64.	**Enormity**	अति, घोर	Extreme seriousness.
	Enormousness	ज्यादा होना	Great in size or scale.
65.	**Ensure**	सुनिश्चित करना	To make sure.
	Insure	बीमा करना	To protect against risk.
	Assure	दिलासा देना	To make certain of.
66.	**Envelop**	(ढ़क देना)	To cover or surround something completely.
	Envelope	(लिफाफा)	A flat usually square paper container for a letter.
67.	**Especially**	विशेष कर	In particular, above all.
	Specially	किसी विशेष अवसर के लिए	For a special purpose.

68.	**Excite**	उत्तेजित करना	To arouse feelings of happiness or enthusiasm.
	Incite	उकसाना / भड़काना	To arouse unpleasant or violent feelings.
69.	**Expedient**	सही/ लाभदायक	Helpful or useful in a particular situation.
	Expeditious	शीघ्र/ फुर्ती से	Prompt.
70.	**Extinct**	विलुप्त	No longer existing.
	Instinct	मूल प्रवृत्ति	Inborn impulse.
71.	**Flair**	जन्मजात प्रवृत्ति	Natural ability.
	Flare	धधकना, फैलना	A burst of flame or light/ to become angry.
72.	**Flaunt**	दिखावा करना	Display ostentatiously/to show off.
	Flout	उल्लंघन करना	Disregard a rule or custom.
73.	**Fortuitous**	आकस्मिक	Happening by chance.
	Fortunate	भाग्यशाली	Lucky.
74.	**Felicity**	प्रसन्नता	A blessing, happiness.
	Facility	सुविधा	Ease or comfort
	Faculty	कार्यशक्ति/ कॉलेज का विभाग /कॉलेज के अध्यापकगण	Ability/departments of college/ the people who teach
75.	**Fatal**	घातक	Deadly
	Fateful	महत्त्वपूर्ण/परन्तु नकारात्मक परिणामयुक्त	Important but with usually negative effect.
76.	**Fain**	खुशी से	Gladly
	Feign	दिखावा करना (जो सच नहीं है)/बहाना बनाना	To pretend to feel something.
77.	**Floor**	फर्श	The flat surface of room on which we walk.
	Ground	जमीन	The surface of earth outside the room.
78.	**Graceful**	भव्य	Handsome or attractive
	Gracious	दयालु	Merciful
79.	**Gate**	द्वार	An entrance
	Gait	चलने का तरीका	A particular way of walking.
80.	**Gourmand**	पेटू	A glutton
	Gourmet	पाक कला का पारखी	A food connoisseur.
81.	**Hear**	सुनना	To receive sound.
	Listen	ध्यान से सुनना	To hear carefully.
82.	**Hoard**	छिपाकर संग्रह करना	To store in a secret place.
	Horde	एक बड़ा समूह	A large group of people.
83.	**Humility**	विनम्रता	The quality of being humble.
	Humiliation	अपमान	Disrespect
84.	**Historic**	महत्त्वपूर्ण	Important
	Historical	ऐतिहासिक	Relating to history
	Histrionic	नाटकीय एवं बढ़ा चढ़ाकर	Dramatic and exaggerated
85.	**Human**	मानव	Relating to man
	Humane	दयालु	Kind

86.	**Illegal**	गैरकानूनी	Against the law
	Illicit	अवैध	Disapproved of by society.
87.	**Incredible**	अविश्वसनीय	Unbelievable
	Incredulous	जो विश्वास न करें	Not ready to believe something/ someone.
88.	**Ingenious**	बढ़िया एवं नई युक्ति भरा	Clever and involving new ideas.
	Ingenuous	निष्कपट, सरल	Honest and sincere.
89.	**Intense**	तीव्र	Extreme and forceful.
	Intensive	गहन	Involving a lot of effort.
90.	**Invent**	आविष्कार करना	To create something which never existed before.
	Discover	खोज करना	To find something for the first time which nobody was aware of.
91.	**Industrial**	उद्योग संबंधी	Relating to industry
	Industrious	मेहनती	Hard-working
92.	**Imperious**	दबंग	Haughty
	Imperial	राजसी	Majestic, relating to empire.
93.	**Incumbent**	जरूरी	To be necessary
	Recumbent	लेटा हुआ	Lying down
94.	**Jealous**	ईर्ष्यालु (जब वस्तु हमारी हो)	When we are afraid of losing the person/ thing we love, we feel jealous.
	Envious	ईर्ष्यालु (जब वस्तु हमारी नहीं हो)	When we wish we had what someone else has, we feel envious. Envy and jealousy are slightly different in meaning.
95.	**Judicial**	न्याय संबंधी	Relating to a judge or justice.
	Judicious	समझदार	Wise, prudent
96.	**Light**	V- जलाना-प्रकाशित करने के लिए N- रोशनी, Adj- हल्का	*Verb*-to start flames in order to spread light/ *Noun*-radiance/ *Adj*-not heavy.
	Burn	V- जलाना-नाश करने के लिए, N- फफोला	*V*-to start flames to destroy something/ *N*-the part of body damaged due to heat.
97.	**Lightening**	उजाला करना, हल्का करना, गोरा करना	To make bright/ less heavy/ pale/ less serious.
	Lightning	बिजली-जो आसमान में दिखती है	A flash of bright light seen in the sky.
	Lighting	बिजली की व्यवस्था	The arrangement of lights.
98.	**Loath**	अनिच्छुक	Reluctant, unwilling
	Loathe	घृणा करना	To hate
99.	**Loose**	ढ़ीला	Not tight.
	Lose	खोना/हारना	Be defeated.
	Loss	घाटा/हानि	The state of not in possession of something or having it less than before.

100. Luxuriant	प्रचुरता में उगना	Strong in growth
Luxurious	विलासितापूर्ण	Very comfortable and expensive.
101. Lovely	प्यारा, सुंदर	Beautiful
Lovable	प्यार करने योग्य	Worthy of love
102. Metal	धातु	A chemical element. Eg-gold, iron etc.
Mettle	क्षमता	Ability.
103. Metre	लम्बाई की इकाई	A unit of length.
Meter	एक यंत्र	A device used to measure the amount of something that is used.
104. Negligent	लापरवाह	Careless
Negligible	नगण्य	Very little
105. Momentary	क्षणिक	Short-lived
Momentous	महत्त्वपूर्ण	Very important
106. Minor	नाबालिग	Underage
Miner	खदान कर्मी	One who works in mines.
107. Militate	प्रतिकूल होना	To hinder
Mitigate	तीव्रता कम करना/शान्त करना	Make less severe.
108. Naval	नेवी संबंधित	Relating to a navy.
Navel	नाभी	Small round part in the middle of the stomach.
109. Notable	ध्यान देने लायक	Important and deserving attention.
Notorious	कुख्यात	Known for bad qualities.
Famous	प्रसिद्ध	Well-known
Eminent	प्रसिद्ध एवं सम्माननीय	Well-known and respected
110. Official	आधिकारिक	Relating to an office.
Officious	सलाह देने के लिए तत्पर	Too eager to tell others what to do.
111. Ordinance	अध्यादेश	A law made by the government.
Ordnance	सेना का साजो-सामान	Military material such as weapons, ammunition etc.
112. Pane	खिड़की/दरवाजे का काँच	A flat piece of glass used in a window/door.
Pain	दर्द	Feeling of physical suffering.
Pains	अथक प्रयास	A lot of efforts.
113. Palate	तालू	The roof of the mouth/ the sense of taste.
Palette	रंग मिलाने का बर्तन	An artist's mixing board.
Pellet	किसी चीज़ का छोटा गोला	A small ball of any substance.
114. Pedal	पैर से चलाने वाला	A foot-operated lever.
Peddle	घूम-घूम कर सामान बेचना	To sell goods by going from one place to another.
115. Perpetrate	करना (गुनाह)	To commit (a crime).
Perpetuate	किसी कार्य/हालात के जारी रहने का कारण बनना	To cause something to continue.

116. Personal	निजी	Private
Personnel	कर्मी	Staff
117. Pore	छेद	Small hole.
Pour	बहना, उड़ेलना	Flow, cause to flow.
118. Practice (N)	अभ्यास	Regular activity.
Practise (V)	अभ्यास करना	To do something regularly.
119. Practicable	व्यवहारिक	Able to be done.
Practical/ Pragmatic	वास्तव में/प्रयोगात्मक	Effective or realistic.
120. Prescribe	सलाह देना (के रूप में)	To recommend
Proscribe	गैर कानूनी करार देना	Forbid or condemn.
121. Proceed	आगे बढ़ना	To continue
Precede	पहले आना	To come before/happen before.
122. Popular	प्रसिद्ध	Liked by all.
Populous	घनी आवादी वाला	Thickly populated.
123. Pray	प्रार्थना करना	To offer prayer to God.
Prey	(V) शिकार करना/(N) शिकार	Hunt and kill/ victim
124. Principal	प्रधानाचार्य/ मुख्य	One who is in charge of a school/ first in order of importance.
Principle	सिद्धान्त	Most important basic idea / moral rule.
125. Quite	पूर्ण/ काफी हद तक	Completely/ upto a large extent
Quiet	चुप	To be silent
Quit	छोड़ देना	to give up
126. Respectable	सम्माननीय	Worthy of respect.
Respectful	सम्मानजनक	Showing respect
Respective	विशिष्ट, अलग-अलग	Particular
127. Resource	संसाधन	Means
Recourse	रास्ता	Resort
128. Regrettable	खेदजनक	Causing regret, undesirable.
Regretful	दुखी	Feeling sorry
129. Rise	उठना/उगना/तरक्की करना	To get up, to progress, to move upward
Raise	उठाना	To lift
Raze	ध्वस्त करना	To demolish
Rage	गुस्सा	Anger
130. Ride	दोपहिया या जानवर की सवारी करना	To sit on an animal or two-wheeler and travel.
Drive	चार-पहिया की सवारी करना	To travel by a four-wheeler.

131. Rout	धराशाही करना	To defeat completely and easily.
Route	रास्ता	Path
Root	जड़	The underground part of a plant.
132. Septic	एक चिकित्सा संबंधी समस्या	A medical term involving sepsis.
Sceptic	संदेही	Doubtful of an idea or belief.
133. See	देखना	Perceive with eyes.
Look	ताकना/नजर डालना	To direct the eyes in order to see.
Watch	देखना (कुछ अंतराल तक)/ नजर रखना	To look at something for a period of time/ to keep an eye on.
Stare	घूरना	To look continuously for a long time with eyes wide open
Peep	झाँकना	To see secretly or through a hole.
Glance	नजर डालना	To give a quick short look.
Glare	गुस्से में घूरना	To stare angrily.
Glimpse	एक झलक देखना	To see someone very briefly.
Glower	गुस्से से देखना	To see angrily.
134. Sever	अलग करना	To break/ to separate.
Amputate	शरीर के किसी बाहरी अंग (हाथ या पैर)को काट कर अलग करना, क्योंकि वह स्थायी रूप से क्षतिग्रस्त हो चुका है	Cut off a body part that is permanently damaged.
Maim	शरीर के किसी अंग को स्थायी रूप से क्षतिग्रस्त करना	To damage any body part permanently.
Severe	तीव्र	Extreme
Sewer	नाला	Drain
135. Story	कहानी	Account of any event.
Storey	तल	Floor
136. Suit	वाद/अभियोग	Action in a law court.
Soot	कालिख	Black substance in smoke.
Suite	रोट	A set of rooms / furniture.
137. Statue	मूर्ति	Image
Statute	लिखित कानून	Written law
138. Straight	सीधा	Extending without a curve.
Strait	जलसंधि	Narrow passage of water.
139. Stationary	स्थिर	Not moving.
Stationery	पैन, कॉपी इत्यादि	Things needed for writing.
140. Sight	दृष्टि/ नजारा	Ability to see/view.
Site	कार्यस्थल	A place of construction.
Cite	उल्लेख करना	To mention.

141. Shear	काटना (बाल, इत्यादि)	To cut off-hair, wool etc.
Sheer	पूर्ण रूप से	Utter, complete
142. Toe	पैर की ऊँगली	Any of the five separate parts at the end of the foot.
Tow	खींच कर गाड़ी ले जाना	To pull a vehicle using a rope or chain tied to another vehicle.
143. Temper	गुस्सा	Anger, rage
Tamper	छेड़-छाड़ करना (किसी चीज से)	To interfere with.
144. Temporary	क्षणिक, तत्कालिक	Short lived
Temporal	सांसारिक	Earthly or worldly
145. Titillate	उत्तेजित करना	Stimulate or excite especially in a sexual way.
Titivate	सुन्दरता बढ़ाना	To make smarter or pretties.
146. Topical	प्रासंगिक/आधुनिक विषय से	Related to present time.
Tropical	उष्ण	With hot climate
147. Vain	बेकार में/घमंडी	Not successful/arrogant.
Vein	नाड़ी	Tube that carries blood to the heart in our body.
148. Verbal	शाब्दिक	Relating to words
Verbose	शब्दों से भरा	Containing more words than necessary
Oral	मौखिक	Spoken
Verbiage	जरूरत से ज्यादा शब्दों भरा जिससे अर्थ समझना कठिन हो जाए	Use of too many words due to which it becomes difficult for one to understand the speech or article.
149. Virtuous	नैतिक रूप से अच्छा	Having good moral qualities
Virtual	आभासीय	In effect, though not in fact
150. Vile	नीच	Immoral
Wile	युक्ति	Tricks
151. Vale	घाटी	Valley
Veil	नकाब, घूँघट	Cover of face
Wail	रोना	Weep
152. Vocation	व्यवसाय	Profession
Vacation	अवकाश	Holidays
153. Violence	हिंसा	Actions that hurt people
Violation	नियम की अवहेलना	Infringement of law
154. Wither	मुरझा जाना	To fade
Whither	कहाँ	Where
Weather	मौसम	Atmospheric condition (of a short period)
Whether	या........या	'Whether ..... or' is a correlative
155. Wave	लहर (N)/ लहराना (V)	Raised mass of water in sea/ to move.
Waive	माफ कर देना (फीस इत्यादि)	To not demand something you have the right to

CHAPTER

26 VOCABULARIES

S.N.	WORD	हिन्दी में अर्थ	Meaning in English
1.	**Abase**	नीचा दिखाना	Degrade.
2.	**Abash**	लज्जित करना	To embarrass.
3.	**Abattoir**	बूचड़ खाना	Place where animals are killed.
4.	**Abdicate**	त्याग देना	Give up.
5.	**Aberrant**	असामान्य	Abnormal.
6.	**Abetment**	दूषप्रेरण	The act of helping someone in wrongdoing.
7.	**Abeyance**	निलंबित अवस्था	Suspended action.
8.	**Abhor**	घृणा करना	Detest, dislike, hate.
9.	**Abject**	बुरी हालत में	Extremely poor or unhappy.
10.	**Abjure**	सौगन्ध खा कर त्याग करना	Renounce upon oath.
11.	**Ablution**	शुद्धि हेतु स्नान	The act of washing oneself.
12.	**Abnegation**	त्याग देना-अधिकार या दावा	To give up a right or a claim.
13.	**Abode**	निवास	The place where someone lives.
14.	**Abolish**	उन्मूलन करना	To put an end to.
15.	**Abominable**	घृणित	Very bad or unpleasant.
16.	**Aboriginal**	आदिवासी	Native.
17.	**Abortive**	निष्फल	Fruitless, futile.
18.	**Abrasive**	घिसने का सामान	Substancc uscd for rubbing.
19.	**Abridge**	संक्षिप्त करना	Shorten.
20.	**Abrogate**	खत्म करना (किसी परम्परा/ कानून को)	Abolish some custom etc.
21.	**Abscission**	चीरा	Cutting off.
22.	**Abscond**	भाग जाना	Depart secretly.
23.	**Absolute**	पूर्ण रूप से	Complete.
24.	**Absolve**	दोष से मुक्त करना	Pardon.
25.	**Abstain**	रोकना, परहेज करना	Refrain from.
26.	**Abstract**	संक्षेप दस्तावेज/सिर्फ भावना के रूप में ही मौजूद	A shortened form of speech/existing as an idea or feeling only.
27.	**Abstruse**	मुश्किल, कठिन	Difficult to understand.

28. **Abysmal** .... बहुत बुरा .... Not measurable, very bad.
29. **Accede** .... मान जाना .... Agree to do.
30. **Acclaim** .... प्रशंसा करना .... Applaud.
31. **Accolade** .... पुरस्कार .... Award of merit.
32. **Accomplice** ...... गुनाह का साथी .... Partner in crime.
33. **Accord** .... सामंजस्य से .... Do something in complete agreement.
34. **Accused** .... आरोपी .... One who is under trial in a court.
35. **Acme** .... शिखर .... Peak.
36. **Acquit** .... बरी करना .... Declare to be not guilty.
37. **Adapt** .... अनुकूल बनाना .... To change to suit different environment.
38. **Adept** .... निपुण .... Proficient.
39. **Adolescent** ...... किशोर .... One who is growing into an adult.
40. **Adulteration** ... मिलावट .... Mixing some undesired commodity.
41. **Adultery** .... विवाहेत्तर संबंध, व्याभिचार .... To have sex outside marriage.
42. **Adverse** .... प्रतिकूल .... Unfavourable.
43. **Aftermath** .... किसी अप्रिय घटना के बाद का समय .... The period which follows an undesired event.
44. **Aghast** .... हत्प्रभ रह जाना .... Sudden feeling of shock and worry.
45. **Agile** .... लचीला .... Able to move your body quickly.
46. **Agony** .... दर्द .... Extreme sufferings.
47. **Aisle** .... सीट के शृँखला के बीच जाने-आने का रास्ता .... Narrow, long space between the two rows of seats.
48. **Alchemist** .... पारस .... One who tries to turn other base metal into gold.
49. **Alimony** .... तलाक पश्चात दी जाने वाली रकम .... Money paid usually to a wife after break-down of marriage.
50. **Altar** .... बेदी .... Table/place where offerings are put in a religious place.
51. **Altercation** ...... वाक युद्ध, कहा-सुनी .... A loud argument.
52. **Ambiguous** ...... अस्पष्ट, द्विअर्थी .... Having more than one possible meaning.
53. **Amenable** .... सुझाव स्वीकार करने को तैयार .... Willing to accept a suggestion.
54. **Amiable** .... दोस्ताना .... Pleasant and friendly behaviour.
55. **Angst** .... चिन्ता .... Great anxiety.
56. **Anguish** .... वेदना, व्यथा .... Extreme unhappiness.
57. **Annotate** .... टिप्पणी .... To add a brief explanation.

58. **Anonymous** ..... गुमनाम .... Made/done by someone unknown.
59. **Antecedent** ...... पूर्वगामी .... Something/someone existing before.
60. **Apathy** .... उदासीनता .... Lack of interest/enthusiasm/ emotion.
61. **Appalling** .... बहुत भयावह .... Very bad and shocking.
62. **Appeasement** .. तुष्टीकरण .... The act of giving advantage to one party.
63. **Archives** .... ऐतिहासिक/ सरकारी दस्तावेज जहाँ रखा जाए . Place where historical records are kept.
64. **Argumentative** बहस करने वाला .... Often arguing or ready to argue.
65. **Articulate** .... अच्छा वक्ता .... A good orator.
66. **Asceticism** ...... सन्यास/ वैराग्य .... Religious beliefs and avoidance of life of pleasure.
67. **Assault** .... मारपीट करना .... A violent attack.
68. **Asset** .... सम्पत्ति .... Valuables.
69. **Atrocities** .... जुल्म .... Violent and cruel act.
70. **Attenuate** .... शान्त करना .... To calm or soothe.
71. **Attrition** .... सनिघर्षण .... The gradual weakening of something.
72. **Augment** .... बढ़ाना .... Add to/increase.
73. **August** .... महत्त्वपूर्ण/राजसी .... Important/Majestic.
74. **Aura** .... आभा .... A feeling or character a person/place seems to have.
75. **Averse** .... नापसंद .... Strong dislike.
76. **Awful** .... अत्यंत बुरा .... Hateful.
77. **Babble** .... बड़बड़ाना .... Talk in a way which is difficult to understand.
78. **Bacchanalian** .. शराब के नशे में मस्ती .... Drunken reverly
79. **Backbite** .... चुगली करना .... To speak something at the back of someone.
80. **Badger** .... परेशान करना .... Annoy.
81. **Badinage** .... मजाक में चिढ़ाना .... playful teasing/banter.
82. **Baffle** .... चकरा देना .... Confuse.
83. **Bait** .... चारा .... Snare, Trap, Decoy.
84. **Baleful** .... घातक, हानिकारक .... Deadly.
85. **Balk** .... अनिच्छुक होना .... To be unwilling to do something.
86. **Balmy** .... सुखदायक गर्म .... Pleasantly warm.
87. **Bane** .... अभिशाप .... Curse.

88. **Banter** .... मजाक में चिढ़ाना .... Conversation which is funny and not serious.
89. **Barb** .... काँटा .... Sharp projection from fish hook.
90. **Barbaric** .... बर्बर .... Savagely cruel.
91. **Bard** .... कवि .... Poet.
92. **Barefaced** .... बेशर्म .... Shameless.
93. **Baroque** .... सजा हुआ .... Highly ornate.
94. **Barrage** .... बाँध .... Structure built across a river.
95. **Beeline** .... सीधी रेखा/रास्ता .... Direct or quick route.
96. **Beget** .... पैदा करना .... To father or produce.
97. **Begrudge** .... बेमन से देना .... To give unwillingly.
98. **Beguile** .... दिशा भ्रमित करना .... Cheat or mislead.
99. **Behemoth** .... बहुत बड़ा जीव .... Huge creature.
100. **Behest** .... के निवेदन/ आदेश पर .... At the request or order of.
101. **Benevolence** ... दया .... Kindness.
102. **Betray** .... धोखा देना .... To be disloyal/ to deceive.
103. **Blackguard** ...... आवारा, अनैतिक व्यक्ति .... A man who has no moral principles.
104. **Blatant** .... बेशर्मी के साथ खुलेआम .... Open and unashamed.
105. **Blister** .... फफोला .... Swellings on skin.
106. **Blizzard** .... बर्फीला तूफान .... Stormy weather.
107. **Blunder** .... बहुत बड़ी गलती .... A big mistake.
108. **Blush** .... शर्म से लाल होना .... To become pink in the face due to shyness.
109. **Boisterous** .... शोर-गुल मचाने वाला, जोश से भरा ..... Noisy and full of energy.
110. **Bombast** .... बढ़ी-चढ़ी बात .... Pompous language with little meaning.
111. **Boost** .... बढ़ाना .... To improve/increase.
112. **Booze** .... शराब पीना .... To take alcoholic drink.
113. **Brickbat** .... बक-झक .... An insult, spoken attack.
114. **Brutal** .... बर्बर .... Savagely violent
115. **Buckle** .... दवाब में टूट जाना .... Crumble under pressure.
116. **Bully** .... परेशान करना/ डराना .... To hurt/frighten someone.
117. **Bunk** .... बिना अनुमति के चले जाना .... To leave without permission.
118. **Butcher** .... हत्या करना .... To kill/murder someone.
119. **Cabal** .... षड्यन्त्र करने वाला समूह .... Group of people who plan secretly.
120. **Cache** .... छिपाने का स्थान .... Hiding place.
121. **Cacophony** ...... शोरगुल .... Harsh mixture of sound.
122. **Cadaver** .... शव .... A dead human body.
123. **Cadence** .... स्वर का उतार चढ़ाव .... Regular rise and fall of voice.
124. **Cahoots** .... षड़यन्त्र .... Acting together generally for a dishonest purpose.

125. Calamity .... संकट .... Disaster.

126. Caldron .... कढ़ाई .... Large kettle.

127. Calibre .... क्षमता .... Ability.

128. Calligraphy .... सुंदर लेखन कला .... Art of writing beautifully.

129. Callous .... निर्दयी .... Cruel.

130. Callow .... अनुभवहीन .... One with little experience or knowledge.

131. Canvass .... घूम-घूम कर वोट माँगना .... Seek votes.

132. Capitalize .... पूँजी उपलब्ध कराना .... To supply money to a business.

133. Capitulate .... आत्मसर्मपण करना .... Surrender.

134. Capricious .... सनकी .... Fickle-minded.

135. Carcass .... मृत शरीर (जानवर का) .... A dead body of a large animal.

136. Cardinal .... प्रमुख .... most important.

137. Careen .... तेजी से आगे बढ़ते हुए बाएं-दाएं हिलना Sway from side to side while moving forward quickly.

138. Carnage .... जनसंहार .... Slaughter/massacre.

139. Casanova .... दिलफेंक .... One who has lots of sexual relationships, philanderer

140. Catastrophe .... विपत्ति, संकट .... A sudden destructive event.

141. Cave (V) .... दवाब में टूट जाना .... Collapse/give in to demands.

Cave (N) .... गुफा .... A large hole on the side of a hill.

142. Censor .... प्रतिबंधित करना .... To ban unacceptable parts.

143. Censure .... निन्दा करना .... Strongly criticise.

144. Chaos .... अव्यवस्था .... Complete disorder.

145. Charismatic .... आर्कषक .... Attractive.

146. Chaste .... पवित्र .... Pure.

147. Chauvinism .... बड़प्पन की भावना (अपनी नस्ल/ मर्द होने पर) .... Feeling of superiority due to race or gender.

148. Cheat .... धोखेबाज/ धोखा देना .... One who cheats or deceives/the act of deceiving.

149. Chide .... डाँटना .... To reprimand and to speak severely to someone.

150. Clamour .... शोर मचा कर माँग या शिकायत करना .. To make a loud complaint or demand.

151. Clandestine .... गुप्त .... Planned/done in sec

152. Clasp .... जोर से थामना .... To hold something firmly.

153. Cloak .... लम्बा चोगा/ छिपाना .... Long gown/ to hide.

154. Coalition .... साझा .... A temporary alliance.
155. Coddle .... कुछ ज्यादा ही देखभाल करना .... To protect something/ someone too much.
156. Collate .... क्रम में रखना, गलती ढूढ़ने हेतु मिलान करना To put in proper order.
157. Collision .... टक्कर.. The act of hitting something with another thing.
158. Combat............ लड़ाई .... A fight especially during a war.
159. Commendable . प्रशंसनीय .... Praiseworthy.
160. Commute .... यात्रा करना जो नियमित हो/ बदल देना ... To make the same journey regularly/ to change.
161. Complement ... पूरक .... A thing that improves.
162. Conceal .... छिपाना .... To hide.
163. Concede .... स्वीकार कर लेना .... Admit to be true.
164. Concurring...... सहमत होना .... To agree with someone.
165. Condolence ..... संवेदना व्यक्त करना .... Sympathy for the family of a person who has recently died.
166. Confrontation टकराव...................................... Fight/argument.
167. Consecrate ...... पवित्र बनाना/पवित्र घोषित करना.......... Make or declare sacred.
168. Conspicuity..... प्रत्यक्ष होना................................. Clarity.
169. Conspirator ..... षड्यंत्रकारी .... One who plans something illegal.
170. Contemplate ... विचार करना .... Think of a particular thing for a long time.
171. Convalesce...... स्वास्थ्य लाभ करना........................ Regain health after illness.
172. Conversant ..... ज्ञान होना.................................... Having knowledge of.
173. Convict............ दोषी सिद्ध करना/दोषसिद्ध व्यक्ति .... One proved guilty/to be proved guilty.
174. Conviviality .... दोस्ताना .... Friendly.
175. Corporal .... शारीरिक .... Bodily.
176. Corpse .... मुर्दा शरीर.................................. A dead body of a person.
177. Corroborate ..... पुष्टि करना.................................. Confirm or support.
178. Countenance... चेहरे का भाव............................. The expression of the face.
179. Couplet .... एक सुर की दो पंक्तियाँ .... Two successive rhyming lines of verse.
180. Cramp .... बाधा डालना/मरोड़ .... Hamper or restraint/painful involuntary tightening of a muscle.
181. Credentials ..... योग्यता एवं अनुभव .... Qualities/documents proving ability and experience.
182. Crooked.......... बेईमान/ सीधा नहीं .... Dishonest/not forming a straight line.

183. **Culminate** .... तक पहुँचना तब खत्म होना .... To reach a point and then finish.
184. **Culprit** .... दोषी .... Someone who has done something wrong.
185. **Curb** .... अंकुश लगाना .... To check/restrain.
186. **Dab hand** .... किसी काम में निपुण .... An expert in something.
187. **Dabble** .... सिर्फ ऐसे ही कोई कार्य करना .... Work in non-serious way.
188. **Daft** .... मूर्ख .... Silly or stupid.
189. **Dainty** .... छोटा एवं सुन्दर .... Small and graceful.
190. **Dally** .... कोई कार्य धीरे-धीरे करना .... Procrastinate/to waste time or do something slowly.
191. **Damsel** .... अविवाहित युवती .... A young unmarried girl.
192. **Dank** .... भीगा हुआ .... Damp/wet.
193. **Dapper** .... साफ-सुथरा .... Neat and tidy.
194. **Dappled** .... चितकबरा .... Spotted.
195. **Daub** .... लेपना .... Smear.
196. **Daunt** .... डराना .... Intimidate, frighten.
197. **Dauntless** .... निडर .... Bold.
198. **Dearth** .... कमी .... Lack of.
199. **Debauched** ...... पथभ्रष्ट (शराब, सेक्स इत्यादि में लिप्त) One who is given to sex, alcohol etc.
200. **Debilitate** .... कमजोर बनाना .... Weaken.
201. **Debonair** .... सजीला/आर्कषक .... Fashionable/Attractive.
202. **Debunk** .... कम महत्वपूर्ण ठहरना .... To show that some thing is less important.
203. **Debut** .... पहला अवसर .... Something performed for the first time.
204. **Decency** .... सभ्य तरीका .... good and moral behavior.
205. **Decimate** .... हत्या करना .... Kill/destroy.
206. **Decipher** .... किसी लिखित दस्तावेज को पढ़ कर अर्थ स्पष्ट करना Decode.
207. **Declivity** .... ढ़ाल .... Downward slope.
208. **Deface** .... बदशक्ल बनाना .... Disfigure.
209. **Defacto** .... वास्तविक .... Existing in fact.
210. **Defeatist** .... निराशावादी .... One who accepts defeat easily.
211. **Deference** .... सम्मान .... Respect.
212. **Defiant** .... अवज्ञाकारी .... Disobedient.
213. **Deforestation** .. जंगल साफ करना .... Cutting down of trees in a large area.
214. **Defuse** .... तनाव कम करना .... Reduce tension.
215. **Deluge** .... बाढ़ .... A large amount of rain/water.

216. Demographer .. जन्म का विवरण रखने वाला .... A person who studies changes in number of births.
217. Denounce .... निन्दा करना .... To criticize strongly.
218. Deplorable ...... घृणित .... Very bad.
219. Deposition ...... बयान.................................... A testimony.
220. Derail .... पटरी से उतरना .... To come off the railway track.
221. Desecration..... पवित्रता भंग करना........................ Treatment of something sacred with disrespect.
222. Desperate........ किसी कार्य या चीज के लिए तीव्र इच्छा . Feeling involving great willingness.
223. Despicable ...... घृणित .... Unpleasant, causing strong feeling of dislike.
224. Detente .... तनाव की कमी .... The easing of hostility between countries.
225. Deterrent .... हत्तोसाहित करने वाला .... Discouragement from action.
226. Detrimental .... नुकसानदायक .... Harmful.
227. Diffuse............ फैल जाना .... Spread over a wide area.
228. Dine .... रात्रि भोज करना .... Eat dinner.
229. Discord .... सामंजस्य की कमी........................ Lack of agreement.
230. Disembarked ... उतरना जहाज से .... To leave a ship/plane after the journey.
231. Disillusion ...... निराशा/मोह भंग........................... Disappointment.
232. Disinterested .. निष्पक्ष.................................... Impartial.
233. Disparagement उपेक्षा .... Insult/abuse.
234. Dispassionate . तटस्थ .... Not influenced by emotion.
235. Dispense with . छुटकारा पाना .... Get rid of or manage without.
236. Disseminate .... फैलना .... Spread widely.
237. Docile .... आज्ञाकारी .... Obedient.
238. Dolorous .... दुखी .... Sad.
239. Draconian .... अत्यंत कठोर............................. Extremely severe.
240. Drain .... बहा देना, नाला............................ (V) removing things; (N) pipes and sewage.
241. Drizzle .... बूँदा-बाँदी होना........................... Rain in very small light drops.
242. Drowsy............ झपकी...................................... Sleepy.
243. Ebb .... घट जाना/ पीछे हटना................... Recede.
244. Ebullient......... उत्साहित .... Very energetic and positive.
245. Eccentric......... सनकी .... Of strange behaviour.
246. Eclectic .... विभिन्न श्रोतो से चुने हुऐ .... Selected from various sources.
247. Ecstasy........... अत्यन्त खुशी .... A state of extreme happiness.
248. Edict.............. राज्य घोषणा .... Official command, order.

249. **Edify** .... शिक्षित करना खास कर नैतिक व आध्यात्मिक विकास के लिए .... To educate morally or spiritually.
250. **Eerie** .... डरावना .... Weird/strange in a frightening way.
251. **Efface** .... मिटा देना .... Wipe out.
252. **Effect** .... परिणाम .... Result.
253. **Effeminate** ...... औरताना गुण .... Having womanly traits.
254. **Effete** .... कमजोर .... Weak and without power.
255. **Effigy** .... पुतला .... A model representing someone, Dummy.
256. **Effluvium** .... बदबू .... Noxious smell.
257. **Effrontery** .... अत्यन्त असम्मान .... Extreme rudeness.
258. **Egalitarian** ...... समतावादी .... Believing all people are equal.
259. **Egregious** .... कुख्यात/बहुत बुरा .... Notorious/extremely bad.
260. **Egress** .... निकासी .... Exit.
261. **Elated** .... खुश .... Overjoyed.
262. **Elicit** .... स्पष्ट करना .... Draw out by discussion.
263. **Elite** .... कुलीन .... A superior group.
264. **Elope** .... भाग जाना (शादी हेतु) .... To leave home secretly to get married.
265. **Elucidate** .... स्पष्ट करना .... To make clear and easy to understand.
266. **Elusive** .... पकड़ में न आनेवाला/अवर्णनीय .... Difficult to find/describe.
267. **Emaciated** .... दुर्बल .... Thin and weak.
268. **Emanate** .... निकालना .... Emitting/ejecting.
269. **Emancipate** ..... मुक्त करना .... Set free.
270. **Embark** .... शुरू करना .... To begin .
271. **Embarrass** ...... शर्मिन्दा करना .... To cause someone to feel uncomfortable.
272. **Embellish** .... सुशोभित करना .... To ornate or decorate.
273. **Embolden** .... साहसी बनाना .... To make someone brave.
274. **Eminent** .... प्रतिष्ठित .... Known and respected .
275. **Emulate** .... बराबरी करना .... Try to be equal.
276. **Endangered** ..... संकटग्रस्त .... To put at risk.
277. **Endear** .... प्रिय बनाना .... To cause someone to be liked.
278. **Enmity** .... दुश्मनी .... Animosity, a feeling of hatred.
279. **Enormity** .... विशालता .... Of very great size or importance.
280. **Enthrall** .... मोहित करना .... Attract.
281. **Enthusiastic** ... उत्साहित .... Causing excitement.
282. **Envisage** .... पर विचार करना .... To expect as a possibility.

283. **Eradicate**	उन्मूलन करना	Remove/destroy completely.
284. **Errand**	दूतकार्य (ऐसा काम जिसमें आना-जाना पड़े)	A short journey to deliver/collect something.
285. **Errant**	पथभ्रष्ट, गुमराह	One who does something wrong.
286. **Escalate**	बढ़ाना	To increase/to expand step by step.
287. **Espouse**	समर्थन करना	Support/adopt a cause or way of life.
288. **Estrange**	त्याग देना	No longer friendly.
289. **Etch**	साफ झलकना	Make clearly defined.
290. **Ethical**	नैतिक	Beliefs which control behaviour.
291. **Eunuch**	हिजड़ा	A person who is neither a man nor a woman.
292. **Exasperate**	क्रोध/ रोष पैदा करना	To irritate
293. **Exceptionable**	आपत्तिजनक	Objectionable.
294. **Exceptional**	अपवाद	Unusual.
295. **Excruciating**	अत्यंत तकलीफदेह	Extremely painful.
296. **Executioner**	जल्लाद	One who carries the job of executing someone.
297. **Exhaust**	खर्च कर देना/थका देना	To spend/to make tired.
298. **Exhilarate**	आनन्दित करना	Cause to feel very happy.
299. **Expostulate**	विरोध प्रकट करना	Disagree strongly.
300. **Extravaganza**	फिजूलखर्ची	Exciting and expensive event.
301. **Fad**	फैशन में होना	A craze.
302. **Falter**	हिचकिचाना	Hesitate.
303. **Fanatic**	कट्टर	Extremely enthusiastic of one's religion, belief etc.
304. **Fancier**	जो जानवरों का प्रजनन करवाता हों	Breeder or dealer of animals.
305. **Farce**	तमाशा के जैसी घटना	An absurd event.
306. **Fatal**	घातक	Having serious and deadly effect.
307. **Fate**	भाग्य	Destiny.
308. **Fateful**	महत्त्वपूर्ण पर दुर्भाग्यपूर्ण	Having important but negative effect.
309. **Fatuous**	मूर्खतापूर्ण	Foolish.
310. **Fauna**	किसी क्षेत्र के जानवर	Animals of a particular area.
311. **Faux pas**	सामाजिक गलती	Word/behaviour that is a social mistake.
312. **Feasible**	व्यवहारिक	Practical.
313. **Feeble**	कमजोर	Weak and without energy.
314. **Feign**	नखरे करना	To pretend.
315. **Felicity**	खुशी	Happiness/ bliss.
316. **Felony**	जघन्य अपराध	A major criminal act.

317. **Feral**	जंगली	Wild.
318. **Ferry**	नदी को पार कराना, नाव	To transport people or goods/a boat for transportation.
319. **Fetter**	बेड़ी अथवा सीमा में रखना	To keep someone within limits.
320. **Fiends**	पिशाच, पिशाच तुल्य	An evil person.
321. **Finesse**	कुशलता	Great skill or style.
322. **Flabbergast**	विस्मित करना	Dumbfound/astonished.
323. **Flare**	भड़कना	To start suddenly such as violence, pain, anger or flash of light.
324. **Flaunt**	दिखावा करना	Display ostentatiously.
325. **Flex**	भुजा का माँस कठोर कर दिखाना	Tighten a muscle.
326. **Flog**	चाबुक या डण्डे से मारना	To beat with a whip or stick.
327. **Flout**	उल्लंघन करना	To disobey rule/law.
328. **Folly**	गलती/बेवकूफी	Foolishness.
329. **Foresee**	पहले से जान जाना	Predicting something.
330. **Fragile**	आसानी से टूट जाने वाला	Which can be easily broken.
331. **Fraught**	अप्रिय चीज़ों से पूर्ण/ ओतप्रोत	Full of unpleasant things.
332. **Frown**	भोहें चढ़ा कर देखना/ गुस्सा करना	Facial expression showing anger/ annoyance.
333. **Furore**	गुस्सा	An outbreak of public anger.
334. **Gag**	मुँह में कुछ ठूँस देना	To put cloth etc in the mouth.
335. **Gallantry**	साहस	Bravery.
336. **Garish**	बहुत अधिक रंगीन	Overbright in colour/gaudy.
337. **Garner**	इकट्ठा करना	Store up, gather.
338. **Gawk**	बेवकूफ की तरह देखना	Stare foolishly.
339. **Genesis**	शुरूआत	The origin of something.
340. **Gigantic**	विशाल	Extremely large.
341. **Glare**	घूरकर देखना	A long angry look.
342. **Glee**	खुशी	Great delight.
343. **Glimmer**	मंद रोशनी/आशा की किरण	A faint light/a slight sign of something good.
344. **Glum**	दुखी/निराश एवं चुप	Disappointed or unhappy and quiet.
345. **Glutton**	पेटू	One who eats too much.
346. **Gourmet**	पाक कला का पारखी	A person who knows a lot about food and cooking.
347. **Grandeur**	भव्य	The quality of being very beautiful and attractive.

348. Grapple........... संघर्ष करना.............................. Wrestle.
349. Grievous.......... तकलीफदेह/ गंभीर .... Having very serious effect or causing pain.
350. Grotesque .... विकृत, भद्दा .... Unpleasant /distorted.
351. Grumble .... बड़बड़ाना (गुस्से में) .... To complain about something in an annoyed way.
352. Guffaw .... ठहाका .... Noisy laughter.
353. Haggard .... थका/बिमार सा .... Looking ill or tired.
354. Hailstorm .... ओले के साथ तूफान....................... A sudden heavy fall of hail.
355. Hallucination .. भ्रम .... To see or feel something or someone that does not exist.
356. Hapless........... बेचारा .... Unlucky/ helpless.
357. Hard hearted ... पत्थर दिल .... A person who is not kind.
358. Harrowing .... परेशान करने वाला........................ Extremely upsetting.
359. Harry .... परेशान करना .... To annoy.
360. Hasten .... जल्दी करना.............................. Hurry and do things quickly.
361. Hatch.............. करना (षड्यंत्र) .... To make (a secret plan).
362. Haughty .... घमंडी .... Arrogant.
363. Hazardous .... खतरनाक.................................. Dangerous.
364. Head Strong .... जिद्दी .... Stubborn.
365. Heckle .... सवाल अथवा वक्तव्य से परेशान करना. To interrupt with loud unfriendly questions or statements.
366. Heinous .... जघन्य .... Atrocious.
367. Heir .... उत्तराधिकारी .... One who legally receives money or title.
368. Hermetic .... वायुरूद्ध .... Air-tight.
369. Hermitage .... मठ .... Home of a hermit.
370. Hideous .... भद्दा .... Extremely ugly/bad.
371. Hobble .... लँगड़ा कर चलना .... To walk in a way as if the leg is injured.
372. Homage .... श्रद्धाँजलि .... Deep respect shown.
373. Honorary .... अवैतनिक .... To work without salary.
374. Honourable ..... आदरणीय .... Respectable.
375. Horde.............. समूह .... A large group of people.
376. Horrendous ..... भयावह.................................... Horrifying.
377. Hulk .... बेडौल..................................... Large and heavy.
378. Hurdle .... रूकावट................................... Obstacle.
379. Hush up .... रफा-दफा करना .... Trying to prevent the discovery of particular facts.

380. **Ideal** .... आदर्श .... Without fault/to be perfect.
381. **Idle** .... बेकार, बिना काम का .... Not working.
382. **Illegal gratification** नाजायज रूप से प्राप्त संतुष्टि .... Unlawful satisfaction.
383. **Illegible** .... अपठनीय .... Which cannot be read.
384. **Illicit** .... अवैध .... Disapproved by the society.
385. **Imbecility** .... मूर्खता .... Stupidity.
386. **Imbibe** .... सोख लेना .... To absorb/receive.
387. **Immerse** .... डुबाना .... To become completely absorbed.
388. **Imminent** .... तुरंत .... Likely to happen very soon.
389. **Immolate** .... जला कर बलि देना .... Offer as a sacrifice by burning.
390. **Immune** .... प्रतिरक्षित होना .... Resistant to.
391. **Immure** .... बन्दी बनाना .... Imprison.
392. **Immutable** .... अपरिवर्तनीय .... Unchangeable.
393. **Impairment** .... अक्षम .... Handicap and disabled.
394. **Impalpable** .... जो आसानी से समझ में न आए .... Difficult to feel or understand.
395. **Impasse** .... अंधा मोड़ .... A deadlock.
396. **Imperialism** .... साम्राज्यवाद .... System in which a country rules other countries.
397. **Implicate** .... किसी अपराध में फँसाना .... To show that someone is involved in a crime.
398. **Impound** .... जब्त कर लेना .... Seize and take legal possession of something.
399. **Impromptu** .... बिना तैयारी के .... Done/said without preparation.
400. **Impulse** .... कुछ करने का आवेग .... Sudden urge to do something.
401. **Impunity** .... दण्ड से रहित .... Freedom from punishment.
402. **Incarnate** .... गानव रूग गें .... In human form.
403. **Incessant** .... लगातार .... Never stopping.
404. **Incision** .... चीरा .... An opening made by a sharp tool.
405. **Incongruous** .... बेमेल .... Unusual/different from others.
406. **Inconspicuous** . जो आसानी से दिखाई न दे .... Not easily noticed or seen.
407. **Incumbent** .... आवश्यक .... Necessary as a duty.
408. **Incur** .... कुछ अप्रिय अनुभव करना जैसे-घाटा .... To experience something usually unpleasant.
409. **Indelible** .... स्थायी .... Unable to be removed.
410. **Indigence** .... गरीबी .... Poverty.
411. **Inducement** .... प्रलोभन .... Act done to persuade someone or something.
412. **Indulge** .... आसक्त होना .... Allow oneself something enjoyable.
413. **Inhibition** .... हिचक .... A feeling preventing one from acting naturally.

414. **Insane** .... पागल .... Mentally ill.
415. **Instigate** .... उकसाना .... To urge to do some action.
416. **Interlocutor** .... वार्तालाप करने वाला .... Someone involved in a conversation.
417. **Intermittent** ... रूक-रूक के .... Not happening regularly or continuously.
418. **Intertwined** ..... गूँथा हुआ .... To be twisted together.
419. **Intimidate** ...... डराना .... Frighten.
420. **Intruder** .... घुसपैठिया .... One who enters a place without permission.
421. **Irony** .... विड़म्बना .... Meaning opposite but in a sarcastic manner.
422. **Irrevocable** ...... जो बदला ना जा सके .... Impossible to change.
423. **Isolate** .... अलग-थलग करना .... To place apart or alone.
424. **Jack** .... उठाना .... To raise something/increase the price.
425. **Jamboree** .... जमावड़ा (खुशी मनाने के लिए) .... A large gathering to have fun.
426. **Jeopardy** .... खतरे में .... In danger.
427. **Jittery** .... परेशान, घबराया हुआ .... Nervous.
428. **Jovial** .... हँसमुख .... Good natured.
429. **Jubilation** .... जश्न .... Rejoicing.
430. **Juncture** .... जोड़ .... Joining point.
431. **knead** .... गूँथना .... To prepare dough.
432. **Knotty** .... जटिल .... Difficult to solve.
433. **Languor** .... शांतिपूर्ण .... Quiet/peaceful.
434. **Lanky** .... लम्बा-पतला .... Long and thin (not attractive).
435. **Latent** .... गुप्त .... Dormant.
436. **Laud** .... तारीफ करना .... To praise.
437. **Laurels** .... सम्मान/ तारीफ .... Honour/praise.
438. **Lax** .... लापरवाह .... Careless.
439. **Lechery** .... विलासिता .... Lustfulness.
440. **Leery** .... शंकित .... Suspicious.
441. **Legend** .... पुरानी और प्रसिद्ध कथा .... Very old and popular story.
442. **Legitimate** ...... जायज .... Allowed by law.
443. **Lenient** .... उदारात्मक .... Not strict.
444. **Lessen** .... कम करना .... To make less strong.
445. **Lethargic** .... आलसी .... Lacking energy/lazy.
446. **Liability** .... दायित्व .... Legally responsible.
447. **Lopsided** .... तिरछा .... With one side lower than the other.
448. **Loquacious** ...... बातूनी .... Talkative/Garrulous.

449. **Lunacy** .... पागलपन .... Insanity.
450. **Macho** .... मर्दाना .... Masculine.
451. **Magnitude** .... तीव्रता .... The large size or importance of something.
452. **Majestic** .... शक्तिशाली/ राजसी .... Powerful/dignified and impressive.
453. **Malady** .... बिमारी .... An illness.
454. **Malcontent** .... असंतुष्ट .... Person dissatisfied with existing state of affairs.
455. **Malign** .... हानिकारक .... Baleful, harmful, Deadly.
456. **Mammoth** .... विशाल .... Huge.
457. **Maniac** .... सनकी .... A person who behaves in an uncontrolled manner.
458. **Manifestation** . अभिव्यक्ति .... Clear to become noticeable.
459. **Marine** .... समुद्रीय .... Related to sea.
460. **Massacre** .... नरसंहार .... An act of killing many people.
461. **Maze** .... जाल .... A complicated set of paths or passages.
462. **Melancholy** .... दुखी .... Sad.
463. **Menace** .... समस्या .... A dangerous or troublesome person/ situation.
464. **Milestone** .... मील का पत्थर .... An important event in the history of someone/something.
465. **Miniscule** .... काफी छोटा .... Very small.
466. **Mirth** .... खुशी .... Laughter, happiness.
467. **Miscreant** .... बदमाश .... One who behaves badly/doesn't obey rules.
468. **Mitigate** .... कम करना .... To make/become less severe.
469. **Momentum** .... संवेग, बल .... The force that keeps motion on.
470. **Monstrous** .... विशाल/ भयावह .... Like a monster (cruel and/or very big).
471. **Morbidity** .... विकृत/ अस्वस्थ .... Unpleasant and strange.
472. **Moron** .... बेवकूफ .... A stupid person.
473. **Mounting** .... बढ़ता हुआ .... Gradually increasing.
474. **Mow** .... कुचल देना .... Kill by knocking down with vehicle.
475. **Mull** .... विचार करना .... To think carefully about something.
476. **Muster** .... एकत्र करना .... Gather together/sum up a feeling.
477. **Mutilate** .... क्षत-विक्षत करना .... To damage severely.
479. **Mythology** .... प्राचीन कथा .... Ancient story.
480. **Myth** .... मिथक/काल्पनिक विचार .... An idea or story that many people believe but that is false.
481. **Nadir** .... सबसे निचला स्तर .... The worst moment/the lowest point.

482. Nape .... गर्दन .... The back of the neck.
483. Nemesis .... प्रतिद्वन्दी जिसे हराना मुश्किल हो .... Rival that is difficult to defeat.
484. Neologism .... किसी शब्द का नया अर्थ .... New meaning.
485. Neophyte .... नौसिखिया .... Beginner, novice.
486. Nexus .... साठ-गांठ .... Connection.
487. Nightmare .... दुस्वप्न .... Frightening dream/an unpleasant experience.
488. Nocturnal .... निशाचर.................................. Occurring/ active at night.
489. Nomad .... अस्थायी आवास वाले जनजाति के सदस्य .... Member of a tribe who travels from place to place.
490. Nonchalant ..... उदासीन/भाव हीन .... Careless/ lacking interest.
491. Oblivion .... विस्मृति.................................. The state of being unaware/ forgotten.
492. Obnoxious .... घृणित .... Unpleasant.
493. Obscene .... अश्लील .... Rude or shocking.
494. Obsessive .... तीव्र इच्छा रखना .... Related to thinking about something constantly.
495. Obsolete .... पुराना.................................... Not in use any more.
496. Obstinate .... हठी .... Stubborn.
497. Occlude .... बंद करना................................. close up or block.
498. Occult .... गुप्त (जादू-टोना से सम्बन्धित) .... Secret, mysterious, relating to magical power.
499. Ogre .... शैतान .... A frightening character of children's stories who eats children.
500. Ombudsman .... लोकपाल .... Officer who deals with complaints.
501. Ominous .... कुछ बुरा होने का आभास .... Suggesting that something unpleasant is likely to happen.
502. Opportunist ..... अवसरवादी .... One who grabs every opportunity.
503. Optimistic .... आशावादी .... One who is hopeful.
504. Orator .... वक्ता .... A skilled speaker.
505. Ordain .... आदेश देना .... Order officially.
506. Ostensible .... दिखावटी .... Showy.
507. Oust .... निकाल देना .... Force out from the position of power.
508. Outrage .... बेइज्जती करना .... Insult/offence.
509. Overestimate .. ज्यादा आकलन करना..................... To think that one is greater than he really is.
510. Palate .... तालु/ स्वाद परखने की शक्ति .... The top part of the inside of your mouth/Appreciation for food or drink.
511. Palatial .... महलनुमा .... A huge and splendid house.

512. Paltry .... मूल्यहीन .... Worthless.
513. Pan .... आलोचना करना .... Criticise harshly.
514. Panacea .... रामवाण .... A remedy for all diseases.
515. Panache .... निपुणता .... Confidence/elegance/style.
516. Pandemic .... व्यापक .... Widespread.
517. Pandemonium . शोर शराबा .... Great confusion/noisy disorder.
518. Panic .... डर .... Sudden uncontrolled fear.
519. Paramount ...... सर्वोच्च .... Supreme, zenith.
520. Parched .... सूखा .... Dried out due to heat.
521. Pariah .... सामाजिक बहिष्कार .... Social outcast.
522. Parley .... सम्मेलन .... Conference.
523. Parochial .... संकीर्ण नजरिया वाला .... Narrow in outlook.
524. Patronage .... संरक्षण .... The support given to an organization.
525. Pawn .... प्यादा .... People of little importance.
526. Peck .... हल्का चुम्बन .... Kiss lightly.
527. Peddler .... रेहड़ी वाला .... One who travels door to door to sell something.
528. Pellet .... छोटा गोला .... A small ball of something.
529. Pelt .... फेंकना .... Throw.
530. Perfidious .... विश्वासघाती .... Unable to be trusted.
531. Persevere .... मेहनत करना (मुश्किलों के बावजूद) ..... Continue inspite of difficulty.
532. Persist .... जारी रहना .... Continue and last.
533. Personify .... मानवीकरण करना .... Represent in human form.
534. Perspire .... पसीना बहाना .... To sweat.
535. Perturb .... तंग करना .... Disturb.
536. Perverse .... विकृत/भ्रष्ट .... Contrary to what is accepted or expected.
537. Pessimist .... निराशावादी .... One who is not hopeful by nature.
538. Pious .... धार्मिक .... Religious.
539. Pivotal .... मुख्य .... Central and important.
540. Plaint .... याचिका .... A legal complaint.
541. Plight .... परेशानी/दुख .... Unpleasant condition.
542. Polygamy .... बहु-विवाह .... To have more that one wife/ husband.
543. Pomp .... धूमधाम .... Splendid and colourful ceremony.
544. Populace .... आम जनता .... Ordinary people.
545. Posthumously . मृत्यु-उपरान्त .... Awarded/published after death.
546. Pragmatic .... व्यवहारिक .... Practical.

547. Precedent .... पूर्वगामी .... An action already taken place/ decision already taken.

548. Precincts .... जहाँ कार इत्यादि ले जाना वर्जित है/ अहाता .... Part of a city where vehicles are not allowed/limits.

549. Predicament ... अप्रिय हालात जिससे निकालना मुश्किल है .... An unpleasant situation, which is difficult to get out of.

550. Prejudice .... पूर्वाग्रह .... Unfair opinion.

551. Preposterous ... बेवकूफी भरा .... Very foolish/ridiculous.

552. Prey .... शिकार .... Victim/an animal hunted by another for food.

553. Proclivity .... झुकाव .... Tendency or inclination.

554. Proliferation ... प्रचुर मात्रा में उत्पन्न होना .... Increasing greatly and suddenly in number.

555. Promising .... आशाजनक .... Showing signs of being successful in future.

556. Propensity .... बुरे बर्ताव के तरफ झुकाव .... Tendency towards behaving badly.

557. Provocative .... उकसाने वाला .... Causing an angry reaction/ inciting.

558. Prudence .... समझदारी .... Wisdom.

559. Pugnacious .... युद्धप्रिय .... Quarrelsome.

560. Punitive .... दण्डात्मक .... Intended as a punishment.

561. Purge .... छुटकारा पाना/ शुद्ध करना .... To get rid of people you don't like/to make free of harmful things.

562. Pyre .... चिता .... A large pile of wood on which a dead body is burnt.

563. Quantum .... किसी चीज की इकाई .... Unit of something.

564. Quell .... रोकना .... To stop something especially by using force.

565. Quench .... बुझाना (प्यास) .... satisfy (thirst).

566. Query .... शंका/सवाल .... A question/doubt.

567. Quiescent .... सुप्त .... Dormant, at rest.

568. Quietude .... शांति .... Tranquility.

569. Quotidian .... साधारण .... Common/ordinary.

570. Racial .... नस्लवाद से संबंधित .... Connected with a particular race or country.

571. Rancor .... नफरत .... Bitterness, hatred.

572. Rankle .... परेशान करना .... Irritate.

573. Rapport .... तालमेल .... Harmony.

574. Ratify .... अंगीकार करना .... Confirm formally by signing it or voting for it.

575. **Ravenous** .... बहुत भुखा .... Extremely hungry.
576. **Raze** .... नष्ट करना .... To destroy.
577. **Rebellious** .... विरोधी .... One who opposes the system.
578. **Rebuff** .... सहायता स्वीकार करने से मना करना..... To refuse a helpful suggestion.
579. **Rebuke** .... बुरी तरह से डॉटना .... Scold harshly.
580. **Recalcitrant** .... उद्दण्ड .... One who is unwilling to obey orders.
581. **Reckless** .... असावधान .... Without caring for the result of an action.
582. **Recluse** .... अकेला .... One who lives alone.
583. **Recuperate** ...... ठीक होना बिमारी के बाद .... To recover from illness.
584. **Redundant** ...... गैर जरूरी .... Unnecessary.
585. **Refute** .... खण्डन करना .... To say/prove that a person opinion is wrong.
586. **Regime** .... शासन .... Rule of.
587. **Reign** .... शासन .... The monarch's period of rule.
588. **Rein** .... लगाम/ लगाम लगाना .... Piece of leather which helps you to control the headgear of a horse/to bridle/to restrain.
589. **Relegate** .... अवनति करना .... Place in a lower position.
590. **Reluctant** .... अनिच्छुक .... Unwilling.
591. **Remorse** .... अफसोस .... Feeling of guilt or regret.
592. **Renewable** ...... नवीनीकरणीय .... Which can be used again and again.
593. **Repent** .... पछताना .... To be sorry for something.
594. **Repercussions** . परिणाम .... Consequence.
595. **Replica** .... हु-ब-हु .... An exact copy of an object.
596. **Reprehensible** . निन्दनीय .... Deserving condemnation.
597. **Reprieve** .... बचाव .... An escape from a bad situation.
598. **Repugnant** ...... प्रतिकूल/ निराशाजनक .... Unpleasant behavior or belief.
599. **Resentment** .... नापसंद .... Feeling of dislike.
600. **Respite** .... बचाव .... Relief from something.
601. **Resurgence** ..... किसी विचारधारा का फिर से सर उठाना .... Revival of ideas which had been forgotten for some time.
602. **Resurrect** .... फिर से जीवित करना .... To bring someone back to life.
603. **Retrieve** .... फिर से प्राप्त करना .... To find and bring back something.
604. **Reverence** .... सम्मान .... Respect.
605. **Rhetoric** .... प्रभावशाली भाषण (परन्तु जरूरी नहीं कि ईमानदार भी) .... Effective speech but not essentially sincere.
606. **Rumour** .... अफवाह .... Piece of news that may or may not be true.

607. **Ruthless** .... क्रूर .... Cruel.
608. **Sacrament** .... धार्मिक कार्य .... An important religious ceremony.
609. **Sadist** .... परपीड़क .... One who obtains pleasure by hurting others.
610. **Salubrious** .... स्वास्थ्य के लिए लाभदायक .... Good for health.
611. **Salvation** .... मोक्ष .... The act of saving someone from danger, loss, sin etc.
612. **Sanctity** .... पवित्रता .... The quality of being holy.
613. **Sanguine** .... आशांवित .... Hopeful.
614. **Sarcasm** .... व्यंग्यकारी .... Scornful remarks.
615. **Scant** .... अपर्याप्त/ कम .... Barely enough.
616. **Scrap** .... टुकड़ा/बकझक .... Small pieces /Argument.
617. **Scum** .... गंदगी (तरल पदार्थ के सतह पर) .... Dirt (on the surface of liquid).
618. **Seasoned** .... परिपक्व .... Having a lot of experience.
619. **Sensuous** .... इन्द्रिय सम्बन्धी (शारीरिक रूप से आकर्षक) .... Relating to physical senses./ Physically attractive.
620. **Severity** .... तीव्रता .... Extremity.
621. **Shambles** .... बुरी हालत में .... A state of confusion/untidiness.
622. **Shirk** .... जी चुराना .... To avoid work/ duty.
623. **Shrewd** .... धूर्त .... Based on clear understanding and judgement.
624. **Shroud** .... छिपाना .... Hide.
625. **Shrug** .... कन्धे उचका कर अनभिज्ञता/उदासीनता जाहिर करना .... To raise and then lower the shoulder to show lack of knowledge/interest.
626. **Site** .... भवन-निर्माण आदि का स्थल .... Place where something is built.
627. **Sizzle** .... काफी गर्म होना .... (of food) make a hissing sound when being fried.
628. **Skeptical** .... सन्देही .... Doubtful.
629. **Slay** .... हत्या करना (हिंसापूर्वक) .... Murder violently.
630. **Solace** .... दिलासा .... Comfort in time of distress.
631. **Solidarity** .... समर्थन .... Support.
632. **Solitary** .... अकेला .... The only person/thing in given place.
633. **Spectre** .... संदेह .... The idea of something unpleasant that may happen in future.
634. **Spinster** .... कुँवारी महिला .... A woman who is not married.
635. **Sporadic** .... अनियमित रूप से .... Occurring at irregular intervals.
636. **Spouse** .... जीवन साथी .... Life partner.
637. **Spurious** .... संदेहास्पद .... False and not what it appears to be.

638. Squirm .... छटपटाना .... To move from side to side in an awkward way because of nervousness, pain etc.

639. Stack .... एक के ऊपर एक रखना .... Pile on one another.

640. Stagger .... लड़खड़ाना .... To walk showing imbalance.

641. Strangle .... गला घोंट कर मारना .... To kill by pressing the throat.

642. Stringent .... कठोर .... Strict and demanding.

643. Stroke .... थपकी/घड़ी की घंटे की घंटी .... An act of hitting/a sound of a striking clock.

644. Subdue .... तीव्रता कम करना .... To reduce the force of something.

645. Substantiate ... वक्तव्य को प्रमाणित करना .... To support a claim.

646. Subterfuge ...... कुछ हासिल करने का गलत तरीका ...... A trick or a dishonest way of achieving something.

647. Subtle .... सूक्ष्म/बारीक लेकिन महत्त्वपूर्ण .... Small but important.

648. Succour .... समय पर सहायता .... Help given to someone in need.

649. Sully .... दाग लगाना .... Stain/to spoil someone's perfect reputation.

650. Sultry .... उमस भरा .... Warm and moist.

651. Sumptuous ...... भरपूर .... Luxurious/showing wealth.

652. Suo-moto .... खुद ही .... On its own.

653. Surge .... तीव्रता से बढ़ना .... A sudden or great increase.

654. Swathe .... कपड़े/जमीन का चौड़ा टुकड़ा .... Broad strip of cloth/land.

655. Sycophancy ..... चापलूसी .... Attempt to win favour by flattery.

656. Symposium ..... विचार-गोष्ठी .... Official meeting.

657. Synchronize .... एक ही समय पर होना .... To (cause to) happen at the same time.

658. Tangible .... जिसे छू कर महसूस किया जा सके ...... Real, which can be touched or experienced.

659. Tawdry .... सस्ता एवं भड़कीला .... Cheap and gaudy.

660. Temerity .... हिम्मत .... Boldness.

661. Temperate ...... संयम रखने वाला .... Self controlled.

662. Tempestuous .. प्रबल भावना से ओत-प्रोत .... Full of strong emotion.

663. Tendentious .... किसी मत का पक्षधर होना .... Supporting a particular opinion.

664. Tenements ...... निवास स्थान .... A large building divided into apartments.

665. Terse .... संक्षिप्त .... Concise/using few words.

666. Thumping .... महत्त्वपूर्ण .... Extremely great or important.

667. **Thunder** .... गर्जन .... Sudden large noise from the sky.
668. **Thunderbolt** .... बिजली का कड़कना एवं बादल का गर्जन A flash of lightening and sound of thunder.
669. **Timid** .... डरपोक .... Lacking courage/ cowardly.
670. **Tiptoe** .... पैरो के ऊँगलियों पर चलना .... To walk on toes with heels not touching the ground.
671. **Tormentor** .... शोषक .... One who causes sufferings.
672. **Tout** .... दलाल .... The act/the person encouraging sale of anything.
673. **Toxic** .... जहरीला .... Poisonous.
674. **Traffic** .... गैर कानूनी चीज का व्यापार .... Illegal trade.
675. **Trail** .... रास्ता / धीरे चलना .... Path/ to follow the path of someone/ to move slowly.
676. **Traitor** .... गद्दार .... A person who is not loyal.
677. **Trauma** .... मानसिक आघात .... Severe emotional shock.
678. **Treason** .... गद्दारी .... The act of being not loyal.
679. **Triumph** .... बड़ी जीत .... A great success.
680. **Twitch** .... फड़कना.................................. Any part of body making sudden, small movement.
681. **Unanimous**...... सर्वसम्मत................................ To agree/support together.
682. **Uncanny** .... विचित्र .... Strange/impossible to explain.
683. **Under-privileged** गरीब....................................... Poor.
684. **Underestimate** कम करके आँकना .... To estimate that one is inferior to what he really is.
685. **Uninterested** ... दिलचस्पी ना होना........................ Not interested.
686. **Unison** .... एक साथ .... Two/more things happening at same time.
687. **Unruly** .... अनियंत्रित .... Not easy to control.
688. **Upbeat** .... आशावादी .... Cheerful, optimistic.
689. **Uproar** .... शोर-शराबा .... A loud noise or disturbance.
690. **Uproot** .... जड़ से उखाड़ देना .... To remove from their home place/ root.
691. **Vague** .... अस्पष्ट .... Not clearly expressed.
692. **Valediction**...... विदाई भाषण .... Speech in which one says goodbye.
693. **Validate**.......... प्रमाणित करना .... Confirm, Ratify.
694. **Vandalism** .... संपत्ति नष्ट करने की क्रिया .... Crime of damaging property.
695. **Veil**................ नकाब/घूँघट .... Thing that hides or disguises.

696. **Vengeance** ...... बदले की भावना .... Revenge.
697. **Vengeful** .... बदले की भावना वाला .... To have strong desire to punish someone who has hurt one or one's dear ones.
698. **Venom** .... जहर .... Poison.
699. **Verbose** .... बातों से भरा .... Using more words than necessary.
700. **Verily** .... सत्यत:/वस्तुत: .... In a completely truthful way.
701. **Vestige** .... अवशेष .... A still existing small part of something.
702. **Veteran** .... अनुभवी .... A person who has a lot of experience.
703. **Vicarious** .... प्रतिनिधिक/सीधे तौर पर नहीं .... Experienced in one's imagination rather than directly.
704. **Vicious** .... बुरा/दुष्ट .... Violent and aggressive.
705. **Victimize** .... सताना .... To treat someone in a cruel and unfair manner.
706. **Vigorous** .... ऊर्जावान.................................. Energetic.
707. **Virtuous** .... नैतिक गुण वाला .... Having good moral qualities.
708. **Volatile** .... क्षणिक .... Likely to change suddenly.
709. **Voluminous** ..... भारी-भरकम .... Loose and full.
710. **Vow** .... कसम .... Solemn promise.
711. **Vulnerable** ...... जिसे आसानी से चोट पहुँचाया जा सकता है। Prone to physical/ emotional hurt.
712. **Vie** .... प्रतिस्पर्धा करना .... To compete with other people to obtain something.
713. **Wan** .... कमजोर.................................... Weak/pale/tired-looking.
714. **Wanderlust** ..... घूमने की इच्छा रखना .... Strong desire to travel.
715. **Whole-heartedly** पूरे दिल से .... With complete interest and enthusiasm.
716. **Witty** .... वाकपटु .... Using words in a clever manner.
717. **Wizard** .... जादुगर .... Magician.
718. **Woes** .... दुख .... Sorrow/distress.
719. **Wretch** .... अभागा .... An unhappy person.
720. **Yawn** .... उबासी लेना .... To breathe taking in a lot of air with mouth open.
721. **Yearn** .... लालसा करना .... Crave.
722. **Zealous** .... उत्साहित .... Enthusiastic, causing excitement.

CHAPTER 27

SYNONYMS

Directions: in questions no. 1 to 274, out of the four alternatives, choose the one which best expresses the meaning of the given word and mark it in the answer sheet.

1. **Irrevocable**
(a) Change
(b) Done
(c) Unalterable
(d) Reversible

2. **Adorn**
(a) Trust
(b) Writer
(c) Suspect
(d) Beautify

3. **Repose**
(a) Place
(b) Keep
(c) Rest
(d) Replace

4. **Commotion**
(a) Cheer
(b) Imbalance
(c) Disturbance
(d) Movement

5. **Nurture**
(a) To encourage
(b) To grow
(c) To see
(d) To maintain

6. **Deny**
(a) Regain
(b) Refuse
(c) Repair
(d) Reduce

7. **Abuse**
(a) Use
(b) Praise
(c) Scorn
(d) Raise

8. **Docile**
(a) Submissive
(b) Stubborn
(c) Strong
(d) Changeable

9. **Considerate**
(a) Agreeable
(b) Kind
(c) Like-minded
(d) Thoughtful

10. **Irresolute**
(a) Undecided
(b) Angry
(c) Ignorant
(d) Firm

11. **Frugal**
(a) Economical
(b) Miserly
(c) Splendid
(d) Hungry

12. **Motive**
(a) Reason
(b) Occasion
(c) Intention
(d) Preparation

13. **Pity**
(a) Offence
(b) Mercy
(c) Kindness
(d) Joy

14. **Quash**
(a) Question
(b) Pledge
(c) Reject
(d) Slash

15. **Restrict**
(a) Curtail
(b) Prohibit
(c) Retain
(d) Retail

16. **Anticipate**
(a) Antagonise
(b) Expect
(c) Accept
(d) Hope

17. **Tremendous**
(a) Awesome
(b) Terrible
(c) Considerable
(d) Excessive

18. **Meticulous**
(a) Correct
(b) Clean
(c) Methodical
(d) Painstaking

19. **Abundant**
(a) Sufficient
(b) Plentiful
(c) Significant
(d) Vibrant

20. **Acquaint**
(a) Arouse
(b) Introduce
(c) Appoint
(d) Acquire

21. **Change**
(a) Alter
(b) Renew
(c) Review
(d) Repeat

22. Surreptitiously
(a) Calmly
(b) Secretly
(c) Suggestively
(d) Quitely

23. Forebode
(a) Alarm
(b) Foretell
(c) Failure
(d) Forefront

24. Genuine
(a) Good
(b) Real
(c) Attractive
(d) Lovable

25. Adverse
(a) Negative
(b) Facilitating
(c) Decorative
(d) Derogative

26. Elastic
(a) Rubbery
(b) Flexible
(c) Expensive
(d) Exciting

27. Vacillate
(a) Waver
(b) Never
(c) Quiver
(d) Queer

28. Impeccable
(a) Perfect
(b) Fair
(c) Faultless
(d) Criminal

29. Impediment
(a) Clear
(b) Ailment
(c) Incapable
(d) Obstruction

30. Advance
(a) Reduce
(b) Halt
(c) Progress
(d) Extend

31. Prognosis
(a) Diagnosis
(b) Forecast
(c) Preface
(d) Identity

32. Poach
(a) Catch
(b) Hunt
(c) Preach
(d) Plunder

33. Repartee
(a) Refuse
(b) Celebrate
(c) Quick witty reply
(d) Question

34. Exhort
(a) Recommend
(b) Coax
(c) Urge
(d) Push

35. Lurid
(a) Happy
(b) Abundant
(c) Bright
(d) Shocking

36. Familiar
(a) Well-known
(b) Familial
(c) Relative
(d) Common

37. Dessert
(a) Wasteland
(b) Abandon
(c) Sweet-dish
(d) Broth

38. Affiliate
(a) Control
(b) Associatc
(c) Copy
(d) Discriminate

39. Explicit
(a) Clear
(b) Obvious
(c) Cautious
(d) Exorbitant

40. Diligent
(a) Intelligent
(b) Energetic
(c) Modest
(d) Industrious

41. Infuriate
(a) Burn
(b) Disgrace
(c) Threaten
(d) Enrage

42. Prospective
(a) Preceded
(b) Prosperous
(c) Perplexed
(d) Possible

43. Lousy
(a) Unbearable
(b) Awful
(c) Loose
(d) Stinking

44. Accentuated
(a) Accent
(b) Devalued
(c) Mitigated
(d) Sharpened

45. Predominantly
(a) Emphatically
(b) Forcefully
(c) Mostly
(d) Profoundly

46. Paucity
(a) Sincerity
(b) Shortfall
(c) Publicity
(d) Downfall

47. Avert
(a) Hide
(b) Obey
(c) Excuse
(d) Avoid

48. Pensive
(a) Careless
(b) Thoughtful
(c) Penitent
(d) Unattached

49. Cordial
(a) Smooth
(b) Friendly
(c) Sophisticated
(d) Reserved

50. Provisional
(a) Casual
(b) Lucky
(c) Visible
(d) Temporary

51. Horrendous
(a) Very huge
(b) Greatly unpleasant
(c) Mildly sincere
(d) Most pleasant

52. Authentic
(a) Admirable
(b) Genuine
(c) Adjustable
(d) None of the above

53. Rectify
(a) Correct
(b) Alter
(c) Erase
(d) Continue

54. Miraculous
(a) Mysterious
(b) Sudden
(c) Amazing
(d) Unexpected

55. Warranty
(a) Threat
(b) Guarantee
(c) Order for arrest
(d) Issue

56. Knave
(a) Emperor
(b) Enchanter
(c) Soldier
(d) Scoundrel

57. Prodigal
(a) Huge
(b) Prodigious
(c) Enormous
(d) Wasteful

58. Impost
(a) Fertilizer
(b) Dispatch
(c) Tax
(d) Postage

59. Coarse
(a) Academic
(b) Grain
(c) Rough
(d) Training

60. Forgo
(a) Renounce
(b) Disown
(c) Leave
(d) Accumulate

61. Recipients
(a) Creators
(b) Donors
(c) Receivers
(d) Instigators

62. Frontier
(a) Edge
(b) Landmark
(c) Boundary
(d) Corner

63. Rout
(a) Death
(b) Defeat
(c) Loss
(d) Crash

64. Irreproachable
(a) Remarkable
(b) Extraordinary
(c) Faultless
(d) Immense

65. Felicity
(a) Prosperity
(b) Honesty
(c) Bliss
(d) Sorrow

66. Judicious
(a) Biased
(b) Sensible
(c) Exact
(d) Honest

67. Transpired
(a) Was communicated
(b) Was discussed
(c) Happened
(d) Conspired

68. Obstinate
(a) Foolish
(b) Unyielding
(c) Unreasonable
(d) Mischievous

69. Sundry
(a) Countless
(b) Various
(c) Certain
(d) Several

70. Menial
(a) Lowly
(b) Tough
(c) Dangerous
(d) Low-paid

71. Impetus
(a) Financial support
(b) Accelerated growth
(c) Retarded growth
(d) Driving force

72. Emulate
(a) Praise
(b) Find out
(c) Follow
(d) Assess

73. Boast
(a) Cry
(b) Abuse
(c) Hate
(d) Brag

74. Mass murder
(a) Patricide
(b) Fratricide
(c) Regicide
(d) Genocide

75. Executioner
(a) Executive engineer
(b) Explorer
(c) Experimenter
(d) One who inflicts capital punishment

76. Maiden speech
(a) Farewell speech
(b) Short speech
(c) First speech
(d) Speech about women

77. Interfere
(a) Meddle
(b) Help
(c) Object
(d) Copy

78. Tedious
(a) Tiresome
(b) Dull
(c) Interesting
(d) Exciting

79. Magnificent
(a) Magnanimous
(b) Modest
(c) Generous
(d) Splendid

80. Spirited
(a) Heated
(b) Drunk
(c) Enthusiastic
(d) Possessed

81. Gloomy
(a) Misty
(b) Morose
(c) Murky
(d) Shadowy

82. Grumble
(a) To scold
(b) To complain
(c) To sheer
(d) To fight

83. Crude
(a) Unrefined
(b) Cruel
(c) Rude
(d) Savage

84. Hostile
(a) Poor
(b) Antagonistic
(c) Delinquent
(d) Reticent

85. Friendly
(a) Gentle
(b) Amiable
(c) Considerate
(d) Industrious

86. Veil
(a) Seclude
(b) Moan
(c) Conceal
(d) Repent

87. Recurrent
(a) Flowing backward
(b) Healing quickly
(c) Happening repeatedly
(d) Timely

88. Peculiar
(a) Same
(b) Strange
(c) Surprising
(d) Tiring

89. Prosper
(a) Cherish
(b) Promote
(c) Thrive
(d) Rich

90. Eminent
(a) Confident
(b) Authentic
(c) Ingenious
(d) Illustrious

91. Fortitude
(a) Composure
(b) Confidence
(c) Courage
(d) Produce

92. Sanitise
(a) Pleasant
(b) Disinfect
(c) Pious
(d) Crazy

93. Favourite
(a) Preferred
(b) Focused
(c) Pleasurable
(d) Disliked

94. Novice
(a) Beginner
(b) Virtuous
(c) Trainer
(d) Learner

95. Adversary
(a) Poverty
(b) Contestant
(c) Opponent
(d) Intruder

96. Dishonour
(a) Infamy
(b) Glory
(c) Uncouth
(d) Wicked

97. Erudite
(a) Scholarly
(b) Friendly
(c) Miserly
(d) Lovely

98. Idea
(a) Comprehension
(b) Notion
(c) Emotion
(d) Gist

99. Takes after
(a) Follows
(b) Comes after
(c) Resembles
(d) Imitates

100. Ill-favoured
(a) Unlucky
(b) Weak in health
(c) Short-tempered
(d) Ugly

101. Homage
(a) Humility
(b) Tribute
(c) Obedience
(d) Allegiance

102. Clue
(a) Hint
(b) Inkling
(c) Intimation
(d) Signal

103. Amazement
(a) Shock
(b) Wander
(c) Surprise
(d) Suspicion

104. Consistency
(a) Constancy
(b) Competence
(c) Permanence
(d) Uniformity

105. Electrifying
(a) Attractive
(b) Fearsome
(c) Exciting
(d) Disturbing

106. Refrain
(a) Dissuade
(b) Desist
(c) Prevent
(d) Curb

107. Merited
(a) Deserved
(b) Encouraged
(c) Prompted
(d) Supported

108. Candid
(a) Overconfident
(b) Frank
(c) Arrogant
(d) Careless

109. Zealous
(a) Ardent
(b) Jealous
(c) Furious
(d) Impatient

110. Industrious
(a) Indolent
(b) Industrial
(c) Hard-working
(d) Economic

111. Feasible
(a) Practical
(b) Rejoice
(c) Accentuate
(d) Accurate

112. Atrocity
(a) Envy
(b) Violence
(c) Jealousy
(d) Absurdity

113. Fortify
(a) Create
(b) Generate
(c) Prohibit
(d) Strengthen

114. Pacify
(a) Calm down
(b) Satisfy
(c) Rouse
(d) Rejoice

115. Barren
(a) Good
(b) Wholesome
(c) Unproductive
(d) Profitable

116. Infamy
(a) Notoriety
(b) Glory
(c) Integrity
(d) Familiarity

117. Intrepid
(a) Hesitant
(b) Fearless
(c) Extrovert
(d) Familiarity

118. Perspicuous
(a) Relevant
(b) Precise
(c) Brief
(d) Clear

119. Sufficient
(a) Full
(b) Complete
(c) Enough
(d) Less

120. Benevolent
(a) Beneficial
(b) Kind
(c) Helpful
(d) Supportive

121. Ancestors
(a) Extinct tribes
(b) Relatives
(c) Forefathers
(d) Old people

122. Embrace
(a) Impress
(b) Except
(c) Embarrass
(d) Accept

123. Meek
(a) Light-hearted
(b) Serious
(c) Submissive
(d) Benign

124. Cajole
(a) Insist
(b) Persuade
(c) Direct
(d) Recommend

125. Fragrance
(a) Taste
(b) Aroma
(c) Sight
(d) Touch

126. Fictitious
(a) False
(b) Frail
(c) Foul
(d) Flattering

127. Obscene
(a) Dirty
(b) Unhealthy
(c) Indecent
(d) Unwanted

128. Imitate
(a) Follow
(b) Copy
(c) Think
(d) Allude

129. Enigmatic
(a) Magnetic
(b) Automatic
(c) Speeding
(d) Puzzling

130. Despondent
(a) Deserted
(b) Dejected
(c) Rejected
(d) Repentant

131. Aversion
(a) Aggression
(b) Assertion
(c) Dislike
(d) Impudence

132. Desperation
(a) Depression
(b) Jubilation
(c) Fascination
(d) Hopelessness

133. Jubilant
(a) Brilliant
(b) Proud
(c) Ecstatic
(d) Gloomy

134. Liberty
(a) Freedom
(b) Equality
(c) Charity
(d) Democracy

135. Blister
(a) Chatter
(b) Travel
(c) Attack
(d) Wound

136. Trauma
(a) Accident
(b) Art form
(c) Type of medicine
(d) Emotional shock

137. Fabulous
(a) Beautiful
(b) Marvellous
(c) Interesting
(d) Charming

138. Laudable
(a) Sincere
(b) Praiseworthy
(c) Benevolent
(d) Welcome

139. Surpass
(a) Outdo
(b) Pass over
(c) Overdo
(d) Pass by

140. Defer
(a) Indifferent
(b) Deft
(c) Differ
(d) Postpone

141. Cease
(a) Begin
(b) Stop
(c) Create
(d) Dull

142. Pious
(a) Religious
(b) Sympathetic
(c) Afraid
(d) Faithful

143. Abandon
(a) Forsake
(b) Keep
(c) Cherish
(d) Enlarge

144. Intimidate
(a) Calm down
(b) View
(c) Leave
(d) Frighten

145. Regard
(a) Respect
(b) Liking
(c) Love
(d) Suspicion

146. Swap
(a) Snap
(b) Exchange
(c) Break
(d) Exclude

147. Prudent
(a) Wise
(b) Cunning
(c) Frank
(d) Severe

148. Genius
(a) A generous person
(b) A foreigner
(c) An intellectual
(d) An athlete

149. Culmination
(a) Conclusion
(b) Climax
(c) Abyss
(d) Cultivation

150. Sporadic
(a) Surviving
(b) Sweeping
(c) Irregular
(d) Persistent

151. Crass
(a) Casual
(b) Formal
(c) Unrefined
(d) Sterile

152. Accomplish
(a) Amass
(b) Acquire
(c) Adhere
(d) Achieve

153. Cursory
(a) Little
(b) Quick
(c) Eager
(d) Tender

154. Envisaged
(a) Ensured
(b) Idealized
(c) Contemplated
(d) Imagined

155. Clandestine
(a) Awkward
(b) Inconsistent
(c) Secret
(d) Ugly

156. Resentment
(a) Annoyance
(b) Dispatch
(c) Disagreement
(d) Dismissal

157. Obdurate
(a) Angry
(b) Calm
(c) Obsessed
(d) Adamant

158. Obscure
(a) Unknown
(b) Neglectful
(c) Occasional
(d) Old

159. Reluctant
(a) Unwilling
(b) Forego
(c) Redundant
(d) Amendable

160. Revelation
(a) Anticipation
(b) Imagination
(c) Revel in
(d) Disclosure

161. Ostracise
(a) Censure
(b) Sentence
(c) Banish
(d) Berate

162. Appalled
(a) Shocked
(b) Saddened
(c) Scared
(d) Alarmed

163. Imbecility
(a) Stupidity
(b) Rusticity
(c) Verbosity
(d) Incoherence

164. Collusion
(a) Conflict
(b) Secret agreement
(c) Consultation
(d) Misunderstanding

165. Hesitant
(a) Antagonistic
(b) Grumbling
(c) Contradict
(d) Undecided

166. Deceptive
(a) Disagreeable
(b) Misleading
(c) Mistake
(d) Debatable

167. Palpable
(a) Obvious
(b) Immense
(c) Sufficient
(d) Hidden

168. Laid-back
(a) Lie in wait
(b) Sorry state
(c) Lame
(d) Easy-going

169. Sauntering
(a) Jogging
(b) Brisk walking
(c) Travelling
(d) Strolling

170. Pompous
(a) Grandiose
(b) Polished
(c) Modest
(d) Skilled

171. Poignant
(a) Showy
(b) Sad
(c) Silly
(d) Snobbish

172. Querulous
(a) Critical
(b) Curious
(c) Quarrelsome
(d) Ambiguous

173. Audacious
(a) Brilliant
(b) Powerful
(c) Bold
(d) Frightening

174. Perilous
(a) Hazardous
(b) Rigorous
(c) Resilient
(d) Requisite

175. Reverie
(a) Determination
(b) Day-dream
(c) Reality
(d) Realization

176. Genial
(a) Cordial
(b) Unselfish
(c) Careful
(d) Specific

177. Accrue
(a) Accumulate
(b) Accommodate
(c) Grow
(d) Suffice

178. Loquacious
(a) Talkative
(b) Slow
(c) Content
(d) Unclear

179. Vindictive
(a) Imaginative
(b) Accusative
(c) Spiteful
(d) Aggressive

180. Inclement
(a) Selfish
(b) Active
(c) Unfavourable
(d) Inactive

181. Hostility
(a) Illness
(b) Enmity
(c) Disturbance
(d) Derogatory

182. Indifferent
(a) Dissimilar
(b) Various
(c) Interference
(d) Unconcerned

183. Condemn
(a) Censure
(b) Despair
(c) Kill
(d) Hit

184. Defect
(a) Loss
(b) Harm
(c) Shortcoming
(d) Delicate

185. Jealous
(a) Envious
(b) Unhappy
(c) Regretful
(d) Remorse

186. Weary
(a) Careless
(b) Shivering
(c) Troubled
(d) Weak

187. Plausible
(a) Pleasing taste
(b) Seemingly true
(c) Manageable
(d) Cannot be proved

188. Creditable
(a) Able to lend money
(b) Bringing praise
(c) Able to repay a loan
(d) Fit to be believed

189. Salient
(a) Most important
(b) Salt-like taste
(c) Pleasing
(d) Satisfactory

190. Fragile
(a) Soft
(b) Smooth
(c) Flexible
(d) Easily broken

191. Reticent
(a) Sensitive
(b) Secretive
(c) Not feeling well
(d) Not saying much

192. Reciprocal
(a) Formal
(b) Favorable
(c) Mutual
(d) Sustainable

193. Apprise
(a) Inform
(b) Estimate
(c) Admire
(d) Require

194. Consensus
(a) Awareness
(b) General agreement
(c) Careful observation
(d) Praiseworthy

195. Unceremonious
(a) Impolite
(b) Informal
(c) Incomplete
(d) Irregular

196. Treason
(a) Absurdity
(b) Disloyalty
(c) Dishonesty
(d) Deception

197. Amiable
(a) Popular
(b) Generous
(c) Friendly
(d) Reasonable

198. Lucid
(a) Fluent
(b) Clear
(c) Musical
(d) Familiar

199. Ravaged
(a) Destroyed
(b) Spoiled
(c) Conquered
(d) Robbed

200. Perplexed
(a) Annoyed
(b) Disappointed
(c) Puzzled
(d) Ruined

201. Anonymity
(a) Reputation
(b) Publicity
(c) Being unknown
(d) Wrong address

202. Ephemeral
(a) Disturbing
(b) Filthy
(c) Short-lived
(d) Poverty-stricken

203. Caption
(a) Joke
(b) Definition
(c) Meaning
(d) Title

204. Battered
(a) Destroyed
(b) Dashed on
(c) Struck hard
(d) Struck off

205. Extravagant
(a) Hardworking
(b) Good
(c) Extraordinary
(d) Spendthrift

206. Redundant
(a) Superfluous
(b) Uninterested
(c) Introspective
(d) Knowledgeable

207. Hindered
(a) Damaged
(b) Disturbed
(c) Obstructed
(d) Protested

208. Concealed
(a) Covered
(b) Closed
(c) Sealed
(d) Hidden

209. Relish
(a) Realize
(b) Taste
(c) Enjoy
(d) Reveal

210. Acute
(a) Dull
(b) Drowsy
(c) Unpleasant
(d) Sharp

211. Solicit
(a) Command
(b) Request
(c) Sympathize
(d) Agree

212. Surmount
(a) Discount
(b) Surround
(c) Overcome
(d) Capture

213. Pertinent
(a) Indirect
(b) Relevant
(c) Direct
(d) Important

214. Nebulous
(a) Revolutionary
(b) Vague
(c) Starting
(d) Idiotic

215. Ubiquitous
(a) Omnipresent
(b) Omnipotent
(c) Omniscient
(d) Affluent

216. Corroborate
(a) Collaborate
(b) Substantiate
(c) Co-operate
(d) Correlate

217. Adequate
(a) Necessary
(b) Sufficient
(c) Procured
(d) Additional

218. Solecism
(a) Abuse
(b) Witty quip
(c) Clever argument
(d) Grammatical error

219. Delirious
(a) Delicious
(b) Pleasing
(c) Desperate
(d) Excited

220. Licentious
(a) Immoral
(b) Intellectual
(c) Moral
(d) Without license

221. Squander
(a) Expensive
(b) Waste
(c) Litter
(d) Economical

222. Abated
(a) Reduced
(b) Vanished
(c) Increased
(d) Stabilized

223. Abrogate
(a) Repeal
(b) Destroy
(c) Delay
(d) Dismiss

224. Abstemious
(a) Resistant
(b) Temperate
(c) Superstitious
(d) Careful

225. Allegiance
(a) Servility
(b) Obedience
(c) Loyalty
(d) Passivity

226. Amicable
(a) Poisonous
(b) Co-operative
(c) Satisfying
(d) Heartening

227. Ample
(a) Meagre
(b) Quantitative
(c) Sufficient
(d) Tasty

228. Baleful
(a) Harmful
(b) Doubtful
(c) Useful
(d) Helpful

229. Benevolence
(a) Ill will
(b) Morbidity
(c) Kindness
(d) Vision

230. Camouflage
(a) Hide
(b) Reveal
(c) Disguise
(d) Pretend

231. Chivalrous
(a) Crude
(b) Gallant
(c) Handsome
(d)Tinkering

232. Covenant
(a)Case
(b) Coupon
(c) Contract
(d) Settlement

233. Dainty
(a)Carefree
(b)Feminine and happy
(c)Delicacy
(d)Small and graceful

234. Deference
(a) Indifference
(b) Sympathy
(c) Respect
(d) Flattery

235. Dormant
(a) Sleeping
(b) Humble
(c) Quick
(d) Active

236. Dramatic
(a) Unprecedented
(b)Thrilling
(c) Spectacular
(d) Effective

237. Dubious
(a) Doubtful
(b) Disputable
(c) Duplicate
(d) Dangerous

238. Duplicity
(a) Repetition
(b) Artlessness
(c) Deception
(d) Cleverness

239. Eternal
(a) Innumerable
(b) Immeasurable
(c) Prolonged
(d) Perpetual

240. Evince
(a) Look
(b) Try
(c) Apply
(d) Show

241. Evoked
(a) Escaped
(b) Called forth
(c) Produced
(d) Summoned

242. Flabbergasted
(a) Scared
(b) Embarrassed
(c) Dumbfounded
(d) Humiliated

243. Flimsy
(a) Weak
(b) Strong
(c) Justified
(d) Impulsive

244. Garish
(a) Unusual
(b) Exciting
(c) Confused
(d) Gaudy

245. Implacable
(a) Relenting
(b) Unappeasable
(c) Dangerous
(d) Courageous

246. Indict
(a) To accuse
(b) Entrapment
(c) Indoctrination
(d) Inducement

247. Indigent
(a) Indian men
(b) Poor
(c) Guilty
(d) Untried

248. Innocuous
(a) Abominable
(b) Harmless
(c) Harmful
(d) Useful

249. Innuendoes
(a) Indications
(b) Inspiring quotes
(c) Witty remarks
(d) Insinuations

250. Insolent
(a) Violent
(b) Polite
(c) Insulting
(d) Frivolous

251. Irreverence
(a) Disrespect
(b) Cruelty
(c) Unkindness
(d) Invalidity

252. Latent
(a)Primitive
(b) Hidden
(c) Potent
(d) Talented

253. Massive
(a) Tall
(b) Large in size
(c) Total
(d) Little

254. Obnoxious
(a) Depressing
(b) Disgusting
(c) Arrogant
(d) Filthy

255. Panacea
(a) Flatter
(b) Praise
(c) Inactivity
(d) Cure-all

256. Pragmatic
(a) Practical
(b) Playful
(c) Causal
(d) Clever

257. Reparation
(a) Compensation
(b) Co-relation
(c) Aspersion
(d) Delegation

258. Salutary
(a) Premature
(b) Terrible
(c) Disastrous
(d) Beneficial

259. Shrink
(a) Contract
(b) Physician
(c) Reduce
(d) Shrivel

260. Soporific
(a) Soothing
(b) Terrific
(c) Supreme

(d) Sleep-inducing

261. Vagary
(a) Lapse of memory
(b) Companionship
(c) gang
(d) impulse

262. Coax
(a) Pacify
(b) Punish
(c) Persuade
(d) Please

263. Renowned
(a) Notorious
(b) Great
(c) Brave
(d) Famous

264. Blaze
(a) Rage
(b) Rush
(c) Fire
(d) Mark

265. Tangential
(a) partly
(b) forcefully
(c) superficial relevance
(d) fitfully

266. Transparent
(a) Translucent
(b) Opaque
(c) Clear
(d) Sharp

267. Fruitless
(a) Successful
(b) barren
(c) Useless
(d) Insufficient

ANSWER KEY

1.	(c)	2.	(d)	3.	(c)	4.	(c)	5.	(b)	6.	(b)	7.	(c)	8.	(a)	9.	(d)	10.	(a)
11.	(b)	12.	(c)	13.	(b)	14.	(c)	15.	(b)	16.	(b)	17.	(d)	18.	(d)	19.	(b)	20.	(b)
21.	(a)	22.	(b)	23.	(b)	24.	(b)	25.	(a)	26.	(b)	27.	(a)	28.	(c)	29.	(d)	30.	(c)
31.	(b)	32.	(b)	33.	(c)	34.	(c)	35.	(d)	36.	(a)	37.	(c)	38.	(b)	39.	(a)	40.	(d)
41.	(d)	42.	(d)	43.	(b)	44.	(d)	45.	(c)	46.	(b)	47.	(d)	48.	(b)	49.	(b)	50.	(d)
51.	(b)	52.	(b)	53.	(a)	54.	(c)	55.	(b)	56.	(d)	57.	(d)	58.	(c)	59.	(c)	60.	(a)
61.	(c)	62.	(c)	63.	(b)	64.	(c)	65.	(c)	66.	(b)	67.	(c)	68.	(b)	69.	(b)	70.	(a)
71.	(d)	72.	(c)	73.	(d)	74.	(d)	75.	(d)	76.	(c)	77.	(a)	78.	(b)	79.	(d)	80.	(c)
81.	(b)	82.	(b)	83.	(a)	84.	(b)	85.	(b)	86.	(c)	87.	(c)	88.	(b)	89.	(c)	90.	(d)
91.	(c)	92.	(b)	93.	(a)	94.	(a)	95.	(c)	96.	(a)	97.	(a)	98.	(b)	99.	(c)	100.	(a)
101.	(b)	102.	(a)	103.	(c)	104.	(d)	105.	(c)	106.	(b)	107.	(a)	108.	(b)	109.	(a)	110.	(c)
111.	(a)	112.	(b)	113.	(d)	114.	(a)	115.	(c)	116.	(a)	117.	(b)	118.	(d)	119.	(c)	120.	(b)
121.	(c)	122.	(d)	123.	(c)	124.	(b)	125.	(b)	126.	(a)	127.	(c)	128.	(b)	129.	(d)	130.	(b)
131.	(c)	132.	(d)	133.	(c)	134.	(a)	135.	(d)	136.	(d)	137.	(b)	138.	(b)	139.	(a)	140.	(d)
141.	(b)	142.	(a)	143.	(a)	144.	(d)	145.	(a)	146.	(b)	147.	(a)	148.	(c)	149.	(b)	150.	(c)
151.	(c)	152.	(d)	153.	(b)	154.	(d)	155.	(c)	156.	(a)	157.	(d)	158.	(a)	159.	(a)	160.	(d)
161.	(c)	162.	(a)	163.	(a)	164.	(b)	165.	(d)	166.	(b)	167.	(a)	168.	(d)	169.	(d)	170.	(a)
171.	(b)	172.	(c)	173.	(c)	174.	(a)	175.	(b)	176.	(a)	177.	(a)	178.	(a)	179.	(c)	180.	(c)
181.	(b)	182.	(d)	183.	(a)	184.	(c)	185.	(a)	186.	(c)	187.	(b)	188.	(b)	189.	(a)	190.	(d)
191.	(d)	192.	(c)	193.	(a)	194.	(b)	195.	(a)	196.	(b)	197.	(c)	198.	(b)	199.	(a)	200.	(c)
201.	(c)	202.	(c)	203.	(d)	204.	(a)	205.	(d)	206.	(a)	207.	(c)	208.	(d)	209.	(c)	210.	(d)
211.	(b)	212.	(c)	213.	(b)	214.	(b)	215.	(a)	216.	(b)	217.	(b)	218.	(d)	219.	(d)	220.	(a)
221.	(b)	222.	(a)	223.	(a)	224.	(d)	225.	(c)	226.	(b)	227.	(c)	228.	(a)	229.	(c)	230.	(c)
231.	(b)	232.	(c)	233.	(d)	234.	(c)	235.	(a)	236.	(c)	237.	(a)	238.	(c)	239.	(d)	240.	(d)
241.	(b)	242.	(c)	243.	(a)	244.	(d)	245.	(b)	246.	(a)	247.	(b)	248.	(b)	249.	(d)	250.	(c)
251.	(a)	252.	(b)	253.	(b)	254.	(b)	255.	(d)	256.	(a)	257.	(a)	258.	(d)	259.	(d)	260.	(d)
261.	(d)	262.	(c)	263.	(d)	264.	(c)	265.	(c)	266.	(c)	267.	(c)						

MEANINGS OF DIFFICULT WORDS IN ALPHABETICAL ORDER

Word	Meaning in English	Meaning in Hindi
Abandon	to give up completely	त्यागना, छोड देना
Abated	reduced	कम किया हुआ
Abominable	extremely unpleasant; disgusting	घिनौना
Abrogate	end a law or an agreement	भंग करना
Abstemious	moderate or restrained	संयमी
Absurdity	state of being ridiculous	बेतुकापन
Abundant	plentiful	प्रचुर, बहुत ज्यादा
Abuse	speak in an insulting and offensive way	अपशब्द कहना
Abyss	chasm or gorge	खाई, दर्रा
Accentuate	make more noticeable or prominent	बल देना
Accomplish	achieve or complete successfully	प्राप्त करना
Accrue	to grow or build up slowly	अर्जित होना
Accumulate	gather together	संग्रह करना
Acquaint	make someone aware of or familiar with	परिचय कराना
Acquire	buy or obtain	अधिकार करना
Acute	sharp or intense	तीव्र, तीखा
Adequate	sufficient	पर्याप्त
Adorn	make more beautiful or attractive	सुंदर बनाना
Advance	move forward	आगे बढ़ना
Adversary	one's opponent	प्रतिद्वंदी, विरोधी
Adverse	unfavorable	प्रतिकूल, विषम
Affilate	officially attach or connect to an organization	संबद्ध करना
Agreeable	appropriate	अनुकूल, उपर्युक्त
Ailment	an illness	रोग, पीड़ा
Allegiance	loyalty	निष्ठा, वफादारी
Allude	suggest indirectly; hint at	इंगित करना, संकेत करना
Amass	Accumulate, gather	एकत्र करना
Amazement	great surprise or wonder	विस्मय, आश्चर्य
Amendable	capable of being corrected by additions	सशोधन योग्य
Amiable	friendly	मैत्रीपूर्ण
Amiable	warm and friendly	सौम्य, प्रिय
Amicable	friendly	मैत्रीपूर्ण, मित्रता
Ample	enough or more than enough	पर्याप्त

Ancestors	forefathers	पूर्वज
Anonymity	namelessness	अज्ञात
Antagonise	cause (someone) to become hostile	दुश्मनी करना
Antagonistic	hostility	विरोधी
Anticipate	expect or predict	आशा करना
Anticipation	expectation or prediction	अपेक्षा, संभावना
Appalled	shocked	आश्चर्यचकित
Apprise	inform or tell	बतलाना, सूचना देना
Arouse	evoke or awaken	जगाना, उकसाना
Aspersion	an attack on the reputation; defamation	लांछन
Assertion	statement or claim	उक्ति, कथन
Atrocity	an extremely wicked or cruel act	क्रूरता, निर्दयता
Audacious	courageous	साहसी
Authentic	of undisputed origin; genuine	विश्वसनीय, सच्चा
Aversion	a strong dislike	घृणा, नफरत
Avert	turn away, avoid	से बचना
Baleful	unfriendly, hostile	हानिकारक
Barren	infertile	बंजर
Barren	unproductive or unfruitful	बंजर भूमि, अनुपजाऊ
Battered	destroyed by repeated blows	नष्ट
Benevolence	Kindness	परोपकार, दयालु
Benevolent	kind and sympathetic	दयालू, परोपकारी
Benign	gentle, kind	सौम्य
Berate	to scold	डाँटना
Blaze	a very large burning fire	ज्वाला, आग
Blister	a small bubble on the skin filled with serum	छाला, फफोला
Boast	an act of talking with excessive pride	डींग हांकना/शेख़ी बघारना
Broth	soup consisting of meat or vegetable chunks	शोरबा
Cajole	to persuade by flattery	फुसलाना, मीठी बातों में फंसाना
Camouflage	clothing that could hide something	छद्म आवरण
Candid	truthful and straightforward, frank	स्पष्टवादी, सच्चा
Capital punishment	the legally authorized killing of someone	मृत्यु दंड
Caption	a title	शीर्षक
Cautious	careful	सतर्क, सावधान
Cease	bring or come to an end	रोकना, समाप्त करना
Censure	express severe disapproval of	निंदा करना
Chatter	incessant trivial talk	बकवास करना

Cherish	protect and care for someone lovingly	लालन-पालन करना
Chivalrous	courteous and gallant	शिष्ट, वीर
Clandestine	kept secret	गुप्त
Clue	a hint	संकेत, सुराग
Coarse	rough or harsh	रूखा
Coax	persuade (someone) by flattery	बहलाना, फुसलाना
Collaborate	to work jointly on an activity	मिलकर कार्य करना
Collusion	secret or illegal cooperation or conspiracy	मिलीभगत
Commotion	confused and noisy disturbance	हलचल, शोर-गूल
Companionship	a feeling of fellowship or friendship	भाईचारा, मित्रता
Composure	calmness	मानसिक संतुलन
Concealed	not revealed	गुप्त
Condemn	criticize or denounce	निंदा, भर्त्सना करना
Conflict	a serious disagreement or clash	झगड़ा, टकराव
Consensus	general agreement	एकमत, आम सहमति
Considerable	significant	महत्वपूर्ण
Considerate	attentive, thoughtful	विचारशील, समझदार
Considerate	thoughtful	विचारशील, समझदार
Consistency	a harmonious uniformity	संगति, सामंजस्य
Conspire	secretly plan to commit an unlawful or harmful act	साजिश करना
Contemplate	inspect or observe	मनन करना, विचार करना
Cordial	warm and friendly	सौहर्दपूर्ण, मैत्रीपूर्ण
Corroborate	confirm or verify	पुष्टि करना, साबित करना
Courageous	brave	निडर, साहसिक
Covenant	an agreement	अनुबंध
Crass	stupid, insensitive	बुद्धिहीन, मूर्ख
Creditable	deserving acknowledgment and praise	श्रेयस्कर, प्रशंसनीय
Crude	impure or unwanted	अपरिष्कृत, कच्चा
Culmination	peak or highest point	चरम बिन्दु
Curb	restrain or keep in check	रोकना
Cursory	hasty and without attention to detail	सतही दृष्टिकोण
Curtail	reduce in extent or quantity	छोटा करना
Dainty	attractively small and delicate	उत्कृष्ट, खुबसूरत
Dashed on	to beat against a surface	दीवार पर टक्कर मारना
Deceptive	misleading	कपटी, भ्रामक
Decorative	ornamental	सजावटी
Defect	imperfection or lack	दोष, त्रुटि

Defer	postpone, delay	विलम्ब करना
Deference	humble submission and respect	सम्मान, आदर
Deft	smart, clever	चतुर, दक्ष
Delegation	a group of representatives	प्रतिनिधि-मंडल
Delinquent	lawbreaker or culprit	अपराधी, दोषी
Delirious	incoherent	समझ में न आने योग्य
Deny	refuse, refuse to accept the truth of something	मना करना, किसी बात की सच्चाई से इंकार करना
Derogative	critical or disrespectful	अपमानजनक
Derogatory	disrespectful	अपमानजनक
Deserted	abandoned	परित्यक्त, त्यागा हुआ
Desist	abstain from doing something	बंद कर देना
Desperation	hopelessness	निराशा
Despondent	in low spirits	निराश, उदास
Dessert	the sweet course eaten at the end of a meal	खाने के बाद की मीठा
Diagnosis	the identification of the nature of an illness	रोग की पहचान
Diligent	hardworking	मेहनती
Disastrous	causing great damage	विनाशकारी, सर्वनाशी
Discriminate	differentiate	भेदभाव करना, अंतर करना
Disgrace	bring shame or discredit	कलंकित करना
Dishonour	loss of reputation or respect	अपमान, निरादर
Disown	refuse to acknowledge	अस्वीकार करना
Dispatch	to send or forward	भेजना, आगे बढ़ाना
Disputable	not established as fact, controversial	संदेहपूर्ण, विवादास्पद
Dissuade	persuade not to do something	मना करना
Docile	submissive	विनम्र
Dormant	inactive, sleeping	निष्क्रिय, सुस्त
Downfall	a loss of power or decline in prosperity	पतन
Dramatic	sudden and striking	नाटकीय
Dubious	vague or suspicious	संदिग्ध, अविश्वसनीय
Duplicity	deceitfulness, double-dealing	छल, कपट
Economical	cheap or inexpensive	किफायती, सस्ता
Ecstatic	expressing overwhelming happiness	उन्मादपूर्ण, अति आनंदित
Elastic	flexible	लचीला
Electrifying	causing strong feelings of enthusiasm and eagerness	उत्तेजित करने वाला, रोमांचक
Embrace	to accept or support	स्वीकार करना
Eminent	famous	प्रख्यात, प्रसिद्ध

Emphatically	in a forceful way	बलपूर्वक
Emulate	imitate or copy	नकल करना
Enchanter	a person who uses magic or sorcery	जादूगर
Enigmatic	mysterious	रहस्यपूर्ण
Entrapment	illegal act of tricking somebody into committing a crime	फंसाना, छल
Envisage	contemplate or conceive of as a possibility	परिकल्पना करना
Ephemeral	lasting for a very short time	अल्पकालिक
Erudite	intellectual	विद्वान
Eternal	existing or continuing forever	अनन्त, निरंतर
Evince	declare or reveal	जताना, बयान करना
Evoke	to bring a feeling	आह्वान करना
Exclude	keep out or deny access	वर्जित करना, निकालना
Executioner	a public official who executes criminals	जल्लाद/फाँसी देने वाला
Exhort	strongly encourage or urge	प्रेरित करना, परामर्श देना
Exorbitant	unreasonably high	अत्याधिक
Explicit	stated clearly and in detail	स्पष्ट, व्यक्त
Extrovert	an outgoing, overt person	बर्हिमुखी
Fabulous	extraordinary	शानदार
Facilitate	make easy or easier	सुविधाजनक बनाना
Familial	relating to a family or its members	परिवारिक
Familiar	well known from long or close association	परिचित
Familiarity	close acquaintance	मेल-जोल, घनिष्ठ परिचय
Fascination	a feeling of great liking	आकर्षण
Fearsome	frightening	डरावना
Feasible	possible to do	संभव, होने योग्य
Felicity	perfect happiness, great joy	परम सुख, आनंद
Fictitious	imaginative, not real	काल्पनिक, अवास्तविक
Filthy	disgustingly dirty, poverty-stricken extremely poor	गंदा, घृणित अत्यंत गरीब
Firm	resolute and determined	दृढ़
Fitfully	not regularly or continuously	अनियमित ढंग से
Flabbergasted	surprised (someone) greatly astonished	आश्चर्यचकित
Flattery	excessive and insincere praise	चापलूसी
Flimsy	lacking physical strength and energy	कमजोर, निर्बल
Forebode	act as a warning of	अपशकुन का संकेत करना
Forefront	the leading or most important position or place	सबसे अगला भाग
Forego	dispense with or give up	त्यागना, छोड़ना
Fortify	to make strong or stronger	मजबूत करना

Fortitude	courage	सहन-शक्ति, साहस
Foul	unfair	अनुचित
Fragile	vulnerable	नाजुक
Fragrance	a pleasant, sweet smell	खुशबु, महक
Frail	weak and delicate	दुर्बल, कमजोर
Fratricide	the killing of one's brother or sister	भाई/बहन की हत्या
Friendly	kind and pleasant	अनुकूल, मित्रतापूर्ण
Frivolous	not having any serious purpose or value	तुच्छ, निरर्थक
Frontier	a line or border separating two countries	सीमा, सरहद
Frugal	sparing or economical	कंजूस
Fruitless	unproductive or useless	निरर्थक, व्यर्थ
Garish	bright and showy	भड़कीला
Generate	to bring about	पैदा करना
Genial	friendly and cheerful	हंसमुख, मिलनसार
Genius	exceptionally intellectual	प्रतिभावान
Genuine	authentic, real	सच्चा, वास्तविक
Gist	the substance or essence	सार, निष्कर्ष
Gloomy	sorrowful or sad	उदासीन, गमगीन
Grumble	complain or protest about something	बड़बड़ाना, असंतोष प्रकट करना
Hesitant	reluctant or unwilling	अनिच्छुक
Hindered	prevented	बाधित
Homage	special honour or respect	श्रद्धांजलि, सम्मान
Horrendous	extremely unpleasant, horrifying, or terrible	भयंकर, डरावना
Hostile	unfriendly, antagonistic	शत्रुतापूर्ण, विरोधी
Hostility	hostile behaviour or opposition	शत्रुता
Humiliated	put to shame	अपमानित
Humility	modesty, humbleness	विनम्रता
Idea	a thought or suggestion	विचार
Idiotic	very stupid	मुर्खतापूर्ण
Ignorant	lacking knowledge or awareness	अनभिज्ञ, अनजान
Ill-favoured	not attractive, ugly	कुरूप, बदसूरत
Imbecility	stupidity	मूर्खता
Imitate	follow, to copy	नकल करना, अनुसरण करना
Immense	extremely large or great	अत्यधिक
Impeccable	faultless, perfect	त्रुटिहीन
Impediment	a hindrance or obstruction	बाधा, अवरोध
Impetus	force or energy	बल
Implacable	unable to be pacified	निर्मम, बेरहम

Impost	a tax of payment	कर, शुल्क
Impudence	impertinence	धृष्टता, बेशर्मी
Impulsive	acting suddenly without thinking carefully	आवेशपूर्ण, क्रोधित
Inclement	(of the weather) unpleasant	कठोर, रूखा
Incoherence	a fact of being not easy to understand	बेतुका, अस्पष्ट
Indict	charge with, accuse of	दोष लगाना
Indifferent	showing no interest	उदासीन
Indigent	poor, needy	गरीब, जरूरतमंद
Indoctrination	process of forcing somebody to accept a particular belief	भरोसा दिलाना
Indolent	lazy	आलसी
Inducement	Motivation	प्रोत्साहन
Industrious	diligent and hard-working	मेहनती, परिश्रमी
Infamy	disgrace or dishonour	बदनामी
Inflict	cause (someone to suffer)	पहुँचाना (पीड़ा इत्यादि)
Infuriate	to make angry	क्रोधित करना
Ingenious	clever, original and inventive	चतुर
Inkling	a slight, uncertain idea about something	आभास, संकेत
Innocuous	harmless	निर्दोष, मासूम
Innuendo	an unpleasant hint	परोक्ष संकेत
Insolent	extremely rude and showing a lack of respect	असभ्य, बदतमीज
Instigator	a person who provokes	भड़काने वाला
Integrity	the state of being whole and undivided	संम्पूर्णता, अखंडता
Interfere	intervene in an activity	हस्तक्षेप करना
Intimation	an indication or information	सूचना, संकेत
Intimidate	frighten	धमकाना, डराना
Intrepid	fearless, adventurous	निडर, बहादूर
Introspective	inward-looking	आत्मविश्लेषी
Intruder	a person who intrudes, trespasser	अनाधिकृत प्रवेश करने वाला
Irreproachable	beyond criticism faultless	त्रुटिहीन
Irresolute	not able to decide what to do	दुविधा में पड़ा हुआ
Irreverence	disrespect	असम्मान, अनादर
Irrevocable	not able to be repeated	जो निरस्त ना किया जा सके
Jealous	envious	ईर्ष्यापूर्ण
Jubilant	expressing great happiness and triumph	उल्लासित
Jubilation	a feeling of great happiness and triumph	आंनदोत्सव
Judicious	showing good judgment	उचित, न्यायपूर्ण
Knave	a dishonest or unscrupulous man	धूर्त, बेईमान

Laid-back	relaxed	शांत
Latent	hidden or concealed	गुप्त, अव्यक्त
Laudable	deserving praise and commendation	प्रंशसनीय
Liberty	freedom	स्वतंत्रता
Licentious	immoral	अनैतिक
Loquacious	talkative	बातूनी
Lousy	very bad, disgusting	घटिया, घिनौना
Lucid	clear and understandable	स्पष्ट, सुबोध
Lurid	dark and shocking	भंयकर, कुत्सित
Magnanimous	very generous or forgiving	उदार
Magnificent	extremely beautiful	शानदार, आलीशान
Maiden speech	the first speech	प्रथम भाषण
Mass murder	the killing of a large number of people	सामूहिक हत्या/नरसंहार
Massive	extremely large	अत्यंत विशाल
Meek	quiet, gentle	नम्र
Menial	not requiring much skill and lacking prestige	हीन, नीचा
Merit	deserve or be worthy of	के योग्य होना
Methodical	orderly systematic	व्यवस्थित
Meticulous	very careful and precise	तीक्ष्ण बुद्धि वाला
Miraculous	amazing or wonderful	अद्भूत
Mischievous	naughty or misbehaving	शरारतपूर्ण
Mitigate	make less severe or serious	कम करना, शांत करना
Moan	expressing pain	विलाप करना
Modest	humble	विनम्र
Morbidity	sickness, illness	अस्वस्थता
Motive	reason, purpose	प्रेरणा, उद्देश्य
Murky	dark and gloomy, especially due to thick mist	अंधकारपूर्ण, धूंधला
Nebulous	not clear	अस्पष्ट
Novicc	new or inexperienced	अनुभवहीन, नौसिखिया
Nurture	bring up, look after	पालन-पोषण करना
Obdurate	determined, obstinate	जिद्दी
Obnoxious	extremely unpleasant	अप्रिय
Obscene	immoral, indecent	अश्लील
Omnipotent	having unlimited power	सर्वशक्तिमान
Omniscient	knowing everything	सर्व-ज्ञान
Ostracise	exclude from a society or group	बहिष्कृत/निष्कासित करना
Outdo	be more successful than	आगे निकल जाना (किसी कार्य में)
Overdo	do something excessively	अति करना

Pacify	to calm	शांत करना
Palpable	easily perceived or understood	स्पष्ट
Panacea	remedy for all difficulties or diseases	कष्ट निवारण, उपचार
Passivity	tolerance	सहनशीलता, धैर्य
Patricide	the killing of one's father	पिता की हत्या
Paucity	scarcity	कमी
Peculiar	strange or odd, unusual	अजीब, अनोखा
Penitent	repentant	पश्चाताप
Pensive	engaged in deep thought	चिंताग्रस्त
Perilous	full of danger	जोखिम
Perplexed	puzzled, confused	उलझन में
Persistent	stubborn	जिद्दी
Perspicuous	clearly expressed and easily understood	सुबोध, स्पष्ट
Persuade	to convince	मनाना, राजी करना
Pertinent	relevant or apposite	उचित, योग्य
Pious	devoutly religious	पवित्र, धार्मिक
Pity	the feeling of sorrow and compassion	दया, करूणा-भाव
Plausible	reasonable and likely to be true	स्वीकार्य, व्यवहारिक
Plunder	loot	लूटना
Poach	illegally hunt	शिकार करना
Poignant	evoking a keen sense of sadness	मार्मिक, उदास
Pompous	excessively elevated or ornate	शानदान, वैभवपूर्ण
Possessed	completely controlled by an evil spirit	बुरी आत्मा के अधीन
Pragmatic	practical and sensible	व्यावहारिक, स्वीकार्य
Preach	deliver a sermon or religious address	धर्म संबंधी शिक्षा देना
Predominantly	mainly, for the most part	मुख्य रूप से
Preface	an introduction	भूमिका
Premature	happening before the normal or expected time	समयपूर्व, असामयिक
Procure	to acquire	प्राप्त करना
Prodigal	extravagant	खर्चीला
Prodigious	enormous or huge	विशाल, बहुत बड़ा
Profoundly	to a profound extent	गंभीरतापूर्वक
Prognosis	the likely course of a disease or ailment	रोग का कारण निर्धारण
Prolonged	continuing for a long time	दीर्घकालीन
Prompt	to assist or encourage	प्रेरित करना
Prospective	expected or expecting to be	भावी, प्रत्याशित
Prosper	make steady progress	समृद्ध, सफल होना
Prosperity	affluence or welfare	समृद्धि, सम्पन्नता

Prosperous	rich; well-to-do	समृद्ध
Provisional	arranged or existing for the present	तत्कालिक
Prudent	wise, sensible	बुद्धिमान, चतुर
Quash	reject or cancel	समाप्त कर देना, खंडन करना
Queer	strange, odd	विचित्र
Querulous	quarrelsome	झगड़ालू, चिड़चिड़ा
Quiver	tremble or shake	काँपना
Rage	uncontrollable anger	क्रोध, गुस्सा
Raise	lift or move to a higher position or level	उठाना, बढ़ाना
Ravaged	severely damaged and devastated	तबाह, नष्ट करना
Recipient	one who receives something	प्राप्तकर्ता, ग्रहण करने वाला
Reciprocal	corresponding or mutual	पारस्परिक
Recommend	advocate, endorse	सिफारिश करना
Rectify	put (something) right, correct	सुधारना
Recurrent	occurring often or repeatedly	बार बार होने वाला
Reduce	make smaller or less	कम करना
Redundant	superfluous or unnecessary	अनावश्यक, व्यर्थ
Refrain	to stop oneself from	बचना
Regard	respect	सम्मान करना
Regicide	the action of killing a king	राजा की हत्या
Rejoice	to feel or show great joy or delight	खुश होना, आनंद मनाना
Relentless	continuing, continual	लगातार
Relish	to enjoy	आनंद लेना
Reluctant	unwilling and hesitant	अनिच्छुक
Renowned	famous	प्रसिद्ध
Reparation	compensation	क्षतिपूर्ति, अदायगी
Repartee	quick, witty reply	हाजिर जवाबी
Repentant	sincere regret and remorse	पछतावा
Rcposc	a state of inactivity; rest	विश्राम
Requisite	necessary	अपेक्षित, आवश्यक
Resentment	bitterness, indignation	नाराजगी, रोष
Resilient	flexible or pliable	लचीला
Restrict	put a limit on	प्रतिबंधित करना
Retail	to sell goods to the public	खुदरा ब्रिकी
Retain	continue to have something	बनाए रखना
Retarded growth	delayed growth	मंद विकास
Reticent	reserved or shy	अल्पभाषी, कम बोलने वाला
Reticent	reserved	कम बोलने वाला

Revel in	enjoy oneself	आनंद लेना
Revelation	disclosure of a previously unknown fact	रहस्योद्घाटन
Reverie	daydream	सपना, कोरी कल्पना
Rigorous	extremely exhaustive	कठिन, सख्त
Rouse	to awaken	जगाना
Rout	an overwhelming defeat, to defeat badly	हार, हराना
Rusticity	the quality of being rustic	गंवारूपन
Salient	noteworthy or significant	मुख्य, महत्वपूर्ण
Salutary	beneficial	लाभदायक
Sanitise	cleaning or sterilizing	स्वच्छ बनाना, कीटाणु रहित करना
Sauntering	a leisurely stroll	इत्मीनान से टहलना
Savage	fierce, violent, and uncontrolled	जंगली, बर्बर
Seclude	separate	अलग करना
Sheer	change course	रास्ता बदलना
Shrink	to be smaller	सिकुड़ना, छोटा होना
Slash	cut with a violent sweeping movement	तेजी से मारना
Snobbish	arrogant or haughty	दंभी, अभिमानी
Solecism	a grammatical mistake in speech or writing	अशुद्ध उच्चारण या व्याकरण
Solicit	ask for or request	विनती करना
Soothing	calm or peaceful	सुखदायक, शांत
Sophisticated	developed to a high degree	सभ्य एवं भव्य
Soporific	tending to induce drowsiness or sleep	निद्राजनक, नींद लाने वाला
Spirited	full of energy	उत्साहयुक्त
Splendid	magnificent, very impressive	शानदार, भव्य
Sporadic	occurring at irregular intervals	छिटपुट, रूक रूक होने वाला
Squander	to waste	व्यर्थ करना, गंवाना
Sterile	incapable of reproducing	बाँझ, बंजर
Strike off	to cut something off	हटा देना
Strike	hit forcibly	जोर से मारना
Stubborn	Obstinate	जिद्दी, हठी
Stubborn	obstinate	जिद्दी
Submissive	meekly obedient or passive	विनम्र
Suggestively	tending to suggest an idea	सांकेतिक रूप से
Sundry	of various kinds, several	विविध, विभिन्न

Surmount	overcome (a difficulty or obstacle)	विजय पाना
Surpass	to be greater than	अधिक होना
Surreptitiously	secretly, stealthily	चोरी-चोरी, चुपके से
Swap	an act of exchanging	अदला-बदली करना
Sympathetic	compassionate or caring	सहानुभूतिपूर्ण
Take after	look like, having same appearance	की तरह दिखना
Tangential	having a slight or indirect connection	ऊपरी तौर से
Tedious	lacking interest or excitement	थकाने वाला
Tinkering	selling or repairing things	मरम्मत
Tiring	wearisome, tiresome	थकावट भरा, थकाऊ
Translucent	semi-transparent	अल्प-पारदर्शी
Transparent	allowing light to pass through	पारदर्शी
Transpire	to happen or occur	होना/पता चलना
Trauma	a deeply distressing or disturbing experience	आघात
Treason	betraying of one's country	राज-द्रोह (देशद्रोह)
Tremendous	very large, great	बहुत अधिक
Ubiquitous	found everywhere	सर्वव्यापी
Unceremonious	rough or abrupt	अनौपचारिक, असभ्य
Uncouth	lacking good manners	गंवार, असभ्य
Unusual	not usual	असामान्य
Vacillate	to be indecisive	निर्णय न ले पाना
Vagary	an unexpected and inexplicable change in behaviour	सनक, आवेग
Veil	conceal or hide	छिपना
Verbosity	the quality of using more words than needed	शब्दों का अनावश्यक प्रयोग
Vibrant	full of energy and enthusiasm	जीवंत
Vindictive	revengeful	प्रतिशोधी
Virtuous	having high moral standards	नैतिक
Warranty	a written guarantee	गांरटी
Weary	tiresome	थका हुआ, सुस्त
Wholesome	healthy	पौष्टिक
Witty quip	verbal humour	मजाकिया
Witty	humorous	हास्यपूर्ण
Zealous	enthusiastic or passionate	उत्साही

28 ANTONYMS

CHAPTER

Directions: In questions no. 1 to 298 choose the word opposite in meaning to the given word and mark it in the answer sheet.

1. **Fastidious**
(a) Fussy
(b) Cooperative
(c) Promising
(d) Adjustable

2. **Shallow**
(a) High
(b) Long
(c) Wide
(d) Deep

3. **Explicit**
(a) Elusive
(b) Allusive
(c) Ambidextrous
(d) Ambiguous

4. **Immune**
(a) Free
(b) Vulnerable
(c) Powerful
(d) Weak

5. **Bleak**
(a) Dull
(b) Dark
(c) Bright
(d) Exposure

6. **Veneration**
(a) Fear
(b) Reverence
(c) Remorse
(d) Disrespect

7. **Insolent**
(a) Ignorant
(b) Proud
(c) Laudable
(d) Humble

8. **Urban**
(a) Rustic
(b) Rural
(c) Civil
(d) Foreign

9. **Incredible**
(a) Possible
(b) Believable
(c) Enjoyable
(d) Imaginary

10. **Concur**
(a) Disagree
(b) Disappear
(c) Disarrange
(d) Discourage

11. **Quiet**
(a) Strong
(b) Pandemonium
(c) Incomplete
(d) Violent

12. **Vague**
(a) Clear
(b) Dull
(c) Unknown
(d) Shady

13. **Inevitable**
(a) Avoidable
(b) Unnecessary
(c) Inseparable
(d) Uncertain

14. **Humility**
(a) Dignity
(b) Cruelty
(c) Anger
(d) Pride

15. **Rapidly**
(a) Lazily
(b) Secretly
(c) Slowly
(d) Firmly

16. **Extol**
(a) Heckle
(b) Censure
(c) Hate
(d) Scold

17. **Make**
(a) Liberate
(b) Break
(c) Emancipate
(d) Bind

18. **Terminate**
(a) Hasten
(b) Depart
(c) Begin
(d) Change

19. **Successor**
(a) Failure
(b) Loser
(c) Predecessor
(d) Predator

20. **Demolish**
(a) Shift
(b) Build
(c) Repeat
(d) Hide

21. **Genial**
(a) Stupid
(b) Stingy
(c) Boorish
(d) Unkind

22. Prevent
(a) Protect
(b) Bleak
(c) Hinder
(d) Induce

23. Plausible
(a) Inplausible
(b) Unplausible
(c) Implausible/ Unbelievable
(d) Displausible

24. Frailty
(a) Energy
(b) Intensity
(c) Vehemence
(d) Strength

25. Flair
(a) Spreading outward
(b) Inability
(c) Spotlight
(d) Taste

26. Collapse
(a) Rise
(b) Handicap
(c) Crush
(d) Crumble

27. Dormant
(a) Acute
(b) Active
(c) Able
(d) Ablaze

28. Anxious
(a) Crafty
(b) Light
(c) Carefree
(d) Careless

29. Hazy
(a) Plain
(b) Light
(c) Clear
(d) Dull

30. Thrifty
(a) Clean
(b) Loyal
(c) Wasteful
(d) Reverent

31. Fantastic
(a) Old
(b) Ordinary
(c) Classic
(d) Rational

32. Innovate
(a) Sell
(b) Buy
(c) Close
(d) Copy

33. Asceticism
(a) Comfort
(b) Luxury
(c) Anti-semitism
(d) Humility

34. Enduring
(a) Fleeting
(b) Painful
(c) Permanent
(d) Long lasting

35. Dissolution
(a) Retribution
(b) Establishment
(c) Persuasion
(d) Compliance

36. Progressive
(a) Repressive
(b) Retrogressive
(c) Repulsive
(d) Aggressive

37. Unnerved
(a) Confident
(b) Nervous
(c) Hopeful
(d) Anxious

38. Vague
(a) Unclear
(b) Sharp
(c) Precise
(d) Actual

39. Harmony
(a) Disagreement
(b) Melody
(c) Confusion
(d) Concord

40. Purposely
(a) Half-heartedly
(b) Timidly
(c) Unintentionally
(d) Hesitatingly

41. Guilty
(a) Innocent
(b) Ignorant
(c) Irreverent
(d) Immature

42. Brave
(a) Sorry
(b) Bold
(c) Timid
(d) Boisterous

43. Duplicity
(a) Complexity
(b) Honesty
(c) Serenity
(d) Originality

44. Opaque
(a) Brilliant
(b) Bright
(c) Transparent
(d) Lustrous

45. Jocular
(a) Merry
(b) Morose
(c) Jugular
(d) Juggler

46. Hinder
(a) Encourage
(b) Acknowledge
(c) Prohibit
(d) Instruct

47. Uncompromising
(a) Courteous
(b) Flexible
(c) Awesome
(d) Soft

48. Zeal
(a) Disinterest
(b) Apathy
(c) Carelessness
(d) Hatred

49. Desecration
(a) Consecration
(b) Discouragement
(c) Despondency
(d) Expectation

50. Shimmering
(a) Gloomy
(b) Glimmering
(c) Refreshing
(d) Repining

51. Far-fetched
(a) Wise
(b) Prudent
(c) Located for
(d) Realistic

52. Takes off
(a) Travels
(b) Falls
(c) Explodes
(d) Lands

53. Niggardly
(a) Hastily
(b) Lavishly
(c) Likely
(d) Gorgeously

54. Melodious
(a) Harmonious
(b) Tuneless
(c) Odious
(d) Mellifluous

55. Advanced
(a) Progressed
(b) Outpaced
(c) Receded
(d) Run back

56. Enlightened
(a) Slander
(b) Bemoan
(c) Ignorant
(d) Before

57. Exceptional
(a) Great
(b) Occasional
(c) Common
(d) Absorbing

58. Permanent
(a) Long
(b) Short
(c) Durable
(d) Temporary

59. Moderate
(a) Abnormal
(b) Weak
(c) Extreme
(d) Separate

60. Diffidence
(a) Boldness
(b) Outspokenness
(c) Fluency
(d) Obstinacy

61. Superficial
(a) Careful
(b) Of surface
(c) Thorough
(d) Casual

62. Reckless
(a) Careful
(b) Frank
(c) Diffident
(d) Smart

63. Scorn
(a) Contempt
(b) Joy
(c) Admiration
(d) Pity

64. Grandiose
(a) Simple
(b) False
(c) Ideal
(d) Proud

65. Trivial
(a) Serious
(b) Violent
(c) Wild
(d) Unimportant

66. Lurid
(a) Dismal
(b) Mild
(c) Murky
(d) Mysterious

67. Loquacious
(a) Reserved
(b) Miserly
(c) Eloquent
(d) Healthy

68. Unscrupulous
(a) Conscientious
(b) Dedicated
(c) Single-minded
(d) Superfluous

69. Confiscate
(a) Produce
(b) Release
(c) Destroy
(d) Exhibit

70. Contaminate
(a) Sanctify
(b) Invigorate
(c) Taint
(d) Purify

71. Often
(a) Usually
(b) Rarely
(c) Sometimes
(d) Occasionally

72. Frugal
(a) Economical
(b) Extravagant
(c) Miserly
(d) Greedy

73. Eminent
(a) Illustrious
(b) Notorious
(c) Intelligent
(d) Known

74. Barbarous
(a) Civilized
(b) Modern
(c) Polite
(d) Praiseworthy

75. Embark upon
(a) Launch
(b) Analyse
(c) Break off
(d) Conclude

76. Falling off
(a) Shrinkage
(b) Erosion
(c) Improvement
(d) Descent

77. Depressed
(a) Satisfied
(b) Elated
(c) Impressed
(d) Affected

78. Yield to
(a) Submit to
(b) Persuade
(c) Resist
(d) Seek terms with

79. Paucity
(a) Overflow
(b) Inflow
(c) Plenty
(d) Grim

80. Conclusive
(a) Powerful
(b) Indecisive
(c) Exclusive
(d) Partial

81. Triggered
(a) Choked
(b) Tapered off
(c) Diluted
(d) Ignited

82. **Parallel**
(a) Divergent
(b) Difficult
(c) Similar
(d) Crooked

83. **Manifested**
(a) Displayed
(b) Concealed
(c) Suppressed
(d) Marked

84. **Blocked**
(a) Facilitated
(b) Started
(c) Checked
(d) Promoted

85. **Vindictive**
(a) Careless
(b) Forgiving
(c) Heedless
(d) Refined

86. **Turncoat**
(a) Loyal
(b) Disappointing
(c) Thrilling
(d) Nail-biting

87. **Inaugurate**
(a) Terminate
(b) Inculcate
(c) Facilitate
(d) Ameliorate

88. **Embellish**
(a) Dishonour
(b) Demolish
(c) Spoil
(d) Suffice

89. **Detest**
(a) Test
(b) Dislike
(c) Like
(d) Interest

90. **Intentional**
(a) Accidental
(b) Undecided
(c) Concentrated
(d) Broken

91. **Commence**
(a) Start
(b) Schedule
(c) Conclude
(d) Dissolve

92. **Expand**
(a) Contract
(b) Contrast
(c) Consist
(d) Controvert

93. **Prosperity**
(a) Propriety
(b) Property
(c) Adversity
(d) Perspicacity

94. **Stimulate**
(a) Encourage
(b) Discourage
(c) Tempt
(d) Instigate

95. **Deliberate**
(a) Unconditional
(b) Unintentional
(c) Unilateral
(d) Emotional

96. **Perilous**
(a) Pitiable
(b) Difficult
(c) Safe
(d) Comfortable

97. **Disputable**
(a) Undisputable
(b) Indisputable
(c) Nondisputable
(d) Adisputable

98. **Audacious**
(a) Cautious
(b) Timid
(c) Rude
(d) Proud

99. **Meticulous**
(a) Unmerited
(b) Unimaginative
(c) Carefree
(d) Careless

100. **Repel**
(a) Attract
(b) Interest
(c) Tempt
(d) Like

101. **Dim**
(a) Transparent
(b) Luminous
(c) Opaque
(d) Dazzling

102. **Genuine**
(a) Genius
(b) Honest
(c) Affected
(d) Fictitious

103. **Ham-fisted**
(a) Simple
(b) Adroit
(c) Difficult
(d) Vague

104. **Implicit**
(a) Explicit
(b) Implied
(c) Explained
(d) Exquisite

105. **Capture**
(a) Catch
(b) Detain
(c) Liberate
(d) Stop

106. **Repulsive**
(a) Attractive
(b) Offensive
(c) Defensive
(d) Pensive

107. **Misery**
(a) Sorry
(b) Careless
(c) Joy
(d) Content

108. **Escalate**
(a) Decrease
(b) Descend
(c) Deliver
(d) Derive

109. **Anarchy**
(a) Curfew
(b) Permanence
(c) Wholesome
(d) Order

110. **Commotion**
(a) Transmission
(b) Tranquility
(c) Transparency
(d) Transition

111. **Monotony**
(a) Enthusiasm
(b) Repetitiveness
(c) Variety
(d) Singularity

112. Latter
(a) Earlier
(b) Before
(c) Later
(d) Former

113. Dynamic
(a) Stable
(b) Still
(c) Lazy
(d) Static

114. Diligent
(a) Intelligent
(b) Lazy
(c) Boastful
(d) Notorious

115. Hereditary
(a) Carried
(b) Acquired
(c) Possessed
(d) Regained

116. Philistine
(a) Cultured
(b) Libertine
(c) Sober
(d) Educated

117. Heretical
(a) Contradictory
(b) Doubtful
(c) Impious
(d) Orthodox

118. Ingest
(a) Disrupt
(b) Disgorge
(c) Dismiss
(d) Display

119. Implicate
(a) Exonerate
(b) Impersonate
(c) Complicate
(d) Impose

120. Laceration
(a) Convalescence
(b) Recuperation
(c) Healing
(d) Palpitation

121. Liberty
(a) Serenity
(b) Slavery
(c) Serfdom
(d) Subordinate

122. Disorderly
(a) Chaotic
(b) Organized
(c) Adjusted
(d) Arranged

123. Elevation
(a) Reduction
(b) Humiliation
(c) Increment
(d) Debasement

124. Glossy
(a) Dull
(b) Shining
(c) Weary
(d) Tired

125. Boon
(a) Dull
(b) Bane
(c) Hurt
(d) Harsh

126. Accomplish
(a) Fail
(b) Improper
(c) Disagreeable
(d) Scatter

127. Famous
(a) Obscure
(b) Eminent
(c) Lenient
(d) Fabulous

128. Orderly
(a) Unclear
(b) Valueless
(c) Chaotic
(d) Incomplete

129. Gloomy
(a) Radiant
(b) Fragrant
(c) Melodious
(d) Illusory

130. Strife
(a) War
(b) Peace
(c) Anger
(d) Woe

131. Isolation
(a) Segregation
(b) Association
(c) Seclusion
(d) Deportation

132. Antique
(a) Common
(b) Recent
(c) Innovative
(d) Youthful

133. Contented
(a) Dissatisfied
(b) Emptied
(c) Happy
(d) Unfriendly

134. Rapid
(a) Happy
(b) Fall
(c) Slow
(d) Abnormal

135. Severe
(a) Sharp
(b) Mild
(c) Important
(d) Cut

136. Initiated
(a) Complicated
(b) Simplified
(c) Concluded
(d) Commenced

137. Consensus
(a) Accept
(b) Opinion
(c) Disagreement
(d) Permission

138. Fatigued
(a) Weakened
(b) Energised
(c) Tired
(d) Activated

139. Autonomy
(a) Slavery
(b) Subordination
(c) Dependence
(d) Submissiveness

140. Flexible
(a) Rigid
(b) Cruel
(c) Humble
(d) Easy

141. Artificial
(a) Artful
(b) Machine-made
(c) Artistic
(d) Natural

142. Delete
(a) Regress
(b) Interpolate
(c) Infer
(d) Include

143. Benefactor
(a) Helper
(b) Victor
(c) Disciple
(d) Enemy

144. Evanescent
(a) Clean
(b) Tight
(c) Eternal
(d) Cheap

145. Barren
(a) Fertile
(b) Rich
(c) Prosperous
(d) Positive

146. Virtue
(a) Vice
(b) Failure
(c) Fault
(d) Offence

147. Nervous
(a) Flawless
(b) Immature
(c) Smooth
(d) Composed

148. Confident
(a) Worried
(b) Pessimistic
(c) Diffident
(d) Depressed

149. Evident
(a) Suspected
(b) Disagreed
(c) Hidden
(d) Unimportant

150. Adamant
(a) Yielding
(b) Permissive
(c) Liberal
(d) Tolerant

151. Professional
(a) Novice
(b) Amateur
(c) Dabbler
(d) Apprentice

152. Callous
(a) Persuasive
(b) Caring
(c) Gentle
(d) Sensitive

153. Cessation
(a) Commencement
(b) Renewal
(c) Ongoing
(d) Interruption

154. Procrastinate
(a) Experiment
(b) Expedite
(c) Exclude
(d) Propagate

155. Potent
(a) Inefficient
(b) Soft
(c) Fragile
(d) Weak

156. Probity
(a) Dishonesty
(b) Timidity
(c) Treachery
(d) Insincerity

157. Gregarious
(a) Recluse
(b) Social
(c) Laudatory
(d) Rustic

158. Sporadic
(a) Surviving
(b) Sweeping
(c) Restrained
(d) Continual

159. Implication
(a) Consideration
(b) Exoneration
(c) Conclusion
(d) Interpretation

160. Apposite
(a) Intemperate
(b) Inappropriate
(c) Indecent
(d) Incriminatory

161. Gregarious
(a) Indecent
(b) Unsociable
(c) Above reproach
(d) Unlovable

162. Chivalry
(a) Cawardish
(b) Discourtesy
(c) Disobedience
(d) Disaffection

163. Dismal
(a) Bright
(b) Indifferent
(c) Fast
(d) Energetic

164. Sanguine temper
(a) Despairing nature
(b) Peaceful temperament
(c) Rude behaviour
(d) Selfish nature

165. Meagre
(a) Extravagant
(b) Abandon
(c) Prosperous
(d) Surplus

166. Imperil
(a) Safeguard
(b) Construct
(c) Create
(d) Brighten

167. Flamboyant
(a) Elaborately
(b) Really
(c) Not showy
(d) Sensibly

168. Consolidated
(a) Disjointed
(b) Broken
(c) Weakened
(d) Lost

169. Chronic
(a) Pathetic
(b) Characteristic
(c) Temporary
(d) Mild

170. Vituperative
(a) Joyous
(b) Laudatory
(c) Critical
(d) Virtuous

171. Awkward
(a) Awful
(b) Satisfactory
(c) Graceful
(d) Easy

172. Smug
(a) Satisfied
(b) Dissatisfied
(c) Serious
(d) Delighted

173. Oppressive
(a) Gentle
(b) Harsh
(c) Smooth
(d) Orderly

174. Obscure
(a) Inconspicuous
(b) Veiled
(c) Clear
(d) Distinct

175. Clinch
(a) Lose
(b) Clasp
(c) Deal
(d) Seal

176. Enervate
(a) Decelerate
(b) Strengthen
(c) Push forward
(d) Aggravate

177. To put up with
(a) To stay together
(b) To talk politely
(c) To dislike
(d) To move along with

178. Autonomous
(a) Self-government
(b) Dependent
(c) Defensive
(d) Neutral

179. Deceitful
(a) Sincere
(b) Useful
(c) Plain
(d) Honest

180. Exonerate
(a) Admit
(b) Release
(c) Convict
(d) Reject

181. Exaggerate
(a) Underwrite
(b) Understate
(c) Ignore
(d) Condemn

182. Controversial
(a) Indisputable
(b) Restrained
(c) Controlled
(d) Appeasing

183. Synthetic
(a) Natural
(b) Plastic
(c) Cosmetic
(d) Apathetic

184. Accord
(a) Disagreement
(b) Welcome
(c) Disrespect
(d) Conformity

185. Infirmity
(a) Employment
(b) Indisposition
(c) Strength
(d) Weakness

186. Feasible
(a) Useful
(b) Impractical
(c) Uneven
(d) Important

187. Deny
(a) Accept
(b) Proceed
(c) Hold
(d) Promote

188. Acquit
(a) Inform
(b) Release
(c) Abuse
(d) Condemn

189. Benediction
(a) Best wishes
(b) Use
(c) Curse
(d) Blessing

190. Affluence
(a) Not being fluent
(b) Poverty
(c) Difficult
(d) Unhealthy

191. Forbid
(a) Defy
(b) Dislike
(c) Permit
(d) Understand

192. Harmonious
(a) Selfish
(b) Aggressive
(c) Mechanical
(d) Discordant

193. Inconspicuous
(a) Open-hearted
(b) Open-minded
(c) Prominent
(d) Smooth

194. Factual
(a) Actual
(b) Idealistic
(c) Unrealistic
(d) Verbal

195. Abandon
(a) Assert
(b) Retain
(c) Produce
(d) Twist

196. Assent
(a) Breakdown
(b) Misunderstand
(c) Dispatch
(d) Disagreement

197. Fickle
(a) Constant
(b) Convenient
(c) Questionable
(d) Faithful

198. Discreet
(a) Worthy
(b) Wishful thinking
(c) Honest
(d) Careless in behaviour

199. Articulate
(a) Unable to understand
(b) Unable to express oneself
(c) Unable to agree
(d) Unable to live

200. Unjust
(a) Serious
(b) Self-centred
(c) Fair-minded
(d) Considerable

201. Humble
(a) Rich
(b) Powerful
(c) Haughty
(d) Strong

202. Exemptions
(a) Generalisation
(b) Liberalisation
(c) Exclusions
(d) Inclusions

203. Prominent
(a) Unknown
(b) Treason
(c) Loyalty
(d) Distrust

204. Alleviate
(a) Intensity
(b) Magnify
(c) Mitigate
(d) Aggravate

205. Disperse
(a) Converge
(b) Smile
(c) Dispense
(d) Sing

206. Ambiguous
(a) Truthful
(b) Lucid
(c) Logical
(d) Systematic

207. Hilarious
(a) Unworthy
(b) Unpleasant
(c) Ill-fated
(d) Serious

208. Tolerance
(a) Loathing
(b) Brawl
(c) Plea
(d) Forbid

209. Steadfast
(a) Staunch
(b) Feeble
(c) Faint
(d) Wavering

210. Conceited
(a) Proud
(b) Honest
(c) Modest
(d) Modern

211. Deterrent
(a) Determinant
(b) Detriment
(c) Encouragement
(d) Enrichment

212. Spurious
(a) Truthful
(b) Authentic
(c) Credible
(d) Original

213. Slander
(a) Gain
(b) Profit
(c) Praise
(d) Loss

214. Reveal
(a) Appeal
(b) Relax
(c) Recover
(d) Conceal

215. Admonish
(a) Condemn
(b) Bless
(c) Praise
(d) Congratulate

216. Adulation
(a) Flattery
(b) Encomium
(c) Confession
(d) Condemnation

217. Affirmation
(a) Denial
(b) Refusal
(c) Opposition
(d) Obstruction

218. Affluent
(a) Poor
(b) Ordinary
(c) Infamous
(d) Backward

219. Agony
(a) Ecstasy
(b) Laughter
(c) Humdrum
(d) Ecstasy

220. Appalling
(a) Shocking
(b) Consoling
(c) Scaring
(d) Horrifying

221. Candid
(a) Frank
(b) Diplomatic
(c) Reserved
(d) Impertinent

222. Camaraderie
(a) Curiosity
(b) Ferocity
(c) Impetuosity
(d) Animosity

223. Convicted
(a) Charged
(b) Relieved
(c) Dismissed
(d) Acquitted

224. Convoluted
(a) Simple
(b) Complicated
(c) Difficult
(d) Majestic

225. Curtail
(a) Lengthen
(b) Shorten
(c) Entail
(d) Close

226. Dense
(a) Scarce
(b) Slim
(c) Sparse
(d) Lean

227. Diminished
(a) Created
(b) Rose
(c) Increased
(d) Lessen

228. Ephemeral
(a) Eternal
(b) Transitory
(c) Mortal
(d) Temporal

229. Escalating
(a) Fixed
(b) Fluctuating
(c) Falling
(d) Reasonable

230. Esteem
(a) Power
(b) Guess
(c) Contempt
(d) Estimate

231. Exotic
(a) Wonderful
(b) Cosmopolitan
(c) Irrelevant
(d) Common

232. Fetter
(a) Restore
(b) Liberate
(c) Exonerate
(d) Distract

233. Flourish
(a) Perish
(b) Degenerate
(c) Decay
(d) Dismiss

234. Futile
(a) Waste
(b) Expensive
(c) Useful
(d) Cheap

235. Garrulous
(a) Vociferous
(b) Eloquent
(c) Taciturn
(d) Vocal

236. Gratuitous
(a) Uncharitable
(b) Grand appearance
(c) Warranted
(d) Being grateful

237. In toto
(a) Bluntly
(b) Partially
(c) Entirely
(d) Strongly

238. Fleeting
(a) Glossy
(b) Perpetual
(c) Aspiring
(d) Sufficient

239. Inert
(a) Active
(b) Lazy
(c) Strong
(d) Resolute

240. Initial
(a) Terminal
(b) Commencing
(c) Delayed
(d) Disastrous

241. Intimidating
(a) Authoritative
(b) Casual
(c) Non-serious
(d) Friendly

242. Jest
(a) Gravity
(b) Grim
(c) Genial
(d) Sport

243. Latent
(a) Unspoken
(b) Later
(c) Implicit
(d) Obvious

244. Maladroit
(a) Authoritative
(b) Skilful
(c) Maladjusted
(d) Malevolent

245. Malevolence
(a) Tenderness
(b) Kindness
(c) Benefiting
(d) Indulgence

246. Malice
(a) Sympathy
(b) Goodwill
(c) Friendship
(d) Attraction

247. Monotonous
(a) Disastrous
(b) Terrifying
(c) Terrible
(d) Interesting

248. Obscene
(a) Disobedient
(b) Decent
(c) Dislocate
(d) Cautious

249. Opposed
(a) Resistant
(b) Against
(c) Favouring
(d) Similar

250. Ostracise
(a) Amuse
(b) Welcome
(c) Entertain
(d) Host

251. Parsimonious
(a) Prodigious
(b) Selfless
(c) Extravagant
(d) Ostentatious

252. Predilection
(a) Acceptance
(b) Attraction
(c) Dislike
(d) Choice

253. Profound
(a) Deep
(b) Superficial
(c) Hollow
(d) Fallow

254. Protean
(a) Amateur
(b) Catholic
(c) Unchanging
(d) Rapid

255. Quiescent
(a) Restless
(b) Exempt
(c) Malignant
(d) Mendicant

256. Perilous
(a) Safe
(b) Developed
(c) Sophisticated
(d) Communicative

257. Revelation
(a) Rejection
(b) Elimination
(c) Concealment
(d) Introduction

258. Repulsion
(a) Attraction
(b) Disapproval
(c) Disparagement
(d) Denigration

259. Segregate
(a) Sever
(b) Unite
(c) Separate
(d) Aggregate

260. Significant
(a) Substantial
(b) Miniscule
(c) Incoherent
(d) Unimportant

261. Despair
(a) Sneer
(b) Compliment
(c) Irony
(d) Hope

262. Validate
(a) Disprove
(b) Authenticate
(c) Ingenuine
(d) Legalise

263. Vicious
(a) Godly
(b) Virtuous
(c) Sublime
(d) Friendly

ANSWER KEY

1. (d)	29. (c)	57. (c)	85. (b)	113. (d)	141. (d)	169. (c)	197. (a)	225. (a)	253. (b)
2. (d)	30. (c)	58. (d)	86. (a)	114. (b)	142. (d)	170. (b)	198. (d)	226. (a)	254. (c)
3. (d)	31. (b)	59. (c)	87. (a)	115. (b)	143. (d)	171. (c)	199. (b)	227. (c)	255. (a)
4. (b)	32. (d)	60. (a)	88. (c)	116. (a)	144. (c)	172. (b)	200. (c)	228. (a)	256. (a)
5. (c)	33. (b)	61. (c)	89. (c)	117. (d)	145. (a)	173. (a)	201. (c)	229. (c)	257. (c)
6. (d)	34. (a)	62. (a)	90. (a)	118. (b)	146. (a)	174. (c)	202. (d)	230. (c)	258. (a)
7. (d)	35. (b)	63. (c)	91. (c)	119. (a)	147. (d)	175. (a)	203. (a)	231. (d)	259. (b)
8. (b)	36. (b)	64. (a)	92. (a)	120. (c)	148. (c)	176. (b)	204. (d)	232. (b)	260. (d)
9. (b)	37. (a)	65. (a)	93. (c)	121. (b)	149. (c)	177. (c)	205. (a)	233. (a)	261. (d)
10. (a)	38. (c)	66. (b)	94. (b)	122. (b)	150. (a)	178. (b)	206. (b)	234. (c)	262. (a)
11. (b)	39. (a)	67. (a)	95. (b)	123. (a)	151. (b)	179. (d)	207. (d)	235. (c)	263. (b)
12. (a)	40. (c)	68. (a)	96. (c)	124. (a)	152. (d)	180. (c)	208. (b)	236. (a)	
13. (a)	41. (a)	69. (b)	97. (b)	125. (b)	153. (a)	181. (b)	209. (d)	237. (b)	
14. (d)	42. (c)	70. (d)	98. (b)	126. (a)	154. (b)	182. (a)	210. (c)	238. (b)	
15. (c)	43. (b)	71. (b)	99. (d)	127. (a)	155. (d)	183. (a)	211. (c)	239. (a)	
16. (b)	44. (c)	72. (b)	100. (a)	128. (c)	156. (a)	184. (a)	212. (b)	240. (a)	
17. (b)	45. (b)	73. (b)	101. (b)	129. (a)	157. (a)	185. (c)	213. (c)	241. (d)	
18. (c)	46. (a)	74. (a)	102. (d)	130. (b)	158. (d)	186. (b)	214. (d)	242. (b)	
19. (c)	47. (b)	75. (d)	103. (b)	131. (b)	159. (b)	187. (a)	215. (c)	243. (d)	
20. (b)	48. (b)	76. (c)	104. (a)	132. (b)	160. (b)	188. (d)	216. (d)	244. (b)	
21. (d)	49. (a)	77. (b)	105. (c)	133. (a)	161. (b)	189. (c)	217. (a)	245. (b)	
22. (d)	50. (b)	78. (c)	106. (a)	134. (c)	162. (a)	190. (b)	218. (a)	246. (b)	
23. (c)	51. (d)	79. (c)	107. (c)	135. (b)	163. (a)	191. (c)	219. (a)	247. (d)	
24. (d)	52. (d)	80. (b)	108. (a)	136. (c)	164. (a)	192. (d)	220. (b)	248. (b)	
25. (b)	53. (b)	81. (a)	109. (d)	137. (c)	165. (d)	193. (c)	221. (c)	249. (c)	
26. (a)	54. (b)	82. (d)	110. (b)	138. (b)	166. (a)	194. (c)	222. (d)	250. (b)	
27. (b)	55. (c)	83. (b)	111. (c)	139. (c)	167. (c)	195. (b)	223. (d)	251. (c)	
28. (c)	56. (c)	84. (a)	112. (d)	140. (a)	168. (a)	196. (d)	224. (a)	252. (c)	

MEANINGS OF DIFFICULT WORDS IN ALPHABETICAL ORDER

Word	Meaning in English	Meaning in Hindi
Abandon	give up completely	छोड़ देना
Ablaze	burning fiercely	जलता हुआ
Absorbing	attentive	तन्मय, सचेत
Accomplish	to achieve or complete successfully.	पूरा करना, प्राप्त करना
Accord	an official agreement or treaty	सहमति
Acknowledge	accept or admit	स्वीकार करना
Acquired	bought or obtained	प्राप्त, अर्जित
Acquit	free from a criminal charge	बरी करना
Acquitted	discharge from a criminal charge	अपराधमुक्त, बरी
Acute	severe or intense	तीक्ष्ण
Adamant	determind	हठी, जिद्दी
Admonish	warn or reprimand	झिडकना, डाँटना
Adroit	clever or skillful	निपुण, दक्ष
Adulation	excessive admiration or praise	खुशामद, चाटुकारिता
Advanced	ahead in development	विकसित
Adversity	difficulties; misfortune.	दुर्भाग्य, विपत्ति
Affirmation	acknowledgment	अभिपुष्टि
Affluence	wealth	समृद्धि
Affluent	wealthy	धनी
Aggravate	To provoke	भड़काना
Agony	extreme physical or mental suffering	यातना
Alleviate	make less severe	शांत करना, मंद करना
Allusive	referring to something	संकेत करता हुआ
Ambidextrous	using both hands equally well	दोनों हाथों को सफलतापूर्वक प्रयोग करने वाला
Ambiguous	not clear	अस्पष्ट
Ameliorate	improve or make better	सुधार करना
Amuse	to entertain	मन बहलाना
Anarchy	disorder due to absence of authority	अराजकता
Animosity	strong hostility	बैर, दुश्मनी
Antique	ancient, very old	प्राचीन, पुरावस्तु
Anti-semitism	hatred of Jewish people	यहूदियों से नफरत की भावना
Anxious	unease; worrisome	चिंतित
Apathetic	uninterested	उदासीन

Apathy	lack of interest	विरक्ति, उदासीनता
Appalling	awful; terrible	डरावना
Appease	to pacify or placate	शांत करना, संतुष्ट करना
Apposite	appropriate; suitable	उचित
Apprentice	a trainee	प्रशिक्षु
Articulate	express (an idea or feeling) fluently coherently	स्पष्ट व्यक्त करना
Artificial	not natural	कृत्रिम
Asceticism	severely self-disciplined and secluded	संन्यास
Assent	express approval or agreement	अनुमति देना
Assert	state a fact confidently attributes	जोर देना
Audacious	courageous; bold	साहसी
Autonomous	having self-government	स्वायत्त, स्वयं-शासन
Autonomy	self-goverenance	स्वराज्य
Awkward	clumsy	भद्दा
Barbarous	cruel, brutal	क्रूर, निर्दयी
Barren	unproductive	बंजर
Bemoan	express discontent	शोक करना
Benediction	bestowing of a blessing	आर्शीवाद, मंगलकामना
Benefactor	benevolent	उपकारी
Bleak	without colour; pale	बेरंग
Blocked	to make the movement impossible	अवरोधित करना, रोकना
Bluntly	abruptly; in a direct way	दो टूक, स्पष्टतया
Boisterous	noisy, energetic, and cheerful	उत्साही
Boon	blessing	वरदान
Boorish	rough and bad-mannered	अशिष्ट, असभ्य
Brave	showing courage	बहादुर
Brawl	noisy fight or quarrel	झगड़ा
Break off	cause to pieces	तोड़ देना
Breakdown	a physical, mental, or nervous collapse,	हत्तोत्साहित होना, खराब होना
Callous	insensitive and cruel	कठोर, क्रुर
Camaraderie	mutual trust and friendship	मित्रता, सौहार्द
Candid	truthful and straightforward, frank	निष्कपट, सच्चा
Capture	to take control; to seize	कब्जा कर लेना
Carefree	free from responsibility	अल्हड़, मस्त
Careless	not giving sufficient attention	लापरवाह
Cautious	careful and attentive	सावधान
Censure	to express severe disapproval	निंदा करना
Cessation	ending or being brought to an end	समाप्ति, रोक

Chaotic	of complete confusion and disorder.	कोलाहलपूर्ण, अराजक
Chivalry	courageousness	साहस, हिम्मत
Choke	cause severe difficulty in breathing	दम घोटना
Chronic	persisting for a long time	पुराना, स्थायी
Clasp	an embrace	आलिंगन, पकड़
Clinch	grapple	पकड़ना, जकड़ लेना
Collapse	falling down	गिरना
Commence	To begin or start	प्रारंभ करना
Commencement	a beginning or start	प्रारंभ, शुरूआत
Commencing	begining	प्रारंभ करना
Commotion	noisy disturbance	हो-हल्ला, शोर-गुल
Complexity	the state of being complicated	जटिलता
Compliance	adherence to the command	अनुपालन, आज्ञाकारिता
Conceal	keep from sight, hide	छिपाना
Concealment	the action of hiding	छिपाना
Conceited	excessively proud of oneself	घमंडी
Conclude	bring to an end	समाप्त करना
Conclusive	decisive; providing an end	अंतिम रूप देना
Concur	to agree	सहमत होना
Confession	admitting of being guilty	दोष स्वीकृति
Confiscate	take or seize	जब्त करना
Conformity	compliance with standards, rules, or laws	अनुपालन, समरूपता
Conscientious	very careful	सजग, विवेकपूर्ण
Consecration	a religious ceremony	धार्मिक अनुष्ठान
Consensus	general agreement	आम सहमति
Considerable	worth consideration	विचारनीय
Consolidated	combined; united	संगठित, सम्मलित
Consoling	giving solace	सांत्वना देना
Contaminate	to make impure	दूषित करना
Contempt	hate or disrespect	नफरत करना
Content	in a state of peaceful happiness.	संतुष्ट
Contented	happy and at ease	संतुष्ट, खुश
Contract	a written or spoken agreement	अनुबंध
Contrast	differ from	के विपरीत होना, अलग होना
Controversial	likely to public disagreement	विवादास्पद
Controvert	deny the truth of (something)	खंडन करना
Convalescence	recovery from an illness	स्वास्थ्य लाभ
Converge	come together	मिलना
Convicted	found guilty	दोषसिद्ध, अपराधी

Convoluted	extremely complex	जटिल
Cosmetic	Related to beauty products	सौन्दर्य संबंधी
Cosmopolitan	familiar with many different countries and culture	विश्व नागरिक
Crooked	bent or twisted	टेढ़ा, मुड़ा हुआ
Crumble	break or fall apart	टुकड़े-टुकडे होना
Curtail	reduce	कम करना, घटाना
Dabbler	an amateur	शौकीया
Dazzling	extremely bright	बहुत चमकीला, चकाचौंध भरा
Debasement	degrading or adulteration	पतन, अवनति
Decay	process of rotting	सड़ना
Deceitful	deceiving or misleading	छली, कपटी
Decelerate	slow down	धीमे करना
Degenerate	decline or deteriorate physically	खत्म हो जाना
Delete	remove	मिटाना
Demolish	to pull or knock down	ध्वस्त करना
Denigration	To make (something or someone) seem less important or valuable	बदनामी
Dense	closely compacted	घना
Deny	refuse to admit the truth	इनकार करना
Dependent	relying on	आश्रित
Deportation	Sending to exile	देश निकाला, निर्वासन
Depressed	in a state of despondency	उदास, निराश
Descend	move or fall downward.	नीचे गिरना, नीचे उतरना
Descent	an action of moving downward	अवरोहण, नीचे गिरना
Desecration	disrespect towards sacred things	असहिष्णुता, अनादर
Despair	loose hope	नाउम्मीद होना
Despondency	loss of hope or courage	निराशा, मायूसी
Detain	Hold or take into custody	रोके रखना, हिरासत में लेना
Determinant	decisive factor	निर्णायक
Deterrent	discouraging	उत्साह भंग करने वाला
Detest	to dislike intensely	घृणा करना
Diffidence	modesty or shyness	संशय, हिचकिचाहट
Diffident	modest or shy	संकोची
Dignity	honour or respect	गरिमा, मर्यादा
Diligent	industrious	परिश्रमी, मेहनती
Diluted	weak or thinner	पतला
Dim	not shining brightly	धुंधला
Diminished	made smaller or less	कम किया हुआ

Diplomatic	marked by tact in dealing with sensitive matters or people	व्यवहार कुशल
Discordant	disagreeing	असंगत, प्रतिकूल
Discreet	careful and prudent	बुद्धिमान
Disgorge	to pour out or eject	उगलना, उड़ेलना
Dismal	depressing	निराशाजनक
Disorderly	untidy	अस्त-व्यस्त
Disparagement	depreciation or derogation	अपमानित या निंदा करना
Disperse	scatter or disseminate	फैलना
Disputable	open to question or debate	विवादास्पद
Dissolution	the closing down or dismissal	विघटन
Dissolve	close down or dismiss	समाप्त करना
Distinct	well-defined and unique	विशिष्ट
Divergent	tending to be in different directions	विभिन्न
Dormant	inactive	निष्क्रिय, शिथिल
Duplicity	deceitfulness; double-dealing	कपट, छल
Durable	long-lasting	टिकाऊ, स्थायी
Dynamic	progressive or constantly changeable	प्रगतिशील, परिवर्तनशील
Economical	using money carefully	किफायती, मितव्ययी
Ecstasy	overwhelming happiness	अति उत्साह
Elated	very happy	प्रसन्न
Elevation	fact of raising	उत्थान, उन्नति
Eloquent	fluent in speaking or writing	लिखने और बोलने में सहज
Elusive	difficult to catch	हाथ न आने वाला
Emancipate	set free	स्वतंत्र करना
Embark upon	to launch	शुरुआत करना
Embellish	to decorate	संवारना, सजाना
Eminent	famous and respected	प्रसिद्ध, सम्माननीय
Encomium	piece of writing that praises someone	तारीफो के पुलींदे
Enduring	continuing or long-lasting	टिकाऊ
Enervate	to weaken	कमजोर करना
Enlightened	having a rational, modern and well-informed outlook	प्रबुद्ध, उन्मुख
Ephemeral	lasting for a very short time	अल्पकालिक
Erosion	the process of gradually wearing away	कटाव, अपरदन
Escalate	increase rapidly	बढ़ाना, अधिक करना
Escalating	increasing rapidly	तीव्र, बढ़ता हुआ
Esteem	respect and admiration	सम्मान
Eternal	lasting or existing forever	चिरकालिक, स्थायी

Evanescent	soon passing out of sight, memory	क्षणभंगुर, अस्थायी
Evident	obvious	प्रत्यक्ष, स्पष्ट
Exaggerate	represent as bigger or greater	बढ़ा-चढ़ा कर कहना
Exceptional	unusual	असाधारण
Exclusion	act of excluding	बहिष्कार
Exempt	free from an obligation	मुक्त
Exemptions	state of being free from an obligation	मुक्ति
Exhibit	to show or display	प्रदर्शित करना
Exonerate	absolve from blame	दोष मुक्त करना
Exonerate	release someone from (a duty or obligation)	मुक्त करना
Exoneration	release or free from blame	दोषमुक्ति, छुटकारा
Exotic	very different, strange, or unusual	अनोखा
Expand	to extend	विस्तार करना
Expedite	speed up or accelerate	शीघ्रता करना
Explicit	clear and detailed	स्पष्ट
Exquisite	extremely beautiful	अति सुंदर
Extol	to praise	प्रशंसा करना
Extravagant	spending money recklessly	फिजूलखर्ची
Fabulous	extraordinary	शानदार
Facilitate	to make easy	सरल बनाना
Factual	truthful, accurate	तथ्यपूर्ण, वास्तविक
Faint	a sudden loss of consciousness	बेहोशी
Falling off	to drop	गिरना, कम होना
Fallow	barren	बंजर
Famous	known	प्रसिद्ध
Fantastic	extremely good, excellent	शानदार
Far-fetched	unlikely and unconvincing	अव्यवहारिक, अवास्तविक
Fastidious	Hard to please	नखरेबाज़
Fatigucd	tired or exhausted	थका हुआ
Feasible	possible to do easily or conveniently	व्यावहारिक, होने योग्य
Feeble	lacking physical strength	दुर्बल, कमजोर
Ferocity	quality of being ferocious	क्रूरता
Fertile	fruitful or productive	उपजाऊ
Fetter	restrain with chains or manacles feudal system to work on his lord's estate	बेड़ी डालना
Fickle	changing frequently	चंचल, अस्थिर
Fictitious	not real or true	काल्पनिक, बनावटी
Flair	a natural talent or ability	प्रतिभा, योग्यता
Flamboyant	showy or elaborate	भड़कीला, आडंबरपूर्ण

Flattery	excessive and insincere praise	खुशामद
Flawless	perfect	त्रुटिरहित
Fleeting	lasting for a very short time	क्षणिक
Flexible	adjustable, not rigid	लचीला
Flourish	to grow	फलना-फूलना
Forbid	refuse to allow (something)	मना करना
Fragrant	having a pleasant or sweet smell.	सुगंधित
Frailty	weakness	निर्बलता, कमजोरी
Frugal	economical with regard to money	मितव्ययी, कंजूस
Fussy	anxious over accuracy to details	नखरेबाज़
Futile	fruitless or pointless	निष्फल, व्यर्थ
Garrulous	excessively talkative	बातूनी
Genial	friendly and kind	हंसमुख
Genuine	true; authentic	वास्तविक, सच्चा
Glimmering	shining faintly with a wavering light	झिलमिलाना, टिमटिमाना
Gloomy	dark or poorly lit	उदासी भरा, अंधकारमय
Glossy	shiny and smooth	चमकदार
Graceful	elegant	सुंदर
Grandiose	impressive or magnificent	अतिसुन्दर, असाधारण
Gratuitous	given or done free of charge	निशुल्क
Gravity	seriousness	गंभीरता
Gregarious	fond of company; sociable	सामाजिक
Grim	unpleasant or shocking	उदास, अप्रिय
Guilty	blameworthy	अपराधी, दोषी
Half-heartedly	lacking spirit or interest	बूझे मन से
Ham-fisted	clumsy; not dextrous	अनाड़ी, बेढ़ंगा
Harmonious	tuneful; not discordant	लयबद्ध, एक स्वर में
Harmony	peaceful existence and agreement	सामंजस्य, सहमति
Hastily	with excessive urgency; hurriedly	शीघ्रतापूर्वक
Haughty	proud and arrogant	अभिमानी, घमंडी
Hazy	vague or opaque	धुंधला
Heckle	to interrupt by aggressive comments	बीच में टोकना, बात काटना
Heedless	lacking care	लापरवाह
Hereditary	conferred by inheritance	अनुवांशिक, पुश्तैनी
Heretical	contrary to orthodox religious doctrine	विधर्मी
Hilarious	extremely amusing	हास्यपूर्ण
Hinder	to obstruct	बाधा डालना
Hollow	having empty space inside	खोखला
Humble	modest	विनम्र

Humdrum	dullness; monotony	नीरस
Humility	modesty humbleness	विनम्रता
Idealistic	of perfect or judicious standard	आदर्शवादी
Ignited	bursting into flames	जलता हुआ
Ignorant	lacking knowledge	अनभिज्ञ
Ill-fated	destined to have bad luck	बदकिस्मत
Illusory	not real	भ्रामक
Illustrious	well known	प्रसिद्ध
Immune	protected; unaffected	प्रतिरक्षित
Imperil	to put in a danger	खतरे में डालना
Impersonate	imitate or copy	नकल करना
Impertinent	not showing proper respect	धृष्ट, अशिष्ट
Impetuosity	rash impulsiveness	उतावलापन
Impious	sinful or wicked	अधर्मी, व्याभिचारी
Implicate	to involve or embroil	फंसाना, उलझाना
Implication	a possible meaning	निहितार्थ, आशय
Implicit	implied or hinted	अंतर्निहित
Impose	force or inflict to accept	थोपना, मढ़ना
In toto	completely or totally	पूर्ण रूप से
Inaugurate	begin or introduce	उद्घाटन, शुभारंभ
Inclusion	the action of including	समावेश
Incoherent	incomprehensible or confusing	बेतुका
Inconspicuous	not attracting attention	तुच्छ, जो उल्लेखनीय न हो
Inconspicuous	unnoticeable	तुच्छ, ध्यान में ना आने वाला
Incredible	unbelievable	अविश्वसनीय
Incriminatory	suggestive of guilt or blame	अभियोग के लायक
Inculcate	instill an idea in mind	कोई बात मन में बैठा लेना
Indecisive	not settling an issue	अनिर्णायक, दुविधा में पड़ा हुआ
Indifferent	uninterested	उदासीन, तटस्थ
Indisposition	reluctance	अनिच्छा, अरूचि
Indisputable	unable to be challenged	निर्विवाद
Inert	not moving, still	स्थिर, गतिहीन
Inevitable	certain to happen, unavoidable	अपरिहार्य
Infer	To conclude	निष्कर्ष निकालना
Infirmity	physical or mental weakness	दुर्बलता
Ingest	to take something into the body	निगलना
Initial	occurring at the beginning	प्रारंभिक
Initiated	started	पहल/आरंभ किया हुआ
Innovate	to introduce something new	अविष्कार करना

Inseparable	unable to be separated	अलग न होने योग्य
Insolent	showing a rude and arrogant lack of respect	असभ्य
Instigate	To initiate or provoke	भड़काना
Intemperate	uncontrolled	असंयमी
Intentional	deliberate	जान-बूझकर किया हुआ
Interpolate	interpolate something to make a remark	लगाना, जोड़ना
Interpretation	explanation of the meaning	व्याख्या
Intimidating	frightening	डरावना
Invigorate	give strength or energy to	मजबूत बनाना
Irreverent	disrespectful	अपमानजनक
Isolation	seclusion, separatedness	अलगाव
Jest	a joke or humour	हंसी-मजाक
Jocular	humorous or playful	हास्यपूर्ण
Juggler	a person who juggles	हाथों की सफाई दिखाने वाला
Jugular	relating to the throat or neck	कंठ संबंधी
Laceration	a deep cut or tear in skin or flesh	घाव, चीरा
Latent	hidden or concealed	छुपा हुआ
Latter	being the second of the two	बाद वाला, दूसरा
Laudable	deserving praise	प्रशंसनीय
Laudatory	expressing praise and commendation.	प्रशंसनीय
Lavishly	extravagantly impressive	संपन्न रूप से
Legalise	make permissible by law.	वैध करना
Lenient	merciful or tolerant	उदार, दयालु
Liberalisation	the act of making less strict	उदारीकरण
Liberate	set free	मुक्त करना
Libertine	Immoral	अनैतिक
Liberty	freedom	स्वतंत्रता, आजादी
Loathing	intense dislike or disgust	घृणा
Loquacious	talkative	बातूनी
Lucid	easy to understand	स्पष्ट अर्थ का
Luminous	bright or shining	प्रकाशमान, चमकीला
Lurid	very vivid in colour,	भड़कीला
lustrous	shining	चमकीला
Magnify	make (something) appear larger	बढ़ाना
Maladjusted	disturbed	विक्षुब्ध
Maladroit	clumsy or awkward	बेढंगा, फुहड़
Malevolent	malicious or hostile	दुर्भावनापूर्ण
Malice	ill will	द्वेष
Malignant	malevolent	दुष्ट, कपटी

Manifest	to display or show matters or people	व्यक्त करना, प्रदर्शन करना
Meagre	scarce	थोड़ा, कम
Mellifluous	sweet; pleasant to hear	मधुर
Melodious	tunefully	मधुर
Melody	something musically satisfying	लय
Mendicant	a beggar	निर्धन, भिखारी
Merry	cheerful and lively	प्रसन्न
Meticulous	very careful and precise	सूक्ष्म/तीक्ष्ण बुद्धि वाला
Misery	a state of great distress	कष्ट, दुर्गति
Mitigate	make less severe or serious	कम करना, शांत करना
Moderate	average	मध्यम
Monotonous	dull, tedious, and repetitious	नीरस, उबाऊ
Monotony	lack of variety and interest	नीरसता, उबाऊ
Morose	sullen and ill-tempered	उदास
Mortal	subjected to death	नश्वर
Murky	dark and gloomy	अंधकारमय, उदासीन
Nervous	easily agitated or anxious	परेशान, घबराया हुआ
Niggardly	not generouly	कंजूसी से
Notorious	infamous	कुख्यात, बदनाम
Notorious	infamous	कुख्यात
Novice	a beginner	नौसिखिया
Obscene	indecent or filthy	अश्लील, गंदा
Obscure	not discovered or known about	अज्ञात
Obscure	not discovered or known about, uncertain	अस्पष्ट
Obstinacy	stubbornness	जिद, हठ
Obstruction	hindrance or intervention	बाधा, रूकावट
Odious	extremely unpleasant, repulsive	घिनौना
Often	frequently, many times	प्रायः
Opaque	not transparent.	अपारदर्शी, धुंधला
Opposed	against	विपक्षी
Oppressive	cruel and unfair	अत्याचारी, दमनकारी
Orderly	neatly and methodically arranged	व्यवस्थित, क्रमबद्ध
Orthodox	conservative or traditional	रूढ़िवादी
Ostentatious	showy or pretentious	आडंम्बरपूर्ण, दिखावटी
Ostracise	exclude (someone) from a society or group outlook	बहिष्कृत करना
Outpace	to surpass	आगे निकल जाना
Outspokenness	frankness	शब्दों की मुखरता

Palpitation	a physical condition in which your heart beats very quickly and in an irregular way	थरथराना, कंपकंपी
Pandemonium	wild and noisy disorder	कोलाहल, शोरगुल
Parallel	equally distant	समानांतर
Parsimonious	miserly, niggardly	कंजूस
Pathetic	arousing pity	दयनीय
Paucity	scarcity	कमी
Pensive	deeply or seriously thoughtful	विचारमग्न, चिंताग्रस्त
Perilous	fraught with danger	जोखिम भरा
Perish	pass from physical life and lose all bodily	नष्ट हो जाना
Permanent	ever lasting	चिरस्थायी
Perpetual	never ending	निरंतर, चिरस्थायी
Perspicacity	wisdom, discernment	सूझ-बूझ, बुद्धिमानी
Persuade	to convince	मनाना, राजी करना
Persuasion	the act of persuading people	मनाना, समझाना-बुझाना
Persuasive	convincing	यकीन दिलाने वाला
Pessimistic	tending to see the darker aspect of life	निराशावादी
Philistine	one who has no liking for art and culture	कला-संस्कृति से नफरत करने वाला
Pitiable	deserving pity	दयनीय
Plain	simple or ordinary	सामान्य
Plausible	reasonable or probable	तार्किक, स्वीकार्य
Plea	petition or request	दलील
Possessed	belonged to or in control	के अधीन, नियंत्रण में
Potent	powerful	प्रबल
Precise	exact or accurate	यथावत्, सटीक
Predator	one who ruthlessly exploits others	शोषण करने वाला
Predecessor	previous or that comes before	पूर्ववर्ती
Predilection	liking, fondness	झुकाव
Prevent	obstruct or hinder	रोकना, निध करना
Probity	honesty and decency	ईमानदारी
Proceed	begin or continue	बढ़ना, चालू करना
Procrastinate	delay or postpone	टालना
Prodigious	enormous or huge	बहुत बड़ा
Profound	showing great knowledge or insight	प्रगाढ़, प्रचुर
Progressive	happening or developing gradually	प्रगतिशील
Prohibit	forbid by law or rule	निषेध करना
Prominent	important; famous	महत्वपूर्ण, प्रसिद्ध
Propagate	spread and promote	प्रचार करना

Propriety	relating to an owner or ownership.	मालिकाना, आधिपत्य संबंधी
Prosperity	richness	समृद्धि
Prosperous	rich	धनी, समृद्ध
Protean	ever-changing or variable	परिवर्तनशील
Prudent	wise and modest	विवेकपूर्ण
Purposely	on purpose; intentionally	जान-बूझकर
Quiescent	inactive or quiet	मौन, स्थिर
Quiet	not talking much	शांत
Radiant	shining or glowing brightly.	चमकीला, प्रकाशमान
Rapid	fast	तीव्र
Rapidly	quickly	तेजी से, शीघ्रता
Realistic	true to life, practical	वास्तविक, यथार्थ
Recede	retreat or go back	पीछे हटना
Reckless	careless	लापरवाह
Recluse	favouring a solitary life	सन्यासी
Recuperation	recovery from illness	रोग से मुक्ति
Regress	returning to a former state	वापस लौटना (पुरानी अवस्था में)
Remorse	deep regret or guilt	पश्चाताप
Repel	to cause dislike	नापसंद करना
Repining	feeling discontent	विलाप करना, शोक मनाना
Repulsion	intense dislike	अरूचि, घृणा
Repulsive	distasteful	अप्रिय, अरुचिकर
Resolute	determined	दृढ़
Retain	continue to have (something)	रखे रहना, बनाए रहना
Retribution	punishment for wrong doing	दण्ड
Retrogressive	causing a return to an earlier state	पुर्व स्थिति में लौटता हुआ
Reveal	make known to others	प्रकट करना
Revelation	disclosure of surprising fact	रहस्योद्घाटन
Reverence	deep respect	सम्मान, आदर
Reverent	respectful	शिष्ट, सम्माननीय
Sanctify	to make holy	शुद्ध करना
Sanguine temper	cheerful mood	हंसमुख व्यक्तित्व
Scorn	contempt, hatred	घृणा
Seclusion	Solitude	अकेलापन, एकांतता
Segregate	isolate or divide	अलग करना, बाँटना
Segregation	Isolation or detachment	अलगाव, पृथक्करण
Serenity	peacefulness	शांति
Serfdom	an agricultural laborer bound under the feudal system to work on his lord's estate	कृषिदासिता

Sever	divide by cutting	काटकर अलग करना
Shallow	of little depth	उथला
Shimmering	a flashing of light	जगमगाना
Shrinkage	the process of becoming smaller in size	सिकुड़न
Significant	noteworthy	महत्वपूर्ण
Singularity	the quality of being one of a kind	विलक्षणता
Slander	make false statements	बदनाम करना
Smug	having an excessive pride in oneself	दंभी
Sneer	make a contemptuous or mocking remark	उपहास करना
Sober	serious and sensible	संयमी, गंभीर
Sparse	thinly dispersed	घना नही होना
Spoil	destroy the value or quality of.	बिगाड़ देना
Sporadic	occurring at irregular intervals	रूक-रूक कर होने वाला
Spurious	fraudulent or fake	नकली, भ्रामक
Staunch	loyal and committed	निष्ठावान
Steadfast	firm and unwavering	दृढ़, अडीग
Stimulate	to trigger or invoke	उत्तेजित करना, उकसाना
Stingy	miserly or not generous	कंजूस
Strife	angry or bitter disagreement	झगड़ा, विवाद
Sublime	of great excellence	उत्कृष्ट
Submissiveness	politeness or humbleness	विनम्रता
Substantial	of considerable importance or size	पर्याप्त
Successor	the one who succeeds	उत्तराधिकारी, बाद में आने वाला
Suffice	be enough or adequate	पूरा करना
Superficial	having little depth	सतही, आधा-अधूरा
Synthetic	made by chemical synthesis	कृत्रिम, बनावटी
Taciturn	reserved	अल्पभाषी
Taint	contaminate or pollute	दुषित करना
Take off	get off the ground,	उड़ना
Taper	cause to diminish in thickness	पतला करना
Temporal	relating to worldly affairs	संसारिक
Tempt	To attract or entice	लुभाना, लालच देना
Terminal	last or concluding	चरम, अंतिम
Terminate	bring to an end	समाप्त करना
Thorough	careful and accurate	तीक्ष्ण बुद्धिमतापूर्ण
Thrifty	frugal	मितव्ययी, कंजूस
To put up with	To tolerate	बर्दाश्त करना
Tolerance	ability or willingness to bear something	सहनशीलता
Tranquillity	peacefulness	शांति

Transition	change or transformation	परिवर्तन
Transitory	not permanent	अस्थायी
Treachery	betrayal of trust	विश्वासघात
Treason	the crime of betraying one's country	राज-द्रोह
Trigger	cause to happen	उकसाना
Trivial	of little value	तुच्छ
Turncoat	a traitor	गद्दार
Uncompromising	unwillingness by changing one's ways or opinions	ढ़ीठ, अडीग
Understate	represent as less important	कम महत्व देना
Underwrite	guarantee financial support	आर्थिक सहायता का वादा करना
Uneven	not level or smooth	अनियमित, उबड़-खाबड़
Unintentionally	done without intention	अनजाने में
Unjust	not just or fair	अनुचित
Unnerved	having no courage or confidence	हतोत्साहित
Unscrupulous	not honest or fair	बेईमान
Urban	related to town	शहरी
Vague	of indefinite meaning	अस्पष्ट
Validate	check or prove the validity or accuracy of (something)	पुष्टि करना
Vehemence	strong feeling; passion	तीव्र भावना
Veiled	covered	ढ़का हुआ
Veneration	great respect	पूज्यभाव, आदर
Verbal	full of words	शब्दों की बहुलता
Vice	immoral or wicked behaviour	दोष, दुष्टता
Vicious	cruel or violent	क्रुर, भष्ट
Victor	A winner	विजेता
Vindictive	having desire for revenge	प्रतिशोधी
Virtue	high moral standards	सदाचार, नैतिक गुण
Virtuous	having high moral standards	भद्र, नेक
Vituperative	bitter and abusive	निंदापूर्ण, अलोचनात्मक
Vociferous	vehement or clamorous	मुखर, कोलाहलकारी
Vulnerable	susceptible	जिसे चोट पहुँचाना आसान हो
Wavering	shaking or quivering	थरथराना, काँपना
Weary	tired or exhausted	थका हुआ
Yield to	to surrender or give way	हार मान लेना, स्वीकार
Yielding	willing to do	मान लेने वाला, जो झुक जाए
Zeal	great energy or enthusiasm	उत्साह, उमंग

CHAPTER

29 ONE WORD SUBSTITUTION

MEANINGS

S.N.	WORD	हिन्दी में अर्थ	Meaning in English
1.	**Abattoir**	कसाईखाना	Place where animals are killed for food.
2.	**Abbot**	मठाधिकारी/ मठाधीश	A man who is the head of a monastery or an abbey.
3.	**Abbreviation**	संक्षेप/ लघुरूप	A shortened form of a word or phrase. Eg:- Engg. for Engineering
4.	**Abdication**	औपचारिक रूप से त्याग देना	To formally give up.
5.	**Ablution**	धार्मिक स्नान	Ritual washing of the body.
6.	**Abstruse**	समझने में मुश्किल	Hard to understand.
7.	**Abundance**	प्रचुरता	A quantity that is more than enough.
8.	**Accentuate**	जोर देना	Give more force or importance to.
9.	**Accomplice**	सह-अपराधी	partner in crime.
10.	**Acronym**	प्रथमाक्षरी नाम	Word formed from initial letters of a name. Eg: MP for Member of Parliament
11.	**Addendum**	परिशिष्ट	Things to be added at the end of a book, notification etc.
12.	**Advertisement**	विज्ञापन	A public notice offering or asking for goods, services etc.
13.	**Afforestation**	वनारोपन	The act of forestation by planting many trees.
14.	**Agenda**	घोषणा पत्र	Items of business for consideration at a meeting.
15.	**Aggressor**	आक्रमणकर्ता	Someone who attacks first.
16.	**Agnosticism**	ईश्वर के अश्तित्व पर शंका	Doubtful about the existence of God.
17.	**Alien**	गैर-नागरिक	One who belongs to different country, race, group or planet.
18.	**Alimony**	तलाक पश्चात् की जीवन वृति	Allowance fixed after divorce to a wife.
19.	**Allegory**	प्रतीक कथा	Story in which ideas are symbolized as people.
20.	**Alliteration**	अनुप्रास	Commencement of adjacent words with the same letter. Eg: Peter Piper picked a peck of pickled peppers.

21. **Altruist** .... परोपकारी .... One who lives and works for the welfare of others.
22. **Amateur** .... गैर-पेशेवर...................... Not professional.
23. **Ambassador** .... राजदूत .... A diplomatic representative of one country in another.
24. **Ambidextrous** .... दोनों हाथों से निपुण .... Equally skillful with each hand.
25. **Ambiguous** .... अस्पष्ट/ दो अर्थो वाला......... Having more than one possible meaning
26. **Amnesia** .... विस्मरण .... Loss of memory.
27. **Amnesty** .... अपराध-क्षमा .... A general pardon to political offenders.
28. **Amphibian** .... उभयचर .... Animals which live both on land and in water.
29. **Amphitheatre** .... अखाड़ा/ रंगभूमि .... A circular building without a roof and with rows of seats that rise in steps around an open space.
30. **Analgesia** .... दर्द की अनुभूति न होना .... The loss of ability to feel pain while still conscious.
31. **Anarchist** .... अराजक .... One who wishes to destroy all established government's law and order.
32. **Anarchy** .... अराजकता .... The absence of government in a country.
33. **Anecdote** .... किस्सा .... Short amusing story about some real person or event.
34. **Anniversary** .... साल गिरह........................ Yearly return of the date of an event.
35. **Annual** .... सालाना .... That which happens once in a year.
36. **Anomaly** .... असाधारण .... Deviation from common rule or standard.
37. **Anonymous** .... गुमनाम........................... A book or a work of art whose author is not known.
38. **Antagonist** .... विरोधी .... One that opposes other.
39. **Antidote** .... जहर-नाशक...................... A medicine to cure the effect of poison.
40. **Aphasia** .... वाचाघात......................... Loss of ability to understand or produce speech.
41. **Apostate** .... धर्म त्यागी .... One who abandons his religious faith.
42. **Aquatic** .... जलीय............................. Animals that live in water.
43. **Arbitrator/ Arbiter** .. मध्यस्थ .... Someone chosen to judge and decide a disputed issue.
44. **Aristocracy** .... कुलीन तंत्र....................... A government by the nobles.
45. **Armistice** .... युद्ध विराम .... The cessation of warfare before a treaty is signed.
46. **Ascetic** .... सन्यासी .... One who practices self denial as a spiritual discipline.
47. **Assassination** .... राजनैतिक कारण से हत्या...... Killing or murder for political reasons.
48. **Astrology** .... ज्योतिष शास्त्र .... Science of the influence of the stars on our destiny.

49. **Astronomy** .... खगोल विज्ञान .... Science of universe with sun, moon, stars and planets.
50. **Atheist** .... नास्तिक .... A person who does not believe in the existence of God.
51. **Audience** .... श्रोता-गण .... An assembly of listeners.
52. **Autobiography** .... आत्म जीवनी .... The life-history of a man written by himself.
53. **Autocracy** .... एकतंत्र........................... A government by one person.
54. **Avaricious** .... लालची........................... One who is greedy.
55. **Bachelorhood** .... कुवांरापन .... The state of being unmarried (of a man).
56. **Bankrupt/Insolvent**. दिवालिया .... A person unable to pay his debts.
57. **Bay** .... खाड़ी .... A part of the sea enclosed by a wide curve of the shore.
58. **Beach** .... समुद्र तट .... A stretch of sand/ stones along the edge of the sea/ lake.
59. **Bellicose** .... लड़ाकू.......................... A person who is fond of fighting.
60. **Belligerent**.............. युद्धरत .... Engaged in war/fight.
61. **Benefactor** .... धर्मोपकारी .... One who gives financial help to a school, hospital, etc.
62. **Bibliophile** .... पुस्तक प्रेमी .... One who loves and collects books.
63. **Biennial** .... द्विवर्षीय .... That happens once in two years.
64. **Biannual** .... साल में दो बार .... That happens twice a year
65. **Bigamy** .... दो विवाह प्रथा .... The custom of having two wives or two husbands.
66. **Bigot** .... कट्टर .... One who is filled with narrow and prejudiced opinion.
67. **Bilingual** .... द्विभाषिय........................ One who can speak two languages.
68. **Biography**................ जीवनी .... The life-history of a man written by someone else.
69. **Biped**......................... दोपाया .... Animal with two-feet.
70. **Blasphemy** .... ईश्वर के खिलाफ बोलना ...... Speaking irreverently about God or sacred things.
71. **Bliss** .... चरमसुख........................ Perfect happiness, ecstasy, euphoria
72. **Bohemian**................. स्वेच्छाचारी .... One who does not follow the usual norms of social life.
73. **Bookworm/Bibliophilic** पुस्तक प्रेमी .... One who is interested in reading books.
74. **Boorish** .... गंवार............................. Person who is rough and ill mannered.
75. **Botany** .... वनस्पति विज्ञान .... The science of vegetable life.
76. **Brittle** .... जो आसानी से टूट जाऐ........ A thing which can be easily broken.
77. **Bureaucracy**............. नौकरशाही .... A government by the officials.
78. **Cabaret**..................... कैबरे नृत्य .... A series of a type of dance performance.
79. **Cabby, Cab driver**.... ट्रैक्सी चालक .... The driver of a taxi cab.
80. **Cacophony** .... कोलाहल........................ Harsh mixture of sound.

81. **Cajole** .... खुशामद करना .... Persuade by flattery.
82. **Calligraphy** .... सुलेखन .... Art of beautiful hand writing.
83. **Cannibal** .... जो अपनी प्रजाति का ही भक्षण करें .... That eats one's own species
84. **Catacomb** .... कब्र/एक दूसरे से संबंधित ..... an underground place where people are buried/ a complex set of interrelated things.
85. **Capsize** .... पलटना .... Overturn in water.
86. **Carnage** .... हत्याकांड .... Killing of large numbers of people.
87. **Carnival** .... मनोरंजन मेला .... Public merry making and feasting.
88. **Cartography** .... मानचित्र कला .... Art of map making.
89. **Catalogue** .... पुस्तक सूची .... List of books and other articles.
90. **Celibate** .... ब्रह्मचारी .... One who has taken a vow not to have sex.
91. **Cemetery** .... कब्रिस्तान .... The place for corpses to be buried.
92. **Centenary** .... शताब्दी .... Hundredth anniversary.
93. **Chronological** .... समय के क्रमानुसार .... According to sequence of time.
94. **Circumlocution** .... घुमा-फिरा के बात करना ...... A roundabout way of speaking.
95. **Cloakroom** .... माल गोदाम .... The place for luggage at a railway station.
96. **Coerce** .... मजबूर करना .... Compel to a course of action.
97. **Cognate** .... एक ही उत्पत्ति के .... Having the same source or origin.
98. **Colleagues** .... सहकर्मी .... Persons working in the same department.
99. **Collusion** .... कपट सन्धि .... Secret agreement for a fraudulent purpose.
100. **Conflagration** .... भीषण अग्निकांड .... Huge destructive fire.
101. **Congregation** .... धर्म-संगति .... Gathering of worshippers.
102. **Congruent** .... सर्वांगसम .... Identical in all respects.
103. **Connoisscur** .... कला का पारखी .... Onc who is wcll-vcrscd in any art.
104. **Conscription** .... अनिवार्य सैनिक सेवा .... Compulsory service in military.
105. **Contagious** .... संक्रामक .... Which spreads by physical touch or contact.
106. **Contemporary** .... समकालीन .... Of the same time.
107. **Contiguous** .... समीपस्थ .... Sharing a common boundary.
108. **Contrite** .... पश्चात्तापी .... Showing deep sorrow for wrong doing.
109. **Convalescence** .... पुनःस्वास्थ्य प्राप्ति के बाद ...... The period of gradual recovery of health after illness.
110. **Conventicle** .... गुप्त व गैरकानूनी धर्मसभा ..... Secret and illegal religious meeting.
111. **Coquette** .... दिलफेंक महिला .... A seductive woman who uses her sex appeal to exploit men.
112. **Coronation** .... राज्याभिषेक .... Ceremony of crowning a king.
113. **Cosmopolitan** .... जो दुनिया में कहीं भी बिना किसी समस्या के रह ले .... A person who feels at home in every part of the world
114. **Credulous** .... सहजविश्वासी .... One who is simple and easily believes whatever is told to him, gullible.

115. **Crematory**	श्मशान घाट	The place where dead bodies are burnt.
116. **Cripple**	अपंग/अपंग बनाना	Someone who is unable to walk normally because of an injury or disability to the legs or back.
117. **Curfew**	कर्फ्यू	An order prohibiting activities/ movements.
118. **Cynosure**	आकर्षण-बिन्दु	Centre of attraction.
119. **Demagogue**	जनोत्तेजक	Political leader who delivers sentimental speeches to seek support of the people.
120. **Democracy**	लोकतंत्र	A government by the people, of the people, and for the people.
121. **Denizen**	निवासी	A person, an animal or a plant that lives, grows or is often found in a particular place.
122. **Depraved**	चरित्र भ्रष्ट	Morally bad or evil.
123. **Deprecate**	विरोध करना	Express disapproval of.
124. **Dermatology**	त्वचा विज्ञान	The study of skin and its diseases.
125. **Despondency**	निराशा	Loss of complete hope.
126. **Destitution**	अभावग्रस्तता	Lacking basic necessities of life.
127. **Detrimental**	हानिकर	Causing harm or damage.
128. **Dexterous**	कुशल	Skilful at handling things.
129. **Diatribe**	कटु-निन्दा	Bitter and violent attack in words or writing.
130. **Dictatorship**	तानाशाही/ निरंकुशता	Government carried on by an absolute ruler, despotism
131. **Diplomacy**	कूटनीति	The skill and policy of a country's statesmen and politicians/ skill in dealing with people.
132. **Discrepancy**	विसंगति	Difference between two things that should be the same.
133. **Dissimulate**	छिपाना	To hide or disguise.
134. **Diurnal**	दैनिक	Of the daytime.
135. **Draper**	कपड़े का कारोबारी	A shopkeeper selling cloth and clothing.
136. **Draw**	अनिर्णित	The result of the match where neither party wins.
137. **Dwarf**	बौना	A person, plant or animal who/which is below the usual size.
138. **Dynasty**	वंश	Succession of rulers belonging to one family.
139. **Eavesdropper**	चुपके से निजी वार्तालाप सुनने वाला	One who witnesses secretly to private conversation
140. **Economical**	किफायती	One who is careful in the use of money/ fuel etc.
141. **Edible**	खाने योग्य	That which is fit to be eaten.
142. **Effeminate**	औरताना गुण होना	A man who is womanish in his habits.

143. Egalitarianism .... समतावाद .... Belief that all people are equal and have the same rights and opportunities.
144. Egoist .... स्वार्थी .... selfish
145. Eligible .... योग्य .... Fit to be chosen; qualified.
146. Emergency .... आपातकाल .... A sudden serious situation requiring immediate action.
147. Emeritus .... ससम्मान सेवामुक्त व्यक्ति ...... One who is honourably discharged from service.
148. Emigrant .... प्रवासी .... A person who goes to another country to live.
149. Emissary .... प्रतिनिधि .... A person sent on a mission (usually official).
150. Epicure .... अच्छा खाने का शौकीन........ Person fond of delicious food.
151. Epidemic .... संक्रामक रोग.................... Disease infecting many people at the same place and time.
152. Epilogue .... नाटक के बाद का भाषण ..... A speech or a poem recited at the end of a play.
153. Episode .... कड़ी/ कथांश .... Part of story (especially of T.V. or Radio show)
154. Episodic .... कभी-कभी होने वाली घटना... Happening only some times and irregularly.
155. Epistle .... धर्मपत्र/ काव्यपत्र .... A letter.
156. Epitaph .... कब्र पर इंगित शब्द............ Words which are inscribed on the grave.
157. Epithet .... उपाधि विशेषक .... Adjective added to a person's name usually to criticise or praise him.
158. Epitome .... सटीक उदाहरण .... A perfect example.
159. Epitomize .... सटीक उदाहरण होना .... To be a perfect example.
160. Equanimity .... धैर्य .... Calmness of mind and temper.
161. Erotica .... अश्लील ग्रन्थ .... Books, pictures, etc. intended to arouse sexual desire.
162. Erudite .... विद्वान .... A learned or scholarly person.
163. Espionage .... जासूसी .... Practice of spying.
164. Eternal .... अनंत .... Existing for ever
165. Etymology .... शब्द-निर्माण विज्ञान............ The science which deals with derivation of words.
166. Euphemism .... कटु शब्दों के स्थान पर कम अप्रिय शब्दों का प्रयोग .. Usage of less offensive words in place of harsh language
167. Euphonious .... सुरीला .... Of pleasant sound.
168. Euphoria .... अत्यन्त खुशी..................... A strong feeling of happiness, ecstasy.
169. Evanescent .... अस्थायी .... Of a very short duration or period./ Ephemeral/Transient
170. Explicable .... विवेचनात्मक .... That which can be explained.
171. Extempore .... बिना तैयारी का भाषण .... A speech delivered without any preparation.
172. Extravaganza .... अतिशयी नाटक .... Activity which takes place in a very elaborate, colourful and expensive way.

173. Fallacy	भ्रम	False or mistaken belief.
174. Fanatic	अति उत्साहित	One who is filled with excessive and mistaken enthusiasm.
175. Fastidious	नखरेबाज	One who is hard to please.
176. Fatal	जानलेवा	Resulting in death, deadly
177. Fatalist	भाग्यवादी	One who believes in destiny.
178. Fauna	प्राणिजात	Animals of a certain region.
179. Feminist	नारीवादी	One who works for the welfare of women.
180. Fiasco	पूर्ण असफलता	Complete failure.
181. Flagstaff	ध्वजदण्ड	A long pole on which a flag is flown.
182. Flora	वनस्पति	All the plants of a particular area or period of time.
183. Fluke	आकस्मिक सफलता	Stroke of good luck.
184. Forgery	जालसाजी	Counterfeiting of document.
185. Fratricide	भ्रातृहत्या	Killing/killer of one's brother.
186. Frenzy	उन्माद	A state of extreme excitement.
187. Frostbite	शीतदंश	Injury to the nose, fingers or toes, caused by extreme cold.
188. Gallery	प्रदर्शनी स्थल	A room or building for showing works of art.
189. Gamble	जुआ खेलना	To play games of chance, for money.
190. Gastronomy	उत्तम आहार विज्ञान	Science and art of preparing and appreciating good food.
191. Genocide	जन संहार	Extermination of a race or community.
192. Geology	भूगर्भ विज्ञान	The science of earth's history and rocks.
193. Germicide	जीवाणु नाशक	A substance that kills germs.
194. Glutton	पेटू	One who eats too much.
195. Gobble	लालची की तरह खाना	Eat fast, noisly and greedily.
196. Gratis/Gratuitous	निःशुल्क	Done or obtained without payment.
197. Gregarious	समूह में रहने वाले	Animals that live in flocks, sociable
198. Hallucinogen	भ्रमित करने की दवा	A drug that causes one to hallucinate.
199. Hedonism	सुखवाद	Belief that the most important thing in the world is pleasure.
200. Henchman	ऐसा सेवक जो गैरकानूनी या हिंसात्मक कार्य भी कर सकता है	Servant who is employed to protect and who can even do things that are illegal or violent
201. Herbivorous	शाकाहारी	Animals that feed on vegetation.
202. Herculean	जिस कार्य में अति परिक्षम या बल की जरूरत हो	Requiring enormous strength or effort.
203. Heterogeneous	विषम	Things which contain elements of different nature.
204. Hexagon	षट्कोण	A plane figure with six sides and angles.

205. Holocaust .... विनाश .... Large scale destruction by fire, inferno, cataclysm, catastrophe disaster

206. Homicide .... मानव हत्या .... Murder of a man.

207. Homogeneous .... समांग .... Things which contain elements of the same nature.

208. Honorary .... अवैतनिक .... A post for which no salary is paid.

209. Horticulture .... बागवानी .... Art of growing vegetables, fruit, etc.

210. Hospitable .... मेहमाननवाज .... Friendly and welcoming to guests.

211. Hypochondria .... काल्पनिक बीमारी .... Imaginary ailments.

212. Iconoclast .... गैर-परम्परावादी .... One who opposes established institutions or beliefs, bohemian

213. Idolatry .... मूर्ति पूजन .... The worship of idols or images.

214. Illegal .... गैरकानूनी .... Contrary to law.

215. Illegible .... अपठनीय .... Incapable of being read.

216. Illicit .... नाजायज .... Prohibited by the society

217. Illiterate .... अनपढ़ .... One who does not know reading and writing.

218. Imaginary .... काल्पनिक .... Existing only in the mind and not in reality.

219. Immigrant .... अप्रवासी .... A person who comes to one's country from another in order to settle there.

220. Immune .... प्रतिरक्षित .... Free from infection.

221. Impalpable .... स्पर्शातीत .... Incapable of being perceived by touch, intangible

222. Impenetrable .... अप्रवेश्य .... That which cannot be penetrated.

223. Imperceptible .... अति सूक्ष्म .... That which cannot be perceived by senses as it is too small or slight.

224. Imperialism .... साम्राज्यवाद .... Policy of extending a country's empire and influence to a less rich or powerful nation.

225. Impertinent .... गुस्ताख .... Not showing proper, rude

226. Impiety .... सम्मान की कमी .... Lack of respect or reverence.

227. Imponderable .... जो सोचा ना जा सके .... That which cannot be guessed or calculated.

228. Imposter .... बहुरूपिया .... One who assumes a character or title that is not his own to deceive others, charlatan

229. Impracticable .... अव्यवहारिक .... Incapable of being practised.

230. Impregnable .... अजेय /अभेद् .... Too strong to be captured or broken into

231. Impulse .... आवेश .... A sudden desire to do something without thinking about he result.

232. Impresario .... संयोजक .... A person who organizes and finances, a concert, a theatre or an opera.

233. Impromptu .... बिना तैयारी का .... Something said or done without preparation, extempore.

234. Impudent .... रूखे व्यवहार वाला .... Rude and not respectful.
235. Impunity .... दंड मुक्ति .... Freedom from punishment.
236. Inaccessible .... जहाँ पहुँचा ना जा सके......... Incapable of being reached.
237. Inadmissible .... अस्वीकार्य .... That which cannot be admitted or allowed.
238. Inaudible .... जो सुनाई ना दे.................. Sound that cannot be heard.
239. Incendiary .... जो आग/ गुस्सा भड़काऐं ...... Designed to cause fire/likely to cause violence.
240. Incombustible .... जो जले नहीं...................... That which cannot be burnt.
241. Incomparable .... अतुलनीय/ अतुल्य .... That which cannot be compared.
242. Incorrigible .... जो सुधारा नहीं जा सकते ...... Incapable of being corrected.
243. Incredible .... अविश्वसनीय .... Which can't be believed.
244. Incurable .... असाध्य .... Which cannot be cured.
245. Indefatigable .... जो थके नहीं .... Incapable of getting tired.
246. Indefensible .... असुरक्षित .... Which cannot be defended.
247. Indelible .... अमिट .... Which cannot be erased or forgotten.
248. Indemnity .... क्षति से सुरक्षा .... Protection against damage or loss.
249. Indestructible .... अनश्वर .... That which cannot be destroyed.
250. Indignant .... अन्याय के कारण क्रुद्ध .... Angry at injustice.
251. Indispensable .... अपरिहार्य .... That without which one can't do.
252. Indivisible .... अविभाज्य.......................... That which cannot be divided.
253. Ineligible .... अयोग्य............................. Not suitable to be elected or selected under the rules.
254. Inevitable .... अटल .... Incapable of being avoided.
255. Inexcusable .... क्षमा ना करने योग्य .... That which cannot be excused.
256. Inexplicable .... अवर्णनीय .... Which cannot be explained.
257. Inexplicit .... अप्रकट .... Not clearly expressed.
258. Inexpressible .... अवर्णनीय .... That which cannot be expressed in words.
259. Infallible .... जो गलती न करें................. One who cannot make mistakes.
260. Infanticide .... शिशुहत्या .... Killing of an infant.
261. Infectious .... संक्रामक .... A disease which spreads through air and water.
262. Inflammable .... ज्वलनशील......................... That catches fire easily, combustible, flammable.
263. Inimitable .... जो अनुकरणीय न हो........... Incapable of being imitated or copied
264. Insecticide .... कीटनाशक .... A substance that kills insects.
265. Insolvent .... दिवालिया .... A person who is unable to pay his debt, bankrupt
266. Insurrection .... बगावत............................. Rising in arms against an established government.
267. Intercede .... दूसरे के स्थान पर दखल देना .. Intervene on behalf of another.
268. Intercept .... रोकना/ पकड़ना.................. To check or stop on way.

269. Intrigue/conspire	साजिश करना	Make or carry out secret planning.
270. Introspection	आत्म निरिक्षण	Examination of one's own thought or feeling.
271. Invincible	अजय	That which cannot be defeated.
272. Invisible	अदृश्य	That which cannot be seen.
273. Invulnerable	सुरक्षित	Incapable of being harmed.
274. Irreconcilable	असंगत	Impossible to find agreement between.
275. Irrecoverable	वापस न मिल सकने योग्य	That which cannot be recovered or regained
276. Irreparable	जिसकी मरम्मद ना की जा सके	Incapable of being repaired.
277. Irrevocable	अपरिवर्तनीय	That which cannot be altered.
278. Itinerant	घुमक्कड़	One who travels from place to place.
279. Journal	अखबार व पत्रिका	A newspaper or magazine that deals with a particular subject or professional activity.
280. Juxtapose	सन्निधान करना	Placing things beside one another.
281. Lagoon	समुद्रताल	Salt water lake separated from the sea by sand banks.
282. Lexicographer	शब्द कोष बनाने वाला	A person who compiles a dictionary.
283. Linguist	बहुभाषाविद् (विदेशी भाषाओं का)	One who speaks many foreign languages.
284. Logic	तर्क	A sensible reason.
285. Maidenhood	कुवाँरापन (लड़की का)	The state of being unmarried (of a girl).
286. Mammals	स्तनपायी	Animals which give birth to babies and feed them with their milk.
287. Manuscript	हस्तलिपि	Matter written by hand.
288. Mariticide	पति हत्या	Killing of one's husband.
289. Martyr	शहीद	One who dies for a noble cause.
290. Masque	डांस-ड्रामा	A play or a dramatic performance in verse, with music, dance and fine costumes.
291. Massacre	नरसंहार	Killing of large numbers of people.
292. Materialist	भौतिकवादी	A person for whom money is the most important consideration.
293. Matins	सुबह की प्रार्थना	Morning prayer.
294. Matricide	मातृहत्या	Killing of one's own mother.
295. Matrimony	विवाह	Marriage.
296. Maxim	कहावत	A short statement of a general truth.
297. Memento	स्मृति चिन्ह	Something kept to remember place or event.
298. Mercenary	जो सिर्फ पैसे के लिए काम करे	One who acts only for money.
299. Metamorphosis	बदलाव	Gradual and complete change in appearance.

300. **Meticulous**	अति सावधान व बारिकियों पर ध्यान देने वाला	Very particular about small details.
301. **Migration**	प्रवास	Movement from one place to another especially in search of livelihood.
302. **Misandrist**	पुरूषद्रोही	One who hates males.
303. **Misanthrope**	मानवता द्रोही	A hater of mankind.
304. **Misogamist**	विवाह से घृणा करने वाला	Hater of marriage.
305. **Misogynist**	महिलाओं से घृणा करने वाला	A hater of womankind.
306. **Misologist**	ज्ञान से घृणा करने वाला	Hater of learning.
307. **Misoneist**	नई चीजों से नफरत करने वाला	Hater of new things.
308. **Missionary**	धर्म प्रचारक	A person sent to teach Christian religion
309. **Monastery**	मठ	Place where monks live.
310. **Monogamy**	एक पत्नी प्रथा	The practice of keeping only one wife.
311. **Mortal**	नश्वर	That will die one day.
312. **Mortuary**	शवगृह	A place where dead bodies are kept before post-mortem.
313. **Mutilation**	अंग-भंग	Cutting off or severely damaging body parts.
314. **Naive**	सीधा-सादा जिसे जीवन का पर्याप्त अनुभव नहीं	Having natural simplicity of nature or without enough experience of life.
315. **Narcotics**	नशीली दवाईयाँ	A medicine that induces sleep.
316. **Naturalism**	प्रकृतिवाद	Adherence or attachment to what is natural.
317. **Neogamist**	नवविवाहित	One who is recently married.
318. **Nepotism**	भाई-भतीजा वाद	Undue favour shown to one's own relatives.
319. **Neurotic**	अत्यंत संवेदनशील या चिंतित	Excessively sensitive, anxious or obsessive.
320. **Newfangled**	नई अनजानी चीज़	Newly developed and unfamiliar.
321. **Nonentity**	अस्तित्वहीन	Person of no importance.
322. **Nonpareil**	अद्वितीय	Person or thing which has no equal, matchless, unrival.
323. **Notorious**	कुख्यात/ बदनाम	Having an evil reputation.
324. **Nuance**	सूक्ष्म भेद	Subtle difference in colour, meaning etc.
325. **Numismatics**	सिक्को की पढ़ाई	The study of coins.
326. **Nursery**	पौधशाला	The place where young plants are grown.
327. **Obscurantist**	ज्ञानोन्नति विरोधी	Person who is opposed to enlightenment or knowledge
328. **Obsequies**	अंतिम संस्कार	Funeral rites.
329. **Obsolete**	पुराना, अब प्रयोग में नहीं	That which is no longer in use.
330. **Octagon**	अष्टकोण	A plane figure with eight sides and angles.

331. **Oligarchy** .... अल्पजनाधिपत्य................. A government by a small group of powerful persons.
332. **Omniform**................. सर्वाकृतिक....................... Having every form or shape.
333. **Omnigenous** .... सब प्रकार का .... Comprising all kinds.
334. **Omnipotent** .... सर्वशक्तिमान .... All-powerful (God).
335. **Omnipresent**........... सर्वविधायमान .... Present everywhere (God).
336. **Omniscient** .... सर्वज्ञानी.......................... Knowing everything (God).
337. **Opaque** .... अपारदर्शी .... That which cannot be seen through.
338. **Optimist** .... आशावादी .... A person who looks to the bright side of things.
339. **Orator** .... वक्ता............................. One who makes an eloquent public speech, Articulate, Eloquent
340. **Orchard**..................... फलों का बगीचा .... A garden of fruits.
341. **Orphan**...................... अनाथ............................ A child whose parents are dead.
342. **Ostracize** .... समाज से निकालना .... To turn out of society.
343. **Oviparous**................. अंड प्रजक .... Bearing eggs and not young ones.
344. **Pacifist** .... शान्ति दूत .... A person who believes in the total abolition of war/ one who preaches peace
345. **Pageant** .... नुमाइश............................ Elaborate public spectacle.
346. **Palatable**.................... स्वादिष्ट............................ Food or drink that has a pleasant taste.
347. **Panacea** .... रामबाण............................ A remedy for all kinds of diseases.
348. **Pandemonium** .... शोरगुल .... A wild and noisy disorder, cacophony
349. **Panegyric** .... प्रशंसा पत्र .... Piece of writing full of praise, encomium
350. **Pantomime** .... मूक अभिनय .... Dramatic performance with dumb show.
351. **Paramour** .... जिस से शारीरिक संबंध हो .... Sexual partner or lover.
352. **Parasite**..................... परजीवी .... One who entirely depends on another.
353. **Parasol** .... रंगीन छाता .... A lady's umbrella.
354. **Parricide** .... माँ व पिता का हत्यारा .... Killing of both the parents.
355. **Patricide** .... पितृहत्या .... Killing of one's own father.
356. **Patrimony** .... पैतृक............................... Inherited from father.
357. **Patriot** .... देशभक्त .... One who loves one's country.
358. **Patronymic** .... पितृ नाम .... Name derived from that of father or ancestor.
359. **Pauper** .... कंगाल .... One who has no means of livelihood.
360. **Peculation** .... गबन .... Use of public money for one's own benefit, embezzlement
361. **Pedantic**.................... ज्ञान दर्शाने वाला लेख .... A style in which a writer makes a display of his knowledge and learning.
362. **Pedestrian** .... पैदल यात्री......................... One who walks on foot.
363. **Peninsula**................. प्रायद्वीप .... Area of land almost surrounded by sea.

364. Pentagon .... पंचभुज .... A plane figure with five sides and angles.
365. Perceptible .... इन्द्रियगोचर .... That can be perceived by the senses.
366. Peroration .... भाषण का समापन भाग .... Concluding part of a speech.
367. Perseverance .... लगन .... Constant efforts to achieve something.
368. Perspicacious .... तिक्ष्ण बुद्धिवाला .... Quick in judging and understanding.
369. Perversion .... विकृति .... Change to something abnormal or unnatural.
370. Pessimist .... निराशावादी .... A person who looks at the dark side of things.
371. Philanderer .... दिलफेंक .... A man who amuses himself by love-making, casanova.
372. Philanthropist .... मानवता प्रेमी .... A lover of mankind.
373. Philatelist .... डाक टिकट संग्राहक .... Collector of stamps.
374. Philistine .... कला के प्रति उदासीन .... Person who is indifferent to art and literature.
375. Philogynist .... औरतों से प्रेम करने वाला ...... A lover of womankind.
376. Philology .... भाषा का अध्ययन .... Science of study of language.
377. Pilgrim .... तीर्थयात्री .... One who travels to a sacred place.
378. Pioneer .... अग्रसर .... One who leads others in any field.
379. Piquant .... मसालेदार/दिलचस्प .... Pleasant or sharp to taste/ interesting.
380. Placard/Poster .... विज्ञापन .... Written or printed things pasted or displayed in public places.
381. Plagiarism .... साहित्यिक चोरी .... The practice of borrowing words and ideas from other authors and using them as one's own; literary theft.
382. Platitude .... घिसी-पिटी बात .... Statement that is obviously true and hence dull or not stimulating.
383. Plutocracy .... कुलीनतंत्र .... A government by a rich and powerful class.
384. Polyandry .... बहुपति प्रथा .... The custom of having more than two husbands at the same time.
385. Polygamy .... बहु-विवाह प्रथा .... The custom of having more than two spouses at the same time.
386. Polyglot .... बहुभाषाविद् .... Person having command over many languages.
387. Polygon .... बहुभुज .... A figure with many angles or sides.
388. Posthumous .... मरणोपरांत .... Received after death.
389. Postscript .... पश्चलेख .... Anything written in a letter after it is signed.
390. Predicament .... अप्रिय व कठिन स्थिति .... Difficult or dangerous situation.
391. Prejudiced .... पूर्वाग्रही .... Be biased against.
392. Premonition .... पूर्वाभास .... Forewarning of an impending danger.
393. Prerogative .... विशेषाधिकार .... Absolute right.
394. Prodigy .... प्रतिभा संपन्न बालक .... A child with unusual or remarkable talent.

395. Prognostication .... भविष्यवाणी .... Act of forecasting by examining present conditions.

396. Prologue .... मंगलाचरण/नाटक के पहले का भाषण ..... A speech or a poem recited at the beginning of a play.

397. Promiscuous .... अति कामुक .... Having a lot of different sexual partners.

398. Proponent .... प्रस्तावक .... Person who proposes something.

399. Propriety .... मर्यादा .... Correct and acceptable moral and social behaviour.

400. Protagonist .... समर्थक/मुख्य पात्र .... An important supporter of an idea or political system/Chief actor or character in a story or drama.

401. Protectorate .... संरक्षित राज्य .... Country under the protection of a more powerful country.

402. Prudent .... समझदार .... Wise, sagacious

403. Pseudonym .... कृत्रिम नाम .... Name taken by an author instead of his real name

404. Punctilious .... अतिशिष्टाचारी .... Very careful to behave correctly.

405. Pyrotechnic .... आतिशबाजी निर्माण-कला ...... Art of making fireworks.

406. Quadruped .... चौपाया .... Four footed-animal.

407. Rebel .... द्रोही .... One who takes up arms against the government.

408. Recapitulate .... संक्षेप में दोहराना .... Repeat the main points.

409. Recluse .... एकांतवासी .... One who lives alone and avoids company.

410. Reconcile .... सुलह .... Bring about harmony or agreement.

411. Reconnaissance ...... किसी स्थान का सैन्य सर्वेक्षण .. Information gathering activity about enemy forces.

412. Red tapism .... लाल फीताशाही .... Too much official formality.

413. Redundancy .... अनावश्यकता .... When something is unnecessary because it is more than what is needed.

414. Regicide .... राजा की हत्या .... Killing of a king.

415. Relegate/Demote ... दर्जा घटाना .... Reduce to a lower position.

416. Reluctant .... अनिच्छुक .... Unwilling

417. Remission .... क्षमा/ वह समय जब कोई बिमारी की तीव्रता कम हो ...... Pardon or forgiveness for breaking religious laws/ a period of time when an illness is less severe

418. Rendezvous .... पूर्व-निश्चित भेंट .... A meeting arranged with someone

419. Renegade .... धर्मपरित्यागी .... Person who changes his religious belief/support to someone else or some other nation.

420. **Repartee** .... हाजिर जवाबी .... Witty and clever answers.
421. **Repercussion** .... दुष्प्रभाव.......................... Ill-effect of some event, action or decision.
422. **Replica** .... प्रतिकृति .... Copy or reproduction of a work of art.
423. **Repository** .... गोदाम/भंडार..................... Place where things are stored for safety.
424. **Republic** .... गणतंत्र .... A political system in which the supreme power lies in a body of citizens who can elect people to represent them.
425. **Requiem** .... शांति-यज्ञ......................... Prayer for the dead.
426. **Restitution** .... खोयी/चोरी हुई वस्तु की वापसी... Return of object stolen or lost.
427. **Retaliate** .... बदला लेना .... Return the same sort of ill-treatment.
428. **Reticent/Taciturn** .. अल्पभाषी......................... Person who does not speak too much.
429. **Retrospective** .... पुर्वगामी .... An effect which has a reference to the past.
430. **Rumour/Hearsay** .... अफवाह.......................... Unverified information.
431. **Sacrilege** .... पवित्र वस्तु का अपमान .... Treating something holy without respect, blasphemy
432. **Sarcasm**..................... ताना............................. Bitter and ironical remark.
433. **Savage** .... क्रूर.............................. Violent and uncivilized.
434. **Scapegoat** .... बलि का बकरा .... One who is blamed for the mistakes of others.
435. **Sceptic**...................... संदेही .... Doubtful.
436. **Screech**..................... चीखना.......................... Cry out in shrill voice.
437. **Scrimmage**............... खींच-तान .... Confused struggle or fight.
438. **Scurry** .... छोटे कदमों से तेजी से चलना .... Move hurriedly with short steps.
439. **Sedition** .... राजसत्ता के विरुद्ध आंदोलन ... Act or speech for inciting the public against the government.
440. **Senility** .... जीर्णावस्था....................... Extreme old age when a man behaves like a fool or tends to forget things, dotage
441. **Siesta** .... दोपहर का आराम.............. Period of rest or sleep after lunch.
442. **Simultaneous** .... साथ-साथ .... Occurring at the same time.
443. **Sinecure**.................... जहाँ कम काम में ज्यादा पैसे मिले... An office for which high salary is paid for little or no work or responsibility.
444. **Smother** .... दम घोंटना .... Kill by suffocation (especially by covering the face with something).
445. **Sojourn** .... थोड़ी देर के लिए रूकना ...... Stay for a short time.
446. **Soliloquy**................... स्वयं से एकांत में बाते करना.. Speaking aloud while alone.
447. **Somnambulist** .... नींद में चलने वाला .... One who walks in sleep.
448. **Somniloquist** .... नींद में बोलने वाला .... One who talks in sleep.
449. **Sonorous** .... सुरीला .... Having a deep and pleasant sound, euphonie.
450. **Sororicide** .... बहन की हत्या .... Killing of one's own sister.

451. **Spendthrift**	फिजूलखर्ची	One who spends one's money recklessly.
452. **Spinster**	कुवाँरी महिला	An unmarried woman.
453. **Spiritualist**	अध्यात्मिक	A person who believes in spiritual things.
454. **Sporadic**	छिटपुट	Occurring irregularly, by fits and starts
455. **Stoic**	तटस्थः	A person who is indifferent to pleasure and pain.
456. **Strangulate**	गला घोंटना	Kill by putting pressure on the throat/ to apply pressure.
457. **Subdue**	काबू में करना	To bring under control.
458. **Subjugate**	अधीन करना	To bring under control.
459. **Suicide**	आत्महत्या	Taking of one's own life.
460. **Supercilious**	घमंडी	Thinking oneself superior to others, conceited, arrogant.
461. **Sycophant**	चापलूस	Person who tries to win a favour by flattering others.
462. **Synagogue**	यहूदी उपासनागृह	Place where Jews worship.
463. **Talkative/Garrulous** .	बातूनी	Person who is fond of talking.
464. **Tantrum**	गुस्से के आवेश	Fit of bad temper or anger.
465. **Teetotaller**	जो शराब से दूर रहे	One who abstains from alcoholic drinks.
466. **Theist**	आस्तिक	A person who believes in existence of God.
467. **Theocracy**	पादरीतंत्र	A government by religious leaders.
468. **Thermometer**	तापमापक यंत्र	An instrument for measuring temperature.
469. **Traitor**	देशद्रोही	One who betrays one's country.
470. **Transgressor**	पापी/ अपराधी	One who violates a rule or law.
471. **Transmigration**	आत्मा का शरीर बदलना	The passage of soul after death from one body to the other.
472. **Transmogrification** .	कायाकल्प	Complete change in appearance or character (especially in a magical or surprising way).
473. **Transparent**	पारदर्शी	That allows the passage of rays of light.
474. **Truant**	कामचोर	One who stays away from school/work without permission.
475. **Truism**	स्वतः सिद्ध	A truth which is often repeated.
476. **Turncoat**	गद्दार	Disloyal, apostate
477. **Unanimous**	एकमत	Consent of all.
478. **Unavoidable**	अपरिहार्य	That which cannot be avoided.

479. Unique .... अनोखा .... The only one of its type.

480. Universal .... विश्वव्यापी........................ Belonging to all parts of the world, ubiquitous

481. Usurper.................... सम्पत्ती हड़पने वाला .... One who grabs somebody's else property or title.

482. Uxoricide .... पत्नी हत्या .... Killing of one's wife.

483. Uxorious/Henpecked जोरू का गुलाम .... Foolishly fond of one's wife.

484. Vacuous .... बुद्धिहीन.......................... Suggesting absence of thought or intellect, stupid, inane.

485. Vendetta .... वंशानुगत/ पुश्तैनी झगड़ा .... Feud in which the relatives of the dead or injured take revenge.

486. Verbatim .... शब्दशः .... Repetition of a writing, word for word.

487. Verbose..................... बातों से भरा .... Using or containing more words than are necessary.

488. Versatile .... बहुमुखी .... One who possesses many talents.

489. Verso .... वामपृष्ठ.......................... Any left hand page of an open book. Note: Recto is right hand page.

490. Vespers .... शाम की प्रार्थना................ Evening prayer in the church. Note: Matin is morning prayer.

491. Veteran..................... अनुभवी .... One who has grown old in or has long experience of (specially military) service or occupation.

492. Vincible .... जिसे जीता जा सके............ That which can be conquered.

493. Vindictive/Vengeful .. प्रतिशोधी......................... Having or showing a desire for revenge.

494. Virulent.................... जहरीला .... Highly poisonous effect, venomous, malignant

495. Viviparous................ सजीव प्रजक .... Bearing living young ones and not eggs.

496. Volte-face .... आकस्मिक परिवर्तन............ Sudden change from one set of beliefs, direction or point of view to another.

497. Voluntary .... स्वेच्छिक......................... Of one's own free will.

498. Voyage .... समुद्री यात्रा..................... Journey by sea.

499. Vulnerable .... आघात योग्य .... That which can be easily damaged or hurt.

500. Widow....................... विधवा .... A woman whose husband is dead.

501. Widower .... विधुर .... A man whose wife is dead.

502. Wreath .... पुष्पहार.......................... Flowers fastened in a circle.

503. Zealot .... कट्टरपंथी .... Person who shows great and uncompromising enthusiasm for a religion, party, cause etc.

30 CHAPTER

ONE WORD SUBSTITUTION

PRACTICE SET

Directions: In question nos.1 to 225, out of the four alternatives, choose the one which can be substituted for the given words/sentence and choose the appropriate alternative which best expresses the sentences.

1. A person who has no money to pay off his debts

(A) Insolvent (B) Poor
(C) Destitute (D) Pauper

2. Words uttered impiously about God

(A) amoral (B) philosophy
(C) logic (D) blasphemy

3. A number of ships.

(a) fleet (b) galaxy
(c) constellation (d) group

4. One who compiles a dictionary

(A) geographer (B) lexicographer
(C) lapidist (D) linguist

5. A test in which cells from diseased organs are removed and tested

(A) Biopsy (B) Autopsy
(C) Operation (D) Amputation

6. A small room in a big house, hotel, ship etc. where glasses, dishes, spoons, food etc. are kept.

(A) Portico (B) Pantry
(C) Mezzanine (D) Kitchen

7. A foreigner who settles in a country.

(A) Immigrant (B) Emigrant
(C) Alien (D) Visitor

8. Doing something according to one's own free will.

(A) Willfully (B) Obligingly
(C) Voluntarily (D) Compulsorily

9. Place that provides refuge

(A) shelter (B) house
(C) country (D) asylum

10. A person who gambles or bets

(A) punter (B) backer
(C) customer (D) client

11. Art of writing for newspapers and magazines

(A) Literature (B) Journalism
(C) Biography (D) Artistry

12. An abandoned child of unknown parents who is found by somebody.

(A) Foundling (B) Sibling
(C) Urchin (D) Orphan

13. Parts of a country behind the coast or a river bank.

(A) Swamps (B) Marshes
(C) Hinterland (D) Isthmuses

14. A written statement about someone's character, usually provided by an employer

(A) testimonial (B) memorandum
(C) certificate (D) license

15. One who does not make mistakes

(A) Pessimist (B) Optimist
(C) Infallible (D) Hypocrite

16. Able to use the left hand and right hand equally well

(A) ambivert (B) ambidextrous
(C) ambivalent (D) ambitious

17. One who hates women

(A) philanthropist (B) ascetic
(C) misogamist (D) misogynist

18. a system of naming things

(A) horticulture (B) miniature
(C) genocide (D) nomenclature

19. A raised passageway in a building

(A) walkway (B) walkout
(C) walkabout (D) walkover

20. A cure for all diseases

(A) laxative (B) panacea
(C) antidote (D) purgative

21. One who cannot speak

(A) deaf (B) dumb
(C) visionless (D) lame

22. Pertaining to cattle

(A) Canine (B) Feline
(C) Bovine (D) Verminous

23. To look at someone in an angry or threatening way

(A) Glower (B) Gnaw
(C) Gnash (D) Grind

24. A post with little work but high salary

(A) Director (B) Trustee
(C) Sinecure (D) Ombudsman

25. Something that causes death

(A) Dangerous (B) Fatal
(C) Brutal (D) Horrible

26. A person who writes decoratively

(A) Calligrapher (B) Colliery
(C) Choreographer (D) Cartographer

27. A person who loves mankind

(A) misanthrope (B) anthropologist
(C) philanthropist (D) mercenary

28. Capable of being interpreted in two ways

(A) confusing (B) unclear
(C) ambiguous (D) ambivert

29. One who has narrow and prejudiced religious views

(A) religious (B) fanatic
(C) bigot (D) god-fearing

30. The action of looking within or into one's own mind

(A) observation (B) examination
(C) introspection (D) introvert

31. To confirm with the help of evidence

(A) corroborate (B) implicate
(C) designate (D) extricate

32. One who is a dabbler in arts, science or literature:

(A) Dilettante (B) Aesthete
(C) Maestro (D) Connoisseur

33. The time between midnight and noon:

(A) Afternoon (B) Antipodes
(C) Ante – meridiem (D) Antenatal

34. Still existing and known :

(A) Extent (B) Extant
(C) Eternal (D) Immanent

35. Fear of height:

(A) Agoraphobia (B) Hydrophobia
(C) Acrophobia (D) Pyrophobia

36. The highest point

(A) zenith (B) height
(C) zeal (D) ridge

37. Feeling inside you which tells you what is right and what is wrong :

(A) cleverness (B) conscience
(C) consciousness (D) fear

38. Release of a prisoner from jail on certain terms and condition

(A) Parole (B) Parley
(C) Pardon (D) Acquittal

39. Loss of memory

(A) Ambrosia (B) Amnesia
(C) Insomnia (D) Forgetting

40. To struggle helplessly

(A) Flounder (B) Founder
(C) Fumble (D) Finger

41. One who tends to take a hopeful view of life

(A) Magnate (B) creator
(C) pacifist (D) optimist

42. Belonging to all parts of the world
(A) Common (B) universal
(C) worldly (D) international

43. To be known for bad acts
(A) Famous (B) notorious
(C) criminal (D) terrorist

44. Words of similar meaning
(A) Homonyms (B) pseudonyms
(C) antonyms (D) synonyms

45. Instrument to measure atmospheric pressure
(A) Metronome (B) compass
(C) pedometer (D) barometer

46. A speech delivered without previous preparation
(A) Soliloquy (B) Extempore
(C) Rhetoric (D) Expression

47. One who pretends to be what he is not
(A) crocodile (B) flatterer
(C) hypocrite (D) counterfeiter

48. Study of heavenly bodies
(A) astrology (B) astronomy
(C) stargazing (D) astrophysics

49. An official call to appear in a court of law
(A) summon (B) notice
(C) memorandum (D) petition

50. To cut apart a person's body
(A) amputate (B) mutilate
(C) ambush (D) mitigate

51. Murder of a brother
(A) Patricide (B) Fratricide
(C) Homicide (D) Parricide

52. One who is filled with excessive and mistaken enthusiasm about his religion
(A) Fatalist (B) Lunatic
(C) Fanatic (D) Stoic

53. A list of items to be transacted at a meeting
(A) Menu (B) Agenda
(C) Minutes (D) Records

54. An involuntary action under a stimulus is described as a
(A) complex (B) reflex
(C) reflection (D) response

55. A continuous process of change is known as
(A) transformation (B) metamorphosis
(C) flux (D) dynamism

56. The use of many words where only a few are necessary.
(A) circumlocution (B) circumspection
(C) circumscription (D) circumvention

57. Circular building or hall with a dome.
(A) edifice (B) palace
(C) rotunda (D) spire

58. One who is a citizen not of a country but of the world.
(A) Bohemian (B) Cosmopolitan
(C) Philanthropist (D) Internationalist

59. An order requiring a person to attend a court.
(A) Courtship (B) Agreement
(C) Subpoena (D) Command

60. An imaginary name assumed by an author for disguise.
(A) Facsimile (B) Surname
(C) Alias (D) Pseudonym

61. An extreme fear of being in a small confined place.
(A) Hydrophobia (B) Paraphernalia
(C) Claustrophobia (D) Progeria

62. An inscription on a tomb.
(A) epitaph (B) crypt
(C) obituary (D) legacy

63. Allowance due to a wife from her husband on separation.
(A) patrimony (B) antimony
(C) parsimony (D) alimony

64. Practice of employing spies in war.
(A) Esplanade (B) Espionage
(C) Espadrille (D) Estrangement

65. A fixed territory in which authority can be exercised.

(A) Jurisdiction (B) judiciary
(C) jurisprudence (D) juristic

66. An appearance of objects often simulating the appearance of water:

(A) image (B) mirage
(C) reflection (D) refraction

67. The art of making fireworks :

(A) Chromatics (B) Numismatics
(C) Pyrotechnics (D) Cosmetics

68. Give off bubbles of gas :

(A) efface (B) effervesce
(C) effloresce (D) effuse

69. A system of governance controlled by persons of high intellectual ability :

(A) oligarchy (B) democracy
(C) meritocracy (D) snobbery

70. Sudden and violent change :

(A) Cataclysm (B) Catalysis
(C) Catacombs (D) Catechism

71. A small waterfall or group of waterfalls flowing down a rocky hill side is called :

(A) Hurricane (B) Stream
(C) Volcano (D) Cascade

72. One who eats human flesh

(A) non-vegetarian (B) vegetarian
(C) cannibal (D) man-eater

73. Instrument which records earth's tremor:

(A) Monograph (B) Geographer
(C) Seismograph (D) Barometer

74. The practice of a woman having more than one husband at the same time:

(A) Polygamy (B) Polyphony
(C) Polyandry (D) Polygyny

75. Specializes in nose diseases :

(A) Otologist (B) Rhinologist
(C) Endocrinologist (D) Gerentologist

76. Boundary of an area

(A) Porch (B) Periphery
(C) Balcony (D) Verandah

77. A war of religions

(A) Calligraphy (B) Contraband
(C) Cavalry (D) Crusade

78. The government by the nobility

(A) Bureaucracy (B) Aristocracy
(C) Autocracy (D) Oligarchy

79. To store and stock

(A) Hail (B) Hide
(C) Hoard (D) Horde

80. Study of relations of organisms to one another and to their surroundings

(A) Biology (B) Ecology
(C) Psychology (D) Physiology

81. A body of persons appointed to hear evidence and give their verdict in trials.

(A) association (B) council
(C) bar (D) jury

82. A person who dishonestly pretends to be somebody else :

(A) Imperialist (B) Impressionist
(C) Implorer (D) Impostor

83. Violent storm:

(A) weather (B) rains
(C) breeze (D) tempest

84. Careful and thorough enquiry :

(A) Investigation (B) Interview
(C) Examination (D) Exploration

85. A situation that stops an activity from progressing :

(A) Bypass (B) Breach
(C) Bottleneck (D) Block head

86. A disease which is spread by direct contact

(A) Contagious (B) Infectious
(C) Epidemic (D) Endemic

87. The study of ancient civilizations

(A) History (B) Anthropology
(C) Ethnology (D) Archaeology

88. An animal story with a moral

(A) Fable (B) Tale
(C) Anecdote (D) Parable

89. A thing likely to be easily broken

(A) vulnerable (B) flexible
(C) brittle (D) delicate

90. Body of singers

(A) Coir (B) Quorum
(C) Quire (D) Choir

91. Very dramatic

(A) Histrionic (B) Hippocratic
(C) Hirsute (D) Hoary

92. A figure of speech by which a thing is spoken of as being that which it only resembles

(A) Metaphor (B) Simile
(C) Personification (D) Alliteration

93. The process by which a person or an organization reduces the amount of money it spends

(A) budgeting (B) retrenchment
(C) saving (D) closure

94. An established principle of practical wisdom :

(A) Marxism (B) Maxim
(C) Neologism (D) Platonism

95. Person with whom one works

(A) contemporary (B) companion
(C) colleague (D) partner

96. Honesty of character

(A) integrity (B) rectitude
(C) honour (D) dignity

97. Expressions of sympathy

(A) congratulation (B) condolence
(C) compliment (D) condemnation

98. An instrument used to record sound

(A) gramophone (B) hydrophone
(C) phonograph (D) megaphone

99. Pertaining to horses

(A) Equine (B) equestrian
(C) equinox (D) equation

100. One who cannot be corrected

(A) Incurable (B) incorrigible
(C) hardened (D) vulnerable

101. Difficult or impossible to read

(A) Illogical (B) illegible
(C) ineligible (D) legible

102. An unexpected piece of good fortune

(A) Turnstile (B) Windfall
(C) Philanthropy (D) Benevolence

103. Those who go on to someone else's land without the owner's permission

(A) Delinquents (B) trespassers
(C) offenders (D) culprits

104. Something that cannot be taken away.

(A) inalienable (B) edible
(C) legible (D) natural

105. Scale used for measuring the strength of an earthquake.

(A) Celsius (B) Newtons
(C) Richter (D) Linear

106. Something kept as a reminder of an event.

(A) Trophy (B) Souvenir
(C) Prize (D) Antique

107. One who practises one of the fine arts:

(A) painter (B) artist
(C) designer (D) architect

108. A general pardon of offenders.

(A) Parley (B) Amnesty
(C) Parole (D) Acquittal

109. Place where wine is made

(A) bakery (B) cloakroom
(C) tannery (D) brewery

110. A paper written by hand

(A) handicraft (B) handiwork
(C) manuscript (D) thesis

111. The art of preserving skin of animals, birds and fish

(A) taxonomy (B) taxidermy
(C) philology (D) seismology

112. Related to moon

(A) solar (B) moony
(C) lunar (D) honeymoon

113. Sum of money to be paid for freeing a person from captivity.

(A) Ransom (B) Compensation
(C) Tribute (D) Penalty

114. Book giving information about every branch of knowledge.
(A) Directory (B) Dictionary
(C) Encyclopedia (D) Dissertation

115. Member of a tribe that wanders from place to place with no fixed home.
(A) Vagabond (B) Nomad
(C) Wanderer (D) Truant

116. Fit to be chosen.
(A) Eligible (B) Capable
(C) Suitable (D) Valuable

117. An animal or plant living in or upon another.
(A) master (B) dependant
(C) insect (D) parasite

118. Strong dislike between two persons
(A) aversion (B) antipathy
(C) apathy (D) despair

119. The killing of a whole group of people
(A) genocide (B) germicide
(C) patricide (D) suicide

120. The plants and vegetation of a region
(A) fauna (B) flora
(C) landscape (D) environment

121. That which is without opposition
(A) unaware (B) verdict
(C) unanimous (D) spontaneous

122. Animal that feeds on plants
(A) Carnivorous (B) Herbivorous
(C) Insectivorous (D) Graminivorous

123. A number of stars grouped together
(A) Orbit (B) Constellation
(C) Solar system (D) Comet

124. Lasting only for a very short while
(A) Transparent (B) Temporal
(C) Temporary (D) Temperate

125. Murder of a man
(A) Regicide (B) Fratricide
(C) Homicide (D) Genocide

126. Use of force or threats to get someone to agree to something
(A) Coercion (B) Conviction
(C) Confession (D) Cajolement

127. A place where gambling is practised
(A) hotel (B) casino
(C) restaurant (D) theatre

128. An object or portion serving as a sample
(A) Specification (B) Spectre
(C) Spectacle (D) Specimen

129. The practice of submitting a proposal to popular vote
(A) Election (B) Reference
(C) Popularity (D) Referendum

130. Code of diplomatic etiquette and precedence
(A) Statesmanship (B) Diplomacy
(C) Hierarchy (D) Protocol

131. To renounce a high position of authority or control
(A) Abduct (B) Abandon
(C) Abort (D) Abdicate

132. Talking about the affairs of other people
(A) teasing (B) gossiping
(C) criticising (D) slandering

133. Medical examination of the body after death
(A) diagnosis (B) irradiation
(C) corpse (D) autopsy

134. A person born or living at the same time as another
(A) corollary (B) accessory
(C) contemporary (D) auxiliary

135. Bad beyond reform
(A) irreversible (B) irrevocable
(C) irredeemable (D) irreparable

136. That which is certain to happen
(A) inevitable (B) invincible
(C) incorrigible (D) immediate

137. The process of deciding the nature of a disease by examination
(A) test (B) perusal
(C) diagnosis (D) operation

138. That which makes it difficult to recognise the presence or real nature of somebody or something.

(A) cover (B) camouflage
(C) pretence (D) mask

139. To bear a hand

(A) interfere (B) join
(C) assist (D) rejoice

140. One who makes an official examination of accounts

(A) auditor (B) accountant
(C) clerk (D) official

141. A government by the officials

(A) Plutocracy (B) Aristocracy
(C) Bureaucracy (D) Monarchy

142. One who offers his services without charging for them

(A) Philanderer (B) Volunteer
(C) Mercenary (D) Missionary

143. A tank where fish or water plants are kept

(A) aviary (B) aquarium
(C) nursery (D) sanatorium

144. Avoiding wastage

(A) economic (B) economical
(C) minimal (D) optimational

145. Sole right to make and sell some invention

(A) Franchise (B) Authorize
(C) Dealership (D) Patent

146. The scientific study of living organisms

(A) Biochemistry (B) Zoology
(C) Organic chemistry (D) Biology

147. One who lives for more than a hundred years

(A) saint (B) meteorologist
(C) demagogue (D) centenarian

148. Detaining and confining someone

(A) Interruption (B) Interrogation
(C) Interment (D) Internment

149. An underhand device resorted to in order to justify misconduct

(A) Subterfuge (B) Manoeuvre
(C) Stratagem (D) Complicity

150. Science of the races of mankind

(A) Genealogy (B) Etiology
(C) Ethnology (D) Sociology

151. Impossible to describe

(A) Miraculous (B) Ineffable
(C) Stupendous (D) Appalling

152. One who criticises popular beliefs which he thinks are mistaken or unwise

(A) Philistine (B) Iconoclast
(C) Imposter (D) Cannibal

153. One who hides away on a ship to obtain a free passage.

(A) Compositor (B) Stoker
(C) Stowaway (D) Shipwright

154. Clues available at a scene

(A) Circumstantial (B) derivative
(C) inferential (D) suggestive

155. An emolument over and above fixed income or salary.

(A) Honorarium (B) Sinecure
(C) Perquisite (D) Prerogative

156. The animals of a particular region.

(A) Flora (B) Museum
(C) Zoo (D) Fauna

157. A person who is physically dependent on a substance.

(A) Criminal (B) Martyr
(C) Gladiator (D) Addict

158. A child born after the death of its father is called.

(A) A deprived child (B) An orphan
(C) A posthumous child (D) A waif

159. A legal agreement by which a person borrows money from a bank usually to buy a house.

(A) Document (B) Mortgage
(C) Lease (D) Invoice

160. Failing to discharge one's duty.

(A) Debacle (B) Dereliction
(C) Determination (D) Deterrent

161. A movement of part of the body to express an idea or feeling.

(A) Jibe (B) Gesture
(C) Pose (D) Mimicry

162. To surround a place with the intention of capturing it

(A) Bivouac (B) Besiege
(C) Invade (D) Intern

163. To send back a person to one's country

(A) Repatriate (B) Expatriate
(C) Migrate (D) Emigrate

164. One who is opposed to intellectual progress

(A) Impostor (B) Chaperon
(C) Prospector (D) Obscurant

165. A woman with dark brown hair

(A) Blonde (B) Brunette
(C) Termagant (D) Coiffure

166. One who has special skill in judging art, music, tastes, etc.

(A) Connoisseur (B) Raconteur
(C) Sybarite (D) Amateur

167. One who devotes his life to the welfare and the interests of other people

(A) Minion (B) Martyr
(C) Altruist (D) Fugitive

168. A place where animals are kept alive, and nearly as possible as in their natural state

(A) Vivarium (B) Orchard
(C) Paddock (D) Zoo

169. One who hates mankind

(A) Misanthropist (B) Misnomer
(C) Misogynist (D) Philanthropist

170. The period between two reigns

(A) Interregnum (B) Interval
(C) Interdict (D) Intercept

171. One who walks in one's sleep.

(A) dreamer (B) somnambulist
(C) neomatic (D) ignorant

172. A place where money is coined.

(A) mint (B) press
(C) treasury (D) bank

173. The house of an Eskimo.

(A) hamlet (B) downy
(C) igloo (D) hut

174. One who collects postage stamp.

(A) philatelist (B) stamp collector
(C) vendor (D) lexicographer

175. What cannot be heard.

(A) inaudible (B) audible
(C) unheard (D) ineffaceable

176. A poem of mourning.

(A) elegy (B) sonnet
(C) lyric (D) epic

177. A game in which no one wins.

(A) abandoned (B) drawn
(C) postponed (D) obsolete

178. Too much official formality.

(A) delayed (B) officiousness
(C) formality (D) red tapism

179. One who knows many languages.

(A) linguist (B) polyglot
(C) stylist (D) debator

180. That which can be carried.

(A) portable (B) edible
(C) potable (D) bearable

181. A writer who steals ideas from others.

(A) plagiarist (B) copier
(C) editor (D) translator

182. Examination of a dead body.

(A) autopsy (B) surgery
(C) operation (D) tanning

183. A speech made to oneself.

(A) dialogue (B) speech
(C) soliloquy (D) monologue

184. A commonplace remark.

(A) platitude (B) ramark
(C) statement (D) epigram

185. That which cannot be captured.

(A) impregnable (B) incorrigible
(C) imperishable (D) invincible

186. The study of birds

(A) ornithology (B) philology
(C) ontology (D) geology

187. An insect with many legs is called.

(A) centipede (B) mammal
(C) herbivorous (D) vertebrate

188. Government in which all religions are honoured.
(A) fanatic (B) secular
(C) catholic (D) progressive

189. One who lives among strangers.
(A) recluse (B) alien
(C) stoic (D) rustic

190. A word no longer in use.
(A) extant (B) obsolete
(C) out-dated (D) nervous

191. A sneering person who always finds faults.
(A) cupid (B) kleptomaniac
(C) cynic (D) crone

192. A place for keeping bees.
(A) aviary (B) apiary
(C) cage (D) nest

193. A long journey, especially by sea.
(A) flight (B) voyage
(C) odyssey (D) safari

194. A short walk for pleasure or exercise.
(A) stroll (B) gallop
(C) jog (D) promenade

195. A place where government or public records are kept.
(A) attic (B) museum
(C) cellar (D) archive

196. A person who kills somebody especially for political reasons.
(A) criminal (B) assassin
(C) murderer (D) hangman

197. A person who opposes another.
(A) soldier (B) fighter
(C) antagonist (D) prophet

198. A person who does not want to see the realities of life and tries to escape.
(A) escapist (B) hovel
(C) plunderer (D) scavenger

199. A person who is very selective, disgusted easily, and is hard to please.
(A) misanthrope (B) fastidious
(C) selector (D) ambiguous

200. A person who can be cheated easily.
(A) credulous (B) faithful
(C) client (D) egoist

201. A sweet music.
(A) lullaby (B) melody
(C) folk song (D) duet

202. A place where everything is perfect.
(A) heaven (B) platoon
(C) cosmos (D) utopia

203. Decision that cannot be taken back.
(A) irrevocable (B) rigid
(C) order (D) brief

204. Fear of strangers.
(A) sitophobia (B) hydrophobia
(C) xenophobia (D) whoopee

205. Physical features of an area.
(A) geography (B) sociology
(C) contour (D) topography

206. Scientific study of fungi.
(A) mycology (B) botany
(C) physiology (D) zoology

207. A funeral bell.
(A) knell (B) replica
(C) windfall (D) call

208. A person who is pure and clean.
(A) immaculate (B) neat
(C) clean (D) irrevocable

209. A person who has just started learning.
(A) novice (B) foreman
(C) supervisor (D) apprentice

210. A person who is appointed by two parties to solve a dispute.
(A) judge (B) arbitrator
(C) advocate (D) barrister

211. A person who wishes to throw over all establishments.
(A) anarchist (B) hooligan
(C) criminal (D) rebel

212. A person who is bad in spelling.
(A) cacographist (B) linguist
(C) calligraphist (D) pedant

213. A person leaving his native country to settle in another.
(A) immigrant (B) emigrant
(C) traveller (D) nomad

214. A person who is always dissatisfied.
(A) heresy (B) malcontent
(C) felon (D) surrogate

215. A person who enters without any invitation.
(A) thief (B) burglar
(C) vandal (D) intruder

216. A person who is talkative.
(A) garrulous (B) faithful
(C) client (D) egoist

217. One who cuts precious stones.
(A) lapidist (B) philatelist
(C) jeweller (D) drover

218. A hospital for recuperation or for the treatment of chronic diseases
(A) sanatorium (B) asylum
(C) farm (D) bedlam

219. A professional rider in horse races
(A) horse rider (B) jockey
(C) screw (D) rider

220. One who champions the cause of women
(A) lover (B) beloved
(C) feminist (D) womanizer

221. A man who hates marriage
(A) polyandrist (B) bigot
(C) misogamist (D) widower

222. Thick skinned animal
(A) pachyderm (B) prehensile
(C) monotreme (D) hand-skinned

223. Cow - like
(A) aquiline (B) bovine
(C) feline (D) vulpine

224. The words with opposite meanings used together
(A) oxymoron (B) irony
(C) pun (D) alliteration

225. Specialist of kidney
(A) nephrologist (B) paediatrist
(C) orthopaedist (D) oncologist

ANSWER KEY

1. (A)	24. (C)	47. (C)	70. (A)	93. (B)	116. (A)	139. (C)	162. (B)	185. (A)	208. (A)
2. (D)	25. (B)	48. (B)	71. (D)	94. (B)	117. (D)	140. (A)	163. (A)	186. (A)	209. (A)
3. (A)	26. (A)	49. (A)	72. (C)	95. (C)	118. (B)	141. (C)	164. (D)	187. (A)	210. (B)
4. (B)	27. (C)	50. (B)	73. (C)	96. (B)	119. (A)	142. (B)	165. (B)	188. (B)	211. (A)
5. (A)	28. (C)	51. (B)	74. (C)	97. (B)	120. (B)	143. (B)	166. (A)	189. (B)	212. (A)
6. (B)	29. (C)	52. (C)	75. (B)	98. (C)	121. (C)	144. (B)	167. (C)	190. (B)	213. (B)
7. (A)	30. (C)	53. (B)	76. (B)	99. (A)	122. (B)	145. (D)	168. (A)	191. (C)	214. (B)
8. (C)	31. (A)	54. (B)	77. (D)	100. (B)	123. (B)	146. (D)	169. (A)	192. (B)	215. (D)
9. (D)	32. (A)	55. (C)	78. (B)	101. (B)	124. (C)	147. (D)	170. (A)	193. (B)	216. (A)
10. (A)	33. (C)	56. (A)	79. (C)	102. (B)	125. (C)	148. (D)	171. (B)	194. (A)	217. (A)
11. (B)	34. (B)	57. (C)	80. (B)	103. (B)	126. (A)	149. (B)	172. (A)	195. (D)	218. (A)
12. (A)	35. (C)	58. (B)	81. (D)	104. (A)	127. (B)	150. (C)	173. (C)	196. (B)	219. (B)
13. (C)	36. (A)	59. (C)	82. (D)	105. (C)	128. (D)	151. (B)	174. (A)	197. (C)	220. (C)
14. (A)	37. (B)	60. (D)	83. (D)	106. (B)	129. (D)	152. (B)	175. (A)	198. (A)	221. (C)
15. (C)	38. (A)	61. (C)	84. (A)	107. (B)	130. (D)	153. (C)	176. (A)	199. (B)	222. (A)
16. (B)	39. (B)	62. (A)	85. (C)	108. (B)	131. (D)	154. (A)	177. (B)	200. (A)	223. (B)
17. (D)	40. (A)	63. (D)	86. (A)	109. (D)	132. (B)	155. (C)	178. (D)	201. (B)	224. (A)
18. (D)	41. (D)	64. (B)	87. (D)	110. (C)	133. (D)	156. (D)	179. (B)	202. (D)	225. (A)
19. (A)	42. (B)	65. (A)	88. (A)	111. (B)	134. (C)	157. (D)	180. (A)	203. (A)	
20. (B)	43. (B)	66. (B)	89. (C)	112. (C)	135. (C)	158. (C)	181. (A)	204. (C)	
21. (B)	44. (D)	67. (C)	90. (D)	113. (A)	136. (A)	159. (B)	182. (A)	205. (D)	
22. (C)	45. (D)	68. (B)	91. (A)	114. (C)	137. (C)	160. (B)	183. (C)	206. (A)	
23. (A)	46. (B)	69. (C)	92. (A)	115. (B)	138. (B)	161. (B)	184. (A)	207. (A)	

CHAPTER

31 IDIOMS AND PHRASES

MEANINGS

S.N.	PHRASES	हिन्दी में अर्थ	Meaning in English
1.	**Achilles' heels**	कमजोर पक्ष	A small but fatal weakness.
2.	**Add fuel to fire**	आग में घी डालना	To make a matter worse.
3.	**An arm chair job**	आसान एवं अच्छी आय वाली नौकरी	Good income job with high comfort.
4.	**An axe to grind**	स्वार्थ से भरा उद्देश्य	Something done for selfish reasons.
5.	**An iron-will**	दृढ़ इच्छा शक्ति	Strong will power.
6.	**An old flame**	पुराना प्यार	A person with whom one had a romantic relationship in the past.
7.	**An old head on young shoulders**	अपनी उम्र से ज्यादा समझदार होना	A child or young person who thinks and talks like an older and experienced person.
8.	**An olive branch/ white flag**	शांति निवेदन	Peace request/ peace treaty.
9.	**Apple of discord**	झगड़े का कारण	Matter of dispute.
10.	**Apple of one's eye**	दुलारा, प्यारा	Very lovable/ dearest onc.
11.	**Apple-pie-order**	बिल्कुल ठीक हालत में	In good condition
12.	**At a loss**	निर्णय न ले पाना	To be unable to decide, not to know what to do.
13.	**At a pinch**	समस्या में होना	In a trouble, in a bad situation
14.	**At arm's length**	दूर रखना (दोस्ती न रखना)	Avoid becoming too friendly.
15.	**At daggers drawn**	कट्टर दुश्मनी होना	To have bitter enmity.
16.	**At ease**	चिन्ता रहित	Free from pain and anxiety.
17.	**At one's finger's tips**	पूर्ण जानकारी होना	To have complete knowledge.
18.	**At one's wits' end**	उलझन में	Puzzled / confused / perplexed.
19.	**At sixes and sevens**	अस्त-व्यस्त	In disorder.
20.	**At stake**	दांव पर	At risk and insecured.
21.	**At the eleventh hour**	अन्तिम समय में	At the last moment.

22.	**Back stairs gossip**	नौकरो के बीच का गपशप	Talk among servants/ unfair talks.
23.	**Bad blood**	शत्रुता	Enmity/ bitter relations.
24.	**Bag and baggage**	बोरिया-बिस्तर समेत	With all belongings.
25.	**Baker's dozen**	संख्या में तेरह	Thirteen in number.
26.	**Be born with a silver spoon in one's mouth**	धनी परिवार में पैदा होना	To be born in a rich family.
27.	**Be in the driving seat**	सारी जिम्मेदारी का भार उठाना	Bearing all responsibilities.
28.	**Bear the brunt of**	परिणाम भुगतना	To bear the main part of something unpleasant.
29.	**Beat about the bush**	घुमा-फिरा कर बातें करना	To talk in a roundabout manner/ circumlocution.
30.	**Beat black and blue**	अत्यधिक पिटाई करना	Beating mercilessly.
31.	**Beat hollow**	काफी आसानी एवं बुरी तरह से पराजित करना	To defeat some one easily and convincingly.
32.	**Beck and call**	आज्ञा में रहना	Ready to obey order instantly.
33.	**Bed of roses**	आनंद से भरपूर	Pleasant situation of comfort.
34.	**Bed of thorns**	दु:ख एवं तकलीफ से भरपूर	A situation of extreme difficulty.
35.	**Beggar description**	अवर्णनीय	Difficult or impossible to describe or explain
36.	**Bell the cat**	जोखिम उठाना	Taking first step at personal risk.
37.	**Between the devil and the deep sea**	दो गंभीर परेशानियों के बीच	Between two difficult situations.
38.	**Big gun**	ऊँची पहुँच वाला व्यक्ति	An influential person
39.	**Bird of passage**	यदा-कदा आनेवाला	One who comes occasionally.
40.	**Bird's eye view**	सरसरी निगाह	Overview.
41.	**Birds of a feather**	एक ही प्रवृति के लोग	People with the same idea, characteristics and interests.
42.	**Bite the dust**	पराजित होना	To be defeated.
43.	**Black sheep**	ऐसा व्यक्ति जो परिवार/टीम के लिए शर्मींदगी का कारण बनें	A person who is regarded as disgrace for his family/ team etc.
44.	**Blind alley**	कार्य जिसमें आगे प्रगति संभव नही	A situation in which no further progress can be made.
45.	**Blind date**	किसी अंजान व्यक्ति से मिलना (प्रेम प्रसंग हेतु)	A meeting between a girl and a boy for love affair, who have not met before.
46.	**Blow one's own trumpet**	अपने मुँह मियाँ मिट्ठू	To praise oneself.
47.	**Blue blood**	शाही व्यक्ति	Royal or aristocratic descent.
48.	**Blue book**	सरकारी रिर्पोट	Government report.

49.	**Body and soul**	पूर्णतया	Entirely.
50.	**Bolt from the blue**	आकस्मिक विपत्ति...............	Unexpected problem.
51.	**Bone of contention**	झगड़े की वस्तु/कारण	Subject of a dispute.
52.	**Boon/blessing in disguise**	छिपा हुआ वरदान	Hidden blessing.
53.	**Bosom friend**	जिगरी दोस्त	Fast friend.
54.	**Break the ice**	चुप्पी तोड़ना......................	To start a conversation.
55.	**Breathe one's last**	मर जाना	To pass away/ to die.
56.	**Broad day light**	दिन-दहाड़े	In day light (when crime cannot be hidden).
57.	**Broken reed**	अविश्वासी व्यक्ति	A weak, unreliable person.
58.	**Brown study**	विचारमग्नता	A state of deep thought.
59.	**Bull in the china shop** ...	जो जगह के अनुकूल न हो	One who is out of place in a delicate situation.
60.	**Burn a hole in the pocket**	शीघ्रता से खर्च करना...........	Money spent quickly.
61.	**Burn one's fingers**	खुद का नुकसान कर बैठना......	To get oneself into trouble.
62.	**Burn the candle at both ends**	अपनी क्षमता अथवा साधन का . अत्याधिक इस्तेमाल करना	To use one's resources or energies to excess.
63.	**Burn the midnight oil** ...	देर रात तक मेहनत करना	Labouring/studying till late night.
64.	**Burning question**	ज्वलन्त प्रश्न	Hot issue.
65.	**Bury the hatchet**	दुश्मनी खत्म करना	To end a hostility.
66.	**By fits and starts**	रुक-रुक कर अनियमित रूप से	Irregularly.
67.	**By hook or by crook**	गलत या सही किसी भी ढंग से..	By any means, right or wrong.
68.	**By leaps and bounds**	दिन दूनी और रात चौगुनी........	At a rapid pace.
69.	**By the skin of one's teeth/ by a whisker**	थोड़े से अंतराल से...............	Narrowly/by a hair breadth
70.	**Carry the coal to newcastle**	बेवजह मेहनत करना	Spending time and energy in doing something that is useless and wastage of energy.
71.	**Cast pearls before swine**	बंदर के हाथ में नारियल .... (किसी वस्तु को ऐसे व्यक्ति को देना जो उसका मूल्य न समझे)	A right thing in the wrong hands.
72.	**Castles in the air**	हवाई किला बनाना..............	Day dream/ a hope or desire unlikely to be realized.
73.	**Cat and dog life**	कलहपूर्ण जीवन	Troublesome life.
74.	**Catch a tartar**...............	शत्रु या बहुत बड़ी परेशानी से ... सामना होना	To encounter a more formidable or stronger opponent.
75.	**Cat's paw**	निजी स्वार्थ के पूर्ति में जिस...... व्यक्ति का प्रयोग किया जाए	A person used by another as a dupe or tool.
76.	**Chew the cud**	मनन करना.......................	To ponder over / meditate.

77. **Chicken hearted**	कायर	Lacking courage / cowardly.
78. **Cock-and-bull story**	मनगढ़ंत कहानी	A concocted story.
79. **Crocodile tears**	दिखावटी आँसू	A false display of grief.
80. **Cross swords**	लड़ना	To quarrel or fight.
81. **Cry for the moon**	किसी असंभव वस्तु की कामना करना	To desire the unattainable.
82. **Cry over spilled milk**	व्यर्थ पछताना	Regret in vain for what cannot be undone.
83. **Cut a sorry figure**	अपने प्रयास से तनिक भी प्रभाव न छोड़ना	To give a poor show.
84. **Cut both ways**	लाभ और हानि एक ही समय में	To have both good and bad effects at the same time
85. **Cut no ice**	कोई असर नहीं डालना	To fail to make an impression.
86. **Cut one's coat according to one's cloth**	अपनी आय के अनुसार व्यय करना	To live within one's means.
87. **Dance to one's tune**	हुक्म का पालन करना	Obeying one's order.
88. **Dark horse**	जो अप्रत्याशित रूप से जीत जाए	One who wins unexpectedly.
89. **Dead letter**	कानून, जो कभी लागू था लेकिन अब लागू नहीं है। जो चिट्ठी गंतव्य तक ना पहुँच पाए	A law or ordinance that is no longer enforced, an undelivered piece of mail
90. **Democle's sword**	सिर पर मंडराता खतरा	Constant threat.
91. **Die a dog's death**	लज्जाजनक मौत मरना	To die a shameful death.
92. **Die in harness**	अपने कार्यावधि के दौरान ही मृत्यु होना	Die while in service.
93. **Dog in the manger**	जो दूसरो को उस सुख का भोग करने नहीं देता है जो उसके किसी काम का नहीं	A person who prevents others from enjoying what he cannot.
94. **Donkey's years**	काफी समय बाद	A long time.
95. **Draw a line**	मर्यादा तय करना	Set a limit.
96. **Duck in a thunder storm**	व्यथा में	In a painful condition.
97. **Eagle eyed**	तेज नजर वाला	With keen eyesight.
98. **Eat humble pie**	शर्मीन्दगी झेलना	To make a humble apology and accept humiliation.
99. **Eat one's words**	शब्द वापस लेना	Take a statement back.
100. **Elbow room**	काम करने की स्वतंत्रता	Sufficient scope to move or function.
101. **End in smoke**	कोई परिणाम न निकलना	Come to nothing.
102. **Escape one's lips**	बोल जाना	Speak unintentionally or unexpectedly.
103. **Fabian policy**	जानबूझकर की गई मन्दगत नीति	Deliberate slow policy/ policy of delaying decisions.

104. Fair and square	निष्पक्ष	In an honest way .
105. Fair sex	नारी जाति	Women.
106. Fair weather friend	सिर्फ सुख में साथ देने वाला मित्र	Selfish friends who are with us only in comfortable situation.
107. Fancy price	मुंहमांगी कीमत	At any cost/ at demanded price.
108. Feather in the cap	अच्छी उप्लब्धि	Additional success.
109. Feather one's nest	अपने पद का लाभ उठा कर कमाई करना, भविष्य के लिए जुगाड़ करना	To enrich oneself by taking advantage of one's position.
110. Fight shy of	टालना	To attempt to avoid a thing or person.
111. Fish in troubled waters	विषम परिस्थिति का लाभ उठाना	To take advantage of the problems of others.
112. Fish out of water	कष्टप्रद अवस्था में	Out of one's usual and comfortable place.
113. Fly in the ointment	असुविधा	A slight unpleasant thing that obstructs the enjoyment of something.
114. Fool's paradise	झुठी उम्मीद में खुश होना	A state of being happy for foolish or unfounded reasons.
115. Forty winks	झपकी	A nap.
116. French leave	बिना सूचना के अनुपस्थित होना	A leave without information or permission.
117. Fringe benefits	वेतन के अलावा मिलने वाला लाभ	An additional benefit apart from salary.
118. From hand to mouth	सिर्फ गुजारा भर	Providing only bare essentials.
119. Gala day	आनंदोत्सव का दिन	Celebration day.
120. Get away with	बच निकलना	To escape.
121. Get down to	काम गंभीरतापूर्वक आरंभ करना	To attend to work seriously.
122. Get into a soup	झंझट में पड़ना	Get into trouble.
123. Get into hot water	समस्या में फँसना	Get into trouble.
124. Get off scot free	अदण्डित निकल जाना	To escape without punishment.
125. Get on one's nerves	तंग करना	To irritate or annoy.
126. Gibble-gabble	मूर्खतापूर्ण वार्तालाप	Foolish talk.
127. Gift of the gab	चतुराईपूर्वक धारा प्रवाह बोलने की शक्ति	Talent for speaking.
128. Give a piece of mind	डाँटना	To rebuke or scold.
129. Go through fire and water	कोई भी खतरा मोल लेना	To brave any danger.

130. Go to dogs	व्यर्थ होना	To deteriorate/ degenerate.
131. Go to rack and ruin	विनाश होना	To decay or get destroyed.
132. Good Samaritan	दयालु व्यक्ति	A person who helps and pays sympathy to those in distress.
133. Grass widow	ऐसी विवाहिता जिस का पति उससे दूर हो	A woman who is separated, divorced or lives apart from her husband.
134. Grease the palm	रिश्वत देना	To bribe.
135. Green room	अभिनेता का भेष-भूषा का कमरा	A lounge in a theatre or studio for the performers to get ready.
136. Grist to the mill	फायदेमंद	Something that can be used for one's advantage.
137. Halcyon days	बीते समय के खुशगवार दिन	Peaceful days of the past
138. Hammer and sickle	समाजवाद का प्रतीक	A symbolic representation of communism in general.
139. Hammer and tongs	बहुत अधिक मेहनत से	With great effort or energy.
140. Hand and glove with	साँठ-गाँठ में	In close co-operation.
141. Hang by a thread	बहुत नाजुक स्थिति में होना	Be in a risky situation.
142. Hard nut to crack	जटिल समस्या/ व्यक्ति	A difficult problem to solve/ A person difficult to understand.
143. Haul over the coals	बुरी तरह से डाँटना	To take to task, to reprimand, to scold badly
144. Have finger in the pie	किसी कार्य में शामिल रहना	To be involved in something.
145. Have one's hands full	भरपूर काम होना	To be completely occupied.
146. Have one's way	अपनी इच्छा के अनुसार	The way one wants.
147. Have several irons in the fire	एक ही समय कई कार्य हाथ में होना	To be involved in many projects or activities at the same time.
148. Hen-pecked husband	जोरू का गुलाम	Admirer of one's own wife in a servile manner.
149. Herculean task	बहुत कठिन कार्य	Task requiring tremendous effort.
150. High and dry	अकेला और वंचित अवस्था में	Alone in a deprived situation
151. High handed	निरंकुश	Overbearing.
152. High living	ऐशो-आराम की जिन्दगी	Living with comfort and luxury
153. Hit below the belt	गलत तरीके से प्रहार करना	To strike unfairly.
154. Hit the jackpot	बड़ी कामयाबी मिलना	Gaining a big/ great success (especially by luck).

155. Hit the nail on the head . सटीक .... To do the right thing or tell what is precisely correct

156. Hobson's choice .... कोई विकल्प न होना .... No alternative.

157. Hole and corner policy .. गुप्त नीति .... Secret policy.

158. Hue and cry .... हो-हल्ला .... Any loud public outcry.

159. Hush money .... किसी बात को गुप्त रखने के लिए दिया जाने वाला पैसा....... Money given to someone to keep something secret.

160. In a nutshell .... संक्षेप में .... In brief.

161. In black and white .... लिखित में .... In printed or written form.

162. In full swing .... पूरे जोरों पर .... At the height of activity.

163. In the blues .... दु:ख/संताप में .... In depression.

164. In the long run .... अन्तत:.......................... Ultimately.

165. In the nick of time .... ठीक समय पर .... At the last possible moment.

166. In the same boat .... एक ही हालात में .... Sharing the same problems.

167. In vogue .... प्रचलित .... In fashion.

168. Ins and outs .... विस्तृत विवरण.................... Full detail.

169. Iron hand/ Iron fist .... कड़ाई से .... Rigorous control.

170. Itching palm .... रिश्वत लेने की आदत होना...... Craving for bribe.

171. Itsy bitsy .... अत्यन्त छोटा .... Very small or tiny.

172. Jack of all trades and master of none .... जो आदमी किसी भी काम में निपुण न हो, लेकिन सभी कार्यों की जानकारी रखता हो .... A person who knows many different kinds of work but is a master of none.

173. Jail bird .... जो जेल में हो या पहले रह चुका हो...................... A person who is or has been confined to jail.

174. Jaundiced eye .... पक्षपातपूर्ण दृष्टिकोण .... To look at something with a prejudiced mind.

175. Judas kiss .... झूठा प्यार .... False love.

176. Jump to a conclusion .... बिना सोचे-समझे नतीजे पर पहुँच जाना .... To come to a conclusion immediately

177. Kangaroo court .... गैर-कानूनी न्यायालय .... An illegal court.

178. Keep one's cards close to one's chest .. किसी बात को छिपाना .... Hiding something.

179. Keep one's fingers crossed .... किसी अच्छी घटना के होने की कामना करना...... To wait expectantly.

180. Keep one's word .... वादा निभाना .... To keep one's promise.

181. Keep the ball rolling ..... जारी रखना .... To maintain the progress of a project or plan.

182. Keep the wolf from the door	दरिद्रता से संघर्ष करना	To avoid poverty/ starvation.
183. Kill two birds with one stone	एक कार्य करके दो समस्याओं से निपट लेना	Doing two things at the same time while effort is made for one
184. Kith and kin	दोस्त एवं संबंधी	Friends and relatives
185. Knit one's brow	त्यौरियाँ चढ़ाना (गुस्सा करना)	To frown.
186. Lady's man	जो महिलाओं के संगत में रहना पसंद करता हो	A man who is fond of the company of women.
187. Lame excuse	असंतोषजनक बहाना	False excuse/ baseless excuse.
188. Left- handed compliment	प्रशंसा के रूप में अपमान	An insult disguised as a compliment.
189. Lion's share	सबसे बड़ा हिस्सा	Large part.
190. Live in an ivory tower	सम्पन्नता में जीना एवं आम लोगों के दुःख से खुद को दूर रखना	Living in comfort and being unaware of realities of others' miseries.
191. Loaves and fishes	व्यक्तिगत लाभ	Material benefit/ Personal profit.
192. Look off colours	अस्वस्थ दिखाई देना	Look ill or unhealthy.
193. Look through coloured glasses	सिर्फ अच्छा-अच्छा देखना	To see only the pleasant things
194. Lump in the throat	गला भर जाना (भावनात्मक क्षण में)	A tight or uncomfortable feeling in throat due to emotions.
195. Mad as a march hare	सिरफिरा	Crazy and insane.
196. Make a clean breast	सच कबूल लेना	To confess especially something bad or illegal.
197. Maiden name	विवाहिता स्त्री का विवाह से पूर्व का नाम	A women's surname before marriage.
198. Maiden speech	प्रथम सार्वजनिक भाषण	First speech.
199. Make a hash of	गड़बड कर देना/ सत्यानाश कर देना	To mess up/ to ruin
200. Make a mountain out of a mole hill	बात का बतंगड़ बनाना	To exaggerate a minor difficulty.
201. Make both ends meet	आय के अंदर ही गुजारा करना	To live within one's means.
202. Make hay while the sun shines	मौके का लाभ उठाना	To take the benefit of an opportunity.
203. Make or mar	बनाना या बिगाड़ना	To make or destroy.
204. Make the best of both the worlds	दोनों हाथ में लड्डू	Getting benefited from both the sides.
205. Make up one's mind	निश्चय करना	To decide.

206. Man of means	समृद्ध व्यक्ति	A wealthy man.
207. Man of iron	दृढ़ इच्छा शक्ति वाला	Man with strong will-power.
208. Man of letters	विद्वान आदमी	Learned person.
209. Man of parts	सुयोग्य/गुणी व्यक्ति	A man of qualities/ a talented person
210. Man of spirit	उत्साहित व्यक्ति	A man full of enthusiasm.
211. Man of straw	चरित्रहीन आदमी या विश्वास .... के लायक नहीं	A weak person.
212. Man of the world	अनुभवी व्यक्ति	An experienced person.
213. Man of word	जुबान का सच्चा	True to one's word.
214. Mare's nest	झूठी अफवाह	A false discovery.
215. Midas touch	जादूई शक्ति (जिस काम में हाथ लगाए वह लाभदायक सिद्ध हो)	A man with extraordinary power or capacity to make any venture profitable.
216. Mince matters	ज्यादा सख्त शब्दों के प्रयोग से बचना	To moderate or restrain one's language.
217. To mind one's P's and Q's	शिष्टाचार का पूरा ध्यान रखना ..	Taking care of etiquettes
218. Miss the beat	अवसर खोना	To lose an opportunity.
219. Mother wit	आम जानकारी	Common sense.
220. Move heaven and earth	आकाश-पाताल एक करना	To try one's best.
221. Much cry and little wool/ Much ado about nothing	ऊँची दुकान, फीका पकवान	Lot of fanfare for something which has very little importance.
222. Narrow escape/ Close Shave	बाल-बाल बचना	To escape by a little margin.
223. Nig-nag	ये एक नस्ल सूचक शब्द है ..... (African-American के लिए नस्ल-सूचक शब्द के रूप में प्रयुक्त शब्द)	A noun used to address a black person (an offensive word)
224. Nine day's wonder	कम समय का सुख (चार .... दिन की चाँदनी)	Something that arouses great interest but for a very short period.
225. Nip in the bud	आरंभ में ही नष्ट कर देना	To put an end to something in its initial stage.
226. Null and void	निरस्त	Ineffective.
227. Nurse a grudge	शत्रुता भाव कायम रखना	Bear resentment for long period.
228. Oily tongue	खुशामद की भाषा	Flattering words.
229. On one's guard	सावधान/सचेत रहना	Vigilant.

230. On one's last legs	खत्म होने की स्थिति में होना	Close to collapsing.
231. Once for all	हमेशा के लिए (काम खत्म करना)	For the last time/ Conclusively.
232. Open question	सवाल जिस का एक से अधिक उत्तर हो सकता है।	A question which may have more than one answer.
233. Palmy days	अच्छे दिन जब फल-फूल रहे हो	Prosperous/ affluent days.
234. Pandora's box	समस्याओं का भंडार (जिससे वाकिफ न हो)	A source of great and unforeseen troubles.
235. Part and parcel	आवश्यक अंग	Inseparable part.
236. Past master	विशेषज्ञ	An expert.
237. Pay the piper	खर्च वहन करना	To bear the cost of something or some service rendered.
238. Pay through one's nose	अत्यधिक खर्च वहन करना	To pay dearly.
239. Penny wise, pound foolish	छोटे खर्च में किफायत करना और बड़ी रकम उड़ाना	Careful about trifles but wasteful in large ventures.
240. Pick up the gauntlet	चुनौती स्वीकार करना	To accept the challenge.
241. Play ducks and drakes	पैसे बर्बाद करना	To waste money.
242. Play second fiddle	निचला स्थान स्वीकारना	To be at a subordinate position.
243. Play truant	बिना इजाजत काम से गायब रहना	To be absent from duty without permission.
244. Poison someone's ears	कान भरना	To speak against one to another.
245. Poke one's nose	टाँग अड़ाना	To Interfere.
246. Pour oil on troubled waters	क्रोध शांत करना	To pacify the matters.
247. Pros and cons	पक्ष और विपक्ष	For and against.
248. Pull ones' legs	टाँग खिंचना (मजाक उड़ाना)	To make fun of or to tease.
249. Pull the wool over somebody's eyes	धोखा देना	To mislead, to cheat
250. Put a spoke in one's wheel	तंग करना/ बाधा उत्पन्न करना	To obstruct.
251. Put in cold storage	काम को लम्बित कर देना	To keep a work pending.
252. Put one's foot down	अपने प्राधिकार को दर्शाना	To act firmly, to assert one's authority
253. Put one's shoulders to the wheel	स्वयं अपने प्रयासो से किसी कार्य को करना	To work vigorously or exert oneself heavily.
254. Put the cart before the horse	कोई काम उल्टे सिरे से प्रारंभ करना	To do things wrongly.

255. Put the cat among pigeons	गलत काम/ बात से काफी लोगो का गुस्सा भड़का देना	To say/ do something that causes trouble or make many very angry.
256. Quarrel with one's bread and butter	जहाँ से रोजी-रोटी मिलती है, वहाँ के वरिष्ठ अधिकारी से लड़ना	To fight with the executive or employer, who is providing one's means of living.
257. Queer fish	अजीब व्यवहार वाला व्यक्ति	Strange person.
258. Rain cats and dogs	तेज बारिश होना	Rain very heavily.
259. Rainy day	आर्थिक कष्ट के दिन	Future time of need, especially financial need.
260. Read between the lines	छिपा हुआ अर्थ समझ जाना	To understand the hidden meaning.
261. Red handed	अपराध करते समय	Exactly while committing a crime or doing something wrong
262. Red letter day	सौभाग्य का अत्यन्त महत्त्वपूर्ण दिन	A memorably important or happy occasion.
263. Red tapism	लाल फीताशाही	Strict adherence to excessive paper work and official formalities.
264. Rest on one's laurels	भूतकाल के उपलब्धि पर निर्भर रहना	Depending on the achievement made in the past.
265. Rhyme or reason	किसी भी कारण से	Sense, logic or reason.
266. Right hand	मुख्य सहायक व्यक्ति	One's most valuable assistant or supporter.
267. Rise like a phoenix from its ashes	बहुत बड़ी समस्या से उबर कर निकल आना	To make a miraculous comeback after a seemingly insurmountable setback.
268. Rock the boat	संतुलन बिगाड़ना	To disturb a situation which was otherwise stable.
269. Rolling stone	जो एक जगह टिक कर नहीं रहता	A person who is unwilling to settle for long at one place.
270. Royal road	आसान रास्ता	An easy or direct way of achieving a desired result.
271. Rule the roost	रोब जमाना	To dominate.
272. Run amuck	सनक सवार होना	Mad with murderous frenzy.
273. Run in the same groove	संबंधो को मधुर बनाए रखना	Maintaining a sweet relationship.
274. Run-of-the mill	सामान्य	Average/ common.
275. Run the gauntlet	बुरे अनुभव से गुजरना	To go through an unpleasant or dangerous experience.

276. Sail under false colours	धोखा देना	To pretend to be something that you are not.
277. Save ones' skin	स्वयं को बचाना	To save oneself.
278. See eye-to-eye	पूर्णत: सहमत होना	Showing agreement/ to agree.
279. See pink elephants	अत्यधिक नशा के कारण उन चीज़ों को देखना जो वास्तव में न हो	Any visual hallucination arising due to intoxication.
280. See red	गुस्से में होना	Be very angry.
281. See through	समझ जाना	Comprehend/ understand.
282. Set at naught	असम्मान करना	To disregard or treat as of no importance.
283. Set one's face against	कड़ा विरोध करना	To oppose with determination.
284. Set one's heart on	बहुत चाहना और लक्ष्य बना लेना	To have as one's ambition to obtain something.
285. Set one's teeth on edge	परेशान करना	To irritate or annoy someone.
286. Set the Thames on fire	आश्चर्यजनक कार्य करना	To achieve something amazing.
287. Shoulder to shoulder	पूर्ण सहयोग के साथ	With united effort.
288. Show white feather	भय प्रदर्शित करना	To show cowardice.
289. Sine die	अनिश्चित काल के लिए	Indefinitely.
290. Sit on the fence	किसी का पक्ष नहीं लेना	Refuse to take side in a dispute.
291. Slip of the tongue	जुबान फिसलना	Spoken unintentionally.
292. Slow coach	आलसी व्यक्ति	A person with lazy approach of working.
293. Small fry	गैर महत्वपूर्ण व्यक्ति	Insignificant person.
294. Smell a rat	कुछ गलत है-ये महसूस कर लेना	To suspect that something wrong has been done.
295. Smooth sailing	परेशानी के बिना	Easy progress.
296. Snake in the grass	आस्तीन का सांप/ कपटी मित्र	A secret enemy.
297. Shake in the shoes	डर से काँपना	To tremble with fear or apprehension.
298. Sow the dragon's teeth	भविष्य के लिए पेरशानी इक्ट्ठा करना	To create future troubles for yourself or others.
299. Speak one's mind	मन की बात करना	Speak what one really thinks.
300. Spick and span	साफ-सुथरा	In order/ neat and clean.
301. Stand on one's own legs	आत्म-निर्भर होना	To be self dependent.
302. Stand/Stick to one's guns	अटल रहना	To be strict and determined.
303. Stand somebody in good stead	लाभदायक सिद्ध होना	To be of great use and benefit to someone.

304. Steal a march	चुपके से लाभ प्राप्त कर लेना	To obtain an advantage by secret means.
305. Step into another's shoes	किसी दूसरे की जगह लेना	To take over a job/responsibility of some other person.
306. Stiff-necked person	ढ़ीट	Stubborn or arrogant.
307. Stir a finger	कोशिश करना	Making effort.
308. Within a stone's throw	बहुत नजदीक	Very near.
309. Street Arabs	बेघर एवं अनाथ	A homeless person (especially who survives by begging).
310. Sum and substance	सारांश	Main idea or gist.
311. Swan song	मरने/ सेवानिवृति के पहले की बिदाई संगीत या समारोह	The last ceremony or farewell.
312. Sweat of one's brow	कड़ी मेहनत	Hard labour.
313. Swelled head	घमंडी	Arrogant, conceited.
314. Sworn enemies	कट्टर दुश्मन	People hating each other a lot.
315. Take away one's breath	भौचक्का कर देना	To overwhelm with surprise.
316. Take by storm	अचानक प्रभावित करना	To surprise unexpectedly.
317. Take into account	पर विचार करना	To consider.
318. Take one at one's word	किसी के कहने पर विश्वास करना	To be convinced of one's sincerity and act in accordance with his/her statement.
319. Take the bull by the horns	संकट का सीधा सामना करना	To adopt the most direct way of facing a difficulty.
320. Take to one's heels	भाग जाना	To run away.
321. Talk big	डींगें मारना	To boast or brag.
322. Talk of the town	चर्चित बात	To be the person or subject everyone is talking about.
323. The printer's devils	छपाई त्रुटि	Error in printing.
324. Think twice	सोच समझ कर निर्णय लेना	To consider carefully before deciding.
325. Through thick and thin	अच्छी-बुरी (सभी परिस्थितियों में)	In good and bad times.
326. Throw cold water upon	हतोत्साहित करना	To discourage.
327. Throw down the gauntlet	चुनौती देना	To challenge.
328. Tooth and nail	पूरी ताकत से	Violently.
329. True to one's salt	वफादार/ नमक हलाल	Loyal person.
330. Turn a deaf ear to	अनसुना करना	Not to pay attention to.
331. Turn over a new leaf	बुरे आचरण छोड़ अच्छी दिशा में पूर्ण रूप से बदलना	To be entirely changed (to be a better person).

332. Turn the corner	किसी कार्य में आये संकटपूर्ण स्थिति से उबर जाना ...	To pass through a critical point in a process.
333. Turn turtle	पलट जाना	To overturn.
334. Turn up one's nose at....	नीचा समझना....................	To treat with contempt.
335. Under the nose of..........	आँखों के सामने, नाक के नीचे .	Right in front of someone.
336. Under the thumb of.......	के वश में होना	Under the power or influence of.
337. Up and doing	काम में सक्रिय रूप से लगना ...	Active in work.
338. Up one's sleeves...........	छिपा के रखी गई वस्तु जिसका प्रयोग जरूरत पड़ने पर करें .	A strategy, idea or resources kept hidden and used whenever required.
339. Uphill task	बहुत कठिन कार्य	Difficult task.
340. Upon one's sweet will....	अपनी इच्छा पर.................	On one's own desire or wish.
341. Ups and downs..............	उतार-चढ़ाव	Good and bad times.
342. Utopian scheme	आदर्श किन्तु कार्यान्वित न होने वाली योजना	A visionary scheme though Impractical.
343. Weather the storm........	समस्या से मुकाबला कर सुरक्षित बाहर निकलना	Survive by coming out of difficulties.
344. Well-to-do.....................	सम्भ्रांत...........................	Affluent, rich
345. Wet blanket	मजा किरकिरा करने वाला	One who spoils the enjoyment.
346. Wheels within wheels ...	जटिल कार्य का और जटिल होना............	A series of intricately connected events
347. White elephant	महंगा परंतु बेकार	Expensive but of no use.
348. White lie	छोटा एवं गैर-महत्त्वपूर्ण झूठ	A minor lie.
349. Will o' the wisp	भ्रामक उम्मीद	Elusive/ unreal.
350. Windfall	ऐसा लाभ जिस की उम्मीद ना हो	Sudden gain received unexpectedly.
351. With a grain of salt	स्वीकार करना लेकिन शंका के साथ	To accept with doubt and not believing it literally.
352. With one accord/ in one voice	एक स्वर में	Unanimously.
353. Wolf in sheep's clothing	मित्रता जताने वाला खतरनाक आदमी	A malicious person in harmless or benevolent disguise.
354. Word for word	शब्दशः...........................	In exactly the same words.
355. Word of mouth	अनौपचारिक व मौखिक	Informal or verbal communication.
356. Yeoman's service	अति उत्तम काम जो खास कर सहायता हेतु किया गया हो	Excellent work done especially to help or support a cause

32 IDIOMS AND PHRASES

CHAPTER

'LET'S USE THEM IN SENTENCES'

1. **Above board** *(honest and straightforward, ईमानदार एवं छल-कपट रहित)*- Gandhi ji was above board and hence had nothing to hide.
2. **Adam's ale** *(pure water, शुद्ध जल)*- In the remotest parts of Rajasthan, people walk miles for Adam's ale.
3. **Add a new feather to one's cap** *(to acquire a new honour or distinction, कोई नया सम्मान प्राप्त करना)*- KD Campus has added a new feather in its cap by starting KD Publication.
4. **Add insult to injury** *(to harm as well as humiliate, जले पर नमक छिड़कना)*- She has added insult to injury by returning the gift and sending a 'get lost' note.
5. **After one's own heart** *(similar to you, जो आप के जैसा ही है)*- Seeing your inclination towards art and literature, I can say that you are clearly a person after my own heart.
6. **An eye wash** *(a pretence, दिखावा)*- The whole investigation was just an eye wash as no one was held guilty.
7. **A hair-breadth escape** *(very narrow escape, बाल-बाल बचना)*- He had a hair-breadth escape when his bike skid on the oil drenched road.
8. **A lost ball in the weeds -** (*completely lost or confused* घबड़ा जाना)– He met with an accident yesterday and became a lost ball in the weeds.
9. **An old flame** *(long time love, पुराना प्यार)*- He saw his old flame in the market yesterday but prudently avoided eye contact.
10. **An old head on young shoulders** *(to be more matured than one's own age, अपनी उम्र से ज्यादा समझदार होना)*- He is an old head on young shoulders as he teaches Physics at a university at a young age of 25 .
11. **As fit as a fiddle** *(strong and healthy, स्वस्थ)*- He feigned illness but I knew that he was as fit as a fiddle.
12. **Assume airs** *(to pretend superiority, बड़प्पन दिखाना)*- After becoming an IAS officer, he has assumed airs.
13. **At large** *(absconding, कानून के गिरफ्त से दूर)*- Many terrorists are at large and posing serious threat to the security of India.

14. **At loggerheads** *(to be at strife, शत्रुता की अवस्था)*- Congress is always at logger heads with the BJP.
15. **At naught** *(to disregard or treat as of no importance, असम्मान करना)*- Leaders today set Gandhiji's ideals at naught.
16. **At odds** *(in disagreement, असहमत होना)*- Various political parties are at odds in the matter of Women Reservation Bill.
17. **At sea** *(to be confused, उलझन में)*- He was at sea when he saw the question paper.
18. **At one's beck and call** *(at service, आज्ञा में हाजिर रहना)*- The servants were always at the beck and call of the rich merchant.
19. **Backstairs influence** *(improper and private influence, ऐसा प्रभाव जो असार्वजनिक हो एवं सही नहीं हो)*- He tried to get a government job by backstairs influence.
20. **Bad egg** *(a worthless person, अवांछनिय व्यक्ति)*- Often a prodigal son of a rich father becomes a bad egg for the society.
21. **Bandy words** *(to argue, जुबान लड़ाना)*- The two neighbours usually bandy words and create a lot of nuisance.
22. **Bank upon** *(depend on, count on, पर निर्भर होना)*- You can bank upon us at the time of need.
23. **Bated breath** *(holding your breath, in anxiety, चिंता इत्यादि से साँस रूकना)*- We waited for the good news outside the delivery room with bated breath.
24. **Caught red-handed** *(to be caught while committing a crime, रंगे हाथ पकड़े जाना)*- My brother felt ashamed when he was caught red handed reading my personal diary.
25. **Be in the bad books of** *(out of favour, कृपा पात्र न होना)*- She is in the bad books of her parents as she went to watch a movie without informing them.
26. **Be in the bad odour of** *(to be out of favour, किसी की बुरी राय में होना)*- A corrupt minister is always in bad odour of the public.
27. **Be in the good books of** *(to be in kind favour, कृपा पात्र होना)*- She is in the good books of her employer as she is very efficient and hardworking.
28. **Be in the good odour of** *(to be in good favour, किसी की अच्छी राय में होना)*- An honest minister is always in the good odour of the public.
29. **Be in the driving seat** *(to take the whole responsibility, सारी जिम्मेदारी का भार उठाना)*- Ramesh is the eldest son and so he is in the driving seat after his father's death.
30. **Bear the palm** *(to be victorious, विजयी होना)*- Our school bore the palm in the dance competition held at the district level.
31. **Beat the air** *(to make useless efforts, व्यर्थ प्रयास करना)*- Trying to reform a hard-core criminal is like beating the air.
32. **Bed of roses** *(an easy and comfortable situation, सरल और आराम की स्थिति)*- The life of the prince was a bed of roses.
33. **Bee in one's bonnet** *(go on talking about something which you think is important, राग अलापना उस बात का जो आप के अनुसार महत्वपूर्ण हो)*- She has a bee in her bonnet about recycling of waste material.
34. **Behind the scene** *(secretly, छिपे रूप में)*- The minister is the mastermind behind the scene and the police are arresting small fries.

35. **Below the belt** *(to strike unfairly, गलत तरीके से प्रहार करना)*- One must compete with others in a fair manner and should not hit anyone below the belt.

36. **Beside oneself** *(to feel extremely nervous or worried, बहुत अधिक चिन्तीत या व्याकुल होना)*- Before any exam I am beside myself.

37. **Beside the mark** *(irrelevant, अप्रासंगिक)*- The judge did not hear any argument that was beside the mark.

38. **Between Scylla and Charybdis** *(between two great dangers, दो कठिन परिस्थितियों के बीच)*- She is between Scylla and Charybdis. If she obeys her mother-in-law she will lose her job and if she does not she will lose her family.

39. **Bid defiance** *(to defy, अवज्ञा करना)*- The army is bidding defiance by going against the government.

40. **Bite the dust** *(to be defeated, हार जाना)*- In every match , the Pakistani team bit the dust.

41. **Blaze the trail** *(to be a pioneer and make path for others, दूसरो के लिए रास्ता बनाना)*- Only a man of iron can blaze the trail.

42. **Blessing in disguise** *(something intrinsically good but having a bad appearance, ऊपर से बुरी दिखने वाली पर वास्तव में अच्छी बात)*- He missed the train but it was a blessing in disguise as the train met with an accident.

43. **Blow one's own trumpet** *(to praise one's ownself, अपनी ही शेखी बघारना)*- Every political party always blows its own trumpet and denounces the other political parties.

44. **Blue stocking** *(an educated intellectual lady, पढ़ी लिखी महिला)*- A blue stocking was rarely found in Medieval India.

45. **Book worm** *(a bibliophilic person, किताबी कीड़ा)*- She is not a book worm but still comes first.

46. **Break the ice** *(to break silence by speaking first, चुप्पी तोड़ना)*- Shyam broke the ice by talking to me after a long time.

47. **Bring down the house** *(receive great applause, भरपूर तारीफ पाना)*- The performance of Lata Mangeshkar brought the house down.

48. **Bring home** *(to explain, समझाना)*- I was unable to bring my views home before my parents.

49. **Bring to book** *(to punish, सजा देना)*- The guilty should be brought to book.

50. **Bring to light** *(to disclose, पता लगाना, छिपी बात को प्रकाश में लाना)*- The CBI has brought many indiscrepancies to light in many high profile cases.

51. **Brow beat** *(to intimidate, डराना)*- The Government must not brow beat the social reformers if they protest against any unjust law.

52. **Burn one's boats** *(point of no return, वापसी का रास्ता बंद कर देना)*- By signing the agreement, he has burnt his boat.

53. **By and by** *(gradually, धीरे-धीरे)*- You will learn the norms of this organization by and by.

54. **By and large** *(on the whole, संपूर्ण रूप से देखने पर)*- My friend is by and large an honest person.

55. **By dint of** *(by means of, के बल पर)*- You can succeed by dint of hard work only.

56. **By fair or foul means** *(by any way right or wrong, सही या गलत किसी भी प्रकार से)*- He will try to get a job by fair or foul means but will ultimately lose his peace of mind.

57. **By the rule of thumb** *(according to practical experience, व्यवहारिक रूप से)*- By rule of thumb we must not allow children to take major decisions.

58. **Call a spade a spade** *(to be frank, मुंहफट बात करना)*- He never hesitated in calling a spade a spade and hence he has few friends.

59. **Call names** *(to abuse, गाली देना)*- He has a bad habit of calling names.

60. **Capital punishment** *(death penalty, मौत की सजा)*- Capital punishment should be abolished as it is the cruelest form of punishment.

61. **Carrot and stick policy** *(reward and punishment policy, इनाम और सजा की पॉलिसी)*- The multinational companies adopt carrot and stick policy to get maximum output.

62. **Carry matters with a high hand** *(to deal with a person strictly, सख्ती से निपटना)*- The police carry matters with a high hand.

63. **Cast a slur** *(to bring disgrace, अपयश का कारण बनना)*- Taking bribe can cast a slur on the honour of your family.

64. **Cave in** *(yield, झुक जाना)*- One must not cave in under pressure or temptation.

65. **Chapter and verse** *(in full detail, पूर्ण विवरण के साथ)*- I cannot narrate the whole incident in chapter and verse.

66. **Cheek by jowl** *(close together, साथ-साथ)*- Many poor people live cheek by jowl in a small room.

67. **Child's play** *(a very easy task, बच्चों का खेल)*- It is not a child's play to address a crowd.

68. **Clinch the issue** *(to clear the controversy, विवाद खत्म करना)*- The college administration clinched the issue by accepting the demands of the students.

69. **Clip one's wings** *(to weaken the power, पर कतरना)*- The PM clipped the wings of some ministers by withdrawing the powers delegated to them.

70. **Close shave** *(a narrow escape, बाल-बाल बचना)*- His family had a close shave in the bus accident.

71. **Cloven hoof** *(symbol of disgrace or evil intention, असम्मान या शैतानी इरादे का प्रतीक)*- Usually some or other leader of the party shows cloven hoof to the leadership.

72. **Cock a snook** *(to show impudent contempt, असम्मान प्रकट करना)*- He refused to accept the award, cocking a snook at the Filmfare Award jury.

73. **Cock sure** *(very sure and certain, सुनिश्चित होना)*- I am cock sure, we will win the match.

74. **Cold reception** *(not a hearty welcome, जो गर्मजोशी से भरा स्वागत नहीं हो)*- We were very unhappy when we were given cold reception at his marriage party.

75. **Come across** *(meet by chance, अचानक मुलाकात होना)*- I came across a problem when I was solving the equation.

76. **Come home to** *(to understand, समझ में आना)*- At last, it came home and we got the correct answer.

77. **Come in handy** *(to be useful, काम का होना)*- This opener comes in handy when we need to open this container.

78. Come to a pass *(to happen, किसी घटना का होना)*- The accident came to pass due to the negligence of the driver.

79. Come true *(to prove true, सही साबित होना)*- My dreams have come true as I have got selected.

80. Cool one's heels *(to be kept waiting, इन्तजार कराया जाना)*- We sat down and cooled our heels for the minister who didn't turn up.

81. Corporal punishment *(bodily punishment, शारीरिक दण्ड)*- Corporal punishment is banned in schools.

82. Count chickens before they are hatched *(To anticipate profit before hand, पहले से लाभ का विश्वास कर लेना)*- Don't dream of profit now as it is futile to count your chickens before they are hatched.

83. Cross one's mind *(to occur to oneself, अचानक दिमाग में आना)*- I was resting when an idea crossed my mind.

84. Curry favour *(to win favour by flattery, खुशामद करके कृपा का पात्र बनना)*- Many developing countries curry favour with America.

85. Curtain lecture *(a private scolding by wife to her husband, अकेले में पति को दी गई डाँट)*- Don't tell me that your father has never got any curtain lecture in his life.

86. Cut both ends *(to argue in support of both sides of the issue, दोनों पक्षो के तरफ से तर्क देना)*- Mahesh always cuts both ends and hence he has no friend.

87. Cut the Gordian knot *(to solve a difficult problem, किसी कठिन समस्या का हल निकालना)*- The national leaders cut the Gordian knot by making India a secular country.

88. Cut throat *(tough, कठीन)*- We face cut throat competition in every field.

89. Damp squib *(complete failure though earlier thought to be exciting, पूर्ण असफलता, जो लगता था उत्तेजनात्मक होगा)*- The performance of team India turned out to be a damp squib.

90. Dance attendance upon *(to be in servile attitude all the time, चापलूसी करना/ हाजिरी बज़ाना)*- The mother-in-law wanted the lady to dance attendance upon her.

91. Dark Horse *(unexpected winner, अप्रत्याशित विजेता)*- An unknown independent candidate came out as a dark horse after the election.

92. Days of reckoning *(a time when the effects of one's past mistakes or misdeeds catch up with one, जब भूतकाल में की गई गल्तियों का असर दिखने लगे)*- You have been manipulating the account for a long time. Now days of reckoning have come.

93. Dead broke *(penniless, दिवालिया)*- Due to recession he has become dead broke.

94. Die-hard *(obstinately resistant to change, परिवर्तन के खिलाफ दृढ़ता से होना)*- He is a die-hard fan of Devanand.

95. Dig one's own grave *(to do something which causes you harm, ऐसा कृत्य जो मुसीबत में डाल दे)*- You are digging your own grave by writing your password in your diary.

96. Dog's life *(very miserable life, कष्टदायक जीवन)*- Due to unchecked inflation, the poor are living a dog's life.

97. Double dealing *(deceitful actions, धोखेबाजी के कार्य)*- The double dealing of the lawyer was exposed by a sting operation.

98. **Double-edged sword** *(act that will harm oneself as well as the others, ऐसा कार्य जो दूसरे को और स्वयं को भी नुकसान पहुंचा सकता है)*- Corruption is a doubled edged sword for the public as well as the Government.

99. **Down and out** *(lacking funds, resources or prospects, फण्ड, संपदा इत्यादि की कमी होना)*- He was down and out when his factory was burnt to the ground.

100. **Down in the mouth** *(filled with melancholy and despondency, दुख एवं निराशा से भरा होना)*- She was down in the mouth when she saw her husband's dead body.

101. **Draconian law** *(extremely severe law, अत्यन्त क्रूर कानून)*- There are still many draconian laws in some countries.

102. **Draw the long bow** *(to tell large stories or to exaggerate, लम्बी कहानियाँ बनाना या बढ़ा-चढ़ा कर कुछ बताना)*- Come to the point. Don't draw a long bow.

103. **Drawn battle / match** *(a battle or match in which no party wins, बराबर की बाजी होना)*- The drawn battle created a lot of excitement till the last ball.

104. **Drop in the ocean** *(very insignificant amount, अत्यन्त ही थोड़ी मात्रा)*- My knowledge about Archeology is only a drop in the ocean.

105. **Ducks and drakes** *(to waste money, पैसे बर्बाद करना)*- I cannot allow you to play ducks and drakes with my hard earned money.

106. **Dutch courage** *(bravery shown under alcoholic influence, शराब के नशे में दिखाये जाना वाला साहस)*- His dutch courage will vanish when he will gain his senses.

107. **Easy money** *(bribe, रिश्वत)*- Many officers make easy money.

108. **Eat one's word** *(to admit that something you said in the past was wrong, ये स्वीकार करना कि कही हुई बात गलत थी)*- Those who said that Amitabh Bachhan's charm was over had to eat their word after the success of Kaun Banega Crorepati.

109. **Egg on** *(to urge somebody to do some thing that is generally wrong, कुछ गलत कार्य करने के लिए प्रोत्साहित करना)*- He egged me on to drive faster.

110. **Eke out** *(to support one's own existence with difficulty and effort or to add (something insufficient), especially with effort, बहुत मुश्किल से कुछ उपलब्ध कराना)*- He is trying *to eke out an income by doing over time.*

111. **Elixir of life** *(nectar of life, जीवन का अमृत)*- Contentment is the elixir of life.

112. **Enough and to spare** *(plentiful, प्रचुर मात्रा में)*- He earns enough and to spare.

113. **Ever and Anon** *(now and then, जब-तब)*- The night was dark and we could hear the howling of dogs ever and anon.

114. **Every dog has his day** *(good fortune comes sooner or later, अच्छा दिन सबका आता है)*- When he bagged three movies in a row, he realized that every dog has his day.

115. **Every inch** *(completely, पूर्ण रूप से)*- She looks every inch a winner.

116. **Eye wash** *(ineffective remedy which is just for show, सिर्फ दिखावे का)*- The committee that was set up to look into the multiple scams was just an eye wash.

117. **See eye-to-eye** *(showing agreement/ to agree, पूर्णत: सहमत होना)*- The two competitors never see eye to eye.

118. **Face the music** *(to face opposition, कठिनाई या विरोध का सामना करना)*- Leaders have to face the music if they do not fulfill promises made by them.

119. Fan the flame *(to aggravate, बदतर बनाना)*- I don't want to fan the flame of the tension brewing between husband and wife.

120. Few and far between *(very rare, बहुत कम)*- The houses in this remote village are few and far away.

121. Fight to the finish *(to fight to the end, आखिरी नतीजे तक लड़ना)*- When she was blamed and sued without any rhyme or reason, she pledged to fight the case to the finish.

122. Fish in troubled waters *(to take advantage of the difficulties of others, दूसरों की परेशानी का लाभ उठाना)*- Many lawyers don't hesitate to fish in troubled waters.

123. Fit to hold a candle to *(match for, equal in quality, बराबरी का होना)*- He is such a miser that he is not fit to hold a candle to such a lavish reception.

124. Flash in the pan *(something or someone that became successful quickly and is unlikely to be repeated, अस्कमात सफलता पाना जो क्षणिक हो और भविष्य में फिर शायद न हो)*- The success of Kumar Gaurav in his debut movie 'Love Story' was a flash in the pan.

125. Flesh and blood *(human nature or physical existence, together with its weaknesses / substance and depth in artistic portrayal, हाड़-माँस का होना/ किसी कला में पायी जाने वाली गहराई)*- These problems are too heavy for mere flesh and blood to handle.

126. Flog a dead horse *(to waste one's energy, बेकार की कोशिश करना)*- Trying to reform a terrorist is like flogging a dead horse.

127. Fly in the face of *(to defy/ to brave/ to withstand, अवज्ञा करना/ साहस से सामना करना)*- The theory about the existence of heaven and hell flies in the face of all logic and common sense.

128. Fly into a passion *(to be enraged, क्रोधित होना)*- He flies into a passion within seconds if someone ignores his instructions.

129. Fool's errand *(a fruitless mission or undertaking, निष्फल कार्य)*- Many projects of Mohammad -bin-Tuglaq were fool's errands.

130. Foot the bill *(bear expenses, खर्च वहन करना)*- You had ordered these tasteless pizzas . Now you will have to foot the bill.

131. For good *(for ever, हमेशा के लिए)* He educated his son and sent him to America for good.

132. For the rainy day *(precaution for emergency, कठिन परिस्थितियों के लिए प्रबन्ध)*- I have kept some money in the bank for the rainy days.

133. Foul Play *(treachery, धोखाधड़ी)*- Foul play destroys the fun of life.

134. French leave *(leave without information, बिना सूचना के अनुपस्थित होना)*- If you take french leave, you will be fined.

135. From the bottom of one's heart *(very sincerely, अन्तर मन से)*- I thanked him from the bottom of my heart for his timely help.

136. Gain ground *(to progress/ advance, तरक्की करना/ वर्चस्व बढ़ाना)*- Due to the misgovernance the opposition is gaining ground.

137. Gentleman at large *(wealthy man with time on his hands, धनी व्यक्ति जिसके पास समय की कमी न हो)*- He is a gentleman at large, the only son of a rich father.

138. Get down to brass tacks *(discuss the basic facts or realities/ to deal with the matter straight, किसी मुख्य विषय पर चर्चा करना)*- After avoiding the thorny questions about tax reforms for months, the ruling party finally got down to brass tacks last week and drafted a preliminary proposal.

139. Get into a scrape *(find oneself in a difficult or awkward situation, खुद को मुश्किल हालात में पाना)*- By signing the bond he will get into a scrape.

140. Get the better of *(to overcome, काबू पा लेना)*- At last he got the better of his problems and opponents.

141. Get wind of *(to know the secret, भेद जान लेना)*- The opposition got the wind of the plans of the ruling party.

142. Gird up the loin *(to be well prepared for some difficult task, किसी कठिन कार्य को करने के लिए कमर कस कर तैयार होना)*- If we all gird up the loin, we can remove illiteracy.

143. Give a wide berth *(to give ample space or distance to avoid an unwanted consequence, किसी अवांछनिय नतीजे से बचने के लिए दूरी बनाये रखना)*- Being an understanding father, you should give a wide berth to your son and wait for the right time to talk to him.

144. Give cold shoulder *(pay no attention to, ध्यान न देना)*- He went to the police for help but they gave him the cold shoulder.

145. Give somebody enough rope (to hang themselves) *(to allow someone to do what he wants to, knowing that he will probably fail or get into trouble, किसी को कुछ करने की अनुमति दे देना ये जानते हुए कि वह असफल हो जाएगा।)*- Don't stop him.Give him enough rope to hang. He will be rejected for his poor performance and will return home.

146. Give the devil his due *(even the wicked person should be given the credit due to him, बुरे आदमी की भी उचित प्रशंसा करना)*- In spite of being so rude, he helped me in need. The devil should be given his due.

147. Give up the ghost *(to die, मर जाना)*- My grandfather gave up the ghost last Sunday.

148. Give vent to *(to express one's thoughts or feelings, अपने विचारों या भावनाओं को प्रकट करना)*- Every Indian is free to give vent to his thoughts.

149. Wool-gathering *(to engage in fanciful daydreaming, मनभावन कल्पना में खोए रहना)*- Work hard. Wool gathering will not help you in any way.

150. Go back on one's word *(to change one's mind about/ repudiate, बात से पीछे हट जाना)*- She has decided to do charity and she should not go back on her word.

151. Go broke *(become bankrupt, दिवालिया होना)*- He has gone broke and is unable to make both ends meet..

152. Whole hog *(the whole way/ completely, पूर्ण रूप से)*- She went the whole hog and checked the account of the whole month in one go.

153. Golden opportunity *(very favourable opportunity or chance, सुनहरा अवसर)*- He missed the golden opportunity by declining the offer.

154. Green horn *(an inexperienced or immature person, especially one who is easily deceived,अनुभवहीन व्यक्ति जिसे बेवकूफ बनाना आसान हो)*- He incurred heavy loss because he relied on the green horn.

155. Hang in balance *(have two equally possible results/ be uncertain, अनिश्चिय की स्थिति)*- After the opposition party won the election, whether or not the new highway will be built, hangs in the balance.

156. Hang over one's head *(to have something bothering or worrying one, परेशानी या समस्या का बने रहना)*- He committed suicide because several court cases hung over his head.

157. Hard and fast *(definite, निश्चित)*- There is no hard and fast rule for solving these numericals.

158. Harp on the same string *(to keep on talking on the same topic, एक ही विषय पर बात करते रहना)*- Some obsessed people have the habit of harping on the same string.

159. In the nick of time *(at the last possible moment, ठीक समय पर)*- I reached the examination hall in the nick of time.

160. Heart and soul *(with complete faith and dedication, सच्चे दिल से)*- He has put heart and soul in his work.

161. Heart to heart *(very frankly, पूरे दिल से, खुले रूप से)*- The two friends had a heart to heart talk when they met after many years.

162. Hen-pecked husband *(admirer of one's own wife in a servile manner, जोरू का गुलाम)*- Every boy boasts, "I will never become a hen pecked husband."

163. Himalayan blunder *(a serious mistake, गंभीर गलती)*- He committed a Himalayan blunder by leaving for work without his body guards and was shot dead.

164. Hit the nail on the head *(to act in the right way, ठीक निशाने पर चोट मारना)*- You have hit the nail on the head by making the bid at the right time.

165. Hold good *(valid/ applicable, लागू/ उचित ठहराना)*- Rule of triple talaq doesn't hold good even in the Islamic countries.

166. Hold one's ground *(to stand firm, दृढ़ता से डटे रहना)*- The Indian soldiers held their ground to the end.

167. Hold one's jaw *(to stop talking, बोलना बन्द होना)*- Please hold your jaw else I shall go away.

168. Hold the fort *(to stand firm on one's position, अपने स्थान पर डटे रहना)*- Our soldiers held the fort and proved their valour.

169. Hold the scales even *(to be impartial, निष्पक्ष रहना)*- The Judge must hold the scales even.

170. Hold water *(to stand up to critical examination, सही साबित होना)*- Your argument does not hold water.

171. Hot water *(trouble, परेशानियां)*- Your cousin is in hot water due to his controversial speech.

172. In a fix *(in a difficult mental state, मानसिक उलझन में)*- He was in a fix when he saw his mother in ICU.

173. In a tight corner *(in difficult situation, मुश्किल हालात में)*- I found myself in a tight corner when I lost my journey ticket.

174. In doldrums *(to be depressed, निराशा में)*- He was found in doldrum when he could not succeed even in his third attempt.

175. In embryo *(immature/ in the making, अविकसित अवस्था में)*- My plan of expanding my business is still in embryo.

176. **In no time** *(in a very short time, थोड़ी ही देर में)*- He can solve any mathematical problem in no time.

177. **In one's teens** *(from thirteen to nineteen years of age, तेरह से उन्नीस साल तक)*- A person in his teens is spirited, full of dreams and optimistic.

178. **In the air** *(in circulation/ in people's thoughts, चर्चा में)*- News of his cold blooded murder is very much in the air.

179. **Down in the dumps** *(unhappy, depressed, दुखी/ निराश)*- He is down in the dumps after his father's death.

180. **In the family way** (pregnant, *गर्भवती)*- She has applied for leave as she is in the family way.

181. **In the good books of** *(to be in favour with a person, पक्ष में करना)*- People usually flatter their boss to remain in their good books.

182. **In the jaws of** *(in the grip of, दांतों के बीच, किसी के कब्जे में)*- The boy was in the jaws of the kidnappers.

183. **In the limelight** *(at the centre of attention, आकर्षण का केन्द्र)*- The life of film stars remain in the lime light.

184. **In the lurch** *(in a difficult and embarrassing position, मुश्किल एवं बीच मंझधार वाली स्थिति में)*- When the experiment failed, the sub-ordinates left the eminent scientist in the lurch.

185. **Melting pot** *(a place where immigrants of different cultures or races form an integrated society, ऐसा स्थान जहाँ अप्रवासी लोग अपनी-अपनी सभ्यता के साथ एक समाज बनाते है)*- With immigrants from all over the world getting an easy passage to India, our country is becoming a melting pot.

186. **In the red** (at a loss/in debt, *घाटे में/कर्ज में)*- The company is in the red due to its unrealistic projects.

187. **In the teeth of** *(facing danger or threats, के विरूद्ध/ खतरे का सामना करना)*- The tribe was in the teeth of starvation.

188. **In the twinkling of an eye** *(in a moment/ in no time, क्षण भर में)*- The house came down in the twinkling of an eye.

189. **To fish in troubled waters** *(to take advantage of the problems of others, विषम परिस्थिति का लाभ उठाना)*- Many self-centred lawyers fish in troubled water.

190. **For all intents and purposes** *(for all practical purposes, हर व्यावहारिक उद्देश्य के लिए)*- This dictionary is useful for all intents and purposes.

191. **Snake in the grass** *(a secret enemy, आस्तीन का सांप/ कपटी मित्र)*- Politicians playing caste based politics are snakes in the grass.

192. **Keep abreast of** *(not to fall behind, पीछे न रह जाना)*- We must keep abreast of the latest developments in technology.

193. **Keep an eye on** *(to watch, नजर रखना)*- It is very necessary for us to keep an eye on our growing children.

194. **Keep an open table** *(to entertain all, सब का स्वागत करना)*- It is not very difficult to keep an open table in a party.

195. Keep at an arm's length *(to keep at a distance, दूरी बना कर रखना)*- You must keep bad habits at arm's length.

196. Keep at bay *(To keep someone at a distance, दूर रखना)*- He held the police at bay with a gun for several hours.

197. Keep body and soul together *(to be able to pay for just those things that you need in order to live, सिर्फ जीवन-यापन भर का जुगाड़ कर पाना)*- They can barely keep body and soul together with their meagre income.

198. Keep the pot boiling *(to keep going on actively, जीवन-यापन जारी रखना)*- One has to keep the pot boiling inspite of all odds one has to face in life.

199. Keep up appearance *(to keep one's prestige/ to maintain outward show, बाहरी दिखावा बनाये रखना)*- Inspite of being bankrupt, he is able to keep up his appearance.

200. Kick one's heels *(wait impatiently to be summoned, बुलावे के लिए बेसब्री से इंतजार करना)*- The whole day we kicked our heels outside the court room.

201. Kick the bucket *(to die, मर जाना)*- He kicked the bucket and left his family in extreme financial difficulty.

202. Kill the fat calf for *(to arrange a lavish reception for someone, किसी का धूमधाम से स्वागत करना)*- India killed the fat calf for the Common Wealth Games.

203. Kiss the dust *(to be humiliated, अपमानित होना)*- In Indo-Pak war our enemies had to kiss the dust.

204. Knock against *(to hit against, टक्कर खाना)*- I couldn't see the transparent door and knocked against it.

205. Lapped in luxury *(brought up in luxury, विलासिता में पलना)*- Great people are generally not lapped in luxury.

206. Laugh in one's sleeves *(to laugh secretly, चुपके से)*- Our neighbours laughed in their sleeves when they saw my grandfather wearing a pair of fashionable goggles.

207. Lead by the nose *(to lead someone by coercion/ to guide someone very carefully, दवाब में या मार्गदर्शन करने हेतु किसी को रास्ता दिखाना)*- *I had to lead him by the nose to the meeting. He will never find his way through the admission form unless you lead him by the nose.*

208. Lead to the altar *(to marry, शादी करने जाना)*- He promised her to lead her to the altar.

209. Leap in the dark *(to do something though there is uncertainty about the outcome, अनिश्चित परिणाम होने पर भी कोई कार्य करना)*- To play lottery is to leap in the dark.

210. Leave no stone unturned *(to make all possible efforts, कोई भी प्रयत्न बाकी न छोड़ना)*- He worked very hard to pass the Civil Services Exams and left no stone unturned.

211. Leave one in the lurch *(to leave one in difficulties, किसी का कठिनाईयों में साथ छोड़ देना)*- He kicked the bucket and left his family in the lurch. (To kick the bucket means to die)

212. Let by-gones be by-gones *(to forget old things, पुरानी बातों को भूल जाना)*- India and Pakistan must start bi-lateral talks and let by-gones be by-gones.

213. Lick the dust *(to get defeated, हार जाना)*- The team licked the dust in the final match.

214. Lie in wait *(wait in hiding to attack, घात लगाये बैठे रहना)*- The policemen were lying in wait for the kidnappers.

215. Live in an ivory tower *(where one can be unaware of the realities of life , जहाँ जीवन की वास्तविकता से दूर रहते हैं)*- The queen lived in an ivory tower and did not know the meaning of poverty.

216. Long and short *(all that can or need be said., सारांश)*- The long and short of the whole discussion will be made available to all in black and white. (In black and white means in written form)

217. Look down upon *(To hate a person, किसी व्यक्ति से घृणा करना)*- I hate those people who look down upon the poor.

218. Lose the day *(to be defeated, हार जाना)*- My favourite football team lost the day.

219. Make a fortune *(To grow rich, धनी बन जाना)*- He made a fortune by selling smuggled goods.

220. Make after *(to pursue or chase, पीछा करना)*- The people made after the chain snatcher and caught him.

221. Make amends *(to compensate, हर्जाना देना)*- He had to make amends for his bad behavior.

222. Make head or tail of *(to understand, समझना)*- The doctor could not make the head or tail of his illness.

223. Make one's mark *(to achieve distinction, अपना प्रभाव छोड़ना)*- India has made its mark in the field of technology.

224. Make out *(to understand, समझ लेना)*- I could not make out what he was saying.

225. Make up the leeway *(struggle out of a bad position, especially by recovering lost time, गवां चुके समय की क्षतिपूर्ति करके बुरे हालात से निकलना)*- The Government will have to make up the leeway by taking remedial actions immediately.

226. Make up one's mind *(To determine, निश्चय करना)*- She has made up her mind to divorce her cruel husband.

227. Make a clean breast *(to confess especially something bad or illegal, किसी गुनाह का सच कबूल लेना)*- After months of lying about the money, he decided to make a clean breast of it and tell the truth.

228. Man in the street *(common man, साधारण व्यक्ति)*- The life of a man in the street has become very difficult because of rising prices.

229. Man of iron *(man with strong will-power, दृढ़ इच्छा शक्ति वाला)*- Nothing can deter a man of iron .

230. Meet half-way *(to be prepared for compromise, समझौते के लिए राजी होना)*- We were ready to meet the other party half way and settle all litigation.

231. Milk of human kindness *(human compassion, मानवता से भरा हृदय)*- Milk of human kindness is necessary for the existence of humanity.

232. Narrow circumstances *(hard days/ poverty, गरीबी के दिन)*- After his father's death, he is living in narrow circumstances.

233. Neither chick nor child *(no child, कोई बच्चे का न होना)*- She feels very lonely because she has neither chick nor child.

234. No love lost *(having no love, किसी प्रकार का प्रेम/मित्रता का न होना)*- There is no love lost between these two neighbours who are fighting an endless court case.

235. Nook and corner *(at every place, प्रत्येक स्थान पर)*- I searched for my book in every nook and corner of the house.

236. Oil someone's hands *(to bribe, रिश्वत देना)*- We should stop oiling the officials' hands.

237. Beauty is only skin deep *(physical beauty is not important, बाहरी सुन्दरता महत्वपूर्ण नहीं)*- She took a wrong decision by not marrying this gentleman. She doesn't know that beauty is only skin deep.

238. On and on *(to continue, जारी रखना)*- She went on and on but nobody listened to her.

239. On the horns of a dilemma *(to face a difficult situation between two problems, मुसीबत में फंसना, दो कठिन अवस्थाओं के बीच में)*- The demolition drive has put many shops on the horns of a dilemma because if they do not shut down, their shops will be sealed and if they do, they lose their means of livelihood.

240. On the wrong side of *(one's age being more than, अधिक उम्र का होना)*- He is on the wrong side of fifty now.

241. Open secret *(known to all, सभी को ज्ञात है)*- He is bankrupt and this is an open secret now.

242. Order of the day *(some common thing of the time, कोई प्रचलित बात)*- Following new fashion is the order of the day.

243. Out of the woods *(out of difficulties, मुसीबत से छुटकारा)*- At last, India came out of the woods and got independence.

244. Pay one back in one's own coin *(tit for tat, जैसे को तैसा)*- The person doing wrong should be paid back in his own coin.

245. Pell-mell *(very fast and not organised, बहुत जल्द और अस्त-व्यस्त तरीके से)*- Everything was done pell-mell as we had no time to prepare.

246. Petticoat-Government *(undue influence of women, स्त्रियों का अनुचित दबाव)*- Petticoat-government may adversely influence your whole project.

247. Pick holes in *(to find fault with, दूसरों में दोष निकालना)*- My boss has the habit of picking holes in our performance.

248. Pin prick *(troubles that are for short time, जो समस्याएं कुछ सिर्फ कुछ समय के लिए हो)*- We should ignore such pin pricks and get on with the job.

249. Play a double game *(to act dubiously, धोखाधाड़ी करना)*- My friend was playing a double game.

250. Play fast and loose *(be unreliable, अविश्वसनीय होना)*- How can you trust a man who plays fast and loose changing his statement every minute?

251. Play one false *(to deceive, किसी को धोखा देना)*- He played her false and married again.

252. Play one's cards well *(to do the correct things to achieve a desired result, समझदारी से काम करना)*- If you play your cards well, you will get selected..

253. Play the fool *(to act foolishly, बेवकूफी करना)*- Why do you play the fool when it comes to spending money?

254. Pocket an insult *(to bear insult, अपमान सहन कर लेना)*- Indians had to pocket much insult during their fight for Independence.

255. Poison one's ears against *(to set a person against another, किसी के विरुद्ध कान भरना)*- She has poisoned the ears of my mother-in-law.

256. Past master *(an expert, किसी क्षेत्र का विशेषज्ञ)*- He is a past master in cheating others.

257. Pour oil on troubled waters *(to pacify the anger of others, क्रोध को शान्त करने का प्रयत्न)*- He solved the matter by pouring oil on troubled waters with his good behaviour.

258. Pull the string *(to exercise secret influence, छिपे रूप से प्रभाव डालना)*- When I saw extreme level of red-tapism in the organization, I had to pull my strings to get my work done.

259. Pull to pieces *(to criticise severely, कटु आलोचना करना)*- The leader of opposition has pulled the ruling party to pieces.

260. Put an end to *(to finish, समाप्त कर देना)*- She has put an end to her project.

261. Put pen to paper *(to start writing, लिखना आरम्भ कर देना)*- In my board examination I put my pen to paper without wasting a second.

262. Put the saddle on the right horse *(to blame the really guilty person, सही अपराधी पर आरोप लगाना)* The court put the saddle on the right horse and passed the right order.

263. Put to the sword *(to kill, मार देना)*- Nadir Shah put even children to the sword.

264. Put up with *(to tolerate, सहन करना)*- Maharana Pratap could not put up with insult.

265. Rank and file *(lower middle class people, साधारण श्रेणी के लोग)*- The extra-ordinary speeches of the great orators cannot be appreciated by the rank and file.

266. Red rag to a bull *(something that will surely produce a violent reaction, निश्चित ही उत्तेजित करने वाली बात)*- The racial comments against the Indians proved to be a red rag to a bull.

267. Rise to the occasion *(to show that you can deal with a difficult situation, ये दिखा देना कि आप मुश्किल हालात का सामना कर सकते है)*- Mahatma Gandhi rose to the occasion and dared the British.

268. Roll up one's sleeves *(to be prepared for hard work, कड़ी मेहनत के लिये तैयार रहना)*- We will have to roll up our sleeves as the time of examination has come.

269. Rub shoulders with *(to meet and spend time with, किसी के निकट सम्पर्क में आना)*- He claims to have rubbed shoulders with Salman Khan during his journey to Sydney.

270. Run down *(reduced in health/ to criticize, स्वास्थ्य में गिरावट/ निन्दा करना)*- I was worried because she looked run down .
Do not run down your friends in public.

271. Run short/ Hard up *(not proving sufficient, shortage of money/ something, किसी चीज/ पैसे की कमी)*- I am running short of money these days.
If you are hard up, you can come to me.

272. Scratch one's head *(to be perplexed, परेशान हो जाना)*- I scratched my head when I saw the puzzles in the PO exam.

273. Screw up one's courage *(to gather courage, साहस बढ़ाना)*- Working women have to screw up their courage to handle eve teasing incidents at their working places.

274. Seal of love *(kiss, चुम्बन)*- They validated their marriage with a seal of love.

275. See the light *(to be born, जन्म लेना)*- Without my son's cooperation, this book would not have seen the light.

276. Set a price on one's head *(to offer reward for killing or helping in the arrest of a criminal, किसी अपराधी को मारने या पकड़वाने में मदद करने पर इनाम की घोषणा)*- The government of America had set price on Osama's head.

277. Show a clean pair of heels *(to run away, भाग जाना)*- The chain snatcher showed a clean pair of heels and the people were unable to catch him.

278. Sink fast *(to deteriorate in quality or condition, बद से बदतर होना)*- The patient was sinking fast.

279. Slip of the pen *(a small unintentional mistake in writing, लिखने में अनजाने में की जाने वाली गलती)*- The slip of the pen created a lot of confusion.

280. Snake in the grass *(some hidden enemy, अज्ञात शत्रु)*- Many leaders are snake in the grass creating disharmony in the society.

281. Sow wild oats *(indulgence in many sexual relationships particularly when one is young, युवावस्था की कई शारीरिक संबंध बनाना)*- Mothers always keeps an eye on their children to see that they do not sow wild oats.

282. Square meal *(full meal, पेट भर भोजन)*- A poor person does not get even one square meal a day.

283. Stand in good stead *(to be of great service, बहुत सहायक होना)*- Your experience will always stand in good stead when you join a full time job.

284. Storm in a tea cup *(much hue and cry over a little matter, छोटी सी बात पर बहुत शोर-गुल करना)*- Do not worry about these complaints. They are just storm in a tea cup.

285. Strain every nerve *(to make every possible effort, हर प्रकार का प्रयत्न करना)*- I strained every nerve to get out of the problem.

286. Sword of Damocles *(an imminent danger, सिर पर लटकी तलवार)*- Terrorism is a sword of Damocles hanging over the whole world.

287. Take a leaf out of another man's book *(to imitate another person, नकल करना)*- He has no originality of thought; he only takes a leaf out of another man's book to make quick money.

288. Take an exception to *(to be offended by something, किसी बात का बुरा मानना)*- She took an exception to his joke.

289. Take into one's head *(to suddenly decide to do something, often silly or surprising, कुछ बेवकूफी भरी हरकत करने का अचानक निर्णय लेना)*- It took into their heads to get married next Sunday.

290. Take pains *(to work hard, कठिन परिश्रम करना)*- She took pains to bring up her children after her husband's death.

291. Take the bull by the horns *(to face danger with courage, खतरे का हिम्मत से सामना करना)*- Bhagat Singh took the bull by the horns and bravely challenged the British empire.

292. Take to one's heels *(to run away, भाग जाना)*- When the police came, the robber took to his heels.

293. Tall talk *(boasting, शेखी मारना)*- One of my friends Rajesh is famous for his tall talks.

294. The Fourth Estate *(the press, प्रेस)*- Today the fourth estate can influence the court proceedings of any case.

295. The knock down price *(very low price, बहुत कम कीमत)*- I bought everything at the mega sale at knock down prices.

296. Sheet anchor *(a person or thing to be relied upon in an emergency, आपातकाल में काम आने वाला व्यक्ति अथवा वस्तु)*- His uncle proved to be his sheet anchor after his father's death.

297. Thick-skinned person *(not easily offended, insensitive, लज्जाहीन या संवेदनहीन व्यक्ति)*- He is such a thick- skinned person that he laughed when people cursed and abused him.

298. Think lightly *(not to be serious about a thing, मजाक के रूप में लेना)*- Don't think lightly. Take your competitors seriously.

299. Throw light on *(to make something easier to understand, किसी विषय पर प्रकाश डालना)*- I wanted to throw light on the pitiful life of the bar dancers.

300. Throw mud at *(try to make a low opinion of someone by saying unpleasant things about him, बदनाम करना)*- Companies should think carefully before slinging mud at someone who may respond with a libel action costing them crores of rupees.

301. Tool in the hands of *(under the authority of another, दूसरे के हाथ में कठपुतली की भांति)*- The whole legal system has become a tool in the hands of the politicians.

302. Turn one's coat *(to change one's party, दल बदल लेना)*- Some leaders are so ambitious that they often turn coat.

303. Turn the tables *(to change the situation completely, स्थिति को बिलकुल बदल देना)*- The ruling party had an easy victory in the last Lok sabha election but inflation and corruption have totally turned the table.

304. Under a cloud *(under suspicious conditions, संदेहपूर्ण स्थिति में)*- Ever since the rumours of corruption started, the former chief minister has been under a cloud .

305. Under the rose *(secretly, गुप्त रूप से)*- He is selling confidential documents under the rose.

306. Under the thumb of (completely under one's power or influence, *किसी के वर्चस्व में दबा होना)*- He is under the thumb of his mother and does not listen to his wife's complaints.

307. Upto the mark *(up to standard, उचित स्तर तक)*- I have to work hard to keep the quality upto the mark.

308. Vexed question *(much debated and discussed, जिस प्रश्न पर काफी बहस हो चुकी हो)*- 'Mercy killing should be granted or not' has become a vexed question.

309. Wash dirty linen in public *(to expose private affairs in public, व्यक्तिगत बातों को बाहर उछालना)*- There is nothing as bad as washing one's dirty linen in public.

310. Wash one's hands of *(to be free from, किसी बात से मुक्त हो जाना)*- Police have washed their hands of the kidnapping case.

311. Wear a long face *(to look gloomy, उदास दिखाई देना)*- Inspite of losing his job, he did not wear a long face.

312. Wild goose chase *(useless efforts, व्यर्थ का प्रयत्न)*- Pakistan's efforts to grab Kashmir have proved to be a wild goose chase.

313. Win laurels *(to win honours, यश प्राप्त करना)*- Sachin won laurels for India.

314. Within a stone's throw *(at a little distance, थोड़ी दूरी पर)*- The Red Fort is within a stone's throw from my house.

315. Without rhyme or reason *(without any justification, अकारण)*- Don't shout at anyone without rhyme or reason.

CHAPTER 33

IDIOMS AND PHRASES

(PRACTICE SET)

Directions : In questions 1 to 300, four alternatives are given for the idiom/ phrase underlined in the sentence. Choose the alternative which best expresses the meaning of the idiom/phrase and mark it in the Answer Sheet.

1. **To strain every nerve**
(A) to make utmost efforts
(B) to feel weak and tired
(C) to be a diligent worker
(D) to be methodical in work

2. **To flog a dead horse**
(A) to whip a dead horse
(B) attempt to do the possible
(C) waste one's efforts
(D) to take advantage of a weakness

3. **To show a clean pair of heels**
(A) to hide (B) to escape
(C) to pursue (D) to follow

4. **To die in harness**
(A) premeditated murder
(B) dying young in an accident
(C) to die while in service
(D) to be taken by surprise

5. **To feather one's nest**
(A) to make a residential house
(B) something that lasts for a short time
(C) to profit in a dishonest way
(D) none of the above

6. **To doctor the accounts**
(A) to make changes in account books
(B) to clear the doctors' bill
(C) to verify the accounts in detail
(D) to manipulate the accounts

7. **She could never measure up to her parent's expectations.**
(A) Reach the level
(B) Work as hard
(C) Assess the amount
(D) Increase her height

8. **The little girl with her flawless performance stole the show.**
(A) Stole something from the show
(B) Crept into the show
(C) Won everybody's praise
(D) Disappeared from the show

9. **The thief was on good terms with the police.**
(A) Kept terms and conditions
(B) Was friendly
(C) Followed the rules
(D) Agreed with them

10. **John's offer of help was turned down by the police.**
(A) Sent back
(B) Twisted around
(C) Refused
(D) Handed over

11. **To be all at sea**
(A) a family voyage
(B) lost and confused
(C) in the middle of the ocean
(D) a string of islands

12. **To take to one's heels**
(A) to walk slowly
(B) to run away
(C) to march forward
(D) to hop and jump

13. **To bite the dust**
(A) eat voraciously
(B) have nothing to eat
(C) eat roots
(D) to fail

14. **A bolt from the blue**
(A) a delayed event
(B) an inexplicable event
(C) an unexpected and unpleasant event
(D) an unpleasant event

15. **Cold comfort**
(A) absurdity
(B) deception
(C) slight satisfaction
(D) foolish proposal

16. **The reputed company is in the red due to the recession.**
(A) making money
(B) losing money
(C) in danger
(D) spending money

17. **When the Principal was entering the class, all my friends quietly disappeared, leaving me alone to face the music.**
(A) to listen to him
(B) to enter into the class
(C) to bear the criticism
(D) to listen to a favourable comment

18. **The Kenyan team proved to be the dark horse in the ICC World Cup Cricket.**
(A) a strong intruder
(B) a skilled team
(C) the most powerful
(D) an unexpected winner

19. **Having no arguments to defend his point, the speaker began to beat about the bush.**
(A) wander across the words
(B) speak in a haphazard manner
(C) speak in a round-about manner
(D) make use of irrelevant reference

20. **They were offered six months' rent in lieu of notice to vacate the building.**
(A) in spite of
(B) in place of
(C) despite of
(D) in addition to

21. **We know that he is the one responsible for the discord but as he is well - connected all we can do is send him to Coventry.**
(A) transfer him
(B) commend him
(C) boycott him
(D) dismiss him

22. **The noble man gave up the ghost.**
(A) left the ghost
(B) lived like a ghost
(C) invited ghost
(D) died

23. **A Prime Minister cannot ride roughshod over his ministerial colleagues for long.**
(A) deal unkindly with
(B) take for granted
(C) be high-handed with
(D) exploit wilfully

24. **He was down in the mouth as he was defeated in the elections.**
(A) unable to speak
(B) very depressed
(C) very angry
(D) very confused

25. **They say, join the Army to drink life to the lees.**
(A) to have the best of fun and fortune
(B) to enjoy a life of drinking and dancing
(C) to have a life full of adventures
(D) to have the best of life

26. **The car in the backyard is proving to be a white elephant.**
(A) very huge item
(B) costly and useless possession
(C) very expensive investment
(D) useful material

27. He takes leave <u>once in a blue moon.</u>
(A) regularly
(B) often
(C) rarely
(D) once a fortnight

28. The meeting has been <u>put off</u> indefinitely.
(A) cancelled
(B) postponed
(C) advanced
(D) announced

29. The rules of the deal are <u>set forth</u> in the brochure.
(A) stated
(B) accepted
(C) contradicted
(D) printed

30. She bought her new house <u>for a song</u>.
(A) very cheaply
(B) on loan
(C) at a loss
(D) very easily

31. Raju had <u>given up</u> doing exercise after surgery.
(A) learned (B) started
(C) continued (D) stopped

32. The chairman tried <u>to get his point across</u>, but the members just wouldn't listen.
(A) give them a lesson
(B) insist on
(C) make them understand
(D) motivate them

33. Ashok had all <u>fair-weather friends</u>.
(A) friends who face difficulties calmly.
(B) favourable friends
(C) friends who desert you in difficulties
(D) reliable friends

34. Since the company has lost a good deal of time and money, you will have <u>to make good the loss</u>.
(A) make a good effort
(B) try to minimize the loss
(C) compensate for the loss
(D) ensure that there are no further losses

35. a damp squib
(A) rainy weather
(B) a disappointing result
(C) a skirt in a laundry
(D) none of the above

36. in cold blood
(A) angrily
(B) deliberately
(C) excitedly
(D) slowly

37. to take someone for a ride
(A) to give a ride to someone
(B) to deceive someone
(C) to be indifferent
(D) to disclose a secret

38. to move heaven and earth
(A) to cause an earthquake
(B) to try everything possible
(C) to pray to all Gods
(D) to travel in a rocket

39. to smell a rat
(A) to smell foul
(B) to see a rat
(C) to chase a rat
(D) to be suspicious

40. The possession of Jerusalem is <u>a bone of contention</u> between Israel and Palestine.
(A) a subject of peace
(B) a subject of trade
(C) a subject of dispute
(D) a subject of exports

41. My friend <u>turned a deaf ear</u> to my tale of loss and refused to help me.
(A) paid no heed
(B) went far away
(C) listened carefully
(D) turned his ear away

42. Helena was <u>over head and ears</u> in love with Demetrius.
(A) carefully (B) completely
(C) brilliantly (D) cautiously

43. Gopi works <u>by fits and starts</u>.
(A) consistently
(B) irregularly
(C) in high spirits
(D) enthusiastically

44. Naresh Goyal had to stand on his feet very early in his life.
(A) to be physically strong
(B) to be independent
(C) to stand erect
(D) to be successful

45. It is high time he came out of his shell.
(A) appeared suddenly
(B) became more sociable
(C) became a loser
(D) removed his clothes

46. Every political party is at present playing to the gallery.
(A) adopting cheap tactics
(B) befooling the common man
(C) fighting for votes
(D) appeasing the masses

47. His blood ran cold when he heard his uncle was murdered.
(A) He was frightened
(B) He was horrified
(C) He was disgusted
(D) He was depressed

48. This is so simple that even a man in the street can understand it.
(A) an ordinary person
(B) an illiterate person
(C) an unknown person
(D) a stranger

49. When he went to claim insurance for his car, the agent said he hadn't a leg to stand on.
(A) had been injured in an accident
(B) was lame
(C) did not have much hope of getting it
(D) would have to wait for some time

50. to cast aspersions
(A) to act as the pillar of support
(B) to raise aspirations
(C) to make unpleasant remarks
(D) to dissolve all the differences

51. on the cards
(A) impossible
(B) shocking
(C) evident
(D) anticipated

52. To turn over a new leaf
(A) to change for the better
(B) to start writing a new book
(C) to work on a novel idea
(D) to clear the garden

53. To keep up one's appearances
(A) to make public appearances now and then.
(B) to maintain one's looks and appearance.
(C) to keep up an outward show of prosperity.
(D) to make it appear that one is not concerned.

54. Off and on
(A) repeatedly
(B) always
(C) occasionally
(D) never

55. To take with a grain of salt
(A) to make more palatable
(B) to take a small quantity of
(C) to make something meaningful
(D) to accept with misgiving

56. To talk through one's hat
(A) to talk carefully
(B) to talk softly
(C) to talk nonsense
(D) to talk secretively

57. Ins and outs
(A) entrances and exits
(B) details and complexities
(C) passages and pathways
(D) rules and regulations

58. The thief passed himself off as a ticket examiner.
(A) described himself
(B) deceived everyone
(C) disguised himself
(D) was regarded

59. A brave soldier will never show the white feather in the face of his enemy.
(A) show signs of cowardice
(B) act arrogantly
(C) show intimacy
(D) act impudently

60. The poor man moved from pillar to post to get money.
(A) went to pillars
(B) went to post
(C) went to money lender
(D) tried his best

61. You have to be tactful in handling the sensitive matters rather than putting the cart before the horse.
(A) treating these indifferently
(B) behaving thoughtlessly
(C) dealing with these in haste
(D) tackling things in the wrong way

62. The boys cried with one voice that the examination should be postponed.
(A) unanimously
(B) vehemently
(C) loudly
(D) strongly

63. The scheme appears worthless at the first blush.
(A) first attempt
(B) first sight
(C) first step
(D) first phase

64. His pronunciation was so bad and his voice so low that the speech he made was all Greek to me.
(A) strange
(B) incomprehensible
(C) inaudible
(D) uninteresting

65. He looked blank when he was informed about his dismissal.
(A) was without any emotion
(B) was puzzled and surprised
(C) was uninterested
(D) was unhappy

66. That fellow trumped up a story
(A) translated
(B) sang with the music of a trumpet
(C) concocted
(D) copied

67. Though he is not a scholar, he wins arguments because he has the gift of the gab.
(A) gifts from many people
(B) a lot of money
(C) talent for speaking
(D) a good memory

68. The A.T.S. set the bait to arrest the terrorists.
(A) laid the trap
(B) announced the reward
(C) set the record
(D) put the bet

69. I have decided to give it a shot.
(A) click a picture
(B) try something
(C) pose for a picture
(D) injure someone

70. He turned a blind eye to his son's pranks.
(A) pretended not to notice
(B) paid special attention to
(C) covered up for
(D) punished severely

71. All his schemes to murder the king ended in smoke.
(A) fructified gradually
(B) came to nothing
(C) were discarded
(D) were partially carried out

72. This fashion of long flowing skirts will run its course.
(A) continue for a long time
(B) become very popular
(C) develop and then come to its usual end
(D) end very soon

73. The police caught the thief red-handed.
(A) in a red uniform
(B) with blood in hands
(C) at the time of committing the crime
(D) after reading the rules

74. I was so disappointed when my close friend left me in the lurch.
(A) went away without waiting for me
(B) helped me in difficult times
(C) abandoned me when I needed help
(D) stopped helping me in emergency

75. His position in the company was on the brink of disaster.
(A) at the top of
(B) at the point of
(C) on the side of
(D) on the back of

76. The car broke down just as it reached the edge of a cliff. It was indeed a close shave.
(A) to share one's brand
(B) very risky
(C) narrow escape from danger
(D) to be happy

77. The parents are in high spirits as their son has got a decent job.
(A) in good position (B) drunk
(C) cheerful (D) shocked

78. When she realised that she had bought a fake product, she knew that her money had gone down the drain.
(A) was lost forever
(B) dropped in the drain
(C) got washed away
(D) her money was safe

79. Even though the new clerk was given a difficult task, he remained cool as a cucumber.
(A) not nervous or emotional
(B) caught cold
(C) was happy
(D) was scared

80. Some people do not grease anybody's palm on any account.
(A) bribe (B) flatter
(C) cheat (D) fight

81. I had to pull strings to put up a good show.
(A) play music
(B) use personal influence
(C) use the instrument
(D) play a song

82. You can easily overcome this situation if you keep your head.
(A) keep faith in
(B) remain calm
(C) believe in
(D) trust the others

83. It is clear that the ideas of both reformers ran in the same groove.
(A) promoted each other
(B) clashed with each other
(C) moved in harmony
(D) moved in different directions

84. This place affords a bird's eye view of the green valley below.
(A) a beautiful view
(B) a narrow view
(C) an overview
(D) an ugly view

85. To foam at one's mouth
(A) to brush properly
(B) to get very angry
(C) to salivate on seeing food
(D) none of the above

86. To feel like a fish out of water
(A) disgusted
(B) uncomfortable
(C) disappointed
(D) homeless

87. At the eleventh hour
(A) too late
(B) too early
(C) immediately
(D) at the last moment

88. to burn one's fingers
(A) to get hurt physically
(B) to suffer financial losses
(C) to find work
(D) to suffer nervous breakdown

89. to add fuel to fire
(A) to investigate (B) to insulate
(C) to initiate (D) to incite

90. To bring to light
(A) to reveal
(B) to conceal
(C) to provide luminescence
(D) to appeal

91. To hit the jackpot
(A) to gamble
(B) to get an unexpected victory
(C) to be wealthy
(D) to make money quickly

92. To burn the candle at both ends
(A) to spend cautiously
(B) to be stingy
(C) to be extravagant
(D) to survive difficulty

93. Status quo
(A) unchanged position
(B) excellent place
(C) unbreakable statue
(D) long queue

94. By fair means or foul
(A) without using common sense
(B) without difficulty
(C) in any way, honest or dishonest
(D) having been instigated

95. at one's beck and call
(A) to attend a call
(B) to be helped by someone
(C) to be useful to someone
(D) to be dominated by someone

96. to explore every avenue
(A) to search all streets
(B) to scout the wilderness
(C) to find adventure
(D) to try every opportunity

97. a red letter day
(A) a dangerous day in one's life
(B) a sorrowful day in one's life
(C) an important or joyful occasion in one's life
(D) both a dangerous and sorrowful day in one's life

98. to have something up one's sleeve
(A) to hide something in the sleeve
(B) to play a magician trick
(C) to have a secret plan
(D) to play hide and seek

99. on the spur of the moment
(A) to act at once
(B) to ride a horse in a race
(C) to act deliberately
(D) to act at the appointed time

100. When my friend was in Kolkata, he <u>ran into</u> an old friend at the theatre.
(A) hit
(B) met accidentally
(C) planned to meet
(D) invited

101. The news of the President's death <u>spread like wild fire</u>.
(A) spread rapidly
(B) caused a major confusion
(C) was a wild rumour
(D) set the nation on fire

102. Going abroad for a holiday was <u>out of the question</u>.
(A) undesirable
(B) impossible
(C) unpleasant
(D) irresistible

103. As a businessman, my father always maintained that his transactions constituted <u>an open book</u>.
(A) an account book always open
(B) a book of open confessions
(C) an opening for new ventures
(D) straight forward and honest dealings

104. The project advanced <u>by leaps and bounds</u>.
(A) rapidly (B) slowly
(C) sharply (D) simply

105. She is <u>too fond of her own voice</u>.
(A) loves singing
(B) very selfish
(C) does not listen properly to anyone else
(D) very talkative

106. Indian police is, on the whole, high handed in dealing with citizens.
(A) kind
(B) overbearing
(C) prompt
(D) adept

107. I take exception to your statement that I am bad tempered.
(A) do not agree
(B) feel unhappy
(C) object
(D) feel angry

108. His speech fell short on the audience.
(A) had no effect
(B) moved the audience
(C) impressed the audience
(D) was quite short

109. The officer called for an explanation from the cashier for the shortage of cash.
(A) asked (B) begged
(C) served a notice (D) demanded

110. We wanted the gift to be a surprise for my mother, but my sister gave the game away.
(A) lost the game
(B) gave out the secret
(C) gave away the gift
(D) withdrew from the plan

111. The actress took cue from her brother and became successful.
(A) some help
(B) a hint
(C) some money
(D) learnt acting

112. Let us have a heart to heart talk to solve this problem.
(A) good talk
(B) emotional talk
(C) frank talk
(D) loving talk

113. To miss the bus
(A) to miss the bus that one regularly takes
(B) to miss an opportunity
(C) to have something to fall back upon
(D) to find fault with others

114. Birds of the same feather
(A) persons of same caste
(B) persons of same colour
(C) birds with same type of feather
(D) persons of same character

115 To fight tooth and nail
(A) to fight a losing battle
(B) to fight heroically
(C) to fight cowardly
(D) to make every possible effort

116. To call a spade a spade
(A) to be frank
(B) to be sly
(C) to be rude
(D) to be diplomatic

117. by putting two and two together
(A) to mix several things
(B) to make an arithmetical calculation
(C) to keep people in pairs
(D) to deduce from given facts

118. to look down one's nose
(A) to show anger
(B) to retaliate
(C) to insult in the presence of others
(D) to regard with contempt

119. to shed crocodile tears
(A) to weep profusely
(B) to pretend grief
(C) to grieve seriously
(D) to mock something

120. To call it a day
(A) to conclude proceedings
(B) to initiate proceedings
(C) to work through the day
(D) None of the above

121. To put up with
(A) to accommodate (B) to adjust
(C) to understand (D) to tolerate

122. To take to heart
(A) to be encouraged
(B) to grieve over
(C) to like
(D) to hate

123. Yeoman's service
(A) medical help
(B) excellent work
(C) social work
(D) hard work

124. to go scot-free
(A) to walk like a native of Scotland
(B) to get something free
(C) to escape without punishment
(D) to save tax

125. to see red
(A) get broke
(B) get angry
(C) feel lucky
(D) become rich

126. in the nick of time
(A) in an unexpected time
(B) after some time
(C) at a time when it was too late
(D) precisely at the right time

127. the stage has been set
(A) the conditions are beyond control
(B) the platform for meeting is ready
(C) the situation is getting worse
(D) the situation is conducive

128. on this side of the grave
(A) outside the grave
(B) by the side of the grave
(C) in this world
(D) before going to grave

129. A man who, while pretending to be your friend, sets a spy to watch your activities is indeed a snake in the grass.
(A) secret enemy
(B) mean fellow
(C) dangerous man
(D) cunning fellow

130. The audience was greatly impressed though I spoke off the cuff.
(A) away from the mike
(B) without preparation
(C) off the subject
(D) about the cuff

131. After listening to the student's statements, the teacher had to eat her words.
(A) withdraw her words
(B) stop speaking
(C) apologize
(D) quarrel

132. to lose ground
(A) to become less powerful
(B) to become less popular
(C) to lose foundation
(D) to be without a leader

133. to make both ends meet
(A) to buy costly articles
(B) live a luxurious life
(C) to live within one's income
(D) to please all people

134. to fall back on
(A) to oppose something important
(B) to suffer an injury on the back in an accident
(C) to fail to do something important in time
(D) to seek support out of necessity

135. to make one's blood boil
(A) to make somebody furious
(B) to develop fever
(C) to get excited
(D) to make someone nervous

136. She decided that she would get this job by hook or by crook.
(A) by compromising or other responsibilities
(B) by impressing the interviewers
(C) by any means, right or wrong
(D) by becoming a specialist in the field

137. In a debate, no one is allowed to sit on the fence.
(A) to avoid taking sides
(B) to insult a speaker
(C) to relax while others speak
(D) to agree with everyone

138. The matter has been sorted out.
(A) revised (B) supported
(C) resolved (D) changed

139. The soldiers carried out the orders of the General very effectively.
(A) exited (B) executed
(C) supported (D) applied

140. They set off by car for Mumbai late in the evening.
(A) started (B) travelled
(C) entered (D) resonated

141. Once his crime was discovered, he had no option but to come clean.
(A) to deny the crime
(B) to confess to the crime
(C) to accuse someone else of the crime
(D) to apologize for the cirme

142. The employees were kept in the dark about the latest developments.
(A) were informed after office hours
(B) were informed when it was too late
(C) were given secret information
(D) were not informed at all

143. When things go wrong, everyone starts passing the buck.
(A) analyses the problem
(B) prepares to resign
(C) pays a bribe
(D) blames someone else

144. To keep the wolf away from the door.
(A) to avoid a bad person
(B) to clean the house
(C) to avoid extreme poverty
(D) to visit the zoo

145. To break the ice
(A) to clear the snow
(B) to start quarreling
(C) to commence an interaction
(D) to revive old enmity

146. Spick and span
(A) neat and clean
(B) hard-working
(C) kitchen implements
(D) calm and quiet

147. The pros and cons
(A) good and evil
(B) first and last
(C) fair and foul
(D) for and against

148. Build castles in the air
(A) waste time (B) daydream
(C) build houses (D) work hard

149. Sought after
(A) highly paid
(B) pursued by
(C) in great demand
(D) with great talent

150. All at sea
(A) very proud (B) overjoyed
(C) puzzled (D) excited

151. To hit below the belt
(A) to punish
(B) to tie with a belt
(C) to hit with a belt
(D) to attack unfairly

152. Pot-luck dinner
(A) dinner where everybody brings something to eat
(B) dinner where everybody brings his food
(C) dinner where only soup is served
(D) dinner where people eat and play games at the same time

153. His friends beat the boy to pay off old scores.
(A) to refund old dues.
(B) to take revenge.
(C) to force him to be a scorer in a match.
(D) because he had not scored well earlier.

154. Chintan is so innocent that he wears his heart on his sleeve.
(A) Wears dress that does not match.
(B) Expresses his feelings openly.
(C) Wears colourful dresses.
(D) Expresses his feelings with the shape of a heart printed on its sleeve.

155. Tagore was a man of letters.
(A) of wide contacts.
(B) an excellent letter dictator.
(C) a great writer of letters.
(D) proficient in literary art.

156. The poor subordinates are made scapegoats by their superiors.
(A) punished for others' misdeeds.
(B) developed poor relations.
(C) treated humbly and respectfully.
(D) scolded with arrogant reactions.

157. She was on the horns of a dilemma as she had either to leave her job or divorce her husband.
(A) in nervous condition
(B) in terrible mood
(C) in difficult situation
(D) in suspense

158. Brown study
(A) to study sincerely
(B) to study uselessly
(C) deep in thought
(D) practical advantage

159. The young boy was kicking his heels inspite of his mother's stern warnings.
(A) playing happily
(B) kicking someone
(C) forced to wait
(D) passing a gesture of disrespect

160. She denied point-blank her involvement in the crime.
(A) directly
(B) desperately
(C) stubbornly
(D) rudely

161. It is hard to strike a bargain with a woman.
(A) to finalize a deal
(B) to negotiate a deal
(C) to negotiate
(D) to deal

162. He took his father's advice to heart.
(A) casually (B) patiently
(C) seriously (D) quietly

163. Can you give me a hand with this luggage?
(A) keep a watch on
(B) handle
(C) provide me with
(D) help me with

164. Fling away
(A) to have an affair (B) to flare up
(C) to throw violently (D) to swing

165. Stick by
(A) to adhere closely
(B) stand by someone
(C) to paste
(D) to pass by

166. Wink at
(A) to tease somebody
(B) to like someone
(C) to pretend not to see
(D) to stare at

167. To be on the wane
(A) to complain
(B) to be sick
(C) to be on boat
(D) to be diminishing

168. To give a person the cold shoulder
(A) to offer someone ice-cream
(B) to be humble
(C) to threaten
(D) to treat coldly

169. To get one's back up
(A) to become irritated or angry
(B) to sit straight
(C) to act proud
(D) to give support

170. To strike oil
(A) to have found an oil well
(B) to have lucky success
(C) to have a close escape
(D) to be unsuccessful

171. To talk shop
(A) to talk a lot
(B) to use phrases peculiar to one's employment
(C) to like to shop
(D) to lie

172. To draw a line
(A) to fix a limit
(B) to caution someone
(C) to be stern
(D) to insult someone

173. A swan song
(A) melodious song
(B) disharmonious display
(C) utterance/statement made just before death or retirement
(D) concocted tale

174. Knit one's brows
(A) to disappoint somebody
(B) to frown
(C) to have a headache
(D) to express discontentment

175. To plough the sands
(A) to be extremely accomplished
(B) to be resourceful
(C) to be dejected
(D) to busy oneself in an unprofitable proposition

176. To rip up old sores
(A) to destroy something
(B) to act cruelly
(C) to reopen a quarrel
(D) to inflict pain on someone

177. To rate soundly
(A) to censure strongly
(B) to acquire heavy profits
(C) to be at peace
(D) to assure somebody

178. To be no spring chicken
(A) to be brave
(B) to be honest
(C) to be no longer young
(D) to be childish

179. To take to one's bed
(A) to be very attached to one's belongings
(B) to lie in bed due to illness
(C) to fight with one's husband
(D) to agree with someone

180. To stand on ceremony
(A) to celebrate an occasion in a grand way
(B) to be extravagant
(C) to get married
(D) to insist on excessive formality

181. To be at sixes and sevens
(A) a state of total confusion and disorder
(B) to be a great success
(C) to be certain
(D) to give away generously

182. To break the ice
(A) a strong man
(B) to start a quarrel
(C) to break the awkward silence
(D) to become violent

183. Put one's foot down
(A) to demand
(B) to take rest
(C) to be firm about something
(D) to do something stupid

184. Backstairs influence
(A) one who is easily influenced
(B) influential person
(C) influence exerted secretly
(D) wife's influence on her husband

185. Long in the tooth
(A) distant journey (B) rather old
(C) ailment (D) young

186. A brazen-faced fellow
(A) cruel person
(B) ugly person
(C) dark-complexioned person
(D) impudent fellow

187. To see pink elephants
(A) to dream
(B) to anticipate luck
(C) to be afraid of
(D) to have hallucination due to excessive alcoholic intake.

188. Elbow room
(A) opportunity for freedom of action
(B) special room for the guest
(C) to give enough space to move or work in
(D) to add a new room to the house

189. French leave
(A) a person who does not take leave
(B) leave without permission
(C) to take long leave
(D) to take a day off and have fun

190. To commit to memory
(A) to learn by heart
(B) to tax one's memory
(C) to be forgetful
(D) to commit oneself totally to a task

191. To burn a hole in the pocket
(A) to steal from someone's pocket
(B) to destroy other's belongings
(C) to be very miserly
(D) money that is spent quickly

192. To bury the hatchet
(A) to have found a treasure
(B) to make peace
(C) to purchase something without discretion
(D) to act in a suspicious manner

193. To beggar description
(A) something of least importance
(B) something beyond description
(C) to describe a beggar
(D) an accurate description

194. To beat the air
(A) efforts that are vain or useless
(B) to be satisfied with one's performance
(C) to be extremely relieved
(D) to be very happy

195. To provide against a rainy day
(A) to provide plentiful
(B) to provide for a possible future, in time of difficulty or need
(C) to store for the family
(D) to store for the rainy season

196. To be all eyes
(A) to be cautious
(B) watching closely and attentively
(C) to be amazed
(D) to be non-plussed

197. Swollen headed
(A) to be suffering from illness
(B) to be conceited
(C) to be narrow-minded
(D) to be dumb

198. To stir up a hornet's nest
(A) to excite the hostility of people
(B) to do some social service
(C) to be totally at a loss in a situation
(D) to be bankrupt

199. My hands are full
(A) I am having a lot of things to carry
(B) I am having lots of money
(C) I am very busy
(D) I am anxious

200. No love lost between them
(A) to have a fight
(B) to dislike each other
(C) to be as friendly as ever
(D) to be upset

201. To be hand and glove with someone
(A) to be social
(B) to be playful
(C) to be annoyed
(D) to be intimate

202. To play fast and loose
(A) to deceive someone
(B) to be agile
(C) say one thing and do another
(D) to be efficient

203. To take stock of
(A) to imagine (B) to supply
(C) to survey (D) to attract

204. A man of straw
(A) a man of no substance
(B) a man without means
(C) a man of character
(D) a generous man

205. Wolf in sheep's clothing
(A) to act on the sly
(B) to be a good actor
(C) to be a hypocrite
(D) to be money-minded or materialistic

206. To cut someone short
(A) to oblige someone
(B) to assist someone
(C) to interrupt someone
(D) to insult someone

207. To stick to one's colours
(A) to refuse to yield
(B) to be patriotic
(C) to be notorious
(D) to be straightforward

208. An old head on young shoulders
(A) to be old before one's age
(B) to be wise beyond one's age
(C) to be youthful in spite of one's old age
(D) to maintain good health

209. To snap one's fingers at
(A) to honour someone
(B) to greet someone
(C) to beckon someone
(D) to treat with contempt

210. Falling foul of
(A) quarrelling with
(B) becoming friends with
(C) being dishonest with
(D) being scared of

211. Harp on the same string
(A) to play music
(B) to dwell tediously on the same subject
(C) to beat someone
(D) to acknowledge

212. Keep a good table
(A) to have an artistic taste
(B) to throw a party
(C) to be a good host
(D) to be extravagant

213. Take up the cudgels
(A) to take notice
(B) to accept a present
(C) to defend someone vigorously
(D) to accept a challenge

214. Splitting hairs
(A) to be worried
(B) to be venturesome
(C) to trouble someone
(D) to dispute over petty points

215. A great hand at
(A) to be a good artist
(B) to be an expert
(C) to be a good player
(D) to be generous

216. To make a pile
(A) to make a fortune
(B) to make a mess
(C) to be absent-minded
(D) to be corrupt

217. Under someone's wing
(A) to work under someone
(B) to be under someone's protection
(C) to be alert
(D) to be in the army

218. To sow one's wild oats
(A) to swear
(B) to be at ease
(C) to engage in youthful excesses
(D) to till the land

219. An olive branch
(A) an offer of peace
(B) an idea
(C) a lady
(D) a wicked person

220. Not worth a rap
(A) worth nothing
(B) very expensive
(C) worth a lot
(D) modestly priced

221. In merry pin
(A) perplexed
(B) merry making
(C) embarrassed
(D) in a cheerful mood

222. To leap the pale
(A) to throw a bucket
(B) to get into debt, to spend more than one's income
(C) to have much of fear
(D) to become pale

223. To cut the Gordian knot
(A) to perform the opening ceremony
(B) to be present at the opening ceremony
(C) to solve a difficult problem
(D) to get a sharp cut

224. To sow the wind and reap the whirlwind
(A) to enjoy the fruits of hard work
(B) to be deprived of one' s reward
(C) to act wisely
(D) to suffer for one's foolish conduct

225. To play possum
(A) to play hide and seek
(B) to feign ignorance or pretend the be sleeping or dead
(C) to cheat somebody
(D) to play seriously

226. A grass widow
(A) a young widow
(B) widow who has illicit relations with men
(C) a woman whose husband is temporarily away from her
(D) a working old woman

227. Mad as a March hare
(A) sane
(B) intoxicated
(C) as mad as a hare in spring
(D) slightly touched in the brain

228. Halcyon days
(A) long days
(B) short days
(C) happy and peaceful days
(D) disturbed days

229. Mother wit
(A) to have an intelligent mother
(B) university
(C) silly
(D) common sense

230. A blind date
(A) a cloudy day
(B) unknown future
(C) meeting with someone you do not know
(D) death-day

231. Much ado about nothing
(A) to take something seriously
(B) to play false
(C) to make a fuss
(D) to add

232. Judas' kiss
(A) wooing
(B) a narrow escape
(C) hypocritical affection
(D) a religious person

233. To have no truck with
(A) have no means of conveyance
(B) scientifically backward
(C) to have no trade with
(D) to have no dealings with

234. To clean the Augean stables
(A) to purge/ clean the administration of its abuses
(B) to buy horses
(C) to sell horses
(D) to improve working conditions

235. A fly in the ointment
(A) to clean a thing
(B) to sterilise
(C) Small annoyance that spoils a pleasant experience.
(D) an unsuccessful attempt

236. Of the deepest dye
(A) of the worst/ extreme type
(B) of the best type
(C) of the most colourless type
(D) of the colourless type

237. To throw up the sponge
(A) to accept the challenge
(B) to forget the past offences
(C) to admit defeat
(D) to send message

238. To rule the roost
(A) to measure the height of something
(B) to measure the depth
(C) to strike with a stick
(D) to dominate

239. Bats in the belfry
(A) to be mad
(B) something needed cleanliness
(C) an impending danger
(D) to be deceived

240. To have a jaundice eye
(A) to have jaundice
(B) to have fever
(C) to be prejudiced
(D) to lose colour

241. Rank and file
(A) Common people
(B) Officers
(C) People of high rank
(D) Army personnel

242. To egg on
(A) to egg on slowly
(B) to destroy slowly
(C) to give a walk over
(D) to instigate/ cause to proceed further

243. To haul over the coals
(A) to walk over the fire
(B) to burn
(C) to scold for something done wrong
(D) to throw into fire

244. To draw a bead on
(A) to say prayers
(B) to count the beads
(C) to do one's best
(D) to take careful aim at

245. Fabian policy
(A) dictatorial policy
(B) democratic policy
(C) systematic policy
(D) policy of cautious persistence

246. To play to the gallery
(A) to try to get the appreciation from the least intelligent people
(B) to try to win appreciation of intelligent people
(C) to play in the gallery
(D) to disturb people sitting in the gallery

247. Pyrrhic victory
(A) Permanent victory
(B) Defeat
(C) Easy victory
(D) Victory at high cost

248. Go the whole hog
(A) to do something thoroughly
(B) sleep
(C) to neglect duty
(D) to mishandle the case

249. To bite one's lips
(A) to feel sorry
(B) to repress one's anger or other emotions
(C) laugh at others
(D) to have doubt

250. To hold someone in leash
(A) to restrain
(B) to be firm
(C) to be unsure
(D) to touch the exact point

251. To cool one's heels
(A) to give a cold treatment to somebody
(B) to be kept waiting for sometime
(C) a closed chapter
(D) a hot issue

252. Bag of bones
(A) a bag full of bones
(B) a dead person
(C) a person about to die
(D) an extremely weak person

253. All moonshine
(A) show
(B) lighted only by moon
(C) false
(D) far from reality

254. To shake the dust off one's feet
(A) to wash feet
(B) to walk fast
(C) to leave a place with a sense of resentment
(D) to rest after a long journey

255. Off hand
(A) Without preparation
(B) Out of hand
(C) Rehearsed
(D) In hand

256. A bird of passage
(A) a flying bird
(B) an unreliable person
(C) one who stays for a short time
(D) bad time

257. Count on
(A) Depend on
(B) as a result of
(C) ceremonially
(D) to wait for the benefactor

258. With a string
(A) not to give any aid
(B) to give unconditional aid
(C) gift or aid with condition
(D) to accept aid

259. To set stores by
(A) to value highly
(B) to hoard a large quantity of something
(C) to set up store
(D) fix a price

260. To draw the long bow
(A) to shoot
(B) to exaggerate
(C) to criticize
(D) to admire

261. To know the ropes
(A) to recognize the lost things
(B) to do rigging
(C) to know the procedure of doing a job
(D) to flog

262. To give the devil his due
(A) to be just to a person even though he does not deserve such treatment
(B) to surrender oneself willingly when one's mistake is detected
(C) to punish an innocent person
(D) to punish a guilty person

263. In the swim
(A) knowing latest current things
(B) to cross a river by a boat
(C) to cross a river by swimming
(D) to be in the river

264. To knuckle under
(A) to be in a crisis
(B) to submit
(C) to take rest
(D) to go to bed

265. To have a dig at
(A) to criticise someone
(B) to sow seeds
(C) to weed out
(D) to praise someone

266. In vogue
(A) in fashion
(B) fair
(C) smooth
(D) total absence

267. Three R's
(A) radiogram, radiograph, radio telescope
(B) rabble, rattle, razzle
(C) reading, writing, arithmetic
(D) rail, radar, raft

268. A wild goose chase
(A) foolish and useless enterprise
(B) to hunt
(C) a violent chase
(D) to speak harshly

269. To rest on one's laurels
(A) to cease to strive for further glory
(B) to be lazy
(C) to be proud of one's victory
(D) to die

270. Raw deal
(A) unjust treatment
(B) unripe fruit
(C) early stage of business
(D) contract not yet finally decided

271. A forlorn hope
(A) a plan which has remote chances of success
(B) hope about unforeseeable future
(C) hope of a single person
(D) hope of a silly person

272. Printer's devil
(A) an apprentice in a printing office
(B) blunder
(C) low type of printed material
(D) delay in printing

273. To call on the carpet
(A) subject to criticism
(B) to summon for a scolding
(C) a heartfelt welcome
(D) on the ground

274. To bring the house down
(A) to appeal greatly to the audience
(B) to pull down a building
(C) to defame one's family
(D) to pass a bill unanimously

275. To have an edge on
(A) to cut with a knife
(B) to threaten to wound
(C) to be slightly better than
(D) to be in a dangerous situation

276. In sackcloth and ashes
(A) to cremate
(B) in a state of great mourning
(C) dirty clothes
(D) cheap clothes

277. To put two and two together
(A) to progress steadily
(B) to compare the debit and credit
(C) to conclude keeping in view the merits and demerits
(D) to oppose as a last resort

278. To weather the storm
(A) to face a crisis
(B) to survive a crisis
(C) to be the victim of a crisis
(D) to create crisis

279. Lump in the throat
(A) to be hoarse
(B) a highly emotional state
(C) food of low type
(D) wind-pipe

280. To fight shy of
(A) to keep aloof from
(B) to fight social evils
(C) to be bold
(D) to fight and win

281. Hobson's choice
(A) lion's share
(B) the best choice
(C) option of taking the one offered or nothing
(D) the last chance

282. To hit it off
(A) to quarrel
(B) to be hostile
(C) to agree or be congenial
(D) to threaten

283. To whitewash
(A) to clean a place
(B) to work hard
(C) to retrieve damaged reputation
(D) to use cosmetics

284. Within an ace of
(A) very close
(B) within one's means
(C) within a narrow circle
(D) near centre

285. To keep an open mind
(A) to remember
(B) to forget
(C) to come to no decision on a subject until one knowns all the facts
(D) to be clear-headed

286. Open question
(A) a question put to all
(B) a question without any generally agreed answer
(C) a permanent problem
(D) a clearly-written/expressed question

287. On one's mettle
(A) roused to do one's best
(B) to put on an overcoat
(C) to safeguard against attack
(D) to use one's own money properly

288. To keep the pot boiling
(A) to earn enough money
(B) to buy one's food
(C) to show anger
(D) to do experiments

289. Grist to one's mill
(A) grain to be ground
(B) useful for one's purpose
(C) income from will
(D) to work one's machine

290. Kangaroo court
(A) a group of kangaroos
(B) the young kangaroo
(C) unofficial court
(D) unofficial estimate

291. Wool gathering
(A) to become a shepherd
(B) to shear sheep
(C) to engage in idle or aimless day dreaming
(D) to live in the countryside

292. Between Scylla and Charybdis
(A) between two hills
(B) between two rivers
(C) between two enemies
(D) between two dangers

293. Achilles' heel
(A) bare-foot
(B) to run fast
(C) to wait on somebody
(D) one's vulnerable or susceptible spot

294. To know which side the bread is buttered on
(A) to know where one's interest lies
(B) to be a glutton
(C) to be fond of rich diet
(D) to know how to increase one's income

295. To eke out
(A) to subtract
(B) to supplement
(C) to etch
(D) to oust

296. To be in the doldrums
(A) to be in low spirits
(B) to be within doors
(C) to praise loudly
(D) to be in a crisis

297. Wild cat strike
(A) a furious attack
(B) strike not approved by the trade union
(C) a strike in which violence is committed
(D) to face a strong enemy

298. Blind alley
(A) blindness due to old age
(B) a dark room
(C) unprofitable action
(D) to continue to make efforts in spite of confusion

299. Tied to the apron strings of
(A) be independent
(B) to be dominated by
(C) to live together
(D) to fall in love with

300. Our school is <u>within a stone's throw</u> from the railway station
(A) Very far-off
(B) with a certain radius
(C) at a short distance
(D) within a dcfinite circumference

ANSWER KEY

1. (A)	31. (D)	61. (D)	91. (D)	121. (B)	151. (D)	181. (A)	211. (B)	241. (A)	271. (A)
2. (C)	32. (C)	62. (A)	92. (C)	122. (B)	152. (B)	182. (C)	212. (C)	242. (D)	272. (A)
3. (B)	33. (C)	63. (B)	93. (A)	123. (B)	153. (B)	183. (C)	213. (C)	243. (C)	273. (B)
4. (C)	34. (C)	64. (B)	94. (C)	124. (C)	154. (B)	184. (C)	214. (D)	244. (D)	274. (A)
5. (C)	35. (B)	65. (A)	95. (D)	125. (B)	155. (D)	185. (B)	215. (B)	245. (D)	275. (C)
6. (D)	36. (A)	66. (C)	96. (D)	126. (D)	156. (A)	186. (D)	216. (A)	246. (A)	276. (B)
7. (A)	37. (B)	67. (C)	97. (C)	127. (D)	157. (C)	187. (D)	217. (B)	247. (D)	277. (C)
8. (C)	38. (B)	68. (A)	98. (C)	128. (C)	158. (C)	188. (C)	218. (C)	248. (A)	278. (B)
9. (B)	39. (D)	69. (B)	99. (A)	129. (A)	159. (C)	189. (B)	219. (A)	249. (B)	279. (B)
10. (C)	40. (C)	70. (A)	100. (B)	130. (B)	160. (A)	190. (A)	220. (A)	250. (A)	280. (A)
11. (B)	41. (A)	71. (B)	101. (A)	131. (A)	161. (A)	191. (D)	221. (D)	251. (B)	281. (C)
12. (B)	42. (B)	72. (C)	102. (B)	132. (B)	162. (C)	192. (B)	222. (B)	252. (D)	282. (C)
13. (D)	43. (B)	73. (C)	103. (D)	133. (C)	163. (D)	193. (B)	223. (C)	253. (D)	283. (C)
14. (C)	44. (B)	74. (C)	104. (A)	134. (D)	164. (C)	194. (A)	224. (D)	254. (C)	284. (A)
15. (C)	45. (B)	75. (B)	105. (D)	135. (A)	165. (A)	195. (B)	225. (B)	255. (A)	285. (C)
16. (C)	46. (D)	76. (C)	106. (B)	136. (C)	166. (C)	196. (B)	226. (C)	256. (C)	286. (B)
17. (C)	47. (A)	77. (C)	107. (C)	137. (A)	167. (D)	197. (B)	227. (C)	257. (A)	287. (A)
18. (D)	48. (A)	78. (A)	108. (A)	138. (C)	168. (D)	198. (A)	228. (C)	258. (C)	288. (A)
19. (C)	49. (C)	79. (A)	109. (D)	139. (B)	169. (A)	199. (C)	229. (D)	259. (A)	289. (B)
20. (B)	50. (C)	80. (A)	110. (B)	140. (A)	170. (B)	200. (B)	230. (C)	260. (B)	290. (C)
21. (C)	51. (D)	81. (B)	111. (B)	141. (B)	171. (B)	201. (D)	231. (C)	261. (C)	291. (C)
22. (D)	52. (A)	82. (B)	112. (C)	142. (D)	172. (A)	202. (C)	232. (C)	262. (A)	292. (D)
23. (C)	53. (C)	83. (C)	113. (B)	143. (D)	173. (C)	203. (C)	233. (D)	263. (A)	293. (D)
24. (B)	54. (C)	84. (C)	114. (D)	144. (C)	174. (B)	204. (A)	234. (A)	264. (B)	294. (A)
25. (C)	55. (D)	85. (C)	115. (D)	145. (C)	175. (D)	205. (C)	235. (C)	265. (A)	295. (B)
26. (B)	56. (C)	86. (B)	116. (A)	146. (A)	176. (C)	206. (C)	236. (A)	266. (A)	296. (A)
27. (C)	57. (B)	87. (D)	117. (D)	147. (D)	177. (A)	207. (A)	237. (C)	267. (C)	297. (B)
28. (B)	58. (C)	88. (B)	118. (D)	148. (B)	178. (C)	208. (B)	238. (D)	268. (A)	298. (C)
29. (A)	59. (A)	89. (D)	119. (B)	149. (C)	179. (B)	209. (D)	239. (A)	269. (A)	299. (B)
30. (A)	60. (D)	90. (A)	120. (A)	150. (C)	180. (D)	210. (A)	240. (C)	270. (A)	300. (C)

CHAPTER

34 SPELLINGS

English is an 'unphonetic' language. Owing to this, we are made to learn spellings in our childhood and regular dictations are conducted is schools.

We have to learn spellings but there are certain rules that help us remember or form the spellings easily.

Rule 1 : If 'y' comes after a consonant, we need to change 'y' into 'i' before adding 'es', 'ed' or 'er'.

This rule is applicable to 'verb', 'noun' and 'adjective'.

Cry (Verb)	cried (V_2, V_3)
Fry (Verb)	fried (V_2, V_3)
Dry (Verb)	dried (V_2, V_3)
Dry (Adj.)	drier, driest
City (Noun)	cities (Pl. Noun)
Country (Noun)	countries (Pl. Noun)
Happy (Adj)	happily (Adverb)
Marry + age	Marriage
Carry + ed	Carried

Rule 2 : If '*y*' comes after a vowel '*y*' is not changed into '*i*'.

Boy (Noun)	Boys (Pl. Noun)
Pray (Verb)	Prayed (V_2, V_3)
Grey (Adj.)	Greyer, Greyest

Exceptions:-

Pay (verb)	Paid (V_2, V_3)
Say (verb)	Said (V_2, V_3)
Lay (verb)	Laid (V_2, V_3)

Rule 3 : A famous saying is **'*i* ' before 'e' except 'c'**. This means '*i* ' comes before '*e* ' but this rule is not applicable when they come after 'c'. '*e*' is not followed by *i,e*. '*C*' is followed by (*e,i.*) This rule is applicable only when the pronunciation of 'ie' and 'ei' is 'ee' as in jeep.

Examples:-

ie	***ei***
achieve	ceiling
belief	conceit
believe	receive
chief	deceit
thief	perceive
grief	receipt
grieve	conceive

Science, efficient, their, beige, foreign, height, neighbour, vein, weight do not follow this rule because here the pronunciation is not 'ee'.

Exceptions:- In the following words the rule is not applicable though the pronunciation is '*ee*'.

seize, protein, surfeit, plabeian, counterfeit

Rule 4 : The verbs that end in '*ie*' take 'ing' only when 'ie' changes into 'y'.

die (verb)	dying
tie (verb)	tying
lie (verb)	lying

Rule 5 : Those words that end in silent '*e* ' take suffix starting with a vowel only after the '*e*' is removed.

Eg:

live + ing › living
hope + ing → hoping
move + ing/ed → moving, moved
drive + ing/er → driving, driver
become + ing → becoming
Shape + ing → Shaping
Argue + ment → argument
Nine + th → ninth
Note + able → notable
Advise + able → advisable
Imagine + ary → imaginary
Desire + ous → desirous

Value + able → valuable
Age + ing → aging
True + ly → truly
Sensible + ly → sensibly
Forcible + ly → forcibly
Gentle + ly → gently
Subtle + ly → subtly
Rove + ing → roving
Fame + ous → famous
Pore + ous → porous
Value + able → valuable
Stone + y → stony
Noise + y → noisy
Whole + ly → wholly
Taste + y → tasty
Ice + y → Icy
Awe + full → Awful

Exceptions:-

Hope + full/less → Hopeful/ hopeless
Awe + some → Awesome
Acknowledge + ment → Acknowledgement
Judge + ment → Judgement
Home + less → Homeless
Manage + able → Manageable
Charge + able → Chargeable
Courage + ous → Courageous
Notice + able → Noticeable

नियम 6 : See the following words. Here 'e' changes into 'i' and then suffix 'ous' is added.

Space + ous = spacious
Vice + ous = vicious
Malice + ous = Malicious
Grace + ous = Gracious
Omen + ous = Ominous

Rule 7 : The words that end in a short vowel and a consonant take a suffix starting with a vowel only after the last consonant is doubled.

beg + ed begged
run + ing running
rob + er robber
sad + er/est sadder, saddest
fit + er/est fitter, fittest
begin + ing beginning
occur + ed occurring
kidnap + er kidnapper

Exceptions:- When a suffix starting with a consonant is added, this rule is not applicable.

bag + $\underbrace{\text{ed}}_{\textit{vowel}}$ bagged ('g' doubled)

bag + $\underbrace{\text{ful}}_{\textit{consonant}}$ bagful ('g' not doubled)
suffix

If Consonant is preceded by a long vowel, the Consonant is doubled.

Eg: Heat + ing → Heating
Beat + en → Beaten

Rule 8 : When suffix 'full' is added to a word, an '*l*' is removed

Eg: Skill + full → skilful
Hand + full → handful
Mouth + full → mouthful
Spoon + full → spoonful
Beauty + full → Beautiful

Rule 9 : '*Q*' is followed by '*u*' for all words of English language.

queue, quiz, queen, tranquil, quest, quarrel

- Some words take double 'uu'. For eg– vacuum, continuum, residuum

Rule 10 : Many spellings of British English are different from American English. We must use spellings as per British English.

U.K.	**U.S.**
Meagre	Meager
Colour	Color
Favour	Favor
Foetus	Fetus
Organisation	Organization
Mileage	Milage

Rule 11 : It two words ending in double '*l*' and joined, one '*l*' is dropped.

Will + full → wilful
Full + fill → fulfil

Rule 12 : If All, well, till, still come as

'prefix' or 'suffix' then one 'l' will be removed.

All+together → Altogether

All+most → Almost   Un+till → Until

In+still → Instill   Dis+till → Distil

Exception: wellbeing, farewell

Rule 13 : It 'ness' is added to a word ending in 'n' then both 'n' remain in the word.

Keen + ness → keenness

Clean + ness → cleanness or cleanliness

Mean + ness → meanness

Rule 14 : Look at the following words. They end in 'c' and if they are to take a 'suffix', then change 'c' into 'ck'.

Panic + ed → panicked

Traffic + ing → trafficking

Picnic + er → picnicker

SILENT LETTERS

- **'h' is silent in**

Daughter, draught, sight, right, bright, height, honour, hour, honest, rhythm, honorary, exhaust, haemorrhage

- **'l' is silent in**

Balm, palm, talk, walk, alms, chalk, calm

- **'k' is silent in**

Knife, know, knee, knight

- **'n' is silent in**

Solemn, autumn, hymn, column

- **'t' is silent in**

Whistle, fasten, hasten, often, hustle, bustle, debut, depot

- **'d' is silent in**

Adjective, adjourn, grudge

- **'w' is silent in**

Write, wrath, wring, wrong, wrap

- **'b' is silent in**

Subtle, debt, debtor, doubt

- **'r' is silent in**

Summer, winter, mother, father, sister, brother

- **'g' is silent in**

Malign, benign, assign, sign, campaign

See how spellings change even when the words are of same origin.

Enemy → enmity

Maintain → Maintenance

Repeat → Repetition

Dexterous → Ambidextrous

Odour → Malodorous

Continue → Continuous

Humour → Humorous

See the difference-

Tomb – कब्र

Tome – किताब

Epitome – perfect example

Note: 'c' never comes in place of 's' in the words given below.

Supersede, Idiosyncrasy, Abstruse

See the difference-

Condemn – deplore/ criticize

Commend – Praise

Comment – Annotation (टिप्पणी)

- **Colonel** does not take 'r'
- **Lieutenant** does not take 'f'
- **Cigar + rette** – Cigarette
- **Superintendent** – Super+in+ten+dent
- **Etiquette**
- **Omelette**

See carefully:– Tuition, Omniscient, Occasion, Millionaire, Liaison, Queue. 'i' comes after 'u' in Tuition. 'c' is in Omniscient. Occasion does not take 'ss'. Millionaire takes 'aire' not 'er' and Liaison takes 'i' after and before 'a'.

Commonly Misspelt Words

Assassination, Calendar, Cemetery, Chauffeur, Committee, Ecstasy, Four, Forty, Nine, Ninth, Twelve, Twelfth, Harass, Forthcoming, Champagne, Lollipop, Millennium, Occasion, Separate, Pneumonia, Diarrhoea

Directions : In questions given below, groups of four words are given. In each group, one word is correctly spelt. Find the correctly spelt word and mark your answer in the Answer-Sheet.

1. (A) Emancipation (B) Emancipasion (C) Emencipation (D) Emansipation
2. (A) Prejudice (B) Prejudise (C) Predjudice (D) Prejudis
3. (A) Surgeon (B) Surjon (C) Surgen (D) Surjun
4. (A) Potatos (B) Potatoes (C) Potatose (D) None of the above
5. (A) Ireversible (B) Irreversible (C) Irrevarsible (D) Irravarsible
6. (A) Independance (B) Independence (C) Independens (D) Indepandance
7. (A) Hypocrisy (B) Hypocresy (C) Hipocrisy (D) Hipocrecy
8. (A) Aeroplane (B) Airoplane (C) Aeroplain (D) Airoplain
9. (A) Loanly (B) Lonly (C) Loneli (D) Lonely
10. (A) Cerimony (B) Ceremoney (C) Ceremony (D) Cerimoney
11. (A) Deceive (B) Decieve (C) Diceive (D) Dicieve
12. (A) Argumeant (B) Argument (C) Arguement (D) Argumant
13. (A) Toom (B) Tuom (C) Tumb (D) Tomb
14. (A) Perusal (B) Perusel (C) Perusil (D) Perucil
15. (A) Diversion (B) Divertion (C) Dieversion (D) Divartion
16. (A) Gestelt (B) Imbrolios (C) Ampasse (D) Recondite
17. (A) Hindrance (B) Corespondence (C) Insurence (D) Assurence
18. (A) adversery (B) adultary (C) Advisory (D) Arbitary
19. (A) Rogeu (B) Colleague (C) Diluge (D) Algea
20. (A) Malignant (B) Impertinant (C) Independant (D) Negligant
21. (A) Supercede (B) Superceed (C) Supersede (D) Superseed
22. (A) Abandant (B) Abendant (C) Abundent (D) Abundant
23. (A) Asassin (B) Assassin (C) Assasin (D) Assassen
24. (A) Foyere (B) Foayer (C) Foyer (D) Fouyer
25. (A) Seperately (B) Separately (C) Seperatley (D) Separatly
26. (A) Pidistrian (B) Pedistrian (C) Pedestrian (D) Pidestrian
27. (A) Budgetery (B) Bugetary (C) Budgetary (D) Budgetry
28. (A) Embarrassed (B) Embarassed (C) Embarrased (D) Embarased
29. (A) Occurence (B) Occurrence (C) Ocurence (D) Occurrance
30. (A) Livelihood (B) Livelyhood (C) Livlihood (D) Livelyhud
31. (A) Volumenous (B) Voluptous (C) Voceferous (D) Virtuous
32. (A) Lision (B) Benine (C) Aqueous (D) Bavine
33. (A) Prolifirate (B) Propitiate (C) Apropriate (D) Apreciate
34. (A) Fragrent (B) Fragmant (C) Flurocent (D) Flamboyant
35. (A) Mammal (B) Mammale (C) Mammath (D) Mambrane
36. (A) Collaborate (B) Comemorate (C) Colate (D) Choclate
37. (A) Circuiteous (B) Clairvoyant (C) Chivelery (D) Cavelcade
38. (A) Severety (B) Sovereignity (C) Superiorty (D) Serenity

39. (A) Cummulative
(B) Comemmorative
(C) Accummulative
(D) Accommodative
40. (A) Benidiction (B) Besmerch
(C) Beneficient (D) Benevolence
41. (A) Parapharnelia (B) Parsimonious
(C) Peccadilo (D) Peadiatrics
42. (A) Measureable (B) Manageable
(C) Marriagable (D) Manoevrable
43. (A) Tussel (B) Tunnle
(C) Tumble (D) Trable
44. (A) Populus (B) Pompuous
(C) Prelious
(D) Presumptuous
45. (A) Impromptue (B) Illustrious
(C) Illusery (D) Impetous
46. (A) Irelevant (B) Irrelavent
(C) Irelevent (D) Irrelevant
47. (A) Seismic (B) Siesmic
(C) Seissmic (D) Seismik
48. (A) Choas (B) Chaos
(C) Chaaos (D) Chaoss
49. (A) Surreptitious (B) Surreptitous
(C) Surreptetious (D) Sureptitious
50. (A) Stealthily (B) Stealthely
(C) Steelthily (D) Stealthilly
51. (A) Acknowlege (B) Acknoledge
(C) Aknowledge (D) Acknowledge
52. (A) Cirtificate (B) Certificate
(C) Cirtifikate (D) Certeficate
53. (A) Mischievous (B) Mischievious
(C) Mischeivous (D) Mischeivious
54. (A) Ordinannce (B) Ordinannce
(C) Ordinance (D) Ordinnence
55. (A) Incidantally (B) Incidantelly
(C) Incidentally (D) Incidentelly
56. (A) Mandatary (B) Circulatory
(C) Temporery (D) Regulatary
57. (A) Convinience (B) Initative
(C) Concesional (D) Exaggerate
58. (A) Diologue (B) Giraffe
(C) Scissor (D) Humourous
59. (A) Asiduous (B) Nefarious
(C) Macaber (D) Loqacious
60. (A) Cortage (B) Damege
(C) Milege (D) Plumage
61. (A) Onvelope (B) Envelope
(C) Envalope (D) Envelap
62. (A) Character (B) Charecter
(C) Charactar (D) Chaerector
63. (A) Drunkeness (B) Drunkenness
(C) Dunnkness (D) Drunkennes
64. (A) Surprise (B) Supprise
(C) Suprise (D) Surprize
65. (A) Comitee (B) Commitee
(C) Committie (D) Committee
66. (A) Secretariel (B) Secreterel
(C) Secreterial (D) Secretarial
67. (A) Aquisition (B) Acquizition
(C) Acquisition (D) Acquisision
68. (A) Vaccation (B) Vocation
(C) Vecation (D) Vecasion
69. (A) Gaurd (B) Gard
(C) Guard (D) Garad
70. (A) Coreigible (B) Coraegible
(C) Correigible (D) Corrigible
71. (A) Aromatic (B) Aurobatic
(C) Antartic (D) Altrustic
72. (A) Misoginist (B) Momentery
(C) Monotheeism (D) Moratorium
73. (A) Assessment (B) Rudiement
(C) Retrenchement
(D) Bereavment
74. (A) Tinker (B) Plumeber
(C) Despacher (D) Sailar
75. (A) Psychiotrist (B) Punctillious
(C) Pursuanse (D) Pseudonym
76. (A) Precarius (B) Preceede
(C) Premier (D) Preperation
77. (A) Corespondent
(B) Commandent
(C) Superintendent
(D) Attendent
78. (A) Imaginery (B) Dictionary
(C) Itinerery (D) Stationerry
79. (A) Pronounciation
(B) Repercution
(C) Rehabilitation
(D) Tution

80. (A) Columen (B) Autumn
(C) Condamm (D) Symptem
81. (A) Relinquish (B) Relenquish
(C) Relinqeush (D) Relinquesh
82. (A) Ecspectation (B) Expactation
(C) Expectation (D) Expectasion
83. (A) Assimilation
(B) Asimillation
(C) Assimillation
(D) Assimmilation
84. (A) Lassivous (B) Lacivoius
(C) Lascivious (D) Lasivious
85. (A) Enemyty (B) Enemity
(C) Enmity (D) Enraety
86. (A) Occasion (B) Occation
(C) Ocasion (D) Occassion
87. (A) Intermitent (B) Intermittant
(C) Intermittent (D) Intermitant
88. (A) Acommodation
(B) Accommodation
(C) Accomodation (D) Acomodation
89. (A) Sovereignty (B) Soveriegnty
(C) Sovereignity (D) Soveriegnity
90. (A) Greivance (B) Grievance
(C) Griveance (D) Grieveance
91. (A) Enterpreneur (B) Entreprenure
(C) Entrepreneur (D) Enterprenure
92. (A) Promiscuous (B) Promescuous
(C) Promiscuos (D) Promiscous
93. (A) Onomatopoeia (B) Onomotopoei
(C) Onomatopoia (D) Onamotipoei
94. (A) Bureacracy (B) Bereaucracy
(C) Buereacracy (D) Bureaucracy
95. (A) Miliionair (B) Millionaire
(C) Millionare (D) Millionair
96. (A) Rumble (B) Rumbble
(C) Stummble (D) Jumbble
97. (A) Nigardlely (B) Niggardly
(C) Nigerdly (D) Nigardly
98. (A) Grammatical (B) Gremmatical
(C) Gramatical (D) Grematical
99. (A) Omitted (B) Ommitted
(C) Ommited (D) Omited
100. (A) Priveiege (B) Familier
(C) Usualy (D) Nuisance
101. (A) Fascimile (B) Facsimile
(C) Facsimele (D) Facksimile
102. (A) Haemorrage (B) Hemorhage
(C) Hemmorage (D) Haemorrhage
103. (A) Hoseire (B) Hosier
(C) Hosair (D) Hasier
104. (A) Punctileous (B) Punctilious
(C) Punktilious (D) Punctileus
105. (A) Clientele (B) Clientale
(C) Cleintele (D) Clientelle
106. (A) Definitely (B) Definately
(C) Definitley (D) Definitly
107. (A) Cemetary (B) Semetary
(C) Cemetery (D) Cemetry
108. (A) Recesion (B) Reccesion
(C) Reccession (D) Recession
109. (A) Desiccation (B) Dessication
(C) Desiccasion (D) Deziccation
110. (A) Inconvenienced
(B) Inconveniensed
(C) Inconvineinced
(D) Inconvenneinced
111. (A) Misdemenour (B) Manoeuvre
(C) Begining (D) Chameloon
112. (A) Irrepairable (B) Irreparable
(C) Irreparabel (D) Irepairable
113. (A) Superfluous (B) Superflous
(C) Superfluos (D) Supperflous
114. (A) Capracious (B) Auspicious
(C) Fallicious (D) Dalicious
115. (A) Inefable (B) Inaccesible
(C) Infallible (D) Invinscible
116. (A) Concomitant
(B) Concommitant
(C) Concommittant
(D) Concommitent
117. (A) Fluorescent (B) Floorescent
(C) Floorascent (D) Flourascent
118. (A) Travelling (B) Remitance
(C) Kidnaping (D) Equiteble
119. (A) Neccessary (B) Temparory
(C) Itinerary (D) Sanguinery
120. (A) Tomorow (B) Tommorow
(C) Tommorrow (D) Tomorrow

121. (A) Superintendent
(B) Superentendent
(C) Suprintendent
(D) Supirentendent

122. (A) Symatry (B) Symmetry
(C) Symetry (D) Symmitry

123. (A) Villain (B) Alleince
(C) Pleintive (D) Sustein

124. (A) Commisioner
(B) Commissioner
(C) Comissioner
(D) Commissionar

125. (A) Asassin (B) Assassin
(C) Assasin (D) Assassen

126. (A) Magnificient (B) Magnifecent
(C) Magnifiscient (D) Magnificent

127. (A) Eccumenikal (B) Ecumenical
(C) Ecuemenicel (D) Ekumanical

128. (A) Aprentice (B) Advertise
(C) Treatice (D) Sencitive

129. (A) Misile (B) Missile
(C) Misille (D) Missiel

130. (A) Abandant (B) Abendent
(C) Abundent (D) Abundant

131. (A) Beneficil (B) Beneficial
(C) Benifical (D) Benificial

132. (A) Avericious (B) Avaricious
(C) Avarisious (D) Averisious

133. (A) Internaly (B) Coldlly
(C) Fortunetely (D) Uniquely

134. (A) Affectionately (B) Afectionately
(C) Affectionnality (D) Affactionately

135. (A) Aprehension (B) Apprihension
(C) Aprihension (D) Apprehension

136. (A) Acquisision (B) Acquisision
(C) Aquisition (D) Acquisition

137. (A) Demanstrative
(B) Attractive
(C) Represantative
(D) Administrative

138. (A) Monarchy (B) Discrapancy
(C) Hieararchy (D) Anorchy

139. (A) Refference (B) Relliance
(C) Occurence (D) Recurrence

140. (A) Descreptive (B) Recepttive
(C) Coopperative (D) Competitive

141. (A) Veterinerian (B) Vaterinerian
(C) Veterinarian (D) Vetarinerian

142. (A) Equilibrium (B) Equalibirium
(C) Ecquilibrium (D) Equilibriam

143. (A) Meritime (B) Marrytime
(C) Marytime (D) Maritime

144. (A) Degression (B) Digresion
(C) Digrestion (D) Digression

145. (A) Presomptous
(B) Presumpchous
(C) Presumtous
(D) Presumptuous

146. (A) Anathemaa (B) Anathima
(C) Anathema (D) Annathema

147. (A) Quiant (B) Quaaint
(C) Quaint (D) Qauint

148. (A) Effervescent (B) Efferescent
(C) Effervesent (D) Efervescent

149. (A) Persuesive (B) Persuasieve
(C) Pursuasive (D) Persuasive

150. (A) Ascendancy (B) Ascendensy
(C) Asscendency (D) Ascenndency

151. (A) Holocaust (B) Holocast
(C) Holocost (D) Halocaust

152. (A) Reverantial (B) Reverential
(C) Revarential (D) Reverentiel

153. (A) Meteculous (B) Meticulous
(C) Metikyulus (D) Meticulus

154. (A) Souvenir (B) Suvenire
(C) Suvenir (D) Souviener

155. (A) Flabergast (B) Flabergust
(C) Flabbergast (D) Fiabbergust

Directions : In Questions given below, four word are given in each question, out of which only one word is wrongly spelt. Find the word and indicate it in the Answer Sheet by blackening the appropriate rectangle.

1. (A) Poignant (B) Relevent (C) Prevalent (D) Malignant
2. (A) Seize (B) Achieve (C) Wierd (D) Leisure
3. (A) Repent (B) Serpent (C) Flagrent (D) Reverent
4. (A) Dining (B) Shining (C) Determining (D) Begining
5. (A) Vendetta (B) Verisimilitude (C) Vicarious (D) Vociferate
6. (A) Embankment (B) Deliberately (C) Preceding (D) Proleferous
7. (A) Inexplicable (B) Inevitable (C) Inextinguishable (D) Inexpressable
8. (A) Representation (B) Verification (C) Amplification (D) Liberalisetion
9. (A) Reference (B) Preference (C) Difference (D) Performence
10. (A) Agreebly (B) Cruelly (C) Doubtfully (D) Fatally
11. (A) Nomenclature (B) Non – interference (C) Nonchalant (D) Commisioned
12. (A) Insolvency (B) Legitimacy (C) Hypocrisy (D) Idiosyncracy
13. (A) Anniversary (B) Bureaucracy (C) Heresy (D) Secresy
14. (A) Malignity (B) Malodorus (C) Malfeasance (D) Malevolent
15. (A) Unaccompanied (B) Unaccusstomed (C) Unadopted (D) Unalloyed
16. (A) Boutique (B) Physique (C) Opaque (D) Obleeque
17. (A) Admitting (B) Budgetting (C) Preferring (D) Travelling
18. (A) Torpedoes (B) Mosquitoes (C) Pianoes (D) Tomatoes
19. (A) Oscillate (B) Deliberate (C) Ennumerate (D) Narrate
20. (A) Hurdle (B) Cuddel (C) Puddle (D) Meddle
21. (A) Composition (B) Grammer (C) Literature (D) Poetry
22. (A) Pneumonia (B) Diarrheoa (C) Xenophobia (D) Amnesia
23. (A) Commission (B) Omission (C) Possession (D) Occassion

Directions : In Questions given below, four word are given in each question, out of which only one word is wrongly spelt. Find the word and indicate it in the Answer Sheet by blackening the appropriate rectangle.

1. (A) Poignant (B) Relevent (C) Prevalent (D) Malignant
2. (A) Seize (B) Achieve (C) Wierd (D) Leisure
3. (A) Repent (B) Serpent (C) Flagrent (D) Reverent
4. (A) Dining (B) Shining (C) Determining (D) Begining
5. (A) Vendetta (B) Verisimilitude (C) Vicarious (D) Vociferate
6. (A) Embankment (B) Deliberately (C) Preceding (D) Proleferous
7. (A) Inexplicable (B) Inevitable (C) Inextinguishable (D) Inexpressable

8. (A) Representation
(B) Verification
(C) Amplification
(D) Liberalisetion

9. (A) Reference (B) Preference
(C) Difference (D) Performence

10. (A) Agreebly (B) Cruelly
(C) Doubtfully (D) Fatally

11. (A) Nomenclature
(B) Non–interference
(C) Nonchalant
(D) Commisioned

12. (A) Insolvency (B) Legitimacy
(C) Hypocrisy (D) Idiosyncracy

13. (A) Anniversary (B) Bureaucracy
(C) Heresy (D) Secresy

14. (A) Malignity (B) Malodorus
(C) Malfeasance (D) Malevolent

15. (A) Unaccompanied
(B) Unaccusstomed
(C) Unadopted (D) Unalloyed

16. (A) Boutique (B) Physique
(C) Opaque (D) Obleeque

17. (A) Admitting (B) Budgetting
(C) Preferring (D) Travelling

18. (A) Torpedoes (B) Mosquitoes
(C) Pianoes (D) Tomatoes

19. (A) Oscillate (B) Deliberate
(C) Ennumerate (D) Narrate

20. (A) Hurdle (B) Cuddel
(C) Puddle (D) Meddle

21. (A) Composition (B) Grammer
(C) Literature (D) Poetry

22. (A) Pneumonia (B) Diarrheoa
(C) Xenophobia (D) Amnesia

23. (A) Commission (B) Omission
(C) Possession (D) Occassion

24. (A) Pronunciation (B) Vaccum
(C) Troublesome (D) Vacuum

25. (A) Successor (B) Marriage
(C) Auctioner (D) Enthusiastic

Answer

Directions : In questions given below, groups of four words are given. In each group, one word is correctly spelt. Find the correctly spelt word and mark your answer in the Answer-Sheet.

1. (A) emancipation
2. (A) prejudice
3. (A) surgeon
4. (B) potatoes
5. (B) irreversible
6. (B) independence
7. (A) hypocrisy
8. (A) aeroplane
9. (D) lonely
10. (C) ceremony
11. (A) deceive
12. (B) Argument
13. (D) tomb
14. (A) perusal
15. (A) diversion
16. (D) recondite

Correct spellings of remaining words:
(A) gestalt
(B) imbroglios
(C) impasse

17. (A) hindrance

Correct spellings of remaining words:
(B) correspondence
(C) insurance
(D) assurance

18. (C) advisory

Correct spellings of remaining words:
(A) adversary
(B) adultery
(D) arbitrary

19. (B) colleague

Correct spellings of remaining words:
(A) rogue
(C) deluge
(D) algae

20. (A) malignant

Correct spellings of remaining words:
(B) impertinent
(C) independent
(D) negligent

21. (C) Supersede
22. (D) Abundant
23. (B) Assassin
24. (C) Foyer
25. (B) Separately
26. (C) Pedestrian
27. (C) Budgetary
28. (A) Embarrassed
29. (B) Occurrence
30. (A) Livelihood
31. (D) Virtuous
32. (C) Aqueous
33. (B) Propitiate
34. (D) Flamboyant
35. (A) Mammal
36. (A) Collaborate

Correct spellings of remaining words:

(B) Commemorate
(C) Collate
(D) Chocolate

37. (B) Clairvoyant
(A) Circuitous
(C) Chivalry
(D) Cavalcade

38. (D) Serenity
Correct spellings of remaining words:
(A) Severity
(B) Sovereignty
(C) Superiority

39. (D) Accommodative
Correct spellings of remaining words:
(A) Cumulative
(B) Commemorative
(C) Accumulative

40. (D) Benevolence
Correct spellings of remaining words:
(A) Benediction
(B) Besmirch
(C) Beneficent

41. (B) Parsimonious
Correct spellings of remaining words:
(A) Paraphernalia
(C) Peccadillo
(D) Pediatrics

42. (B) Manageable
Correct spellings of remaining words:
(A) Measurable
(C) Marriageable
(D) Maneuverable

43. (C) Tumble
Correct spellings of remaining words:
(A) Tussle
(B) Tunnel
(D) Treble

44. (D) Presumptuous
Correct spellings of remaining words:
(A) Populous
(B) Pompous
(C) Perilous

45. (B) Illustrious
Correct spellings of remaining words:
(A) Impromptu
(C) Illusory
(D) Impetuous

46. (D) Irrelevant
47. (A) Seismic
48. (B) Chaos
49. (A) Surreptitious
50. (A) Stealthily
51. (D) Acknowledge
52. (B) Certificate
53. (A) Mischievous
54. (C) Ordinance
55. (C) Incidentally
56. (B) Circulatory
Correct spellings of remaining words:
(A) Mandatory
(C) Temporary
(D) Regulatory

57. (D) Exaggerate
Correct spellings of remaining words:
(A) Convenience
(B) Initiative
(C) Concessional

58. (B) Giraffe
Correct spellings of remaining words:
(A) Dialogue
(C) Scissors
(D) Humorous

59. (B) Nefarious
Correct spellings of remaining words:
(A) Assiduous
(C) Macabre
(D) Loquacious

60. (D) Plumage
Correct spellings of remaining words:
(A) Cortege
(B) Damage
(C) Mileage

61. (B) Envelope
62. (A) Character
63. (B) Drunkenness
64. (A) Surprise
65. (D) Committee
66. (D) Secretarial
67. (C) Acquisition
68. (B) Vocation
69. (C) Guard
70. (D) Corrigible
71. (A) Aromatic
Correct spellings of remaining words:
(B) Aerobatic
(C) Antarctic
(D) Altruistic

72. (D) Moratorium
(A) Misogynist
(B) Momentary
(C) Monotheism

73. (A) Assessment
Correct spellings of remaining words:
(B) Rudiment
(C) Retrenchment
(D) Bereavement

74. (A) Tinker
Correct spellings of remaining words:
(B) Plumber
(C) Dispatcher
(D) Sailor

75. (D) Pseudonym
Correct spellings of remaining words:
(A) Psychiatrist
(B) Punctilious
(C) Pursuance

76. (C) Premier
Correct spellings of remaining words:
(A) Precarious
(B) Precede
(C) Preparation

77. (C) Superintendent
Correct spellings of remaining words:

(A) Correspondent
(B) Commandant
(D) Attendant

78. (B) Dictionary
Correct spellings of remaining words:
(A) Imaginary
(C) Itinerary
(D) Stationery

79. (C) Rehabilitation
Correct spellings of remaining words:
(A) Pronunciation
(B) Repercussion
(D) Tuition

80. (B) Autumn
Correct spellings of remaining words:
(A) Column
(C) Condemn
(D) Symptom

81. (A) Relinquish
82. (C) Expectation
83. (A) Assimilation
84. (C) Lascivious
85. (C) Enmity
86. (A) Occasion
87. (C) Intermittent
88. (B) Accommodation
89. (A) Sovereignty
90. (B) Grievance
91. (C) Entrepreneur
92. (A) Promiscuous
93. (A) Onomatopoeia
94. (D) Bureaucracy
95. (B) Millionaire
96. (A) Rumble
97. (B) Niggardly
98. (A) Grammatical
99. (A) Omitted
100. (D) Nuisance
Correct spellings of remaining words:
(A) Privilege
(B) Familiar
(C) Usually

101. (B) Facsimile
102. (D) Haemorrhage
103. (B) Hosier
104. (B) Punctilious
105. (A) Clientele
106. (A) Definitely
107. (C) Cemetery
108. (D) Recession
109. (A) Desiccation
110. (A) Inconvenienced
111. (B) Manoeuvre
Correct spellings of remaining words:
(A) Misdemeanour
(C) Beginning
(D) Chameleon

112. (B) Irreparable
113. (A) Superfluous
114. (B) Auspicious
Correct spellings of remaining words:
(A) Capricious
(C) Fallacious
(D) Delicious

115. (C) Infallible
Correct spellings of remaining words:
(A) Ineffable
(B) Inaccessible
(D) Invincible

116. (A) Concomitant
117. (A) Fluorescent
118. (A) Travelling
Correct spellings of remaining words:
(B) Remittance
(C) Kidnapping
(D) Equitable

119. (C) Itinerary
(A) Necessary
(B) Temporary
(D) Sanguinary

120. (D) Tomorrow
121. (A) Superintendent
122. (B) Symmetry
123. (A) Villain
Correct spellings of remaining words:
(B) Alliance
(C) Plaintive
(D) Sustain

124. (B) Commissioner
125. (B) Assassin
126. (D) Magnificent
127. (B) Ecumenical
128. (B) Advertise
Correct spellings of remaining words:
(A) Apprentice
(C) Treatise
(D) Sensitive

129. (B) Missile
130. (D) Abundant
131. (B) Beneficial
132. (B) Avaricious
133. (D) Uniquely
Correct spellings of remaining words:
(A) Internally
(B) Coldly
(C) Fortunately

134. (A) Affectionately
135. (D) Apprehension
136. (D) Acquisition
137. (B) Attractive
Correct spellings of remaining words:
(A) Demonstrative
(C) Representative
(D) Administrative

138. (A) Monarchy
Correct spellings of remaining words:
(B) Discrepancy
(C) Hierarchy
(D) Anarchy

139. (D) Recurrence
Correct spellings of remaining words:
(A) Reference
(B) Reliance
(C) Occurrence

140. (D) Competitive
Correct spellings of remaining words:

(A) Descriptive
(B) Receptive
(C) Cooperative
141. (C) Veterinarian
142. (A) Equilibrium
143. (D) Maritime
144. (D) Digression
145. (D) Presumptuous
146. (C) Anathema
147. (C) Quaint
148. (A) Effervescent
149. (D) Persuasive
150. (A) Ascendancy
151. (A) Holocaust
152. (B) Reverential
153. (B) Meticulous
154. (A) Souvenir
155. (C) Flabbergast

Directions : In Questions given below, four word are given in each question, out of which only one word is wrongly spelt. Find the word and indicate it in the Answer Sheet by blackening the appropriate rectangle.

Answer

With correct spellings of the misspelt words-

1. (B) Relevant
2. (C) Weird
3. (C) Flagrant
4. (D) Beginning
5. (D) Vociferate
6. (D) Proliferate
7. (D) Inexpressible
8. (D) Liberalization
9. (D) Performance
10. (A) Agreeably
11. (D) Commissioned
12. (D) Idiosyncrasy
13. (D) Secrecy
14. (B) Malodorous
15. (B) Unaccustomed
16. (D) Oblique
17. (B) Budgeting
18. (C) Pianos
19. (C) Enumerate
20. (B) Cuddle
21. (B) Grammar
22. (B) Diarrhoea
23. (D) Occasion
24. (B) Vacuum
25. (C) Auctioneer

MEANING OF SOME WORDS GIVEN IN THE ASSIGNMENT

S.No.	WORDS	MEANING IN HINDI	MEANING IN ENGLISH
1.	Abundant	प्रचुरता में	Plentiful
2.	Accommodative	समाविष्ट करने वाला	Adjusting
3.	Accumulative	संचयी	The act of collecting
4.	Acknowledge	स्वीकार करना (कि किसी बात की जानकारी है)	To admit the Knowledge of
5.	Acquisition	प्राप्त/कब्जे में करना	To get hold of
6.	Adultery	विवाहेतर संबंध	Extra-marital affairs
7.	Adversary	प्रतिद्वंदी	Opponent
8.	Alliance	गठबंधन	Association
9.	Altruistic	परोपकारी	Unselfish devotion towards welfare of others
10.	Anarchy	अराजकता	Lawlessness
11.	Anathema	नफरत	Abhorrence, hatred
12.	Apprehension	आशंका	Suspicion
13.	Apprentice	जो किसी दक्ष व्यक्ति के मार्गदर्शन में कार्य करता है	Helper, Trainee
14.	Aqueous	तरल/जलीय	Watery
15.	Arbitrary	मनमाना	As per one's will or caprice
16.	Aromatic	खुशबुदार	Perfumed
17.	Ascendancy	अधिपत्य	The state of being on a position of power
18.	Assassin	राजनैतिक कारणों से हत्या करने वाला	One who kills for political reason
19.	Assessment	आकलन	Evalutation
20.	Assiduous	मेहनती	Diligent/hard-working

21.	Assimilation	आत्मसाव	To absorb into system
22.	Auspicious	शुभ	That brings good luck
23.	Avaricious	लालची	Greedy
24.	Benediction	आर्शीवाद	Blessings
25.	Benevolence	दया	Kindness
26.	Bereavement	मातम	Mourning
27.	Besmirch	बदनाम करना	To defame
28.	Bureaucracy	नौकरशाही	Ruled by Government officials
29.	Capricious	सनकी	Of weird behaviour
30.	Cavalcade	काफिला	A procession of vehicles, ships etc
31.	Cemetery	कब्रिस्तान	Burial ground
32.	Chivalry	वीर व सभ्य	Gallant and courteous
33.	Circuitous	घुमावदार	Round-about
34.	Clairvoyant	दूरदर्शी	Able to see beyond the range of ordinary perception, farsightedness
35.	Clientele	उपभोगताओं का समूह	A body of clients
36.	Collaborate	साथ-साथ काम करना	The act of working together
37.	Collate	जमा करना	To collect
38.	Commemorate	के याद में मनाना	To celebrate in the memory of
39.	Concomitant	सहयोगी	Accompanying
40.	Condemn	निन्दा करना	Criticize
41.	Convenience	सुविधा	Facility
42.	Corrigible	जो सुधारा जा सकता है	That can be corrected
43.	Cortege	नौकर-चाकर का समूह/जूलुस (विशेषकर अंतिम संस्कार के लिए ले जाने वाली)	Retinue/Procession especially funeral procession
44.	Cuddle	आलिंगन करना	Hug, embrace
45.	Cumulative	बढ़ाने वाला	Increasing by successive addition
46.	Deceive	धोखा देना	To cheat
47.	Delicious	स्वादिष्ट	Pleasant to taste
48.	Deluge	बाढ़	Flood
49.	Desiccation	सुखा कर देने वाला	The act of drying up/dehydration
50.	Digression	भटक जाना	Departure from the subject
51.	Discrepancy	असमानता	Difference
52.	Diversion	दिशा परिवर्तन	The act of changing the direction
53.	Ecumenical	वृहत प्रभाव डालने वाला	World wide in effect
54.	Effervescent	बुलबुलो से भरा/उल्लासपूर्ण	Fizzy/vibrant
55.	Emancipation	मुक्ति	Liberation/freedom
56.	Enmity	दुश्मनी	Hostility, Animosity
57.	Entrepreneur	व्यापारी	Business man/capitalist
58.	Enumerate	सूचीबद्ध करना	To specify one after the other
59.	Equitable	निष्पक्ष	Fair/reasonable

60.	Exaggerate	बढ़ा-चढ़ा कर पेश करना	To overstate
61.	Expectation	उम्मीद	Hope
62.	Facsimile	हू-ब-हू	Exact copy
63.	Fallacious	झूठ/भ्रामक	Untrue, misleading
64.	Flabbergast	हक्का-बक्का	Extremely surprised
65.	Flagrant	अत्यन्त शर्मनाक	Blatant, brazen
66.	Flamboyant	दिखावा करने वाला	Showy
67.	Fluorescent	चमकदार	Shining, glowing
68.	Foyer	हॉल के बाहर की खुली जगह	An entrance, hallway
69.	Gestalt	कार्यकारी यूनिट	Functional unit
70.	Grievance	शिकायत	Complaint
71.	Hierarchy	पदानुक्रम	Chain of people in authority according to their post.
72.	Hindrance	रूकावट	Obstruction
73.	Holocaust	सर्वनाश	Devastation, Cataclysm, Catastrophe
74.	Humorous	विनोदी	Entertaining, amusing
75.	Hypocrisy	पाखंड	Showing the character that is fake
76.	Idiosyncrasy	सनक	Eccentricity, weird behaviour
77.	Illusory	भ्रामक	Deceptive
78.	Illustrious	प्रसिद्ध व सफल	Famous and successful
79.	Imbroglios	लज्जाजनक हालात	Embarrassing situation
80.	Impasse	गतिरोध/रूकावट	Deadlock
81.	Impertinent	अशिष्ट	Rude and not showing respect
82.	Impetuous	लापरवाह/आवेगशील	Rash, Impulsive
83.	Impromptu	बिना तैयारी के	Without preparation, extempore
84.	Inaccessible	जहाँ पहुँचा ना जा सके	Where one cannot reach
85.	Incidentally	गैर-इरादतन	Without intention
86.	Inconvenienced	तकलीफ होना	Troubled
87.	Ineffable	अवर्णणनीय	That cannot be described
88.	Inexpressible	अवर्णणनीय	That cannot be described or expressed
89.	Infallible	जो गलती ना करें	One who cannot make mistakes
90.	Initiative	पहल	Introductory step
91.	Intermittent	रूक-रूक कर	Irregular
92	Invincible	अजय	That cannot be defeated
93.	Irrelevant	अप्रासंगिक	Not related to
94.	Irreparable	जो मरम्मद ना किया जा सके	That cannot be repaired
95.	Irreversible	जो परिवर्तित ना किया जा सके	That cannot be altered
96.	Mischievous	शरारती	Naughty
97.	Itinerary	यात्राक्रम	Schedule of a tour
98.	Lascivious	अश्लील	Obscene
99.	Liberalization	आजादी	Freedom

100.	Loquacious	बातूनी	Talkative/Garrulous
101.	Macabre	भयावह	Gruesome/horrible
102.	Magnificent	भव्य	Splendid
103.	Malignant	अहितकर	Evil, wicked
104.	Malodorous	बदबूदार	Of bad odour
105.	Mandatory	अनिवार्य	Compulsory
106.	Maneuverable	जो चतुराई/दक्षता से संभाल लिया जा सकता है	That can be managed with skill or tactics
107.	Maritime	समुद्र संबंधित	Relating to sea
108.	Meticulous	अतिसावधान	Careful
109.	Millionaire	लखपति	Very rich
111.	Misdemeanour	दुव्यवहार	Misbehaviour
112.	Misogynist	महिलाओं से नफरत करने वाला	One who hates women
113.	Momentary	क्षणिक	Short-lived
114.	Monarchy	राजतंत्र	King's rule
115.	Monotheism	एकेश्वरवाद	Belief in one god
116.	Moratorium	विलम्ब जो आदेश के तहत हो	An authorized period of delay
117.	Nefarious	दुष्ट	Evil, wicked
118.	Niggardly	कंजूस	Miserly
119.	Nuisance	समस्या	Problem
120.	Omitted	मिटा हुआ	Removed
121.	Onomatopoeia	ध्वनि पर आधारित शब्द	A word formed from the sound that it produces. Eg-hiss, pop etc.
122.	Ordinance	कानून	Statute
123.	Paraphernalia	औजार	Miscellaneous equipment
124.	Parsimonious	कंजूस	Miser, stingy
125.	Peccadillo	गुनाह	Sin
126.	Pedestrian	पैदल यात्री	One who travels on foot
127.	Pediatrics	बच्चों का डाक्टर	Doctor of children
128.	Perilous	खतरनाक	Dangerous
129.	Persuasive	राजी कर लेने वाला	Convincing
130.	Perusal	निरीक्षण	Careful examination
131.	Plaintive	याचक	One who has filed legal plaint
132.	Plumage	पंख	Feathers of a bird
133.	Pompous	दिखावा करने वाला	Showy
134.	Populous	भीड़ भरा	Crowded
135.	Precarious	अस्थिर	Unstable
136.	Precede	के पहले आना	To come before
137.	Prejudice	पक्षपातपूर्ण	Partiality
138.	Presumptuous	धृष्ट	Self assuming/too bold
139.	Privilege	विशेषाधिकार	Special right
140.	Proliferate	संख्या में बढ़ जाना	Multiply

141.	Promiscuous	अनैतिक	Immoral
142.	Propitiate	तुष्टी करना	Appease
143.	Pseudonym	जो नाम सिर्फ लेखन के लिए लेखक ने रखा हो	Assumed named taken by an author
144.	Punctilious	सावधानी से भरा	Careful
145.	Pursuance	अनुसरण	Follow
146.	Quaint	विचित्र पर सुन्दर	Unusual but pretty
147.	Recession	मंदी	Slump/decline
148.	Recondite	छिपा हुआ	Concealed
149.	Recurrence	दुबारा होना	To occur again
150.	Rehabilitation	पुनः स्थापन	Restoration to the former state
151.	Relevant	प्रसंगिक	Related to
152.	Relinquish	त्याग देना	Forsake
153.	Remittance	भुगतान	Payment/allowance
154.	Repercussion	नतीजा	Consequence
155.	Retrenchment	खर्चे में कटौती	Reduction of expenditure
156.	Reverential	सम्मानीय	Respectful
157.	Rogue	बदमाश	Scoundrel
158.	Rudiment	प्रारंभिक तथ्य	The simplest and most basic facts
159.	Rumble	घड़घड़ाना	To make a low, heavy continuous sound
160.	Sanguinary	रक्तपातपूर्ण	Murderoues
161.	Serenity	शांति	Calmness
162.	Severity	तीव्रता	Harshness, strictness
163.	Souvenir	याद दिलाने वाला	That reminds
164.	Sovereignty	प्रभुत्व संपन्नता	Freedom from external control
165.	Superfluous	जरूरत से ज्यादा	More than what is needed
166.	Supersede	निरस्त कर उसकी जगह लेना	To nullify and take its place
167.	Sustain	टिकना	To uphold, survive
168.	Symmetry	एक सा	Similarity of structure
169.	Tinker	ठठेरा	One who mends houshold utensils
170.	Tomb	कब्र	Burial chamber
171.	Treble	उच्च ध्वनि	Shrill voice
172.	Tumble	लुढकना	To roll over
173.	Tunnel	सुरंग	Passageway
174.	Tussle	द्वंद	Scuffle
175.	Uniquely	अलग हट कर	Of different kind, unmatched
176.	Virtuous	अच्छाई	Good quality
177.	Vocation	रोजगार	Occupation
178.	Vociferous	शोरगुलपूर्ण	Marked by an insistent outcry
179.	Weird	विचित्र	Strange